SEVEN CENTURIES
OF VERSE

SEVEN CENTURIES OF VERSE

English & American;

*FROM THE EARLY ENGLISH LYRICS
TO THE PRESENT DAY*

Selected and Edited by A. J. M. SMITH

MICHIGAN STATE UNIVERSITY

Second Edition, Revised and Enlarged

NEW YORK
CHARLES SCRIBNER'S SONS

COPYRIGHT NOTICES AND ACKNOWLEDGMENTS

Since this page cannot legibly accommodate all the copyright notices, the opposite page and the pages following it constitute an extension of the copyright page.

Thanks are due the following copyright owners and publishers for permission to reprint certain poems in this anthology:

G. BELL & SONS, LTD.—for the quotation from *The Poet's Tongue* by W. H. Auden and John Garrett, by permission of the publisher, G. Bell & Sons, Ltd.

BRANDT & BRANDT—for "Oh, Sleep forever in the Latmian Cave" from *Fatal Interview* by Edna St. Vincent Millay, published by Harper & Brothers, copyright, 1931, by Edna St. Vincent Millay; for "who's most afraid of death? thou" from *XLI Poems* by E. E. Cummings, published in *Collected Poems* by Harcourt, Brace & Co., copyright, 1925, by E. E. Cummings.

CHATTO & WINDUS—for "Strange Meeting" "Greater Love" and "Insensibility" by Wilfred Owen by permission of the publishers; for "The Groundhog" by Richard Eberhart, by permission of the publishers, Chatto & Windus Ltd.

CLARENDON PRESS—for "Nightingales," "The north wind came up yesternight," "Eros," "London Snow" and "A Passerby" by Robert Bridges from the *Shorter Poems of Robert Bridges*, by permission of the Clarendon Press, Oxford.

iv

TO MY WIFE

PREFACE

IT is gratifying that the welcome accorded *Seven Centuries of Verse* in so many universities and colleges should now make possible the publication of a new, enlarged, edition. While the basic plan of the book and the purpose for which it is intended remain the same it has been found possible to increase the number of poems included by more than a hundred and thus to give a more adequate representation of eighteenth century poetry than the earlier edition attempted and to strengthen the modern section by adding a number of important poets—among them William Carlos Williams, Edward Thomas, and Robert Lowell—and increasing the representation of such significant writers as Robert Frost, Wallace Stevens, Marianne Moore, and Ezra Pound. Among the additions are such great, if difficult, poems as Gerard Manley Hopkins' *Wreck of the Deutschland*, Robert Frost's *Directive*, T. S. Eliot's *The Dry Salvages*, and Dylan Thomas's *Ballad of the Long-Legged Bait*. In order to preserve the balance of the book and to avoid duplicating material that is usually studied in Survey courses, I have omitted several lengthy and in some respects unwieldy pieces. It is hoped that most teachers and students will find the additional songs from *Comus* and the choruses from *Samson Agonistes* a compensation for *Paradise Lost*, Book I, which is usually encountered in other courses, while Dryden's *MacFlecknoe* and Burns's *Tam O'Shanter* present difficulties that are distracting rather than challenging in an introductory course. The omission of the two latter poems is made up for by a characteristic sampling of the work of Prior, Gay, Swift, Christopher Smart, and John Clare.

The purpose of the book (we repeat from the Preface to the original edition) is to place in the hands of college students a representative selection of the best poems in the English language and to illustrate the most important types and forms of poetry. At the same time, the arrangement is chronological, and an effort has been made to proportion the selections so as to suggest the main outlines of the historical development of English and American poetry. Although the minor poets have not been neglected, the emphasis is on the major figures, and room has been found for an unusual number of important long poems. Among these are Chaucer's *Prologue* and *Nun's Priest's Tale*, Spenser's *Epithalamion*, Pope's *Rape of the Lock*, Blake's *Auguries of Inno-*

cence, Keats' *Eve of St. Agnes*, Eliot's *Ash Wednesday* and (in this new edition) one of the *Four Quartets*. There is in every section, it is hoped, sufficient material to enable the student to acquire some understanding of the intellectual temper of an age as it is expressed in verse.

The "Statements by Poets and Critics" included in Appendix One have proved so useful that they have been augmented by additional material quoted from the writings of Pope, Dr. Johnson, Coleridge, Arnold, Santayana, Yeats, and Auden. A section on Figurative Language has been added to the critical helps in Appendix Two.

Many of the poems included here will no doubt be familiar to students as well as teachers, for the best poetry is still the best no matter how often it appears in anthologies. To seek for freshness or novelty at the expense of excellence or historical significance is not the object of the compiler of a standard collection. Fortunately, however, English poetry is so rich and varied that one can find in every age little-known poems that are as well worth knowing as many much more widely appreciated classics. Milton's sonnet "I did but prompt the age" speaks to us every bit as pertinently as the fine and famous sonnet on his blindness, and Dryden's *Secular Masque* fits our mood better than the magnificent *Alexander's Feast*. I hope the reader will find a number of fresh and unfamiliar poems to place beside poems that are better known but no better, so that the pleasure of surprise may sometimes supplant the "shock of recognition."

No book such as this would be complete if the poetry of today were neglected. I have, therefore, tried to include a body of modern verse that is not only interesting in itself but representative of the few major poets and characteristic of the intellectual and spiritual temper of our age. The work of Hardy, Housman, the later Yeats, Eliot, and Auden stands in the first rank. The classicism of Robinson and Frost, the apocalyptic romanticism of D. H. Lawrence and Hart Crane, the distinguished craftsmanship of Wallace Stevens, Ezra Pound, and Marianne Moore, the intensely-felt war poetry of Wilfred Owen and its later counterpart in Stephen Spender—all these have been allowed to testify to the variety and richness of twentieth century English and American poetry. Two of the younger poets, Robert Lowell and Dylan Thomas, bring the book to a close and suggest the twofold path—that of metaphysical wit and that of apocalyptic romanticism—which lies ahead.

It remains to thank the friends and authorities, whose assistance and advice, generously given, were of incalculable value to the editor. I wish to thank teachers throughout the United States who have generously offered suggestions. A particular word of thanks must be given to Miss Winifred Lynskey of Purdue University. Miss Lynskey was consulted frequently while the material was being assembled, and her understanding of poetry and of the problems connected with the teaching of poetry gave a special distinction to her counsel. My friends and colleagues, Professor Russell B. Nye, Professor Wallace B. Moffett, and Professor Herbert Weisinger, of the English Department, Michigan State University, assisted me in special problems and have given me much friendly encouragement. So also has Dr. Marshall McLuhan, of St. Michael's College, University of Toronto. I wish to acknowledge also the kindly and unsparing assistance of Mr. Thomas J. B. Walsh of Charles Scribner's Sons, and his staff. To my wife I owe thanks for her aid in matters of mechanical detail and for the taste, intelligence, and severity which made her critical judgments a court of last appeal in this new edition as in the first.

I also thank the various authors and publishers who have given their permission to reprint copyrighted material. Detailed acknowledgment of such permissions is made on the copyright page.

A. J. M. S.

Michigan State University,
East Lansing

CONTENTS

PART ONE

The Middle Ages and Early Renascence

EARLY LYRICS OF UNKNOWN AUTHORSHIP

GEOFFREY CHAUCER (1340?–1400)

ENGLISH & SCOTTISH POPULAR BALLADS

PART TWO

The Elizabethan Age

THOMAS CAMPION (1567–1620)

AUTHOR UNKNOWN

PART THREE

The Seventeenth Century

JOHN DONNE (1572–1631)

BEN JONSON (1572–1637)

JOHN WEBSTER (1580?–1630?)

WILLIAM BROWNE, OF TAVISTOCK (1591?–1643)

ROBERT HERRICK (1591–1674)

GEORGE HERBERT (1593–1633)

JAMES SHIRLEY (1596–1666)

EDMUND WALLER (1606–1687)

JOHN MILTON (1608–1674)

PART FOUR

The Eighteenth Century

THOMAS GRAY (1716–1771)

WILLIAM COLLINS (1721–1759)

CHRISTOPHER SMART (1722–1770)

OLIVER GOLDSMITH (1728–1774)

WILLIAM COWPER (1731–1800)

WILLIAM BLAKE (1757–1827)

PART FIVE

The Romantic Period

PART SIX

The Victorian Age

PART SEVEN

The Modern Period

VACHEL LINDSAY (1879–1931)

WALLACE STEVENS (1879–1955)

WILLIAM CARLOS WILLIAMS (1883–)

D. H. LAWRENCE (1885–1930)

EZRA POUND (1885–)

EDWARD THOMAS (1878–1917)

RUPERT BROOKE (1887–1915)

ROBINSON JEFFERS (1887–)

APPENDIX ONE

POETRY, ITS NATURE AND PURPOSE:
A SERIES OF STATEMENTS BY POETS AND CRITICS

CONTENTS xxxv

APPENDIX TWO

VERSIFICATION AND KINDRED TOPICS

INTRODUCTION

MANY of the poems included in this book are simple and direct, but many of them also are complex and difficult. A body of poetry such as this, which is the accumulated wisdom of a race, deals with the deepest and most serious experiences of life; and in doing so it makes use of the widest variety of the rich and subtle resources of language. We should not expect such poetry to be immediately easy to understand. We should, indeed, be willing to give to the study of a mature poem the same diligent and loving care that a student of music gives to a sonata of Mozart or Beethoven. Yet if the reader will recognize certain fundamental facts about the purpose, nature, and technique of poetry he will avoid some rather widespread misconceptions, and may discover that the reading of poetry is less difficult and more exciting than he imagined. At the risk of seeming dogmatic let me put down briefly what I think it is useful to know if we wish to read a poem accurately and with pleasure.

1. A poem is a highly organized, complex, and unified re-creation of an experience. It is not merely the description of an experience, it is itself an experience; and it awakens in the mind of the receptive reader an experience analogous to the one in the mind of the poet which was ultimately responsible for the creation of the poem. "Experience" here may mean anything—a field of daffodils dancing in the sunshine, indignation on hearing the news of a religious massacre in Switzerland, delight in a marvelous or dramatic action, or the scorn and hatred felt for a vicious fool. If the poem is a vast structure like *Paradise Lost*, the "experience" would be an immense complex of feelings and attitudes embracing the whole world of sensation and ideas: it would be, in other words, "Milton's philosophy."

2. The full meaning of a poem is much more than the bare literal meaning of the sentences of which it is made up, though the complete meaning cannot be rightly apprehended unless the logical, grammatical sense is first correctly understood. Indeed, even in poems in which the logical sense is of minor importance (Shakespeare's *Full fathom five*, for instance) what that sense is needs to be known before it can be dismissed or relegated to its proper place. It is important, therefore, to examine carefully poems in which there is a complex grammatical structure—those of Shakespeare,

Donne, Milton, Browning, and Hopkins, among others—and it is important also to consider the exact meaning (or meanings) of the individual words, especially archaic words or words that have altered their meaning or their connotation.

3. Words are the raw material of poems, and in a poem words are used to their full capacity. The literal meaning plays its necessary part, but the associations and suggestions that surround all but a few of our words are deliberately sought after and made to play a part in modifying and expanding the meaning. Then the sounds of syllables and combinations of syllables * are made to play upon our senses in such a way as to affect our emotions and put us into a state of receptivity in which we experience the meaning of the poem with our feelings.

4. But the appeal of a poem is to the eye of the mind, as well as to the ear. It exercises the imagination, the power to recognize, create, and interpret images. Much of the language of poetry is figurative language; that is, perceptions, feelings, and ideas are presented concretely and in terms of other things. This makes for vividness, intensity, and speed. But the reader must be careful, after perceiving the figure or image for what it is and enjoying it for its own sake, not to interpret literally what is intended figuratively. Figurative language may be fresh, vivid, and exciting, but its interpretation requires tact and intelligence. One of the great practical advantages of reading poetry with attention is that it forces you to rub away the dull mist of habit and see things and the unsuspected relations of things with a new and clearer vision.

5. In a poem experience is usually being criticized and interpreted as well as being expressed. The poet's attitude towards the experience—both emotionally and intellectually—is conveyed by his tone. "Tone" is difficult to define. It is like the expression on a face or the tone of voice which betrays or expresses feeling. It is conveyed by the choice of words and the ordering of phrases, but above all by the rhythm. Often the fullest "meaning" of a poem is the poet's attitude, and the clue to this is the tone.

6. A final thing to remember is that a poem is a whole, a unity, an organized pattern. Its meaning (that is, Itself—cp. "A poem should not mean, but be") can only be apprehended when all the factors that go into it have been taken into account—its plain literal sense, its sounds, images, and figures, its tone and its structure. If

* See Appendix 2, "Sound and Sense."

at first we read it analytically, we must not fail to read it syntheti-cally at last. Our final response to the various aspects of experience which form the unique entity of the poem, that is what the poem is for us. We should try to make it as good as the poet made it. To do so is to read creatively.

From all this it should be clear that the way to approach the reading of a poem is with a mind free from preconceptions and bias. The poetic impulse is one of the most natural in the world. Its fundamental principle is simply this: Excitement finds an inevitable and natural expression in rhythm, and rhythm in turn communicates excitement. This can be easily demonstrated by such elementary poems as *General William Booth Enters into Heaven* or *The Daffodils*, but it is a principle underlying each of Shake-speare's sonnets and every paragraph of *Paradise Lost*. The com-munication of feelings and ideas by means of images and the evalu-ation of experience in terms of emotion—two of the characteristic tricks of the poet—are what we are actually all doing in everyday life. Whatever a human being is capable of feeling or thinking or imagining is the scope of poetry, and to select a corner of experi-ence and impose upon it the order of art is the act of a poet. There are no restrictions on the subjects available for poetry. Virgil wrote a poem on cattle-breeding, Donne on a flea, Herrick on the flounce of a petticoat, Horace, Pope, and Karl Shapiro on theories of criticism, Burns on a louse crawling up a lady's bonnet in church. A subject in itself may be trivial or apparently unpoetic; it is what the poet does with it that turns it into poetry.

When the subject is a great one—the justification of God's ways to man, the struggle between good and evil in the human heart, the longing for immortality—and the poet brings to it a commen-surate mastery of all the resources of language, then we are in the presence of a work of art which, whether large or small, ranks with the glories of the human mind. The study of such a work has a practical value. What that is has been well stated by Shelley: "A man to be greatly good, must imagine intensely and comprehen-sively; he must put himself in the place of another and of many others; the pains and pleasures of his species must become his own. . . . Whatever strengthens and purifies the affections, enlarges the imagination, and adds spirit to sense, is useful."

Never more useful—do we need to add?—than at the present crisis in world affairs, never a more essential part of education than here and now.

PART ONE
Middle Ages and Early Renascence

EARLY LYRICS OF
UNKNOWN AUTHORSHIP

SUMER IS ICUMEN IN

Sumer is icumen in,
   Lhudè sing cuccu;
Groweth sed and bloweth med
   And springth the wudè nu.
     Sing cuccu!
Awè bleteth after lomb,
   Lhouth after calvè cu;
Bulluc sterteth, buckè verteth;
   Murie sing cuccu.
     Cuccu, cuccu,
   Wel singès thu, cuccu,
   Ne swik thu naver nu.
Sing cuccu nu! Sing cuccu!
Sing cuccu! Sing cuccu nu!

ADAM LAY I-BOWNDYN

Adam lay i-bownden,
   bowndyn in a bond,
Fowre thowsand wynter
   thowt he not to long;

And al was for an appil,   5
   an appil that he tok,
As clerkès fyndyn wretyn
   in here Book.

Lhude: loudly. **Med:** meadow. **Nu:** now. **Awe:** ewe. **Lhouth:** lows.
Sterteth: leaps. **Verteth:** breaks wind. **Swik:** stop. **Clerkes:** scholars. **Here:**
their.

Ne hadde the appil takè ben,
 the appil taken ben,   10
Ne hadde never our lady
 a ben hevenè qwen.

Blessid be the tyme
 that appil takè was!
Therefor we mown syngyn   15
 Deo gracias.

QUID PETIS, O FILY?

 "Quid petis, o fily?"
 "Mater dulcissima, ba-ba!"
 "Quid petis, o fili?"
 "Michi plausus oscula da-da!"

So laughyng in lap leyde,
 So pretyly, so pertly,
So passyngly well a-payd,
 Ful softly and full soberly
Unto her swet son she said: 5
  "Quid petis," etc.

The moder full manerly and mekly as a mayd,
Lokyng on her lytill son so laughyng in lap layd,
So pretyly, so partly, so passingly well apayd,
So passyngly wel apayd,   10
  Full softly and full soberly
Unto her son she saide,
Unto her son saide:
  "Quid petis," etc.

I mene this by Mary, our Makers moder of myght, 15
Full lovely lookyng on our Lord, the lanterne of
 lyght,
Thus saying to our Savior; this saw I in my syght.

UBI SUNT QUI ANTE NOS
FUERUNT?

Were beth they that biforen us weren,
Houndes ladden and havekes beren,
  And hadden feld and wode?
    The riche levedies in here bour,
    That wereden gold in here tressour,   5
  With here brighte rode;

Eten and drounken, and maden hem glad;
Here lif was al with gamen y-lad,
  Men kneleden hem biforen;
    They beren hem wel swithe heye;   10
    And in a twincling of an eye
  Here soules weren forloren.

Were is that lawhing and that song,
That trayling and that proude gong,
  Tho havekes and tho houndes?   15
    Al that joye is went away,
    That wele is comen to weylaway
  To manye harde stoundes.

Here paradis they nomen here,
And nou they lyen in helle y-fere;   20
  The fyr hit brennes evere.
    Long is ay, and long is o,
    Long is wy, and long is wo;
  Thennes ne cometh they nevere.

I HAVE A YONG SUSTER

I have a yong suster
  fer beyondyn the se;
Many be the drowryis
  that che sente me.

Ubi sunt, etc.: Where are those who were before us? **Havekes:** hawks.
Levedies: ladies. **Tressour:** headdress. **Hem:** them. **Here:** their. **Lawhing:**
laughing. **Trayling:** traveling. **Gong:** going. **Drowryis:** keepsakes.

Che sente me the cherye   5
    withoutyn ony ston,
And so che dede dowe
    withoutyn ony bon.

Sche sente me the brere
    withoutyn ony rynde,   10
Sche bad me love my lemman
    withoute longyng.

How shuld ony cherye
    be withoute ston?
And how shuld ony dowe   15
    ben withoute bon?

How shuld ony brere
    ben withoute rynde?
How shuld I love my lemman
    without longyng?   20

Quan the cherye was a flour,
    than hadde it non ston;
Quan the dowe was an ey,
    than hadde it non bon.

Quan the brere was onbred,   25
    than hadde it non rynd;
Quan the mayden hayt that che lovit,
    che is without longyng.

I SING OF A MAIDEN

I sing of a maiden
    That is makeles;
King of all kings
    To her son she ches.

He came al so still   5
    There his mother was,
As dew in April
    That falleth on the grass.

Dowe: dove. **Lemman:** sweetheart. **Ey:** egg. **Makeles:** mateless, matchless.
Ches: chose.

He came al so still
 To his mother's bour,   10
As dew in April
 That falleth on the flour.

He came al so still
 There his mother lay,
As dew in April   15
 That falleth on the spray.

Mother and maiden
 Was never none but she;
Well may such a lady
 Goddes mother be.   20

WESTERN WIND, WHEN WILT THOU BLOW

Western wind, when wilt thou blow,
The small rain down can rain?
Christ, if my love were in my arms,
And I in my bed again!

THE BAILEY BEARETH THE BELL AWAY

The maidens came
When I was in my mother's bower,
I had all that I would.
 The bailey beareth the bell away;
 The lily, the rose, the rose I lay.

The silver is white, red is the gold;
The robes they lay in fold.
 The bailey beareth the bell away;
 The lily, the rose, the rose I lay.

And through the glass window shines the sun.
How should I love, and I so young?
 The bailey beareth the bell away;
 The lily, the rose, the rose I lay.

THE FALCON

Lully, lulley! lully, lulley!
The faucon hath borne my make away!

He bare him up, he bare him down,
He bare him into an orchard brown.

In that orchard there was an halle,   5
That was hangèd with purple and pall.

And in that hall there was a bed,
It was hangèd with gold so red.

And in that bed there li'th a knight,
His woundès bleeding day and night.   10

At that bed's foot there li'th a hound,
Licking the blood as it runs down.

By that bed-side kneeleth a may,
And she weepeth both night and day.

And at that bed's head standeth a stone,   15
Corpus Christi written thereon.

Lully, lulley! lully, lulley!
The faucon hath borne my make away.

A LYKE-WAKE DIRGE

This ae nighte, this ae nighte,
    —Every nighte and alle,
Fire and fleet and candle-lighte,
    And Christe receive thy saule.

When thou from hence away art past,   5
    —Every nighte and alle,
To Whinny-muir thou com'st at last:
    And Christe receive thy saule.

Make: mate. **May:** maid. **Lyke-wake:** watch-night.

If ever thou gavest hosen and shoon,
    —*Every nighte and alle,*   10
Sit thee down and put them on:
    And Christe receive thy saule.

If hosen and shoon thou ne'er gav'st nane
    —*Every nighte and alle,*
The whinnes sall prick thee to the bare bane;   15
    And Christe receive thy saule.

From Brig o' Dread when thou may'st pass,
    —*Every nighte and alle,*
To Purgatory fire thou com'st at last;
    And Christe receive thy saule.   20

If ever thou gavest meat or drink,
    —*Every nighte and alle,*
The fire sall never make thee shrink;
    And Christe receive thy saule.

If meat or drink thou ne'er gav'st nane,   25
    —*Every nighte and alle,*
The fire will burn thee to the bare bane;
    And Christe receive thy saule.

This ae nighte, this ae nighte,
    —*Every nighte and alle,*   30
Fire and fleet and candle-lighte,
    And Christe receive thy saule.

JOLLY GOOD ALE AND OLD

I cannot eat but little meat,
    My stomach is not good;
But sure I think that I can drink
    With him that wears a hood.
Though I go bare, take ye no care,   5
    I nothing am a-cold;
I stuff my skin so full within
    Of jolly good ale and old,

Back and side go bare, go bare;
Both foot and hand go cold;   10
But, belly, God send thee good ale enough,
Whether it be new or old.

I love no roast but a nut-brown toast,
    And a crab laid in the fire;
A little bread shall do me stead;   15
    Much bread I not desire.
No frost nor snow, no wind, I trow,
    Can hurt me if I wold;
I am so wrapped and thoroughly lapped
    Of jolly good ale and old.   20
        Back and side go bare, go bare, etc.

And Tib, my wife, that as her life
    Loveth well good ale to seek,
Full oft drinks she till ye may see
    The tears run down her cheek: 25
Then doth she trowl to me the bowl
    Even as a maltworm should,
And saith, "Sweetheart, I took my part
    Of this jolly good ale and old."
        Back and side go bare, go bare, etc.   30

Now let them drink till they nod and wink,
    Even as good fellows should do;
They shall not miss to have the bliss
    Good ale doth bring men to;
And all poor souls that have scoured bowls   35
    Or have them lustily trolled,
God save the lives of them and their wives,
    Whether they be young or old.
        Back and side go bare, go bare;
        Both foot and hand go cold;   40
        But, belly, God send thee good ale enough,
        Whether it be new or old.

Crab: crab apple.

GEOFFREY CHAUCER (1340?–1400)

BALADE

Hyd, Absolon, thy gilte tresses clere;
Ester, ley thou thy meknesse al a-doun;
Hyd, Jonathas, al thy frendly manere;
Penalopee, and Marcia Catoun,
Mak of your wyfhod no comparisoun;   5
Hyde ye your beautes, Isoude and Eleyne,
Alceste is here, that al that may desteyne.

Thy faire bodye, lat hit nat appere,
Lavyne; and thou, Lucresse of Rome toun,
And Polixene, that boghte love so dere,   10
Eek Cleopatre, with al thy passioun,
Hyde ye your trouthe in love and your renoun;
And thou, Tisbe, that hast for love swich peyne:
Alceste is here, that al that may desteyne.

Herro, Dido, Laudomia, alle in-fere,   15
Eek Phyllis, hanging for thy Demophoun,
And Canace, espyed by thy chere,
Ysiphile, betrayed with Jasoun,
Mak of your trouthe in love no bost ne soun;
Nor Ypermistre or Adriane, ne pleyne;   20
Alceste is here, that al that may desteyne.

Hyd: hide. **Gilte:** golden. **Clere:** bright. **Desteyne:** bedim. **Swich:** such.
Peyne: distress. **In-fere:** together. **Eek:** also. **Espyed:** disclosed. **Chere:** appearance. **Bost:** boast. **Soun:** sound. **Pleyne:** lament.

PROLOGUE TO THE
CANTERBURY TALES

Whan that Aprille with his shoures soote
The droghte of March hath perced to the roote,
And bathed every veyne in swich licour
Of which vertu engendred is the flour;
Whan Zephirus eek with his sweete breeth   5

1. **Soote:** sweet   5. **Zephirus:** the west wind
3. **Swich:** such

Inspired hath in every holt and heeth
The tendre croppes, and the yonge sonne
Hath in the Ram his half cours yronne,
And smale foweles maken melodye,
That slepen al the nyght with open eye   10
(So priketh hem nature in hir corages):
Than longen folk to goon on pilgrymages,
And palmeres for to seken straunge strondes,
To ferne halwes, kouthe in sondry londes;
And specially from every shires ende   15
Of Engelond to Caunterbury they wende,
The holy blisful martir for to seke,
That hem hath holpen whan that they were seeke.

Bifel that, in that sesoun on a day,
In Southwerk at the Tabard as I lay   20
Redy to wenden on my pilgrymage
To Caunterbury with ful devout corage,
At nyght was come into that hostelrye
Wel nyne and twenty in a compaignye,
Of sondry folk, by aventure yfalle   25
In felaweshipe, and pilgrymes were they alle,
That toward Caunterbury wolden ryde.
The chambres and the stables weren wyde,
And wel we weren esed atte beste.
And shortly, whan the sonne was to reste,   30
So hadde I spoken with hem everichon,
That I was of hir felaweshipe anon,
And made forward erly for to ryse,
To take oure wey ther as I yow devyse.

But nathelees, whil I have tyme and space,   35
Er that I ferther in this tale pace,
Me thynketh it acordant to resoun
To telle yow al the condicioun
Of ech of hem, so as it semed me,

8. **Ram:** Aries, a sign of the Zodiac
9. **Foweles:** birds
11. **Priketh:** inspires
    Corages: hearts
13. **Palmeres:** pilgrims
    Straunge strondes: foreign
      shores
14. **Ferne halwes:** distant shrines
    Kouthe: well-known

17. **Martir:** St. Thomas à Becket
18. **Seeke:** sick
25. **Aventure:** chance
28. **Wyde:** spacious
29. **Esed:** entertained
34. **Devyse:** tell

And whiche they weren, and of what degree,   40
And eek in what array that they were inne:
And at a Knyght than wol I first bigynne.

A Knyght ther was, and that a worthy man,
That fro the tyme that he first bigan
To riden out, he loved chivalrye   45
Trouthe and honour, fredom and curteisye.
Ful worthy was he in his lordes werre,
And ther-to hadde he riden, no man ferre,
As wel in Cristendom as in hethenesse,
And evere honoured for his worthynesse.   50
   At Alisaundre he was whan it was wonne.
Ful ofte tyme he hadde the bord bigonne
Aboven alle nacions in Pruce.
In Lettow hadde he reysed and in Ruce,
No Cristen man so ofte of his degree.   55
In Gernade at the seege eek hadde he be
Of Algezir, and riden in Belmarye.
At Lyeys was he and at Satalye,
Whan they were wonne; and in the Grete See
At many a noble armee hadde he be.   60
At mortal batailles hadde he been fiftene,
And foghten for oure feith at Tramyssene
In lystes thries, and ay slayn his foo.
This ilke worthy knyght hadde been also
Som-tyme with the lord of Palatye,   65
Agayn another hethen in Turkye.
   And evere-moore he hadde a sovereyn prys;
And though that he were worthy, he was wys,
And of his port as meke as is a mayde.
He nevere yet no vileynye ne sayde   70
In al his lyf un-to no maner wight.
He was a verray, parfit gentil knyght.
   But for to tellen yow of his array,
Hise hors were goode, but he was nat gay.

46. **Fredom:** generosity
47. **Lordes werre:** king's war
48. **Ferre:** farther
51. **Alesaundre:** Alexandria
52. **The bord bigonne:** presided at the head of the table
53. **Pruce:** Prussia
54. **Reysed:** campaigned
55. **Ruce:** Russia
59. **Grete Sea:** the Mediterranean
63. **Lystes:** lists
64. **Ilke:** same
67. **Prys:** reputation
72. **Verray:** true

Of fustian he wered a gypoun 75
Al bismotered with his habergeoun,
For he was late ycome from his viage,
And wente for to doon his pilgrymage.

With hym ther was his sone, a yong Squyer,
A lovere and a lusty bachelor, 80
With lokkes crulle, as they were leyd in presse.
Of twenty yeer of age he was, I gesse.
  Of his stature he was of evene lengthe,
And wonderly delyvere, and of greet strengthe.
And he hadde been som-tyme in chivachye 85
In Flaundres, in Artoys, and Picardye,
And born hym wel, as of so litel space,
In hope to stonden in his lady grace.
  Embrouded was he, as it were a meede
Al ful of fresshe floures, white and reede. 90
Syngynge he was, or floytynge, al the day;
He was as fressh as is the monthe of May.
Short was his gowne, with sleves longe and wyde.
Wel koude he sitte on hors and faire ryde.
He koude songes make and wel endite, 95
Juste and eek daunce, and wel purtreye and write.
So hoote he lovede, that by nyghtertale
He slepte namoore than dooth a nyghtyngale.
  Curteys he was, lowely, and servysable,
And carf biforn his fader at the table. 100

A Yeman hadde he and servantz namo
At that tyme, for hym liste ryde so;
And he was clad in coote and hood of grene.
A sheef of pecok arwes bright and kene
Under his belt he bar ful thriftily, 105
(Wel koude he dresse his takel yemanly:
His arwes drouped noght with fetheres lowe),
And in his hand he bar a myghty bowe.

75. **Fustian:** coarse cloth
   Gypoun: vest
76. **Bismotered:** stained
   Habergeoun: coat of mail
81. **Crulle:** curled
84. **Delyvere:** agile
85. **Chivachye:** cavalry raids

89. **Embrouded:** embroidered
91. **Floytynge:** playing the flute
96. **Juste:** joust
97. **By nyghtertale:** at night
102. **Hym liste ryde so:** he chooses to ride so
103. **Arwes:** arrows

A not heed hadde he, with a broun visage.
Of wodecraft wel koude he al the usage. 110
Upon his arm he bar a gay bracer,
And by his syde a swerd and a bokeler,
And on that oother syde a gay daggere,
Harneysed wel and sharp as poynt of spere,
A Cristofre on his brest of silver shene. 115
An horn he bar, the bawdryk was of grene;
A forster was he, soothly, as I gesse.

Ther was also a nonne, a Prioresse,
That of hir smylyng was ful symple and coy;
Hir gretteste ooth was but by Seint Loy; 120
And she was cleped Madame Eglentyne.
Ful wel she soong the servyce dyvyne,
Entuned in hir nose ful semely,
And Frenssh she spak ful faire and fetisly,
After the scole of Stratford-atte-Bowe, 125
For Frenssh of Parys was to hire unknowe.
At mete wel ytaught was she with alle:
She let no morsel from hir lippes falle,
Ne wette hir fyngres in hir sauce depe.
Wel koude she carie a morsel and wel kepe 130
That no drope ne fille up-on hir brest.
In curteisie was set ful muchel hir lest.
Hir over lippe wyped she so clene
That in hir coppe ther was no ferthyng sene
Of grece, whan she dronken hadde hir draughte. 135
Ful semely after hir mete she raughte.
And sikerly she was of greet desport,
And ful plesaunt, and amyable of port,
And peyned hire to countrefete cheere
Of court, and to been estatlich of manere, 140

109. **Not heed:** a head brown and grizzled like a nut
114. **Harneysed:** mounted
115. **A Cristofre:** an image of the patron saint of archers
116. **Bawdryk:** belt
117. **Forster:** forester, game-keeper
120. **Seint Loy:** St. Louis
121. **Cleped:** called
124. **Fetisley:** elegantly
132. **In curteisie . . . hir list:** she set great store by good manners
134. **Ferthyng:** particle
136. **Raughte:** reached
137. **Sikerly:** certainly
139. **Peyned . . . court:** she took pains to imitate courtly manners
140. **Estatlich:** stately

And to been holden digne of reverence.
But, for to speken of hir conscience,
She was so charitable and so pitous
She wolde wepe, if that she sawe a mous
Caught in a trappe, if it were deed or bledde.   145
Of smale houndes hadde she, that she fedde
With rosted flessh, or mylk and wastel breed.
But soore wepte she if oon of hem were deed,
Or if men smoot it with a yerde smerte;
And al was conscience and tendre herte.   150
Ful semely hir wympel pynched was;
Hir nose tretys, hir eyen greye as glas,
Hir mouth ful smal, and ther-to softe and reed;
But sikerly she hadde a fair forheed:
It was almoost a spanne brood, I trowe;   155
For, hardily, she was nat undergrowe.
Ful fetys was hir cloke, as I was war.
Of smal coral aboute hir arm she bar
A peyre of bedes, gauded al with grene,
And there-on heng a brooch of gold ful shene,   160
On which ther was first writen a crowned A,
And after *Amor vincit omnia.*

Another Nonne with hire hadde she,
That was hir chapeleyne, and preestes thre.

A Monk ther was, a fair for the maistrye,   165
An outridere, that lovede venerye,
A manly man, to been an abbot able.
Ful many a deyntee hors hadde he in stable,
And whanne he rood, men myghte his brydel heere
Gynglen in a whistlynge wynd as cleere,   170
And eek as loude, as dooth the chapel belle,
Ther-as this lord was kepere of the celle.
The reule of Seint Maure or of Seint Beneit,

---

147. **Wastel bread:** fine white bread
149. **Yerde:** stick
       Smerte: smartly
151. **Pynched:** pleated
152. **Tretys:** shapely
156. **Hardily:** certainly

162. **Amor . . . omnia:** Love conquers all
165. **A fair for the maistrye:** a very fine one
166. **Outridere:** an inspector of monastic property
       Venerye: hunting

By cause that it was old and somdel streit,—
This ilke Monk leet olde thynges pace,   175
And heeld after the newe world the space.
He yaf nat of that text a pulled hen,
That seith that hunters been nat holy men,
Ne that a monk whan he is recchelees,
Is likned til a fissh that is waterlees—   180
This is to seyn, a monk out of his cloystre;
But thilke text heeld he nat worth an oystre,
And I seyde his opinioun was good.
What sholde he studie and make hym-selven wood,
Upon a book in cloystre alwey to poure,   185
Or swynken with his handes, and laboure,
As Austyn bit? How shal the world be served?
Lat Austyn have his swynk to hym reserved!
Therfore he was a prikasour aright;
Grehoundes he hadde, as swift as fowel in flight;   190
Of prikyng and of huntyng for the hare
Was al his lust, for no cost wolde he spare.
   I seigh his sleves ypurfiled at the hond
With grys, and that the fyneste of a lond;
And, for to festne his hood under his chyn,   195
He hadde of gold wroght a ful curious pyn;
A love knotte in the gretter ende ther was.
His heed was balled, that shoon as any glas,
And eek his face, as he hadde been enoynt.
He was a lord ful fat and in good poynt;   200
Hise eyen stepe, and rollynge in his heed,
That stemed as a forneys of a leed;
His bootes souple, his hors in greet estat.
   Now certeynly he was a fair prelat;
He was nat pale as a forpyned goost.   205
A fat swan loved he best of any roost.
His palfrey was as broun as is a berye.

174. **Somdel streit:** somewhat strict
176. **Space:** meantime
184. **Wood:** mad
186. **Swynken:** work
187. **Austyn:** St. Augustine
     Bit: bid
189. **Prikasour:** an enthusiastic horseman
192. **Lust:** pleasure, desire
193. **Seigh:** saw
     Ypurfiled: trimmed
194. **Grys:** gray fur
200. **Poynt:** condition
201. **Stepe:** deep set
202. **Stemed:** shone
     Forneys of a leed: fire under a cauldron

A Frere ther was, a wantowne and a merye,
A lymytour, a ful solempne man.
In alle the ordres foure is noon that kan   210
So muche of daliaunce and fair langage.
He hadde maad ful many a mariage
Of yonge wommen at his owene cost.
  Un-to his ordre he was a noble post.
Ful wel biloved and famulier was he   215
With frankeleyns over al in his contree,
And with worthy wommen of the toun;
For he hadde power of confessioun,
As seyde hym-self, moore than a curat,
For of his ordre he was licenciat.   220
Ful swetely herde he confessioun,
And pleasaunt was his absolucioun;
He was an esy man to yeve penaunce,
Ther-as he wiste to have a good pitaunce.
For un-to a poure ordre for to yive   225
Is signe that a man is wel yshryve;
For if he yaf, he dorste make avaunt,
He wiste that a man was repentaunt;
For many a man so hard is of his herte,
He may not wepe, al-thogh hym soore smerte.   230
Ther-fore in stede of wepynge and preyeres,
Men moote yeve silver to the poure freres.
  His typet was ay farsed ful of knyves
And pynnes, for to yeven faire wyves.
And certeynly he hadde a murye note;   235
Wel koude he synge and pleyen on a rote;
Of yeddynges he bar outrely the prys.
His nekke whit was as the flour de lys;
Ther-to he strong was as a champioun.
  He knew the tavernes wel in every toun,   240
And every hostiler and tappestere
Bet than a lazar or a beggestere;

209. **Lymytour:** a friar licensed to   227. **Avaunt:** boast
  beg in a limited territory   233. **Typet:** cape
210. **Kan:** knew   **Ay farsed:** always stuffed
216. **Frankeleyns:** rich country   236. **Rote:** a stringed instrument
  squires   237. **Yeddynges:** ballads
224. **Ther-as:** where   241. **Tappestere:** barmaid
  Wiste: knew   242. **Lazar:** leper
  Pitaunce: gift   **Beggestere:** beggar woman

For un-to swich a worthy man as he
Accorded nat, as by his facultee,
To have with sike lazars aqueyntaunce.   245
It is nat honeste, it may nat avaunce
For to deelen with no swich poraille,
But al with riche and selleres of vitaille.
And over-al, ther as profit sholde arise,
Curteys he was and lowely of servyse.   250
Ther was no man no wher so vertuous.
He was the beste beggere in his hous,
For thogh a wydwe hadde noght a sho,
So plesant was his *In principio*,
Yet wolde he have a ferthyng, er he wente.   255
His purchas was wel bettre than his rente.
And rage he koude, as it were right a whelpe.
   In lovedayes ther koude he muchel helpe:
For ther he was nat lyk a cloystrer
With a threadbare cope, as is a poure scoler,   260
But he was lyk a maister or a pope.
Of double worstede was his semycope,
That rounded as a belle out of the presse.
   Somewhat he lipsed, for his wantownesse,
To make his Englissh sweete up-on his tonge;   265
And in his harpyng, whan that he hadde songe,
Hise eyen twynkled in his heed aright,
As doon the sterres in the frosty nyght.
This worthy lymytour was cleped Huberd.

   A Marchant was ther with a forked berd,   270
In motlee, and hye on hors he sat,
Up-on his heed a Flaundryssh bevere hat,
His bootes clasped faire and fetisly.
   Hise resons he spak ful solempnely,
Sownynge alwey th' encrees of his wynnyng.   275
He wolde the see were kept for any thyng

246. **Honeste:** respectable
247. **Poraille:** poor trash
248. **Vitaille:** victuals
254. **In principio:** In the beginning, first words of St. John's gospel
256. **Purchas:** graft
258. **Lovedays:** days set aside for the settlement of disputes by law

262. **Semycope:** short cape
264. **Lipsed:** lisped
274. **Resons:** opinions
275. **Sownynge:** relating to
276. **Wolde:** wished
     See: sea

Bitwixe Middelburgh and Orewelle.
Wel koude he in eschaunge sheeldes selle.
　　This worthy man ful wel his wit bisette:
Ther wiste no wight that he was in dette,　　　　　280
So estatly was he of his governaunce,
With his bargaynes and with his chevysaunce.
　　For sothe he was a worthy man with alle,
But, sooth to seyn, I noot how men hym calle.

　　A Clerk ther was of Oxenford also,　　　　　285
That un-to logyk hadde longe ygo.
　　As leene was his hors as is a rake,
And he was nat right fat, I undertake,
But looked holwe, and ther-to sobrely.
Ful thredbare was his overeste courtepy;　　　　　290
For he hadde geten hym yet no benefice,
Ne was so worldly for to have office.
For hym was levere have at his beddes heed
Twenty bookes, clad in blak or reed,
Of Aristotle and his philosophie,　　　　　295
Than robes riche, or fithele, or gay sautrie.
　　But al be that he was a philosophre,
Yet hadde he but litel gold in cofre;
But al that he myghte of his frendes hente,
On bookes and on lernynge he it spente,　　　　　300
And bisily gan for the soules preye
Of hem that yaf hym wher-with to scoleye.
　　Of studie took he moost cure and moost heede.
Noght oo word spak he moore than was neede,
And that was seid in forme and reverence,　　　　　305
And short and quyk and ful of heigh sentence.
Sownynge in moral vertu was his speche,
And gladly wolde he lerne and gladly teche.

　　A Sergeant of the Lawe, war and wys,
That often hadde been at the Parvys,　　　　　310
Ther was also, ful riche of excellence.

---

278. Sheeldes: French currency
282. Chevysaunce: business dealings, rackets
284. Noot: know not
286. Ygo: begun
290. Courtepy: short coat

296. Fithele or gay sautrie: fiddling or merry music
299. Hente: get
302. Scoleye: study
310. Parvys: convention of lawyers

Discreet he was and of greet reverence—
He seemed swich, hise wordes weren so wyse.
 Justice he was ful often in assise,
By patente and by pleyn commissioun.   315
For his science and for his heigh renoun,
Of fees and robes hadde he many oon.
So greet a purchasour was nowher noon;
Al was fee symple to hym in effect,
His purchasyng myghte nat been infect.   320
 Nowher so bisy a man as he ther nas,
And yet he semed bisier than he was.
 In termes hadde he caas and doomes alle,
That from the tyme of Kyng William were falle.
Ther-to he koude endite, and make a thyng,   325
Ther koude no wight pynchen at his writyng;
And every statut koude he pleyn by roote.
 He rood but hoomly in a medlee coote,
Girt with a ceynt of silk, with barres smale;
Of his array telle I no lenger tale.   330

A Frankeleyn was in his compaignye;
Whit was his berd as is the dayesye;
Of his complexioun he was sangwyn.
Wel loved he by the morwe a sop in wyn.
To lyven in delyt was evere his wone,   335
For he was Epicurus owene sone,
That heeld opynyoun that pleyn delit
Was verray felicitee parfit.
 An housholdere, and that a greet, was he;
Seint Julyan he was in his contree.   340
His breed, his ale, was alweys after oon;
A bettre envyned man was nevere noon.
Withoute bake mete was nevere his hous,
Of fissh and flessh, and that so plentevous,
It snewed in his hous of mete and drynke.   345

318. **Purchasour:** buyer of land
319. **Fee symple:** absolute possession
320. **Infect:** defective in title
323. **Caas and doomes:** cases and judgments
325. **Thyng:** legal document
329. **Ceynt:** girdle

335. **Wone:** custom
341. **After oon:** up to the same high standard
342. **Envyned:** well stocked with wine
345. **Snewed:** snowed

Of alle deyntees that men koude thynke
After the sondry sesons of the yeer,
So chaunged he his mete and his soper.
Ful many a fat partrich hadde he in muwe,
And many a breem and many a luce in stuwe.   350
Wo was his cook, but if his sauce were
Poynaunt and sharp, and redy al his geere.
His table dormaunt in his halle alway
Stood redy-covered al the longe day.
 At sessions ther he was lord and sire;   355
Ful ofte tyme he was knyght of the shire.
An anlaas and a gipser al of silk
Heeng at his girdel, whit as morne mylk.
A shirreve hadde he been, and a countour;
Was nowher swich a worthy vavasour.   360

 An Haberdasshere and a Carpenter,
A Webbe, a Dyere, and a Tapycer—
And they were clothed alle in oo lyveree
Of a solempne and a greet fraternytee.
Ful fressh and newe hir geere apiked was;   365
Hir knyves were chaped noght with bras,
But al with silver; wroght ful clene and wel
Hir girdles and hir pouches everydel.
Wel semed ech of hem a fair burgeys
To sitten in a yeldehalle on a deys.   370
Everych for the wisdom that he kan,
Was shaply for to been an alderman.
For catel hadde they ynogh and rente,
And eek hir wyves wolde it wel assente;
And elles certeyn were they to blame: 375
It is ful fair to been ycleped madame,
And goon to vigilies al bifore,
And have a mantel roialliche ybore.

349. **Muwe:** cage or pen
350. **Stuwe:** fishpond
353. **Dormaunt:** fixed
357. **Anlaas:** dagger
 Gipser: purse
359. **Shirreve:** sheriff
 Countour: accountant
360. **Vavasour:** country squire

362. **Webbe:** weaver
 Tapycer: tapestry maker
365. **Apiked:** adorned
366. **Hir:** their
370. **Yeldehalle:** guildhall, town hall
 Deys: dais
373. **Catel:** chattels, property
376. **Ycleped:** called
377. **Vigilies:** watch night services

A Cook they hadde with hem for the nones,
To boille the chiknes with the marybones,   380
And poudre marchaunt tart, and galyngale.
Wel koude he knowe a draughte of Londoun ale.
He koude rooste, and sethe, and broille, and frye,
Maken mortreux, and wel bake a pye.
But greet harm was it, as it thoughte me,   385
That on his shyne a mormal hadde he,
For blankmanger that made he with the beste.

A Shipman was ther, wonyng fer by weste:
For aught I woot, he was of Dertemouthe.
He rood upon a rouncy, as he kouthe,   390
In a gowne of faldyng to the knee.
A daggere hangynge on a laas hadde he
Aboute his nekke, under his arm adoun.
The hoote somer had maad his hewe al broun.
And certeynly he was a good felawe;   395
Ful many a draughte of wyn hadde he drawe
Fro Burdeuxward, whil that the chapman sleep.
Of nyce conscience took he no keep.
If that he faught, and had the hyer hond,
By water he sente hem hoom to every lond.   400
But of his craft to rekene wel his tydes,
His stremes and his daungers hym bisydes,
His herberwe, and his moone, his lodemenage,
Ther nas noon swich from Hulle to Cartage.
Hardy he was, and wys to undertake;   405
With many a tempest hadde his berd been shake.
He knew alle the havenes, as they were,
Fro Gootland to the cape of Fynystere,
And every cryke in Britaigne and in Spayne.
His barge ycleped was the Mawdelayne.   410

With us ther was a Doctour of Phisik;
In al this world ne was ther noon hym lyk,

---

381 **Poudre marchaunt:** a tart fla-
     voring powder
381. **Galyngale:** a spice
384. **Mortreux:** stew
386. **Mormal:** canker
388. **Wonyng:** dwelling
389. **Woot:** know

390. **Rouncy:** nag
     As he kouthe: as best he could
391. **Faldyng:** coarse wool
392. **Laas:** cord
400. **By water . . . hoom:** made them
     walk the plank
403. **Lodemenage:** pilot's craft

To speke of phisik and of surgerye,
For he was grounded in astronomye.
He kepte his pacient a ful greet deel   415
In houres by his magik natureel.
Wel koude he fortunen the ascendent
Of hise ymages for his pacient.
He knew the cause of every maladye,
Were it of hoot, or coold, or moyste, or drye,   420
And where engendred, and of what humour.
He was a verray, parfit practisour.
    The cause yknowe, and of his harm the roote,
Anon he yaf the sike man his boote.
Ful redy hadde he hise apothecaries,   425
To sende hym drogges and his letuaries,
For ech of hem made oother for to wynne:
Hir frendshipe nas nat newe to begynne.
    Wel knew he the olde Esculapius,
And Deïscorides, and eek Rusus,   430
Old Ypocras, Haly, and Galyen,
Serapion, Razis, and Avycen,
Averrois, Damascien, and Constantyn,
Bernard, and Gatesden, and Gilbertyn.
    Of his diete mesurable was he,   435
For it was of no superfluitee,
But of greet norissynge and digestible.
His studie was but litel on the Bible.
    In sangwyn and in pers he clad was al,
Lyned with taffata and with sendal;   440
And yet he was but esy of dispence;
He kepte that he wan in pestilence.
For gold in phisik is a cordial,
Therfore he loved gold in special.

    A good Wyf was ther of biside Bathe,   445
But she was som del deef, and that was scathe.
    Of clooth makyng she hadde swich an haunt,
She passed hem of Ypres and of Gaunt.

416. **Magik natureel:** astrology
417. **Fortunen the ascendent:** cast
    the horoscope
424. **Boote:** help
426. **Letuaries:** remedies

439. **Sangwyn:** red
    Pers: blue-gray
440. **Sendel:** thin silk
445. **Biside:** just outside
446. **Scathe:** a pity
447. **Haunt:** knack

In al the parisshe wyf ne was ther noon
That to the offrynge bifore hire sholde goon;   450
And if ther dide, certeyn so wrooth was she,
That she was out of alle charitee.
Hir coverchiefs ful fyne were of ground;
I dorste swere they weyeden ten pound
That on a Sonday weren up-on hir heed.
Hir hosen weren of fyn scarlet reed,
Ful streite yteyd, and shoes ful moyste and newe.
Boold was hir face, and fair, and reed of hewe.
    She was a worthy womman al hir lyve;
Housbondes at chirche dore she hadde fyve,   460
With-outen oother compaignye in youthe,—
But ther-of nedeth nat to speke as nouthe.
    And thries hadde she been at Jerusalem;
She hadde passed many a straunge strem;
At Rome she hadde been, and at Boloyne,   465
In Galice at Seint Jame, and at Coloyne.
She koude muche of wandrynge by the weye.
Gat tothed was she, soothly for to seye.
    Upon an amblere esily she sat,
Ywympled wel, and on hir heed an hat   470
As brood as is a bokeler or a targe;
A foot mantel aboute hir hipes large,
And on hir feet a peyre of spores sharpe.
In felawshipe wel koude she laughe and carpe.
Of remedies of love she knew par chaunce,   475
For she koude of that art the olde daunce.

    A good man was ther of religioun,
And was a poure Persoun of a toun,
But riche he was of holy thoght and werk.
He was also a lerned man, a clerk,   480
That Cristes gospel trewely wolde preche;
His parisshens devoutly wolde he teche.
Benygne he was, and wonder diligent,
And in adversitee ful pacient,
And swich he was preved ofte sithes.   485

462. **As nouthe:** at present   485. **Preved:** proved
474. **Carpe:** talk   **Ofte sithes:** many times
476. **The old daunce:** she knew all
       the tricks of the game

Ful looth were hym to cursen for his tithes,
But rather wolde he yeven, out of doute,
Un-to his poure parisshens aboute
Of his offrynge and eek of his substaunce.
He koude in litel thyng have suffisaunce.   490
Wyd was his parisshe, and houses fer asonder,
But he ne lafte nat, for reyn ne thonder,
In siknesse nor in meschief, to visite
The ferreste in his parisshe, muche and lite,
Up-on his feet, and in his hond a staf.   495
This noble ensample to his sheep he yaf,
That first he wroghte, and afterward he taughte.
Out of the gospel he tho wordes caughte,
And this figure he added eek ther-to,
That if gold ruste, what sholde iren do?   500
For if a preest be foule, on whom we truste,
No wonder is a lewed man to ruste;
And shame it is, if a preest take keep,
A shiten shepherde and a clene sheep.
Wel oghte a preest ensample for to yive,   505
By his clennesse, how that his sheep sholde lyve.
   He sette nat his benefice to hyre,
And leet his sheep encombred in the myre,
And ran to Londoun, un-to Seint Poules,
To seken hym a chauntrye for soules,   510
Or with a bretherhede to been withholde;
But dwelte at hoom, and kepte wel his folde,
So that the wolf ne made it nat myscarye;
He was a shepherde and noght a mercenarye.
   And thogh he hooly were and vertuous,   515
He was noght to synful men despitous,
Ne of his speche daungerous ne digne,
But in his techyng discreet and benigne.
To drawen folk to hevene by fairnesse,
By good ensample, this was his bisynesse,   520
But it were any persone obstinat,

486. **Cursen:** excommunicate
487. **Yeven:** give
494. **Muche and lite:** high and low
502. **Lewed:** ignorant
508. **Leet:** left
510. **A chauntrye for soules:** an en- dowment for singing requiem masses
511. **Bretherhede:** a guild
   Withholde: hired as chaplain
517. **Daungerous ne digne:** stand- offish nor disdainful

What so he were, of heigh or lowe estat,
Hym wolde he snybben sharply for the nonys.
   A bettre preest I trowe that nowher noon ys.
He wayted after no pompe and reverence,   525
Ne maked hym a spiced conscience,
But Cristes loore, and his apostles twelve,
He taughte, but first he folwed it hym-selve.

   With him ther was a Plowman, was his brother,
That hadde y-lad of dong ful many a fother.   530
A trewe swynkere and a good was he,
Lyvynge in pees and parfit charitee.
God loved he best with al his hoole herte
At alle tymes, though hym gamed or smerte,
And thanne his neighebore right as hym-selve.   535
He wolde thresshe, and ther-to dyke and delve,
For Cristes sake, for every poure wight,
With-outen hire, if it lay in his myght.
His tithes payde he ful faire and wel,
Bothe of his propre swynk and his catel.   540
In a tabard he rood upon a mere.

   Ther was also a Reve, and a Millere,
A Somnour, and a Pardoner, also,
A Maunciple, and my-self: ther were namo.

   The Miller was a stout carl for the nones,   545
Ful big he was of brawn, and eek of bones;
That proved wel, for over-al ther he cam,
At wrastlynge he wolde have alwey the ram.
He was short sholdred, brood, a thikke knarre;
Ther was no dore that he nolde heve of harre,   550

530. **Y-lad . . . fother:** had drawn many a load of manure
531. **Swynkere:** worker
534. **Gamed or smerte:** pleased or pained
536. **Dyke:** dig a ditch
541. **Tabard:** plain loose coat
542. **Reve:** manager of a country estate
543. **Somnour:** a process server for an ecclesiastical court

Pardoner: a seller of Papal indulgences
544. **Maunciple:** purchasing agent for a college or an inn of court
545. **Stout . . . nones:** an exceedingly strong fellow
549. **A thikke knarre:** a knotted, thickset churl
550. **Heve of harre:** heave off its hinges

Or breke it at a rennyng, with his heed.
His berd as any sowe or fox was reed,
And ther-to brood as though it were a spade.
Upon the cop right of his nose he hade
A werte, and ther-on stood a tuft of herys,   555
Reed as the bristles of a sowes erys;
His nosethirles blake were and wyde.
A swerd and a bokeler bar he by his syde.
    His mouth as greet was as a greet fourneys.
He was a jangler and a goliardeys,   560
And that was moost of synne and harlotries.
    Wel koude he stelen corn and tollen thries;
And yet he hadde a thombe of gold, pardee.
    A whit cote and a blew hood wered hee.
A baggepipe wel koude he blowe and sowne,   565
And therwithal he broghte us out of towne.

    A gentil Maunciple was ther of a temple,
Of which achatours myghte take exemple
For to be wys in byynge of vitaille;
For wheither that he payde or took by taille,   570
Algate he wayted so in his achaat,
That he was ay biforn and in good staat.
Now is nat that of God a ful fair grace
That swich a lewed mannes wit shal pace
The wisdom of an heep of lerned men?   575
Of maistres hadde he mo than thries ten,
That weren of lawe expert and curious,
Of whiche ther were a dozeyne in that hous
Worthy to been stywardes of rente and lond
Of any lord that is in Engelond,   580
To make hym lyve by his propre good,
In honour detteles, but if he were wood,

---

554. **Cop:** top
555. **Werte:** wart
556. **Erys:** ears
557. **Nosethirles:** nostrils
560. **Jangler:** babbler
    Goliardeys: rough jester
562. **Stelen . . . thries:** steal corn and
    charge a triple toll for grind-
    ing it

563. **He . . . gold:** he was honest—
    for a miller
568. **Achatours:** buyers
570. **By taille:** on credit
571. **Algate . . . achaat:** in every
    way he watched so in his
    buying
577. **Curious:** skillful
582. **Wood:** mad

Or lyve as scarsly as hym list desire;
And able for to helpen al a shire
In any caas that myghte falle or happe;   585
And yet this Maunciple sette hir aller cappe.

The Reve was a sclendre, colerik man.
His berd was shave as neigh as ever he kan;
His heer was by his erys ful round yshorn;
His top was dokked lyk a preest byforn.   590
Ful longe were his legges and ful lene,
Ylik a staf ther was no calf ysene.
    Wel koude he kepe a gerner and a bynne;
Ther was noon auditour koude on hym wynne.
Wel wiste he by the droghte and by the reyn   595
The yeldynge of his seed and of his greyn.
His lordes sheep, his neet, his dayerye
His swyn, his hors, his stoor, and his pultrye,
Was hoolly in this Reves governynge,
And by his covenant yaf the rekenynge,   600
Syn that his lord was twenty yeer of age.
Ther koude no man brynge hym in arrerage.
Ther nas baillif, ne hierde, ne oother hyne,
That he ne knew his sleighte and his covyne:
They were adrad of hym as of the deeth.   605
    His wonyng was ful faire upon an heeth,
With grene trees shadwed was his place.
He koude bettre than his lord purchace.
Ful riche he was astored pryvely:
His lord wel koude he plesen subtilly,   610
To yeve and lene hym of his owene good,
And have a thank, and yet a coote and hood.
    In youthe he hadde lerned a good myster:
He was a wel good wrighte, a carpenter.
    This Reve sat up-on a full good stot,   615
That was al pomely grey and highte Scot.

583. **Scarsly as hym list:** economi-
    cally as it pleases him to
586. **Sette . . . cappe:** made fools of
    all of them
593. **Gerner:** granary
597. **Neet:** cattle
598. **Stoor:** stock
601. **Syn:** since

603. **Hierde:** herdsman
    Hyne: farm laborer
604. **Covyne:** deceitfulness
611. **Lene:** lend
613. **Myster:** craft
615. **Stot:** stallion
616. **Pomely:** dappled
    Highte: was called

A long surcote of pers up-on he hade,
And by his syde he baar a rusty blade.
Of Northfolk was this Reve of which I telle,
Biside a toun men clepen Baldeswelle.   620
Tukked he was as is a frere aboute,
And evere he rood the hyndreste of oure route.

    A Somnour was ther with us in that place,
That hadde a fyr-reed cherubynnes face,
For saucefleem he was, with eyen narwe.   625
As hoot he was and lecherous as a sparwe;
With scaled browes blake, and piled berd;
Of his visage children were aferd.
Ther nas quyk silver, lytarge, ne brymstoon,
Boras, ceruce, ne oille of tartre noon,   630
Ne oynement that wolde clense and byte,
That hym myghte helpen of his whelkes white,
Nor of the knobbes sittynge on his chekes.
    Wel loved he garlek, oynons, and eek lekes,
And for to drynke strong wyn, reed as blood.   635
Thanne wolde he speke and crye as he were wood;
And whan that he wel dronken hadde the wyn,
Thanne wolde he speke no word but Latyn.
A fewe termes hadde he, two or thre,
That he had lerned out of som decre—   640
No wonder is: he herde it al the day—
And eek ye knowen wel how that a jay
Kan clepen "Watte" as wel as kan the pope.
But who so koude in oother thyng hym grope,
Thanne hadde he spent al his philosophie;   645
Ay "Questio quid juris" wolde he crie.
    He was a gentil harlot and a kynde;
A bettre felawe sholde men noght fynde.
He wolde suffre for a quart of wyn
A good felawe to have his concubyn   650
A twelf monthe, and excuse hym atte fulle.

---

624. **Fyr . . . face:** fire-red face of a
    cherub
625. **Saucefleem:** afflicted with a dis-
    ease
627. **Piled berd:** thin beard
632. **Whelkes:** pimples

644. **Grope:** test
646. **"Questio . . . juris":** the ques-
    tion is what part of the law
    is involved
647. **Harlot:** rascal

Ful pryvely a fynch eek koude he pulle.
And if he foond owher a good felawe,
He wolde techen hym to have noon awe,
In swich caas, of the ercedekenes curs,   655
But if a mannes soule were in his purs;
For in his purs he sholde ypunysshed be.
"Purs is the ercedekenes helle," seyde he.
But wel I woot he lyed right in dede;
Of cursyng oghte ech gilty man hym drede,   660
For curs wol slee right as assoillyng savith,
And also war hym of a *Significavit!*
    In daunger hadde he at his owene gyse
The yonge gerles of the diocise,
And knew hir counseil, and was al hir reed.   665
    A gerland hadde he set up-on his heed
As greet as it were for an ale stake;
A bokeler hadde he maad hym of a cake.

    With hym ther rood a gentil Pardoner
Of Rouncival, his freend and his comper,   670
That streight was comen fro the court of Rome.
Ful loude he soong, "Com hider, love, to me!"
This Somnour bar to hym a stif burdoun,
Was nevere trompe of half so greet a soun.
    This Pardoner hadde heer as yelow as wex,   675
But smothe it heeng as dooth a strike of flex;
By ounces henge his lokkes that he hadde,
And ther-with he his shuldres overspradde;
But thynne it lay, by colpons oon and oon;
But hood, for jolitee, wered he noon,   680
For it was trussed up in his walet.
Hym thoughte he rood al of the newe jet;

652. **Fynch . . . pulle:** seduce
653. **Owher:** anywhere
658. **Ercedekenes:** archdeacon's
661. **Assoiling savith:** absolution
    saves
662. **War . . . Significavit!:** Let him
    beware of a writ of arrest!
663. **Daunger:** control
    Gyse: way
664. **Yonge gerles:** young of both
    sexes

665. **Reed:** adviser
666. **Gerland:** wreath
667. **Ale stake:** sign of an alehouse
670. **Comper:** comrade
673. **Bar . . . burdoun:** accompanied
    him with a strong bass
676. **Strike:** bunch
677. **Ounces:** thin strands
679. **Colpons:** shreds
682. **Jet:** fashion

Dischevelee, save his cappe, he rood al bare.
Swiche glarynge eyen hadde he as an hare.
    A vernycle hadde he sowed up-on his cappe.   685
His walet biforn hym in his lappe,
Bret-ful of pardoun, comen from Rome al hoot.
    A voys he hadde as smal as hath a goot.
No berd hadde he, ne nevere sholde have,
As smothe it was as it were late yshave: 690
I trowe he were a geldyng or a mare.
    But of his craft, fro Berwyk into Ware,
Ne was ther swich another pardoner.
For in his male he hadde a pilwe beer,
Which that he seyde was Our Lady veyl;   695
He seyde he hadde a gobet of the seyl
That Seint Peter hadde, whan that he wente
Up-on the see, til Jesu Crist hym hente.
He hadde a croys of latoun ful of stones,
And in a glas he hadde pigges bones.   700
But with thise relikes, whan that he fond
A poure persoun dwellyng up-on lond,
Up-on a day he gat hym moore moneye
Than that the persoun gat in monthes tweye.
And thus, with feyned flaterye and japes,   705
He made the persoun and the peple his apes.
    But trewely to tellen, atte laste,
He was in chirche a noble ecclesiaste.
Wel koude he rede a lessoun or a storie,
But alderbest he song an offertorie;   710
For wel he wiste, whan that song was songe,
He moste preche and wel affile his tonge
To wynne silver, as he ful wel koude;
Ther-fore he song the murierly and loude.

    Now have I told yow soothly, in a clause,   715
Th' estaat, th' array, the nombre, and eek the cause

685. **Vernycle:** reproduction of St. Veronica's handkerchief bearing Christ's face
687. **Bret-ful of pardoun:** brimful of pardons
694. **Male:** bag
Pilwe-beer: pillowcase
696. **Gobet:** piece

697. **Hente:** caught
699. **Croys of latoun:** cross of latten, a metal much like brass
702. **Up-on lond:** in the country
705. **Japes:** tricks
710. **Alderbest:** best of all
711. **Wiste:** knew

Why that assembled was this compaignye
In Southwerk, at this gentil hostelrye
That highte the Tabard, faste by the Belle.
But now is tyme to yow for to telle   720
How that we baren us that ilke nyght,
Whan we were in that hostelrie alyght;
And after wol I telle of oure viage,
And al the remenant of oure pilgrymage.
  But first I pray yow, of youre courteisye,   725
That ye n'arette it nat my vileynye,
Thogh that I pleynly speke in this matere,
To telle yow hir wordes and hir cheere,
Ne thogh I speke hir wordes proprely.
For this ye knowen also wel as I,   730
Who-so shal telle a tale after a man,
He moot reherce as neigh as evere he kan
Everich a word, if it be in his charge,
Al speke he nevere so rudeliche and large,
Or ellis he moot telle his tale untrewe,   735
Or feyne thyng, or fynde wordes newe.
He may nat spare, al-thogh he were his brother,
He moot as wel seye o word as another.
Crist spak hym-self ful brode in holy writ,
And wel ye woot, no vileynye is it.   740
Eek Plato seith, who-so kan hym rede,
The wordes mote be cosyn to the dede.
  Also I pray yow to foryeve it me,
Al have I nat set folk in hir degree
Here in this tale, as that they sholde stonde: 745
My wit is short, ye may wel understonde.
  Greet cheere made oure Hoost us everichon,
And to the soper sette he us anon.
He served us with vitaille at the beste;
Strong was the wyn, and wel to drynke us leste.   750

722. **Alyght:** alighted
726. **N'arette . . . vileynye:** blame it
  not on my lack of good breed-
  ing
728. **Hir cheere:** their behavior
729. **Proprely:** exactly as they spoke
733. **Everich a:** every single

734. **Al:** although
  Rudeliche and large: rudely
  and broadly
736. **Feyne thing:** make something
  up
739. **Brode:** plainly
742. **Cosyn:** cousin
748. **Anon:** at once
750. **Us leste:** it pleased us

A semely man oure Hoost was with-alle
For to been a marchal in an halle.
A large man he was with eyen stepe,
A fairer burgeys was ther noon in Chepe,
Boold of his speche, and wys, and wel ytaught,   755
And of manhode hym lakked right naught.
Eke ther-to he was right a murye man,
And after soper pleyen he bigan,
And spak of myrthe amonges othere thynges,
Whan that we hadde maad oure rekenynges,   760
And seyde thus, "Now, lordynges, trewely,
Ye been to me right welcome, hertely;
For by my trouthe, if that I shal not lye,
I saugh nat this yeer so murye a compaignye
At ones in this herberwe as is now.   765
Fayn wolde I doon yow myrthe, wiste I how.
And of a myrthe I am right now bythoght,
To doon yow ese, and it shal coste noght.
    "Ye goon to Caunterbury—God yow spede,
The blisful martir quyte yow youre mede!   770
And wel I woot, as ye goon by the weye,
Ye shapen yow to talen and to pleye;
For trewely, confort ne myrthe is noon
To ryde by the weye domb as a stoon;
And ther-fore wol I maken yow disport,   775
As I seyde erst, and doon yow som confort.
And if yow liketh alle, by oon assent,
For to stonden at my juggement,
And for to werken as I shal yow seye,
Tomorwe, whan ye riden by the weye,   780
Now, by my fader soule that is deed,
But ye be murye, I wol yeve yow myn heed!
Hoold up youre hondes, with-outen moore speche."
    Our conseil was nat longe for to seche;
Us thoughte it was nat worth to make it wys,   785
And graunted hym with-outen moore avys,
And bad hym seye his voirdit as hym leste.
    "Lordynges," quod he, "now herkneth for the beste;

---

753. **Eyen stepe:** protruding eyes   764. **Saugh:** saw
754. **Chepe:** Cheapside, the business   765. **Herbewe:** lodging
     district of London   786. **Avys:** deliberation
762. **Hertely:** heartily   787. **Voirdit:** verdict

But taketh it not, I pray yow, in desdeyn;
This is the poynt, to speken short and pleyn,   790
That ech of yow, to shorte with oure weye,
In this viage shal telle tales tweye
To Caunterburyward, I mene it so,
And homward he shal tellen othere two,
Of adventures that whilom have bifalle.   795
And which of yow that bereth hym best of alle,
That is to seyn, that telleth in this caas
Tales of best sentence and moost solaas,
Shal have a soper at oure aller cost
Here in this place, sittyng by this post,   800
Whan that we come agayn fro Caunterbury.
And for to make yow the moore mury,
I wol my-self goodly with yow ryde,
Right at myn owene cost, and be your gyde
And who-so wole my juggement withseye   805
Shal paye al that we spende by the weye.
And if ye vouche sauf that it be so,
Tel me anoon, with-outen wordes mo,
And I wol erly shape me ther-fore."
    This thyng was graunted, and oure othes swore   810
With ful glad herte, and preyden hym also
That he wolde vouche sauf for to do so,
And that he wolde been oure governour,
And of oure tales juge and reportour,
And sette a soper at a certeyn prys,   815
And we wol reuled been at his devys
In heigh and lough; and thus by oon assent
We been acorded to his juggement.
And ther-upon the wyn was fet anoon;
We dronken, and to reste wente echon,   820
With-outen any lenger taryynge.
    Amorwe, whan that day bigan to sprynge,
Up roos oure Hoost, and was oure aller cok,
And gadred us togidre in a flok,
And forth we riden, a litel moore than pas,   825
Unto the wateryng of Seint Thomas;

798. **Sentence:** instruction
    Solaas: entertainment
799. **Oure aller cost:** the cost of us
    all

810. **Swore:** were sworn
816. **Devys:** direction
817. **In . . . lough:** in all respects
819. **Fet:** fetched

And there oure Hoost bigan his hors areste,
And seyde, "Lordynges, herkneth, if yow leste:
Ye woot youre forward, and I it yow recorde.
If evensong and morwesong acorde,   830
Lat se now who shal telle the firste tale.
As evere moot I drynke wyn or ale,
Who so be rebel to my juggement
Shal paye for al that by the wey is spent.
Now draweth cut, er that we ferre twynne;   835
He which that hath the shorteste shal bigynne.
"Sir Knyght," quod he, "my mayster and my lord,
Now draweth cut, for that is myn acord.
Cometh neer," quod he, "my lady Prioresse,
And ye, sire Clerk, lat be youre shamefastnesse,   840
Ne studieth noght; ley hond to, every man!"
   Anoon to drawen every wight bigan,
And shortly for to tellen as it was,
Were it by aventure, or sort, or cas,
The sothe is this, the cut fil to the Knyght,   845
Of which ful blithe and glad was every wight,
And telle he moste his tale, as was resoun,
By forward and by composicioun,
As ye han herd; what nedeth wordes mo ?
   And whan this goode man saugh that it was so,   850
As he that wys was and obedient
To kepe his forward by his free assent,
He seyde, "Syn I shal bigynne the game,
What, welcome be the cut, a Goddes name!
Now lat us ryde, and herkneth what I seye."   855
And with that word we ryden forth oure weye,
And he bigan with right a murye cheere
His tale anoon, and seyde as ye may heere.

829. **Forward:** agreement   840. **Shamefastnesse:** shyness
     Recorde: recall   841. **Studieth:** meditate
835. **Ferrer twynne:** set out farther 845. **Sothe:** truth
838. **Draweth cut:** draw lots   848. **Composicioun:** agreement

THE NUN'S PRIEST'S TALE

A poure widwe, somdel stape in age,
Was whilom dwellynge in a narwe cotage,
Biside a grove, stondyng in a dale.

This widwe, of which I telle yow my tale,
Syn thilke day that she was last a wyf, 5
In pacience ladde a ful symple lyf,
For litel was hire catel and hire rente.
By housbondrye of swich as God hire sente
She foond hire-self, and eek hire doghtren two.
Thre large sowes hadde she, and namo, 10
Thre kyn, and eek a sheep that highte Malle.
Ful sooty was hire bour, and eek hire halle,
In which she eet ful many a sklendre meel.
Of poynaunt sauce hir neded never a deel.
No deyntee morsel passed thurgh hir throte; 15
Hir diete was acordant to hir cote.
Repleccioun ne made hire nevere syk;
Attempree diete was al hir phisyk,
And exercise, and hertes suffisaunce.
The goute lette hire no-thyng for to daunce, 20
N'apoplexie shente nat hir heed
No wyn ne drank she, neither whit ne reed;
Hir bord was served moost with whit and blak,
Milk and broun breed, in which she foond no lak,
Seynd bacoun, and som-tyme an ey or tweye, 25
For she was, as it were, a maner deye.
    A yeerd she hadde, enclosed al aboute
With stikkes, and a drye dych with-oute,
In which she hadde a cok, heet Chauntecleer;
In al the land of crowyng nas his peer. 30
His voys was murier than the myrie orgon
On massedayes that in the chirche gon.
Wel sikerer was his crowyng in his logge
Than is a clokke or any abbey orlogge.
By nature he knew ech ascensioun 35
Of the equinoxial in thilke toun;
For when degrees fiftene were ascended,
Thanne krew he, that it myghte nat ben amended.
His comb was redder than the fyn coral,
And batailled as it were a castel wal. 40

7. **Rente:** income	26. **Manner:** sort of
9. **Foond:** provided for	**Deye:** dairy woman
20. **Lette:** prevented	29. **Heet:** called
21. **Shente:** split	33. **Sikerer:** more certain
25. **Ey:** egg	34. **Orlogge:** clock

His byle was blak, and as the jeet it shoon;
Lyk asure were hise legges and his toon;
Hise nayles whitter than the lylye flour,
And lyk the burned gold was his colour.
This gentil cok hadde in his governaunce   45
Sevene hennes for to doon al his plesaunce,
Whiche were hise sustres and his paramours,
And wonder lyke to hym as of colours;
Of whiche the faireste hewed on hire throte
Was cleped faire damoysele Pertelote.   50
Curteys she was, discreet, and debonaire,
And compaignable, and bar hir-self so faire,
Syn thilke day that she was seven nyght oold,
That trewely she hath the herte in hoold
Of Chauntecleer, loken in every lith;   55
He loved hire so that wel was hym ther-with.
But swich a joye was it to here hem synge,
Whan that the brighte sonne gan to sprynge,
In swete acord, "My leef is faren in londe!"
For thilke tyme, as I have understonde,   60
Beestes and briddes koude speek and synge.
    And so bifel, that in a dawenynge,
As Chauntecleer among hise wyves alle
Sat on his perche, that was in the halle,
And next hym sat this faire Pertelote,   65
This Chauntecleer gan gronen in his throte,
As man that in his dreem is drecched soore.
    And whan that Pertelote thus herde hym rore,
She was agast, and seyde, "Herte deere,
What eyleth yow, to grone in this manere?   70
Ye ben a verray slepere, fy, for shame!"
    And he answerde, and seyde thus, "Madame,
I prey yow that ye take it nat agrief.
By God, me mette I was in swich meschief
Right now, that yet myn herte is soore afright.   75
Now God," quod he, "my swevene recche aright,

41. **Byle:** bill
42. **Toon:** toes
50. **Cleped:** called
55. **Lith:** limb
59. **My leef is faren in londe:** my
    love has gone to the country

67. **Drecched:** troubled
74. **Me mette:** I dreamed
76. **Swevene:** dream
    Recche: interpret

And kepe my body out of foul prisoun!
Me mette how that I romed up and doun
With-inne oure yeerd, where-as I say a beest
Was lyk an hound, and wolde han maad areest   80
Up-on my body, and han had me deed.
His colour was bitwixe yelow and reed,
And tipped was his tayl and bothe hise erys
With blak, unlik the remenaunt of hise herys,
His snowte smal, with glowyng eyen tweye   85
Yet of his look for fere almoost I deye;
This caused me my gronyng, doutelees."
      "Avoy!" quod she, "fy on yow, hertelees!
Allas!" quod she, "for by that God above,
Now han ye lost myn herte and al my love!   90
I kan nat love a coward, by my feith!
For, certes, what so any womman seith,
We alle desiren, if it myghte be,
To han housbondes hardy, wise, and fre,
And secree, and no nygard, ne no fool,   95
Ne hym that is agast of every tool,
Ne noon avauntour, by that God above!
How dorste ye seyn, for shame, un-to youre love
That any thyng myghte make yow aferd?
Have ye no mannes herte, and han a berd?   100
      "Allas! and konne ye ben agast of swevenys?
No thyng, God woot, but vanytee in swevene is.
Swevenes engendren of replexions,
And ofte of fume, and of complexions,
Whan humours ben to habundant in a wight.   105
      "Certes this dreem which ye han met to-nyght,
Comth of the grete superfluytee
Of youre rede colera, pardee,
Which causeth folk to dreden in hir dremes
Of arwes, and of fyr with rede lemes,   110
Of rede bestes, that they wol hem byte,
Of contek, and of whelpes grete and lyte;
Right as the humour of malencolie

---

81. **Deed:** dead
95. **Secree:** discreet
97. **Avauntour:** boaster
105. **Humours:** a medical term; the four humours were blood,

phlegm, yellow bile and black bile
106. **Met:** dreamed
    To-nyght: last night

Causeth ful many a man in sleep to crie
For fere of blake beres, or boles blake,   115
Or elles blake develes wol hem take.
   "Of othere humours koude I telle also,
That werken many a man in sleep ful wo;
But I wol passe as lightly as I kan.
   "Lo Catoun, which that was so wys a man,   120
Seyde he nat thus, 'Ne do no fors of dremes?'
   "Now sire," quod she, "whan we fle fro the bemes,
For Goddes love, as taak some laxatif;
Up peril of my soule and of my lif,
I conseille yow the beste, I wol nat lye,   125
That bothe of colere and of malencolye
Ye purge yow; and for ye shal nat tarye,
Thogh in this toun is noon apothecarye,
I shal my-self to herbes techen yow,
That shul ben for youre heele and for youre prow;   130
And in oure yerd tho herbes shal I fynde
The wiche han of hire propretee, by kynde,
To purge yow bynethe and eek above.
Foryet nat this, for Goddes owene love!
Ye ben ful colerik of complexioun.   135
Ware the sonne in his ascensioun
Ne fynde yow nat replet of humours hote;
And if it do, I dar wel leye a grote,
That ye shul have a fevere terciane,
Or an agu, that may be youre bane.   140
A day or two ye shul have digestyves
Of wormes, er ye take youre laxatyves
Of lauriol, centaure, and fumetere,
Or elles of ellebor, that groweth there,
Of katapuce, or of gaitrys beryis,   145
Of herbe yve, growyng in oure yerd, ther merye is;
Pekke hem up right as they growe and ete hem in.
Be myrie, housbonde, for youre fader kyn!
Dredeth no dreem, I kan sey yow namoore."
   "Madame," quod he, "graunt mercy of youre loore.
But nathelees, as touchyng Daun Catoun,   151
That hath of wisdom swich a gret renoun,
Thogh that he bad no dremes for to drede,

---

115. **Boles:** bulls   140. **Bane:** death
121. **Do no fors of:** pay no heed to

By God, men may in olde bokes rede
Of many a man, moore of auctoritee   155
Than evere Catoun was, so mote I thee,
That al the revers seyn of his sentence,
And han wel founden by experience
That dremes ben significaciouns
As wel of joye as of tribulaciouns   160
That folk enduren in this lyf present.
Ther nedeth make of this noon argument:
The verray preeve sheweth it in dede.
   "Oon of the gretteste auctor that man rede
Seith thus, that whilom two felawes wente   165
On pilgrymage, in a ful good entente;
And happed so, they coomen in a toun,
Where as ther was swich congregacioun
Of peple, and eek so streit of herbergage,
That they ne founde as muche as a cotage   170
In which they bothe myghte ylogged be.
Wherfore they mosten of necessitee,
As for that nyght, departen compaignye;
And ech of hem gooth to his hostelrye,
And took his loggyng as it wolde falle.   175
That oon of hem was logged in a stalle,
Fer in a yeerd, with oxen of the plough,
That oother man was logged wel ynough,
As was his aventure or his fortune,
That us governeth alle as in commune.   180
   "As so bifel that, longe er it were day,
This man mette in his bed, ther as he lay,
How that his felawe gan up-on hym calle,
And seyde, 'Allas! for in an oxes stalle
This nyght I shal be mordred ther I lye.   185
Now help me, deere brother or I dye!
In alle haste com to me!' he sayde.
   "This man out of his sleep for feere abrayde;
But whan that he was wakned of his sleep,
He turned hym, and took of this no keep.   190
Hym thoughte his dreem nas but a vanytee.
Thus twies in his slepyng dremed he.
And atte thridde tyme yet his felawe

157. **Revers:** opposite   179. **Aventure:** chance
157. **Sentence:** opinion   188. **Abrayde:** started up

Cam, as hym thoughte, and seyde, 'I am now slawe!
Bihoold my blody woundes, depe and wyde!   195
Arys up erly in the morwe tyde,
And at the west gate of the toun,' quod he,
'A carte ful of donge ther shaltow se,
In which my body is hid ful pryvely;
Do thilke carte aresten boldely.   200
My gold caused my mordre, sooth to seyn.'
And tolde hym every poynt how he was slayn,
With a ful pitous face, pale of hewe.
And truste wel, his dreem he fond ful trewe,
For on the morwe, as soone as it was day,   205
To his felawes in he took the way;
And whan that he cam to this oxes stalle,
After his felawe he bigan to calle.
    "The hostiler answerde hym anon,
And seyde, 'Sire, youre felawe is agon;   210
As soone as day he wente out of the toun.'
    "This man gan fallen in suspecioun,
Remembrynge on hise dremes that he mette,
And forth he gooth, no lenger wolde he lette,
Unto the west gate of the toun, and fond   215
A dong-carte, wente as it were to donge lond,
That was arrayed in the same wise
As ye han herd the dede man devyse.
And with an hardy herte he gan to crye
Vengeaunce and justice of this felonye: 220
'My felawe mordred is this same nyght,
And in this carte here he lyth gapyng upright.
I crye out on the mynystres,' quod he,
'That sholden kepe and reulen this citee.
Harrow! allas! heere lith my felawe slayn!'   225
What sholde I moore un-to this tale sayn?
The peple out sterte, and caste the cart to grounde,
And in the myddel of the dong they founde
The dede man, that mordred was al newe.
    "O blisful God, that art so just and trewe,   230
Lo, how that thow biwreyest mordre alway!
Mordre wol out, that se we day by day.

---

194. **Slawe:** slain   206. **In:** inn
198. **Donge:** manure   218. **Devyse:** describe
200. **Aresten:** stop   223. **Mynysteres:** officers of justice

Mordre is so wlatsom and abhomynable
To God, that is so just and resonable,
That he ne wol nat suffre it heled be;   235
Though it abyde a yeer, or two, or thre,
Mordre wol out, this is my conclusioun.
And right anon ministres of that toun
Han hent the cartere, and so soore hym pyned,
And eek the hostiler so soore engyned,   240
That they biknewe hir wikkednesse anon,
And were an-hanged by the nekke bon.
  "Heere may men seen that dremes ben to drede.
And, certes, in the same book I rede,
Right in the nexte chapitre after this—   245
I gabbe nat so have I joye or blys—
  "Two men that wolde han passed over see,
For certeyn cause, in-to a fer contree,
If that the wynd ne hadde ben contrarie,
That made hem in a citee for to tarie,   250
That stood ful myrie up-on an haven syde.
But on a day, agayn the even-tyde,
The wynd gan chaunge, and blew right as hem leste.
Jolif and glad they wente un-to reste,
And casten hem ful erly for to saille.   255
  "But herkneth, to that o man fil a greet mervaille:
That oon of hem, in slepyng as he lay,
Hym mette a wonder dreem, agayn the day;
Hym thoughte a man stood by his beddes syde,
And hym comanded that he sholde abyde,   260
And seyde hym thus, 'If thow tomorwe wende,
Thow shalt be dreynt; my tale is at an ende.'
  "He wook, and tolde his felawe what he mette,
And preyde hym his viage to lette;
As for that day, he preyde hym to abyde.   265
  "His felawe, that lay by his beddes syde,
Gan for to laughe, and scorned hym ful faste.
'No dreem,' quod he, 'may so myn herte agaste
That I wol lette for to do my thynges.
I sette nat a straw by thy dremynges,   270
For swevenes ben but vanytees and japes.

---

235. **Heled:** hidden
240. **Engyned:** racked
241. **Biknewe:** confessed

252. **Agayn:** towards
262. **Dreynt:** drowned

Men dreme alday of owles and of apes,
And of many a maze ther-with-al;
Men dreme of thyng that nevere was ne shal.
But sith I see that thow wolt here abyde,   275
And thus forslewthen wilfully thy tyde,
God woot, it reweth me; and have good day.'
And thus he took his leve, and wente his way.
But er that he hadde half his cours yseyled,
Noot I nat why, ne what meschaunce it eyled,   280
But casuelly the shippes botme rente,
And ship and man under the water wente
In sighte of othere shippes it bisyde,
That with hem seyled at the same tyde.
And therfore, faire Pertelote so deere,   285
By swiche ensamples olde maystow leere
That no man sholde been to recchelees
Of dremes, for I sey thee, doutelees,
That many a dreem ful soore is for to drede.
  "Lo, in the lyf of Seint Kenelm I rede,   290
That was Kenulphus sone, the noble kyng
Of Mercenrike, how Kenelm mette a thyng.
A lite er he was mordred, on a day,
His mordre in his avysioun he say.
His norice hym expowned every del   295
His swevene, and bad hym for to kepe hym wel
For traisoun, but he nas but sevene yeer old,
And therfore litel tale hath he told
Of any dreem, so holy was his herte.
By God! I hadde levere than my sherte   300
That ye hadde rad his legende, as have I.
Dame Pertelote, I sey yow trewely,
Macrobeus that writ the avysioun
In Affrike of the worthy Cipioun,
Affermeth dremes, and seith that they ben   305
Warnynge of thynges that men after sen.
  "And forther-moore, I pray yow, looketh wel
In the Olde Testament, of Danyel,
If he heeld dremes any vanytee.

---

276. **Forslewthen:** wasted through   293. **Lite er:** a little before
     sloth   294. **Say:** saw
280. **Noot I nat:** I know not   295. **Norice:** nurse
287. **Recchelees:** unmindful

"Rede eek of Joseph, and there shul ye see   310
Wher dremes be som-tyme—I sey nat alle—
Warnynge of thynges that shul after falle.
    "Looke of Egipte the kyng, Daun Pharao,
His bakere and his butiller also,
Wher they ne felte noon effect in dremes.   315
Who-so wol seke actes of sondry remes
May rede of dremes many a wonder thyng.
    "Lo Cresus, which that was of Lyde kyng,
Mette he nat that he sat up-on a tree,
Which signified he sholde an-hanged be?   320
    "Lo heere Andromacha, Ectores wyf,
That day that Ector sholde lese his lyf,
She dremed on the same nyght biforn,
How that the lyf of Ector sholde be lorn,
If thilke day he wente in-to bataille;   325
She warned hym, but it myghte nat availle;
He wente for to fighte nathelees,
But he was slayn anon of Achilles.
But thilke tale is al to long to telle,
And eek it is ny day, I may nat dwelle.   330
Shortly I seye, as for conclusioun,
That I shal han of this avysioun
Adversitee; and I seye forther-moor,
That I ne telle of laxatyves no stoor,
For they ben venymes, I woot it wel;   335
I hem deffye, I love hem never a del!
    "Now lat us speke of myrthe, and stynte al this.
Madame Pertelote, so have I blis,
Of o thyng God hath sent me large grace:
For whan I se the beautee of youre face,   340
Ye ben so scarlet reed aboute youre eyen,
It maketh al my drede for to dyen;
For also siker as In principio,
Mulier est hominis confusio—
    "Madame, the sentence of this Latyn is,   345
'Woman is mannes joye and al his blis.'
For whan I feele a nyght youre softe syde,
Al be it that I may nat on you ryde,

316. **Remes:** realms   334. **Ne . . . stoor:** set no store by
324. **Lorn:** lost   344. **Mulier est, etc.:** Woman is
327. **Nathelees:** nevertheless   man's ruin

For that oure perche is maad so narwe, allas!
I am so ful of joye and of solas,   350
That I deffye bothe swevene and dreem!"
And with that word he fley doun fro the beem,
For it was day, and eke hise hennes alle,
And with a chuk he gan hem for to calle,
For he hadde founde a corn lay in the yerd.   355
Real he was, he was namoore aferd;
He fethered Pertelote twenty tyme,
And trad as ofte, er it was pryme.
He looketh as it were a grym leoun,
And on hise toos he rometh up and doun,   360
Hym deyned nat to sette his foot to grounde.
He chukketh, whan he hath a corn yfounde,
And to hym rennen thanne hise wyves alle.
Thus real, as a prince is in his halle,
Leve I this Chauntecleer in his pasture,   365
And after wol I telle his aventure.
   Whan that the monthe in which the world bigan,
That highte March, whan God first maked man,
Was complet, and passed were also,
Syn March bigan, thritty dayes and two,   370
Bifel that Chauntecler in al his pryde,
Hise sevene wyves walkyng hym bisyde,
Caste up hise eyen to the brighte sonne,
That in the signe of Taurus hadde yronne
Twenty degrees and oon, and som-what moore,   375
And knew by kynde, and by noon oother loore,
That it was pryme, and krew with blisful stevene.
"The sonne," he seyde, "is clomben up on hevene
Fourty degrees and oon, and moore ywis.
Madame Pertelote, my worldes blis,   380
Herkneth thise blisful briddes how they synge,
And se the fresshe floures how they sprynge!
Ful is myn herte of revel and solas!"
But sodeynly him fil a sorweful cas;
For evere the latter ende of joye is wo.   385
God woot that worldly joye is soone ago;

356. **Real:** royal
358. **Pryme:** 6 A.M. or the period between 6 and 9

376. **By kynde:** by instinct
377. **Stevene:** voice
386. **Woot:** knows

And if a rethor koude faire endite,
He in a cronycle saufly myghte it write,
As for a sovereyn notabilitee.
Now every wys man, lat hym herkne me: 390
This storie is also trewe, I undertake,
As is the book of Launcelot de Lake,
That wommen holde in ful gret reverence.
Now wol I torne agayn to my sentence.
    A colfox, ful of sly iniquitee,   395
That in the grove hadde woned yeres three,
By heigh ymaginacioun forncast,
The same nyght thurgh-out the hegges brast
In-to the yerd, ther Chauntecleer the faire
Was wont, and eek hise wyves, to repaire;   400
And in a bed of wortes stille he lay,
Til it was passed undren of the day,
Waitynge his tyme on Chauntecleer to falle,
As gladly doon thise homycides alle,
That in awayt liggen to mordre men.   405
O false mordrour, lurkynge in thy den!
O newe Scariot, newe Genyloun!
False dissimilour, O Greek Synoun,
That broghtest Troye al outrely to sorwe!
O Chauntecleer, acursed be that morwe   410
That thow in-to the yerd flaugh fro the bemes!
Thow were ful wel ywarned by thy dremes,
That thilke day was perilous to thee.
But what that God forwoot moot nedes be,
After the opynyoun of certeyn clerkis.   415
Witnesse on hym that any parfit clerk is,
That in scole is greet altercacioun
In this matere, and greet disputisoun,
And hath ben of an hundred thousand men.
But I ne kan nat bulte it to the bren,   420
As kan the holy doctour Augustyn,
Or Boece, or the bisshop Bradwardyn,
Wheither that Goddes worthy forewityng

387. **Rethor:** rhetorician
394. **Sentence:** subject
396. **Woned:** lived
398. **Hegges:** hedges

402. **Undren:** mid-morning
416. **Clerk:** scholar
417. **Scole:** university
423. **Forewityng:** foreknowledge

Streyneth me nedely for to doon a thyng—
"Nedely" clepe I symple necessitee—   425
Or ellis, if fre choys be graunted me
To do that same thyng, or do it noght,
Though God forwoot it, er that it was wroght;
Or if his wityng streyneth never a del
But by necessitee condicionel.   430
I wol nat han to do of swich matere;
My tale is of a cok, as ye may heere,
That took his conseil of his wyf, with sorwe,
To walken in the yerd up-on that morwe
That he hadde met the dreem that I yow tolde.   435
Wommens conseils ben ful ofte colde;
Wommanes conseil broghte us first to wo,
And made Adam fro Paradys to go,
Ther as he was ful myrie and wel at ese.
But for I noot to whom it myghte displese,   440
If I conseil of wommen wolde blame,
Passe over, for I seyde it in my game.
Rede auctours, where they trete of swich matere,
And what they seyn of wommen ye may heere.
Thise ben the cokkes wordes, and nat myne;   445
I kan noon harm of no womman devyne.
    Faire in the sond, to bathe hire myrily,
Lith Pertelote, and alle hir sustres by,
Agayn the sonne, and Chauntecleer so free
Song myrier than the mermayde in the see;   450
For Phisiologus seith sikerly,
How that they syngen wel and myrily.
    And so bifel that, as he caste his eye
Among the wortes, on a boterflye,
He was war of this fox that lay ful lowe.   455
No-thyng ne liste hym thanne for to crowe,
But cryde anon, "Cok! cok!" and up he sterte,
As man that was affrayed in his herte.
For naturelly a beest desireth flee
Fro his contrarie, if he may it see,   460
Though he nevere erst hadde seyn it with his eye.
    This Chauntecleer, whan he gan hym espye,
He wolde han fled, but that the fox anon

424. **Streyneth:** constrains   436. **Colde:** off the mark
425. **Nedely:** necessarily

Seyde, "Gentil sire, allas! wher wol ye gon?
Be ye affrayed of me that am youre freend?   465
Now, certes, I were worse than a feend,
If I to yow wolde harm or vileynye!
I am nat come youre conseil for t'espye,
But trewely, the cause of my comynge
Was oonly for to herkne how that ye synge.   470
For trewely, ye han as myrie a stevene
As any aungel hath, that is in hevene.
Ther-with ye han in musyk moore feelynge
Than hadde Boece, or any that kan synge.
My lord youre fader—God his soule blesse!—   475
And eek youre moder, of hire gentillesse,
Han in myn hous yben, to my greet ese;
And, certes, sire, ful fayn wolde I yow plese.
    "But for men speke of syngynge, I wol seye,
So mote I brouke wel myne eyen tweye,   480
Save ye, I herde nevere man so synge
As dide youre fader in the morwenynge.
Certes, it was of herte, al that he song.
And for to make his voys the moore strong,
He wolde so peyne hym, that with bothe hise eyen   485
He moste wynke, so loude he wolde cryen,
And stonden on his tiptoon ther-with-al,
And strecche forth his nekke long and smal.
And eek he was of swich discrecioun,
That ther nas no man in no regioun   490
That hym in song or wisdom myghte passe.
I have wel rad in Daun Burnel the Asse,
Among his vers, how that ther was a cok,
For a preestes sone yaf hym a knok
Up-on his leg, whil he was yong and nyce,   495
He made hym for to lese his benefice.
But certeyn, ther nys no comparisoun
Bitwix the wisdom and discrecioun
Of youre fader and of his subtiltee.
Now syngeth, sire, for seinte Charitee!   500
Lat se, konne ye youre fader countrefete?"
    This Chauntecleer hise wynges gan to bete,
As man that koude his traysoun nat espie,

480. **Brouke:** have the use of
495. **Nyce:** foolish

496. **Lese his benefice:** the cock
      failed to wake him

So was he ravysshed with his flaterie.
    Allas! ye lordes, many a fals flatour   505
Is in youre court, and many a losengeour,
That plesen yow wel moore, by my feith,
Than he that soothfastnesse un-to yow seith.
Redeth Ecclesiaste of flaterye;
Beth war, ye lordes, of hir trecherye.   510
This Chauntecler stood hye up-on his toos,
Strecchynge his nekke, and heeld hise eyen cloos,
And gan to crowe loude for the nones.
And Daun Russell the fox stirte up atones,
And by the gargat hente Chauntecleer,   515
And on his bak toward the wode hym beer,
For yet ne was ther no man that hym sewed.
    O destynee, that mayst nat ben eschewed!
Allas, that Chauntecleer fleigh fro the bemes!
Allas, his wif ne roghte nat of dremes!   520
And on a Friday fil al this meschaunce.
    O Venus, that art goddesse of plesaunce,
Syn that thy servant was this Chauntecleer,
And in thy servyce dide al his power,
Moore for delit, than world to multiplie,   525
Why woldestow suffre hym on thy day to dye?
    O Gaufred, deere maister soverayn,
That, whan thy worthy kyng, Richard, was slayn
With shot, compleynedest his deth so soore,
Why ne hadde I now thy sentence and thy loore, 530
The Friday for to chide, as diden ye?
For on a Friday, soothly, slayn was he.
Thanne wolde I shewe yow how that I koude pleyne
For Chauntecleres drede and for his peyne.
    Certes, swich cry ne lamentacioun   535
Was nevere of ladyes maad whan Ylioun
Was wonne, and Pirrus with his streite swerd,
Whanne he hadde hent Kyng Priam by the berd,
And slayn hym, as seith us *Eneydos*,
As maden alle the hennes in the cloos,   540
Whan they hadde seyn of Chauntecleer the sighte.

---

506. **Losengeour:** flatterer
508. **Soothfastnesse:** truth

515. **Gargat:** throat
     Hente: seize
517. **Sewed:** pursued

But sovereynly Dame Pertelote shrighte,
Ful louder than dide Hasdrubales wyf,
Whan that hire housbonde, hadde lost his lyf,
And that the Romayns hadden brend Cartage: 545
She was so ful of torment and of rage,
That wilfully in-to the fyr she sterte,
And brende hir-selven with a stedefast herte.
  O woful hennes, right so cryden ye,
As whan that Nero brende the citee   550
Of Rome, cryden senatours wyves,
For that hir housbondes losten alle hire lyves;
With-outen gilt this Nero hath hem slayn.
Now wol I turne to my tale agayn.
  The sely widwe, and eek hire doghtres two,   555
Herden thise hennes crye and maken wo,
And out atte dores stirten they anon,
And syen the fox toward the grove gon,
And bar up-on his bak the cok away,
And criden, "Out! harrow! and weilaway!   560
Ha! ha! the fox!" and after hym they ran,
And eek with staves many another man.
Ran Colle oure dogge, and Talbot, and Gerland,
And Malkyn, with a distaf in hire hand;
Ran cow and calf, and eek the verray hogges,   565
So fered for berkyng of the dogges
And showtynge of the men and wommen eek,
They ronne so, hem thoughte hir herte breek.
They yelleden as fendes doon in helle;
The dokes cryden as men wolde hem quelle;   570
The gees for feere flowen over the trees;
Out of the hyve cam the swarm of bees.
So hydous was the noyse, a! *benedicitee!*
Certes, he Jakke Straw, and his meynee,
Ne made nevere shoutes half so shrille,   575
Whan that they wolden any Flemyng kille,
As thilke day was maad up-on the fox.
Of bras they broghten bemes, and of box,
Of horn, of boon, in whiche they blewe and powped,
And ther-with-al they skryked and they howped.   580

542. **Shrighte:** shrieked
555. **Sely:** simple
570. **Quelle:** kill

578. **Bemes:** trumpets
      Box: of boxwood

It semed as that hevene sholde falle!
Now, goode men, I prey yow herkneth alle:
   Lo, how Fortune turneth sodeynly
The hope and pryde eek of hire enemy!
This cok, that lay up-on the foxes bak,   585
In al his drede un-to the fox he spak,
And seyde, "Sire, if that I were as ye,
Yit sholde I seyn, as wys God helpe me,
'Turneth agayn, ye proude cherles alle!
A verray pestilence up-on yow falle!   590
Now I am come un-to this wodes syde,
Maugree youre heed, the cok shal here abyde.
I wol hym ete, in feith, and that anon!' "
   The fox answerde, "In feith, it shal be done."
And as he spak that word, al sodeynly   595
This cok brak from his mouth delyverly,
And hye up-on a tree he fley anon.
And whan the fox say that he was gon,
   "Allas!" quod he, "O Chauntecleer, allas!
I have to yow," quod he, "ydoon trespas,   600
In as muche as I maked yow aferd,
Whan I yow hente, and broghte out of the yerd.
But, sire, I dide it in no wikke entente.
Com doun, and I shal telle yow what I mente.
I shal seye sooth to yow, God help me so!"   605
   "Nay thanne," quod he, "I shrewe us bothe two!
And first I shrewe my-self, bothe blood and bones,
If thow bigile me any ofter than ones.
Thow shalt namoore, thurgh thy flaterye,
Do me to synge and wynke with myn eye,   61c
For he that wynketh, whan he sholde see,
Al wilfully, God lat hym nevere thee!"
   "Nay," quod the fox, "but God yeve hym meschaunce,
That is so undiscreet of governaunce,
That jangleth whan he sholde holde his pees."   615
   Lo, swich it is for to be reccheless
And necligent, and truste on flaterye.
   But ye that holden this tale a folye,
As of a fox, or of a cok and hen,
Taketh the moralitee, goode men.   620

592. **Maugree:** in spite of   612. **Thee:** thrive
596. **Delverly:** agilely

For Seint Poul seith, that al that writen is,
To oure doctryne it is ywrite, ywis:
Taketh the fruyt, and lat the chaf be stille.
Now, goode God, if that it be thy wille,
As seith my lord, so make us alle goode men,   625
And brynge us to his heye blisse! *Amen.*

English and Scottish Popular Ballads

SIR PATRICK SPENS

The king sits in Dumferling toune,
    Drinking the blude-reid wine:
O quhar will I get guid sailor,
    To sail this schip of mine?

Up and spak an eldern knicht,   5
    Sat at the king's richt knee:
Sir Patrick Spens is the best sailor
    That sails upon the sea.

The king has written a braid letter,
    And signed it wi' his hand;   10
And sent it to Sir Patrick Spens,
    Was walking on the sand.

The first line that Sir Patrick red,
    A loud lauch lauchèd he:
The next line that Sir Patrick red,   15
    The teir blinded his ee.

O quhar is this has don this deid,
    This ill deid don to me;
To send me out this time o' the yeir,
    To sail upon the sea?   20

Mak haste, mak haste, my mirry men all,
    Our good schip sails the morn.
O say na sae, my master deir,
    For I feir a deadlie storme.

Late late yestreen I saw the new moone   25
   Wi' the auld moone in hir arme;
And I feir, I feir, my deir master,
   That we will come to harme.

O our Scots nobles wer richt laith
   To weet their cork-heild schoone;   30
But lang owre a' the play were played,
   Their hats they swam aboone.

O lang, lang may the ladies stand
   Wi' their fans into their hand,
Or e'er they see Sir Patrick Spens   35
   Come sailing to the land.

O lang, lang, may the ladies stand
   Wi' their gold kems in their hair,
Waiting for their ain deir lords,
   For they'll see them na mair.   40

Have owre, have owre to Aberdour,
   It's fifty fadom deip:
And thair lies guid Sir Patrick Spens,
   Wi' the Scots lords at his feit.

THE WIFE OF USHER'S WELL

There lived a wife at Usher's Well,
   And a wealthy wife was she;
She had three stout and stalwart sons,
   And sent them o'er the sea.

They hadna been a week from her,   5
   A week but barely ane,
Whan word came to the carline wife
   That her three sons were gane.

They hadna been a week from her,
   A week but barely three,   10
When word came to the carlin wife
   That her sons she'd never see.

Carlin wife: old woman.

"I wish the wind may never cease,
   Nor fashes in the flood,
Till my three sons come hame to me,   15
   In earthly flesh and blood."

It fell about the Martinmass,
   When nights are lang and mirk,
The carlin wife's three sons came hame,
   And their hats were o' the birk.   20

It neither grew in syke nor ditch,
   Nor yet in ony sheugh;
But at the gates o' Paradise,
   That birk grew fair eneugh.

"Blow up the fire, my maidens,   25
   Bring water from the well;
For a' my house shall feast this night,
   Since my three sons are well."

And she has made to them a bed,
   She's made it large and wide,   30
And she's taen her mantle her about,
   Sat down at the bed-side.

Up then crew the red, red cock,
   And up and crew the gray;
The eldest to the youngest said,   35
   " 'T is time we were away."

The cock he hadna crawd but once,
   And clapp'd his wings at a',
When the youngest to the eldest said,
   "Brother, we must awa.   40

"The cock doth craw, the day doth daw,
   The channerin worm doth chide;
Gin we be mist out o' our place,
   A sair pain we maun bide.

Birk: birch. **Sheugh:** furrow. **Gin:** if.

"Fare ye weel, my mother dear!   45
    Fareweel to barn and byre!
And fare ye weel, the bonny lass
    That kindles my mother's fire!"

THOMAS THE RHYMER

True Thomas lay on Huntlie bank;
    A ferlie he spied wi' his e'e;
And there he saw a ladye bright
    Come riding doun by Eildon Tree.

Her skirt was o' the grass-green silk,   5
    Her mantle o' the velvet fyne;
At ilka tett o' her horse's mane
    Hung fifty siller bells and nine.

True Thomas he pu'd aff his cap,
    And louted low doun on his knee: 10
"Hail to thee, Mary, Queen of Heaven!
    For thy peer on earth could never be."

"O no, O no, Thomas," she said,
    "That name does not belang to me;
I'm but the Queen o' fair Elfland,   15
    That am hither come to visit thee.

"Harp and carp, Thomas," she said;
    "Harp and carp along wi' me;
And if ye dare to kiss my lips,
    Sure of your bodie I will be."   20

"Betide me weal, betide me woe,
    That weird shall never daunten me."
Syne he has kissed her rosy lips,
    All underneath the Eildon Tree.

"Now ye maun go wi' me," she said,   25
    "True Thomas, ye maun go wi' me;
And ye maun serve me seven years,
    Thro' weal or woe as may chance to be."

Ferlie: wonder.

She's mounted on her milk-white steed,
   She's ta'en true Thomas up behind;   30
And aye, whene'er her bridle rang,
   The steed gaed swifter than the wind.

O they rade on, and farther on,
   The steed gaed swifter than the wind;
Until they reached a desert wide,   35
   And living land was left behind.

"Light down, light down now, true Thomas,
   And lean your head upon my knee;
Abide ye here a little space,
   And I will show you ferlies three.   40

"O see ye not yon narrow road,
   So thick beset wi' thorns and briars?
That is the Path of Righteousness,
   Though after it but few inquires.

"And see ye not yon braid, braid road,   45
   That lies across the lily leven?
That is the Path of Wickedness,
   Though some call it the Road to Heaven.

"And see ye not yon bonny road
   That winds about the fernie brae?   50
That is the road to fair Elfland,
   Where thou and I this night maun gae.

"But, Thomas, ye sall haud your tongue,
   Whatever ye may hear or see;
For speak ye word in Elfyn-land,   55
   Ye'll ne'er win back to your ain countrie."

O they rade on, and farther on,
   And they waded rivers abune the knee;
And they saw neither sun nor moon,
   But they heard the roaring of the sea.   60

It was mirk, mirk night, there was nae starlight,
   They waded thro' red blude to the knee;

For a' the blude that's shed on the earth
   Rins through the springs o' that countrie.

Syne they came to a garden green,   65
   And she pu'd an apple frae a tree:
"Take this for thy wages, true Thomas;
   It will give thee the tongue that can never lee."

"My tongue is my ain," true Thomas he said;
   "A gudely gift ye wad gie to me!   70
I neither dought to buy or sell
   At fair or tryst where I might be.

"I dought neither speak to prince or peer,
   Nor ask of grace from fair ladye!"
"Now haud thy peace, Thomas," she said,   75
   "For as I say, so must it be."

He has gotten a coat of the even cloth,
   And a pair o' shoon of the velvet green;
And till seven years were gane and past,
   True Thomas on earth was never seen.   80

KEMP OWYNE

Her mother died when she was young,
   Which gave her cause to make great moan;
Her father married the warst woman
   That ever lived in Christendom.

She servèd her with foot and hand,   5
   In every thing that she could dee,
Till once, in an unlucky time,
   She threw her in ower Craigy's sea.

Says, "Lie you there, dove Isabel,
   And all my sorrows lie with thee;   10
Till Kemp Owyne come ower the sea,
   And borrow you with kisses three:
Let all the warld do what they will,
   Oh borrowed shall you never be."

Kemp: champion. **Borrowed:** ransomed, set free from enchantment.

Her breath grew strang, her hair grew lang,   15
   And twisted thrice about the tree,
And all the people, far and near,
   Thought that a savage beast was she.

These news did come to Kemp Owyne,
   Where he lived far beyond the sea;   20
He hasted him to Craigy's sea,
   And on the savage beast look'd he.

Her breath was strang, her hair was lang,
   And twisted was about the tree,
And with a swing she came about: 25
   "Come to Craigy's sea, and kiss with me.

"Here is a royal belt," she cried,
   "That I have found in the green sea;
And while your body it is on,
   Drawn shall your blood never be;   30
But if you touch me, tail or fin,
   I vow my belt your death shall be."

He steppèd in, gave her a kiss,
   The royal belt he brought him wi';
Her breath was strang, her hair was lang,   35
   And twisted twice about the tree,
And with a swing she came about:
   "Come to Craigy's sea, and kiss with me.

"Here is a royal ring," she said,
   "That I have found in the green sea;   40
And while your finger it is on,
   Drawn shall your blood never be;
But if you touch me, tail or fin,
   I swear my ring your death shall be."

He steppèd in, gave her a kiss,   45
   The royal ring he brought him wi';
Her breath was strang, her hair was lang,
   And twisted ance about the tree,
And with a swing she came about:
   "Come to Craigy's sea, and kiss with me.   50

"Here is a royal brand," she said,
　"That I have found in the green sea;
And while your body it is on,
　Drawn shall your blood never be;
But if you touch me, tail or fin,　　　　　　　　55
　I swear my brand your death shall be."

He steppèd in, gave her a kiss,
　The royal brand he brought him wi';
Her breath was sweet, her hair grew short,
　And twisted nane about the tree;　　　　　　　60
And smilingly she came about,
　As fair a woman as fair could be.

CLERK SAUNDERS

Clerk Saunders and may Margaret
　Walk'd owre yon garden green;
And deep and heavy was the love
　That fell thir twa between.

"A bed, a bed," Clerk Saunders said,　　　　　　5
　"A bed for you and me!"
"Fye na, fye na," said may Margaret,
　"Till anes we married be!"

"Then I'll take the sword frae my scabbard
　And slowly lift the pin;　　　　　　　　　　10
And you may swear, and save your aith,
　Ye ne'er let Clerk Saunders in.

"Take you a napkin in your hand,
　And tie up baith your bonnie e'en,
And you may swear, and save your aith,　　　　　15
　Ye saw me na since late yestreen."

It was about the midnight hour,
　When they asleep were laid,
When in and came her seven brothers,
　Wi' torches burning red;　　　　　　　　　20

When in and came her seven brothers,
   Wi' torches burning bright:
They said, "We hae but one sister,
   And behold her lying with a knight!"

Then out and spake the first o' them,   25
   "I bear the sword shall gar him dee."
And out and spake the second o' them,
   "His father has nae mair but he."

And out and spake the third o' them,
   "I wot that they are lovers dear."   30
And out and spake the fourth o' them,
   "They hae been in love this mony a year."

Then out and spake the fifth o' them,
   "It were great sin true love to twain."
And out and spake the sixth o' them,   35
   "It were shame to slay a sleeping man."

Then up and gat the seventh o' them,
   And never a word spake he;
But he has striped his bright brand
   Out through Clerk Saunders' fair body.   40

Clerk Saunders he started, and Margaret she turn'd
   Into his arms as asleep she lay;
And sad and silent was the night
   That was atween thir twae.

And they lay still and sleepit sound   45
   Until the day began to daw';
And kindly she to him did say,
   "It is time, true love, you were awa'."

But he lay still, and sleepit sound,
   Albeit the sun began to sheen;   50
She look'd atween her and the wa',
   And dull and drowsie were his e'en.

Then in and came her father dear;
   Said, "Let a' your mourning be;

I'll carry the dead corse to the clay,   55
    And I'll come back and comfort thee."

"Comfort weel your seven sons,
    For comforted I will never be:
I ween 'twas neither knave nor loon
    Was in the bower last night wi' me."   60

The clinking bell gaed through the town,
    To carry the dead corse to the clay;
And Clerk Saunders stood at may Margaret's
        window,
    I wot, an hour before the day.

"Are ye sleeping, Margaret?" he says,   65
    "Or are ye waking presently?
Give me my faith and troth again,
    I wot, true love, I gied to thee."

"Your faith and troth ye sall never get,
    Nor our true love sall never twin,   70
Until ye come within my bower,
    And kiss me cheik and chin."

"My mouth it is full cold, Marg'ret;
    It has the smell, now, of the ground;
And if I kiss thy comely mouth,   75
    Thy days of life will not be lang.

"O cocks are crowing a merry midnight;
    I wot the wild fowls are boding day;
Give me my faith and troth again,
    And let me fare me on my way."   80

"Thy faith and troth thou sallna get,
    And our true love sall never twin,
Until ye tell what comes o' women,
    I wot, who die in strong traivelling?"

"Their beds are made in the heavens high,   85
    Down at the foot of our good Lord's knee,
Weel set about wi' gillyflowers;
    I wot, sweet company for to see.

"O cocks are crowing a merry midnight;
    I wot the wild fowls are boding day;   90
The psalms of heaven will soon be sung,
    And I, ere now, will be miss'd away."

Then she has taken a crystal wand,
    And she has stroken her troth thereon;
She has given it him out at the shot-window,   95
    Wi' mony a sad sigh and heavy groan.

"I thank ye, Marg'ret; I thank ye, Marg'ret;
    And ay I thank ye heartily;
Gin ever the dead come for the quick,
    Be sure, Marg'ret, I'll come for thee."   100

It's hosen and shoon, and gown alone,
    She climb'd the wall, and follow'd him,
Until she came to the green forest,
    And there she lost the sight o' him.

"Is there ony room at your head, Saunders?   105
    Is there ony room at your feet?
Or ony room at your side, Saunders,
    Where fain, fain, I wad sleep?"

"There's nae room at my head, Marg'ret,
    There's nae room at my feet;   110
My bed it is fu' lowly now,
    Amang the hungry worms I sleep.

"Cauld mould is my covering now,
    But and my winding-sheet;
The dew it falls nae sooner down   115
    Than my resting-place is weet.

"But plait a wand o' bonny birk,
    And lay it on my breast;
And shed a tear upon my grave,
    And wish my saul gude rest."   120

Then up and crew the red, red cock,
    And up and crew the gray;

" 'Tis time, 'tis time, my dear Marg'ret,
   That you were going away.

"And fair Marg'ret, and rare Marg'ret,   125
   And Marg'ret o' veritie,
Gin e'er ye love another man,
   Ne'er love him as ye did me."

THE CHERRY-TREE CAROL

Joseph was an old man,
   And an old man was he,
When he wedded Mary,
   In the land of Galilee.

Joseph and Mary walked   5
   Through an orchard good,
Where was cherries and berries,
   So red as any blood.

Joseph and Mary walked
   Through an orchard green,   10
Where was berries and cherries,
   As thick as might be seen.

O then bespoke Mary,
   So meek and so mild:
"Pluck me one cherry, Joseph,   15
   For I am with child."

O then bespoke Joseph,
   With words most unkind:
"Let him pluck thee a cherry
   That brought thee with child."   20

O then bespoke the babe,
   Within his mother's womb:
"Bow down then the tallest tree,
   For my mother to have some."

Then bowed down the highest tree   25
   Unto his mother's hand;

Then she cried, "See, Joseph,
    I have cherries at command."

O then bespoke Joseph:
    "I have done Mary wrong;   30
But cheer up, my dearest,
    And be not cast down."

Then Mary plucked a cherry,
    As red as the blood,
Then Mary went home   35
    With her heavy load.

Then Mary took her babe,
    And sat him on her knee,
Saying, "My dear son, tell me
    What this world will be."   40

"O I shall be as dead, mother,
    As the stones in the wall;
O the stones in the streets, mother,
    Shall mourn for me all.

"Upon Easter-day, mother,   45
    My uprising shall be;
O the sun and the moon, mother,
    Shall both rise with me."

THE TWA CORBIES

As I was walking all alane,
I heard twa corbies making a mane;
The tane unto the t' other say,
"Where sall we gang and dine today?"

"In behint yon auld fail dyke,   5
I wot there lies a new-slain knight;
And naebody kens that he lies there,
But his hawk, his hound, and lady fair.

Corbies: ravens. **Wot:** know.

"His hound is to the hunting gane,
His hawk to fetch the wild-fowl hame,   10
His lady's ta'en another mate,
So we may mak our dinner sweet.

"Ye'll sit on his white hause-bane,
And I'll pick out his bonny blue een;
Wi' ae lock o' his gowden hair   15
We'll theek our nest when it grows bare.

"Mony a one for him makes mane,
But nane sall ken where he is gane;
O'er his white banes when they are bare,
The wind sall blaw for evermair."   20

THE THREE RAVENS

There were three ravens sat on a tree,
They were as black as they might be.

The one of them said to his make,
"Where shall we our breakfast take?"

"Down in yonder greene field   5
There lies a knight slain under his shield;

"His hounds they lie down at his feet,
So well they their master keep;

"His hawks they flie so eagerly,
There's no fowl dare him come nigh."   10

Down there comes a fallow doe
As great with young as she might go.

She lift up his bloudy head
And kist his wounds that were so red.

She got him up upon her back   15
And carried him to earthen lake.

Earthen lake: the grave.

She buried him before the prime,
She was dead herself ere evensong time.

God send every gentleman
Such hounds, such hawks, and such a leman.   20

LORD RANDAL

"O where ha you been, Lord Randal, my son?
And where ha you been, my handsome young man?"
"I ha been at the greenwood; mother, mak my bed soon,
For I'm wearied wi huntin, and fain wad lie down."

"An wha met ye there, Lord Randal, my son?   5
An wha met you there, my handsome young man?"
"O I met wi my true-love; mother, mak my bed soon,
For I'm wearied wi huntin, and fain wad lie down."

"And what did she give you, Lord Randal, my son?
And what did she give you, my handsome young man?"   10
"Eels fried in a pan; mother, mak my bed soon,
For I'm wearied wi huntin, and fain wad lie down."

"And wha gat your leavins, Lord Randal, my son?
And wha gat your leavins, my handsome young man?"
"My hawks and my hounds; mother, mak my bed soon,   15
For I'm wearied wi huntin, and fain wad lie down."

"And what becam of them, Lord Randal, my son?
And what becam of them, my handsome young man?"
"They swelled and they died; mother, mak my bed soon,
For I'm wearied wi huntin, and fain wad lie down."   20

"O I fear you are poisoned, Lord Randal, my son!
I fear you are poisoned, my handsome young man!"
"O yes, I am poisoned, mother, mak my bed soon,
For I'm sick at the heart, and I fain wad lie down."

"What d' ye leave to your mother, Lord Randal, my son?   25
What d' ye leave to your mother, my handsome young
     man?"

Leman: mistress.

"Four and twenty milk kye; mother, mak my bed soon,
For I'm sick at the heart, and I fain wad lie down."

"What d' ye leave to your sister, Lord Randal, my son?
What d' ye leave to your sister, my handsome young man?"   30
"My gold and my silver; mother, mak my bed soon,
For I'm sick at the heart, and I fain wad lie down."

"What d' ye leave to your brother, Lord Randal, my son?
What d' ye leave to your brother, my handsome young
     man?"
"My houses and my lands; mother, mak my bed soon,   35
For I'm sick at the heart, and I fain wad lie down."

"What d' ye leave to your true-love, Lord Randal, my son?
What d' ye leave to your true-love, my handsome young
     man?"
"I leave her hell and fire; mother, mak my bed soon,
For I'm sick at the heart, and I fain wad lie down."   40

EDWARD, EDWARD

I

"Why does your brand sae drop wi' blude,
     Edward, Edward?
Why does your brand sae drop wi' blude,
     And why sae sad gang ye, O?"—
"O I hae kill'd my hawk sae gude,   5
     Mither, mither;
O I hae kill'd my hawk sae gude,
     And I had nae mair but he, O."

II

"Your hawk's blude was never sae red,
     Edward, Edward;   10
Your hawk's blude was never sae red,
     My dear son, I tell thee, O."—
"O I hae kill'd my red-roan steed,
     Mither, mither;
O I hae kill'd my red-roan steed,   15
     That erst was sae fair and free, O."

III

"Your steed was auld, and ye hae got mair,
    Edward, Edward;
Your steed was auld, and ye hae got mair;
    Some other dule ye dree, O." 20
"O I hae kill'd my father dear,
    Mither, mither;
O I hae kill'd my father dear,
    Alas, and wae is me, O!"

IV

"And whatten penance will ye dree for that, 25
    Edward, Edward?
Whatten penance will ye dree for that?
    My dear son, now tell me, O."—
I'll set my feet in yonder boat,
    Mither, mither; 30
"I'll set my feet in yonder boat,
    And I'll fare over the sea, O."

V

"And what will ye do wi' your tow'rs and your ha',
    Edward, Edward?
And what will ye do wi' your tow'rs and your ha', 35
    That were sae fair to see, O?"—
"I'll let them stand till they doun fa',
    Mither, mither;
I'll let them stand till they doun fa',
    For here never mair maun I be, O." 40

VI

"And what will ye leave to your bairns and your wife,
    Edward, Edward?
And what will ye leave to your bairns and your wife,
    When ye gang owre the sea, O?"—
"The warld's room: let them beg through life, 45
    Mither, mither;
The warld's room: let them beg through life;
    For them never mair will I see, O."

VII

"And what will ye leave to your ain mither dear,
   Edward, Edward? 50
And what will ye leave to your ain mither dear,
   My dear son, now tell me, O?"—
"The curse of hell frae me sall ye bear,
   Mither, mither;
The curse of hell frae me sall ye bear: 55
   Sic counsels ye gave to me, O!"

HELEN OF KIRCONNELL

I wish I were where Helen lies,
Night and day on me she cries;
O that I were where Helen lies,
   On fair Kirconnell lea!

Curst be the heart that thought the thought, 5
And curst the hand that fired the shot,
When in my arms burd Helen dropt,
   And died to succour me!

O think na ye my heart was sair,
When my Love dropp'd and spak nae mair! 10
There did she swoon wi' meikle care,
   On fair Kirconnell lea.

As I went down the water side,
None but my foe to be my guide,
None but my foe to be my guide, 15
   On fair Kirconnell lea;

I lighted down my sword to draw,
I hackèd him in pieces sma',
I hackèd him in pieces sma',
   For her sake that died for me. 20

O Helen fair, beyond compare!
I'll mak a garland o' thy hair,

Burd: maid. **Meikle**: much.

Shall bind my heart for evermair,
   Until the day I die!

O that I were where Helen lies!   25
Night and day on me she cries;
Out of my bed she bids me rise,
   Says, "Haste, and come to me!"

O Helen fair! O Helen chaste!
If I were with thee, I'd be blest,   30
Where thou lies low and taks thy rest,
   On fair Kirconnell lea.

I wish my grave were growing green,
A winding-sheet drawn owre my e'en,
And I in Helen's arms lying,   35
   On fair Kirconnell lea.

I wish I were where Helen lies!
Night and day on me she cries;
And I am weary of the skies,
   For her sake that died for me.   40

JOHN SKELTON (1460?–1529)

TO MISTRESS MARGARET HUSSEY

   Merry Margaret,
      As midsummer flower,
   Gentle as falcon
   Or hawk of the tower:
   With solace and gladness,   5
   Much mirth and no madness,
   All good and no badness;
      So joyously,
      So maidenly,
      So womanly   10
   Her demeaning
   In every thing,
   Far, far passing
   That I can indite,

Or suffice to write   15
Of merry Margaret
  As midsummer flower,
Gentle as falcon
Or hawk of the tower.
  As patient and still   20
And as full of good will
As fair Isaphill,
Coliander,
Sweet pomander,
Good Cassander,   25
Steadfast of thought,
Well made, well wrought,
Far may be sought
Ere that he can find
So courteous, so kind   30
As merry Margaret,
  This midsummer flower,
Gentle as falcon
Or hawk of the tower.

TO MISTRESS ISABEL PENNELL

By Saint Mary, my lady,
Your mammy and your daddy
Brought forth a goodly baby.

My maiden Isabel,
Reflaring rosabel,   5
The flagrant camomel,

The ruddy rosary,
The sovereign rosemary,
The pretty strawberry,

The columbine, the nept,   10
The jelofer well set,
The proper violet;

Reflaring: redolent. **Flagrant:** fragrant. **Nept:** mint. **Jelofer:** gillyflower.

Ennewèd your colour
Is like the daisy flower
After the April shower.   15

Star of the morrow gray,
The blossom on the spray,
The freshest flower of May,

Maidenly demure,
Of womanhood the lure;   20
Wherefore I you assure,

It were an heavenly health,
It were an endless wealth,
A life for God himself,

To hear this nightingale   25
Among the birdès small
Warbling in the vale,

Dug, dug,
Jug, jug!
Good year and good luck!   30
With Chuck, chuck, chuck, chuck!

WILLIAM CORNISH (14—?–1523)

DESIRE

The knight knock'd at the castle gate;
The lady marvell'd who was thereat.

To call the porter he would not blin;
The lady said he should not come in.

The portress was a lady bright;   5
Strangèness that lady hight.

She asked him what was his name;
He said: Desire, your man, madame.

Ennewed: tinted. **Blin:** cease. **Hight:** was called.

She said: Desire, what do ye here?
He said: Madame, as your prisonere.   10

He was counsell'd to brief a bill,
And show my lady his own will.

Kindness, said she, would it bear,
And Pity, said she, would be there.

Thus how they did we cannot say;   15
We left them there and went our way.

STEPHEN HAWES (1475?–1523?)

THE EPITAPH OF GRAUNDE AMOURE

O mortal folk! you may behold and see
  How I lie here, sometime a mighty knight;
The end of joy and all prosperity
  Is death at last, thorough his course and might;
  After the day there cometh the dark night;   5
    For though the day be never so long,
    At last the bells ringeth to evensong.

And my self called La Graunde Amoure,
  Seeking adventure in the worldly glory,
For to attain the riches and honour,   10
  Did think full little that I should here lie,
  Till death did mate me full right privily.
    Lo what I am! and whereto you must!
    Like as I am so shall you be all dust.

Then in your mind inwardly despise   15
  The brittle world, so full of doubleness,
With the vile flesh, and right soon arise
  Out of your sleep of mortal heaviness;
  Subdue the devil with grace and meekness,
    That after your life frail and transitory   20
    You may then live in joy perdurably.

Brief a bill: draw up a petition.

SIR THOMAS WYATT (1503–1542)

THE HIND

Whoso list to hunt, I know where is an hind,
But as for me, *helas!* I may no more.
The vain travail hath wearied me so sore,
I am of them that furthest come behind.
Yet may I, by no means, my wearied mind
Draw from the deer; but as she fleeth afore
Fainting I follow. I leave off therefore,
Since in a net I seek to hold the wind.
Who list her hunt, I put him out of doubt,
As well as I, may spend his time in vain;
And graven with diamonds in letters plain
There is written, her fair neck round about,
Noli me tangere, for Caesar's I am,
And wild for to hold, though I seem tame.

THEY FLEE FROM ME

They flee from me, that sometime did me seek,
With naked foot stalking in my chamber.
I have seen them gentle, tame, and meek,
That now are wild, and do not remember
That sometime they put themselves in danger   5
To take bread at my hand; and now they range
Busily seeking with a continual change.

Thankèd be fortune it hath been otherwise
Twenty times better; but once, in special,
In thin array, after a pleasant guise,   10
When her loose gown from her shoulders did fall,
And she me caught in her arms long and small,
Therewithal sweetly did me kiss,
And softly said, Dear heart, how like you this?

It was no dream; I lay broad waking: 15
But all is turnèd thorough my gentleness

The Hind: Anne Boleyn. **Caesar:** Henry VIII.

Into a strange fashion of forsaking;
And I have leave to go of her goodness,
And she also to use newfangleness.
But since that I so kindely am servèd,   20
How like you this, what hath she now deservèd?

21. This line is as printed in Tottel's *Miscellany* (1557). In the manuscript version it runs "I would fain know what she hath deserved." Tottel's fine emendation may have had Wyatt's sanction.

HENRY HOWARD, EARL OF SURREY
(1517?–1547)

DESCRIPTION OF SPRING, WHEREIN EACH THING RENEWS SAVE ONLY THE LOVER

The soote season that bud and bloom forth brings
With green hath clad the hill and eke the vale,
The nightingale with feathers new she sings,
The turtle to her make hath told her tale.
Summer is come, for every spray now springs,
The hart hath hung his old head on the pale,
The buck in brake his winter coat he flings,
The fishes float with new repairèd scale,
The adder all her slough away she slings,
The swift swallow pursueth the flyès smale,
The busy bee her honey now she mings,—
Winter is worn, that was the flowers' bale:
And thus I see, among these pleasant things
Each care decays—and yet my sorrow springs.

Soote: sweet. Eke: also. Turtle: turtle dove. Make: mate. Mings: mixes

PART TWO

The Elizabethan Age

EDMUND SPENSER (1552?–1599)
From *AMORETTI*

lxviii

Most glorious Lord of lyfe, that on this day
Didst make thy triumph over death and sin,
And having harrowd hell, didst bring away
Captivity thence captive, us to win:
This joyous day, deare Lord, with joy begin,
And grant that we, for whom thou diddest dye,
Being with thy deare blood clene washt from sin,
May live for ever in felicity:
And that thy love we weighing worthily,
May likewise love thee for the same againe;
And for they sake, that all lyke deare didst buy,
May love with one another entertayne.
So let us love, deare love, lyke as we ought:
Love is the lesson which the Lord us taught.

lxx

Fresh Spring the herald of loves mighty king,
In whose cote-armour richly are displayd
All sorts of flowers the which on earth do spring,
In goodly colours glorious arrayd,
Goe to my love, where she is carelesse layd,
Yet in her winters bowre, not well awake;
Tell her the joyous time will not be staid,
Unlesse she doe him by the forelock take;
Bid her therefore her selfe soone ready make
To wayt on Love amongst his lovely crew,
Where every one that misseth then her make
Shall be by him amearst with penance dew.
Make haste therefore, sweet love, whilest it is prime;
For none can call againe the passed time.

lxxv

One day I wrote her name upon the strand,
But came the waves and washed it away:
Agayne I wrote it with a second hand,
But came the tyde, and made my paynes his pray.
Vayne man, sayde she, that doest in vaine assay
A mortal thing so to immortalize,
For I my selve shall lyke to this decay,
And eek my name bee wyped out lykewize.
Not so, (quod I) let baser things devize
To dy in dust, but you shall live by fame:
My verse your vertues rare shall eternize,
And in the hevens wryte your glorious name.
Where whenas death shall al the world subdew,
Our love shall live, and later life renew.

EPITHALAMION

Ye learnèd sisters, which have oftentimes
Beene to me ayding, others to adorne,
Whom ye thought worthy of your gracefull rymes,
That even the greatest did not greatly scorne
To heare theyr names sung in your simple layes,   5
But joyèd in theyr praise;
And when ye list your owne mishaps to mourne,
Which death, or love, or fortunes wreck did rayse,
Your string could soone to sadder tenor turne,
And teach the woods and waters to lament   10
Your dolefull dreriment:
Now lay those sorrowful complaints aside,
And having all your heads with girland crowned,
Helpe me mine owne loves prayses to resound;
Ne let the same of any be envide: 15
So Orpheus did for his owne bride:
So I unto my selfe alone will sing;
The woods shall to me answer, and my eccho ring.
Early, before the worlds light giving lampe
His golden beame upon the hils doth spred,   20
Having disperst the nights unchearefull dampe,
Doe ye awake, and, with fresh lustyhed,

Epithalamion: a song or ode in praise of a bride and bridegroom.

Go to the bowre of my belovèd love,
   My truest turtle dove:
Bid her awake; for Hymen is awake,   25
And long since ready forth his maske to move,
With his bright tead that flames with many a flake,
And many a bachelor to waite on him,
   In theyr fresh garments trim.
Bid her awake therefore, and soone her dight,   30
For lo! the wishèd day is come at last,
That shall, for al the paynes and sorrowes past,
Pay to her usury of long delight:
   And whylest she doth her dight,
Doe ye to her of joy and solace sing,   35
That all the woods may answer, and your eccho ring.

Bring with you all the nymphes that you can heare,
Both of the rivers and the forrests greene,
And of the sea that neighbours to her neare,
Al with gay girlands goodly wel beseene.   40
And let them also with them bring in hand
   Another gay girland,
For my fayre love, of lillyes and of roses,
Bound truelove wize with a blew silke riband.
And let them make great store of bridale poses,   45
And let them eeke bring store of other flowers,
   To deck the bridale bowers.
And let the ground whereas her foot shall tread,
For feare the stones her tender foot should wrong,
Be strewed with fragrant flowers all along,   50
And diapred lyke the discolored mead.
Which done, doe at her chamber dore awayt,
   For she will waken strayt;
The whiles doe ye this song unto her sing
The woods shall to you answer, and your eccho ring.   55

Ye nymphes of Mulla, which with careful heed
The silver scaly trouts doe tend full well,
And greedy pikes which use therein to feed,
(Those trouts and pikes all others doo excel)
And ye likewise which keepe the rushy lake,   60
   Where none doo fishes take,

27. **Tead:** a whitethorn torch used in Roman marriage processions.

Bynd up the locks the which hang scatterd light,
And in his waters, which your mirror make,
Behold your faces as the christall bright,
That when you come whereas my love doth lie,   65
   No blemish she may spie.
And eke ye lightfoot mayds which keepe the dere
That on the hoary mountayne use to towre,
And the wylde wolves, which seeke them to devoure,
With your steele darts doo chace from coming neer,   70
   Be also present heere,
To helpe to decke her, and to help to sing,
That all the woods may answer, and your eccho ring.

Wake now, my love, awake! for it is time:
The rosy Morne long since left Tithones bed,   75
All ready to her silver coche to clyme,
And Phœbus gins to shew his glorious hed.
Hark how the cheerefull birds do chaunt theyr laies,
   And carroll of loves praise!
The merry larke hir mattins sings aloft,   80
The thrush replyes, the mavis descant playes,
The ouzell shrills, the ruddock warbles soft,
So goodly all agree, with sweet consent,
   To this dayes merriment.
Ah! my deere love, why doe ye sleepe thus long,   85
When meeter were that ye should now awake,
T'awayt the comming of your joyous make,
And hearken to the birds love-learnèd song,
   The deawy leaves among?
For they of joy and pleasance to you sing,   90
That all the woods them answer, and theyr eccho ring.

My love is now awake out of her dreame,
And her fayre eyes, like stars that dimmèd were
With darksome cloud, now shew theyr goodly beams
More bright then Hesperus his head doth rere.   95
Come now, ye damzels, daughters of delight,
   Helpe quickly her to dight.
But first come ye, fayre Houres, which were begot,
In Joves sweet paradice, of Day and Night,
Which doe the seasons of the year allot,   100

82. **Ruddock:** robin redbreast.

And al that ever in this world is fayre
   Do make and still repayre.
And ye three handmayds of the Cyprian Queene,
The which doe still adorne her beauties pride,
Helpe to addorne my beautifullest bride: 105
And as ye her array, still throw betweene
   Some graces to be seene:
And as ye use to Venus, to her sing,
The whiles the woods shal answer, and your eccho ring.

Now is my love all ready forth to come: 110
Let all the virgins therefore well awayt,
And ye fresh boyes, that tend upon her groome,
Prepare your selves, for he is comming strayt.
Set all your things in seemely good aray,
   Fit for so joyfull day,   115
The joyfulst day that ever sunne did see.
Faire Sun, shew forth thy favourable ray,
And let thy lifull heat not fervent be,
For feare of burning her sunshyny face,
   Her beauty to disgrace.   120
O fayrest Phœbus, father of the Muse,
If ever I did honour thee aright,
Or sing the thing that mote thy mind delight,
Doe not thy servants simple boone refuse,
But let this day, let this one day be myne,   125
   Let all the rest be thine.
Then I thy soverayne prayses loud wil sing,
That all the woods shal answer, and theyr eccho ring.

Harke how the minstrels gin to shrill aloud
Their merry musick that resounds from far,   130
The pipe, the tabor, and the trembling croud,
That well agree withouten breach or jar.
But most of all the damzels doe delite,
   When they their tymbrels smyte,
And thereunto doe daunce and carrol sweet,   135
That all the sences they doe ravish quite,
The whyles the boyes run up and downe the street,
Crying aloud with strong confusèd noyce,
   As if it were one voyce.

118. **Lifull:** lifeful, vital.   131. **Croud:** violin.

'Hymen, Iö Hymen, Hymen,' they do shout,   140
That even to the heavens theyr shouting shrill
Doth reach, and all the firmament doth fill;
To which the people, standing all about,
As in approvance doe thereto applaud,
  And loud advaunce her laud,   145
And evermore they 'Hymen, Hymen' sing,
That al the woods them answer, and theyr eccho ring.

Loe! where she comes along with portly pace,
Lyke Phœbe, from her chamber of the east,
Arysing forth to run her mighty race,   150
Clad all in white, that seemes a virgin best.
So well it her beseemes, that ye would weene
  Some angell she had beene.
Her long loose yellow locks lyke golden wyre,
Sprinckled with perle, and perling flowres atweene,   155
Doe lyke a golden mantle her attyre,
And being crownèd with a girland greene,
  Seeme lyke some mayden queene.
Her modest eyes, abashèd to behold
So many gazers as on her do stare,   160
Upon the lowly ground affixèd are;
Ne dare lift up her countenance too bold,
But blush to heare her prayses sung so loud,
  So farre from being proud.
Nathlesse doe ye still loud her prayses sing,   165
That all the woods may answer, and your eccho ring.

Tell me, ye merchants daughters, did ye see
So fayre a creature in your towne before,
So sweet, so lovely, and so mild as she,
Adornd with beautyes grace and vertues store?   170
Her goodly eyes lyke saphyres shining bright,
  Her forehead yvory white,
Her cheekes lyke apples which the sun hath rudded,
Her lips lyke cherryes charming men to byte,
Her breast like to a bowle of creame uncrudded,   175
  Her paps lyke lyllies budded,
Her snowie necke lyke to a marble towre,
And all her body like a pallace fayre,

175. **Uncrudded:** uncurdled.

Ascending uppe, with many a stately stayre,
To honors seat and chastities sweet bowre.   180
Why stand ye still, ye virgins, in amaze,
   Upon her so to gaze,
Whiles ye forget your former lay to sing,
To which the woods did answer, and your eccho ring.

But if ye saw that which no eyes can see,   185
The inward beauty of her lively spright,
Garnisht with heavenly guifts of high degree,
Much more then would ye wonder at that sight,
And stand astonisht lyke to those which red
   Medusaes mazeful hed.   190
There dwels sweet Love and constant Chastity,
Unspotted Fayth, and comely Womanhood,
Regard of Honour, and mild Modesty;
There Vertue raynes as queene in royal throne,
   And giveth lawes alone,   195
The which the base affections doe obay,
And yeeld theyr services unto her will;
Ne thought of thing uncomely ever may
Thereto approch to tempt her mind to ill.
Had ye once seene these her celestial threasures,   200
   And unrevealèd pleasures,
Then would ye wonder, and her prayses sing,
That al the woods should answer, and your eccho ring.

Open the temple gates unto my love,
Open them wide that she may enter in,   205
And all the postes adorne as doth behove,
And all the pillours deck with girlands trim,
For to receyve this saynt with honour dew,
   That commeth in to you.
With trembling steps and humble reverence,   210
She commeth in before th' Almighties view:
Of her, ye virgins, learne obedience,
When so ye come into those holy places,
   To humble your proud faces.
Bring her up to th' high altar, that she may   215
The sacred ceremonies there partake,
The which do endlesse matrimony make;

189. **Red:** saw.

And let the roring organs loudly play
The praises of the Lord in lively notes,
 The whiles with hollow throates   220
The choristers the joyous antheme sing,
That al the woods may answere, and their eccho ring.

Behold, whiles she before the altar stands,
Hearing the holy priest that to her speakes,
And blesseth her with his two happy hands,   225
How the red roses flush up in her cheekes,
And the pure snow with goodly vermill stayne,
 Like crimson dyde in grayne:
That even th' angels, which continually
About the sacred altare doe remaine,   230
Forget their service and about her fly,
Ofte peeping in her face, that seemes more fayre,
 The more they on it stare.
But her sad eyes, still fastened on the ground,
Are governèd with goodly modesty,   235
That suffers not one looke to glaunce awry,
Which may let in a little thought unsownd.
Why blush ye, love, to give to me your hand,
 The pledge of all our band?
Sing, ye sweet angels Alleluya sing,   240
That all the woods may answere, and your eccho ring.

Now al is done; bring home the bride againe,
Bring home the triumph of our victory,
Bring home with you the glory of her gaine,
With joyance bring her and with jollity.   245
Never had man more joyfull day then this,
Whom heaven would heape with blis.
Make feast therefore now all this live long day;
This day for ever to me holy is;
Poure out the wine without restraint or stay,   250
Poure not by cups, but by the belly full,
Poure out to all that wull,
And sprinkle all the postes and wals with wine,
That they may sweat, and drunken be withall.
Crowne ye God Bacchus with a coronall.   255
And Hymen also crowne with wreathes of vine;
And let the Graces daunce unto the rest,

For they can doo it best:
The whiles the maydens doe theyr carroll sing,
The which the woods shal answer, and theyr eccho ring.   260

Ring ye the bels, ye yong men of the towne,
And leave your wonted labors for this day:
This day is holy; doe ye write it downe,
That ye for ever it remember may.
This day the sunne is in his chiefest hight,   265
With Barnaby the bright,
From whence declining daily by degrees,
He somewhat loseth of his heat and light,
When once the Crab behind his back he sees.
But for this time it ill ordainèd was,   270
To chose the longest day in all the yeare,
And shortest night, when longest fitter weare:
Yet never day so long, but late would passe.
Ring ye the bels, to make it weare away,
And bonefires make all day,   275
And daunce about them, and about them sing:
That all the woods may answer, and your eccho ring.

Ah! when will this long weary day have end,
And lende me leave to come unto my love?
How slowly do the houres theyr numbers spend!   280
How slowly does sad Time his feathers move!
Hast thee, O fayrest planet, to thy home
Within the westerne foame:
Thy tyrèd steedes long since have need of rest.
Long though it be, at last I see it gloome,   285
And the bright evening star with golden creast
Appeare out of the east.
Fayre childe of beauty, glorious lampe of love,
That all the host of heaven in rankes doost lead,
And guydest lovers through the nightes dread,   290
How chearefully thou lookest from above,
And seemst to laugh atweene thy twinkling light,
As joying in the sight
Of these glad many, which for joy doe sing,
That all the woods them answer, and their eccho ring!   295

266. **Barnaby the bright:** St. Barnabas's Day, June 11.
269. **Crab:** a sign of the Zodiac.

Now ceasse, ye damsels, your delights forepast;
Enough is it that all the day was youres:
Now day is doen, and night is nighing fast:
Now bring the bryde into the brydall boures
The night is come, now soone her disaray,   300
And in her bed her lay;
Lay her in lillies and in violets,
And silken courteins over her display,
And odoured sheetes, and Arras coverlets.
Behold how goodly my faire love does ly,   305
In proud humility!
Like unto Maia, when as Jove her tooke
In Tempe, lying on the flowry gras,
Twixt sleepe and wake, after she weary was
With bathing in the Acidalian brooke.   310
Now it is night, ye damsels may be gon,
And leave my love alone.
And leave likewise your former lay to sing:
The woods no more shal answere, nor your eccho ring.

Now welcome, night! thou night so long expected, 315
That long daies labour doest at last defray,
And all my cares, which cruell Love collected,
Hast sumd in one, and cancellèd for aye:
Spread thy broad wing over my love and me,
That no man may us see,   320
And in thy sable mantle us enwrap,
From feare of perrill and foule horror free.
Let no false treason seeke us to entrap,
Nor any dread disquiet once annoy
The safety of our joy: 325
But let the night be calme and quietsome,
Without tempestuous storms or sad afray:
Lyke as when Jove with fayre Alcmena lay,
When he begot the great Tirynthian groome:
Or lyke as when he with thy selfe did lie,   330
And begot Majesty.
And let the mayds and yongmen cease to sing:
Ne let the woods them answer, nor theyr eccho ring.

Let no lamenting cryes, nor dolefull teares,
Be heard all night within, nor yet without: 335

Ne let false whispers, breeding hidden feares,
Breake gentle sleepe with misconceivèd dout.
Let no deluding dreames, nor dreadful sights,
Make sudden sad affrights;
Ne let house-fyres, nor lightnings helplesse harmes,   340
Ne let the Pouke, nor other evill sprights,
Ne let mischivous witches with theyr charmes,
Ne let hob goblins, names whose sense we see not,
Fray us with things that be not.
Let not the shriech oule, nor the storke be heard   345
Nor the night raven that still deadly yels,
Nor damnèd ghosts cald up with mighty spels,
Nor griesly vultures make us once affeard:
Ne let th' unpleasant quyre of frogs still croking
Make us to wish theyr choking.   350
Let none of these theyr drery accents sing;
Ne let the woods them answer, nor theyr eccho ring.

But let stil Silence trew night watches keepe,
That sacred Peace may in assurance rayne,
And tymely Sleep, when it is tyme to sleepe,   355
May poure his limbs forth on your pleasant playne,
The whiles an hundred little wingèd loves,
    Like divers fethered doves,
Shall fly and flutter round about our bed,
And in the secret darke, that none reproves,   360
Their prety stealthes shall worke, and snares shal spread
To filch away sweet snatches of delight,
    Conceald through covert night.
Ye sonnes of Venus, play your sports at will:
For greedy Pleasure, careless of your toyes,   365
Thinks more upon her paradise of joyes,
Then what ye do, albe it good or ill.
All night therefore attend your merry play,
    For it will soone be day:
Now none doth hinder you, that say or sing,   370
Ne will the woods now answer, nor your eccho ring.

Who is the same which at my window peepes?
Or whose is that faire face that shines so bright?
Is it not Cinthia, she that never sleepes,

341. **Pouke:** Puck, Robin Goodfellow. 374. **Cinthia:** goddess of the moon.

But walkes about high heaven al the night?   375
O fayrest goddesse, do thou not envy
   My love with me to spy:
For thou likewise didst love, though now unthought,
And for a fleece of woll, which privily
The Latmian shephard once unto thee brought,   380
   His pleasures with thee wrought.
Therefore to us be favorable now;
And sith of wemens labours thou hast charge,
And generation goodly dost enlarge,
Encline thy will t' effect our wishful vow,   385
And the chast wombe informe with timely seed,
   That may our comfort breed:
Till which we cease our hopefull hap to sing,
Ne let the woods us answere, nor our eccho ring.

And thou, great Juno, which with awful might   390
The lawes of wedlock still dost patronize,
And the religion of the faith first plight
With sacred rites hast taught to solemnize,
And eeke for comfort often callèd art
   Of women in their smart,   395
Eternally bind thou this lovely band,
And all thy blessings unto us impart.
And thou, glad Genius, in whose gentle hand
The bridale bowre and geniall bed remaine,
   Without blemish or staine,   400
And the sweet pleasures of theyr loves delight
With secret ayde doest succour and supply,
Till they bring forth the fruitful progeny,
Send us the timely fruit of this same night.
And thou, fayre Hebe, and thou, Hymen free,   405
   Grant that it may so be.
Til which we cease your further prayse to sing,
Ne any woods shal answer, nor your eccho ring.

And ye high heavens, the temple of the gods,
In which a thousand torches flaming bright   410
Doe burne, that to us wretched earthly clods
In dreadful darknesse lend desirèd light,
And all ye powers which in the same remayne,

380. **Latmian shephard:** Endymion.

More then we men can fayne,
Poure out your blessing on us plentiously,   415
And happy influence upon us raine,
That we may raise a large posterity,
Which from the earth, which they may long possesse
　　With lasting happinesse,
Up to your haughty pallaces may mount,   420
And for the guerdon of theyr glorious merit,
May heavenly tabernacles there inherit,
Of blessed saints for to increase the count.
So let us rest sweet love, in hope of this,
And cease till then our tymely joyes to sing: 425
The woods no more us answer, nor our eccho ring.

Song, made in lieu of many ornaments
With which my love should duly have bene dect,
Which cutting off through hasty accidents,
Ye would not stay your dew time to expect,   430
　　But promist both to recompens,
Be unto her a goodly ornament,
And for short time an endlesse moniment.

SIR WALTER RALEGH (1552?–1618)

WALSINGHAME

"As you came from the holy land
　　Of Walsinghame,
Met you not with my true love
　　By the way as you came?"

"How shall I know your true love,   5
　　That have met many a one
As I went to the holy land,
　　That have come, that have gone?"

"She is neither white nor brown,
　　But as the heavens fair,   10
There is none hath a form so divine
　　In the earth or the air."

"Such an one did I meet, good Sir,
    Such an angelic face,
Who like a queen, like a nymph did appear   15
    By her gait, by her grace."

"She hath left me here alone,
    All alone as unknown,
Who sometime did me lead with herself,
    And me loved as her own."   20

"What's the cause that she leaves you alone
    And a new way doth take,
Who loved you once as her own
    And her joy did you make?"

"I have loved her all my youth,   25
    But now old as you see,
Love likes not the falling fruit
    From the withered tree.

"Know that Love is a careless child,
    And forgets promise past;   30
He is blind, he is deaf when he list
    And in faith never fast.

"His desire is a dureless content
    And a trustless joy;
He is won with a world of despair   35
    And is lost with a toy."

"Of womenkind such indeed is the love
    Or the word love abused,
Under which many childish desires
    And conceits are excused.   40

"But love is a durable fire
    In the mind ever burning;
Never sick, never old, never dead,
    From itself never turning."

THE LIE

Go, soul, the body's guest,
  Upon a thankless arrant:
Fear not to touch the best;
  The truth shall be thy warrant.
    Go, since I needs must die,   5
    And give the world the lie.

Say to the court, it glows
  And shines like rotten wood;
Say to the church, it shows
  What's good, and doth no good: 10
    If church and court reply,
    Then give them both the lie.

Tell potentates, they live
  Acting by others' action,
Not loved unless they give,   15
  Not strong but by a faction:
    If potentates reply,
    Give potentates the lie.

Tell men of high condition
  That manage the estate,   20
Their purpose is ambition,
  Their practice only hate:
    And if they once reply,
    Then give them all the lie.

Tell them that brave it most,   25
  They beg for more by spending,
Who, in their greatest cost,
  Seek nothing but commending:
    And if they make reply,
    Then give them all the lie.   30

Tell zeal it wants devotion;
  Tell love it is but lust;
Tell time it is but motion;
  Tell flesh it is but dust:

2. **Arrant:** errand

And wish them not reply,   35
  For thou must give the lie.

Tell age it daily wasteth;
  Tell honour how it alters;
Tell beauty how she blasteth;
  Tell favour how it falters: 40
    And as they shall reply,
    Give every one the lie.

Tell wit how much it wrangles
  In tickle points of niceness;
Tell wisdom she entangles   45
  Herself in over-wiseness:
    And when they do reply,
    Straight give them both the lie.

Tell physic of her boldness;
  Tell skill it is prevention;   50
Tell charity of coldness;
  Tell law it is contention:
    And as they do reply,
    So give them still the lie.

Tell fortune of her blindness;   55
  Tell nature of decay;
Tell friendship of unkindness;
  Tell justice of delay:
    And if they will reply,
    Then give them all the lie.   60

Tell arts they have no soundness,
  But vary by esteeming;
Tell schools they want profoundness,
  And stand too much on seeming:
    If arts and schools reply,   65
    Give arts and schools the lie.

Tell faith it's fled the city;
  Tell how the country erreth;
Tell, manhood shakes off pity;
  Tell, virtue least preferreth: 70

And if they do reply
Spare not to give the lie.

So when thou hast, as I
　Commanded thee, done blabbing,
Although to give the lie　　　　　　　　　　75
　Deserves no less than stabbing,
　　Stab at thee he that will,
　　No stab the soul can kill.

EVEN SUCH IS TIME

Even such is time, that takes in trust
　Our youth, our joys, our all we have,
And pays us but with earth and dust;
　Who, in the dark and silent grave,
When we have wandered all our ways,
Shuts up the story of our days.
But from this earth, this grave, this dust,
My God shall raise me up, I trust.

JOHN LYLY (1553–1606)

CUPID AND CAMPASPE

Cupid and my Campaspe played
At cards for kisses; Cupid paid.
He stakes his quiver, bow, and arrows,
His mother's doves and team of sparrows;
Loses them too; then down he throws
The coral of his lip, the rose
Growing on's cheek (but none knows how);
With these the crystal of his brow,
And then the dimple of his chin;
All these did my Campaspe win.
At last he set her both his eyes;
She won, and Cupid blind did rise.
O Love, has she done this to thee?
What shall, alas! become of me?

SIR PHILIP SIDNEY (1554–1586)

LOVING IN TRUTH

Loving in truth, and fain in verse my love to show,
That she, dear she, might take some pleasure of my pain,
Pleasure might cause her read, reading might make her know,
Knowledge might pity win, and pity grace obtain,
I sought fit words to paint the blackest face of woe,
Studying inventions fine, her wits to entertain,
Oft turning others' leaves, to see if thence would flow
Some fresh and fruitful showers upon my sun-burn'd brain.
But words came halting forth, wanting Invention's stay;
Invention, Nature's child, fled step-dame Study's blows;
And others' feet still seem'd but strangers in my way.
Thus, great with child to speak, and helpless in my throes,
Biting my truant pen, beating myself for spite—
Fool, said my Muse to me, Look in thy heart and write.

WITH HOW SAD STEPS, O MOON

With how sad steps, O Moon, thou climb'st the skies,
How silently, and with how wan a face!
What! may it be that even in heav'nly place
That busy archer his sharp arrows tries?
Sure, if that long-with-love-acquainted eyes
Can judge of love, thou feel'st a lover's case.
I read it in thy looks; thy languisht grace
To me, that feel the like, thy state descries.
Then, ev'n of fellowship, O Moon, tell me,
Is constant love deem'd there but want of wit?
Are beauties there as proud as here they be?
Do they above love to be lov'd, and yet
Those lovers scorn whom that love doth possess?
Do they call virtue there ungratefulness?

MY TRUE-LOVE HATH MY HEART

My true-love hath my heart, and I have his,
By just exchange one for another given:
I hold his dear, and mine he cannot miss,

There never was a better bargain driven:
  My true-love hath my heart, and I have his.

His heart in me keeps him and me in one,
My heart in him his thoughts and senses guides:
He loves my heart, for once it was his own,
I cherish his because in me it bides:
  My true-love hath my heart, and I have his.

LEAVE ME, O LOVE

Leave me, O Love, which reachest but to dust;
And thou, my mind, aspire to higher things;
Grow rich in that which never taketh rust;
Whatever fades, but fading pleasure brings.
Draw in thy beams, and humble all thy might
To that sweet yoke where lasting freedoms be;
Which breaks the clouds, and opens forth the light,
That doth both shine and give us sight to see.
O, take fast hold! let that light be thy guide
In this small course which birth draws out to death—
And think how evil becometh him to slide,
Who seeketh heaven, and comes of heavenly breath.
  Then farewell, world; thy uttermost I see:
  Eternal Love, maintain thy life in me.

FULKE GREVILLE, LORD BROOKE
(1554–1628)

O WEARISOME CONDITION OF
HUMANITY

O wearisome condition of humanity!
Born under one law, to another bound:
Vainly begot, and yet forbidden vanity,
Created sick, commanded to be sound:
What meaneth Nature by these diverse laws,   5
Passion and Reason, self-division's cause?

Is it the mark or majesty of Power
To make offences that it may forgive?
Nature herself doth her own self deflower
To hate those errors she herself doth give.   10
But how should man think that he may not do,
If Nature did not fail, and punish too?

Tyrant to others, to herself unjust,
Only commands things difficult and hard,
Forbids us all things which it knows is lust,   15
Makes easy pains, unpossible reward.
If Nature did not take delight in blood,
She would have made more easy ways to good.

GEORGE PEELE (1558?–1597)

THE SONG AT THE WELL

*(Enter Zantippa with a pitcher to the well. A head comes up with
ears of corn, and she combs them in her lap.)*

VOICE

Gently dip, but not too deep,
For fear you make the golden beard to weep.
Fair maiden, white and red,
Comb me smooth, and stroke my head,
And thou shalt have some cockell-bread.

*(A second head comes up full of gold, which she combs into
her lap.)*

SECOND HEAD

Gently dip, but not too deep,
For fear thou make the golden beard to weep.
Fair maiden, white and red,
Comb me smooth and stroke my head,
And every hair a sheaf shall be,
And every sheaf a golden tree.

BETHSABE'S SONG

Hot sun, cool fire, tempered with sweet air,
Black shade, fair nurse, shadow my white hair:
Shine, sun; burn, fire; breathe, air, and ease me;
Black shade, fair nurse, shroud me and please me:
Shadow, my sweet nurse, keep me from burning,
Make not my glad cause, cause of mourning.
    Let not my beauty's fire
    Inflame unstaid desire,
    Nor pierce any bright eye
    That wand'reth lightly.

SAMUEL DANIEL (1562?–1619)

ARE THEY SHADOWS THAT WE SEE?

    Are they shadows that we see?
    And can shadows pleasure give?
    Pleasures only shadows be
    Cast by bodies we conceive,
    And are made the things we deem,
    In those figures which they seem.
But these pleasures vanish fast,
Which by shadows are exprest:
    Pleasures are not, if they last,
    In their passing, is their best.
    Glory is most bright and gay
    In a flash, and so away.
Feed apace then, greedy eyes,
On the wonder you behold.
    Take it sudden as it flies
    Though you take it not to hold:
When your eyes have done their part,
Thought must length it in the heart.

MARK ALEXANDER BOYD (1563–1601)

SONET

Fra bank to bank, fra wood to wood I rin
Ourhailit with my feeble fantasie
Like til a leaf that fallis from a tree
Or til a reed ourblawin with the wind,

Two gods guides me, the ane of them is blin,
Yea, and a bairn brocht up in vanitie,
The next a wife ingenrit of the sea
And lichter nor a dauphin with her fin.

Unhappy is the man for evermair
That tills the sand and sawis in the air,

But twice unhappier is he, I lairn,
That feidis in his heart a mad desire
And follows on a woman throw the fire
Led by a blind and teachit by a bairn.

MICHAEL DRAYTON (1563–1631)

THE PARTING

Since there's no help, come, let us kiss and part;
Nay, I have done, you get no more of me;
And I am glad, yea glad with all my heart,
That thus so cleanly I myself can free.
Shake hands for ever, cancel all our vows,
And, when we meet at any time again,
Be it not seen in either of our brows
That we one jot of former love retain.
Now at the last gasp of Love's latest breath,

Ourhailit: carried away	**Lichter:** lighter, more unstable, more
Blin: blind	capricious
Wife: woman	**Dauphin:** dolphin
Ingenrit: engendered	**Sawis:** sows
	Feidis: feeds

When, his pulse failing, Passion speechless lies,
When Faith is kneeling by his bed of death,
And Innocence is closing up his eyes,
   Now if thou wouldst, when all have given him over,
   From death to life thou might'st him yet recover.

CHRISTOPHER MARLOWE (1564–1593)

THE PASSIONATE SHEPHERD TO HIS LOVE

Come live with me and be my Love,
And we will all the pleasures prove
That valleys, groves, hills and fields,
Woods or steepy mountain yields.

And we will sit upon the rocks   5
Seeing the shepherds feed their flocks,
By shallow rivers, to whose falls
Melodious birds sing madrigals.

And I will make thee beds of roses
And a thousand fragrant posies,   10
A cap of flowers, and a kirtle
Embroidered all with leaves of myrtle.

A gown made of the finest wool,
Which from our pretty lambs we pull,
Fair linèd slippers for the cold,   15
With buckles of the purest gold.

A belt of straw and ivy buds,
With coral clasps and amber studs:
And if these pleasures may thee move,
Come live with me and be my love.   20

The shepherd swains shall dance and sing
For thy delight each May-morning:
If these delights thy mind may move,
Then live with me and be my love.

THE NYMPH'S REPLY TO THE SHEPHERD

(by Sir Walter Ralegh)

If all the world and love were young,
And truth in every shepherd's tongue,
These pretty pleasures might me move
To live with thee and be thy love.

But time drives flocks from field to fold,   5
When rivers rage and rocks grow cold,
And Philomel becometh dumb;
The rest complain of cares to come.

The flowers do fade, and wanton fields
To wayward Winter reckoning yields;   10
A honey tongue, a heart of gall,
Is fancy's spring, but sorrow's fall.

Thy gowns, thy shoes, thy beds of roses,
Thy cap, thy kirtle, and thy posies
Soon break, soon wither, soon forgotten,   15
In folly ripe, in reason rotten.

Thy belt of straw and ivy buds,
Thy coral clasps and amber studs,
All these in me no means can move
To come to thee and be thy love.   20

But could youth last and love still breed,
Had joys no date nor age no need,
Then these delights my mind might move
To live with thee and be thy love.

WILLIAM SHAKESPEARE (1564–1616)

SONNETS

XVIII

Shall I compare thee to a Summer's day?
Thou art more lovely and more temperate:
Rough winds do shake the darling buds of May,
And Summer's lease hath all too short a date:
Sometime too hot the eye of heaven shines,
And often is his gold complexion dimm'd;
And every fair from fair sometime declines,
By chance or nature's changing course untrimm'd:
But thy eternal Summer shall not fade
Nor lose possession of that fair thou ow'st;
Nor shall Death brag thou wander'st in his shade,
When in eternal lines to time thou grow'st:
  So long as men can breathe, or eyes can see,
  So long lives this, and this gives life to thee.

XXIX

When, in disgrace with Fortune and men's eyes,
I all alone beweep my outcast state,
And trouble deaf heaven with my bootless cries,
And look upon myself, and curse my fate,
Wishing me like to one more rich in hope,
Featured like him, like him with friends possest,
Desiring this man's art and that man's scope,
With what I most enjoy contented least;
Yet in these thoughts myself almost despising—
Haply I think on thee: and then my state,
Like to the Lark at break of day arising
From sullen earth, sings hymns at Heaven's gate;
  For thy sweet love rememb'red such wealth brings
  That then I scorn to change my state with Kings.

XXX

When to the sessions of sweet silent thought
I summon up remembrance of things past,
I sigh the lack of many a thing I sought,
And with old woes new wail my dear time's waste:

Then can I drown an eye, unused to flow,
For precious friends hid in death's dateless night,
And weep afresh love's long-since-cancell'd woe,
And moan th' expense of many a vanish'd sight:
Then can I grieve at grievances foregone,
And heavily from woe to woe tell o'er
The sad account of fore-bemoanèd moan,
Which I new pay as if not paid before.
    But if the while I think on thee, dear friend,
    All losses are restored and sorrows end.

XXXIII

Full many a glorious morning have I seen
Flatter the mountain-tops with sovereign eye,
Kissing with golden face the meadows green,
Gilding pale streams with heavenly alchemy;
Anon permit the basest clouds to ride
With ugly rack on his celestial face,
And from the forlorn world his visage hide,
Stealing unseen to west with this disgrace:
Even so my sun one early morn did shine
With all-triumphant splendour on my brow;
But out, alack! he was but one hour mine;
The region cloud hath mask'd him from me now.
    Yet him for this my love no whit disdaineth;
    Suns of the world may stain when heaven's sun
      staineth.

LV

Not marble, nor the gilded monuments
Of princes, shall outlive this powerful rhyme;
But you shall shine more bright in these contents
Than unswept stone besmear'd with sluttish time.
When wasteful war shall statues overturn,
And broils root out the work of masonry,
Nor Mars his sword nor war's quick fire shall burn
The living record of your memory.
'Gainst death and all-oblivious enmity
Shall you pace forth; your praise shall still find room
Even in the eyes of all posterity
That wears this world out to the ending doom.
    So, till the judgement that yourself arise,
    You live in this, and dwell in lovers' eyes.

LX

Like as the waves make towards the pebbled shore,
So do our minutes hasten to their end;
Each changing place with that which goes before,
In sequent toil all forwards do contend.
Nativity, once in the main of light,
Crawls to maturity, wherewith being crown'd,
Crooked eclipses 'gainst his glory fight,
And Time that gave doth now his gift confound.
Time doth transfix the flourish set on youth
And delves the parallels in beauty's brow,
Feeds on the rarities of nature's truth,
And nothing stands but for his scythe to mow:
    And yet to times in hope my verse shall stand,
    Praising thy worth, despite his cruel hand.

LXIV

When I have seen by Time's fell hand defaced
The rich proud cost of outworn buried age;
When sometime lofty towers I see down-razed
And brass eternal slave to mortal rage;
When I have seen the hungry ocean gain
Advantage on the kingdom of the shore,
And the firm soil win of the watery main,
Increasing store with loss and loss with store;
When I have seen such interchange of state,
Or state itself confounded to decay;
Ruin hath taught me thus to ruminate,
That Time will come and take my love away.
    This thought is as a death, which cannot choose
    But weep to have that which it fears to lose.

LXV

Since brass, nor stone, nor earth, nor boundless sea,
But sad mortality o'er-sways their power,
How with this rage shall beauty hold a plea,
Whose action is no stronger than a flower?
O, how shall summer's honey breath hold out
Against the wrackful siege of battering days,
When rocks impregnable are not so stout,
Nor gates of steel so strong, but Time decays?
O fearful meditation! where, alack,

Shall Time's best jewel from Time's chest lie hid?
Or what strong hand can hold his swift foot back?
Or who his spoil of beauty can forbid?
   O, none, unless this miracle have might,
   That in black ink my love may still shine bright.

LXVI

Tired with all these, for restful death I cry,—
As, to behold Desert a beggar born,
And needy Nothing trimm'd in jollity,
And purest Faith unhappily forsworn,
And gilded Honour shamefully misplaced,
And maiden Virtue rudely strumpeted,
And right Perfection wrongfully disgraced,
And Strength by limping sway disablèd,
And Art made tongue-tied by Authority,
And Folly doctor-like controlling Skill,
And simple Truth miscall'd Simplicity,
And captive Good attending captain Ill:
   Tired with all these, from these would I be gone,
   Save that, to die, I leave my love alone.

LXXI

No longer mourn for me when I am dead
Than you shall hear the surly sullen bell
Give warning to the world that I am fled
From this vile world, with vilest worms to dwell:
Nay, if you read this line, remember not
The hand that writ it; for I love you so
That I in your sweet thoughts would be forgot
If thinking on me then should make you woe.
O, if, I say, you look upon this verse
When I perhaps compounded am with clay,
Do not so much as my poor name rehearse,
But let your love even with my life decay,
   Lest the wise world should look into your moan
   And mock you with me after I am gone.

LXXIII

That time of year thou mayst in me behold
When yellow leaves, or none, or few, do hang
Upon those boughs which shake against the cold,

Bare ruin'd choirs, where late the sweet birds sang.
In me thou see'st the twilight of such day
As after sunset fadeth in the west,
Which by and by black night doth take away,
Death's second self, that seals up all in rest.
In me thou see'st the glowing of such fire
That on the ashes of his youth doth lie,
As the death-bed whereon it must expire,
Consumed with that which it was nourish'd by.
    This thou perceivest, which makes thy love more
       strong,
    To love that well which thou must leave ere long.

CVI

When in the chronicle of wasted time
I see descriptions of the fairest wights,
And beauty making beautiful old rhyme
In praise of ladies dead and lovely knights,
Then, in the blazon of sweet beauty's best,
Of hand, of foot, of lip, of eye, of brow,
I see their antique pen would have express'd
Even such a beauty as you master now.
So all their praises are but prophecies
Of this our time, all you prefiguring;
And, for they look'd but with divining eyes,
They had not skill enough your worth to sing:
    For we, which now behold these present days,
    Have eyes to wonder, but lack tongues to praise.

CVII

Not mine own fears, nor the prophetic soul
Of the wide world dreaming on things to come,
Can yet the lease of my true love control,
Supposed as forfeit to a confined doom.
The mortal moon hath her eclipse endured,
And the sad augurs mock their own presage;
Incertainties now crown themselves assured,
And peace proclaims olives of endless age.
Now with the drops of this most balmy time
My love looks fresh, and Death to me subscribes,
Since, spite of him, I'll live in this poor rhyme,
While he insults o'er dull and speechless tribes:

And thou in this shalt find thy monument,
When tyrants' crests and tombs of brass are spent.

CXVI

Let me not to the marriage of true minds
Admit impediments. Love is not love
Which alters when it alteration finds,
Or bends with the remover to remove:
O, no! it is an ever-fixèd mark,
That looks on tempests and is never shaken;
It is the star to every wand'ring bark,
Whose worth's unknown, although his heighth be taken.
Love's not Time's fool, though rosy lips and cheeks
Within his bending sickle's compass come;
Love alters not with his brief hours and weeks,
But bears it out even to the edge of doom:—
    If this be error and upon me proved,
    I never writ, nor no man ever loved.

CXXIX

Th' expense of spirit in a waste of shame
Is lust in action; and till action, lust
Is perjur'd, murd'rous, bloody, full of blame,
Savage, extreme, rude, cruel, not to trust:
Enjoy'd no sooner but despised straight;
Past reason hunted, and no sooner had,
Past reason hated, as a swallow'd bait
On purpose laid to make the taker mad:
Mad in pursuit and in possession so;
Had, having, and in quest to have, extreme;
A bliss in proof, and prov'd, a very woe;
Before, a joy propos'd; behind, a dream.
    All this the world well knows; yet none knows well
    To shun the heaven that leads men to this hell.

CXXX

My mistress' eyes are nothing like the sun;
Coral is far more red than her lips red;
If snow be white, why then her breasts are dun;
If hairs be wires, black wires grow on her head.
I have seen roses damask'd, red and white,
But no such roses see I in her cheeks;

And in some perfumes is there more delight
Than in the breath that from my mistress reeks.
I love to hear her speak, yet well I know
That music hath a far more pleasing sound;
I grant I never saw a goddess go;
My mistress, when she walks, treads on the ground:
    And yet, by heaven, I think my love as rare
    As any She belied with false compare.

CXLVI

Poor soul, the center of my sinful earth,
Thrall to these rebel powers that thee array,
Why dost thou pine within and suffer dearth,
Painting thy outward walls so costly gay?
Why so large cost, having so short a lease,
Dost thou upon thy fading mansion spend?
Shall worms, inheritors of this excess,
Eat up thy charge? Is this thy body's end?
Then, soul, live thou upon thy servant's loss,
And let that pine to aggravate thy store;
Buy terms divine in selling hours of dross;
Within be fed, without be rich no more:
    So shalt thou feed on Death, that feeds on men,
    And Death once dead, there's no more dying then.

SONGS FROM THE PLAYS

WHO IS SILVIA?

(From *Two Gentlemen of Verona*)

Who is Silvia? what is she,
    That all our swains commend her?
Holy, fair, and wise is she;
    The heaven such grace did lend her,
That she might admirèd be.   5

Is she kind as she is fair?
    For beauty lives with kindness.

Array: accuse, arraign, impose upon.
Aggravate: make greater.

Love doth to her eyes repair,
    To help him of his blindness,
And, being helped, inhabits there.   10

Then to Silvia let us sing,
    That Silvia is excelling;
She excels each mortal thing
    Upon the dull earth dwelling:
To her let us garlands bring.   15

WHEN DAISIES PIED
(From *Love's Labour's Lost*)

When daisies pied and violets blue
    And lady-smocks all silver-white
And cuckoo buds of yellow hue
    Do paint the meadows with delight,
The cuckoo then on every tree,   5
Mocks married men; for thus sings he,
                "Cuckoo!
Cuckoo, cuckoo!" Oh word of fear,
Unpleasing to a married ear!

When shepherds pipe on oaten straws,   10
    And merry larks are ploughmen's clocks,
When turtles tread, and rooks, and daws,
    And maidens bleach their summer smocks,
The cuckoo then, on every tree,
Mocks married men; for thus sings he,   15
                "Cuckoo!
Cuckoo, cuckoo!" Oh word of fear,
Unpleasing to a married ear!

WHEN ICICLES HANG BY THE WALL
(From *Love's Labour's Lost*)

When icicles hang by the wall,
    And Dick the shepherd blows his nail,
And Tom bears logs into the hall,
    And milk comes frozen home in pail,

When blood is nipp'd, and ways be foul,   5
Then nightly sings the staring owl,
     To-whit!
To-who!—a merry note,
While greasy Joan doth keel the pot.

When all aloud the wind doth blow,
  And coughing drowns the parson's saw,
And birds sit brooding in the snow,
  And Marian's nose looks red and raw,
When roasted crabs hiss in the bowl,
Then nightly sings the staring owl,   15
     To-whit!
To-who!—a merry note,
While greasy Joan doth keel the pot.

NOW THE HUNGRY LION ROARS

(From *A Midsummer Night's Dream*)

Now the hungry lion roars,
  And the wolf behowls the moon;
Whilst the heavy ploughman snores,
  All with weary task fordone.
Now the wasted brands do glow,   5
  Whilst the screech-owl, screeching loud,
Puts the wretch that lies in woe
  In remembrance of a shroud.
Now it is the time of night
  That the graves, all gaping wide,   10
Every one lets forth his sprite,
  In the churchway paths to glide.
And we fairies, that do run
  By the triple Hecate's team,
From the presence of the sun,   15
  Following darkness like a dream,
Now are frolic; not a mouse
Shall disturb this hallowed house:
I am sent with broom before,
To sweep the dust behind the door.   20

TELL ME WHERE IS FANCY BRED
(From *The Merchant of Venice*)

Tell me where is fancy bred,
Or in the heart or in the head?
How begot, how nourishèd?
   Reply, reply.
It is engender'd in the eyes,
With gazing fed; and fancy dies
In the cradle where it lies.
   Let us all ring fancy's knell:
   I'll begin it,—Ding, dong, bell.

SIGH NO MORE LADIES
(From *Much Ado About Nothing*)

Sigh no more, ladies, sigh no more!
   Men were deceivers ever,
One foot in sea and one on shore,
   To one thing constant never:
Then sigh not so, but let them go,   5
   And be you blithe and bonny,
Converting all your sounds of woe
   Into Hey nonny, nonny!

Sing no more ditties, sing no moe
   Of dumps so dull and heavy!   10
The fraud of men was ever so,
   Since summer first was leavy:
Then sigh not so, but let them go,
   And be you blithe and bonny,
Converting all your sounds of woe   15
   Into Hey nonny, nonny!

UNDER THE GREENWOOD TREE
(From *As You Like It*)

Under the greenwood tree
Who loves to lie with me
And turn his merry note
Unto the sweet bird's throat

Come hither! come hither! come hither!   5
  Here shall he see
   No enemy
But winter and rough weather.

  Who doth ambition shun
  And loves to live i' the sun,   10
  Seeking the food he eats
  And pleased with what he gets,
Come hither! come hither! come hither!
  Here shall he see
   No enemy   15
But winter and rough weather.

BLOW, BLOW, THOU WINTER WIND
(From *As You Like It*)

  Blow, blow, thou winter wind!
  Thou art not so unkind
  As man's ingratitude;
  Thy tooth is not so keen,
  Because thou art not seen,   5
   Although thy breath be rude.

Heigh ho! sing heigh ho! unto the green holly:
Most friendship is feigning, most loving mere folly:
  Then, heigh ho, the holly!
  This life is most jolly.   10

  Freeze, freeze, thou bitter sky!
  That dost not bite so nigh
   As benefits forgot;
  Though thou the waters warp,
  Thy sting is not so sharp   15
   As friend remembered not.

Heigh ho! sing, heigh ho! etc.

COME AWAY, DEATH
(From *Twelfth Night*)

Come away, come away, Death!
  And in sad cypress let me be laid;
Fly away, fly away, breath;
  I am slain by a fair cruel maid.
My shroud of white, stuck all with yew,   5
      O, prepare it!
My part of death, no one so true
      Did share it.

Not a flower, not a flower sweet,
  On my black coffin let there be strown;   10
Not a friend, not a friend greet
  My poor corpse, where my bones shall be
    thrown:
A thousand thousand sighs to save,
      Lay me, O, where
Sad true lover never find my grave,   15
      To weep there!

O MISTRESS MINE
(From *Twelfth Night*)

O Mistress mine, where are you roaming?
O stay and hear! your true-love's coming
  That can sing both high and low;
Trip no further, pretty sweeting:
Journeys end in lovers meeting
  Every wise man's son doth know.

What is love? 'tis not hereafter;
Present mirth hath present laughter;
  What's to come is still unsure:
In delay there lies no plenty:
Then come kiss me, Sweet-and-twenty,
  Youth's a stuff will not endure.

TAKE, O! TAKE THOSE LIPS AWAY
(From *Measure for Measure*)

Take, O! take those lips away,
  That so sweetly were forsworn,
And those eyes, the break of day,
  Lights that do mislead the morn;
But my kisses bring again,
    Bring again,
Seals of love, but sealed in vain,
    Sealed in vain.

HARK, HARK! THE LARK
(From *Cymbeline*)

Hark, hark! the lark at heaven's gate sings,
  And Phœbus 'gins arise,
His steeds to water at those springs
  On chaliced flowers that lies;
And winking Mary-buds begin
  To ope their golden eyes:
With every thing that pretty is,
  My lady sweet, arise!
    Arise, arise!

FEAR NO MORE THE HEAT O' THE SUN
(From *Cymbeline*)

Fear no more the heat o' the sun,
  Nor the furious winter's rages;
Thou thy worldly task hast done,
  Home art gone, and ta'en thy wages:
Golden lads and girls all must,   5
As chimney-sweepers, come to dust.

Fear no more the frown o' the great;
  Thou art past the tyrant's stroke;
Care no more to clothe and eat;
  To thee the reed is as the oak: 10

The Sceptre, Learning, Physic, must
All follow this, and come to dust.

Fear no more the lightning-flash,
    Nor th' all-dreaded thunder-stone;
Fear not slander, censure rash;   15
    Thou hast finished joy and moan:
All lovers young, all lovers must
Consign to thee, and come to dust.

No exorciser harm thee!
Nor no witchcraft charm thee!   20
Ghost unlaid forbear thee!
Nothing ill come near thee!
Quiet consummation have;
And renownèd be thy grave!

WHERE THE BEE SUCKS
(From *The Tempest*)

Where the bee sucks, there suck I:
In a cowslip's bell I lie;
There I couch, when owls do cry:
On the bat's back I do fly
After summer merrily.
    Merrily, merrily, shall I live now,
    Under the blossom that hangs on the bough!

FULL FATHOM FIVE
(From *The Tempest*)

Full fathom five thy father lies;
    Of his bones are coral made;
Those are pearls that were his eyes:
    Nothing of him that doth fade
But doth suffer a sea-change
Into something rich and strange.
Sea-nymphs hourly ring his knell:
                            Ding-dong.
Hark! now I hear them,—Ding-dong, bell.

THE PHŒNIX AND THE TURTLE

Let the bird of loudest lay
 On the sole Arabian tree,
 Herald sad and trumpet be,
To whose sound chaste wings obey.

But thou shrieking harbinger,   5
 Foul precurrer of the fiend,
 Augur of the fever's end,
To this troop come thou not near.

From this session interdict
 Every fowl of tyrant wing   10
 Save the eagle, feathered king.
Keep the obsequy so strict.

Let the priest in surplice white
 That defunctive music can,
 Be the death-divining swan,   15
Lest the requiem lack his right.

And thou, treble-dated crow,
 That thy sable gender mak'st
 With the breath thou giv'st and tak'st,
'Mongst our mourners shalt thou go.   20

Here the anthem doth commence:—
 Love and constancy is dead;
 Phœnix and the turtle fled
In a mutual flame from hence.

So they loved, as love in twain   25
 Had the essence but in one;
 Two distincts, division none;
Number there in love was slain.

Hearts remote, yet not asunder;
 Distance, and no space was seen   30
 'Twixt the turtle and his queen:
But in them it were a wonder.

Turtle: turtle dove.

So between them love did shine,
 That the turtle saw his right
  Flaming in the phœnix' sight;   35
Either was the other's mine.

Property was thus appalled,
 That the self was not the same;
  Single nature's double name
Neither two nor one was called.   40

Reason, in itself confounded,
 Saw division grow together;
  To themselves yet either neither;
Simple were so well compounded,

That it cried, "How true a twain   45
 Seemeth this concordant one!
  Love hath reason, reason none
If what parts can so remain."

Whereupon it made this threne
 To the phœnix and the dove,   50
  Co-supremes and stars of love,
As chorus to their tragic scene.

THRENOS

Beauty, truth, and rarity,
Grace in all simplicity,
Here enclosed in cinders lie.   55

Death is now the phœnix' nest;
And the turtle's loyal breast
To eternity doth rest,

Leaving no posterity:
'Twas not their infirmity,   60
It was married chastity.

Truth may seem, but cannot be;
Beauty brag, but 'tis not she;
Truth and beauty buried be.

To this urn let those repair   65
That are either true or fair;
For these dead birds sigh a prayer.

THOMAS CAMPION (1567–1620)

CHERRY-RIPE

There is a garden in her face
  Where roses and white lilies grow;
A heavenly paradise is that place,
  Wherein all pleasant fruits do flow.
    There cherries grow which none may buy   5
    Till "Cherry-ripe" themselves do cry.

Those cherries fairly do inclose
  Of orient pearl a double row,
Which when her lovely laughter shows,
  They look like rosebuds filled with snow;   10
    Yet them nor peer nor prince can buy
    Till "Cherry-ripe" themselves do cry.

Her eyes like angels watch them still;
  Her brows like bended bows do stand,
Threat'ning with piercing frowns to kill   15
  All that attempt with eye or hand
    Those sacred cherries to come nigh,
    Till "Cherry-ripe" themselves do cry.

ROSE-CHEEKED LAURA

  Rose-cheeked Laura, come,
Sing, thou smoothly with thy beauty's
Silent music, either other
    Sweetly gracing.

  Lovely forms do flow   5
From concent divinely framèd;
Heav'n is music, and thy beauty's
    Birth is heavenly.

These dull notes we sing
Discords need for helps to grace them;   10
Only beauty purely loving
    Knows no discord,

But still moves delight,
Like clear springs renewed by flowing,   15
Ever perfect, ever in them-
    selves eternal.

VIVAMUS MEA LESBIA ATQUE AMEMUS

My sweetest Lesbia, let us live and love;
And though the sager sort our deeds reprove,
Let us not weigh them. Heaven's great lamps do dive
Into their west, and straight again revive;
But soon as once set is our little light,   5
Then must we sleep one ever-during night.

If all would lead their lives in love like me,
Then bloody swords and armour should not be;
No drum nor trumpet peaceful sleeps should move,
Unless alarm came from the camp of Love.   10
But fools do live and waste their little light,
And seek with pain their ever-during night.

When timely death my life and fortune ends,
Let not my hearse be vext with mourning friends;
But let all lovers, rich in triumph, come,   15
And with sweet pastimes grace my happy tomb.
And, Lesbia, close up thou my little light,
And crown with love my ever-during night.

WHEN TO HER LUTE CORINNA SINGS

When to her lute Corinna sings,
Her voice revives the leaden strings,
And doth in highest notes appear,
As any challenged Echo clear;
But when she doth of mourning speak,
E'en with her sighs the strings do break.

And as her lute doth live or die,
Led by her passion, so must I!
For when of pleasure she doth sing,
My thoughts enjoy a sudden spring;
But if she doth of sorrow speak,
E'en from my heart the strings do break.

KIND ARE HER ANSWERS

Kind are her answers,
But her performance keeps no day;
Breaks time, as dancers
From their own music when they stray.
All her free favours   5
And smooth words wing my hopes in vain.
O! did ever voice so sweet but only feign?
Can true love yield such delay,
Converting joy to pain?

Lost is our freedom,   10
When we submit to women so:
Why do we need them
When, in their best they work our woe?
There is no wisdom
Can alter ends, by Fate prefixt.   15
O! why is the good of man with evil mixt?
Never were days yet called two,
But one night went betwixt.

YOUNG AND SIMPLE THOUGH I AM

Young and simple though I am,
I have heard of Cupid's name:
Guess I can what thing it is
Men desire when they do kiss.
Smoke can never burn, they say,   5
But the flames that follow may.

I am not so foul or fair
To be proud nor to despair;

Yet my lips have oft observed
Men that kiss them press them hard,   10
As glad lovers use to do
When their new-met loves they woo.

Faith, 'tis but a foolish mind,
Yet methinks, a heat I find,
Like thirstlonging, that doth bide   15
Ever on my weaker side,
Where they say my heart doth move.
Venus, grant it be not love.

If it be, alas, what then?
Were not women made for men?   20
As good 'twere a thing were past
That must needs be done at last.
Roses that are over-blown,
Grow less sweet, then fall alone.

Yet not churl, nor silken gull,   25
Shall my maiden blossom pull;
Who shall not I soon can tell;
Who shall, would I could as well!
This I know, whoe'er he be,
Love he must or flatter me.   30

WHEN THOU MUST HOME

When thou must home to shades of underground,
    And there arrived, a new admirèd guest,
The beauteous spirits do engirt thee round,
    White Iope, blithe Helen and the rest,
To hear the stories of thy finished love
From that smooth tongue, whose music hell can move:

Then wilt thou speak of banqueting delights,
    Of masks and revels which sweet youth did make,
Of tourneys and great challenges of knights,
    And all these triumphs for thy beauty's sake.
When thou hast told these honours done to thee,
Then tell, O! tell, how thou didst murder me.

AUTHOR UNKNOWN

TOM O' BEDLAM'S SONG

From the hag and hungry goblin
  That into rags would rend ye,
And the spirit that stands by the naked man
  In the book of moons, defend ye,
That of your five sound senses   5
  You never be forsaken,
Nor wander from yourselves with Tom,
  Abroad to beg your bacon.
    While I do sing: Any food,
      Any feeding, drink, or clothing?   10
    Come, dame or maid, be not afraid,
      Poor Tom will injure nothing.

Of thirty bare years have I
  Twice twenty been enragèd,
And of forty been three times fifteen   15
  In durance soundly cagèd
On the lordly lofts of Bedlam,
  With stubble soft and dainty,
Brave bracelets strong, sweet whips, ding-dong,
  With wholesome hunger plenty.   20
    And now I sing: Any food,
      Any feeding, drink, or clothing?
    Come, dame or maid, be not afraid,
      Poor Tom will injure nothing.

With a thought I took for Maudlin,   25
  And a cruse of cockle pottage,
With a thing thus tall, sky bless you all,
  I befell into this dotage.
I slept not since the Conquest,
  Till then I never wakèd,   30
Till the roguish boy of love where I lay
  Me found and stripped me naked.

17. **Bedlam:** Bethlehem Hospital (for the insane)
31. **Roguish boy:** Cupid

And now I sing: Any food,
　　Any feeding, drink, or clothing?
Come, dame or maid, be not afraid,　　　　　35
　　Poor Tom will injure nothing.

When I short have shorn my sour-face,
　　And swigged my horny barrel,
In an oaken inn I pound my skin,
　　As a suit of gilt apparel.　　　　　　　　40
The moon's my constant mistress,
　　And the lowly owl my morrow;
The flaming drake and the night-crow make
　　Me music to my sorrow.
　　　While I do sing: Any food,　　　　　　45
　　　　Any feeding, drink, or clothing?
　　　Come, dame or maid, be not afraid,
　　　　Poor Tom will injure nothing.

The palsy plagues my pulses,
　　When I prig your pigs or pullen,　　　　　50
Your culvers take, or matchless make
　　Your chanticleer or sullen.
When I want provant, with Humphrey
　　I sup, and when benighted,
I repose in Powles with waking souls,　　　　55
　　Yet never am affrighted.
　　　But I do sing: Any food,
　　　　Any feeding, drink, or clothing?
　　　Come, dame or maid, be not afraid,
　　　　Poor Tom will injure nothing.　　　　60

I know more than Apollo,
　　For oft when he lies sleeping,
I see the stars at bloody wars
　　In the wounded welkin weeping,
The moon embrace her shepherd,　　　　　65
　　And the queen of love her warrior,
While the first doth horn the star of morn,
　　And the next the heavenly Farrier.

50. **Prig:** steal
　　Pullen: poultry
53. **Humphrey:** to dine with Duke
　　Humphrey—to go hungry

55. **Powles:** St. Paul's churchyard
68. **Farrier:** Vulcan, the husband of
　　the queen of love, Venus

While I do sing: Any food,
　Any feeding, drink, or clothing?　　　　　70
Come, dame or maid, be not afraid,
　Poor Tom will injure nothing.

The gipsy Snap and Pedro
　Are none of Tom's comradoes.
The punk I scorn, and the cutpurse sworn,　　75
　And the roaring boys' bravadoes.
The meek, the white, the gentle,
　Me handle, touch, and spare not;
But those that cross Tom Rhinoceros
　Do what the panther dare not.　　　　　80
　　Although I sing: Any food,
　　　Any feeding, drink, or clothing?
　　Come, dame or maid, be not afraid,
　　　Poor Tom will injure nothing.

With an host of furious fancies　　　　　85
　Whereof I am commander,
With a burning spear and a horse of air
　To the wilderness I wander.
By a knight of ghosts and shadows
　I summoned am to tourney　　　　　90
Ten leagues beyond the wide world's end,
　Methinks it is no journey.
　　Yet will I sing: Any food,
　　　Any feeding, drink, or clothing?
　　Come, dame or maid, be not afraid,　　95
　　　Poor Tom will injure nothing.

PART THREE
The Seventeenth Century

JOHN DONNE (1572–1631)

SONG

Go and catch a falling star,
  Get with child a mandrake root,
Tell me where all past years are,
  Or who cleft the devil's foot,
Teach me to hear mermaids singing,   5
Or to keep off envy's stinging,
       And find
       What wind
Serves to advance an honest mind.

If thou be'st born to strange sights,   10
  Things invisible to see,
Ride ten thousand days and nights,
  Till age snow white hairs on thee.
Thou, when thou return'st, wilt tell me,
All strange wonders that befell thee,   15
       And swear,
       No where
Lives a woman true and fair.

If thou find'st one, let me know;
  Such a pilgrimage were sweet.   20
Yet do not, I would not go,
  Though at next door we might meet:
Though she were true when you met her,
And last till you write your letter,
       Yet she   25
       Will be
False, ere I come, to two or three.

THE CANONIZATION

For Godsake hold your tongue and let me love,
  Or chide my palsy or my gout,
My five gray hairs or ruin'd fortune flout,
  With wealth your state, your mind with Arts improve,
    Take you a course, get you a place,   5
    Observe His Honour, or His Grace,
Or the King's real, or his stamped face
  Contemplate, what you will, approve,
  So you will let me love.

Alas, alas, who's injur'd by my love?   10
  What merchant's ships have my sighs drown'd?
Who says my tears have overflow'd his ground?
  When did my colds a forward spring remove?
    When did the heats which my veins fill
    Add one more to the plaguey Bill?   15
Soldiers find wars, and Lawyers find out still
  Litigious men, which quarrels move,
  Though she and I do love.

Call us what you will, we are made such by love;
  Call her one, me another fly,   20
We are tapers too, and at our own cost die,
  And we in us find th' Eagle and the Dove.
    The Phoenix riddle hath more wit
    By us, we two being one, are it.
So to one neutral thing both sexes fit,   25
  We die and rise the same, and prove
  Mysterious by this love.

We can die by it, if not live by love,
  And if unfit for tombs and hearse
Our legend be, it will be fit for verse;   30
  And if no piece of Chronicle we prove,
    We'll build in sonnets pretty rooms;
    As well a well-wrought urn becomes
The greatest ashes, as half-acre tombs,
  And by these hymns, all shall approve   35
  Us *Canoniz'd* for Love:

And thus invoke us; You whom reverend love
  Made one another's hermitage;
You, to whom love was peace, that now is rage;
   Who did the whole world's soul contract, and drove   40
    Into the glasses of your eyes
    (So made such mirrors and such spies
That they did all to you epitomize,)
  Countries, Towns, Courts: Beg from above
  A pattern of your love!   45

THE SUN RISING

    Busy old fool, unruly Sun,
    Why dost thou thus,
Through windows, and through curtains, call on us?
Must to thy motions lovers' seasons run?
    Saucy pedantic wretch, go chide   5
    Late school-boys and sour prentices,
  Go tell court-huntsmen that the King will ride,
  Call country ants to harvest offices;
Love, all alike, no season knows nor clime,
Nor hours, days, months, which are the rags of time.   10

    Thy beams so reverend and strong
    Why shouldst thou think?
I could eclipse and cloud them with a wink,
But that I would not lose her sight so long.
    If her eyes have not blinded thine,   15
    Look, and to-morrow late tell me,
  Whether both th' Indias of spice and mine
  Be where thou left'st them, or lie here with me.
Ask for those Kings whom thou saw'st yesterday,
And thou shalt hear, All here in one bed lay.   20

    She's all States, and all Princes I;
    Nothing else is;
Princes do but play us; compared to this,
All honour's mimic, all wealth alchemy.
    Thou, Sun, art half as happy as we,   25
    In that the world's contracted thus;

Thine age asks ease, and since thy duties be
To warm the world, that's done in warming us.
Shine here to us, and thou art everywhere;
This bed thy center is, these walls thy sphere. 30

THE GOOD-MORROW

I wonder, by my troth, what thou and I
Did, till we loved? were we not wean'd till then?
But suck'd on country pleasures, childishly?
Or snorted we in the Seven Sleepers' den?
'Twas so; but this, all pleasures fancies be; 5
If ever any beauty I did see,
Which I desired, and got, 'twas but a dream of thee.

And now good-morrow to our waking souls,
Which watch not one another out of fear;
For love all love of other sights controls, 10
And makes one little room an everywhere.
Let sea-discoverers to new worlds have gone;
Let maps to other worlds on worlds have shown;
Let us possess one world; each hath one, and is one.

My face in thine eye, thine in mine appears, 15
And true plain hearts do in the faces rest;
Where can we find two better hemispheres
Without sharp north, without declining west?
Whatever dies, was not mix'd equally;
If our two loves be one, or thou and I 20
Love so alike that none do slacken, none can die.

THE ECSTACY

Where, like a pillow on a bed,
    A pregnant bank swell'd up, to rest
The violet's reclining head,
    Sat we two, one another's best.
Our hands were firmly cemented 5
    With a fast balm, which thence did spring;
Our eye-beams twisted, and did thread
    Our eyes upon one double string.

So to'entergraft our hands, as yet
   Was all the means to make us one;   10
And pictures in our eyes to get
   Was all our propagation.
As, 'twixt two equal armies, Fate
   Suspends uncertain victory,
Our souls (which to advance their state,   15
   Were gone out) hung 'twixt her and me.
And whilst our souls negotiate there,
   We like sepulchral statues lay;
All day, the same our postures were,
   And we said nothing, all the day.   20
If any, so by love refined,
   That he soul's language understood,
And by good love were grown all mind,
   Within convenient distance stood,
He (though he knew not which soul spake,   25
   Because both meant, both spake the same)
Might thence a new concoction take,
   And part far purer than he came.
This ecstasy doth unperplex
   (We said) and tell us what we love;   30
We see by this, it was not sex;
   We see, we saw not, what did move:
But as all several souls contain
   Mixture of things they know not what,
Love these mix'd souls doth mix again,   35
   And makes both one, each this, and that.
A single violet transplant,
   The strength, the colour, and the size,
(All which before was poor and scant)
   Redoubles still, and multiples.   40
When love with one another so
   Interinanimates two souls,
That abler soul, which thence doth flow,
   Defects of loneliness controls.
We then, who are this new soul, know,   45
   Of what we are composed, and made,
For th' atomies of which we grow
   Are souls, whom no change can invade.
But O alas! so long, so far,
   Our bodies why do we forbear?   50

They are ours, though they are not we; we are
   Th' intelligences, they the spheres.
We owe them thanks, because they thus
   Did us, to us, at first convey,
Yielded their forces, sense, to us,   55
   Nor are dross to us, but allay.
On man heaven's influence works not so,
   But that it first imprints the air;
So soul into the soul may flow,
   Though it to body first repair.   60
As our blood labours to beget
   Spirits, as like souls as it can;
Because such fingers need to knit
   That subtle knot, which makes us man;
So must pure lovers' souls descend   65
   T'affections, and to faculties,
Which sense may reach and apprehend,
   Else a great prince in prison lies.
To'our bodies turn we then, that so
   Weak men on love reveal'd may look;   70
Love's mysteries in souls do grow,
   But yet the body is his book.
And if some lover, such as we,
   Have heard this dialogue of one,
Let him still mark us, he shall see   75
   Small change when we're to bodies gone.

THE ANNIVERSARY

   All Kings, and all their favourites,
   All glory of honours, beauties, wits,
The Sun itself, which makes times, as they pass,
Is elder by a year now than it was
When thou and I first one another saw.   5
All other things to their destruction draw,
   Only our love hath no decay;
This no to-morrow hath, nor yesterday;
Running it never runs from us away,
But truly keeps his first, last, everlasting day.   10

Two graves must hide thine and my corse;
   If one might, death were no divorce.
Alas! as well as other princes, we
—Who prince enough in one another be—
Must leave at last in death these eyes and ears,   15
Oft fed with true oaths, and with sweet salt tears;
   But souls where nothing dwells but love
(All other thoughts being inmates) then shall prove
This, or a love increasèd there above,
When bodies to their graves, souls from their graves remove.   20

   And then we shall be throughly blest;
   But we no more than all the rest.
Here upon earth we're Kings, and none but we
Can be such Kings, nor of such subjects be.
Who is so safe as we? where none can do   25
Treason to us, except one of us two.
   True and false fears let us refrain,
Let us love nobly, and live, and add again
Years and years unto years, till we attain
To write threescore; this is the second of our reign.   30

ON HIS MISTRESS

By our first strange and fatal interview,
By all desires which thereof did ensue,
By our long starving hopes, by that remorse
Which my words' masculine persuasive force
Begot in thee, and by the memory   5
Of hurts which spies and rivals threatened me,
I calmly beg; but by thy father's wrath,
By all pains, which want and divorcement hath,
I conjure thee; and all the oaths which I
And thou have sworn to seal joint constancy,   10
Here I unswear, and overswear them thus:
Thou shalt not love by ways so dangerous.
Temper, O fair love, love's impetuous rage,
Be my true mistress still, not my feigned page;
I'll go, and by thy kind leave, leave behind   15
Thee, only worthy to nurse in my mind
Thirst to come back; oh, if thou die before,

My soul from other lands to thee shall soar.
Thy else almighty beauty cannot move
Rage from the seas, nor thy love teach them love,　20
Nor tame wild Boreas' harshness; thou hast read
How roughly he in pieces shiverèd
Fair Orithea, whom he swore he loved.
Fall ill or good, 'tis madness to have proved
Dangers unurged; feed on this flattery,　25
That absent lovers one in th' other be.
Dissemble nothing, not a boy, nor change
Thy body's habit, nor mind's; be not strange
To thyself only; all will spy in thy face
A blushing womanly discovering grace.　30
Richly clothed apes are called apes; and as soon
Eclipsed as bright, we call the moon the moon.
Men of France, changeable chameleons,
Spitals of diseases, shops of fashions,
Love's fuelers, and the rightest company　35
Of players which upon the world's stage be,
Will quickly know thee, and no less, alas!
Th' indifferent Italian, as we pass
His warm land, well content to think thee page,
Will hunt thee with such lust and hideous rage　40
As Lot's fair guests were vexed. But none of these,
Nor spongy hydroptic Dutch shall thee displease,
If thou stay here. Oh, stay here! for, for thee,
England is only a worthy gallery
To walk in expectation, till from thence　45
Our greatest King call thee to his presènce.
When I am gone, dream me some happiness,
Nor let thy looks our long hid love confess,
Nor praise, nor dispraise me, nor bless nor curse
Openly love's force, nor in bed fright thy nurse　50
With midnight's startings, crying out, Oh, oh
Nurse, oh, my love is slain, I saw him go
O'er the white Alps alone; I saw him, I,
Assailed, fight, taken, stabbed, bleed, fall, and die.
Augur me better chance, except dread Jove　55
Think it enough for me to'have had thy love.

A VALEDICTION FORBIDDING MOURNING

As virtuous men pass mildly away,
　And whisper to their souls to go,
Whilst some of their sad friends do say,
　The breath goes now, and some say, No:

So let us melt, and make no noise,　　　　5
　No tear-floods, nor sigh-tempests move;
'Twere profanation of our joys
　To tell the laity our love.

Moving of th' earth brings harms and fears,
　Men reckon what it did, and meant;　　10
But trepidation of the spheres,
　Though greater far, is innocent.

Dull sublunary lovers' love
　(Whose soul is sense) cannot admit
Absence, because it doth remove　　　　15
　Those things which elemented it.

But we by a love so much refined
　That ourselves know not what it is,
Inter-assurèd of the mind,
　Care less eyes, lips and hands to miss.　　20

Our two souls therefore, which are one,
　Though I must go, endure not yet
A breach, but an expansion,
　Like gold to airy thinness beat.

If they be two, they are two so　　　　25
　As stiff twin compasses are two;
Thy soul, the fix'd foot, makes no show
　To move, but doth, if th' other do.

And though it in the centre sit,
　Yet, when the other far doth roam,　　30
It leans, and hearkens after it,
　And grows erect, as that comes home.

Such wilt thou be to me, who must,
  Like th' other foot, obliquely run;
Thy firmness makes my circle just,   35
  And makes me end where I begun.

THE RELIC

When my grave is broke up again
Some second guest to entertain,
  (For graves have learn'd that womanhead
  To be to more than one a bed)
    And he that digs it, spies   5
A bracelet of bright hair about the bone,
    Will he not let'us alone,
And think that there a loving couple lies,
Who thought that this device might be some way
To make their souls, at the last busy day,   10
Meet at this grave, and make a little stay?

  If this fall in a time, or land,
  Where mis-devotion doth command,
    Then he that digs us up will bring
    Us to the Bishop and the King,   15
      To make us Relics; then
Thou shalt be a Mary Magdalen, and I
      A something else thereby;
All women shall adore us, and some men;
And since at such time, miracles are sought,   20
I would have that age by this paper taught
What miracles we harmless lovers wrought.

  First, we lov'd well and faithfully,
  Yet knew not what we lov'd, nor why,
    Difference of sex no more we knew   25
    Than our Guardian Angels do;
      Coming and going, we
Perchance might kiss, but not between those meals;
      Our hands ne'er touch'd the seals
Which nature, injur'd by late law, sets free: 30
These miracles we did; but now alas,
All measure, and all language, I should pass
Should I tell what a miracle she was.

HOLY SONNETS

VII

At the round earth's imagined corners, blow
Your trumpets, angels, and arise, arise
From death, you numberless infinities
Of souls, and to your scattered bodies go;
All whom the flood did, and fire shall o'erthrow;
All whom war, dearth, age, agues, tyrannies,
Despair, law, chance, hath slain, and you whose eyes
Shall behold God, and never taste death's woe.
But let them sleep, Lord, and me mourn a space,
For, if above all these, my sins abound,
'Tis late to ask abundance of Thy grace,
When we are there; here on this lowly ground,
Teach me how to repent; for that's as good
As if Thou hadst sealed my pardon, with Thy blood.

X

Death, be not proud, though some have callèd thee
Mighty and dreadful, for thou art not so;
For those whom thou think'st thou dost overthrow
Die not, poor Death; nor yet canst thou kill me.
From rest and sleep, which but thy pictures be,
Much pleasure; then from thee much more must flow;
And soonest our best men with thee do go—
Rest of their bones and souls' delivery!
Thou'rt slave to fate, chance, kings, and desperate men,
And dost with poison, war, and sickness dwell;
And poppy or charms can make us sleep as well
And better than thy stroke. Why swell'st thou then?
One short sleep past, we wake eternally,
And Death shall be no more: Death, thou shalt die.

XIII

What if this present were the world's last night?
Mark in my heart, O Soul, where thou dost dwell,
The picture of Christ crucified, and tell
Whether that countenance can thee afright:
Tears in his eyes quench the amazing light,
Blood fills his frowns, which from his pierc'd head fell.

And can that tongue adjudge thee unto hell,
Which pray'd forgiveness for his foes' fierce spite?
No, no; but as in my idolatry
I said to all my profane mistresses,
Beauty, of pity, foulness only is
A sign of rigour: so I say to thee,
To wicked spirits are horrid shapes assign'd,
This beauteous form assures a piteous mind.

XIV

Batter my heart, three personed God; for you
As yet but knock, breathe, shine, and seek to mend;
That I may rise and stand, o'erthrow me and bend
Your force to break, blow, burn and make me new.
I, like an usurped town, to another due,
Labour to admit you, but Oh, to no end;
Reason, your viceroy in me, me should defend,
But is captived and proves weak or untrue.
Yet dearly I love you and would be loved fain,
But am betrothed unto your enemy:
Divorce me, untie or break that knot again,
Take me to you, imprison me, for I
Except you enthrall me, never shall be free,
Nor ever chaste, except you ravish me.

A HYMN TO GOD THE FATHER

I

Wilt Thou forgive that sin where I begun,
  Which is my sin, though it were done before?
Wilt Thou forgive those sins, through which I run,
  And do run still, though still I do deplore?
    When Thou hast done, Thou hast not done,   5
     For I have more.

II

Wilt Thou forgive that sin by which I have won
  Others to sin, and made my sin their door?
Wilt Thou forgive that sin which I did shun
  A year or two, but wallowed in a score?
    When Thou hast done, Thou hast not done,   10
     For I have more.

III

I have a sin of fear, that when I have spun
  My last thread, I shall perish on the shore;
Swear by Thyself, that at my death Thy Son   15
  Shall shine as he shines now, and heretofore;
  And, having done that, Thou hast done:
    I fear no more.

BEN JONSON (1572–1637)

TO CELIA

Drink to me only with thine eyes,
  And I will pledge with mine;
Or leave a kiss but in the cup,
  And I'll not look for wine.
The thirst that from the soul doth rise,   5
  Doth ask a drink divine:
But might I of Jove's nectar sup,
  I would not change for thine.

I sent thee late a rosy wreath,
  Not so much honouring thee   10
As giving it a hope that there
  It could not withered be.
But thou thereon didst only breathe,
  And sent'st it back to me:
Since when it grows, and smells, I swear,   15
  Not of itself, but thee.

SONG: TO CELIA

Come, my Celia, let us prove,
While we may, the sports of love;
Time will not be ours for ever:
He at length our good will sever.
Spend not then his gifts in vain: 5
Suns that set, may rise again;
But if once we lose this light,

'Tis with us perpetual night.
Why should we defer our joys?
Fame and rumour are but toys.   10
Cannot we delude the eyes
Of a few poor household spies?
Or his easier ears beguile,
Thus removèd by our wile?
'Tis no sin love's fruits to steal,   15
But the sweet theft to reveal:
To be taken, to be seen,
These have crimes accounted been.

THE TRIUMPH OF CHARIS

See the Chariot at hand here of Love,
   Wherein my Lady rideth!
Each that draws is a swan or a dove,
   And well the car Love guideth.
As she goes, all hearts do duty   5
     Unto her beauty;
And enamour'd do wish, so they might
     But enjoy such a sight,
That they still were to run by her side,
Through swords, through seas, whither she would ride. 10

Do but look on her eyes, they do light
   All that Love's world compriseth!
Do but look on her hair, it is bright
   As Love's star when it riseth!
Do but mark, her forehead's smoother   15
     Than words that soothe her;
And from her arch'd brows such a grace
     Sheds itself through the face,
As alone there triumphs to the life
All the gain, all the good, of the elements' strife. 20

Have you seen but a bright lily grow
   Before rude hands have touch'd it?
Have you mark'd but the fall of the snow
   Before the soil hath smutch'd it?
Have you felt the wool of beaver,   25

Or swan's down ever?
Or have smelt of the bud of the brier,
　　Or the nard in the fire?
Or have tasted the bag of the bee?
O so white, O so soft, O so sweet is she!　　　　30

SLOW, SLOW, FRESH FOUNT

Slow, slow, fresh fount, keep time with my salt tears;
　Yet slower, yet; O faintly, gentle springs;
List to the heavy part the music bears,
　Woe weeps out her division when she sings.
　　　Droop herbs and flowers,
　　　Fall grief in showers,
　　　Our beauties are not ours.
　　　　O, I could still,
Like melting snow upon some craggy hill,
　　　Drop, drop, drop, drop,
Since Nature's pride is now a withered daffodil.

TO THE MEMORY OF MY BELOVED, THE AUTHOR, MASTER WILLIAM SHAKESPEARE

To draw no envy, Shakespeare, on thy name,
Am I thus ample to thy book and fame;
While I confess thy writings to be such
As neither man nor Muse can praise too much.
'Tis true, and all men's suffrage. But these ways　　　5
Were not the paths I meant unto thy praise;
For silliest ignorance on these may light,
Which, when it sounds at best, but echoes right;
Or blind affection, which doth ne'er advance
The truth, but gropes, and urgeth all by chance;　　　10
Or crafty malice might pretend this praise,
And think to ruin, where it seemed to raise.
These are, as some infamous bawd or whore
Should praise a matron. What could hurt her more?
But thou art proof against them, and indeed,　　　15
Above the ill fortune of them, or the need.
I therefore will begin. Soul of the age!

The applause, delight, the wonder of our stage!
My Shakespeare, rise! I will not lodge thee by
Chaucer, or Spenser, or bid Beaumont lie   20
A little further, to make thee a room;
Thou art a monument without a tomb,
And art alive still while thy book doth live
And we have wits to read and praise to give.
That I not mix thee so, my brain excuses,   25
I mean with great, but disproportioned Muses;
For if I thought my judgment were of years,
I should commit thee surely with thy peers,
And tell how far thou didst our Lyly outshine,
Or sporting Kyd, or Marlowe's mighty line.   30
And though thou hadst small Latin and less Greek,
From thence to honor thee I would not seek
For names; but call forth thundering Aeschylus,
Euripides, and Sophocles to us;
Pacuvius, Accius, him of Cordova dead,   35
To life again, to hear thy buskin tread,
And shake a stage; or, when thy socks were on,
Leave thee alone for the comparison
Of all that insolent Greece or haughty Rome
Sent forth, or since did from their ashes come.   40
Triumph, my Britain, thou hast one to show
To whom all scenes of Europe homage owe.
He was not of an age, but for all time!
And all the Muses still were in their prime,
When, like Apollo, he came forth to warm   45
Our ears, or like a Mercury to charm!
Nature herself was proud of his designs
And joyed to wear the dressing of his lines,
Which were so richly spun, and woven so fit,
As, since, she will vouchsafe no other wit.   50
The merry Greek, tart Aristophanes,
Neat Terence, witty Plautus, now not please,
But antiquated and deserted lie,
As they were not of Nature's family.
Yet must I not give Nature all; thy art,   55
My gentle Shakespeare, must enjoy a part.

36. **Buskin:** high-heeled boot worn   37. **Sock:** low-heeled slipper worn
    by Greek tragic actors; hence,   by Greek comic actors; a sym-
    a symbol of tragedy   bol of comedy

For though the poet's matter Nature be,
His art doth give the fashion; and, that he
Who casts to write a living line, must sweat
(Such as thine are) and strike the second heat   60
Upon the Muses' anvil; turn the same
(And himself with it) that he thinks to frame,
Or, for the laurel, he may gain a scorn;
For a good poet's made, as well as born.
And such wert thou! Look how the father's face   65
Lives in his issue; even so the race
Of Shakespeare's mind and manners brightly shines
In his well-turnèd, and true-filèd lines;
In each of which he seems to shake a lance,
As brandished at the eyes of ignorance.   70
Sweet Swan of Avon! what a sight it were
To see thee in our waters yet appear,
And make those flights upon the banks of Thames,
That so did take Eliza, and our James!
But stay, I see thee in the hemisphere   75
Advanced, and made a constellation there!
Shine forth, thou star of poets, and with rage
Or influence, chide or cheer the drooping stage,
Which, since thy flight from hence, hath mourned like night,
And despairs day, but for thy volume's light.   80

77. **Rage:** Poetic inspiration, enthusiasm

AN ODE TO HIMSELF

Where dost thou careless lie,
    Buried in ease and sloth?
Knowledge that sleeps doth die;
    And this security,
      It is the common moth   5
That eats on wits and arts, and destroys them both.

Are all the Aonian springs
    Dried up? Lies Thespia waste?
Doth Clarius' harp want strings,
    That not a nymph now sings?   10
      Or droop they as disgraced,
To see their seats and bowers by chattering pies defaced?

If hence thy silence be,
 As 'tis too just a cause,
Let this thought quicken thee: 15
Minds that are great and free
 Should not on fortune pause;
'Tis crown enough to virtue still, her own applause.

What though the greedy fry
 Be taken with false baits   20
Of worded balladry,
And think it poesy?
 They die with their conceits,
And only piteous scorn upon their folly waits.

Then take in hand thy lyre;   25
 Strike in thy proper strain;
With Japhet's line aspire
Sol's chariot for new fire
 To give the world again;
Who aided him will thee, the issue of Jove's brain. 30

And, since our dainty age
 Cannot endure reproof,
Make not thyself a page
To that strumpet the stage;
 But sing high and aloof,
         35
Safe from the wolf's black jaw, and the dull ass's hoof.

TO HEAVEN

Good and great God! can I not think of thee,
 But it must straight my melancholy be?
Is it interpreted in me disease,
 That, laden with my sins, I seek for ease?
O be thou witness, that the reins dost know 5
 And hearts of all, if I be sad for show;
And judge me after, if I dare pretend
 To aught but grace, or aim at other end.
As thou art all, so be thou all to me,
 First, midst, and last, converted One and Three! 10
My faith, my hope, my love; and, in this state,

My judge, my witness, and my advocate!
Where have I been this while exiled from thee,
 And whither rapt, now thou but stoop'st to me?
Dwell, dwell here still! O, being everywhere,   15
 How can I doubt to find thee ever here?
I know my state, both full of shame and scorn,
 Conceived in sin, and unto labor born,
Standing with fear, and must with horror fall,
 And destined unto judgment, after all.   20
I feel my griefs too, and there scarce is ground
 Upon my flesh t' inflict another wound;
Yet dare I not complain or wish for death
 With holy Paul, lest it be thought the breath
Of discontent; or that these prayers be   25
 For weariness of life, not love of thee.

JOHN WEBSTER (1580?–1630?)

CALL FOR THE ROBIN REDBREAST

Call for the robin redbreast and the wren,
Since o'er shady groves they hover,
And with leaves and flowers do cover
The friendless bodies of unburied men.
Call unto his funeral dole
The ant, the field-mouse, and the mole,
To rear him hillocks that shall keep him warm,
And, when gay tombs are robbed, sustain no harm;
But keep the wolf far thence, that's foe to men,
For with his nails he'll dig them up again.

WILLIAM BROWNE, OF TAVISTOCK (1591?–1643)

ON THE COUNTESS DOWAGER OF PEMBROKE

Underneath this sable hearse
Lies the subject of all verse:
Sidney's sister, Pembroke's mother:
Death, ere thou hast slain another
Fair and learned and good as she,
Time shall throw a dart at thee.

IN OBITUM M.S., X MAII, 1614

May! be thou never graced with birds that sing,
    Nor Flora's pride!
In thee all flowers and roses spring,
    Mine only died.

ROBERT HERRICK (1591–1674)

THE ARGUMENT OF HIS BOOK

I sing of Brooks, of Blossoms, Birds, and Bowers:
Of April, May, of June, and July-Flowers.
I sing of May-poles, Hock-carts, Wassails, Wakes,
Of Bride-grooms, Brides, and of their Bridal-cakes.
I write of Youth, of Love, and have access
By these, to sing of cleanly-wantonness.
I sing of Dews, of Rains, and piece by piece
Of Balm, of Oil, of Spice, and Amber-Greece.
I sing of Times trans-shifting; and I write
How Roses first came red, and Lilies white.
I write of Groves, of Twilights, and I sing
The Court of Mab, and of the Fairy-King.
I write of Hell; I sing (and ever shall)
Of Heaven, and hope to have it after all.

CORINNA'S GOING A-MAYING

Get up, get up for shame! The blooming morn
Upon her wings presents the god unshorn.
    See how Aurora throws her fair,
    Fresh-quilted colors through the air.
    Get up, sweet slug-a-bed, and see   5
    The dew bespangling herb and tree!
Each flower has wept and bowed toward the east
Above an hour since, yet you not drest;
    Nay! not so much as out of bed?
    When all the birds have matins said   10

And sung their thankful hymns, 'tis sin,
  Nay, profanation, to keep in,
Whenas a thousand virgins on this day
Spring sooner than the lark, to fetch in May.

Rise and put on your foliage, and be seen   15
To come forth, like the springtime, fresh and green,
  And sweet as Flora. Take no care
  For jewels for your gown or hair.
  Fear not; the leaves will strew
  Gems in abundance upon you.   20
Besides, the childhood of the day has kept
Against you come, some orient pearls unwept.
  Come, and receive them while the light
  Hangs on the dew-locks of the night;
  And Titan on the eastern hill   25
  Retires himself, or else stands still
Till you come forth! Wash, dress, be brief in praying;
Few beads are best when once we go a-Maying.

Come, my Corinna, come; and coming, mark
How each field turns a street, each street a park, 30
  Made green and trimmed with trees! see how
  Devotion gives each house a bough
  Or branch! each porch, each door, ere this,
  An ark, a tabernacle is,
Made up of white-thorn neatly interwove,   35
As if here were those cooler shades of love.
  Can such delights be in the street
  And open fields, and we not see't?
  Come, we'll abroad; and let's obey
  The proclamation made for May,   40
And sin no more, as we have done, by staying;
But, my Corinna, come, let's go a-Maying.

There's not a budding boy or girl this day
But is got up and gone to bring in May.
  A deal of youth ere this is come   45
  Back, and with white-thorn laden home.
  Some have dispatched their cakes and cream,
  Before that we have left to dream;
And some have wept and wooed, and plighted troth,

And chose their priest, ere we can cast off sloth.   50
  Many a green-gown has been given,
  Many a kiss, both odd and even;
  Many a glance, too, has been sent
  From out the eye, love's firmament;
Many a jest told of the keys betraying   55
This night, and locks picked; yet we're not a-Maying!

Come, let us go, while we are in our prime,
And take the harmless folly of the time!
  We shall grow old apace, and die
  Before we know our liberty.   60
  Our life is short, and our days run
  As fast away as does the sun.
And, as a vapor or a drop of rain,
Once lost, can ne'er be found again,
  So when or you or I are made   65
  A fable, song, or fleeting shade,
  All love, all liking, all delight
  Lies drowned with us in endless night.
Then, while time serves, and we are but decaying,
Come, my Corinna, come, let's go a-Maying.   70

TO THE VIRGINS, TO MAKE MUCH OF TIME

  Gather ye rose-buds while ye may,
    Old Time is still a-flying:
  And this same flower that smiles today,
    Tomorrow will be dying.

  The glorious lamp of heaven, the Sun,   5
    The higher he's a-getting
  The sooner will his race be run,
    And nearer he's to setting.

  That age is best which is the first,
    When youth and blood are warmer;   10
  But being spent, the worse, and worst
    Times, still succeed the former.

Then be not coy, but use your time;
   And while ye may, go marry:
For having lost but once your prime,   15
   You may for ever tarry.

TO DAFFODILS

Fair Daffodils, we weep to see
   You haste away so soon:
As yet the early-rising Sun
   Has not attain'd his noon.
     Stay, stay,   5
   Until the hasting day
     Has run
   But to the even-song;
And, having pray'd together, we
   Will go with you along.   10

We have short time to stay, as you,
   We have as short a Spring!
As quick a growth to meet decay
   As you, or any thing.
     We die,   15
   As your hours do, and dry
     Away
   Like to the Summer's rain;
Or as the pearls of morning's dew
   Ne'er to be found again.   20

THE NIGHT-PIECE, TO JULIA

Her eyes the glow-worm lend thee;
The shooting stars attend thee;
   And the elves also,
   Whose little eyes glow
Like the sparks of fire, befriend thee.   5

No Will-o'-the-wisp mislight thee,
Nor snake or slow-worm bite thee;
   But on, on thy way
   Not making a stay,
Since ghost there's none to affright thee.   10

Let not the dark thee cumber;
What though the moon does slumber?
    The stars of the night
    Will lend thee their light
Like tapers clear without number.   15

Then, Julia, let me woo thee,
Thus, thus to come unto me;
    And when I shall meet
    Thy silv'ry feet,
My soul I'll pour into thee.   20

UPON JULIA'S CLOTHES

Whenas in silks my Julia goes
Then, then (methinks) how sweetly flows
That liquefaction of her clothes.

Next, when I cast mine eyes and see
That brave vibration each way free;
O how that glittering taketh me!

DELIGHT IN DISORDER

A sweet disorder in the dress
Kindles in clothes a wantonness:
A lawn about the shoulders thrown
Into a fine distraction,
An erring lace, which here and there
Enthralls the crimson stomacher,
A cuff neglectful, and thereby
Ribbands to flow confusedly,
A winning wave (deserving note)
In the tempestuous petticoat,
A careless shoe-string, in whose tie
I see a wild civility,
Do more bewitch me, than when art
Is too precise in every part.

THE CHEAT OF CUPID: or, THE UNGENTLE GUEST

One silent night of late,
  When every creature rested,
Came one unto my gate,
  And knocking, me molested.

Who's that (said I) beats there,   5
  And troubles thus the sleepy?
Cast off (said he) all fear,
  And let not locks thus keep ye,

For I a Boy am, who
  By moonless nights have swerved;   10
And all with show'rs wet through,
  And e'en with cold half starved.

I pitiful arose,
  And soon a taper lighted;
And did myself disclose   15
  Unto the lad benighted.

I saw he had a bow,
  And wings too, which did shiver;
And looking down below,
  I spy'd he had a quiver.   20

I to my chimney's shine
  Brought him (as Love professes)
And chaf'd his hands with mine,
  And dry'd his dropping tresses:

But when he felt him warm'd,   25
  Let's try this bow of ours,
And string if they be harm'd,
  Said he, with these late show'rs.

Forthwith his bow he bent,
  And wedded string and arrow,   30
And struck me that it went
  Quite through my heart and marrow.

Then laughing loud, he flew
   Away, and thus said flying,
Adieu, mine Host, adieu,
   I'll leave thy heart a-dying.

35

A CHILD'S GRACE

Here a little child I stand,
Heaving up my either hand;
Cold as Paddocks though they be,
Here I lift them up to Thee,
For a Benizon to fall
On our meat, and on us all. Amen.

HIS PRAYER TO BEN JONSON

When I a verse shall make,
   Know I have prayed thee,
For old religion's sake,
   Saint Ben, to aid me.

Make the way smooth for me,
   When I, thy Herrick,
Honouring thee, on my knee
   Offer my lyric.

Candles I'll give thee,
   And a new altar;
And thou, Saint Ben, shalt be
   Writ in my psalter.

THE BAD SEASON MAKES THE POET SAD

Dull to myself, and almost dead to these
My many fresh and fragrant mistresses:
Lost to all music now, since everything
Puts on the semblance here of sorrowing.
Sick is the land to th' heart, and doth endure
More dangerous faintings by her desp'rate cure.

But if that golden age would come again,
And Charles here rule, as he before did reign;
If smooth and unperplexed the seasons were,
As when the sweet Maria livèd here;
I should delight to have my curls half drowned
In Tyrian dews, and head with roses crowned;
And once more yet, ere I am laid out dead,
Knock at a star with my exalted head.

A THANKSGIVING TO GOD, FOR HIS HOUSE

Lord, Thou hast given me a cell
    Wherein to dwell,
A little house, whose humble roof
    Is weather-proof;
Under the spars of which I lie   5
    Both soft, and dry;
Where Thou my chamber for to ward
    Hast set a guard
Of harmless thoughts, to watch and keep
    Me, while I sleep.   10
Low is my porch, as is my fate,
    Both void of state;
And yet the threshold of my door
    Is worn by th' poor,
Who thither come, and freely get   15
    Good words, or meat;
Like as my parlor, so my hall
    And kitchen's small:
A little buttery, and therein
    A little bin,   20
Which keeps my little loaf of bread
    Unchipped, unflead:
Some brittle sticks of thorn or briar
    Make me a fire,
Close by whose living coal I sit,   25
    I glow like it.
Lord, I confess too, when I dine,
    The pulse is Thine,
And all those other bits, that be
    There placed by Thee;   30

The worts, the purslain, and the mess
    Of water cress,
Which of Thy kindness Thou hast sent;
    And my content
Make those, and my beloved beet,   35
    To be more sweet.
'Tis Thou that crown'st my glittering hearth
    With guiltless mirth;
And giv'st me wassail bowls to drink,
    Spiced to the brink.   40
Lord, 'tis Thy plenty-dropping hand,
    That soils my land;
And giv'st me, for my bushel sown,
    Twice ten for one:
Thou mak'st my teeming hen to lay   45
    Her egg each day:
Besides my healthful ewes to bear
    Me twins each year:
The while the conduits of my kine
    Run cream (for wine).   50
All these, and better Thou dost send
    Me, to this end,
That I should render, for my part,
    A thankful heart;
Which, fired with incense, I resign,   55
    As wholly Thine;
But the acceptance, that must be,
    My Christ, by Thee.

HIS CREED

I do believe that die I must,
And be return'd from out my dust:
I do believe that when I rise,
Christ I shall see, with these same eyes:
I do believe that I must come,   5
With others, to the dreadful Doom:
I do believe the bad must go
From thence, to everlasting woe:
I do believe the good, and I,
Shall live with Him eternally: 10

I do believe I shall inherit
Heaven, by Christ's mercies, not my merit:
I do believe the One in Three,
And Three in perfect Unity:
Lastly, that JESUS is a Deed   15
Of Gift from God: *And here's my Creed.*

GEORGE HERBERT (1593–1633)

THE COLLAR

I struck the board, and cry'd, No more;
        I will abroad!
What? shall I ever sigh and pine?
My lines and life are free; free as the road,
   Loose as the winde, as large as store,
     Shall I be still in suit?   5
   Have I no harvest but a thorn
   To let me blood, and not restore
What I have lost with cordial fruit?
      Sure there was wine   10
   Before my sighs did dry it: there was corn
    Before my tears did drown it.
   Is the year only lost to me?
    Have I no bays to crown it?
No flowers, no garlands gay? all blasted?   15
     All wasted?
  Not so, my heart: but there is fruit,
    And thou hast hands.
  Recover all thy sigh-blown age
On double pleasures: leave thy cold dispute   20
Of what is fit, and not; forsake thy cage,
    Thy rope of sands,
Which petty thoughts have made, and made to thee
  Good cable, to enforce and draw,
    And be thy law,   25
  While thou didst wink and wouldst not see.
    Away; take heed:
    I will abroad.
Call in thy death's head there: tie up thy fears.
    He that forbears   30

> To suit and serve his need,
>> Deserves his load.
> But as I rav'd and grew more fierce and wild
>> At every word,
> Me thought I heard one calling, *Child:*   35
>> And I replied, *My Lord.*

REDEMPTION

Having been tenant long to a rich Lord,
>> Not thriving, I resolved to be bold,
>> And make a suit unto him, to afford
A new small-rented lease, and cancell th' old.

In heaven at his manour I him sought:
>> They told me there, that he was lately gone
>> About some land, which he had dearly bought
Long since on earth, to take possession.

I straight return'd, and knowing his great birth,
>> Sought him accordingly in great resorts;
>> In cities, theatres, gardens, parks, and courts:
At length I heard a ragged noise and mirth

>> Of thieves and murderers: there I him espied,
>> Who straight, *Your suit is granted*, said, & died.

PEACE

Sweet peace, where dost thou dwell? I humbly crave,
>> Let me once know.
> I sought thee in a secret cave,
>> And ask'd, if Peace were there.
A hollow wind did seem to answer, No: 5
>> Go seek elsewhere.

I did; and going did a rainbow note:
>> Surely, thought I,
> This is the lace of Peace's coat:
>> I will search out the matter.   10
But while I lookt the clouds immediately
>> Did break and scatter.

Then went I to a garden and did spy
    A gallant flower,
  The crown Imperiall: Sure, said I,   15
    Peace at the root must dwell.
But when I digg'd, I saw a worm devoure
    What show'd so well.

At length I met a rev'rend good old man;
    Whom when for Peace   20
  I did demand, he thus began:
    There was a Prince of old
At Salem dwelt, who liv'd with good increase
    Of flock and fold.

He sweetly liv'd; yet sweetnesse did not save   25
    His life from foes.
  But after death out of his grave
    There sprang twelve stalks of wheat;
Which many wondring at, got some of those
    To plant and set.   30

It prosper'd strangely, and did soon disperse
    Through all the earth:
  For they that taste it do rehearse,
    That vertue lies therein;
A secret vertue, bringing peace and mirth   35
    By flight of sinne.

Take of this grain, which in my garden grows,
    And grows for you;
  Make bread of it: and that repose
    And peace, which ev'rywhere   40
With so much earnestness you do pursue
    Is only there.

THE CHURCH-FLOOR

Mark you the floor? that square and speckled stone,
    Which looks so firm and strong,
      Is *Patience*:

And th' other black and grave, wherewith each one
    Is checker'd all along,   5
        Humility:

The gentle rising, which on either hand
    Leads to the Quire above,
        Is *Confidence:*

By the sweet cement, which in one sure band   10
    Ties the whole frame, is *Love*
        And *Charity.*

  Hither sometimes Sin steals, and stains,
  The marbles' neat and curious veins:
But all is cleansed when the marble weeps.   15
  Sometimes Death, puffing at the door,
  Blows all the dust about the floor:
But while he thinks to spoil the room, he sweeps.
  Blest be the Architect, whose art
  Could build so strong in a weak heart.   20

LOVE

Love bade me welcome; yet my soul drew back,
    Guilty of dust and sin.
But quick-ey'd Love, observing me grow slack
    From my first entrance in,
Drew nearer to me, sweetly questioning   5
    If I lacked anything.

A guest, I answer'd, worthy to be here.
    Love said, You shall be he.
I, the unkind, ungrateful? Ah, my dear,
    I cannot look on Thee.   10
Love took my hand, and smiling, did reply,
    Who made the eyes but I?

Truth, Lord, but I have marred them: let my shame
    Go where it doth deserve.
And know you not, says Love, who bore the blame? 15
    My dear, then I will serve.
You must sit down, says Love, and taste my meat:
    So I did sit and eat.

THE PULLEY

When God at first made man,
Having a glass of blessings standing by—
Let us (said he) pour on him all we can;
Let the world's riches, which dispersed lie,
  Contract into a span.   5

So strength first made a way,
Then beauty flow'd, then wisdom, honour, pleasure:
When almost all was out, God made a stay,
Perceiving that, alone of all His treasure,
  Rest in the bottom lay.   10

For if I should (said he)
Bestow this jewel also on My creature,
He would adore My gifts instead of Me,
And rest in Nature, not the God of Nature:
  So both should losers be.   15

Yet let him keep the rest,
But keep them with repining restlessness;
Let him be rich and weary, that at least,
If goodness lead him not, yet weariness
  May toss him to My breast.   20

DISCIPLINE

Throw away thy rod,
Throw away thy wrath;
   O my God,
Take the gentle path.

For my heart's desire   5
Unto thine is bent;
   I aspire
To a full consent.

Not a word or look
I affect to own,   10
   But by book,
And thy book alone.

Though I fail, I weep;
Though I halt in pace,
   Yet I creep   15
To the throne of grace.

Then let wrath remove,
Love will do the deed;
   For with love
Stony hearts will bleed.   20

Love is swift of foot;
Love's a man of war,
   And can shoot,
And can hit from far.

Who can 'scape his bow?   25
That which wrought on thee,
   Brought thee low,
Needs must work on me.

Throw away thy rod:
Though man frailties hath,   30
   Thou art God;
Throw away thy wrath.

LIFE

I made a posie, while the day ran by:
Here will I smell my remnant out, and tie
   My life within this band.
But time did beckon to the flowers, and they
By noon most cunningly did steal away   5
   And wither'd in my hand.

My hand was next to them, and then my heart:
I took, without more thinking, in good part
   Time's gentle admonition:
Who did so sweetly death's sad taste convey,   10
Making my mind to smell my fatal day,
   Yet sug'ring the suspicion.

Farewell, dear flowers, sweetly your time ye spent,
Fit, while ye liv'd, for smell or ornament,
  And after death for cures.   15
I follow straight without complaints or grief,
Since, if my scent be good, I care not if
  It be as short as yours.

VIRTUE

Sweet day, so cool, so calm, so bright,
The bridal of the earth and sky:
The dew shall weep thy fall to-night;
  For thou must die.

Sweet rose, whose hue angry and brave   5
Bids the rash gazer wipe his eye:
Thy root is ever in its grave,
  And thou must die.

Sweet spring, full of sweet days and roses,
A box where sweets compacted lie;   10
My music shews ye have your closes,
  And all must die.

Only a sweet and virtuous soul,
Like season'd timber, never gives;
But though the whole world turn to coal,   15
  Then chiefly lives.

JAMES SHIRLEY (1596–1666)

DEATH THE LEVELLER

The glories of our blood and state
 Are shadows, not substantial things;
There is no armour against Fate;
 Death lays his icy hand on kings:
   Sceptre and crown   5
   Must tumble down,
And in the dust be equal made
With the poor crookèd scythe and spade.

Some men with swords may reap the field,
　And plant fresh laurels where they kill; 10
But their strong nerves at last must yield;
　They tame but one another still:
　　　Early or late
　　　They stoop to fate,
And must give up their murmuring breath 15
When they, pale captives, creep to death.

The garlands wither on your brow;
　Then boast no more your mighty deeds!
Upon Death's purple altar now
　See where the victor-victim bleeds. 20
　　　Your heads must come
　　　To the cold tomb:
Only the actions of the just
Smell sweet and blossom in their dust.

EDMUND WALLER (1606–1687)

GO, LOVELY ROSE

　　　Go, lovely rose—
Tell her that wastes her time and me
　　　That now she knows,
When I resemble her to thee,
How sweet and fair she seems to be. 5

　　　Tell her that's young,
And shuns to have her graces spied,
　　　That hadst thou sprung
In deserts where no men abide,
Thou must have uncommended died. 10

　　　Small is the worth
Of beauty from the light retired:
　　　Bid her come forth,
Suffer herself to be desired,
And not blush so to be admired. 15

Then die—that she
The common fate of all things rare
    May read in thee:
How small a part of time they share
That are so wondrous sweet and fair.   20

JOHN MILTON (1608–1674)

AT A SOLEMN MUSIC

Blest pair of Sirens, pledges of Heav'n's joy,
Sphere-born harmonious sisters, Voice and Verse,
Wed your divine sounds, and mixt power employ,
Dead things with inbreath'd sense able to pierce;
And to our high-rais'd phantasy present   5
That undisturbèd song of pure concent,
Aye sung before the sapphire-coloured throne
To him that sits thereon
With saintly shout and solemn jubilee;
Where the bright Seraphim in burning row   10
Their loud uplifted angel trumpets blow,
And the Cherubic host in thousand quires
Touch their immortal harps of golden wires,
With those just Spirits that wear victorious palms,
Hymns devout and holy psalms   15
Singing everlastingly:
That we on Earth, with undiscording voice,
May rightly answer that melodious noise;
As once we did, till disproportion'd sin
Jarr'd against nature's chime, and with harsh din   20
Broke the fair music that all creatures made
To their great Lord, whose love their motion sway'd
In perfect diapason, whilst they stood
In first obedience, and their state of good.
O may we soon again renew that song,   25
And keep in tune with Heaven, till God ere long
To his celestial consort us unite,
To live with him, and sing in endless morn of light.

ON TIME

Fly envious Time, till thou run out thy race,
Call on the lazy leaden-stepping hours,
Whose speed is but the heavy Plummet's pace;
And glut thy self with what thy womb devours,
Which is no more than what is false and vain,   5
And merely mortal dross;
So little is our loss,
So little is thy gain.
For when as each thing bad thou hast entomb'd,
And last of all, thy greedy self consum'd,   10
Then long Eternity shall greet our bliss
With an individual kiss;
And Joy shall overtake us as a flood,
When every thing that is sincerely good
And perfectly divine,   15
With Truth, and Peace, and Love shall ever shine
About the supreme Throne
Of him, t'whose happy-making sight alone,
When once our heav'nly-guided soul shall climb,
Then all this Earthy grossness quit,   20
Attir'd with Stars, we shall for ever sit,
Triumphing over Death, and Chance, and thee O Time.

ON THE MORNING OF CHRIST'S NATIVITY

This is the Month, and this the happy morn
Wherein the Son of Heav'n's eternal King,
Of wedded Maid, and Virgin Mother born,
Our great Redemption from above did bring;
For so the holy Sages once did sing,   5
   That he our deadly forfeit should release,
And with his Father work us a perpetual peace.

That glorious Form, that Light unsufferable,
And that far-beaming blaze of Majesty,
Wherewith he wont at Heav'n's high Council-Table,   10
To sit the midst of Trinal Unity,

10. **Wont:** was accustomed

He laid aside; and here with us to be,
    Forsook the Courts of everlasting Day,
And chose with us a darksome House of mortal Clay.

Say Heav'nly Muse, shall not thy sacred vein   15
Afford a Present to the Infant God?
Hast thou no verse, no hymn, or solemn strain,
To welcome him to this his new abode,
Now while the Heav'n, by the Sun's team untrod,
    Hath took no print of the approaching light,   20
And all the spangled host keep watch in squadrons bright?

See how from far upon the Eastern road
The Star-led Wizards haste with odours sweet!
O run, prevent them with thy humble ode,
And lay it lowly at his blessed feet!   25
Have thou the honour first, thy Lord to greet,
    And join thy voice unto the Angel Quire,
From out his secret Altar toucht with hallow'd fire.

THE HYMN

It was the Winter wild,
While the Heav'n-born child   30
    All meanly wrapt in the rude manger lies;
Nature in awe to him
Had doff't her gawdy trim,
    With her great Master so to sympathize:
It was no season then for her   35
To wanton with the Sun her lusty Paramour.

Only with speeches fair
She woo's the gentle Air
    To hide her guilty front with innocent Snow,
And on her naked shame,   40
Pollute with sinful blame
    The Saintly Veil of Maiden white to throw,
Confounded, that her Maker's eyes
Should look so near upon her foul deformities.

But he, her fears to cease,   45
Sent down the meek-ey'd Peace:

23. **Wizards:** wise men   24. **Prevent:** anticipate

She, crown'd with Olive green, came softly sliding
Down through the turning sphere,
His ready Harbinger;
   With Turtle wing the amorous clouds dividing,   50
And waving wide her myrtle wand,
She strikes a universal Peace through Sea and Land.

No War, or Battle's sound,
Was heard the World around,
   The idle Spear and Shield were high up hung,   55
The hooked Chariot stood
Unstained with hostile blood,
   The Trumpet spake not to the armed throng,
And Kings sate still with awful eye,
As if they surely knew their sovran Lord was by.   60

But peaceful was the night
Wherein the Prince of light
   His reign of peace upon the earth began:
The Winds, with wonder whist,
Smoothly the waters kist,   65
   Whispering new joyes to the milde Ocean,
Who now hath quite forgot to rave,
While Birds of Calm sit brooding on the charmed wave.

The Stars with deep amaze
Stand fixt in steadfast gaze,   70
   Bending one way their precious influence,
And will not take their flight,
For all the morning light,
   Or *Lucifer* that often warn'd them thence;
But in their glimmering Orbs did glow,   75
Until their Lord himself bespake, and bid them go.

And though the shady gloom
Had given day her room,
   The Sun himself with-held his wonted speed
And hid his head for shame,
As his inferior flame   80

50. **Turtle:** turtle dove
56. **Hooked:** with knives on the axles

64. **Whist:** hushed
74. **Lucifer:** the Morning Star

The new enlightn'd world no more should need;
He saw a greater Sun appear
Than his bright Throne, or burning Axletree could bear.

The Shepherds on the Lawn,
Or ere the point of dawn,   85
  Sate simply chatting in a rustic row;
Full little thought they then
That the mighty *Pan*
  Was kindly come to live with them below;
Perhaps their loves, or else their sheep,   90
Was all that did their silly thoughts so busy keep—

When such music sweet
Their hearts and ears did greet,
  As never was by mortal finger strook,
Divinely-warbl'd voice   95
Answering the stringed noise,
  As all their souls in blissful rapture took:
The Air, such pleasure loath to lose,
With thousand echoes still prolongs each heav'nly close.

Nature, that heard such sound   100
Beneath the hollow round
  Of *Cynthia's* seat, the Airy region thrilling,
Now was almost won
To think her part was done,
  And that her reign had here its last fulfilling;   105
She knew such harmony alone
Could hold all Heav'n and Earth in happier union.

At last surrounds their sight
A Globe of circular light,
  That with long beams the shame-fac't night array'd; 110
The helmed Cherubim
And sworded Seraphim
  Are seen in glittering ranks with wings displayed,
Harping in loud and solemn quire,
With unexpressive notes to Heav'ns new-born Heir.   115

91. **Silly:** simple   115. **Unexpressive:** inexpressible
99. **Close:** conclusion of a musical
    phrase

Such Music (as 'tis said)
Before was never made,
 But when of old the sons of morning sung,
While the Creator great
His Constellations set,   120
 And the well-ballanc't world on hinges hung,
And cast the dark foundations deep,
And bid the welt'ring waves their oozy channel keep.

Ring out, ye crystal spheres:
Once bless our human ears   125
 (If ye have power to touch our senses so)
And let your silver chime
Move in melodious time;
 And let the Base of Heav'n's deep Organ blow,
And with your ninefold harmony   130
Make up full consort to th'Angelic symphony.

For if such holy Song
Enwrap our fancy long,
 Time will run back, and fetch the age of gold,
And speckl'd vanity   135
Will sicken soon and die,
 And leprous sin will melt from earthly mould,
And Hell itself will pass away,
And leave her dolorous mansions to the peering day.

Yea Truth, and Justice, then   140
Will down return to men,
 Orb'd in a Rain-bow; and like glories wearing
Mercy will sit between,
Thron'd in Celestial sheen,
 With radiant feet the tissued clouds down steering, 145
And Heav'n, as at some Festival,
Will open wide the Gates of her high Palace Hall.

---

124. Spheres: according to Ptolemaic astronomy eight concentric transparent spheres surrounded the Earth as center. These were the spheres of moon, sun, and planets. A ninth, outermost sphere was called the *primum mobile*. The revolution of the spheres was supposed to cause exquisite music too refined for earthly ears.

131. Consort: accord

But wisest Fate says No,
This must not yet be so;
   The Babe lies yet in smiling Infancy,   150
That on the bitter cross
Must redeem our loss,
   So both himself and us to glorify:
Yet first to those ychain'd in sleep,
The wakeful trump of doom must thunder through the deep,

With such a horrid clang   156
As on mount *Sinai* rang
   While the red fire, and smold'ring clouds out brake:
The aged Earth aghast
With terror of that blast,   160
   Shall from the surface to the center shake;
When, at the world's last session,
The dreadful Judge in middle Air shall spread his throne.

And then at last our bliss
Full and perfect is,   165
   But now begins; for from this happy Day
Th'old Dragon under ground
In straiter limits bound,
   Not half so far casts his usurped sway,
And, wroth to see his Kingdom fail,   170
Swinges the scaly Horror of his folded tail.

The Oracles are dumb;
No voice or hideous hum
   Runs through the arched roof in words deceiving.
Apollo from his shrine   175
Can no more divine,
   With hollow shriek the steep of *Delphos* leaving.
No nightly trance, or breathed spell,
Inspires the pale-ey'd Priest from the prophetic cell.

The lonely mountains o'er,   180
And the resounding shore,
   A voice of weeping heard, and loud lament;
From haunted spring, and dale
Edg'd with poplar pale,

The parting Genius is with sighing sent;   185
With flow'r-inwov'n tresses torn,
The Nymphs in twilight shade of tangled thickets mourn.

In consecrated Earth,
And on the holy Hearth,
   The *Lars*, and *Lemures*, moan with midnight plaint;   190
In Urns, and Altars round.
A drear and dying sound
   Affrights the *Flamens* at their service quaint;
And the chill Marble seems to sweat,
While each peculiar power foregoes his wonted seat.   195

Peor, and *Baalim*,
Forsake their Temples dim,
   With that twice-batter'd god of *Palestine*;
And mooned *Ashtaroth*,
Heav'ns Queen and Mother both,   200
   Now sits not girt with Tapers' holy shine;
The Libyc *Hammon* shrinks his horn;
In vain the *Tyrian* Maids their wounded *Thammuz* mourn.

And sullen *Moloch*, fled,
Hath left in shadows dread   205
   His burning Idol all of blackest hue;
In vain with Cymbals' ring
They call the grisly King
   In dismal dance about the furnace blue;
The brutish gods of *Nile* as fast,   210
Isis and *Orus*, and the Dog *Anubis*, haste.

Nor is *Osiris* seen
In *Memphian* Grove, or Green,
   Trampling the unshow'r'd Grass with lowings loud,
Nor can he be at rest   215
Within his sacred chest;
   Naught but profoundest Hell can be his shroud;
In vain with Timbrel'd Anthems dark
The sable-stoled Sorcerers bear his worshipt Ark.

190. **Lars and Lemures:** Roman   193. **Flamens:** priests
    spirits of the dead

He feels from *Juda*'s Land 220
The dreaded Infant's hand;
 The rays of *Bethlehem* blind his dusky eyn.
Nor all the Gods beside
Longer dare abide,
 Not *Typhon* huge ending in snaky twine: 225
Our Babe to shew his Godhead true,
Can in his swaddling bands control the damned crew.

So when the Sun in bed,
Curtain'd with cloudy red,
 Pillows his chin upon an Orient wave, 230
The flocking shadows pale,
Troop to th'infernal Jail,
 Each fetter'd Ghost slips to his several grave,
And the yellow-skirted *Fays*,
Fly after the Night-steeds, leaving their Moon-lov'd maze. 235

But see, the Virgin blest
Hath laid her Babe to rest.
 Time is our tedious Song should here have ending:
Heav'ns youngest teemed Star
Hath fixt her polisht Car, 240
 Her sleeping Lord with Handmaid Lamp attending:
And all about the Courtly Stable,
Bright-harness't Angels sit in order serviceable.

L'ALLEGRO

Hence, loathed Melancholy,
 Of Cerberus and blackest Midnight born,
In Stygian cave forlorn
 'Mongst horrid shapes, and shrieks, and sights unholy!
Find out some uncouth cell 5
 Where brooding Darkness spreads his jealous wings
And the night-raven sings;
 There under ebon shades, and low-browed rocks
As ragged as thy locks,
 In dark Cimmerian desert ever dwell. 10
But come, thou goddess fair and free,
In heaven yclept Euphrosyne,

And by men, heart-easing Mirth,
Whom lovely Venus at a birth
With two sister Graces more 15
To ivy-crowned Bacchus bore;
Or whether (as some sager sing)
The frolic wind that breathes the spring,
Zephyr, with Aurora playing,
As he met her once a-Maying— 20
There on beds of violets blue
And fresh-blown roses washed in dew
Filled her with thee, a daughter fair,
So buxom, blithe, and debonair.

   Haste thee, Nymph, and bring with thee 25
Jest and youthful Jollity,
Quips and Cranks and wanton Wiles,
Nods and Becks and wreathed Smiles,
Such as hang on Hebe's cheek
And love to live in dimple sleek; 30
Sport that wrinkled Care derides,
And Laughter holding both his sides.
Come, and trip it as you go
On the light fantastic toe;
And in thy right hand lead with thee 35
The mountain-nymph, sweet Liberty;
And if I give thee honor due
Mirth, admit me of thy crew,
To live with her, and live with thee
In unreproved pleasures free; 40
To hear the lark begin his flight
And singing startle the dull night
From his watch-tower in the skies,
Till the dappled dawn doth rise;
Then to come, in spite of sorrow, 45
And at my window bid good-morrow
Through the sweetbriar, or the vine,
Or the twisted eglantine:
While the cock with lively din
Scatters the rear of darkness thin, 50
And to the stack, or the barn-door,
Stoutly struts his dames before:
Oft listening how the hounds and horn
Cheerly rouse the slumbering morn,

From the side of some hoar hill, 55
Through the high wood echoing shrill;
Sometime walking, not unseen,
By hedge-row elms, on hillocks green,
Right against the eastern gate
Where the great Sun begins his state, 60
Robed in flames and amber light,
The clouds in thousand liveries dight;
While the ploughman, near at hand,
Whistles o'er the furrowed land,
And the milkmaid singeth blithe, 65
And the mower whets his scythe,
And every shepherd tells his tale
Under the hawthorn in the dale.
   Straight mine eye hath caught new pleasures
Whilst the landscape round it measures: 70
Russet lawns, and fallows gray,
Where the nibbling flocks do stray;
Mountains, on whose barren breast
The laboring clouds do often rest;
Meadows trim with daisies pied, 75
Shallow brooks, and rivers wide.
Towers and battlements it sees
Bosomed high in tufted trees,
Where perhaps some beauty lies,
The cynosure of neighboring eyes. 80
Hard by, a cottage chimney smokes
From betwixt two aged oaks,
Where Corydon and Thyrsis met
Are at their savoury dinner set
Of herbs, and other country messes 85
Which the neat-handed Phillis dresses;
And then in haste her bower she leaves,
With Thestylis to bind the sheaves;
Or, if the earlier season lead,
To the tanned haycock in the mead. 90
   Sometimes with secure delight
The upland hamlets will invite,
When the merry bells ring round,

62. **Dight:** arrayed   80. **Cynosure:** the North Star,
                                               hence whatever attracts by
                                               beauty and brightness

And the jocund rebecks sound
To many a youth and many a maid,   95
Dancing in the chequered shade;
And young and old come forth to play
On a sunshine holy-day,
Till the livelong daylight fail:
Then to the spicy nut-brown ale,   100
With stories told of many a feat:
How faery Mab the junkets eat:—
She was pinched, and pulled, she said;
And he, by friar's lantern led,
Tells how the drudging Goblin sweat   105
To earn his cream-bowl duly set,
When in one night, ere glimpse of morn,
His shadowy flail hath threshed the corn
That ten day-laborers could not end;
Then lies him down the lubber fiend,   110
And, stretched out all the chimney's length,
Basks at the fire his hairy strength;
And crop-full out of doors he flings,
Ere the first cock his matin rings.
Thus done the tales, to bed they creep,   115
By whispering winds soon lulled asleep.
Towered cities please us then
And the busy hum of men,
Where throngs of knights and barons bold,
In weeds of peace, high triumphs hold,   120
With store of ladies, whose bright eyes
Rain influence, and judge the prize
Of wit or arms, while both contend
To win her grace, whom all commend.
There let Hymen oft appear   125
In saffron robe, with taper clear,
And pomp, and feast, and revelry,
With mask, and antique pageantry;
Such sights as youthful poets dream
On summer eves by haunted stream.   130
Then to the well-trod stage anon,
If Jonson's learned sock be on,
Or sweetest Shakespeare, Fancy's child,
Warble his native wood-notes wild.

94. **Rebecks:** fiddles   120. **Weeds:** clothes

    And ever against eating cares 135
Lap me in soft Lydian airs,
Married to immortal verse,
Such as the meeting soul may pierce,
In notes with many a winding bout
Of linked sweetness long drawn out, 140
With wanton heed and giddy cunning,
The melting voice through mazes running,
Untwisting all the chains that tie
The hidden soul of harmony;
That Orpheus' self may heave his head 145
From golden slumber, on a bed
Of heaped Elysian flowers, and hear
Such strains as would have won the ear
Of Pluto, to have quite set free
His half-regained Eurydice. 150
    These delights if thou canst give,
Mirth, with thee I mean to live.

IL PENSEROSO

    Hence, vain deluding Joys,
      The brood of Folly without father bred!
    How little you bestead
      Or fill the fixed mind with all your toys!
    Dwell in some idle brain, 5
      And fancies fond with gaudy shapes possess
    As thick and numberless
      As the gay motes that people the sunbeams,
    Or likest hovering dreams,
      The fickle pensioners of Morpheus' train. 10
But hail, thou goddess sage and holy,
Hail, divinest Melancholy!
Whose saintly visage is too bright
To hit the sense of human sight,
And therefore to our weaker view 15
O'erlaid with black, staid Wisdom's hue;
Black, but such as in esteem
Prince Memnon's sister might beseem,
Or that starred Ethiop queen that strove

3. **Bestead:** avail   6. **Fond:** foolish

To set her beauty's praise above   20
The sea-nymphs, and their powers offended.
Yet thou art higher far descended:
Thee bright-haired Vesta long of yore
To solitary Saturn bore;
His daughter she; in Saturn's reign   25
Such mixture was not held a stain:
Oft in glimmering bowers and glades
He met her, and in secret shades
Of woody Ida's inmost grove,
While yet there was no fear of Jove.   30
   Come, pensive Nun, devout and pure,
Sober, steadfast, and demure,
All in a robe of darkest grain
Flowing with majestic train,
And sable stole of cypress lawn   35
Over thy decent shoulders drawn.
Come, but keep thy wonted state,
With even step, and musing gait,
And looks commercing with the skies,
Thy rapt soul sitting in thine eyes: 40
There, held in holy passion still,
Forget thyself to marble, till
With a sad leaden downward cast
Thou fix them on the earth as fast.
And join with thee calm Peace, and Quiet,   45
Spare Fast, that oft with gods doth diet,
And hears the Muses in a ring
Aye round about Jove's altar sing:
And add to these retired Leisure
That in trim gardens takes his pleasure:—   50
But first and chiefest, with thee bring
Him that yon soars on golden wing
Guiding the fiery-wheeled throne,
The cherub Contemplation;
And the mute Silence hist along,   55
'Less Philomel will deign a song
In her sweetest saddest plight,
Smoothing the rugged brow of Night,
While Cynthia checks her dragon yoke
Gently o'er the accustomed oak.   60

55. **Hist along:** call silently

Sweet bird, that shunn'st the noise of folly,
Most musical, most melancholy!
Thee, chauntress, oft the woods among
I woo, to hear thy even-song;
And missing thee, I walk unseen   65
On the dry smooth-shaven green,
To behold the wandering Moon
Riding near her highest noon,
Like one that had been led astray
Through the heaven's wide pathless way,   70
And oft, as if her head she bowed,
Stopping through a fleecy cloud.
   Oft, on a plat of rising ground,
I hear the far-off curfew sound
Over some wide-water'd shore,   75
Swinging slow with sullen roar;
Or, if the air will not permit,
Some still removed place will fit,
Where glowing embers through the room
Teach light to counterfeit a gloom;   80
Far from all resort of mirth,
Save the cricket on the hearth,
Or the bellman's drowsy charm
To bless the doors from nightly harm.
   Or let my lamp at midnight hour   85
Be seen in some high lonely tower,
Where I may oft out-watch the Bear
With thrice-great Hermes, or unsphere
The spirit of Plato, to unfold
What worlds or what vast regions hold   90
The immortal mind that hath forsook
Her mansion in this fleshly nook;
And of those Daemons that are found
In fire, air, flood, or underground,
Whose power hath a true consent   95
With planet, or with element.
Sometime let gorgeous Tragedy
In sceptered pall come sweeping by,
Presenting Thebes, or Pelops' line,
Or the tale of Troy divine;   100
Or what (though rare) of later age
Ennobled hath the buskined stage.

But, O sad Virgin, that thy power
Might raise Musaeus from his bower,
Or bid the soul of Orpheus sing   105
Such notes as, warbled to the string,
Drew iron tears down Pluto's cheek
And made Hell grant what Love did seek!
Or call up him that left half-told
The story of Cambuscan bold,   110
Of Camball, and of Algarsife,
And who had Canace to wife,
That owned the virtuous ring and glass,
And of the wondrous horse of brass,
On which the Tartar king did ride;   115
And if aught else great bards beside
In sage and solemn tunes have sung,
Of tourneys, and of trophies hung,
Of forests, and enchantments drear,
Where more is meant than meets the ear.   120
    Thus, Night, oft see me in thy pale career,
Till civil-suited Morn appear,
Not tricked and frounced as she was wont
With the Attic boy to hunt,
But kerchiefed in a comely cloud   125
While rocking winds are piping loud,
Or ushered with a shower still,
When the gust hath blown his fill,
Ending on the rustling leaves
With minute-drops from off the eaves.   130
And when the sun begins to fling
His flaring beams, me, goddess, bring
To arched walks of twilight groves,
And shadows brown, that Sylvan loves,
Of pine, or monumental oak,   135
Where the rude axe, with heaved stroke,
Was never heard the nymphs to daunt
Or fright them from their hallowed haunt.
There in close covert by some brook
Where no profaner eye may look,   140
Hide me from day's garish eye,
While the bee with honeyed thigh,
That at her flowery work doth sing,

123. **Frounced:** curled

And the waters murmuring,
With such consort as they keep, 145
Entice the dewy-feathered Sleep;
And let some strange mysterious dream
Wave at his wings in airy stream
Of lively portraiture displayed,
Softly on my eyelids laid: 150
And, as I wake, sweet music breathe
Above, about, or underneath,
Sent by some spirit to mortals good,
Or the unseen Genius of the wood.
    But let my due feet never fail 155
To walk the studious cloister's pale
And love the high-embowed roof,
With antique pillars massy proof
And storied windows richly dight,
Casting a dim religious light: 160
There let the pealing organ blow
To the full-voiced quire below
In service high and anthems clear,
As may with sweetness, through mine ear,
Dissolve me into ecstasies, 165
And bring all Heaven before mine eyes.
    And may at last my weary age
Find out the peaceful hermitage,
The hairy gown and mossy cell
Where I may sit and rightly spell 170
Of every star that heaven doth shew,
And every herb that sips the dew;
Till old experience do attain
To something like prophetic strain.
    These pleasures, Melancholy, give, 175
And I with thee will choose to live.

156. **Pale:** boundary

LYCIDAS

Yet once more, O ye laurels, and once more,
Ye myrtles brown, with ivy never sere,
I come to pluck your berries harsh and crude,
And with forced fingers rude
Shatter your leaves before the mellowing year. 5

Bitter constraint and sad occasion dear
Compels me to disturb your season due:
For Lycidas is dead, dead ere his prime,
Young Lycidas, and hath not left his peer.
Who would not sing for Lycidas? he knew   10
Himself to sing, and build the lofty rhyme.
He must not float upon his watery bier
Unwept, and welter to the parching wind,
Without the meed of some melodious tear.
　　Begin then, Sisters of the sacred well   15
That from beneath the seat of Jove doth spring;
Begin, and somewhat loudly sweep the string;
Hence with denial vain and coy excuse:
So may some gentle Muse
With lucky words favor my destined urn;   20
And as he passes, turn
And bid fair peace be to my sable shroud.
　　For we were nursed upon the self-same hill,
Fed the same flock by fountain, shade, and rill.
Together both, ere the high lawns appeared   25
Under the opening eye-lids of the Morn,
We drove a-field, and both together heard
What time the gray-fly winds her sultry horn,
Battening our flocks with the fresh dews of night;
Oft till the star, that rose at evening bright,   30
Toward heaven's descent had sloped his westering wheel.
Meanwhile the rural ditties were not mute;
Tempered to the oaten flute,
Rough Satyrs danced, and Fauns with cloven heel
From the glad sound would not be absent long;   35
And old Damoetas loved to hear our song.
　　But, O! the heavy change, now thou art gone,
Now thou art gone, and never must return!
Thee, Shepherd, thee the woods and desert caves,
With wild thyme and the gadding vine o'ergrown,   40
And all their echoes, mourn:
The willows and the hazel copses green
Shall now no more be seen
Fanning their joyous leaves to thy soft lays.
As killing as the canker to the rose,   45
Or taint-worm to the weanling herds that graze,
Or frost to flowers, that their gay wardrobe wear

When first the white-thorn blows;
Such, Lycidas, thy loss to shepherd's ear.
   Where were ye, Nymphs, when the remorseless deep   50
Closed o'er the head of your loved Lycidas?
For neither were ye playing on the steep
Where your old bards, the famous Druids, lie,
Nor on the shaggy top of Mona high,
Nor yet where Deva spreads her wizard stream.   55
Ay me! I fondly dream
"Had ye been there,"—for what could that have done?
What could the Muse herself that Orpheus bore,
The Muse herself, for her enchanting son,
Whom universal nature did lament,   60
When by the rout that made the hideous roar
His gory visage down the stream was sent,
Down the swift Hebrus to the Lesbian shore?
   Alas! what boots it with uncessant care
To tend the homely, slighted, shepherd's trade   65
And strictly meditate the thankless Muse?
Were it not better done, as others use,
To sport with Amaryllis in the shade,
Or with the tangles of Neaera's hair?
Fame is the spur that the clear spirit doth raise   70
(That last infirmity of noble mind)
To scorn delights, and live laborious days;
But the fair guerdon when we hope to find,
And think to burst out into sudden blaze,
Comes the blind Fury with the abhorred shears   75
And slits the thin-spun life. "But not the praise,"
Phoebus replied, and touched my trembling ears:
"Fame is no plant that grows on mortal soil,
Nor in the glistering foil
Set off to the world, nor in broad rumor lies: 80
But lives and spreads aloft by those pure eyes
And perfect witness of all-judging Jove;
As he pronounces lastly on each deed,
Of so much fame in heaven expect thy meed."
   O fountain Arethuse, and thou honored flood,   85
Smooth-sliding Mincius, crowned with vocal reeds,
That strain I heard was of a higher mood.
But now my oat proceeds,
And listens to the herald of the sea

That came in Neptune's plea; 90
He asked the waves, and asked the felon winds,
What hard mishap hath doomed this gentle swain?
And questioned every gust of rugged wings
That blows from off each beaked promontory:
They knew not of his story; 95
And sage Hippotades their answer brings,
That not a blast was from his dungeon strayed;
The air was calm, and on the level brine
Sleek Panope with all her sisters played.
It was that fatal and perfidious bark, 100
Built in the eclipse, and rigged with curses dark,
That sunk so low that sacred head of thine.
    Next Camus, reverend sire, went footing slow,
His mantle hairy, and his bonnet sedge,
Inwrought with figures dim, and on the edge 105
Like to that sanguine flower inscribed with woe.
"Ah! who hath reft," quoth he, "my dearest pledge?"
Last came, and last did go
The Pilot of the Galilean lake;
Two massy keys he bore of metals twain 110
(The golden opes, the iron shuts amain);
He shook his mitred locks, and stern bespake:
"How well could I have spared for thee, young swain,
Enow of such, as for their bellies' sake
Creep and intrude and climb into the fold! 115
Of other care they little reckoning make
Than how to scramble at the shearers' feast,
And shove away the worthy bidden guest.
Blind mouths! that scarce themselves know how to hold
A sheep-hook, or have learned aught else the least 120
That to the faithful herdman's art belongs!
What recks it them? What need they? They are sped;
And when they list, their lean and flashy songs
Grate on their scrannel pipes of wretched straw;
The hungry sheep look up, and are not fed, 125
But, swol'n with wind and the rank mist they draw,
Rot inwardly, and foul contagion spread:
Besides what the grim wolf with privy paw
Daily devours apace, and nothing said:
—But that two-handed engine at the door 130
Stands ready to smite once, and smite no more."

Return, Alpheus; the dread voice is past
That shrunk thy streams; return, Sicilian Muse,
And call the vales, and bid them hither cast
Their bells and flowerets of a thousand hues. 135
Ye valleys low, where the mild whispers use
Of shades, and wanton winds, and gushing brooks
On whose fresh lap the swart star sparely looks;
Throw hither all your quaint enameled eyes
That on the green turf suck the honeyed showers, 140
And purple all the ground with vernal flowers.
Bring the rathe primrose that forsaken dies,
The tufted crow-toe, and pale jessamine,
The white pink, and the pansy freaked with jet,
The glowing violet, 145
The musk-rose, and the well-attired woodbine,
With cowslips wan that hang the pensive head,
And every flower that sad embroidery wears;
Bid amaranthus all his beauty shed,
And daffadillies fill their cups with tears 150
To strew the laureate hearse where Lycid lies.
For so to interpose a little ease,
Let our frail thoughts dally with false surmise.
Ay me! whilst thee the shores and sounding seas
Wash far away, where'er thy bones are hurled; 155
Whether beyond the stormy Hebrides
Where thou, perhaps, under the whelming tide,
Visit'st the bottom of the monstrous world;
Or whether thou, to our moist vows denied,
Sleep'st by the fable of Bellerus old, 160
Where the great Vision of the guarded mount
Looks toward Namancos and Bayona's hold.
Look homeward, Angel, now, and melt with ruth:
And, O ye dolphins, waft the hapless youth!
Weep no more, woeful shepherds, weep no more, 165
For Lycidas, your sorrow, is not dead,
Sunk though he be beneath the watery floor;
So sinks the day-star in the ocean bed,
And yet anon repairs his drooping head,
And tricks his beams, and with new-spangled ore 170
Flames in the forehead of the morning sky:
So Lycidas sunk low, but mounted high
Through the dear might of Him that walked the waves;

Where, other groves and other streams along,
With nectar pure his oozy locks he laves, 175
And hears the unexpressive nuptial song
In the blest kingdoms meek of joy and love.
There entertain him all the saints above
In solemn troops, and sweet societies,
That sing, and singing in their glory move, 180
And wipe the tears for ever from his eyes.
Now, Lycidas, the shepherds weep no more;
Henceforth thou art the Genius of the shore
In thy large recompense, and shalt be good
To all that wander in that perilous flood. 185
  Thus sang the uncouth swain to the oaks and rills,
While the still morn went out with sandals gray;
He touched the tender stops of various quills,
With eager thought warbling his Doric lay:
And now the sun had stretched out all the hills, 190
And now was dropt into the western bay.
At last he rose, and twitched his mantle blue:
Tomorrow to fresh woods, and pastures new.

SONGS from *COMUS*

I

The star that bids the shepherd fold
Now the top of heaven doth hold;
And the gilded car of day
His glowing axle doth allay
In the steep Atlantic stream; 5
And the slope sun his upward beam
Shoots against the dusky pole,
Pacing toward the other goal
Of his chamber in the east.
Meanwhile, welcome joy and feast, 10
Midnight shout and revelry,
Tipsy dance and jollity.
Braid your locks with rosy twine,
Dropping odours, dropping wine.
Rigour now is gone to bed; 15
And Advice with scrupulous head,
Strict Age, and sour Severity,
With their grave saws, in slumber lie.

We, that are of purer fire,
Imitate the starry choir,   20
Who, in their nightly watchful spheres,
Lead in swift round the months and years.
The sounds and seas, with all their finny drove,
Now to the moon in wavering morrice move;
And on the tawny sands and shelves   25
Trip the pert fairies and the dapper elves.
By dimpled brook and fountain-brim,
The wood-nymphs, decked with daisies trim,
Their merry wakes and pastimes keep:
What hath night to do with sleep?   30
Night hath better sweets to prove;
Venus now wakes, and wakens Love.
Come, let us our rites begin;
'Tis only daylight that makes sin,
Which these dun shades will ne'er report.   35
Hail, goddess of nocturnal sport,
Dark-veiled Cotytto, t' whom the secret flame
Of midnight torches burns! mysterious dame,
That ne'er art called but when the dragon womb
Of Stygian darkness spits her thickest gloom,   40
And makes one blot of all the air!
Stay thy cloudy ebon chair,
Wherein thou ridest with Hecat', and befriend
Us thy vowed priests, till utmost end
Of all thy dues be done, and none left out;   45
Ere the blabbing eastern scout,
The nice Morn on th' Indian steep,
From her cabined loop-hole peep,
And to the tell-tale Sun descry
Our concealed solemnity.   50
Come, knit hands, and beat the ground
In a light fantastic round.

II

Sweet Echo, sweetest nymph, that liv'st unseen
    Within thy airy shell
    By slow Meander's margent green,
And in the violet-embroidered vale
    Where the love-lorn nightingale   5
Nightly to thee her sad song mourneth well:

Canst thou not tell me of a gentle pair
  That likest thy Narcissus are?
    O, if thou have
  Hid them in some flowery cave,   10
    Tell me but where,
Sweet Queen of Parley, Daughter of the Sphere!
So may'st thou be translated to the skies,
And give resounding grace to all Heav'n's harmonies!

III

Sabrina fair,
  Listen where thou art sitting
Under the glassy, cool, translucent wave,
  In twisted braids of lilies knitting
  The loose train of thy amber-dropping hair;   5
    Listen for dear honor's sake,
    Goddess of the silver lake,
      Listen and save!

Listen, and appear to us,
In name of great Oceanus,   10
By the earth-shaking Neptune's mace,
And Tethys' grave majestic pace;
By hoary Nereus' wrinkled look,
And the Carpathian wizard's hook;
By scaly Triton's winding shell,   15
And old sooth-saying Glaucus' spell;
By Leucothea's lovely hands,
And her son that rules the strands;
By Thetis' tinsel-slippered feet,
And the songs of Sirens sweet;   20
By dead Parthenopè's dear tomb,
And fair Ligea's golden comb,
Wherewith she sits on diamond rocks
Sleeking her soft alluring locks;
By all the nymphs that nightly dance   25
Upon thy streams with wily glance;
Rise, rise, and heave thy rosy head
From thy coral-paven bed,
And bridle in thy headlong wave,
Till thou our summons answered have.   30
            Listen and save!

(Sabrina rises, attended by water-nymphs, and sings.)

> By the rushy-fringed bank,
> Where grows the willow and the osier dank,
>   My sliding chariot stays,
> Thickset with agate, and the azurn sheen   35
>   Of turquoise blue, and emerald green
>   That in the channel strays,
>   Whilst from off the waters fleet
>   Thus I set my printless feet
>   O'er the cowslip's velvet head,   40
>   That bends not as I tread,
>   Gentle swain at thy request
>   I am here.

IV

To the ocean now I fly
And those happy climes that lie
Where day never shuts his eye,
Up in the broad fields of the sky.
There I suck the liquid air,   5
All amidst the gardens fair
Of Hesperus, and his daughters three
That sing about the golden tree.
Along the crispèd shades and bowers
Revels the spruce and jocund Spring;   10
The Graces and the rosy-bosomed Hours
Thither all their bounties bring.
That there eternal Summer dwells,
And west winds with musky wing
About the cedarn alleys fling   15
Nard and cassia's balmy smells.
Iris there with humid bow
Waters the odorous banks, that blow
Flowers of more mingled hue   20
Than her purfled scarf can shew,
And drenches with Elysian dew
(List, mortals, if your ears be true)
Beds of hyacinth and roses,
Where young Adonis oft reposes,   25
Waxing well of his deep wound,

In slumber soft, and on the ground
Sadly sits th' Assyrian queen.
But far above, in spangled sheen,
Celestial Cupid, her famed son, advanced   30
Holds his dear Psyche, sweet entranced
After her wandering labours long,
Till free consent the gods among
Make her his eternal bride,
And from her fair unspotted side   35
Two blissful twins are to be born,
Youth and Joy; so Jove hath sworn.
    But now my task is smoothly done:
I can fly, or I can run
Quickly to the green earth's end,   40
Where the bowed welkin slow doth bend,
And from thence can soar as soon
To the corners of the moon.
    Mortals, that would follow me,
Love Virtue; she alone is free.   45
She can teach ye how to climb
Higher than the sphery chime;
Or, if Virtue feeble were,
Heaven itself would stoop to her.

HOW SOON HATH TIME

How soon hath Time, the subtle thief of youth,
    Stol'n on his wing my three-and-twentieth year!
My hasting days fly on with full career,
    But my late spring no bud or blossom shew'th.
Perhaps my semblance might deceive the truth,
    That I to manhood am arriv'd so near,
    And inward ripeness doth much less appear,
    That some more timely-happy spirits indu'th.
Yet it be less or more, or soon or slow,
    It shall be still in strictest measure ev'n,
    To that same lot, however mean or high,
Toward which Time leads me, and the will of Heav'n;
    All is, if I have grace to use it so,
    As ever in my great Taskmaster's eye.

WHEN I CONSIDER HOW MY LIGHT IS SPENT

When I consider how my light is spent
  Ere half my days in this dark world and wide,
  And that one talent which is death to hide
  Lodged with me useless, though my soul more bent
To serve therewith my Maker, and present
  My true account, lest he returning chide,
  Doth God exact day-labor, light denied?
  I fondly ask. But Patience, to prevent
That murmur, soon replies, God doth not need
  Either man's work or his own gifts. Who best
  Bear his mild yoke, they serve him best. His state
Is kingly: Thousands at his bidding speed,
  And post o'er land and ocean without rest;
  They also serve who only stand and wait.

TO OLIVER CROMWELL

Cromwell, our chief of men, that through a cloud,
  Not of war only, but detractions rude;
  Guided by faith and matchless fortitude
  To peace and truth thy glorious way hast plough'd,
And on the neck of crowned Fortune proud
  Hast rear'd God's trophies, and his work pursu'd,
  While Derwent stream with blood of Scots imbru'd,
  And Dunbar field resound thy praises loud,
And Worcester's laureate wreath; yet much remains
  To conquer still; peace hath her victories
  No less renown'd than war; new foes arise
Threat'ning to bind our souls in secular chains:
  Help us to save free conscience from the paw
  Of hireling wolves, whose gospel is their maw.

ON THE LATE MASSACRE IN PIEMONT

Avenge, O Lord, thy slaughter'd saints, whose bones
  Lie scatter'd on the Alpine mountains cold,
  Ev'n them who kept thy truth so pure of old
  When all our fathers worship't stocks and stones,

Forget not: in Thy book record their groans
 Who were Thy sheep and in their ancient fold
 Slain by the bloody Piemontese, that roll'd
 Mother with infant down the rocks. Their moans
The vales redoubl'd to the hills, and they
 To heav'n. Their martyr'd blood and ashes sow
 O'er all th' Italian fields where still doth sway
The triple Tyrant: that from these may grow
 A hundred-fold, who having learnt Thy way
 Early may fly the Babylonian woe.

ON THE DETRACTION WHICH FOLLOWED UPON MY WRITING CERTAIN TREATISES

A book was writ of late called *Tetrachordon*,
 And woven close, both matter, form, and style;
 The subject new: it walked the town a while,
 Numbering good intellects; now seldom pored on.
Cries the stall-reader, Bless us! what a word on
 A title-page is this! and some in file
 Stand spelling false, while one might walk to Mile-
End Green. Why is it harder, sirs, than Gordon,
Colkitto, or Macdonnel, or Galasp?
 Those rugged names to our like mouths grow sleek,
 That would have made Quintilian stare and gasp.
Thy age, like ours, O soul of Sir John Cheek,
 Hated not learning worse than toad or asp,
 When thou taught'st Cambridge and King Edward
 Greek.

ON THE SAME

I did but prompt the age to quit their clogs
 By the known rules of ancient liberty,
 When straight a barbarous noise environs me
 Of owls and cuckoos, asses, apes, and dogs;
As when those hinds that were transformed to frogs
 Railed at Latona's twin-born progeny,
 Which after held the Sun and Moon in fee.
 But this is got by casting pearl to hogs,

That bawl for freedom in their senseless mood,
    And still revolt when truth would set them free.
    Licence they mean when they cry liberty;
For who loves that must first be wise and good:
    But from that mark how far they rove we see,
    For all this waste of wealth and loss of blood.

ON HIS DECEASED WIFE

Methought I saw my late espoused Saint
    Brought to me like *Alcestis* from the grave,
    Whom *Jove's* great son to her glad husband gave,
    Rescu'd from death by force though pale and faint.
Mine as whom washt from spot of child-bed taint,
    Purification in the old Law did save,
    And such, as yet once more I trust to have
    Full sight of her in Heaven without restraint,
Came vested all in white, pure as her mind:
    Her face was veil'd, yet to my fancied sight,
    Love, sweetness, goodness, in her person shin'd
So clear, as in no face with more delight.
    But O as to embrace me she enclin'd
    I wak'd, she fled, and day brought back my night.

CHORUSES from *SAMSON AGONISTES*

I

Many are the sayings of the wise,
In ancient and in modern books enrolled,
Extolling patience as the truest fortitude,
And to the bearing well of all calamities,
All chances incident to man's frail life,   5
Consolatories writ
With studied argument, and much persuasion sought,
Lenient of grief and anxious thought.
But with th' afflicted in his pangs their sound
Little prevails, or rather seems a tune   10
Harsh, and of dissonant mood from his complaint,
Unless he feel within
Some source of consolation from above,

Secret refreshings that repair his strength
And fainting spirits uphold.   15
   God of our fathers! what is Man,
That thou towards him with hand so various—
Or might I say contrarious?—
Temper'st thy providence through his short course:
Not evenly, as thou rul'st   20
The angelic orders, and inferior creatures mute,
Irrational and brute?
Nor do I name of men the common rout,
That, wandering loose about,
Grow up and perish as the summer fly,   25
Heads without name, no more remembered;
But such as thou hast solemnly elected,
With gifts and graces eminently adorned,
To some great work, thy glory,
And people's safety, which in part they effect.   30
Yet toward these, thus dignified, thou oft,
Amidst their height of noon,
Changest thy countenance and thy hand, with no regard
Of highest favours past
From thee on them, or them to thee of service.   35
   Nor only dost degrade them, or remit
To life obscured, which were a fair dismission,
But throw'st them lower than thou didst exalt them high—
Unseemly falls in human eye,
Too grievous for the trespass or omission;   40
Oft leav'st them to the hostile sword
Of heathen and profane, their carcases
To dogs and fowls a prey, or else captived,
Or to the unjust tribunals, under change of times,
And condemnation of the ingrateful multitude.   45
If these they scape, perhaps in poverty
With sickness and disease thou bow'st them down,
Painful diseases and deformed,
In crude old age;
Though not disordinate, yet causeless suffering   50
The punishment of dissolute days. In fine,
Just or unjust alike seem miserable,
For oft alike both come to evil end.
So deal not with this once thy glorious champion,
The image of thy strength, and mighty minister.   55

What do I beg? how hast thou dealt already!
Behold him in this state calamitous, and turn
His labours, for thou canst, to peaceful end.

II

O, how comely it is, and how reviving
To the spirits of just men long oppressed,
When God into the hands of their deliverer
Puts invincible might,
To quell the mighty of the earth, th' oppressor,   5
The brute and boisterous force of violent men,
Hardy and industrious to support
Tyrannic power, but raging to pursue
The righteous, and all such as honour truth!
He all their ammunition   10
And feats of war defeats,
With plain heroic magnitude of mind
And celestial vigour armed;
Their armouries and magazines contemns,
Renders them useless, while   15
With wingèd expedition
Swift as the lightning glance he executes
His errand on the wicked, who, surprised,
Lose their defence, distracted and amazed.
    But patience is more oft the exercise   20
Of saints, the trial of their fortitude,
Making them each his own deliverer,
And victor over all
That tyranny or fortune can inflict.
Either of these is in thy lot,   25
Samson, with might endued
Above the sons of men; but sight bereaved
May chance to number thee with those
Whom patience finally must crown.

III

All is best, though we oft doubt
What th' unsearchable dispose
Of Highest Wisdom brings about,
And ever best found in the close.
Oft he seems to hide his face,   5
But unexpectedly returns,

And to his faithful champion hath in place
Bore witness gloriously; whence Gaza mourns,
And all that band them to resist
His uncontrollable intent.   10
His servants he, with new acquist
Of true experience from this great event,
With peace and consolation hath dismissed,
And calm of mind, all passion spent.

SIR JOHN SUCKLING (1609–1642)

OUT UPON IT! I HAVE LOVED

Out upon it! I have loved
　Three whole days together;
And am like to love three more,
　If it prove fair weather.

Time shall moult away his wings,   5
　Ere he shall discover
In the whole wide world again
　Such a constant lover.

But the spite on 't is, no praise
　Is due at all to me;   10
Love with me had made no stays,
　Had it any been but she.

Had it any been but she,
　And that very face,
There had been at least ere this   15
　A dozen dozen in her place.

A BALLAD UPON A WEDDING

I tell thee, Dick, where I have been,
Where I the rarest things have seen,
　Oh, things without compare!
Such sights again cannot be found
In any place on English ground,   5
　Be it at wake or fair.

At Charing Cross, hard by the way
Where we (thou know'st) do sell our hay,
   There is a house with stairs;
And there I did see coming down   10
Such folk as are not in our town,
   Forty, at least, in pairs.

Amongst the rest, one pest'lent fine
(His beard no bigger, though, than thine)
   Walked on before the rest.   15
Our landlord looks like nothing to him;
The king (God bless him!), 'twould undo him
   Should he go still so dressed.

At course-a-park, without all doubt,
He should have been the first taken out   20
   By all the maids i' the town,
Though lusty Roger there had been,
Or little George upon the Green,
   Or Vincent of the Crown.

But wot you what? the youth was going   25
To make an end of all his wooing;
   The parson for him stayed.
Yet by his leave, for all his haste,
He did not so much wish all past,
   Perchance, as did the maid.   30

The maid (and thereby hangs a tale),
For such a maid no Whitsun-ale
   Could ever yet produce;
No grape, that's kindly ripe, could be
So round, so plump, so soft as she,   35
   Nor half so full of juice.

Her finger was so small the ring
Would not stay on, which they did bring;
   It was too wide a peck:
And to say truth (for out it must),   40
It looked like the great collar, just,
   About our young colt's neck.

Her feet beneath her petticoat,
Like little mice stole in and out,
   As if they feared the light;
But oh, she dances such a way,   45
No sun upon an Easter day
   Is half so fine a sight!

He would have kissed her once or twice,
But she would not, she was so nice,   50
   She would not do't in sight;
And then she looked as who should say,
I will do what I list to-day,
   And you shall do't at night.

Her cheeks so rare a white was on,   55
No daisy makes comparison
   (Who sees them is undone),
For streaks of red were mingled there,
Such as are on a Catherine pear
   (The side that's next the sun).   60

Her lips were red, and one was thin
Compared to that was next her chin
   (Some bee had stung it newly);
But, Dick, her eyes so guard her face
I durst no more upon them gaze   65
   Than on the sun in July.

Her mouth so small, when she does speak,
Thou'dst swear her teeth her words did break,
   That they might passage get;
But she so handled still the matter,   70
They came as good as ours, or better,
   And are not spent a whit.

If wishing should be any sin,
The parson himself had guilty been
   (She looked that day so purely);
And did the youth so oft the feat   75
At night, as some did in conceit,
   It would have spoiled him, surely.

Passion o' me, how I run on!
There's that that would be thought upon,   80
   I trow, besides the bride.
The business of the kitchen's great,
For it is fit that man should eat,
   Nor was it there denied.

Just in the nick the cook knocked thrice,   85
And all the waiters in a trice
   His summons did obey;
Each serving-man, with dish in hand,
Marched boldly up, like our trained band,
   Presented, and away.   90

When all the meat was on the table,
What man of knife or teeth was able
   To stay to be entreated?
And this the very reason was—
Before the parson could say grace,   95
   The company was seated.

Now hats fly off, and youths carouse;
Healths first go round, and then the house;
   The bride's came thick and thick:
And when 'twas named another's health,   100
Perhaps he made it hers by stealth;
   And who could help it, Dick?

O' the sudden up they rise and dance;
Then sit again and sigh and glance;
   Then dance again and kiss;   105
Thus several ways the time did pass,
Till every woman wished her place,
   And every man wished his!

By this time all were stolen aside
To counsel and undress the bride,   110
   But that he must not know;
But yet 'twas thought he guessed her mind,
And did not mean to stay behind
   Above an hour or so.

When in he came, Dick, there she lay 115
Like new-fallen snow melting away
   ('Twas time, I trow, to part);
Kisses were now the only stay,
Which soon she gave, as who would say,
   "God be wi' ye, with all my heart." 120

But just as heavens would have to cross it,
In came the bridesmaids with the posset.
   The bridegroom eat in spite,
For had he left the women to't, 125
It would have cost two hours to do't,
   Which were too much that night.

At length the candle's out, and now
All that they had not done, they do.
   What that is, who can tell?
But I believe it was no more 130
Than thou and I have done before
   With Bridget and with Nell.

SONG

When, dearest, I but think of thee,
Methinks all things that lovely be
Are present, and my soul delighted;
For beauties that from worth arise
Are like the grace of deities,
Still present with us, tho' unsighted.

Thus whilst I sit, and sigh the day
With all his borrowed lights away,
Till night's black wings do overtake me,
Thinking on thee, thy beauties then,
As sadder lights do sleepy men,
So they by their bright rays awake me.

Thus absence dies, and dying proves
No absence can subsist with loves
That do partake of fair perfection;
Since in the darkest night they may,

By love's quick motion, find a way
To see each other by reflection.

The waving sea can with each flood
Bathe some high promont, that has stood
Far from the main up in the river:
Oh think not then but love can do
As much, for that's an ocean too,
Which flows not every day, but ever.

RICHARD CRASHAW (1613?–1649)

IN THE HOLY NATIVITY OF OUR LORD GOD

A Hymn Sung as by the Shepherds

Chorus

Come, we shepherds, whose blest sight
Hath met Love's noon in Nature's night;
Come, lift we up our loftier song
And wake the sun that lies too long.

To all our world of well-stol'n joy   5
He slept, and dreamt of no such thing;
   While we found out heaven's fairer Eye
And kissed the cradle of our King.
   Tell him he rises now, too late
To show us aught worth looking at.   10

   Tell him we now can show him more
Than he e'er showed to mortal sight;
   Than he himself e'er saw before;
Which to be seen needs not his light.
   Tell him, Tityrus, where th' hast been   15
Tell him, Thyrsis, what th' hast seen.

Tityrus.   Gloomy night embraced the place
   Where the noble infant lay,
    The babe looked up and showed his face;
   In spite of darkness, it was day.   20
    It was thy day, sweet! and did rise
Not from the east, but from thine eyes.

CHORUS.   It was thy day, sweet, etc.

THYRSIS.   Winter chid aloud; and sent
  The angry North to wage his wars.   25
   The North forgot his fierce intent;
  And left perfumes instead of scars.
   By those sweet eyes' persuasive powers,
  Where he meant frost he scattered flowers.

CHORUS.   By those sweet eyes', etc.   30

BOTH.   We saw thee in thy balmy nest,
  Young dawn of our Eternal Day!
   We saw thine eyes break from their east
  And chase the trembling shades away.
   We saw thee, and we blest the sight, 35
  We saw thee by thine own sweet light.

CHORUS.   We saw thee, etc.

TITYRUS.   Poor World, said I, what wilt thou do
  To entertain this starry stranger?
   Is this the best thou canst bestow?
  A cold, and not too cleanly, manger? 40
   Contend, ye powers of heaven and earth,
  To fit a bed for this huge birth!

CHORUS.   Contend ye powers, etc.

THYRSIS.   Proud World, said I; cease your contest
  And let the mighty babe alone;   45
   The phœnix builds the phœnix' nest,
  Love's architecture is his own;
   The babe whose birth embraves this morn,
  Made his own bed e'er he was born.

CHORUS.   The babe whose, etc.   50

TITYRUS.   I saw the curled drops, soft and slow,
  Come hovering o'er the place's head;
   Off'ring their whitest sheets of snow
  To furnish the fair infant's bed.

Forbear, said I; be not too bold.   55
Your fleece is white, but 't is too cold.

CHORUS.   Forbear, said I, etc.

THYRSIS.   I saw the obsequious seraphim
        Their rosy fleece of fire bestow,
            For well they now can spare their wings,   60
        Since heaven itself lies here below.
            Well done, said I; but are you sure
        Your down so warm, will pass for pure?

CHORUS.   Well done, said I, etc.

TITYRUS.   No, no, your king's not yet to seek   65
        Where to repose his royal head;
            See, see how soon his new-bloomed cheek
        'Twixt's mother's breasts is gone to bed!
            Sweet choice, said we! no way but so
        Not to lie cold, yet sleep in snow.   70

CHORUS.   Sweet choice, said we, etc.

BOTH.   We saw thee in thy balmy nest,
        Bright dawn of our Eternal Day!
            We saw thine eyes break from their east
        And chase the trembling shades away.   75
            We saw thee, and we blest the sight,
        We saw thee by thine own sweet light.

CHORUS.   We saw thee, etc.

FULL CHORUS

Welcome all wonders in one sight!
Eternity shut in a span,   80
    Summer in winter, day in night,
Heaven in earth, and God in man.
    Great Little One, whose all-embracing birth
Lifts earth to heaven, stoops heaven to earth!

Welcome, though nor to gold nor silk,   85
To more than Cæsar's birthright is;
 Two sister-seas of virgin-milk
With many a rarely-tempered kiss
 That breathes at once both maid and mother,
Warms in the one, cools in the other.   90

Welcome, though not to those gay flies
Gilded i' the beams of earthly kings,
 Slippery souls in smiling eyes,
But to poor shepherds, homespun things,
 Whose wealth's their flock, whose wit's to be   95
Well read in their simplicity.

Yet when young April's husband showers
Shall bless the fruitful Maia's bed,
 We'll bring the first-born of her flowers
To kiss thy feet and crown thy head.   100
 To thee, dread Lamb! Whose love must keep
The shepherds, more than they the sheep.

To Thee, meek Majesty! soft King
Of simple graces and sweet loves!
 Each of us his lamb will bring,   105
Each his pair of silver doves!
 Till burnt at last in fire of thy fair eyes,
Ourselves become our own best sacrifice!

A SONG

Lord, when the sense of thy sweet grace
Sends up my soul to seek thy face,
Thy blessed eyes breed such desire,
I dy in love's delicious Fire.
 O love, I am thy SACRIFICE.
Be still triumphant, blessed eyes.
Still shine on me, fair suns! that I
Still may behold, though still I dy.

Though still I dy, I live again;
Still longing so to be still slain,

So gainful is such loss of breath,
I dy even in desire of death.
   Still live in me this loving strife
Of living DEATH & dying LIFE.
For while thou sweetly slayest me
Dead to myself, I live in Thee.

RICHARD LOVELACE (1618–1658)

TO LUCASTA, GOING TO THE WARS

Tell me not, Sweet, I am unkind,
   That from the nunnery
Of thy chaste breast and quiet mind
   To war and arms I fly.

True, a new mistress now I chase,
   The first foe in the field;
And with a stronger faith embrace
   A sword, a horse, a shield.

Yet this inconstancy is such
   As thou too shalt adore;
I could not love thee, Dear, so much,
   Loved I not Honor more.

TO ALTHEA, FROM PRISON

When Love with unconfined wings
   Hovers within my Gates;
And my divine *Althea* brings
   To whisper at the Grates:
When I lie tangled in her hair,
   And fetter'd to her eye;
The *Gods* that wanton in the Air,
   Know no such Liberty.

When flowing Cups run swiftly round
  With no allaying Thames,
Our careless heads with Roses bound,
  Our hearts with Loyal Flames;
When thirsty grief in Wine we steep,
  When Healths and draughts go free,
Fishes that tipple in the Deep,
  Know no such Liberty.

When (like committed Linnets) I
  With shriller throat shall sing
The sweetness, Mercy, Majesty,
  And glories of my KING;
When I shall voice aloud, how Good
  He is, how Great should be;
Inlarged Winds that curl the Flood,
  Know no such Liberty.

Stone Walls do not a Prison make,
  Nor Iron Bars a Cage;
Minds innocent and quiet take
  That for an Hermitage;
If I have freedom in my Love,
  And in my soul am free;
Angels alone that soar above,
  Enjoy such liberty.

ANDREW MARVELL (1621–1678)

TO HIS COY MISTRESS

Had we but world enough, and time,
This coyness, lady, were no crime.
We would sit down, and think which way
To walk, and pass our long love's day.
Thou by the Indian Ganges' side   5
Should'st rubies find: I by the tide
Of Humber would complain. I would
Love you ten years before the Flood,

And you should, if you please, refuse
Till the conversion of the Jews.   10
My vegetable love should grow
Vaster than empires, and more slow.
An hundred years should go to praise
Thine eyes, and on thy forehead gaze:
Two hundred to adore each breast: 15
But thirty thousand to the rest;
An age at least to every part,
And the last age should show your heart.
For, lady, you deserve this state,
Nor would I love at lower rate.   20
    But at my back I always hear
Time's wingèd chariot hurrying near:
And yonder all before us lie
Deserts of vast eternity.
Thy beauty shall no more be found;   25
Nor, in thy marble vault, shall sound
My echoing song: then worms shall try
That long-preserved virginity,
And your quaint honor turn to dust,
And into ashes all my lust.   30
The grave's a fine and private place,
But none, I think, do there embrace.
    Now, therefore, while the youthful hue
Sits on thy skin like morning dew,
And while thy willing soul transpires   35
At every pore with instant fires,
Now let us sport us while we may;
And now, like amorous birds of prey,
Rather at once our Time devour,
Than languish in his slow-chapt power.   40
Let us roll all our strength and all
Our sweetness up into one ball,
And tear our pleasures with rough strife
Thorough the iron gates of life.
Thus, though we cannot make our sun   45
Stand still, yet we will make him run.

THE GARDEN

How vainly men themselves amaze
To win the palm, the oak, or bays;
And their incessant labors see
Crowned from some single herb, or tree,
Whose short and narrow-vergèd shade 5
Does prudently their toils upbraid;
While all flowers and all trees do close
To weave the garlands of repose!

Fair Quiet, have I found thee here,
And Innocence, thy sister dear? 10
Mistaken long, I sought you then
In busy companies of men.
Your sacred plants, if here below,
Only among the plants will grow;
Society is all but rude 15
To this delicious solitude.

No white nor red was ever seen
So amorous as this lovely green.
Fond lovers, cruel as their flame,
Cut in these trees their mistress' name: 20
Little, alas! they know or heed
How far these beauties hers exceed!
Fair trees! wheres'e'er your barks I wound
No name shall but your own be found.

When we have run our passion's heat, 25
Love hither makes his best retreat.
The gods, that mortal beauty chase,
Still in a tree did end their race;
Apollo hunted Daphne so,
Only that she might laurel grow; 30
And Pan did after Syrinx speed,
Not as a nymph, but for a reed.

What wondrous life is this I lead!
Ripe apples drop about my head;
The luscious clusters of the vine 35
Upon my mouth do crush their wine;

The nectarine, and curious peach,
Into my hands themselves do reach;
Stumbling on melons, as I pass,
Ensnared with flowers, I fall on grass.   40

Meanwhile, the mind, from pleasure less,
Withdraws into its happiness:
The mind, that ocean where each kind
Does straight its own resemblance find;
Yet it creates, transcending these,   45
Far other worlds, and other seas;
Annihilating all that's made
To a green thought in a green shade.

Here at the fountain's sliding foot,
Or at some fruit-tree's mossy root,   50
Casting the body's vest aside,
My soul into the boughs does glide:
There like a bird it sits, and sings,
Then whets and combs its silver wings;
And, till prepared for longer flight,   55
Waves in its plumes the various light.

Such was that happy garden-state,
While man there walked without a mate:
After a place so pure and sweet,
What other help could yet be meet?   60
But 'twas beyond a mortal's share
To wander solitary there:
Two paradises 'twere in one,
To live in paradise alone.

How well the skillful gardener drew   65
Of flowers, and herbs, this dial new;
Where, from above, the milder sun
Does through a fragrant zodiac run;
And, as it works, the industrious bee
Computes its time as well as we.   70
How could such sweet and wholesome hours
Be reckoned but with herbs and flowers!

THE PICTURE OF LITTLE T. C. IN A
PROSPECT OF FLOWERS

See with what simplicity
This nymph begins her golden days!
In the green grass she loves to lie,
And there with her fair aspect tames
The wilder flowers, and gives them names,   5
But only with the roses plays,
      And them does tell
What colour best becomes them, and what smell.

Who can foretell for what high cause
This darling of the gods was born?   10
Yet this is she whose chaster laws
The wanton Love shall one day fear,
And, under her command severe,
See his bow broke and ensigns torn.
      Happy, who can   15
Appease this virtuous enemy of man!

O then let me in time compound
And parley with those conquering eyes,
Ere they have tried their force to wound;
Ere with their glancing wheels they drive   20
In triumph over hearts that strive,
And them that yield but more despise:
      Let me be laid
Where I may see thy glories from some shade.

Meantime, whilst every verdant thing   25
Itself does at thy beauty charm,
Reform the errors of the Spring:
Make that the tulips may have share
Of sweetness, seeing they are fair;
And roses of their thorns disarm;   30
      But most procure
That violets may a longer age endure.

But O, young beauty of the woods,
Whom nature courts with fruits and flowers,

Gather the flowers, but spare the buds,   35
Lest Flora, angry at thy crime
To kill her infants in their prime,
Do quickly make th' example yours;
      And, ere we see,
Nip in the blossom all our hopes and thee.   40

BERMUDAS

Where the remote Bermudas ride
In th' ocean's bosom unespy'd,
From a small boat that rowed along,
The list'ning winds receiv'd this song:

"What should we do but sing His praise,   5
That led us through the watery maze,
Unto an isle so long unknown,
And yet far kinder than our own?
Where He the huge sea-monsters wracks,
That lift the deep upon their backs.   10
He lands us on a grassy stage,
Safe from the storms, and prelate's rage.
He gave us this eternal spring,
Which here enamels everything,
And sends the fowls to us in care,   15
On daily visits through the air.
He hangs in shades the orange bright,
Like golden lamps in a green night,
And does in the pomegranates close
Jewels more rich than Ormus shows.   20
He makes the figs our mouths to meet,
And throws the melons at our feet.
But apples plants of such a price,
No tree could ever bear them twice.
With cedars, chosen by His hand,   25
From Lebanon, he stores the land,
And makes the hollow seas, that roar
Proclaim the ambergris on shore.
He cast (of which we rather boast)
The Gospel's pearl upon our coast   30
And in these rocks for us did frame

A temple, where to sound His name.
Oh let our voice His praise exalt,
Till it arrive at Heaven's vault,
Which thence (perhaps) rebounding, may   35
Echo beyond the Mexique Bay."

    Thus sung they, in the English boat,
An holy and a cheerful note;
And all the way, to guide their chime,
With falling oars they kept the time.   40

THE DEFINITION OF LOVE

My love is of a birth as rare
As 'tis for object strange and high:
It was begotten by Despair
Upon Impossibility.

Magnanimous Despair alone   5
Could show me so divine a thing,
Where feeble Hope could ne'er have flown
But vainly flapt its tinsel wing.

And yet I quickly might arrive
Where my extended soul is fixt,   10
But Fate does iron wedges drive,
And always crowds itself betwixt.

For Fate with jealous eye does see
Two perfect loves, nor lets them close:
Their union would her ruin be,   15
And her tyrannic pow'r depose.

And therefore her decrees of steel
Us as the distant poles have plac'd,
(Though Love's whole world on us does wheel)
Not by themselves to be embrac'd   20

Unless the giddy heaven fall
And earth some new convulsion tear,
And, us to join, the world should all
Be cramp'd into a planisphere.

As lines so loves oblique may well   25
Themselves in every angle greet;
But ours so truly parallel,
Though infinite can never meet.

Therefore the love which doth us bind,
But Fate so enviously debars,   30
Is the conjunction of the mind,
And opposition of the stars.

HENRY VAUGHAN (1622–1695)

THE WORLD

I saw Eternity the other night,
Like a great Ring of pure and endless light,
   All calm, as it was bright;
And round beneath it, Time in hours, days, years,
   Driven by the spheres,   5
Like a vast shadow moved: in which the world
   And all her train were hurled.
The doting lover in his quaintest strain
   Did there complain;
Near him, his lute, his fancy, and his flights,   10
   Wit's sour delights,
With gloves, and knots, the silly snares of pleasure,
   Yet his dear treasure,
All scattered lay, while he his eyes did pore
   Upon a flower.   15

The darksome statesman, hung with weights and woe,
Like a thick midnight-fog, moved there so slow,
   He did not stay, nor go;
Condemning thoughts—like sad eclipses—scowl
   Upon his soul,   20
And clouds of crying witnesses without
   Pursued him with one shout.
Yet digged the mole, and lest his ways be found,
   Worked under ground,
Where he did clutch his prey; but one did see   25
   That policy;

Churches and altars fed him; perjuries
  Were gnats and flies;
It rained about him blood and tears; but he
  Drank them as free.   30

The fearful miser on a heap of rust
Sate pining all his life there, did scarce trust
  His own hands with the dust,
Yet would not place one piece above, but lives
  In fear of thieves.   35
Thousands there were as frantic as himself
  And hugged each one his pelf;
The downright epicure placed heaven in sense,
  And scorned pretence;
While others, slipped into a wide excess,   40
  Said little less;
The weaker sort slight, trivial wares enslave,
  Who think them brave;
And poor, despisèd Truth sat counting by
  Their victory.   45

Yet some, who all this while did weep and sing,
And sing, and weep, soared up into the Ring;
  But most would use no wing.
O fools (said I) thus to prefer dark night
  Before true light!   50
To live in grots and caves, and hate the day
  Because it shows the way,
The way, which from this dead and dark abode
  Leads up to God,
A way where you might tread the sun, and be   55
  More bright than he.
But as I did their madness so discuss,
  One whispered thus,
"This Ring the Bridegroom did for none provide,
  But for His bride."

John, Cap. 2, Ver. 16, 17.

All that is in the world, the lust of the flesh, the lust of the eyes, and the pride of life, is not of the father, but is of the world.

And the world passeth away, and the lusts thereof, but he that doth the will of God abideth for ever.

THE RETREAT

Happy those early days, when I
Shined in my angel-infancy!
Before I understood this place
Appointed for my second race,
Or taught my soul to fancy ought   5
But a white, celestial thought;
When yet I had not walked above
A mile or two from my first love;
And looking back, at that short space,
Could see a glimpse of his bright face;   10
When on some gilded cloud or flower
My gazing soul would dwell an hour,
And in those weaker glories spy
Some shadows of eternity;
Before I taught my tongue to wound   15
My conscience with a sinful sound,
Or had the black art to dispense
A several sin to every sense,
But felt through all this fleshy dress
Bright shoots of everlastingness.   20
  O how I long to travel back,
And tread again that ancient track!
That I might once more reach that plain,
Where first I left my glorious train;
From whence the enlightened spirit sees   25
That shady City of Palm trees.
But ah! my soul with too much stay
Is drunk, and staggers in the way!
Some men a forward motion love,
But I by backward steps would move;   30
And, when this dust falls to the urn,
In that state I came, return.

THE NIGHT

John 3:2

Through that pure virgin-shrine,
That sacred veil drawn o'er thy glorious noon,
That men might look and live, as glow-worms shine

    And face the moon:
Wise Nicodemus saw such light   5
As made him know his God by night.

    Most blest believer he!
Who in that land of darkness and blind eyes
Thy long-expected healing wings could see
    When thou didst rise,   10
    And, what can never more be done,
    Did at midnight speak with the Sun!

    O who will tell me, where
He found thee at that dead and silent hour?
What hallowed solitary ground did bear   15
    So rare a flower
    Within whose sacred leaves did lie
    The fulness of the Deity?

    No mercy-seat of gold,
No dead and dusty cherub, nor carved stone,   20
But his own living works did my Lord hold
    And lodge alone;
    Where trees and herbs did watch and peep
    And wonder, while the Jews did sleep.

    Dear Night! this world's defeat;   25
The stop to busy fools; care's check and curb;
The day of spirits; my soul's calm retreat
    Which none disturb!
    Christ's progress, and his prayer-time;
    The hours to which high Heaven doth chime.   30

    God's silent, searching flight:
When my Lord's head is fill'd with dew and all
His locks are wet with the clear drops of night;
    His still, soft call;
    His knocking-time; the soul's dumb watch,   35
    When spirits their fair kindred catch.

    Were all my loud, evil days
Calm and unhaunted as is thy dark tent,

Whose peace but by some angel's wing or voice
    Is seldom rent;   40
  Then I in heaven all the long year
  Would keep, and never wander here.

  But living where the sun
Doth all things wake, and where all mix and tire
Themselves and others, I consent and run   45
    To every mire;
  And by this world's ill-guiding light,
  Err more than I can do by night.

  There is in God (some say)
A deep, but dazzling darkness; as men here   50
Say it is late and dusky, because they
    See not all clear.
  O for that night! where I in him
  Might live invisible and dim.

ASCENSION-HYMN

They are all gone into the world of light!
  And I alone sit lingring here;
Their very memory is fair and bright,
  And my sad thoughts doth clear.

It glows and glitters in my cloudy breast
  Like stars upon some gloomy grove,
Or those faint beams in which this hill is drest,
  After the Sun's remove.

I see them walking in a Air of glory,
  Whose light doth trample on my days:
My days, which are at best but dull and hoary,
  Mere glimmering and decays.

O holy hope! and high humility,
  High as the Heavens above!
These are your walks, and you have shew'd them me
  To kindle my cold love.

Dear, beauteous death! the Jewel of the Just,
   Shining no where, but in the dark;
What mysteries do lie beyond thy dust;
   Could man outlook that mark!

He that hath found some fledg'd birds nest, may know
   At first sight, if the bird be flown;
But that fair Well, or Grove he sings in now,
   That is to him unknown.

And yet, as Angels in some brighter dreams
   Call to the soul, when man doth sleep:
So some strange thoughts transcend our wonted themes,
   And into glory peep.

If a star were confin'd into a Tomb
   Her captive flames must needs burn there;
But when the hand that lockt her up, gives room,
   She'll shine through all the sphere.

O Father of eternal life, and all
   Created glories under thee!
Resume thy spirit from this world of thrall
   Into true liberty.

Either disperse these mists, which blot and fill
   My perspective as they pass,
Or else remove me hence unto that hill,
   Where I shall need no glass.

THOMAS TRAHERNE (1636?–1674)

WONDER

How like an angel came I down!
   How bright are all things here!
When first among his works I did appear,
   Oh, how their glory did me crown!
The world resembled his eternity,
     In which my soul did walk;
   And ev'rything that I did see
     Did with me talk.

5

The skies in their magnificence,
    The lovely lively air,   10
Oh, how divine, how soft, how sweet, how fair!
    The stars did entertain my sense,
And all the works of God so bright and pure,
      So rich and great, did seem,
    As if they ever must endure   15
      In my esteem.

A native health and innocence
    Within my bones did grow,
And while my God did all his glories show,
    I felt a vigor in my sense   20
That was all spirit; I within did flow
      With seas of life like wine;
    I nothing in the world did know,
      But 'twas divine.

Harsh rugged objects were concealed;   25
    Oppressions, tears, and cries,
Sins, griefs, complaints, dissensions, weeping eyes,
    Were hid, and only things revealed
Which heavenly spirits and the angels prize:
      The state of innocence   30
    And bliss, not trades and poverties,
      Did fill my sense.

The streets seemed paved with golden stones,
    The boys and girls all mine—
To me how did their lovely faces shine!   35
    The sons of men all holy ones,
In joy and beauty then appeared to me;
      And ev'rything I found,
    While like an angel I did see,
      Adorned the ground.   40

Rich diamonds, and pearl, and gold
    Might ev'rywhere be seen;
Rare colors, yellow, blue, red, white, and green,
    Mine eyes on ev'ry side behold;

All that I saw a wonder did appear,   45
   Amazement was my bliss,
That and my wealth met ev'rywhere;
   No joy to this!

Cursed, ill-devised proprieties,
   With envy, avarice,   50
And fraud, those fiends that spoil ev'n paradise,
   Were not the object of mine eyes;
Nor hedges, ditches, limits, narrow bounds,
   I dreamt not aught of those,
But in surveying all men's grounds   55
   I found repose.

For property itself was mine,
   And hedges, ornaments,
Walls, houses, coffers, and their rich contents,
   To make me rich combine.   60
Clothes, costly jewels, laces, I esteemed
   My wealth, by others worn,
For me they all to wear them seemed,
   When I was born.

JOHN DRYDEN (1631–1700)

ALEXANDER'S FEAST; or, THE POWER OF MUSIC

AN ODE IN HONOR OF ST. CECILIA'S DAY

1

'Twas at the royal feast, for Persia won
   By Philip's warlike son:
  Aloft in awful state
  The godlike hero sate
   On his imperial throne: 5
 His valiant peers were placed around;
Their brows with roses and with myrtles bound
  (So should desert in arms be crowned).
The lovely Thaïs, by his side,
Sate like a blooming Eastern bride   10

In flower of youth and beauty's pride.
    Happy, happy, happy pair!
      None but the brave,
      None but the brave,
  None but the brave deserves the fair.   15

CHORUS

Happy, happy, happy pair!
  None but the brave,
  None but the brave,
None but the brave deserves the fair.

2

Timotheus, placed on high   20
  Amid the tuneful choir,
With flying fingers touched the lyre:
  The trembling notes ascend the sky,
    And heavenly joys inspire.
  The song began from Jove,   25
  Who left his blissful seats above
  (Such is the power of mighty love).
  A dragon's fiery form belied the god:
  Sublime on radiant spires he rode,
  When he to fair Olympia pressed;   30
  And while he sought her snowy breast:
  Then, round her slender waist he curled,
And stamped an image of himself, a sovereign of the world.
  The listening crowd admire the lofty sound;
  "A present deity," they shout around;   35
  "A present deity," the vaulted roofs rebound:
    With ravished ears
    The monarch hears,
    Assumes the god,
    Affects to nod,   40
And seems to shake the spheres.

CHORUS

    With ravished ears
    The monarch hears,
    Assumes the god,
    Affects to nod,   45
And seems to shake the spheres.

3

The praise of Bacchus then the sweet musician sung,
    Of Bacchus ever fair and ever young:
        The jolly god in triumph comes;
        Sound the trumpets; beat the drums;   50
          Flushed with a purple grace
          He shows his honest face:
Now give the hautboys breath; he comes, he comes!
        Bacchus, ever fair and young,
          Drinking joys did first ordain;   55
        Bacchus' blessings are a treasure,
        Drinking is the soldier's pleasure:
          Rich the treasure,
          Sweet the pleasure,
        Sweet is pleasure after pain.   60

CHORUS

        Bacchus' blessings are a treasure,
        Drinking is the soldier's pleasure;
          Rich the treasure,
          Sweet the pleasure,
        Sweet is pleasure after pain.   65

4

Soothed with the sound, the king grew vain;
    Fought all his battles o'er again;
And thrice he routed all his foes, and thrice he slew the slain.
    The master saw the madness rise;
    His glowing cheeks, his ardent eyes;   70
    And, while he heaven and earth defied,
    Changed his hand, and checked his pride.
      He chose a mournful Muse,
      Soft pity to infuse:
    He sung Darius great and good,   75
      By too severe a fate,
    Fallen, fallen, fallen, fallen,
      Fallen from his high estate,
    And weltering in his blood;
    Deserted, at his utmost need,   80
    By those his former bounty fed;
    On the bare earth exposed he lies,
    With not a friend to close his eyes.

With downcast looks the joyless victor sate,
    Revolving in his altered soul   85
        The various turns of chance below;
    And, now and then, a sigh he stole;
    And tears began to flow.

CHORUS

    Revolving in his altered soul
        The various turns of chance below;   90
    And, now and then, a sigh he stole;
    And tears began to flow.

5

The mighty master smiled to see
That love was in the next degree:
'Twas but a kindred sound to move,   95
For pity melts the mind to love.
    Softly sweet, in Lydian measures,
    Soon he soothed his soul to pleasures.
"War," he sung, "is toil and trouble;
Honor, but an empty bubble;   100
    Never ending, still beginning,
Fighting still, and still destroying:
    If the world be worth thy winning,
    Think, O think it worth enjoying;
    Lovely Thaïs sits beside thee,   105
    Take the good the gods provide thee."
The many rend the skies with loud applause;
So Love was crowned, but Music won the cause.
    The prince, unable to conceal his pain,
        Gazed on the fair   110
        Who caused his care,
    And sighed and looked, sighed and looked,
    Sighed and looked, and sighed again:
At length, with love and wine at once oppressed,
The vanquished victor sunk upon her breast.   115

CHORUS

    The prince, unable to conceal his pain,
        Gazed on the fair
        Who caused his care,

And sighed and looked, sighed and looked,
Sighed and looked, and sighed again: 120
At length, with love and wine at once oppressed,
The vanquished victor sunk upon her breast.

6

Now strike the golden lyre again:
A louder yet, and yet a louder strain.
Break his bands of sleep asunder,   125
And rouse him, like a rattling peal of thunder!
    Hark, hark! the horrid sound
        Has raised up his head:
        As awaked from the dead,
        And amazed, he stares around.   130
"Revenge, revenge!" Timotheus cries,
    "See the Furies arise!
    See the snakes that they rear,
    How they hiss in their hair,
And the sparkles that flash from their eyes!   135
    Behold a ghastly band,
    Each a torch in his hand!
Those are Grecian ghosts, that in battle were slain,
        And unburied remain
        Inglorious on the plain: 140
        Give the vengeance due
        To the valiant crew!
Behold how they toss their torches on high,
        How they point to the Persian abodes,
And glittering temples of their hostile gods!"   145
The princes applaud, with a furious joy;
And the king seized a flambeau with zeal to destroy;
        Thaïs led the way,
        To light him to his prey,
And, like another Helen, fired another Troy.   150

CHORUS

And the king seized a flambeau with zeal to destroy;
        Thaïs led the way,
        To light him to his prey,
And, like another Helen, fired another Troy.

7

Thus, long ago,   155
Ere heaving bellows learned to blow,
While organs yet were mute;
Timotheus, to his breathing flute,
And sounding lyre,
Could swell the soul to rage, or kindle soft desire.   160
At last, divine Cecilia came,
Inventress of the vocal frame;
The sweet enthusiast, from her sacred store,
Enlarged the former narrow bounds,
And added length to solemn sounds,   165
With nature's mother wit, and arts unknown before.
Let old Timotheus yield the prize,
Or both divide the crown;
He raised a mortal to the skies,
She drew an angel down.   170

GRAND CHORUS

At last, divine Cecilia came,
Inventress of the vocal frame;
The sweet enthusiast, from her sacred store,
Enlarged the former narrow bounds,
And added length to solemn sounds,   175
With nature's mother wit, and arts unknown before.
Let old Timotheus yield the prize,
Or both divide the crown;
He raised a mortal to the skies,
She drew an angel down.   180

TO THE MEMORY OF MR. OLDHAM

Farewell, too little and too lately known,
Whom I began to think and call my own:
For sure our souls were near allied, and thine
Cast in the same poetic mold with mine.
One common note on either lyre did strike,   5
And knaves and fools we both abhorred alike.
To the same goal did both our studies drive:

The last set out the soonest did arrive.
Thus Nisus fell upon the slippery place,
Whilst his young friend performed and won the race.   10
O early ripe! to thy abundant store
What could advancing age have added more?
It might (what nature never gives the young)
Have taught the numbers of thy native tongue.
But satire needs not those, and wit will shine   15
Through the harsh cadence of a rugged line.
A noble error, and but seldom made,
When poets are by too much force betray'd.
Thy generous fruits, though gathered ere their prime,
Still showed a quickness; and maturing time   20
But mellows what we write to the dull sweets of rhyme.
Once more, hail, and farewell! farewell, thou young,
But ah! too short, Marcellus of our tongue!
Thy brows with ivy and with laurels bound;
But Fate and gloomy night encompass thee around.   25

PROLOGUE TO *AURENG-ZEBE*

Our author, by experience, finds it true,
'Tis much more hard to please himself than you;
And out of no feign'd modesty, this day
Damns his laborious trifle of a play:
Not that it's worse than what before he writ,   5
But he has now another taste of wit;
And, to confess a truth, (though out of time,)
Grows weary of his long-lov'd mistress, Rhyme.
Passion's too fierce to be in fetters bound,
And nature flies him like enchanted ground.   10
What verse can do, he has perform'd in this,
Which he presumes the most correct of his;
But spite of all his pride, a secret shame
Invades his breast at Shakespeare's sacred name:
Aw'd when he hears his godlike Romans rage,   15
He, in a just despair, would quit the stage;
And to an age less polish'd, more unskill'd,
Does, with disdain, the foremost honours yield.
As with the greater dead he dares not strive,

He would not match his verse with those who live: 20
Let him retire, betwixt two ages cast,
The first of this, and hindmost of the last.
A losing gamester, let him sneak away;
He bears no ready money from the play.
The fate which governs poets thought it fit 25
He should not raise his fortunes by his wit.
The clergy thrive, and the litigious bar;
Dull heroes fatten with the spoils of war:
All southern vices, Heav'n be prais'd, are here;
But wit's a luxury you think too dear. 30
When you to cultivate the plant are loath,
'Tis a shrewd sign 'twas never of your growth;
And wit in northern climates will not blow,
Except, like orange trees, 'tis hous'd from snow.
There needs no care to put a playhouse down, 35
'Tis the most desert place of all the town:
We and our neighbours, to speak proudly, are
Like monarchs, ruin'd with expensive war;
While, like wise English, unconcern'd you sit,
And see us play the tragedy of wit. 40

LINES PRINTED UNDER THE ENGRAVED
PORTRAIT OF MILTON, 1688

Three poets, in three distant ages born,
Greece, Italy, and England did adorn.
The first in loftiness of thoughts surpassed,
The next in majesty, in both the last.
The force of Nature could no farther go;
To make a third she joined the former two.

SONG OF VENUS

Fairest Isle, all Isles Excelling,
 Seat of Pleasures, and of Loves;
Venus, here, will choose her Dwelling,
 And forsake her Cyprian Groves.

Cupid from his Fav'rite Nation, 5
    Care and Envy will Remove;
Jealousie, that poysons Passion,
    And Despair that dies for Love.

Gentle Murmurs, sweet Complaining,
    Sighs that blow the Fire of Love; 10
Soft Repulses, kind Disdaining,
    Shall be all the Pains you prove.

Every Swain shall pay his Duty,
    Grateful every Nymph shall prove;
And as these Excel in Beauty, 15
    Those shall be Renown'd for Love.

THE LADY'S SONG

A choir of bright beauties in spring did appear,
To choose a May-lady to govern the year.
All the nymphs were in white, and the shepherds in green,
The garland was giv'n, and Phillis was Queen;
But Phillis refused it, and sighing did say,
I'll not wear a garland while Pan is away.

While Pan and fair Syrinx are fled from our shore,
The graces are banished, and love is no more.
The soft god of pleasure that warmed our desires,
Has broken his bow, and extinguished his fires;
And vows that himself and his mother will mourn,
Till Pan and fair Syrinx in triumph return.

Forbear your addresses, and court us no more,
For we will perform what the Deity swore.
But if you dare think of deserving our charms,
Away with your sheephooks and take to your arms;
Then laurels and myrtles your brows shall adorn,
When Pan and his son and fair Syrinx return.

THE SECULAR MASQUE

(*Enter Janus.*)

JANUS: Chronos, Chronos, mend thy pace:
An hundred times the rolling Sun
Around the Radiant Belt has run
   In his revolving race.
Behold, behold, the goal in sight;   5
Spread thy fans, and wing thy flight.

(*Enter Chronos, with a scythe in his hand, and a great globe on his back, which he sets down at his entrance.*)

CHRONOS: Weary, weary of my weight,
Let me, let me drop my freight,
   And leave the World behind.
    I could not bear   10
    Another year,
   The load of human-kind.

(*Enter Momus, laughing.*)

MOMUS: Ha! ha! ha! Ha! ha! ha! well hast thou done
   To lay down thy pack,
   And lighten thy back.   15
The World was a fool, e'er since it begun,
And since neither Janus, nor Chronos, nor I
   Can hinder the crimes
   Or mend the bad times,
'Tis better to laugh than to cry.   20

Cho. of all 3. '*Tis better to laugh than to cry.*

JANUS: Since Momus comes to laugh below,
Old Time, begin the show,
That we may see, in every Scene,
What changes in this Age have been.   25
CHRONOS: Then, Goddess of the Silver Bow, begin.

(*Horns, or Hunting-music within. Enter Diana.*)

DIANA:	With horns and with hounds I waken the day,
	And hye to my woodland walks away:
	I tuck up my robe, and am buskined soon,
	And tie to my forehead a waxing Moon. 30
	I course the fleet stag, unkennel the fox,
	And chase the wild goats o'er summits of rocks:
	With shouting and hooting we pierce thro' the sky,
	And Echo turns hunter, and doubles the cry.

Cho. of all: *With shouting and hooting, &c.*   35

JANUS: Then our age was in its prime:
CHRONOS: Free from rage.
DIANA: And free from crime.
MOMUS: A very merry, dancing, drinking,
         Laughing, quaffing, and unthinking time.   40

Cho. of all: *Then our age, &c.*

                    (*Dance of Diana's attendants.*)

                    (*Enter Mars.*)

MARS: Inspire the vocal brass, inspire;
         The World is past its infant age:
           Arms and honour,
           Arms and honour,   45
         Set the martial mind on fire,
         And kindle manly rage.
           Mars has looked the sky to red;
         And Peace, the lazy Good, is fled.
           Plenty, Peace, and Pleasure fly;   50
             The sprightly green
           In woodland-walks no more is seen;
         The sprightly green has drunk the Tyrian dye.

Cho. of all: *Plenty, Peace, &c.*

MARS: Sound the trumpet, beat the drum;   55
           Through all the World around,
           Sound a Reveille, sound, sound,
         The Warrior-God is come.

Cho. of all: *Sound the trumpet, &c.*

MOMUS: Thy sword within the scabbard keep,   60
        And let Mankind agree;
      Better the World were fast asleep,
        Than kept awake by thee.
      The fools are only thinner,
        With all our cost and care;   65
      But neither side a winner,
        For things are as they were.

Cho. of all: *The fools are only, &c.*

(*Enter Venus.*)

VENUS: Calms appear when storms are past;
      Love will have his hour at last: 70
      Nature is my kindly care;
      Mars destroys, and I repair;
      Take me, take me, while you may,
      Venus comes not ev'ry day.

Cho. of all: *Take her, take her, &c.*

CHRONOS: The World was then so light,
      I scarcely felt the weight;
      Joy rul'd the day, and Love the night.
      But since the Queen of Pleasure left the ground,
        I faint, I lag,   80
        And feebly drag
      The pond'rous Orb around.
MOMUS: All, all of a piece throughout:
  Pointing to Diana: Thy chase had a beast in view;
      to Mars: Thy wars brought nothing about;   85
      to Venus: Thy lovers were all untrue.
JANUS: 'Tis well an old Age is out.
CHRONOS: And time to begin a new.

Cho. of all: *All, all of a piece throughout:*
      Thy chase had a beast in view;   90
      Thy wars brought nothing about;
      Thy lovers were all untrue.
      'Tis well an old Age is out,
      And time to begin a new.

(*Dance of Huntsmen, Nymphs, Warriors, and Lovers.*)

PART FOUR

The Eighteenth Century

MATTHEW PRIOR (1664–1749)

A BETTER ANSWER (TO CLOE JEALOUS)

Dear Cloe, how blubbered is that pretty face!
   Thy cheek all on fire, and thy hair all uncurled!
Prithee quit this caprice; and (as old Falstaff says)
   Let us e'en talk a little like folks of this world.

How canst thou presume, thou hast leave to destroy   5
   The beauties, which Venus but lent to thy keeping?
Those looks were designed to inspire love and joy;
   More ordinary eyes may serve people for weeping.

To be vexed at a trifle or two that I writ,
   Your judgment at once and my passion you wrong: 10
You take that for fact which will scarce be found wit:
   Od's life! must one swear to the truth of a song?

What I speak, my fair Cloe, and what I write, shows
   The difference there is betwixt nature and art;
I court others in verse, but I love thee in prose;   15
   And they have my whimsies, but thou hast my heart.

The god of us verse-men (you know, child), the Sun,
   How after his journeys he sets up his rest;
If at morning o'er earth 'tis his fancy to run,
   At night he reclines on his Thetis's breast.   20

So when I am wearied with wandering all day,
   To thee my delight in the evening I come;
No matter what beauties I saw in my way—
   They were but my visits, but thou art my home.

Then finish, dear Cloe, this pastoral war;   25
   And let us like Horace and Lydia agree:
For thou art a girl as much brighter than her,
   As he was a poet sublimer than me.

TO A CHILD OF QUALITY

FIVE YEARS OLD, MDCCIV, THE AUTHOR THEN FORTY

Lords, knights, and squires, the numerous band
    That wear the fair Miss Mary's fetters,
Were summoned by her high command,
    To show their passions by their letters.

My pen among the rest I took,   5
    Lest those bright eyes that cannot read
Should dart their kindling fires, and look
    The power they have to be obeyed.

Nor quality nor reputation
    Forbid me yet my flame to tell;   10
Dear five years old befriends my passion,
    And I may write till she can spell.

For while she makes her silkworms beds
    With all the tender things I swear,
Whilst all the house my passion reads   15
    In papers round her baby hair,

She may receive and own my flame,
    For, though the strictest prudes should know it,
She'll pass for a most virtuous dame,
    And I for an unhappy poet.   20

Then too, alas! when she shall tear
    The lines some younger rival sends,
She'll give me leave to write, I fear,
    And we shall still continue friends.

For, as our different ages move,   25
    'Tis so ordained, (would Fate but mend it!)
That I shall be past making love,
    When she begins to comprehend it.

ON CRITICS

IN IMITATION OF ANACREON

Let 'em Censure: what care I?
The Herd of Criticks I defie.
Let the Wretches know, I write
Regardless of their Grace, or Spight.
No, no: the Fair, the Gay, the Young   5
Govern the Numbers of my Song.
All that They approve is sweet:
And All is Sense, that They repeat.
   Bid the warbling Nine retire:
Venus, String thy Servant's Lyre: 10
Love shall be my endless Theme:
Pleasure shall triumph over Fame:
And when these Maxims I decline,
Apollo, may Thy Fate be Mine:
May I grasp at empty Praise;   15
And lose the Nymph, to gain the Bays.

JONATHAN SWIFT (1667–1745)

A DESCRIPTION OF THE MORNING

Now hardly here and there an hackney-coach
Appearing, showed the ruddy morn's approach.
Now Betty from her master's bed had flown,
And softly stole to discompose her own;
The slip-shod 'prentice from his master's door   5
Had pared the dirt, and sprinkled round the floor.
Now Moll had whirled her mop with dexterous airs,
Prepared to scrub the entry and the stairs.
The youth with broomy stumps began to trace
The kennel-edge, where wheels had worn the place.   10
The small-coal man was heard with cadence deep,
Till drowned in shriller notes of chimney-sweep:
Duns at his lordship's gate began to meet;
And brickdust Moll had screamed through half the street.
The turnkey now his flock returning sees,   15

Duly let out a-nights to steal for fees:
The watchful bailiffs take their silent stands,
And schoolboys lag with satchels in their hands.

DESCRIPTION OF A CITY SHOWER

Careful observers may foretell the Hour
(By sure Prognostics) when to dread a Show'r:
While Rain depends, the pensive Cat gives o'er
Her Frolics, and pursues her Tail no more.
Returning Home at Night, you'll find the Sink   5
Strike your offended Sense with double Stink.
If you be wise, then go not far to Dine;
You'll spend in Coach-hire more than save in Wine.
A coming Show'r your shooting Corns presage,
Old Aches throb, your hollow Tooth will rage.   10
Saunt'ring in Coffee-house is Dulman seen;
He damns the Climate, and complains of Spleen.

Meanwhile the South, rising with dabbled Wings,
A sable Cloud athwart the Welkin flings,
That swill'd more Liquor than it could contain,   15
And like a Drunkard gives it up again.
Brisk Susan whips her Linen from the Rope,
While the first drizzling Show'r is born aslope,
Such is that Sprinkling which some careless Quean
Flirts on you from her Mop, but not so clean.   20
You fly, invoke the Gods; then turning, stop
To rail; she, singing, still whirls on her Mop.
Not yet the Dust had shunn'd th' unequal Strife
But, aided by the Wind, fought still for Life;
And wafted with its Foe by violent Gust.   25
'Twas doubtful which was Rain, and which was Dust.
Ah! where must needy Poet seek for Aid,
When Dust and Rain at once his Coat invade,
His only Coat, where Dust, confus'd with Rain,
Roughen the Nap and leave a mingled Stain.   30

Now in contiguous Drops the Flood comes down,
Threat'ning with Deluge this Devoted Town.
To Shops in Crowds the daggled Females fly,

Pretend to cheapen Goods, but nothing buy.
The Templer spruce, while ev'ry Spout's a-broach,   35
Stays till 'tis fair, yet seems to call a Coach.
The tuck'd-up Sempstress walks with hasty Strides,
While Streams run down her oil'd Umbrella's Sides.
Here various Kinds by various Fortunes led
Commence Acquaintance underneath a Shed.   40
Triumphant Tories and desponding Whigs
Forget their Feuds, and join to save their Wigs.

  Box'd in a Chair the Beau impatient sits,
While Spouts run clatt'ring o'er the Roof by Fits;
And ever and anon with frightful Din   45
The Leather sounds; he trembles from within.
So when Troy Chair-men bore the Wooden Steed,
Pregnant with Greeks, impatient to be freed,
(Those Bully Greeks, who, as the Moderns do,
Instead of paying Chair-men, run them thro'.)   50
Laoco'n struck the Outside with his Spear,
And each imprison'd Hero quak'd for Fear.

  Now from all Parts the swelling Kennels flow,
And bear their Trophies with them as they go:
Filth of all Hues and Odours seem to tell   55
What Street they sail'd from, by their Sight and Smell.
They, as each Torrent drives, with rapid Force
From Smithfield, or St. Pulchre's shape their Course,
And in huge Confluent join at Snow-Hill Ridge,
Fall from the Conduit prone to Holborn-Bridge.   60
Sweepings from Butchers' Stalls, Dung, Guts, and Blood,
Drown'd Puppies, stinking Sprats, all drench'd in Mud,
Dead Cats and Turnip-Tops come tumbling down the
    Flood.

A SATYRICAL ELEGY ON THE DEATH OF
A LATE FAMOUS GENERAL,[1] 1722

His Grace! impossible! what, dead!
Of old age, too, and in his bed!
And could that mighty warrior fall,
And so inglorious, after all?

[1] The Duke of Marlborough

Well, since he's gone, no matter how,   5
The last loud trump must wake him now;
And, trust me, as the noise grows stronger,
He'd wish to sleep a little longer.
And could he be indeed so old
As by the newspapers we're told?   10
Threescore, I think, is pretty high;
'Twas time, in conscience he should die!
This world he cumber'd long enough;
He burnt his candle to the snuff;
And that's the reason, some folks think,   15
He left behind so great a stink.
Behold his funeral appears,
Nor widow's sighs, nor orphan's tears,
Wont at such times each heart to pierce,
Attend the progress of his hearse.   20
And what of that? his friends may say,
He had those honours in his day.
True to his profit and his pride,
He made them weep before he died.
   Come hither, all ye empty things,   25
Ye bubbles raised by breath of kings!
Who float upon the tide of state;
Come hither, and behold your fate.
Let Pride be taught by this rebuke,
How very mean a thing's a duke;   30
From all his ill-got honours flung,
Turn'd to that dirt from whence he sprung.

CLEVER TOM CLINCH GOING TO BE HANGED

As clever Tom Clinch, while the rabble was bawling,
Rode stately through Holbourn, to die in his calling;
He stopt at the George for a bottle of sack,
And promis'd to pay for it when he'd come back.
His waistcoat and stockings, and breeches were white,   5
His cap had a new cherry ribbon to ty't.
The maids to the doors and the balconies ran,
And said, lack-a-day! he's a proper young man.
But, as from the windows the ladies he spy'd,
Like a beau in the box, he bow'd low on each side;   10

And when his last speech the loud hawkers did cry,
He swore from his cart, it was all a damn'd lye.
The hangman for pardon fell down on his knee;
Tom gave him a kick in the guts for his fee.
Then said, I must speak to the people a little,   15
But I'll see you all damn'd before I will Whittle.
My honest friend Wild, may he long hold his place,
He lengthen'd my life with a whole year of grace.
Take courage, dear comrades, and be not afraid,
Nor slip this occasion to follow your trade.   20
My conscience is clear, and my spirits are calm,
And thus I go off without pray'r-book or psalm.
Then follow the practice of clever Tom Clinch,
Who hung like a hero and never would flinch.

JOHN GAY (1685–1732)

DAMON AND CUPID

The sun was now withdrawn,
   The shepherds home were sped;
The moon wide o'er the lawn
   Her silver mantle spread;
When Damon stay'd behind,   5
   And saunter'd in the grove:
"Will ne'er a nymph be kind,
   And give me love for love?

"Oh! those were golden hours,
   When Love, devoid of cares,   10
In all Arcadia's bowers
   Lodg'd swains and nymphs by pairs!
But now from wood and plain
   Flies ev'ry sprightly lass:
No joys for me remain,   15
   In shades, or on the grass."

The wingèd boy draws near,
   And thus the swain reproves:
"While Beauty revell'd here,
   My game lay in the groves;   20

At Court I never fail
  To scatter round my arrows;
Men fall as thick as hail,
  And maidens love like sparrows.

"Then, swain, if me you need,   25
  Straight lay your sheep-hook down;
Throw by your oaten reed,
  And haste away to town.
So well I'm known at Court,
  None asks where Cupid dwells;   30
But readily resort
  To Bellenden's or Lepell's."

SONG FROM *THE BEGGAR'S OPERA*

Air: *Over the hills and far away, etc.*

MACHEATH.   Were I laid on Greenland's coast,
               And in my arms embraced my lass;
               Warm amidst eternal frost,
               Too soon the half year's night would pass.

POLLY.   Were I sold on Indian soil,   5
               Soon as the burning day was closed,
               I could mock the sultry toil,
               When on my charmer's breast reposed.

MACHEATH.   And I would love you all the day,
POLLY.   Every night would kiss and play,   10
MACHEATH.   If with me you'd fondly stray
BOTH.   Over the hills and far away.

MY OWN EPITAPH

Life is a jest; and all things show it:
I thought so once; but now I know it.

GEORGE BERKELEY (1685–1753)

ON THE PROSPECT OF PLANTING ARTS
AND LEARNING IN AMERICA

The Muse, disgusted at an age and clime
    Barren of every glorious theme,
In distant lands now waits a better time,
    Producing subjects worthy fame:

In happy climes where from the genial sun   5
    And virgin earth such scenes ensue,
The force of art by nature seems outdone,
    And fancied beauties by the true:

In happy climes, the seat of innocence,
    Where nature guides and virtue rules,   10
Where men shall not impose for truth and sense
    The pedantry of courts and schools:

There shall be sung another golden age,
    The rise of empire and of arts,
The good and great inspiring epic rage,   15
    The wisest heads and noblest hearts.

Not such as Europe breeds in her decay;
    Such as she bred when fresh and young,
When heavenly flame did animate her clay,
    By future poets shall be sung.   20

Westward the course of empire takes its way;
    The four first acts already past,
A fifth shall close the drama with the day;
    Time's noblest offspring is the last.

ALEXANDER POPE (1688–1744)

ODE ON SOLITUDE

Happy the man whose wish and care
 A few paternal acres bound,
Content to breathe his native air,
  In his own ground.

Whose herds with milk, whose fields with bread,   5
 Whose flocks supply him with attire,
Whose trees in summer yield him shade,
  In winter fire.

Blest, who can unconcern'dly find
 Hours, days, and years slide soft away,   10
In health of body, peace of mind,
  Quiet by day,

Sound sleep by night; study and ease,
 Together mixt; sweet recreation;
And Innocence, which most does please   15
  With meditation.

Thus let me live, unseen, unknown,
 Thus unlamented let me die,
Steal from the world, and not a stone
  Tell where I lie.   20

TO A YOUNG LADY: ON HER LEAVING THE TOWN AFTER THE CORONATION

As some fond Virgin, whom her mother's care
Drags from the Town to wholesome Country air,
Just when she learns to roll a melting eye,
And hear a spark, yet think no danger nigh;
From the dear man unwilling she must sever,   5
Yet takes one kiss before she parts forever:
Thus from the world fair Zephalinda flew,
Saw others happy, and with sighs withdrew;

Not that their pleasures caus'd her discontent,
She sigh'd not that they stay'd, but that she went.   10
   She went, to plain-work and to purling brooks,
Old-fashioned halls, dull Aunts, and croaking rooks:
She went from op'ra, park, assembly, play,
To morning walks, and pray'rs three hours a day;
To part her time 'twixt reading and bohea,   15
To muse, and spill her solitary tea,
Or o'er cold coffee trifle with the spoon,
Count the slow clock, and dine exact at noon;
Divert her eyes with pictures in the fire,
Hum half a tune, tell stories to the squire;   20
Up to her godly garret after sev'n,
There starve and pray, for that's the way to heav'n.
   Some Squire, perhaps, you take delight to rack;
Whose game is Whisk, whose treat a toast in sack;
Who visits with a gun, presents you birds,   25
Then gives a smacking buss, and cries,—No words!
Or with his hound comes hollowing from the stable,
Makes love with nods, and knees beneath a table;
Whose laughs are hearty, tho' his jests are coarse,
And loves you best of all things—but his horse.   30
   In some fair ev'ning, on your elbow laid,
You dream of Triumphs in the rural shade;
In pensive thought recall the fancy'd scene,
See Coronations rise on ev'ry green;
Before you pass th' imaginary sights   35
Of Lords, and Earls, and Dukes, and garter'd Knights,
While the spread fan o'ershades your closing eyes;
Then give one flirt, and all the vision flies.
Thus vanish sceptres, coronets, and balls,
And leave you in lone woods, or empty walls.   40
   So when your Slave, at some dear idle time,
(Not plagu'd with head-aches, or the want of rhyme)
Stands in the streets, abstracted from the crew,
And while he seems to study, thinks of you;
Just when his fancy points your sprightly eyes,   45
Or sees the blush of Parthenissa rise,
Gay pats my shoulder, and you vanish quite,
Streets, Chairs, and Coxcombs rush upon my sight;
Vex'd to be still in town, I knit my brow,
Look sour, and hum a song—as you may now.   50

THE RAPE OF THE LOCK

CANTO I

What dire offense from am'rous causes springs,
What mighty contests rise from trivial things,
I sing—This verse to CARYL, Muse! is due:
This, even Belinda may vouchsafe to view:
Slight is the subject, but not so the praise,   5
If She inspire, and He approve my lays.
  Say what strange motive, Goddess! could compel
A well-bred Lord t' assault a gentle Belle?
O say what stranger cause, yet unexplored,
Could make a gentle Belle reject a Lord?   10
In tasks so bold, can little men engage,
And in soft bosoms dwells such mighty Rage?
  Sol through white curtains shot a tim'rous ray,
And oped those eyes that must eclipse the day:
Now lap-dogs give themselves the rousing shake,   15
And sleepless lovers, just at twelve, awake:
Thrice rung the bell, the slipper knocked the ground,
And the pressed watch returned a silver sound.
Belinda still her downy pillow prest,
Her guardian Sylph prolonged the balmy rest: 20
'Twas He had summoned to her silent bed
The morning-dream that hovered o'er her head;
A Youth more glitt'ring than a Birth-night Beau,
(That even in slumber caused her cheek to glow)
Seemed to her ear his winning lips to lay,   25
And thus in whispers said, or seemed to say:
  Fairest of mortals, thou distinguished care
Of thousand bright Inhabitants of Air!
If e'er one vision touched thy infant thought,
Of all the Nurse and all the Priest have taught;   30
Of airy Elves by moonlight shadows seen,
The silver token, and the circled green,
Or virgins visited by Angel-powers,
With golden crowns and wreaths of heav'nly flowers;
Hear and believe! thy own importance know,   35
Nor bound thy narrow views to things below.
Some secret truths, from learnèd pride concealed,
To Maids alone and Children are revealed:

What though no credit doubting Wits may give?
The Fair and Innocent shall still believe.   40
Know, then, unnumbered Spirits round thee fly,
The light Militia of the lower sky:
These, though unseen, are ever on the wing,
Hang o'er the Box, and hover round the Ring.
Think what an equipage thou hast in Air,   45
And view with scorn two Pages and a Chair.
As now your own, our beings were of old,
And once inclosed in Woman's beauteous mould;
Thence, by a soft transition, we repair
From earthly Vehicles to these of air.   50
Think not, when Woman's transient breath is fled,
That all her vanities at once are dead;
Succeeding vanities she still regards,
And though she plays no more, o'erlooks the cards.
Her joy in gilded Chariots, when alive,   55
And love of Ombre, after death survive.
For when the Fair in all their pride expire,
To their first Elements their Souls retire:
The Sprites of fiery Termagants in Flame
Mount up, and take a Salamander's name.   60
Soft yielding minds to Water glide away,
And sip, with Nymphs, their elemental Tea.
The graver Prude sinks downward to a Gnome,
In search of mischief still on Earth to roam.
The light Coquettes in Sylphs aloft repair,   65
And sport and flutter in the fields of Air.
    Know further yet; whoever fair and chaste
Rejects mankind, is by some Sylph embraced:
For Spirits, freed from mortal laws, with ease
Assume what sexes and what shapes they please.   70
What guards the purity of melting Maids,
In courtly balls, and midnight masquerades,
Safe from the treach'rous friend, the daring spark,
The glance by day, the whisper in the dark,
When kind occasion prompts their warm desires,   75
When music softens, and when dancing fires?
'Tis but their Sylph, the wise Celestials know,
Though Honor is the word with Men below.
    Some nymphs there are, too conscious of their face,
For life predestined to the Gnomes' embrace.   80

These swell their prospects and exalt their pride,
When offers are disdained, and love denied:
Then gay Ideas crowd the vacant brain,
While Peers, and Dukes, and all their sweeping train,
And Garters, Stars, and Coronets appear,   85
And in soft sounds, Your Grace salutes their ear.
'Tis these that early taint the female soul,
Instruct the eyes of young Coquettes to roll,
Teach Infant-cheeks a bidden blush to know,
And little hearts to flutter at a Beau.   90
   Oft, when the world imagine women stray,
The Sylphs through mystic mazes guide their way,
Through all the giddy circle they pursue,
And old impertinence expel by new.
What tender maid but must a victim fall   95
To one man's treat, but for another's ball?
When Florio speaks what virgin could withstand,
If gentle Damon did not squeeze her hand?
With varying vanities, from every part,
They shift the moving Toyshop of their heart;   100
Where wigs with wigs, with sword-knots sword-knots strive,
Beaux banish beaux, and coaches coaches drive.
This erring mortals Levity may call;
Oh blind to truth! the Sylphs contrive it all.
   Of these am I, who thy protection claim,   105
A watchful sprite, and Ariel is my name.
Late, as I ranged the crystal wilds of air,
In the clear Mirror of thy ruling Star
I saw, alas! some dread event impend,
Ere to the main this morning sun descend,   110
But heaven reveals not what, or how, or where:
Warned by the Sylph, oh pious maid, beware!
This to disclose is all thy guardian can:
Beware of all, but most beware of Man!
   He said; when Shock, who thought she slept too long,   115
Leaped up, and waked his mistress with his tongue.
'Twas then, Belinda, if report say true,
Thy eyes first opened on a Billet-doux;
Wounds, Charms, and Ardors were no sooner read,
But all the Vision vanished from thy head.   120
   And now, unveiled, the Toilet stands displayed,
Each silver Vase in mystic order laid.

First, robed in white, the Nymph intent adores,
With head uncovered, the Cosmetic powers.
A heav'nly image in the glass appears,   125
To that she bends, to that her eyes she rears;
Th' inferior Priestess, at her altar's side,
Trembling begins the sacred rites of Pride.
Unnumbered treasures ope at once, and here
The various off'rings of the world appear;   130
 From each she nicely culls with curious toil,
And decks the Goddess with the glitt'ring spoil.
This casket India's glowing gems unlocks,
And all Arabia breathes from yonder box.
The Tortoise here and Elephant unite,   135
Transformed to combs, the speckled, and the white.
Here files of pins extend their shining rows,
Puffs, Powders, Patches, Bibles, Billet-doux.
Now awful Beauty puts on all its arms;
The fair each moment rises in her charms,   140
Repairs her smiles, awakens every grace,
And calls forth all the wonders of her face;
Sees by degrees a purer blush arise,
And keener lightnings quicken in her eyes.
The busy Sylphs surround their darling care,   145
These set the head, and those divide the hair,
Some fold the sleeve, whilst others plait the gown;
And Betty's praised for labors not her own.

CANTO II

Not with more glories, in th' etherial plain,
The Sun first rises o'er the purpled main,
Than, issuing forth, the rival of his beams
Launched on the bosom of the silver Thames.
Fair Nymphs, and well-drest Youths around her shone,   5
But every eye was fixed on her alone.
On her white breast a sparkling Cross she wore,
Which Jews might kiss, and Infidels adore.
Her lively looks a sprightly mind disclose,
Quick as her eyes, and as unfixed as those: 10
Favors to none, to all she smiles extends;
Oft she rejects, but never once offends.
Bright as the sun, her eyes the gazers strike,
And, like the sun, they shine on all alike.

Yet graceful ease, and sweetness void of pride, 15
Might hide her faults, if Belles had faults to hide:
If to her share some female errors fall,
Look on her face, and you'll forget 'em all.
　This Nymph, to the destruction of mankind,
Nourished two Locks, which graceful hung behind 20
In equal curls, and well conspired to deck
With shining ringlets the smooth iv'ry neck.
Love in these labyrinths his slaves detains,
And mighty hearts are held in slender chains.
With hairy springes we the birds betray, 25
Slight lines of hair surprise the finny prey,
Fair tresses man's imperial race ensnare,
And beauty draws us with a single hair.
　　Th' advent'rous Baron the bright locks admired;
He saw, he wished, and to the prize aspired. 30
Resolved to win, he meditates the way,
By force to ravish, or by fraud betray;
For when success a Lover's toil attends,
Few ask, if fraud or force attained his ends.
　　For this, ere Phœbus rose, he had implored 35
Propitious heaven, and every power adored,
But chiefly Love—to Love an Altar built,
Of twelve vast French Romances, neatly gilt.
There lay three garters, half a pair of gloves;
And all the trophies of his former loves; 40
With tender Billet-doux he lights the pyre,
And breathes three am'rous sighs to raise the fire.
Then prostrate falls, and begs with ardent eyes
Soon to obtain, and long possess the prize:
The powers gave ear, and granted half his prayer, 45
The rest, the winds dispersed in empty air.
　　But now secure the painted vessel glides,
The sun-beams trembling on the floating tides:
While melting music steals upon the sky,
And softened sounds along the waters die; 50
Smooth flow the waves, the Zephyrs gently play,
Belinda smiled, and all the world was gay.
All but the Sylph—with careful thoughts opprest,
Th' impending woe sat heavy on his breast.
He summons strait his Denizens of air; 55
The lucid squadrons round the sails repair:

Soft o'er the shrouds aërial whispers breathe,
That seemed but Zephyrs to the train beneath.
Some to the sun their insect-wings unfold,
Waft on the breeze, or sink in clouds of gold;   60
Transparent forms, too fine for mortal sight,
Their fluid bodies half dissolved in light,
Loose to the wind their airy garments flew,
Thin glitt'ring textures of the filmy dew,
Dipt in the richest tincture of the skies,   65
Where light disports in ever-mingling dyes,
While every beam new transient colors flings,
Colors that change whene'er they wave their wings.
Amid the circle, on the gilded mast,
Superior by the head, was Ariel placed;   70
His purple pinions opening to the sun,
He raised his azure wand, and thus begun:
    Ye Sylphs and Sylphids, to your chief give ear!
Fays, Fairies, Genii, Elves, and Dæmons, hear!
Ye know the spheres and various tasks assigned   75
By laws eternal to th' aërial kind.
Some in the fields of purest Æther play,
And bask and whiten in the blaze of day.
Some guide the course of wand'ring orbs on high,
Or roll the planets through the boundless sky.   80
Some less refined, beneath the moon's pale light
Pursue the stars that shoot athwart the night,
Or suck the mists in grosser air below,
Or dip their pinions in the painted bow,
Or brew fierce tempests on the wintry main,   85
Or o'er the glebe distil the kindly rain.
Others on earth o'er human race preside,
Watch all their ways, and all their actions guide:
Of these the chief the care of Nations own,
And guard with Arms divine the British Throne.   90
    Our humbler province is to tend the Fair,
Not a less pleasing, though less glorious care;
To save the powder from too rude a gale,
Nor let th' imprisoned essences exhale;
To draw fresh colors from the vernal flowers;   95
To steal from rainbows e'er they drop in showers
A brighter wash; to curl their waving hairs,
Assist their blushes, and inspire their airs;

Nay oft, in dreams, invention we bestow,
To change a Flounce, or add a Furbelow.   100
    This day, black Omens threat the brightest Fair,
That e'er deserved a watchful spirit's care;
Some dire disaster, or by force, or slight;
But what, or where, the fates have wrapt in night.
Whether the nymph shall break Diana's law,   105
Or some frail China jar receive a flaw;
Or stain her honor or her new brocade;
Forget her prayers, or miss a masquerade;
Or lose her heart, or necklace, at a ball;
Or whether Heaven has doomed that Shock must fall. 110
Haste, then, ye spirits! to your charge repair:
The flutt'ring fan be Zephyretta's care;
The drops to thee, Brillante, we consign;
And, Momentilla, let the watch be thine;
Do thou, Crispissa, tend her fav'rite Lock;   115
Ariel himself shall be the guard of Shock.
    To fifty chosen Sylphs, of special note,
We trust th' important charge, the Petticoat:
Oft have we known that seven-fold fence to fail,
Though stiff with hoops, and armed with ribs of whale; 120
Form a strong line about the silver bound,
And guard the wide circumference around.
    Whatever spirit, careless of his charge,
His post neglects, or leaves the fair at large,
Shall feel sharp vengeance soon o'ertake his sins,   125
Be stopped in vials, or transfixed with pins;
Or plunged in lakes of bitter washes lie,
Or wedged whole ages in a bodkin's eye:
Gums and Pomatums shall his flight restrain,
While clogged he beats his silken wings in vain;   130
Or Alum styptics with contracting power
Shrink his thin essence like a riveled flower:
Or, as Ixion fixed, the wretch shall feel
The giddy motion of the whirling Mill,
In fumes of burning Chocolate shall glow,   135
And tremble at the sea that froths below!
    He spoke; the spirits from the sails descend;
Some, orb in orb, around the nymph extend;
Some thrid the mazy ringlets of her hair;
Some hang upon the pendants of her ear: 140

With beating hearts the dire event they wait,
Anxious, and trembling for the birth of Fate.

CANTO III

Close by those meads, forever crowned with flowers,
Where Thames with pride surveys his rising towers,
There stands a structure of majestic frame,
Which from the neighb'ring Hampton takes its name.
Here Britain's statesmen oft the fall foredoom 5
Of foreign Tyrants and of Nymphs at home;
Here thou, great ANNA! whom three realms obey,
Dost sometimes counsel take—and sometimes Tea.
   Hither the heroes and the nymphs resort,
To taste awhile the pleasures of a Court; 10
In various talk th' instructive hours they past,
Who gave the ball, or paid the visit last;
One speaks the glory of the British Queen,
And one describes a charming Indian screen;
A third interprets motions, looks, and eyes; 15
At every word a reputation dies.
Snuff, or the fan, supply each pause of chat,
With singing, laughing, ogling, *and all that.*
   Meanwhile, declining from the noon of day,
The sun obliquely shoots his burning ray; 20
The hungry Judges soon the sentence sign,
And wretches hang that jury-men may dine;
The merchant from th' Exchange returns in peace,
And the long labors of the Toilet cease.
Belinda now, whom thirst of fame invites, 25
Burns to encounter two advent'rous Knights,
At Ombre singly to decide their doom;
And swells her breast with conquests yet to come.
Straight the three bands prepare in arms to join,
Each band the number of the sacred nine. 30
Soon as she spreads her hand, th' aërial guard
Descend, and sit on each important card:
First Ariel perched upon a Matadore,
Then each, according to the rank they bore;
For Sylphs, yet mindful of their ancient race, 35
Are, as when women, wondrous fond of place.
   Behold, four Kings in majesty revered,
With hoary whiskers and a forky beard;

And four fair Queens whose hands sustain a flower,
Th' expressive emblem of their softer power;   40
Four Knaves in garbs succinct, a trusty band,
Caps on their heads, and halberts in their hand;
And particolored troops, a shining train,
Draw forth to combat on the velvet plain.
　　The skilful Nymph reviews her force with care: 45
Let Spades be trumps! she said, and trumps they were.
　　Now move to war her sable Matadores,
In show like leaders of the swarthy Moors.
Spadillio first, unconquerable Lord!
Led off two captive trumps, and swept the board.   50
As many more Manillio forced to yield,
And marched a victor from the verdant field.
Him Basto followed, but his fate more hard
Gained but one trump and one Plebeian card.
With his broad sabre next, a chief in years,   55
The hoary Majesty of Spades appears,
Puts forth one manly leg, to sight revealed,
The rest, his many-colored robe concealed.
The rebel Knave, who dares his prince engage,
Proves the just victim of his royal rage.   60
Even mighty Pam, that Kings and Queens o'erthrew
And mowed down armies in the fights of Lu,
Sad chance of war! now destitute of aid,
Falls undistinguished by the victor spade!
　　Thus far both armies to Belinda yield;   65
Now to the Baron fate inclines the field.
His warlike Amazon her host invades,
Th' imperial consort of the crown of Spades.
The Club's black Tyrant first her victim died,
Spite of his haughty mien, and barb'rous pride: 70
What boots the regal circle on his head,
His giant limbs, in state unwieldy spread;
That long behind he trails his pompous robe,
And, of all monarchs, only grasps the globe?
　　The Baron now his Diamonds pours apace;   75
Th' embroidered King who shows but half his face,
And his refulgent Queen, with powers combined
Of broken troops an easy conquest find.
Clubs, Diamonds, Hearts, in wild disorder seen,
With throngs promiscuous strow the level green.   80

Thus when dispersed a routed army runs,
Of Asia's troops, and Afric's sable sons,
With like confusion different nations fly,
Of various habit, and of various dye,
The pierced battalions dis-united fall,   85
In heaps on heaps; one fate o'erwhelms them all.
　　The Knave of Diamonds tries his wily arts,
And wins (oh shameful chance!) the Queen of Hearts.
At this, the blood the virgin's cheek forsook,
A livid paleness spreads o'er all her look;   90
She sees, and trembles at th' approaching ill,
Just in the jaws of ruin, and Codille.
And now (as oft in some distempered State)
On one nice Trick depends the general fate.
An Ace of Hearts steps forth: The King unseen   95
Lurked in her hand, and mourned his captive Queen:
He springs to Vengeance with an eager pace,
And falls like thunder on the prostrate Ace.
The nymph exulting fills with shouts the sky;
The walls, the woods, and long canals reply.   100
　　Oh thoughtless mortals! ever blind to fate,
Too soon dejected, and too soon elate.
Sudden, these honors shall be snatched away,
And cursed for ever this victorious day.
　　For lo! the board with cups and spoons is crowned,   105
The berries crackle, and the mill turns round;
On shining Altars of Japan they raise
The silver lamp; the fiery spirits blaze:
From silver spouts the grateful liquors glide,
While China's earth receives the smoking tide: 110
At once they gratify their scent and taste,
And frequent cups prolong the rich repast.
Straight hover round the Fair her airy band;
Some, as she sipped, the fuming liquor fanned,
Some o'er her lap their careful plumes displayed,   115
Trembling, and conscious of the rich brocade.
Coffee (which makes the politician wise,
And see through all things with his half-shut eyes)
Sent up in vapors to the Baron's brain
New Stratagems, the radiant Lock to gain.   120
Ah cease, rash youth! desist ere 'tis too late,
Fear the just Gods, and think of Scylla's Fate!

Changed to a bird, and sent to flit in air,
She dearly pays for Nisus' injured hair!
　But when to mischief mortals bend their will,　　　125
How soon they find fit instruments of ill!
Just then, Clarissa drew with tempting grace
A two-edged weapon from her shining case:
So Ladies in Romance assist their Knight,
Present the spear, and arm him for the fight.　　　130
He takes the gift with rev'rence, and extends
The little engine on his fingers' ends;
This just behind Belinda's neck he spread,
As o'er the fragrant steams she bends her head.
Swift to the Lock a thousand Sprites repair,　　　135
A thousand wings, by turns, blow back the hair;
And thrice they twitched the diamond in her ear;
Thrice she looked back, and thrice the foe drew near.
Just in that instant, anxious Ariel sought
The close recesses of the Virgin's thought;　　　140
As on the nosegay in her breast reclined,
He watched th' Ideas rising in her mind,
Suddenly he viewed, in spite of all her art,
An earthly Lover lurking at her heart.
Amazed, confused, he found his power expired,　　　145
Resigned to fate, and with a sigh retired.
　The Peer now spreads the glitt'ring Forfex wide,
T' inclose the Lock; now joins it, to divide.
Even then, before the fatal engine closed,
A wretched Sylph too fondly interposed;　　　150
Fate urged the shears, and cut the Sylph in twain,
(But airy substance soon unites again)
The meeting points the sacred hair dissever
From the fair head, forever, and forever!
　Then flashed the living lightning from her eyes,　　　155
And screams of horror rend th' affrighted skies.
Not louder shrieks to pitying heaven are cast,
When husbands, or when lap-dogs breathe their last;
Or when rich China vessels fall'n from high,
In glitt'ring dust and painted fragments lie!　　　160
　Let wreaths of triumph now my temples twine,
(The victor cried) the glorious Prize is mine!
While fish in streams, or birds delight in air,
Or in a coach and six the British Fair,

As long as *Atalantis* shall be read,   165
Or the small pillow grace a Lady's bed,
While visits shall be paid on solemn days,
When num'rous wax-lights in bright order blaze,
While nymphs take treats, or assignations give,
So long my honor, name, and praise shall live!   170
What Time would spare, from Steel receives its date,
And monuments, like men, submit to fate!
Steel could the labor of the Gods destroy,
And strike to dust th' imperial towers of Troy;
Steel could the works of mortal pride confound,   175
And hew triumphal arches to the ground.
What wonder then, fair nymph! thy hairs should feel,
The conq'ring force of unresisted steel?

CANTO IV

But anxious cares the pensive nymph oppressed,
And secret passions labored in her breast.
Not youthful kings in battle seized alive,
Not scornful virgins who their charms survive,
Not ardent lovers robbed of all their bliss,   5
Not ancient ladies when refused a kiss,
Not tyrants fierce that unrepenting die,
Not Cynthia when her manteau's pinned awry,
E'er felt such rage, resentment, and despair,
As thou, sad Virgin! for thy ravished Hair.   10
    For, that sad moment, when the Sylphs withdrew
And Ariel weeping from Belinda flew,
Umbriel, a dusky, melancholy sprite,
As ever sullied the fair face of light,
Down to the central earth, his proper scene,   15
Repaired to search the gloomy Cave of Spleen.
    Swift on his sooty pinions flits the Gnome,
And in a vapour reached the dismal dome.
No cheerful breeze this sullen region knows,
The dreaded East is all the wind that blows.   20
Here in a grotto, sheltered close from air,
And screened in shades from day's detested glare,
She sighs forever on her pensive bed,
Pain at her side, and Megrim at her head.
    Two handmaids wait the throne: alike in place,   25
But diff'ring far in figure and in face.

Here stood Ill-nature like an ancient maid,
Her wrinkled form in black and white arrayed;
With store of prayers, for mornings, nights, and noons,
Her hand is filled; her bosom with lampoons.   30
  There Affectation, with a sickly mien,
Shows in her cheek the roses of eighteen,
Practised to lisp, and hang the head aside,
Faints into airs, and languishes with pride,
On the rich quilt sinks with becoming woe,   35
Wrapt in a gown, for sickness, and for show.
The fair ones feel such maladies as these,
When each new night-dress gives a new disease.
  A constant Vapor o'er the palace flies;
Strange phantoms rising as the mists arise;   40
Dreadful, as hermit's dreams in haunted shades,
Or bright, as visions of expiring maids.
Now glaring fiends, and snakes on rolling spires,
Pale specters, gaping tombs, and purple fires:
Now lakes of liquid gold, Elysian scenes,   45
And crystal domes, and angels in machines.
  Unnumbered throngs on every side are seen,
Of bodies changed to various forms by Spleen.
Here living Tea-pots stand, one arm held out,
One bent; the handle this, and that the spout: 50
A Pipkin there, like Homer's Tripod walks;
Here sighs a Jar, and there a Goose-pie talks;
Men prove with child, as powerful fancy works,
And maids turned bottles, call aloud for corks.
  Safe past the Gnome through this fantastic band,   55
A branch of healing Spleenwort in his hand.
Then thus addressed the power: 'Hail, wayward Queen!
Who rule the sex to fifty from fifteen:
Parent of vapors and of female wit,
Who give th' hysteric or poetic fit,   60
On various tempers act by various ways,
Make some take physic, others scribble plays;
Who cause the proud their visits to delay,
And send the godly in a pet to pray.
A nymph there is, that all thy power disdains,   65
And thousands more in equal mirth maintains.
But oh! if e'er thy Gnome could spoil a grace,
Or raise a pimple on a beauteous face,

Like Citron-waters matrons' cheeks inflame,
Or change complexions at a losing game;   70
If e'er with airy horns I planted heads,
Or rumpled petticoats, or tumbled beds,
Or caus'd suspicion when no soul was rude,
Or discomposed the head-dress of a Prude,
Or e'er to costive lap-dog gave disease,   75
Which not the tears of brightest eyes could ease:
Hear me, and touch Belinda with chagrin,
That single act gives half the world the spleen.'
   The Goddess with a discontented air
Seems to reject him, though she grants his prayer.   80
A wondrous Bag with both her hands she binds,
Like that where once Ulysses held the winds;
There she collects the force of female lungs,
Sighs, sobs, and passions, and the war of tongues.
A Vial next she fills with fainting fears,   85
Soft sorrows, melting griefs, and flowing tears.
The Gnome rejoicing bears her gifts away,
Spreads his black wings, and slowly mounts to day.
   Sunk in Thalestris' arms the nymph he found,
Her eyes dejected and her hair unbound.   90
Full o'er their heads the swelling bag he rent,
And all the Furies issued at the vent.
Belinda burns with more than mortal ire,
And fierce Thalestris fans the rising fire.
'Oh wretched maid!' she spread her hands, and cried,   95
(While Hampton's echoes, 'Wretched maid!' replied)
'Was it for this you took such constant care
The bodkin, comb, and essence to prepare?
For this your locks in paper durance bound,
For this with torturing irons wreathed around?   100
For this with fillets strained your tender head,
And bravely bore the double loads of lead?
Gods! shall the ravisher display your hair,
While the Fops envy, and the Ladies stare!
Honor forbid! at whose unrivaled shrine   105
Ease, pleasure, virtue, all our sex resign.
Methinks already I your tears survey,
Already hear the horrid things they say,
Already see you a degraded toast,
And all your honor in a whisper lost!   110

How shall I, then, your helpless fame defend?
'Twill then be infamy to seem your friend!
And shall this prize, th' inestimable prize,
Exposed through crystal to the gazing eyes,
And heightened by the diamond's circling rays,   115
On that rapacious hand forever blaze?
Sooner shall grass in Hyde-park Circus grow,
And wits take lodgings in the sound of Bow;
Sooner let earth, air, sea, to Chaos fall,
Men, monkeys, lap-dogs, parrots, perish all!'   120
   She said; then raging to Sir Plume repairs,
And bids her Beau demand the precious hairs:
(Sir Plume of amber snuff-box justly vain,
And the nice conduct of a clouded cane)
With earnest eyes, and round unthinking face,   125
He first the snuff-box opened, then the case,
And thus broke out—'My Lord, why, what the devil?
Z—ds! damn the lock! 'fore Gad, you must be civil!
Plague on't! 'tis past a jest—nay prithee, pox!
Give her the hair'—he spoke, and rapped his box.   130
   'It grieves me much' (replied the Peer again)
'Who speaks so well should ever speak in vain.
But by this Lock, this sacred Lock I swear,
(Which never more shall join its parted hair;
Which never more its honors shall renew,   135
Clipped from the lovely head where late it grew)
That while my nostrils draw the vital air,
This hand, which won it, shall for ever wear.'
He spoke, and speaking, in proud triumph spread
The long-contended honours of her head.   140
   But Umbriel, hateful Gnome! forbears not so;
He breaks the Vial whence the sorrows flow.
Then see! the nymph in beauteous grief appears,
Her eyes half-languishing, half-drowned in tears;
On her heaved bosom hung her drooping head,   145
Which, with a sigh, she raised; and thus she said.
   'Forever cursed be this detested day,
Which snatched my best, my fav'rite curl away!
Happy! ah ten times happy had I been,
If Hampton-Court these eyes had never seen!   150
Yet am not I the first mistaken maid,
By love of Courts to numerous ills betrayed.

Oh had I rather un-admired remained
In some lone isle, or distant Northern land;
Where the gilt Chariot never marks the way,   155
Where none learn Ombre, none e'er taste Bohea!
There kept my charms concealed from mortal eye,
Like roses, that in deserts bloom and die.
What moved my mind with youthful Lords to roam?
Oh had I stayed, and said my prayers at home!   160
'Twas this, the morning omens seemed to tell,
Thrice from my trembling hand the patch-box fell;
The tott'ring China shook without a wind,
Nay, Poll sat mute, and Shock was most unkind!
A Sylph too warned me of the threats of fate,   165
In mystic visions, now believed too late!
See the poor remnants of these slighted hairs!
My hands shall rend what even thy rapine spares:
These in two sable ringlets taught to break,
Once gave new beauties to the snowy neck;   170
The sister-lock now sits uncouth, alone,
And in its fellow's fate foresees its own;
Uncurled it hangs, the fatal shears demands,
And tempts once more, thy sacrilegious hands.
Oh hadst thou, cruel! been content to seize   175
Hairs less in sight, or any hairs but these!'

CANTO V

She said: the pitying audience melt in tears.
But Fate and Jove had stopped the Baron's ears.
In vain Thalestris with reproach assails,
For who can move when fair Belinda fails?
Not half so fixed the Trojan could remain,   5
While Anna begged and Dido raged in vain.
Then grave Clarissa graceful waved her fan;
Silence ensued, and thus the nymph began.
   'Say why are Beauties praised and honored most,
The wise man's passion, and the vain man's toast?   10
Why decked with all that land and sea afford,
Why Angels called, and Angel-like adored?
Why round our coaches crowd the white-gloved Beaux,
Why bows the side-box from its inmost rows;
How vain are all these glories, all our pains,   15
Unless good sense preserve what beauty gains:

That men may say, when we the front-box grace:
"Behold the first in virtue as in face!"
Oh! if to dance all night, and dress all day,
Charmed the small-pox, or chased old-age away;   20
Who would not scorn what housewife's cares produce,
Or who would learn one earthly thing of use?
To patch, nay ogle, might become a Saint,
Nor could it sure be such a sin to paint.
But since, alas! frail beauty must decay,   25
Curled or uncurled, since Locks will turn to grey;
Since painted, or not painted, all shall fade,
And she who scorns a man, must die a maid;
What then remains but well our power to use,
And keep good-humor still whate'er we lose?   30
And trust me, dear! good-humor can prevail,
When airs, and flights, and screams, and scolding fail.
Beauties in vain their pretty eyes may roll;
Charms strike the sight, but merit wins the soul.'
    So spoke the Dame, but no applause ensued;   35
Belinda frowned, Thalestris called her Prude.
'To arms, to arms!' the fierce Virago cries,
And swift as lightning to the combat flies.
All side in parties, and begin th' attack;
Fans clap, silks rustle, and tough whalebones crack;   40
Heroes' and Heroines' shouts confus'dly rise,
And bass and treble voices strike the skies.
No common weapons in their hands are found,
Like Gods they fight, nor dread a mortal wound.
    So when bold Homer makes the Gods engage,   45
And heavenly breasts with human passions rage;
'Gainst Pallas, Mars; Latona, Hermes arms;
And all Olympus rings with loud alarms:
Jove's thunder roars, heaven trembles all around,
Blue Neptune storms, the bellowing deeps resound: 50
Earth shakes her nodding towers, the ground gives way,
And the pale ghosts start at the flash of day!
    Triumphant Umbriel on a sconce's height
Clapped his glad wings, and sat to view the fight:
Propped on their bodkin spears, the Sprites survey   55
The growing combat, or assist the fray.
    While through the press enraged Thalestris flies,
And scatters death around from both her eyes,

A Beau and Witling perished in the throng,
One died in metaphor, and one in song.   60
'O cruel nymph! a living death I bear,'
Cried Dapperwit, and sunk beside his chair.
A mournful glance Sir Fopling upwards cast,
'Those eyes are made so killing'—was his last.
Thus on Mæander's flowery margin lies   65
Th' expiring Swan, and as he sings he dies.
    When bold Sir Plume had drawn Clarissa down,
Chloe stepped in, and killed him with a frown;
She smiled to see the doughty hero slain,
But, at her smile, the Beau revived again.   70
    Now Jove suspends his golden scales in air,
Weighs the Men's wits against the Lady's hair;
The doubtful beam long nods from side to side;
At length the wits mount up, the hairs subside.
    See, fierce Belinda on the Baron flies,   75
With more than usual lightning in her eyes:
Nor feared the Chief th' unequal fight to try,
Who sought no more than on his foe to die.
But this bold Lord with manly strength endued,
She with one finger and a thumb subdued: 80
Just where the breath of life his nostrils drew,
A charge of Snuff the wily virgin threw;
The Gnomes direct, to every atom just,
The pungent grains of titillating dust.
Sudden, with starting tears each eye o'erflows,   85
And the high dome re-echoes to his nose.
    Now meet thy fate, incensed Belinda cried,
And drew a deadly bodkin from her side.
(The same, his ancient personage to deck,
Her great great grandsire wore about his neck,   90
In three seal-rings; which after, melted down,
Formed a vast buckle for his widow's gown:
Her infant grandame's whistle next it grew,
The bells she jingled, and the whistle blew;
Then in a bodkin graced her mother's hairs,   95
Which long she wore, and now Belinda wears.)
    'Boast not my fall' (he cried) 'insulting foe!
Thou by some other shalt be laid as low,
Nor think, to die dejects my lofty mind:
All that I dread is leaving you behind!   100

Rather than so, ah let me still survive,
And burn in Cupid's flames—but burn alive.'
   'Restore the Lock!' she cries; and all around
'Restore the Lock!' the vaulted roofs rebound.
Not fierce Othello in so loud a strain   105
Roared for the handkerchief that caused his pain.
But see how oft ambitious aims are crossed,
And chiefs contend till all the prize is lost!
The Lock, obtained with guilt, and kept with pain,
In every place is sought, but sought in vain: 110
With such a prize no mortal must be blest,
So heaven decrees! with heaven who can contest?
   Some thought it mounted to the Lunar sphere,
Since all things lost on earth are treasured there.
There Hero's wits are kept in pond'rous vases,   115
And beau's in snuff-boxes and tweezer-cases.
There broken vows and death-bed alms are found,
And lovers' hearts with ends of riband bound,
The courtier's promises, and sick man's prayers,
The smiles of harlots, and the tears of heirs,   120
Cages for gnats, and chains to yoke a flea,
Dried butterflies, and tomes of casuistry.
   But trust the Muse—she saw it upward rise,
Though marked by none but quick, poetic eyes:
(So Rome's great founder to the heavens withdrew,   125
To Proculus alone confessed in view)
A sudden Star, it shot through liquid air,
And drew behind a radiant trail of hair.
Not Berenice's Locks first rose so bright,
The heavens bespangling with disheveled light.   130
The Sylphs behold it kindling as it flies,
And pleased pursue its progress through the skies.
   This the Beau monde shall from the Mall survey,
And hail with music its propitious ray.
This the blest Lover shall for Venus take,   135
And send up vows from Rosamonda's lake.
This Partridge soon shall view in cloudless skies,
When next he looks through Galileo's eyes;
And hence th' egregious wizard shall foredoom
The fate of Louis, and the fall of Rome.   140
   Then cease, bright Nymph! to mourn thy ravished hair,
Which adds new glory to the shining sphere!

Not all the tresses that fair head can boast,
Shall draw such envy as the Lock you lost.
For, after all the murders of your eye,   145
When, after millions slain, yourself shall die:
When those fair suns shall set, as set they must,
And all those tresses shall be laid in dust,
This Lock, the Muse shall consecrate to fame,
And 'midst the stars inscribe Belinda's name.   150

ELEGY TO THE MEMORY
OF AN UNFORTUNATE LADY

What beck'ning ghost, along the moon-light shade
Invites my steps, and points to yonder glade?
'Tis she!—but why that bleeding bosom gor'd,
Why dimly gleams the visionary sword?
Oh ever beauteous, ever friendly! tell,   5
Is it, in heav'n, a crime to love too well?
To bear too tender, or too firm a heart,
To act a Lover's, or a Roman's part?
Is there no bright reversion in the sky,
For those who greatly think, or bravely die?   10
    Why bade ye else, ye Pow'rs! her soul aspire
Above the vulgar flight of low desire?
Ambition first sprung from your blest abodes;
The glorious fault of Angels and of Gods;
Thence to their images on earth it flows,   15
And in the breasts of Kings and Heroes glows.
Most souls, 't is true, but peep out once an age,
Dull sullen pris'ners in the body's cage:
Dim lights of life, that burn a length of years
Useless, unseen, as lamps in sepulchres;   20
Like Eastern Kings, a lazy state they keep,
And close confin'd to their own palace, sleep.
    From these perhaps (ere nature bade her die)
Fate snatch'd her early to the pitying sky.
As into air the purer spirits flow,   25
And sep'rate from their kindred dregs below;
So flew the soul to its congenial place,
Nor left one virtue to redeem her Race.
    But thou, false guardian of a charge too good,

Thou, mean deserter of thy brother's blood!   30
See on these ruby lips the trembling breath,
These cheeks now fading at the blast of death:
Cold is that breast which warm'd the world before,
And those love-darting eyes must roll no more.
Thus, if Eternal justice rules the ball,   35
Thus shall your wives, and thus your children fall;
On all the line a sudden vengeance waits,
And frequent herses shall besiege your gates.
There passengers shall stand, and pointing say,
(While the long fun'rals blacken all the way)   40
"Lo these were they, whose souls the Furies steel'd,
And curs'd with hearts unknowing how to yield."
Thus unlamented pass the proud away,
The gaze of fools, and pageant of a day!
So perish all, whose breast ne'er learn'd to glow   45
For others good, or melt at others woe.
    What can atone (oh ever-injur'd shade!)
Thy fate unpity'd, and thy rites unpaid?
No friend's complaint, no kind domestic tear
Pleas'd thy pale ghost, or grac'd thy mournful bier.   50
By foreign hands thy dying eyes were clos'd,
By foreign hands thy decent limbs compos'd,
By foreign hands thy humble grave adorn'd,
By strangers honour'd, and by strangers mourn'd!
What tho' no weeping Loves thy ashes grace,   55
Nor polish'd marble emulate thy face?
What tho' no sacred earth allow thee room,
Nor hallow'd dirge be mutter'd o'er thy tomb?
Yet shall thy grave with rising flow'rs be drest,
And the green turf lie lightly on thy breast: 60
There shall the morn her earliest tears bestow,
There the first roses of the year shall blow;
While Angels with their silver wings o'ershade
The ground, now sacred by the reliques made.
    So peaceful rests, without a stone, a name,   65
What once had beauty, titles, wealth, and fame.
How lov'd, how honour'd once, avails thee not,
To whom related, or by whom begot;
A heap of dust alone remains of thee,
'Tis all thou art, and all the proud shall be!   70
    Poets themselves must fall, like those they sung,

Deaf the prais'd ear, and mute the tuneful tongue.
Ev'n he, whose soul now melts in mournful lays,
Shall shortly want the gen'rous tear he pays;
Then from his closing eyes thy form shall part,   75
And the last pang shall tear thee from his heart,
Life's idle business at one gasp be o'er,
The Muse forgot, and thou be lov'd no more!

ENGRAVED ON THE COLLAR OF A DOG, WHICH I GAVE TO HIS ROYAL HIGHNESS

I am his Highness' dog at Kew;
Pray tell me, sir, whose dog are you?

THE BALANCE OF EUROPE

Now Europe's balanc'd, neither Side prevails;
For nothing's left in either of the Scales.

EPITAPH
INTENDED FOR SIR ISAAC NEWTON

Nature, and Nature's laws, lay hid in night,
God said, *Let Newton be!* And all was light.

SAMUEL JOHNSON (1709–1784)

PROLOGUE SPOKEN BY MR. GARRICK AT THE OPENING OF THE THEATRE IN DRURY-LANE, 1747

When Learning's triumph o'er her barb'rous foes
First rear'd the stage, immortal Shakespeare rose;
Each change of many-colour'd life he drew,
Exhausted worlds, and then imagin'd new:
Existence saw him spurn her bounded reign,   5
And panting Time toil'd after him in vain:
Her pow'rful strokes presiding Truth impress'd,
And unresisted Passion storm'd the breast.

Then Jonson came, instructed from the School,
To please in method, and invent by rule;   10
His studious patience and laborious art,
By regular approach essay'd the heart;
Cold Approbation gave the ling'ring bays,
For those who durst not censure, scarce could praise.
A mortal born, he met the general doom,   15
But left, like Egypt's kings, a lasting tomb.

    The wits of Charles found easier ways to fame,
Nor wish'd for Jonson's Art, or Shakespeare's Flame;
Themselves they studied, as they felt, they writ;
Intrigue was plot, obscenity was wit.   20
Vice always found a sympathetic friend;
They pleas'd their age, and did not aim to mend.
Yet bards like these aspir'd to lasting praise,
And proudly hop'd to pimp in future days.
Their cause was gen'ral, their supports were strong,   25
Their slaves were willing, and their reign was long;
Till Shame regain'd the post that Sense betray'd,
And Virtue call'd Oblivion to her aid.

    Then crush'd by rules, and weaken'd as refin'd,
For years the pow'r of Tragedy declin'd;   30
From bard to bard the frigid caution crept,
Till Declamation roar'd, while Passion slept.
Yet still did Virtue deign the stage to tread,
Philosophy remain'd, though Nature fled.
But forc'd at length her ancient reign to quit,   35
She saw great Faustus lay the ghost of Wit:
Exulting Folly hail'd the joyful day,
And Pantomime and Song confirm'd her sway.

    But who the coming changes can presage,
And mark the future periods of the Stage?   40
Perhaps if skill could future times explore,
New Behns, new Durfeys, yet remain in store.
Perhaps, where Lear has rav'd and Hamlet died,
On flying cars new sorcerers may ride.
Perhaps, for who can guess th'effects of chance?   45
Here Hunt may box, or Mahomet may dance.

    Hard is his lot, that here by Fortune plac'd,
Must watch the wild vicissitudes of taste;
With ev'ry meteor of caprice must play,
And chase the new-blown bubbles of the day.   50

Ah! let not censure term our fate or choice,
The stage but echoes back the public voice.
The drama's laws the drama's patrons give,
For we that live to please, must please to live.
   Then prompt no more the follies you decry,   55
As tyrants doom their tools of guilt to die;
'Tis yours this night to bid the reign commence
Of rescu'd Nature, and reviving Sense;
To chase the charms of sound, the pomp of show,
For useful mirth, and salutary woe;   60
Bid scenic virtue form the rising age,
And Truth diffuse her radiance from the stage.

THOMAS GRAY (1716–1771)

ODE ON A DISTANT PROSPECT OF ETON COLLEGE

Ye distant spires, ye antique towers,
That crown the watery glade,
Where grateful Science still adores
Her Henry's holy shade;
And ye, that from the stately brow   5
Of Windsor's heights the expanse below
Of grove, of lawn, of mead survey,
Whose turf, whose shade, whose flowers among
Wanders the hoary Thames along
His silver-winding way.   10

   Ah happy hills, ah pleasing shade,
Ah fields beloved in vain,
Where once my careless childhood strayed,
A stranger yet to pain!
I feel the gales, that from ye blow,   15
A momentary bliss bestow,
As waving fresh their gladsome wing
My weary soul they seem to soothe,
And, redolent of joy and youth,
To breathe a second spring.   20

Say, Father Thames, for thou hast seen
Full many a sprightly race
Disporting on thy margent green
The paths of pleasure trace,
Who foremost now delight to cleave   25
With pliant arm thy glassy wave?
The captive linnet which enthrall?
What idle progeny succeed
To chase the rolling circle's speed,
Or urge the flying ball?   30

While some on earnest business bent
Their murmuring labours ply
'Gainst graver hours, that bring constraint
To sweeten liberty;
Some bold adventurers disdain   35
The limits of their little reign,
And unknown regions dare descry;
Still as they run they look behind,
They hear a voice in every wind,
And snatch a fearful joy.   40

Gay hope is theirs by fancy fed,
Less pleasing when possest;
The tear forgot as soon as shed,
The sunshine of the breast;
Theirs buxom health of rosy hue,   45
Wild wit, invention ever-new,
And lively cheer of vigour born;
The thoughtless day, the easy night,
The spirits pure, the slumbers light,
That fly the approach of morn.   50

Alas, regardless of their doom,
The little victims play!
No sense have they of ills to come,
Nor care beyond to-day;
Yet see how all around 'em wait   55
The ministers of human Fate,
And black Misfortune's baleful train!
Ah, show them where in ambush stand,
To seize their prey, the murtherous band!
Ah, tell them they are men!   60

These shall the fury Passions tear,
The vultures of the mind,
Disdainful Anger, pallid Fear,
And Shame that skulks behind;
Or pining Love shall waste their youth,   65
Or Jealousy with rankling tooth,
That inly gnaws the secret heart,
And Envy wan, and faded Care,
Grim-visaged comfortless Despair,
And Sorrow's piercing dart.   70

Ambition this shall tempt to rise,
Then whirl the wretch from high,
To bitter Scorn a sacrifice,
And grinning Infamy.
The stings of Falsehood those shall try,   75
And hard Unkindness' altered eye,
That mocks the tear it forced to flow;
And keen Remorse with blood defiled,
And moody Madness laughing wild
Amid severest woe.   80

Lo! in the vale of years beneath
A grisly troop are seen,
The painful family of Death,
More hideous than their queen.
This racks the joints, this fires the veins,   85
That every labouring sinew strains,
Those in the deeper vitals rage;
Lo, Poverty, to fill the band,
That numbs the soul with icy hand,
And slow-consuming Age.   90

To each his sufferings; all are men,
Condemned alike to groan,
The tender for another's pain,
The unfeeling for his own.
Yet ah! why should they know their fate?   95
Since sorrow never comes too late,
And happiness too swiftly flies.
Thought would destroy their paradise.
No more; where ignorance is bliss,
'Tis folly to be wise.   100

ON THE DEATH OF A FAVOURITE CAT,
DROWNED IN A TUB OF GOLD FISHES

'Twas on a lofty vase's side,
Where China's gayest art had dy'd
  The azure flowers, that blow;
Demurest of the tabby kind,
The pensive Selima reclin'd,
  Gazed on the lake below.   5

Her conscious tail her joy declar'd;
The fair round face, the snowy beard,
  The velvet of her paws,
Her coat, that with the tortoise vies,   10
Her ears of jet, and emerald eyes,
  She saw; and purr'd applause.

Still had she gaz'd; but 'midst the tide
Two angel forms were seen to glide,
  The Genii of the stream: 15
Their scaly armour's Tyrian hue
Thro' richest purple to the view
  Betray'd a golden gleam.

The hapless Nymph with wonder saw:
A whisker first and then a claw,   20
  With many an ardent wish,
She stretch'd in vain to reach the prize.
What female heart can gold despise?
  What Cat's averse to fish?

Presumptuous Maid! with looks intent   25
Again she stretch'd, again she bent,
  Nor knew the gulf between.
(Malignant Fate sat by, and smil'd)
The slipp'ry verge her feet beguil'd,
  She tumbled headlong in.   30

Eight times emerging from the flood
She mew'd to ev'ry watery God,
  Some speedy aid to send.

No Dolphin came, no Nereid stirr'd:
Nor cruel Tom, nor Susan heard.   35
  A Fav'rite has no friend!

From hence, ye Beauties, undeceiv'd,
Know, one false step is ne'er retriev'd,
  And be with caution bold.
Not all that tempts your wand'ring eyes   40
And heedless hearts, is lawful prize;
  Nor all, that glisters, gold.

ELEGY

WRITTEN IN A COUNTRY CHURCHYARD

The Curfew tolls the knell of parting day,
  The lowing herd wind slowly o'er the lea,
The plowman homeward plods his weary way,
  And leaves the world to darkness and to me.

Now fades the glimmering landscape on the sight,   5
  And all the air a solemn stillness holds,
Save where the beetle wheels his droning flight,
  And drowsy tinklings lull the distant folds;

Save that from yonder ivy-mantled tower
  The moping owl does to the moon complain   10
Of such, as wandering near her secret bower,
  Molest her ancient solitary reign.

Beneath those rugged elms, that yew-tree's shade,
  Where heaves the turf in many a mouldering heap,
Each in his narrow cell for ever laid,   15
  The rude Forefathers of the hamlet sleep.

The breezy call of incense-breathing Morn,
  The swallow twittering from the straw-built shed,
The cock's shrill clarion, or the echoing horn,
  No more shall rouse them from their lowly bed.   20

For them no more the blazing hearth shall burn,
  Or busy housewife ply her evening care:

No children run to lisp their sire's return,
  Or climb his knees the envied kiss to share.

Oft did the harvest to their sickle yield,   25
  Their furrow oft the stubborn glebe has broke;
How jocund did they drive their team afield!
  How bowed the woods beneath their sturdy stroke!

Let not Ambition mock their useful toil,
  Their homely joys, and destiny obscure;   30
Nor Grandeur hear with a disdainful smile
  The short and simple annals of the poor.

The boast of heraldry, the pomp of power,
  And all that beauty, all that wealth e'er gave,
Awaits alike the inevitable hour.   35
  The paths of glory lead but to the grave.

Nor you, ye Proud, impute to These the fault,
  If Memory o'er their Tomb no Trophies raise,
Where through the long-drawn aisle and fretted vault
  The pealing anthem swells the note of praise.   40

Can storied urn or animated bust
  Back to its mansion call the fleeting breath?
Can Honor's voice provoke the silent dust,
  Or Flattery sooth the dull cold ear of Death?

Perhaps in this neglected spot is laid   45
  Some heart once pregnant with celestial fire;
Hands, that the rod of empire might have swayed,
  Or waked to ecstasy the living lyre.

But Knowledge to their eyes her ample page
  Rich with the spoils of time did ne'er unroll;   50
Chill Penury repressed their noble rage,
  And froze the genial current of the soul.

Full many a gem of purest ray serene,
  The dark unfathomed caves of ocean bear:
Full many a flower is born to blush unseen,   55
  And waste its sweetness on the desert air.

Some village-Hampden, that with dauntless breast
    The little Tyrant of his fields withstood;
Some mute inglorious Milton here may rest,
    Some Cromwell guiltless of his country's blood.   60

The applause of listening senates to command,
    The threats of pain and ruin to despise,
To scatter plenty o'er a smiling land,
    And read their history in a nation's eyes,

Their lot forbade: nor circumscribed alone   65
    Their growing virtues, but their crimes confin'd;
Forbade to wade through slaughter to a throne,
    And shut the gates of mercy on mankind,

The struggling pangs of conscious truth to hide,
    To quench the blushes of ingenuous shame,   70
Or heap the shrine of Luxury and Pride
    With incense kindled at the Muse's flame.

Far from the madding crowd's ignoble strife,
    Their sober wishes never learned to stray;
Along the cool sequestered vale of life   75
    They kept the noiseless tenor of their way.

Yet even these bones from insult to protect,
    Some frail memorial still erected nigh,
With uncouth rhymes and shapeless sculpture decked,
    Implores the passing tribute of a sigh.   80

Their name, their years, spelt by the unlettered muse,
    The place of fame and elegy supply:
And many a holy text around she strews,
    That teach the rustic moralist to die.

For who to dumb Forgetfulness a prey,   85
    This pleasing anxious being e'er resigned,
Left the warm precincts of the cheerful day,
    Nor cast one longing lingering look behind?

On some fond breast the parting soul relies,
    Some pious drops the closing eye requires;   90

Ev'n from the tomb the voice of Nature cries,
Ev'n in our Ashes live their wonted Fires.

For thee, who mindful of the unhonoured Dead
Dost in these lines their artless tale relate,
If chance, by lonely contemplation led,   95
Some kindred Spirit shall inquire thy fate,

Haply some hoary-headed Swain may say,
"Oft have we seen him at the peep of dawn
Brushing with hasty steps the dews away
To meet the sun upon the upland lawn.   100

"There at the foot of yonder nodding beech
That wreathes its old fantastic roots so high,
His listless length at noontide would he stretch,
And pore upon the brook that babbles by.

"Hard by yon wood, now smiling as in scorn,   105
Muttering his wayward fancies he would rove,
Now drooping, woeful wan, like one forlorn,
Or crazed with care, or crossed in hopeless love.

"One morn I missed him on the customed hill,
Along the heath and near his favorite tree;   110
Another came; nor yet beside the rill,
Nor up the lawn, nor at the wood was he;

"The next with dirges due in sad array
Slow through the church-way path we saw him borne.
Approach and read (for thou can'st read) the lay,   115
Graved on the stone beneath yon agèd thorn."

THE EPITAPH

Here rests his head upon the lap of earth
A youth to fortune and to fame unknown.
Fair Science frowned not on his humble birth,
And Melancholy marked him for her own.   120

Large was his bounty, and his soul sincere,
Heaven did a recompense as largely send:
He gave to Misery all he had, a tear,
He gained from Heaven ('twas all he wished) a friend.

No farther seek his merits to disclose,   125
  Or draw his frailties from their dread abode,
(There they alike in trembling hope repose)
  The bosom of his Father and his God.

ON LORD HOLLAND'S SEAT NEAR MARGATE, KENT

Old and abandon'd by each venal friend
  Here Holland took the pious resolution
To smuggle some few years and strive to mend
  A broken character and constitution.
On this congenial spot he fix'd his choice,   5
  Earl Godwin trembled for his neighbouring sand,
Here Seagulls scream and cormorants rejoice,
  And Mariners tho' shipwreckt dread to land,
Here reign the blustring north and blighting east,
  No tree is heard to whisper, bird to sing,   10
Yet nature cannot furnish out the feast,
  Art he invokes new horrors still to bring:
Now mouldring fanes and battlements arise,
  Arches and turrets nodding to their fall,
Unpeopled palaces delude our eyes,   15
  And mimick desolation covers all.
Ah, said the sighing Peer, had Bute been true
  Nor Shelburn's, Rigby's, Calcraft's friendship vain,
Far other scenes than these had bless'd our view
  And realis'd the ruins that we feign.   20
Purg'd by the sword and beautifyed by fire,
  Then had we seen proud London's hated walls,
Owls might have hooted in St. Peters Quire,
  And foxes stunk and litter'd in St. Pauls.

Lord Holland: a corrupt and discredited politician forced into retirement.

6. **Sand:** the Goodwin sands, dangerous quicksands on which many ships had been wrecked.

6. **Earl Godwin:** the Saxon earl after whom the sands were named. He trembled lest Holland should steal them.

20. **Realised the ruins:** had he remained in a position of influence in the government he would have brought ruin to London instead of harmlessly building mock ruins on the Kentish coast.

WILLIAM COLLINS (1721–1759)

ODE TO EVENING

If aught of oaten stop, or pastoral song,
May hope, chaste Eve, to soothe thy modest ear,
    Like thy own solemn springs,
    Thy springs and dying gales,

O nymph reserved, while now the bright-hair'd sun   5
Sits in yon western tent, whose cloudy skirts,
    With brede ethereal wove,
    O'erhang his wavy bed:

Now air is hushed, save where the weak-eyed bat,
With short shrill shriek, flits by on leathern wing,   10
    Or where the beetle winds
    His small but sullen horn,

As oft he rises 'midst the twilight path,
Against the pilgrim borne in heedless hum.
    Now teach me, maid composed,   15
    To breathe some softened strain,

Whose numbers, stealing through thy dark'ning vale
May not unseemly with its stillness suit,
    As, musing slow, I hail
    Thy genial lov'd return!   20

For when thy folding-star arising shews
His paly circlet, at his warning lamp
    The fragrant Hours, the elves
    Who slept in flow'rs the day,

And many a nymph who wreaths her brows with sedge,   25
And sheds the fresh'ning dew, and, lovelier still
    The pensive Pleasures sweet,
    Prepare thy shadowy car.

Then lead, calm vot'ress, where some sheety lake
Cheers the lone heath, or some time-hallowed pile   30
    Or upland fallows grey
    Reflect its last cool gleam.

But when chill blust'ring winds, or driving rain,
Forbid my willing feet, be mine the hut
 That from the mountain's side   35
 Views wilds, and swelling floods,

And hamlets brown, and dim-discover'd spires,
And hears their simple bell, and marks o'er all
 Thy dewy fingers draw
 The gradual dusky veil.   40

While Spring shall pour his show'rs, as oft he wont,
And bathe thy breathing tresses, meekest Eve;
 While Summer loves to sport
 Beneath thy ling'ring light;

While sallow Autumn fills thy lap with leaves;   45
Or Winter, yelling through the troublous air,
 Affrights thy shrinking train,
 And rudely rends thy robes;

So long, sure-found beneath the sylvan shed,
Shall Fancy, Friendship, Science, rose-lipp'd Health,   50
 Thy gentlest influence own,
 And hymn thy fav'rite name!

ODE

WRITTEN IN THE BEGINNING OF THE YEAR 1746

How sleep the brave who sink to rest,
By all their country's wishes blessed!
When Spring, with dewy fingers cold,
Returns to deck their hallow'd mould,
She there shall dress a sweeter sod
Than Fancy's feet have ever trod.

By fairy hands their knell is rung;
By forms unseen their dirge is sung;
There Honour comes, a pilgrim grey,
To bless the turf that wraps their clay;
And Freedom shall awhile repair,
To dwell, a weeping hermit, there!

CHRISTOPHER SMART (1722–1770)

FOR I WILL CONSIDER MY CAT JEOFFREY

from
JUBILATE AGNO

For I will consider my Cat Jeoffrey.

For he is the servant of the Living God, duly and daily serving him.

For at the First glance of the glory of God in the East he worships in his way.

For is this done by wreathing his body seven times round with elegant quickness.

For then he leaps up to catch the musk, which is the blessing of God upon his prayer.

For he rolls upon prank to work it in.   5

For having done duty and received blessing he begins to consider himself.

For this he performs in ten degrees.

For first he looks upon his fore-paws to see if they are clean.

For secondly he kicks up behind to clear away there.   10

For thirdly he works it upon stretch with the fore-paws extended.

For fourthly he sharpens his paws by wood.

For fifthly he washes himself.

For sixthly he rolls upon wash.

For Seventhly he fleas himself, that he may not be interrupted upon the beat.   15

For Eighthly he rubs himself against a post.

For Ninthly he looks up for his instructions.

For Tenthly he goes in quest of food.

For having consider'd God and himself he will consider his neighbour.

For if he meets another cat he will kiss her in kindness.   20

For when he takes his prey he plays with it to give it a chance.

For one mouse in seven escapes by his dallying.

For when his day's work is done his business more properly begins.

For he keeps the Lord's watch in the night against the adversary.

For he counteracts the powers of darkness by his electrical skin & glaring eyes.   25

For he counteracts the Devil, who is death, by brisking about the life.

For in his morning orisons he loves the sun and the sun loves him.
For he is of the tribe of Tiger.
For the Cherub Cat is a term of the Angel Tiger.
For he has the subtlety and hissing of a serpent, which in goodness
he suppresses.   30
For he will not do destruction, if he is well fed, neither will he spit
without provocation.
For he purrs in thankfulness, when God tells him he's a good Cat.
For he is an instrument for the children to learn benevolence upon.
For every house is incomplete without him and a blessing is lack-
ing in the spirit.
For the Lord commanded Moses concerning the cats at the de-
parture of the Children of Israel from Egypt.   35
For every family had one cat at least in the bag.
For the English Cats are the best in Europe.
For he is the cleanest in the use of his fore-paws of any quadrupede.
For the dexterity of his defence is an instance of the love of God
to him exceedingly.
For he is the quickest to his mark of any creature.   40
For he is tenacious of his point.
For he is a mixture of gravity and waggery.
For he knows that God is his Saviour.
For there is nothing sweeter than his peace when at rest.
For there is nothing brisker than his life when in motion.   45
For he is of the Lord's poor and so indeed is he called by benevo-
lence perpetually—Poor Jeoffrey! poor Jeoffrey! the rat has bit
thy throat.
For I bless the name of the Lord Jesus that Jeoffrey is better.
For the divine spirit comes about his body to sustain it in com-
plete cat.
For his tongue is exceedingly pure so that it has in purity what it
wants in music.
For he is docile and can learn certain things.   50
For he can set up with gravity which is patience upon approbation.
For he can fetch and carry, which is patience in employment.
For he can jump over a stick which is patience upon proof positive.
For he can spraggle upon waggle at the word of command.
For he can jump from an eminence into his master's bosom.   55
For he can catch the cork and toss it again.
For he is hated by the hypocrite and miser.
For the former is afraid of detection.
For the latter refuses the charge.

For he camels his back to bear the first notion of business.   60
For he is good to think on, if a man would express himself neatly.
For he made a great figure in Egypt for his signal services.
For he killed the Ichneumon-rat very pernicious by land.
For his ears are so acute that they sting again.
For from this proceeds the passing quickness of his attention.   65
For by stroking of him I have found out electricity.
For I perceived God's light about him both wax and fire.
For the Electrical fire is the spiritual substance, which God sends
    from heaven to sustain the bodies both of man and beast.
For God has blessed him in the variety of his movements.
For, tho he cannot fly, he is an excellent clamberer.   70
For his motions upon the face of the earth are more than any other
    quadrupede.
For he can tread to all the measures upon the music.
For he can swim for life.
For he can creep.

OLIVER GOLDSMITH (1728–1774)

WHEN LOVELY WOMAN STOOPS TO FOLLY

When lovely woman stoops to folly,
    And finds too late that men betray,
What charm can soothe her melancholy,
    What art can wash her guilt away?

The only art her guilt to cover,
    To hide her shame from every eye,
To give repentance to her lover,
    And wring his bosom, is—to die.

EDMUND BURKE

(From *Retaliation*)

Here lies our good Edmund, whose genius was such,
We scarcely can praise it or blame it too much;
Who, born for the universe, narrowed his mind,
And to party gave up what was meant for mankind:

Though fraught with all learning, yet straining his throat   5
To persuade Tommy Townshend to lend him a vote;
Who, too deep for his hearers, still went on refining,
And thought of convincing, while they thought of dining;
Though equal to all things, for all things unfit;
Too nice for a statesman, too proud for a wit;   10
For a patriot too cool; for a drudge disobedient;
And too fond of the right to pursue the expedient.
In short, 'twas his fate, unemployed or in place, sir,
To eat mutton cold, and cut blocks with a razor.

DAVID GARRICK

(From *Retaliation*)

  Here lies David Garrick—describe me who can
An abridgement of all that was pleasant in man:
As an actor, confessed without rival to shine;
As a wit, if not first, in the very first line;
Yet, with talents like these, and an excellent heart,   5
The man had his failings—a dupe to his art.
Like an ill-judging beauty, his colors he spread,
And beplastered with rouge his own natural red.
On the stage he was natural, simple, affecting;
'Twas only that when he was off he was acting.   10
With no reason on earth to go out of his way,
He turned and he varied full ten times a day:
Though secure of our hearts, yet confoundedly sick
If they were not his own by finessing and trick:
He cast off his friends, as a huntsman his pack,   15
For he knew when he pleased he could whistle them back.
Of praise a mere glutton, he swallowed what came,
And the puff of a dunce, he mistook it for fame;
Till his relish grown callous, almost to disease,
Who peppered the highest was surest to please.   20
But let us be candid, and speak out our mind;
If dunces applauded, he paid them in kind.
Ye Kenricks, ye Kellys, and Woodfalls so grave,
What a commerce was yours while you got and you gave!
How did Grub Street re-echo the shouts that you raised,   25
While he was be-Rosciused, and you were be-praised!

But peace to his spirit, wherever it flies,
To act as an angel and mix with the skies;
Those poets who owe their best fame to his skill
Shall still be his flatterers, go where he will;   30
Old Shakespeare receive him with praise and with love,
And Beaumonts and Bens be his Kellys above.

WILLIAM COWPER (1731–1800)

THE POPLAR FIELD

The poplars are felled; farewell to the shade
And the whispering sound of the cool colonnade;
The winds play no longer and sing in the leaves,
Nor Ouse on his bosom their image receives.

Twelve years have elapsed since I first took a view   5
Of my favourite field, and the bank where they grew;
And now in the grass behold they are laid,
And the tree is my seat that once lent me a shade.

The blackbird has fled to another retreat
Where the hazels afford him a screen from the heat,   10
And the scene where his melody charmed me before
Resounds with his sweet-flowing ditty no more.

My fugitive years are all hasting away,
And I must ere long lie as lowly as they
With a turf on my breast, and a stone at my head,   15
Ere another such grove shall arise in its stead.

'Tis a sight to engage me, if anything can,
To muse on the perishing pleasures of man;
Though his life be a dream, his enjoyments, I see,
Have a being less durable even than he.   20

EPITAPH ON A HARE

Here lies, whom hound did ne'er pursue,
    Nor swifter greyhound follow,
Whose foot ne'er tainted morning dew,
    Nor ear heard huntsman's halloo.

Old Tiney, surliest of his kind,   5
  Who, nursed with tender care,
And to domestic bounds confined,
  Was still a wild Jack-hare.

Though duly from my hand he took
  His pittance every night,   10
He did it with a jealous look,
  And, when he could, would bite.

His diet was of wheaten bread,
  And milk, and oats, and straw;
Thistles, or lettuces instead,   15
  With sand to scour his maw.

On twigs of hawthorn he regaled,
  On pippins' russet peel,
And when his juicy salads failed,
  Sliced carrot pleased him well.   20

A Turkey carpet was his lawn,
  Whereon he loved to bound,
To skip and gambol like a fawn,
  And swing his rump around.

His frisking was at evening hours,   25
  For then he lost his fear,
But most before approaching showers
  Or when a storm drew near.

Eight years and five round-rolling moons
  He thus saw steal away,   30
Dozing out all his idle noons,
  And every night at play.

I kept him for his humour's sake,
  For he would oft beguile
My heart of thoughts that made it ache,   35
  And force me to a smile.

But now beneath his walnut shade
  He finds his long last home,

And waits, in snug concealment laid,
Till gentler Puss shall come.   40

He, still more aged, feels the shocks
From which no care can save,
And, partner once of Tiney's box,
Must soon partake his grave.

LIGHT SHINING OUT OF DARKNESS

God moves in a mysterious way,
His wonders to perform;
He plants his footsteps in the sea,
And rides upon the storm.

Deep in unfathomable mines   5
Of never failing skill,
He treasures up his bright designs,
And works his sovereign will.

Ye fearful saints fresh courage take;
The clouds ye so much dread   10
Are big with mercy, and shall break
In blessings on your head.

Judge not the Lord by feeble sense,
But trust him for his grace;
Behind a frowning providence,   15
He hides a smiling face.

His purposes will ripen fast,
Unfolding every hour:
The bud may have a bitter taste,
But sweet will be the flower.   20

Blind unbelief is sure to err,
And scan his work in vain;
God is his own interpreter,
And he will make it plain.

WILLIAM BLAKE (1757–1827)

TO THE MUSES

Whether on Ida's shady brow,
  Or in the chambers of the East,
The chambers of the Sun, that now
  From ancient melody have ceased;

Whether in Heaven ye wander fair,   5
  Or the green corners of the earth,
Or the blue regions of the air
  Where the melodious winds have birth;

Whether on crystal rocks ye rove,
  Beneath the bosom of the sea,   10
Wandering in many a coral grove;
  Fair Nine, forsaking Poetry;

How have you left the ancient love
  That bards of old enjoyed in you!
The languid strings do scarcely move,   15
  The sound is forced, the notes are few!

SONG

How sweet I roam'd from field to field,
  And tasted all the summer's pride,
Till I the Prince of Love beheld
  Who in the sunny beams did glide.

He show'd me lilies for my hair,   5
  And blushing roses for my brow;
He led me through his gardens fair,
  Where all his golden pleasures grow.

With sweet May-dews my wings were wet,
  And Phœbus fir'd my vocal rage;   10
He caught me in his silken net,
  And shut me in his golden cage.

He loves to sit and hear me sing,
 Then, laughing, sports and plays with me;
Then stretches out my golden wing,   15
 And mocks my loss of liberty.

SONGS OF INNOCENCE

Introduction

Piping down the valleys wild,
Piping songs of pleasant glee,
On a cloud I saw a child,
And he laughing said to me:

"Pipe a song about a Lamb!"   5
So I piped with merry cheer.
"Piper, pipe that song again";
So I piped: he wept to hear.

"Drop thy pipe, thy happy pipe;
Sing thy songs of happy cheer!"   10
So I sung the same again,
While he wept with joy to hear.

"Piper, sit thee down and write
In a book, that all may read."
So he vanish'd from my sight;   15
And I pluck'd a hollow reed,

And I made a rural pen,
And I stain'd the water clear,
And I wrote my happy songs
Every child may joy to hear.   20

THE LAMB

 Little Lamb, who made thee?
 Dost thou know who made thee?
Gave thee life, & bid thee feed
By the stream & o'er the mead;
Gave thee clothing of delight,   5
Softest clothing, wooly, bright;

Gave thee such a tender voice,
Making all the vales rejoice?
  Little Lamb, who made thee?
  Dost thou know who made thee? 10

  Little Lamb, I'll tell thee
  Little Lamb, I'll tell thee:
He is callèd by thy name,
For he calls himself a Lamb.
He is meek, & he is mild; 15
He became a little child.
I a child, & thou a lamb,
We are callèd by his name.
  Little Lamb, God bless thee!
  Little Lamb, God bless thee! 20

THE LITTLE BLACK BOY

My mother bore me in the southern wild,
And I am black, but O! my soul is white;
White as an angel is the English child,
But I am black, as if bereav'd of light.

My mother taught me underneath a tree, 5
And sitting down before the heat of day,
She took me on her lap and kissed me,
And pointing to the East, began to say:

"Look on the rising sun: there God does live,
And gives his light, and gives his heat away, 10
And flowers and trees and beasts and men receive
Comfort in morning, joy in the noonday.

"And we are put on earth a little space,
That we may learn to bear the beams of love;
And these black bodies and this sunburnt face 15
Is but a cloud, and like a shady grove.

"For when our souls have learn'd the heat to bear,
The cloud will vanish, we shall hear his voice,
Saying, 'Come out from the grove, my love & care,
And round my golden tent like lambs rejoice.'" 20

Thus did my mother say, and kissed me,
And thus I say to little English boy:
When I from black, and he from white cloud free,
And round the tent of God like lambs we joy,

I'll shade him from the heat till he can bear   25
To lean in joy upon our Father's knee;
And then I'll stand and stroke his silver hair,
And be like him, and he will then love me.

THE TYGER

Tyger! Tyger! burning bright
In the forests of the night,
What immortal hand or eye
Could frame thy fearful symmetry?

In what distant deeps or skies   5
Burnt the fire of thine eyes?
On what wings dare he aspire?
What the hand dare seize the fire?

And what shoulder, & what art,
Could twist the sinews of thy heart?   10
And when thy heart began to beat,
What dread hand? & what dread feet?

What the hammer? what the chain?
In what furnace was thy brain?
What the anvil? what dread grasp   15
Dare its deadly terrors clasp?

When the stars threw down their spears,
And water'd heaven with their tears,
Did he smile his work to see?
Did he who made the Lamb make thee?   20

Tyger! Tyger! burning bright
In the forests of the night,
What immortal hand or eye,
Dare frame thy fearful symmetry?

AH! SUN-FLOWER

Ah, Sun-flower! weary of time,
Who countest the steps of the Sun;
Seeking after that sweet golden clime
Where the traveller's journey is done;

Where the Youth pined away with desire,
And the pale Virgin shrouded in snow,
Arise from their graves, and aspire
Where my Sun-flower wishes to go.

THE SICK ROSE

O Rose, thou art sick!
The invisible worm
That flies in the night,
In the howling storm,

Has found out thy bed
Of crimson joy:
And his dark, secret love
Does thy life destroy.

LONDON

I wander thro' each charter'd street,
Near where the charter'd Thames does flow,
And mark in every face I meet
Marks of weakness, marks of woe.

In every cry of every Man,   5
In every Infant's cry of fear,
In every voice, in every ban,
The mind-forg'd manacles I hear.

How the Chimney-sweeper's cry
Every black'ning Church appalls;   10
And the hapless Soldier's sigh
Runs in blood down Palace walls.

But most thro' midnight streets I hear
How the youthful Harlot's curse
Blasts the new born Infant's tear,   15
And blights with plagues the Marriage hearse.

THE LITTLE VAGABOND

Dear Mother, dear Mother, the Church is cold,
But the Ale-house is healthy & pleasant & warm;
Besides I can tell where I am used well,
Such usage in Heaven will never do well.

But if at the Church they would give us some Ale,   5
And a pleasant fire our souls to regale,
We'd sing and we'd pray all the live-long day,
Nor ever once wish from the Church to stray.

Then the Parson might preach, & drink, & sing,
And we'd be as happy as birds in the spring;   10
And modest Dame Lurch, who is always at Church,
Would not have bandy children, nor fasting, nor birch.

And God, like a father rejoicing to see
His children as pleasant and happy as he,
Would have no more quarrel with the Devil or the
      Barrel,   15
But kiss him, & give him both drink and apparel.

THE GARDEN OF LOVE

I went to the Garden of Love,
And saw what I never had seen:
A Chapel was built in the midst,
Where I used to play on the green.

And the gates of this Chapel were shut,
And 'Thou shalt not' writ over the door;
So I turn'd to the Garden of Love
That so many sweet flowers bore;

And I saw it was fillèd with graves,
And tomb-stones where flowers should be:
And Priests in black gowns were walking their rounds,
And binding with briars my joys & desires.

I ASKED A THIEF

I asked a thief to steal me a peach:
He turn'd up his eyes.
I ask'd a lithe lady to lie her down:
Holy & meek she cries.
As soon as I went an angel came:
He wink'd at the thief
And smil'd at the dame,
And without one word spoke
Had a peach from the tree,
And 'twixt earnest & joke
Enjoy'd the Lady.

FROM *MILTON*

And did those feet in ancient time
  Walk upon England's mountains green?
And was the holy Lamb of God
  On England's pleasant pastures seen?

And did the Countenance Divine   5
  Shine forth upon our clouded hills?
And was Jerusalem builded here
  Among these dark Satanic mills?

Bring me my Bow of burning gold!
  Bring me my Arrows of desire!   10
Bring me my Spear: O clouds, unfold!
  Bring me my Chariot of fire!

I will not cease from Mental Fight,
  Nor shall my Sword sleep in my hand,
Till we have built Jerusalem   15
  In England's green and pleasant land.

SCOFFERS

Mock on, mock on, Voltaire, Rousseau,
Mock on, mock on; 'tis all in vain;
You throw the sand against the wind,
And the wind blows it back again.

And every sand becomes a gem,
Reflected in the beams divine;
Blown back, they blind the mocking eye,
But still in Israel's paths they shine.

The atoms of Democritus
And Newton's particles of light
Are sands upon the Red Sea shore
Where Israel's tents do shine so bright.

AUGURIES OF INNOCENCE

To see a World in a Grain of Sand
And a Heaven in a Wild flower,
Hold Infinity in the palm of your hand,
And Eternity in an hour.

A Robin Redbreast in a Cage   5
Puts all Heaven in a Rage.
A dove-house filled with Doves & Pigeons
Shudders Hell through all its regions.
A dog starved at his Master's Gate
Predicts the ruin of the State.   10
A Horse misused upon the Road
Calls to Heaven for Human blood.
Each outcry of the hunted Hare
A fibre from the Brain does tear.
A Skylark wounded in the wing,   15
A Cherubim does cease to sing;
The Game Cock clipped and armed for fight
Does the Rising Sun affright.
Every Wolf's & Lion's howl
Raises from Hell a Human Soul.   20

The wild Deer, wandering here & there,
Keeps the Human Soul from Care.
The Lamb misused breeds Public Strife
And yet forgives the Butcher's knife.
The Bat that flits at close of Eve   25
Has left the Brain that won't Believe.
The Owl that calls upon the Night
Speaks the Unbeliever's fright.
He who shall hurt the little Wren
Shall never be beloved by Men.   30
He who the Ox to wrath has moved
Shall never be by Woman loved.
The wanton Boy that kills the Fly
Shall feel the Spider's enmity.
He who torments the Chafer's Sprite   35
Weaves a Bower in endless Night.
The Caterpillar on the Leaf
Repeats to thee thy Mother's grief.
Kill not the Moth nor Butterfly,
For the Last Judgment draweth nigh.   40
He who shall train the Horse to war
Shall never pass the Polar Bar.
The Beggar's Dog & Widow's Cat,
Feed them & thou wilt grow fat.
The Gnat that sings his Summer's Song   45
Poison gets from Slander's tongue.
The poison of the Snake & Newt
Is the sweat of Envy's Foot.
The poison of the Honey Bee
Is the Artist's Jealousy.   50
The Prince's Robes & Beggar's Rags
Are Toadstools on the Miser's Bags.
A Truth that's told with bad intent
Beats all the Lies you can invent.
It is right it should be so;   55
Man was made for Joy & Woe;
And when this we rightly know,
Through the World we safely go.
Joy & Woe are woven fine,
A Clothing for the Soul divine.   60
Under every grief & pine
Runs a joy with silken twine.

The Babe is more than Swadling Bands;
Throughout all these Human Lands
Tools were made, & Born were hands,   65
Every Farmer understands.
Every Tear from Every Eye
Becomes a Babe in Eternity;
This is caught by Females bright,
And returned to its own delight.   70
The Bleat, the Bark, Bellow, & Roar
Are Waves that beat on Heaven's Shore.
The Babe that weeps the Rod beneath
Writes Revenge in realms of Death.
The Beggar's Rags, fluttering in Air,   75
Does to Rags the Heavens tear.
The Soldier, armed with Sword & Gun,
Palsied strikes the Summer's Sun.
The poor Man's Farthing is worth more
Than all the Gold on Afric's Shore.   80
One Mite wrung from the Lab'rer's hands
Shall buy & sell the Miser's Lands;
Or, if protected from on high,
Does that whole Nation sell & buy.
He who mocks the Infant's Faith   85
Shall be mocked in Age & Death.
He who shall teach the Child to Doubt
The rotting Grave shall ne'er get out.
He who respects the Infant's faith
Triumphs over Hell & Death.   90
The Child's Toys and the Old Man's Reasons
Are the Fruits of the Two Seasons.
The Questioner, who sits so sly,
Shall never know how to Reply.
He who replies to words of Doubt   95
Doth put the Light of Knowledge out.
The Strongest Poison ever known
Came from Caesar's Laurel Crown.
Naught can Deform the Human Race
Like to the Armour's iron brace.   100
When Gold and Gems adorn the Plow
To peaceful Arts shall Envy bow.
A Riddle, or the Cricket's Cry,
Is to Doubt a fit Reply.

The Emmet's Inch & Eagle's Mile 105
Make Lame Philosophy to smile.
He who Doubts from what he sees
Will ne'er Believe, do what you Please.
If the Sun & Moon should Doubt,
They'd immediately Go Out. 110
To be in a Passion you Good may do,
But no Good if a Passion is in you.
The Whore & Gambler, by the State
Licensed, build that Nation's Fate.
The Harlot's cry from Street to Street 115
Shall weave Old England's winding Sheet.
The Winner's shout, the Loser's Curse,
Dance before dead England's Hearse.
Every Night and every Morn
Some to Misery are Born. 120
Every Morn and every Night
Some are Born to Sweet Delight.
Some are Born to Sweet Delight,
Some are Born to Endless Night.
We are led to Believe a Lie 125
When we see not Through the Eye,
Which was Born in a Night to perish in a Night,
When the Soul slept in Beams of Light.
God appears, & God is light,
To those poor souls who dwell in Night, 130
But does a Human Form Display
To those who Dwell in Realms of Day.

ROBERT BURNS (1759–1796)

SCOTS WHA HAE

Scots, wha hae wi' Wallace bled,
Scots, wham Bruce has aften led;
Welcome to your gory bed,
   Or to victorie!
Now's the day, and now's the hour; 5
See the front o' battle lour;
See approach proud Edward's power—
   Chains and slaverie!

Wha will be a traitor knave?
Wha can fill a coward's grave?   10
Wha sae base as be a slave?
   Let him turn and flee!
Wha for Scotland's king and law
Freedom's sword will strongly draw,
Freeman stand or freeman fa',   15
   Let him follow me!

By oppression's woes and pains!
By your sons in servile chains!
We will drain our dearest veins,
   But they shall be free!   20
Lay the proud usurpers low!
Tyrants fall in every foe!
Liberty's in every blow!—
   Let us do or die!

A RED, RED ROSE

O my Luve's like a red, red rose,
   That's newly sprung in June:
O my Luve's like the melodie
   That's sweetly play'd in tune.

As fair art thou, my bonnie lass,   5
   So deep in luve am I;
And I will luve thee still, my Dear,
   Till a' the seas gang dry.

Till a' the seas gang dry, my Dear,
   And the rocks melt wi' the sun: 10
And I will luve thee still, my Dear,
   While the sands o' life shall run.

And fare thee weel, my only Luve!
   And fare thee weel, awhile!
And I will come again, my Luve,   15
   Tho' it were ten thousand mile!

AE FOND KISS

Ae fond kiss, and then we sever!
Ae farewell, and then forever!
Deep in heart-wrung tears I'll pledge thee;
Warring sighs and groans I'll wage thee.
Who shall say that Fortune grieves him 5
While the star of hope she leaves him?
Me, nae cheerfu' twinkle lights me,
Dark despair around benights me.

I'll ne'er blame my partial fancy;
Naething could resist my Nancy: 10
But to see her was to love her,
Love but her and love forever.
Had we never loved sae kindly,
Had we never loved sae blindly,
Never met, or never parted, 15
We had ne'er been broken-hearted.

Fare-thee-weel, thou first and fairest!
Fare-thee-weel, thou best and dearest!
Thine be ilka joy and treasure,
Peace, enjoyment, love, and pleasure! 20
Ae fond kiss, and then we sever;
Ae farewell, alas, forever!
Deep in heart-wrung tears I'll pledge thee;
Warring sighs and groans I'll wage thee.

TO A MOUSE, ON TURNING UP HER NEST
WITH THE PLOUGH, NOVEMBER, 1785

Wee, sleekit, cow'rin', tim'rous beastie,
O what a panic's in thy breastie!
Thou need na start awa sae hasty,
   Wi' bickering brattle!
I wad be laith to rin an' chase thee 5
   Wi' murd'ring pattle!

I'm truly sorry man's dominion
Has broken Nature's social union,
An' justifies that ill opinion
        Which makes thee startle   10
At me, thy poor earth-born companion,
        An' fellow-mortal!

I doubt na, whiles, but thou may thieve;
What then? poor beastie, thou maun live!
A daimen-icker in a thrave   15
        'S a sma' request:
I'll get a blessin' wi' the lave,
        And never miss 't!

Thy wee bit housie, too, in ruin!
Its silly wa's the win's are strewin'!   20
An' naething, now, to big a new ane,
        O' foggage green!
An' bleak December's winds ensuin',
        Baith snell an' keen!

Thou saw the fields laid bare and waste,   25
An' weary winter comin' fast,
An' cozie here, beneath the blast,
        Thou thought to dwell,
Till crash! the cruel coulter past
        Out-thro' thy cell.   30

That wee bit heap o' leaves an' stibble
Has cost thee money a weary nibble!
Now thou's turn'd out, for a' thy trouble,
        But house or hald,
To thole the winter's sleety dribble,   35
        An' cranreuch cauld!

But, Mousie, thou art no thy lane,
In proving foresight may be vain:

---

15. **Daimen-icker in a thrave:** a few ears out of the sheaf
17. **Lave:** leavings
21. **Big:** build
24. **Snell:** bitter
36. **Cranreuch:** hoar-frost

The best laid schemes o' mice an' men
      Gang aft a-gley,   40
An' lea'e us nought but grief an' pain
      For promis'd joy.

Still thou art blest compar'd wi' me!
The present only toucheth thee:
But oh! I backward cast my e'e   45
      On prospects drear!
An' forward tho' I canna see,
      I guess an' fear!

40. **A-gley**: askew

JOHN BARLEYCORN

A Ballad

There were three Kings into the east
    Three Kings both great and high,
And they hae sworn a solemn oath
    John Barleycorn should die.

They took a plough and ploughed him down,   5
    Put clods upon his head,
And they hae sworn a solemn oath
    John Barleycorn was dead.

But the cheerfu' Spring came kindly on,
    And show'rs began to fall;
John Barleycorn got up again,   10
    And sore surprised them all.

The sultry suns of Summer came,
    And he grew thick and strong,
His head weel armed wi' pointed spears,   15
    That no one should him wrong.

The sober Autumn entered mild,
    When he grew wan and pale;
His bending joints and drooping head
    Showed he began to fail.   20

His colour sickened more and more,
 He faded into age;
And then his enemies began
 To shew their deadly rage.

They've ta'en a weapon, long and sharp,   25
 And cut him by the knee;
Then tied him fast upon a cart,
 Like a rogue for forgerie.

They laid him down upon his back,
 And cudgelled him full sore;   30
They hung him up before the storm,
 And turned him o'er and o'er.

They fillèd up a darksome pit
 With water to the brim,
They heavèd in John Barleycorn,   35
 There let him sink or swim.

They laid him out upon the floor,
 To work him further woe,
And still, as signs of life appeared,
 They tossed him to and fro.   40

They wasted, o'er a scorching flame,
 The marrow of his bones;
But a miller used him worst of all,
 For he crushed him between two stones.

And they hae ta'en his very heart's blood,   45
 And drank it round and round;
And still the more and more they drank,
 Their joy did more abound.

John Barleycorn was a hero bold,
 Of noble enterprise,   50
For if you do but taste his blood,
 'Twill make your courage rise;

'Twill make a man forget his woe;
 'Twill heighten all his joy:

'Twill make the widow's heart to sing,   55
   Tho' the tear were in her eye.

Then let us toast John Barleycorn,
   Each man a glass in hand;
And may his great posterity
   Ne'er fail in old Scotland.   60

TO A LOUSE, ON SEEING ONE
ON A LADY'S BONNET AT CHURCH

   Ha! where ye gaun, ye crowlan ferlie!
Your impudence protects you sairly:
I canna say but ye strunt rarely,
       Owre gawze and lace;
Tho' faith, I fear ye dine but sparely,   5
       On sic a place.

   Ye ugly, creepan, blastet wonner,
Detested, shunn'd, by saunt an' sinner,
How daur ye set your fit upon her,
       Sae fine a Lady!   10
Gae somewhere else and seek your dinner,
       On some poor body.

   Swith, in some beggar's haffet squattle;
There ye may creep, and sprawl, and sprattle,
Wi' ither kindred, jumping cattle,   15
       In shoals and nations;
Whare horn nor bane ne'er daur unsettle,
       Your thick plantations.

   Now haud you there, ye're out o' sight,
Below the fatt'rels, snug and tight,   20
Na faith ye yet! ye'll no be right,
       Till ye've got on it,
The vera tapmost, towrin height
       O' Miss's bonnet.

1. **Ferlie:** wonder   13. **Haffet:** temple

My sooth! right bauld ye set your nose out, 25
As plump an' gray as onie grozet:
O for some rank, mercurial rozet,
   Or fell, red smeddum,
I'd gie you sic a hearty dose o't,
   Wad dress your droddum! 30

I wad na been surpriz'd to spy
You on an auld wife's flainen toy;
Or aiblins some bit duddie boy,
   On's wylecoat;
But Miss'i fine Lunardi, fye! 35
   How daur ye do't?

O Jenny dinna toss your head,
An' set your beauties a' abread!
Ye little ken what cursed speed
   The blastie's makin! 40
Thae winks and finger-ends, I dread,
   Are notice takin!

O wad some Pow'r the giftie gie us
To see oursels as others see us!
It wad frae monie a blunder free us 45
   An' foolish notion:
What airs in dress an' gait wad lea'e us,
   And ev'n Devotion!

26. **Grozet:** gooseberry   32. **Fainen:** flannel
27. **Rozet:** rosin   **Toy:** old-fashioned head-dress
28. **Smeddum:** powder   33. **Aiblins:** perhaps
30. **Droddum:** breech

ADDRESS TO THE UNCO GUID, OR THE
RIGIDLY RIGHTEOUS

My son, these maxims make a rule,
 And lump them ay thegither:
The rigid righteous is a fool,
 The rigid wise anither;
The cleanest corn that e'er was dight,
 May hae some pyles o' caff in;
So ne'er a fellow-creature slight
 For random fits o' daffin.
     Solomon. *Eccles.*, vii, 16.

O ye wha are sae guid yoursel,
   Sae pious and sae holy,
Ye've nought to do but mark and tell
   Your neibor's fauts and folly!
Whase life is like a weel-gaun mill,   5
   Supplied wi' store o' water;
The heapet happer's ebbing still,
   And still the clap plays clatter.

Hear me, ye venerable core,
   As counsel for poor mortals,   10
That frequent pass douce Wisdom's door,
   For glaikit Folly's portals;
I, for their thoughtless, careless sakes,
   Would here propone defenses—
Their donsie tricks, their black mistakes,   15
   Their failings and mischances.

Ye see your state wi' theirs compared,
   And shudder at the niffer;
But cast a moment's fair regard—
   What maks the mighty differ?   20
Discount what scant occasion gave,
   That purity ye pride in,
And (what's aft mair than a' the lave)
   Your better art o' hidin'.

Think, when your castigated pulse   25
   Gies now and then a wallop,
What ragings must his veins convulse,
   That still eternal gallop!
Wi' wind and tide fair i' your tail,
   Right on ye scud your seaway;   30
But in the teeth o' baith to sail,
   It makes an unco leeway.

See Social-life and Glee sit down,
   All joyous and unthinking,
Till, quite transmogrified, they're grown   35
   Debauchery and Drinking.
O would they stay to calculate
   Th' eternal consequences;

Or your more dreaded hell to state,
   Damnation of expenses!   40

Ye high, exalted, virtuous Dames,
   Tied up in godly laces,
Before ye gie poor Frailty names,
   Suppose a change o' cases;
A dear loved lad, convenience snug,   45
   A treacherous inclination—
But, let me whisper i' your lug,
   Ye're aiblins nae temptation.

Then gently scan your brother man,
   Still gentler sister woman;
Though they may gang a kennin wrang,   50
   To step aside is human.
One point must still be greatly dark,
   The moving Why they do it;
And just as lamely can ye mark   55
   How far perhaps they rue it.

Who made the heart, 'tis He alone
   Decidedly can try us;
He knows each chord, its various tone,
   Each spring its various bias.   60
Then at the balance let's be mute,
   We never can adjust it;
What's done we partly may compute,
   But know not what's resisted.

PART FIVE

The Romantic Period

WILLIAM WORDSWORTH
(1770–1850)

THE DAFFODILS

I wandered lonely as a cloud
That floats on high o'er vales and hills,
When all at once I saw a crowd,
A host of golden daffodils;
Beside the lake, beneath the trees,   5
Fluttering and dancing in the breeze.

Continuous as the stars that shine
And twinkle on the milky way,
They stretched in never-ending line
Along the margin of a bay: 10
Ten thousand saw I at a glance,
Tossing their heads in sprightly dance.

The waves beside them danced; but they
Out-did the sparkling waves in glee.
A poet could not but be gay,   15
In such a jocund company:
I gazed—and gazed—but little thought
What wealth the show to me had brought:

For oft, when on my couch I lie
In vacant or in pensive mood,   20
They flash upon that inward eye
Which is the bliss of solitude;
And then my heart with pleasure fills,
And dances with the daffodils.

THE SOLITARY REAPER

Behold her, single in the field,
Yon solitary Highland Lass!
Reaping and singing by herself;
Stop here, or gently pass!
Alone she cuts and binds the grain,   5
And sings a melancholy strain;
O listen! for the Vale profound
Is overflowing with the sound.

No Nightingale did ever chant
More welcome notes to weary bands   10
Of travellers in some shady haunt,
Among Arabian sands:
A voice so thrilling ne'er was heard
In spring-time from the Cuckoo-bird,
Breaking the silence of the seas   15
Among the farthest Hebrides.

Will no one tell me what she sings?—
Perhaps the plaintive numbers flow
For old, unhappy, far-off things,
And battles long ago: 20
Or is it some more humble lay,
Familiar matter of to-day?
Some natural sorrow, loss, or pain,
That has been, and may be again?

Whate'er the theme, the maiden sang   25
As if her song could have no ending;
I saw her singing at her work,
And o'er the sickle bending;—
I listened, motionless and still;
And, as I mounted up the hill,   30
The music in my heart I bore
Long after it was heard no more.

TO A BUTTERFLY

I've watched you now a full half-hour,
Self-pois'd upon that yellow flower;
And, little Butterfly, indeed
I know not if you sleep or feed.
How motionless!—not frozen seas   5
More motionless; and then
What joy awaits you, when the breeze
Hath found you out among the trees,
And calls you forth again!

This plot of Orchard-ground is ours;   10
My trees they are, my Sister's flowers;
Here rest your wings when they are weary;
Here lodge as in a sanctuary.
Come often to us, fear no wrong;
Sit near us on the bough—   15
We'll talk of sunshine and of song,
And summer days when we were young;
Sweet childish days, that were as long
As twenty days are now.

STEPPING WESTWARD

While my Fellow-traveller and I were walking by the side of Loch
Katrine, one fine evening after sunset, in our road to a Hut where, in the
course of our Tour, we had been hospitably entertained some weeks before,
we met, in one of the loneliest parts of that solitary region, two well-dressed
Women, one of whom said to us, by way of greeting, "What, you are stepping westward?"

"What, you are stepping westward?"—"Yea."
—'T would be a wildish destiny,
If we, who thus together roam
In a strange Land, and far from home,
Were in this place the guests of Chance: 5
Yet who would stop, or fear to advance,
Though home or shelter he had none,
With such a sky to lead him on?

The dewy ground was dark and cold;
Behind, all gloomy to behold;   10

And stepping westward seemed to be
A kind of heavenly destiny:
I liked the greeting; 'twas a sound
Of something without place or bound;
And seemed to give me spiritual right   15
To travel through that region bright.

The voice was soft, and she who spake
Was walking by her native lake:
The salutation had to me
The very sound of courtesy: 20
Its power was felt; and while my eye
Was fixed upon the glowing sky,
The echo of the voice enwrought
A human sweetness with the thought
Of travelling through the world that lay   25
Before me in my endless way.

LUCY GRAY; OR, SOLITUDE

Oft I had heard of Lucy Gray:
And, when I crossed the wild,
I chanced to see at break of day
The solitary child.

No mate, no comrade Lucy knew;   5
She dwelt on a wide moor,
—The sweetest thing that ever grew
Beside a human door!

You yet may spy the fawn at play,
The hare upon the green;   10
But the sweet face of Lucy Gray
Will never more be seen.

"To-night will be a stormy night—
You to the town must go;
And take a lantern, Child, to light   15
Your mother through the snow."

"That, Father! will I gladly do:
'Tis scarcely afternoon—
The minster-clock has just struck two,
And yonder is the moon!"   20

At this the father raised his hook,
And snapped a faggot-band;
He plied his work;—and Lucy took
The lantern in her hand.

Not blither is the mountain roe: 25
With many a wanton stroke
Her feet disperse the powdery snow,
That rises up like smoke.

The storm came on before its time:
She wandered up and down;   30
And many a hill did Lucy climb:
But never reached the town.

The wretched parents all that night
Went shouting far and wide;
But there was neither sound nor sight   35
To serve them for a guide.

At daybreak on a hill they stood
That overlooked the moor;
And thence they saw the bridge of wood,
A furlong from their door.   40

They wept—and, turning homeward, cried,
"In heaven we all shall meet";
—When in the snow the mother spied
The print of Lucy's feet.

Then downwards from the steep hill's edge   45
They tracked the footmarks small;
And through the broken hawthorn hedge,
And by the long stone-wall;

And then an open field they crossed:
The marks were still the same;   50

They tracked them on, nor ever lost;
And to the bridge they came.

They followed from the snowy bank
Those footmarks, one by one,
Into the middle of the plank;   55
And further there were none!

—Yet some maintain that to this day
She is a living child;
That you may see sweet Lucy Gray
Upon the lonesome wild.   60

O'er rough and smooth she trips along,
And never looks behind;
And sings a solitary song
That whistles in the wind.

THREE YEARS SHE GREW

Three years she grew in sun and shower,
Then Nature said, "A lovelier flower
On earth was never sown;
This child I to myself will take;
She shall be mine, and I will make   5
A lady of my own.

"Myself will to my darling be
Both law and impulse: and with me
The girl, in rock and plain,
In earth and heaven, in glade and bower,   10
Shall feel an overseeing power
To kindle or restrain.

"She shall be sportive as the fawn
That wild with glee across the lawn
Or up the mountain springs;   15
And hers shall be the breathing balm,
And hers the silence and the calm
Of mute insensate things.

"The floating clouds their state shall lend
To her; for her the willow bend; 20
Nor shall she fail to see
Even in the motions of the storm
Grace that shall mold the maiden's form
By silent sympathy.

"The stars of midnight shall be dear 25
To her; and she shall lean her ear
In many a secret place
Where rivulets dance their wayward round,
And beauty born of murmuring sound
Shall pass into her face. 30

"And vital feelings of delight
Shall rear her form to stately height,
Her virgin bosom swell;
Such thoughts to Lucy I will give
While she and I together live 35
Here in this happy dell."

Thus Nature spake.—The work was done.—
How soon my Lucy's race was run!
She died, and left to me
This heath, this calm and quiet scene; 40
The memory of what has been,
And never more will be.

A SLUMBER DID MY SPIRIT SEAL

A slumber did my spirit seal;
    I had no human fears:
She seem'd a thing that could not feel
    The touch of earthly years.

No motion has she now, no force;
    She neither hears nor sees;
Roll'd round in earth's diurnal course,
    With rocks, and stones, and trees.

ODE

Intimations of Immortality from Recollections of Early Childhood

I

There was a time when meadow, grove, and stream,
The earth, and every common sight,
    To me did seem
    Apparelled in celestial light,
The glory and the freshness of a dream.   5
It is not now as it hath been of yore;—
    Turn wheresoe'er I may,
      By night or day,
The things which I have seen I now can see no more.

II

    The Rainbow comes and goes,   10
    And lovely is the Rose;
    The Moon doth with delight
Look round her when the heavens are bare;
    Waters on a starry night
    Are beautiful and fair;   15
    The sunshine is a glorious birth;
    But yet I know, where'er I go,
That there hath past away a glory from the earth.

III

Now, while the birds thus sing a joyous song,
    And while the young lambs bound   20
      As to the tabor's sound,
To me alone there came a thought of grief:
A timely utterance gave that thought relief,
    And I again am strong:
The cataracts blow their trumpets from the steep;   25
No more shall grief of mine the season wrong;
I hear the Echoes through the mountains throng,
The Winds come to me from the fields of sleep,
    And all the earth is gay;
      Land and sea   30

Give themselves up to jollity,
  And with the heart of May
Doth every Beast keep holiday;—
  Thou Child of Joy,
Shout round me, let me hear thy shouts, thou
    happy Shepherd-boy!   35

IV

Ye blessed Creatures, I have heard the call
  Ye to each other make; I see
The heavens laugh with you in your jubilee;
  My heart is at your festival,
    My head hath its coronal,   40
The fulness of your bliss, I feel—I feel it all.
      Oh evil day! if I were sullen
      While Earth herself is adorning,
        This sweet May-morning,
      And the Children are culling   45
        On every side,
      In a thousand valleys far and wide,
      Fresh flowers; while the sun shines warm,
And the Babe leaps up on his Mother's arm:—
      I hear, I hear, with joy I hear!   50
      —But there's a Tree, of many, one,
A single Field which I have looked upon,
Both of them speak of something that is gone;
        The Pansy at my feet
        Doth the same tale repeat: 55
Whither is fled the visionary gleam?
Where is it now, the glory and the dream?

V

Our birth is but a sleep and a forgetting:
The Soul that rises with us, our life's Star,
      Hath had elsewhere its setting,   60
        And cometh from afar:
      Not in entire forgetfulness,
      And not in utter nakedness,
But trailing clouds of glory do we come
        From God, who is our home: 65
Heaven lies about us in our infancy!

Shades of the prison-house begin to close
    Upon the growing Boy,
But He beholds the light, and whence it flows,
    He sees it in his joy;   70
The Youth, who daily farther from the east
    Must travel, still is Nature's Priest,
    And by the vision splendid
    Is on his way attended;
At length the Man perceives it die away,   75
And fade into the light of common day.

VI

Earth fills her lap with pleasures of her own;
Yearnings she hath in her own natural kind,
And, even with something of a Mother's mind,
    And no unworthy aim,   80
    The homely Nurse doth all she can
To make her Foster-child, her Inmate Man,
    Forget the glories he hath known,
And that imperial palace whence he came.

VII

Behold the Child among his new-born blisses,   85
A six years' Darling of a pigmy size!
See, where 'mid work of his own hand he lies,
Fretted by sallies of his mother's kisses,
With light upon him from his father's eyes!
See, at his feet, some little plan or chart,   90
Some fragment from his dream of human life,
Shaped by himself with newly-learnèd art;
    A wedding or a festival,
    A mourning or a funeral;
        And this hath now his heart,   95
    And unto this he frames his song:
        Then will he fit his tongue
To dialogues of business, love, or strife;
    But it will not be long
    Ere this be thrown aside,   100
    And with new joy and pride
The little Actor cons another part;

Filling from time to time his "humorous stage"
With all the Persons, down to palsied Age,
That Life brings with her in her equipage;   105
    As if his whole vocation
    Were endless imitation.

VIII

Thou, whose exterior semblance doth belie
    Thy Soul's immensity;
Thou best Philosopher, who yet dost keep   110
Thy heritage, thou Eye among the blind,
That, deaf and silent, read'st the eternal deep,
Haunted for ever by the eternal mind,—
    Mighty Prophet! Seer blest!
    On whom those truths do rest,   115
Which we are toiling all our lives to find,
In darkness lost, the darkness of the grave;
Thou, over whom thy Immortality
Broods like the Day, a Master o'er a Slave,
A Presence which is not to be put by;   120
    To whom the grave
Is but a lonely bed without the sense or sight
    Of day or the warm light,
A place of thought where we in waiting lie;
Thou little Child, yet glorious in the might   125
Of heaven-born freedom on thy being's height,
Why with such earnest pains dost thou provoke
The years to bring the inevitable yoke,
Thus blindly with thy blessedness at strife?
Full soon thy Soul shall have her earthly freight,   130
And custom lie upon thee with a weight,
Heavy as frost, and deep almost as life!

IX

    O joy! that in our embers
    Is something that doth live,
    That nature yet remembers   135
    What was so fugitive!
The thought of our past years in me doth breed
Perpetual benediction: not indeed
For that which is most worthy to be blest—

Delight and liberty, the simple creed   140
Of Childhood, whether busy or at rest,
With new-fledged hope still fluttering in his breast:--
    Not for these I raise
    The song of thanks and praise;
    But for those obstinate questionings   145
    Of sense and outward things,
    Fallings from us, vanishings;
    Blank misgivings of a Creature
Moving about in worlds not realised,
High instincts before which our mortal Nature   150
Did tremble like a guilty Thing surprised:
    But for those first affections,
    Those shadowy recollections,
    Which, be they what they may,
Are yet the fountain-light of all our day,   155
Are yet a master-light of all our seeing;
    Uphold us, cherish, and have power to make
Our noisy years seem moments in the being
Of the eternal Silence: truths that wake,
    To perish never: 160
Which neither listlessness, nor mad endeavour,
    Nor Man nor Boy,
Nor all that is at enmity with joy,
Can utterly abolish or destroy!
    Hence in a season of calm weather   165
    Though inland far we be,
Our Souls have sight of that immortal sea
    Which brought us hither,
    Can in a moment travel thither,
And see the Children sport upon the shore,   170
And hear the mighty waters rolling evermore.

X

Then sing, ye Birds, sing, sing a joyous song!
    And let the young Lambs bound
    As to the tabor's sound!
We in thought will join your throng,   175
    Ye that pipe and ye that play,
    Ye that through your hearts to-day
    Feel the gladness of the May!

What though the radiance which was once so bright
Be now for ever taken from my sight,   180
    Though nothing can bring back the hour
Of splendour in the grass, of glory in the flower;
       We will grieve not, rather find
       Strength in what remains behind;
       In the primal sympathy   185
       Which having been must ever be;
       In the soothing thoughts that spring
       Out of human suffering;
       In the faith that looks through death,
In years that bring the philosophic mind.   190

XI

And O, ye Fountains, Meadows, Hills, and Groves,
Forebode not any severing of our loves!
Yet in my heart of hearts I feel your might;
I only have relinquished one delight
To live beneath your more habitual sway.   195
I love the Brooks which down their channels fret,
Even more than when I tripped lightly as they;
The innocent brightness of a new-born Day
      Is lovely yet;
The Clouds that gather round the setting sun   200
Do take a sober colouring from an eye
That hath kept watch o'er man's mortality;
Another race hath been, and other palms are won.
Thanks to the human heart by which we live,
Thanks to its tenderness, its joys, and fears,   205
To me the meanest flower that blows can give
Thoughts that do often lie too deep for tears.

LINES COMPOSED A FEW MILES ABOVE
TINTERN ABBEY

Five years have past; five summers, with the length
Of five long winters! and again I hear
These waters, rolling from their mountain-springs
With a soft inland murmur.—Once again
Do I behold these steep and lofty cliffs,   5

That on a wild secluded scene impress
Thoughts of more deep seclusion, and connect
The landscape with the quiet of the sky.
The day is come when I again repose
Here, under this dark sycamore, and view   10
These plots of cottage-ground, these orchard-tufts,
Which at this season, with their unripe fruits,
Are clad in one green hue, and lose themselves
'Mid groves and copses. Once again I see
These hedge-rows, hardly hedge-rows, little lines   15
Of sportive wood run wild: these pastoral farms,
Green to the very door; and wreaths of smoke
Sent up, in silence, from among the trees!
With some uncertain notice, as might seem
Of vagrant dwellers in the houseless woods,   20
Or of some Hermit's cave, where by his fire
The Hermit sits alone.
               These beauteous forms,
Through a long absence, have not been to me
As is a landscape to a blind man's eye:
But oft, in lonely rooms, and 'mid the din   25
Of towns and cities, I have owed to them
In hours of weariness, sensations sweet,
Felt in the blood, and felt along the heart;
And passing even into my purer mind,
With tranquil restoration:—feelings too   30
Of unremembered pleasure: such, perhaps,
As have no slight or trivial influence
On that best portion of a good man's life,
His little, nameless, unremembered acts
Of kindness and of love. Nor less, I trust,   35
To them I may have owed another gift,
Of aspect more sublime; that blessed mood,
In which the burden of the mystery,
In which the heavy and the weary weight
Of all this unintelligible world,   40
Is lightened:—that serene and blessed mood,
In which the affections gently lead us on,—
Until, the breath of this corporeal frame
And even the motion of our human blood
Almost suspended, we are laid asleep   45
In body, and become a living soul:

While with an eye made quiet by the power
Of harmony, and the deep power of joy,
We see into the life of things.
                                    If this
Be but a vain belief, yet, oh!—how oft—   50
In darkness and amid the many shapes
Of joyless daylight; when the fretful stir
Unprofitable, and the fever of the world,
Have hung upon the beatings of my heart—
How oft, in spirit, have I turned to thee,   55
O sylvan Wye! thou wanderer thro' the woods,
How often has my spirit turned to thee!
    And now, with gleams of half extinguished thought,
With many recognitions dim and faint,
And somewhat of a sad perplexity,   60
The picture of the mind revives again:
While here I stand, not only with the sense
Of present pleasure, but with pleasing thoughts
That in this moment there is life and food
For future years. And so I dare to hope,   65
Though changed, no doubt, from what I was when first
I came among these hills; when like a roe
I bounded o'er the mountains, by the sides
Of the deep rivers, and the lonely streams,
Wherever nature led: more like a man   70
Flying from something that he dreads, than one
Who sought the thing he loved. For nature then
(The coarser pleasures of my boyish days,
And their glad animal movements all gone by)
To me was all in all.—I cannot paint   75
What then I was. The sounding cataract
Haunted me like a passion: the tall rock,
The mountain, and the deep and gloomy wood,
Their colours and their forms, were then to me
An appetite; a feeling and a love,   80
That had no need of a remoter charm,
By thought supplied, nor any interest
Unborrowed from the eye.—That time is past,
And all its aching joys are now no more,
And all its dizzy raptures. Not for this   85
Faint I, nor mourn nor murmur; other gifts
Have followed; for such loss, I would believe,

Abundant recompense. For I have learned
To look on nature, not as in the hour
Of thoughtless youth; but hearing oftentimes   90
The still, sad music of humanity,
Nor harsh nor grating, though of ample power
To chasten and subdue. And I have felt
A presence that disturbs me with the joy
Of elevated thoughts; a sense sublime   95
Of something far more deeply interfused,
Whose dwelling is the light of setting suns,
And the round ocean, and the living air,
And the blue sky, and in the mind of man;
A motion and a spirit, that impels   100
All thinking things, all objects of all thought,
And rolls through all things. Therefore am I still
A lover of the meadows and the woods,
And mountains; and of all that we behold
From this green earth; of all the mighty world   105
Of eye, and ear,—both what they half create,
And what perceive; well pleased to recognize
In nature and the language of the sense,
The anchor of my purest thoughts, the nurse,
The guide, the guardian of my heart, and soul   110
Of all my moral being.
                Nor perchance,
If I were not thus taught, should I the more
Suffer my genial spirits to decay:
For thou art with me here upon the banks
Of this fair river; thou my dearest Friend,   115
My dear, dear Friend; and in thy voice I catch
The language of my former heart, and read
My former pleasures in the shooting lights
Of thy wild eyes. Oh! yet a little while
May I behold in thee what I was once,   120
My dear, dear Sister! and this prayer I make,
Knowing that Nature never did betray
The heart that loved her; 'tis her privilege,
Through all the years of this our life, to lead
From joy to joy: for she can so inform   125
The mind that is within us, so impress
With quietness and beauty, and so feed
With lofty thoughts, that neither evil tongues,

Rash judgments, nor the sneers of selfish men,
Nor greetings where no kindness is, nor all   130
The dreary intercourse of daily life,
Shall e'er prevail against us, or disturb
Our cheerful faith that all which we behold
Is full of blessings. Therefore let the moon
Shine on thee in thy solitary walk;   135
And let the misty mountain-winds be free
To blow against thee: and, in after years,
When these wild ecstasies shall be matured
Into a sober pleasure; when thy mind
Shall be a mansion for all lovely forms,   140
Thy memory be as a dwelling-place
For all sweet sounds and harmonies; oh! then,
If solitude, or fear, or pain, or grief,
Should be thy portion, with what healing thoughts
Of tender joy wilt thou remember me,   145
And these my exhortations! Nor, perchance—
If I should be where I no more can hear
Thy voice, nor catch from thy wild eyes these gleams
Of past existence—wilt thou then forget
That on the banks of this delightful stream   150
We stood together; and that I, so long
A worshipper of Nature, hither came
Unwearied in that service: rather say
With warmer love—oh! with far deeper zeal
Of holier love. Nor wilt thou then forget,   155
That after many wanderings, many years
Of absence, these steep woods and lofty cliffs,
And this green pastoral landscape, were to me
More dear, both for themselves and for thy sake!

THE WORLD IS TOO MUCH WITH US

The world is too much with us; late and soon,
Getting and spending, we lay waste our powers:
Little we see in Nature that is ours;
We have given our hearts away, a sordid boon!
This Sea that bares her bosom to the moon;
The winds that will be howling at all hours,
And are up-gathered now like sleeping flowers;

For this, for everything, we are out of tune;
It moves us not.—Great God! I'd rather be
A Pagan suckled in a creed outworn;
So might I, standing on this pleasant lea,
Have glimpses that would make me less forlorn;
Have sight of Proteus rising from the sea;
Or hear old Triton blow his wreathèd horn.

UPON WESTMINSTER BRIDGE

Earth has not anything to show more fair:
Dull would he be of soul who could pass by
A sight so touching in its majesty:
This City now doth, like a garment, wear
The beauty of the morning; silent, bare,
Ships, towers, domes, theatres, and temples lie
Open unto the fields, and to the sky;
All bright and glittering in the smokeless air.
Never did sun more beautifully steep
In his first splendour valley, rock, or hill;
Ne'er saw I, never felt, a calm so deep!
The river glideth at his own sweet will:
Dear God! the very houses seem asleep;
And all that mighty heart is lying still!

LONDON, 1802

Milton! thou shouldst be living at this hour;
England hath need of thee; she is a fen
Of stagnant waters: altar, sword, and pen,
Fireside, the heroic wealth of hall and bower,
Have forfeited their ancient English dower
Of inward happiness. We are selfish men;
Oh! raise us up, return to us again;
And give us manners, virtue, freedom, power.
Thy soul was like a Star, and dwelt apart:
Thou hadst a voice whose sound was like the sea:
Pure as the naked heavens, majestic, free,
So didst thou travel on life's common way,
In cheerful godliness; and yet thy heart
The lowliest duties on herself did lay.

THOUGHT OF A BRITON ON THE SUBJUGATION
OF SWITZERLAND

Two Voices are there; one is of the sea,
One of the mountains; each a mighty Voice:
In both from age to age thou didst rejoice,
They were thy chosen music, Liberty!
There came a Tyrant, and with holy glee
Thou fought'st against him; but hast vainly striven:
Thou from thy Alpine holds at length art driven,
Where not a torrent murmurs heard by thee.
Of one deep bliss thine ear hath been bereft:
Then cleave, O cleave to that which still is left;
For, high-souled Maid, what sorrow would it be
That mountain floods should thunder as before,
And ocean bellow from his rocky shore,
And neither awful Voice be heard by thee!

MUTABILITY

From low to high doth dissolution climb,
And sink from high to low, along a scale
Of awful notes, whose concord shall not fail;
A musical but melancholy chime,
Which they can hear who meddle not with crime,
Nor avarice, nor over-anxious care.
Truth fails not; but her outward forms that bear
The longest date do melt like frosty rime
That in the morning whiten'd hill and plain
And is no more; drop like the tower sublime
Of yesterday, which royally did wear
His crown of weeds, but could not even sustain
Some casual shout that broke the silent air,
Or the unimaginable touch of Time.

IT IS A BEAUTEOUS EVENING, CALM AND FREE

It is a beauteous evening, calm and free;
The holy time is quiet as a nun
Breathless with adoration; the broad sun
Is sinking down in its tranquillity;

The gentleness of heaven broods o'er the sea:
Listen! the mighty Being is awake,
And doth with his eternal motion make
A sound like thunder—everlastingly.
Dear child! dear girl! that walkest with me here,
If thou appear untouched by solemn thought,
Thy nature is not therefore less divine:
Thou liest in Abraham's bosom all the year,
And worship'st at the Temple's inner shrine,
God being with thee when we know it not.

SURPRISED BY JOY—IMPATIENT AS THE WIND

Surprised by joy—impatient as the wind—
I turned to share the transport—O! with whom
But Thee, deep buried in the silent tomb,
That spot which no vicissitude can find!
Love, faithful love, recall'd thee to my mind—
But how could I forget thee? Through what power,
Even for the least division of an hour,
Have I been so beguiled as to be blind
To my most grievous loss?—That thought's return
Was the worst pang that sorrow ever bore,
Save one, one only, when I stood forlorn,
Knowing my heart's best treasure was no more;
That neither present time nor years unborn
Could to my sight that heavenly face restore.

SIR WALTER SCOTT (1771–1832)

BONNY DUNDEE

To the Lords of Convention 'twas Claver'se who spoke,
'Ere the King's crown shall fall, there are crowns to be broke;
So let each Cavalier who loves honour and me,
Come follow the bonnet of Bonny Dundee.

Chorus

Come fill up my cup, come fill up my can, 5
Come saddle your horses, and call up your men;
Come open the West Port and let me gang free,
And it's room for the bonnets of Bonny Dundee!

Dundee he is mounted, he rides up the street,
The bells are rung backward, the drums they are beat; 10
But the Provost, douce man, said, "Just e'en let him be,
The Gude Town is weel quit of that Deil of Dundee."

"Away to the hills, to the caves, to the rocks—
Ere I own a usurper, I'll couch with the fox—
And tremble, false Whigs, in the midst of your glee, 15
You have not seen the last of my bonnet and me!"

He waved his proud hand, and the trumpets were blown,
The kettle-drums clashed, and the horsemen rode on,
Till on Ravelston's cliffs, and on Clermiston's lee,
Died away the wild war-notes of Bonny Dundee. 20

Chorus

Come fill up my cup, come fill up my can,
Come saddle the horses and call up the men,
Come open your gates, and let me gae free,
For it's up with the bonnets of Bonny Dundee.

PROUD MAISIE

Proud Maisie is in the wood,
    Walking so early;
Sweet Robin sits on the bush,
    Singing so rarely.

"Tell me, thou bonny bird, 5
    When shall I marry me?"—
"When six braw gentlemen
    Kirkward shall carry ye."

"Who makes the bridal bed,
    Birdie, say truly?"— 10

"The gray-headed sexton
    That delves the grave duly.

"The glow-worm o'er grave and stone
    Shall light thee steady.
The owl from the steeple sing,   15
    'Welcome, proud lady.'"

SAMUEL TAYLOR COLERIDGE
(1772–1834)

THE FRUIT PLUCKER

Encinctured with a twine of leaves,
That leafy twine his only dress,
A lovely Boy was plucking fruits,
By moonlight, in a wilderness.
The moon was bright, the air was free,   5
And fruits and flowers together grew
On many a shrub and many a tree:
And all put on a gentle hue,
Hanging in the shadowy air
Like a picture rich and rare.   10

It was a climate where, they say,
The night is more beloved than day.

But who that beauteous Boy beguiled,
That beauteous Boy to linger here?
Alone, by night, a little child,   15
In place so silent and so wild—
Has he no friend, no loving mother near?

KUBLA KHAN

In Xanadu did Kubla Khan
A stately pleasure-dome decree:
Where Alph, the sacred river, ran
Through caverns measureless to man

Down to a sunless sea.   5
So twice five miles of fertile ground
With walls and towers were girdled round:
And here were gardens bright with sinuous rills
Where blossomed many an incense-bearing tree;
And here were forests ancient as the hills,   10
Enfolding sunny spots of greenery.
But oh! that deep romantic chasm which slanted
Down the green hill athwart a cedarn cover!
A savage place! as holy and enchanted
As e'er beneath a waning moon was haunted   15
By woman wailing for her demon-lover!
And from this chasm, with ceaseless turmoil seething,
As if this earth in fast thick pants were breathing,
A mighty fountain momently was forced;
Amid whose swift half-intermitted burst   20
Huge fragments vaulted like rebounding hail,
Or chaffy grain beneath the thresher's flail:
And 'mid these dancing rocks at once and ever
It flung up momently the sacred river.
Five miles meandering with a mazy motion   25
Through wood and dale the sacred river ran,
Then reached the caverns measureless to man,
And sank in tumult to a lifeless ocean:
And 'mid this tumult Kubla heard from far
Ancestral voices prophesying war!   30

The shadow of the dome of pleasure
    Floated midway on the waves;
Where was heard the mingled measure
    From the fountain and the caves.
It was a miracle of rare device,   35
A sunny pleasure-dome with caves of ice!

A damsel with a dulcimer
In a vision once I saw:
It was an Abyssinian maid,
And on her dulcimer she play'd,   40
Singing of Mount Abora.
Could I revive within me
Her symphony and song,
To such a deep delight 'twould win me,

That with music loud and long,⠀⠀⠀⠀⠀⠀⠀⠀⠀45
I would build that dome in air,
That sunny dome! those caves of ice!
And all who heard should see them there,
And all should cry, Beware! Beware!
His flashing eyes, his floating hair!⠀⠀⠀⠀⠀⠀50
Weave a circle round him thrice,
And close your eyes with holy dread,
For he on honey-dew hath fed,
And drunk the milk of Paradise.

THE RIME OF THE ANCIENT MARINER

PART THE FIRST

*An ancient
Mariner
meeteth three
Gallants bidden
to a wedding-
feast, and de-
taineth one.*

It is an ancient Mariner,
And he stoppeth one of three.
'By thy long grey beard and glittering eye,
Now wherefore stopp'st thou me?

The Bridegroom's doors are opened wide,⠀⠀⠀5
And I am next of kin;
The guests are met, the feast is set:
May'st hear the merry din.'

He holds him with his skinny hand,
'There was a ship,' quoth he.⠀⠀⠀⠀⠀⠀⠀⠀⠀10
'Hold off! unhand me, greybeard loon!'
Eftsoons his hand dropt he.

*The Wedding-
Guest is spell-
bound by the
eye of the old
sea-faring man,
and constrained
to hear his tale.*

He holds him with his glittering eye—
The Wedding-Guest stood still,
And listens like a three years' child:⠀⠀⠀⠀15
The Mariner hath his will.

The Wedding-Guest sat on a stone:
He cannot choose but hear;
And thus spake on that ancient man,
The bright-eyed Mariner.⠀⠀⠀⠀⠀⠀⠀⠀⠀⠀20

'The ship was cheered, the harbour cleared,
Merrily did we drop
Below the kirk, below the hill,
Below the lighthouse top.

The Sun came up upon the left,   25
Out of the sea came he!
And he shone bright, and on the right
Went down into the sea.

The Mariner
tells how the
ship sailed
southward with
a good wind
and fair
weather, till it reached the line.

Higher and higher every day,
Till over the mast at noon—'   30
The Wedding-Guest here beat his breast,
For he heard the loud bassoon.

The Wedding-
Guest heareth
the bridal
music; but the Mariner continueth his tale.

The Bride hath paced into the hall,
Red as a rose is she;
Nodding their heads before her goes   35
The merry minstrelsy.

The Wedding-Guest he beat his breast,
Yet he cannot choose but hear;
And thus spake on that ancient man,
The bright-eyed Mariner.   40

'And now the storm-blast came, and he
Was tyrannous and strong:
He struck with his o'ertaking wings,
And chased us south along.

The ship drawn
by a storm
toward the
South Pole.

With sloping masts and dipping prow,   45
As who pursued with yell and blow
Still treads the shadow of his foe
And forward bends his head,
The ship drove fast, loud roared the blast,
And southward aye we fled.   50

And now there came both mist and snow
And it grew wondrous cold:
And ice, mast-high, came floating by,
As green as emerald.

The land of ice,
and of fearful
sounds, where
no living thing
was to be seen.

And through the drifts the snowy clifts   55
Did send a dismal sheen:
Nor shapes of men nor beasts we ken—
The ice was all between.

The ice was here, the ice was there,
The ice was all around: 60
It cracked and growled, and roared and howled,
Like noises in a swound!

Till a great sea-
bird, called the
Albatross, came
through the
snow-fog, and
was received
with great joy
and hospitality.

At length did cross an Albatross:
Thorough the fog it came;
As if it had been a Christian soul,   65
We hailed it in God's name.

It ate the food it ne'er had eat,
And round and round it flew.
The ice did split with a thunder-fit;
The helmsman steered us through!   70

And lo! the
Albatross
proveth a bird
of good omen,
and followeth
the ship as it
returned north-
ward through
fog and float-
ing ice.

And a good south wind sprung up behind;
The Albatross did follow,
And every day, for food or play,
Came to the mariners' hollo!

In mist or cloud, on mast or shroud,   75
It perched for vespers nine;
Whiles all the night, through fog-smoke white,
Glimmered the white moonshine.'

The ancient
Mariner inhos-
pitably killeth
the pious bird
of good omen.

'God save thee, ancient Mariner!
From the fiends that plague thee thus!—   80
Why look'st thou so?'—'With my crossbow
I shot the Albatross.

PART THE SECOND

'The Sun now rose upon the right:
Out of the sea came he,
Still hid in mist, and on the left   85
Went down into the sea.

And the good south wind still blew behind,
But no sweet bird did follow,
Nor any day for food or play
Came to the mariners' hollo!   90

And I had done a hellish thing,
And it would work 'em woe:
For all averred, I had killed the bird
That made the breeze to blow.
Ah wretch! said they, the bird to slay,   95
That made the breeze to blow!

His shipmates cry out against the ancient Mariner for killing the bird of good luck.

Nor dim nor red, like God's own head,
The glorious Sun uprist:
Then all averred, I had killed the bird
That brought the fog and mist.   100
'Twas right, said they, such birds to slay,
That bring the fog and mist.

But when the fog cleared off, they justify the same, and thus make themselves accomplices in the crime.

The fair breeze blew, the white foam flew,
The furrow followed free;
We were the first that ever burst   105
Into that silent sea.

The fair breeze continues; the ship enters the Pacific Ocean and sails northward, even till it reaches the Line.

Down dropt the breeze, the sails dropt down,
'Twas sad as sad could be;
And we did speak only to break
The silence of the sea!   110

The ship hath been suddenly becalmed.

All in a hot and copper sky,
The bloody Sun, at noon,
Right up above the mast did stand,
No bigger than the Moon.

Day after day, day after day,   115
We stuck, nor breath nor motion;
As idle as a painted ship
Upon a painted ocean.

Water, water, everywhere,
And all the boards did shrink;   120
Water, water, everywhere,
Nor any drop to drink.

And the Albatross begins to be avenged.

The very deep did rot: O Christ!
That ever this should be!
Yea, slimy things did crawl with legs   125
Upon the slimy sea.

About, about, in reel and rout
The death-fires danced at night;
The water, like a witch's oils,
Burnt green, and blue, and white.   130

A Spirit had followed them; one of the invisible inhabitants of this planet, neither

And some in dreams assurèd were
Of the Spirit that plagued us so;
Nine fathom deep he had followed us
From the land of mist and snow.

departed souls nor angels; concerning whom the learned Jew, Josephus, and the Platonic Constantinopolitan, Michael Psellus, may be consulted. They are very numerous, and there is no climate or element without one or more.

And every tongue, through utter drought,   135
Was withered at the root;
We could not speak, no more than if
We had been choked with soot.

The shipmates, in their sore distress, would fain throw the whole guilt on the ancient

Ah! well-a-day! what evil looks
Had I from old and young!   140
Instead of the cross, the Albatross
About my neck was hung.

Mariner: in sign whereof they hang the dead sea-bird round his neck.

PART THE THIRD

'There passed a weary time. Each throat
Was parched and glazed each eye.
A weary time! a weary time!   145
How glazed each weary eye!

The ancient Mariner beholdeth a sign in the element afar off.

When looking westward, I beheld
A something in the sky.

At first it seemed a little speck,
And then it seemed a mist;   150
It moved and moved, and took at last
A certain shape, I wist.

A speck, a mist, a shape, I wist!
And still it neared and neared:
As if it dodged a watersprite,   155
It plunged and tacked and veered.

With throats unslaked, with black lips baked,
We could not laugh nor wail;
Through utter drought all dumb we stood!
I bit my arm, I sucked the blood,   160
And cried, A sail! a sail!

At its nearer approach it seemeth him to be a ship; and at a dear ransom he freeth his speech from the bonds of thirst.

With throats unslaked, with black lips baked,
Agape they heard me call:
Gramercy! they for joy did grin,
And all at once their breath drew in,   165
As they were drinking all.

A flash of joy;

See! See! (I cried) she tacks no more!
Hither to work us weal;
Without a breeze, without a tide,
She steadies with upright keel!   170

And horror follows. For can it be a ship that comes onward without wind or tide?

The western wave was all a-flame.
The day was well-nigh done!
Almost upon the western wave
Rested the broad bright Sun;
When that strange shape drove suddenly   175
Betwixt us and the Sun.

And straight the Sun was flecked with bars,
(Heaven's Mother send us grace!)
As if through a dungeon-grate he peered
With broad and burning face.   180

It seemeth him but the skeleton of a ship.

Alas! (thought I, and my heart beat loud)
How fast she nears and nears!
Are those her sails that glance in the Sun,
Like restless gossameres!

Are those her ribs through which the Sun   185
Did peer, as through a grate?
And is that Woman all her crew?

And its ribs are seen as bars on the face of the setting Sun. The Spectre-

Woman and her Death-mate, and no other on board the skeleton ship.

Is that a Death? and are there two?
Is Death that woman's mate?

Like vessel, like crew!

Her lips were red, her looks were free,   190
Her locks were yellow as gold:
Her skin was as white as leprosy,
The Nightmare Life-in-Death was she,
Who thicks man's blood with cold.

Death and Life-in-Death have diced for the ship's crew, and she (the latter) winneth the ancient Mariner.

The naked hulk alongside came   195
And the twain were casting dice;
"The game is done! I've won, I've won!"
Quoth she, and whistles thrice.

No twilight within the courts of the Sun.

The Sun's rim dips; the stars rush out:
At one stride comes the dark;   200
With far-heard whisper, o'er the sea,
Off shot the spectre-bark.

We listened and looked sideways up!
Fear at my heart, as at a cup,
My life-blood seemed to sip!   205
The stars were dim, and thick the night,
The steersman's face by his lamp gleamed white;
From the sails the dew did drip—

At the rising of the Moon,

Till clomb above the eastern bar
The hornèd Moon, with one bright star   210
Within the nether tip.

One after another,

One after one, by the star-dogged Moon,
Too quick for groan or sigh,
Each turned his face with a ghastly pang,
And cursed me with his eye.   215

His shipmates drop down dead;

Four times fifty living men,
(And I heard nor sigh nor groan)
With heavy thump, a lifeless lump,
They dropped down one by one.

But Life-in-Death begins her work on the ancient Mariner.

The souls did from their bodies fly,—   220
They fled to bliss or woe!
And every soul, it passed me by,
Like the whizz of my cross-bow!'

PART THE FOURTH

'I fear thee, ancient Mariner!
I fear thy skinny hand!   225
And thou art long, and lank, and brown,
As is the ribbed sea-sand.

I fear thee and thy glittering eye,
And thy skinny hand, so brown.'—
'Fear not, fear not, thou Wedding-Guest!   230
This body dropt not down.

Alone, alone, all, all alone,
Alone on a wide wide sea!
And never a saint took pity on
My soul in agony.   235

The many men, so beautiful!
And they all dead did lie:
And a thousand thousand slimy things
Lived on; and so did I.

I looked upon the rotting sea,   240
And drew my eyes away;
I looked upon the rotting deck,
And there the dead men lay.

I looked to Heaven, and tried to pray;
But or ever a prayer had gusht,   245
A wicked whisper came, and made
My heart as dry as dust.

I closed my lids, and kept them close,
And the balls like pulses beat;
For the sky and the sea and the sea and the sky,
Lay like a load on my weary eye,   251
And the dead were at my feet.

The cold sweat melted from their limbs,
Nor rot nor reek did they;
The look with which they looked on me   255
Had never passed away.

The Wedding-Guest feareth that a spirit is talking to him;

But the ancient Mariner assureth him of his bodily life, and proceedeth to relate his horrible penance.

He despiseth the creatures of the calm.

And envieth that they should live, and so many lie dead.

But the curse liveth for him in the eye of the dead men.

An orphan's curse would drag to hell
A spirit from on high;
But oh! more horrible than that
Is a curse in a dead man's eye!   260
Seven days, seven nights, I saw that curse,
And yet I could not die.

In his loneliness and fixedness he yearneth towards the journeying Moon, and the Stars

The moving Moon went up the sky,
And nowhere did abide:
Softly she was going up,   265
And a star or two beside—

that still sojourn, yet still move onward; and everywhere the blue sky belongs to them, and is their appointed rest, and their native country and their own natural homes, which they enter unannounced, as lords that are certainly expected and yet there is a silent joy at their arrival.

Her beams bemocked the sultry main,
Like April hoar-frost spread;
But where the ship's huge shadow lay,
The charmèd water burnt away   270
A still and awful red.

By the light of the Moon he beholdeth God's creatures of the great calm.

Beyond the shadow of the ship,
I watched the water-snakes:
They moved in tracks of shining white,
And when they reared, the elfish light   275
Fell off in hoary flakes.

Within the shadow of the ship
I watched their rich attire:
Blue, glossy green, and velvet black,
They coiled and swam; and every track   280
Was a flash of golden fire.

Their beauty and their happiness.

He blesseth them in his heart.

O happy living things! no tongue
Their beauty might declare:
A spring of love gushed from my heart,
And I blessed them unaware: 285
Sure my kind saint took pity on me,
And I blessed them unaware.

The spell begins to break.

The selfsame moment I could pray;
And from my neck so free
The Albatross fell off, and sank   290
Like lead into the sea.

PART THE FIFTH

'O sleep! it is a gentle thing,
Beloved from pole to pole!
To Mary Queen the praise be given!
She sent the gentle sleep from Heaven,   295
That slid into my soul.

The silly buckets on the deck,
That had so long remained,
I dreamt that they were filled with dew;
And when I awoke, it rained.   300

By grace of the holy Mother, the ancient Mariner is refreshed with rain.

My lips were wet, my throat was cold,
My garments all were dank;
Sure I had drunken in my dreams,
And still my body drank.

I moved, and could not feel my limbs: 305
I was so light—almost
I thought that I had died in sleep,
And was a blessèd ghost.

And soon I saw a roaring wind:
It did not come anear;   310
But with its sound it shook the sails,
That were so thin and sere.

He heareth sounds and seeth strange sights and com motions in the sky and the element.

The upper air burst into life!
And a hundred fire-flags sheen,
To and fro they were hurried about!   315
And to and fro, and in and out,
The wan stars danced between.

And the coming wind did roar more loud,
And the sails did sigh like sedge;
And the rain poured down from one black cloud;
The Moon was at its edge.   321

The thick black cloud was cleft, and still
The Moon was at its side:

Like waters shot from some high crag,
The lightning fell with never a jag,   325
A river steep and wide.

The bodies of
the ship's crew
are inspired,
and the ship
moves on;

The loud wind never reached the ship,
Yet now the ship moved on!
Beneath the lightning and the Moon
The dead men gave a groan.   33c

They groaned, they stirred, they all uprose,
Nor spake, nor moved their eyes;
It had been strange, even in a dream,
To have seen those dead men rise.

The helmsman steered, the ship moved on;   335
Yet never a breeze up blew;
The mariners all 'gan work the ropes,
Where they were wont to do;
They raised their limbs like lifeless tools—
We were a ghastly crew.   340

The body of my brother's son
Stood by me, knee to knee:
The body and I pulled at one rope,
But he said nought to me.'

'I fear thee, ancient Mariner!'   345
'Be calm, thou Wedding-Guest!

but not by the
souls of the
men, nor by
daemons of
earth or middle
air, but by a
blessed troop of
angelic spirits,
sent down by
the invocation
of the guardian
saint.

'Twas not those souls that fled in pain,
Which to their corses came again,
But a troop of spirits blest:

For when it dawned—they dropt their arms, 350
And clustered round the mast;
Sweet sounds rose slowly through their mouths,
And from their bodies passed.

Around, around, flew each sweet sound,
Then darted to the Sun;   355
Slowly the sounds came back again,
Now mixed, now one by one.

Sometimes a-dropping from the sky
I heard the skylark sing;
Sometimes all little birds that are,   360
How they seemed to fill the sea and air
With their sweet jargoning!

And now 'twas like all instruments,
Now like a lonely flute;
And now it is an angel's song,   365
That makes the Heavens be mute.

It ceased; yet still the sails made on
A pleasant noise till noon,
A noise like of a hidden brook
In the leafy month of June,   370
That to the sleeping woods all night
Singeth a quiet tune.

Till noon we quietly sailed on,
Yet never a breeze did breathe:
Slowly and smoothly went the ship,   375
Moved onward from beneath.

Under the keel nine fathom deep,
From the land of mist and snow,
The Spirit slid: and it was he
That made the ship to go.   380
The sails at noon left off their tune,
And the ship stood still also.

The lonesome Spirit from the South Pole carries on the ship as far as the Line, in obedience to the angelic troop, but still requireth vengeance.

The Sun, right up above the mast,
Had fixed her to the ocean:
But in a minute she 'gan stir,   385
With a short uneasy motion—
Backwards and forwards half her length
With a short uneasy motion.

Then, like a pawing horse let go,
She made a sudden bound: 390
It flung the blood into my head,
And I fell down in a swound.

The Polar Spirit's fellow daemons, the invisible inhabitants of the element, take part in his wrong; and two of them relate, one to the other, that penance long and heavy for the ancient Mariner hath been accorded to the Polar Spirit, who returneth southward.

How long in that same fit I lay,
I have not to declare;
But ere my living life returned,   395
I heard and in my soul discerned
Two voices in the air.

"Is it he?" quoth one, "Is this the man?
By Him who died on cross,
With his cruel bow he laid full low   400
The harmless Albatross.

The Spirit who bideth by himself
In the land of mist and snow,
He loved the bird that loved the man
Who shot him with his bow."   405

The other was a softer voice,
As soft as honeydew:
Quoth he, "The man hath penance done,
And penance more will do."

PART THE SIXTH

First Voice

' "But tell me, tell me! speak again,   410
Thy soft response renewing—
What makes that ship drive on so fast?
What is the ocean doing?"

Second Voice

"Still as a slave before his lord,
The Ocean hath no blast;   415
His great bright eye most silently
Up to the Moon is cast—

If he may know which way to go;
For she guides him smooth or grim.
See, brother, see! how graciously   420
She looketh down on him."

First Voice

' "But why drives on that ship so fast,
Without or wave or wind?"

Second Voice

"The air is cut away before,
And closes from behind.   425

Fly, brother, fly! more high, more high!
Or we shall be belated:
For slow and slow that ship will go,
When the Mariner's trance is abated."

I woke, and we were sailing on   430
As in a gentle weather:
'Twas night, calm night, the Moon was high;
The dead men stood together.

All stood together on the deck,
For a charnel-dungeon fitter: 435
All fixed on me their stony eyes,
That in the Moon did glitter.

The pang, the curse, with which they died,
Had never passed away:
I could not draw my eyes from theirs,   440
Nor turn them up to pray.

And now this spell was snapt: once more
I viewed the ocean green,
And looked far forth, yet little saw
Of what had else been seen—   445

Like one that on a lonesome road
Doth walk in fear and dread,
And having once turned round walks on,
And turns no more his head;
Because he knows a frightful fiend   450
Doth close behind him tread.

The Mariner hath been cast into a trance; for the angelic power causeth the vessel to drive northward faster than human life could endure.

The supernatural motion is retarded; the Mariner awakes, and his penance begins anew.

The curse is finally expiated.

But soon there breathed a wind on me,
Nor sound nor motion made:
Its path was not upon the sea,
In ripple or in shade.   455

It raised my hair, it fanned my cheek
Like a meadow-gale of spring—
It mingled strangely with my fears,
Yet it felt like a welcoming.

Swiftly, swiftly flew the ship,   460
Yet she sailed softly too:
Sweetly, sweetly blew the breeze—
On me alone it blew.

And the ancient Mariner beholdeth his native country.

Oh! dream of joy! is this indeed
The lighthouse top I see?   465
Is this the hill? is this the kirk?
Is this mine own countree?

We drifted o'er the harbour-bar,
And I with sobs did pray—
O let me be awake, my God!   470
Or let me sleep alway.

The harbour-bay was clear as glass,
So smoothly was it strewn!
And on the bay the moonlight lay,
And the shadow of the Moon.   475

The rock shone bright, the kirk no less,
That stands above the rock:
The moonlight steeped in silentness
The steady weathercock.

And the bay was white with silent light,   480
Till rising from the same,

The angelic spirits leave the dead bodies, and appear in their own forms of light.

Full many shapes, that shadows were,
In crimson colours came.

A little distance from the prow
Those crimson shadows were: 485

I turned my eyes upon the deck—
O, Christ! what saw I there!

Each corse lay flat, lifeless and flat,
And, by the holy rood!
A man all light, a seraph-man,   490
On every corse there stood.

This seraph-band, each waved his hand:
It was a heavenly sight!
They stood as signals to the land,
Each one a lovely light;   495

This seraph-band, each waved his hand,
No voice did they impart—
No voice; but oh! the silence sank
Like music on my heart.

But soon I heard the dash of oars,   500
I heard the Pilot's cheer;
My head was turned perforce away,
And I saw a boat appear.

The Pilot and the Pilot's boy,
I heard them coming fast: 505
Dear Lord in Heaven! it was a joy
The dead men could not blast.

I saw a third—I heard his voice:
It is the Hermit good!
He singeth loud his godly hymns   510
That he makes in the wood.
He'll shrieve my soul, he'll wash away
The Albatross's blood.

PART THE SEVENTH

'This Hermit good lives in that wood   The Hermit of
Which slopes down to the sea.   515   the wood
How loudly his sweet voice he rears!
He loves to talk with the marineres
That come from a far countree.

He kneels at morn, and noon, and eve—
He hath a cushion plump: 520
It is the moss that wholly hides
The rotted old oak-stump.

The skiff-boat neared: I heard them talk,
"Why this is strange, I trow!
Where are those lights so many and fair,   525
That signal made but now?"

"Strange, by my faith!" the Hermit said—
"And they answered not our cheer!
The planks look warped! and see those sails,
How thin they are and sere!   530
I never saw aught like to them,
Unless perchance it were
Brown skeletons of leaves that lag
My forest-brook along;
When the ivy-tod is heavy with snow,   535
And the owlet whoops to the wolf below,
That eats the she-wolf's young."

"Dear Lord! it hath a fiendish look—"
(The Pilot made reply)
"I am a-feared"—"Push on, push on!"   540
Said the Hermit cheerily.

The boat came closer to the ship,
But I nor spake nor stirred;
The boat came close beneath the ship,
And straight a sound was heard.   545

Under the water it rumbled on,
Still louder and more dread:
It reached the ship, it split the bay;

The ship went down like lead.

Stunned by that loud and dreadful sound,   550
Which sky and ocean smote,
Like one that hath been seven days drowned

My body lay afloat;
But swift as dreams, myself I found
Within the Pilot's boat.   555

The ancient
Mariner is saved
in the Pilot's
boat.

Upon the whirl, where sank the ship,
The boat spun round and round;
And all was still, save that the hill
Was telling of the sound.

I moved my lips—the Pilot shrieked   560
And fell down in a fit;
The holy Hermit raised his eyes,
And prayed where he did sit.

I took the oars: the Pilot's boy,
Who now doth crazy go,   565
Laughed loud and long, and all the while
His eyes went to and fro.
"Ha! ha!" quoth he, "full plain I see,
The Devil knows how to row."

And now, all in my own countree,   570
I stood on the firm land!
The Hermit stepped forth from the boat,
And scarcely he could stand.

"O shrieve me, shrieve me, holy man!"
The Hermit crossed his brow.   575
"Say quick," quoth he, "I bid thee say—
What manner of man art thou?"

The ancient
Mariner ear-
nestly entreateth
the Hermit to
shrive him; and
the penance of
life falls on him.

Forthwith this frame of mine was wrenched
With a woeful agony,
Which forced me to begin my tale;   580
And then it left me free.

Since then, at an uncertain hour,
That agony returns:
And till my ghastly tale is told,
This heart within me burns.   585

And ever and
anon through-
out his future
life an agony
constraineth

him to travel
from land to
land,

I pass, like night, from land to land;
I have strange power of speech;
That moment that his face I see,
I know the man that must hear me:
To him my tale I teach.   590

What loud uproar bursts from that door!
The wedding-guests are there:
But in the garden-bower the Bride
And Bride-maids singing are:
And hark the little vesper bell,   595
Which biddeth me to prayer!

O Wedding-Guest! this soul hath been
Alone on a wide wide sea:
So lonely 'twas, that God Himself
Scarce seemèd there to be.   600

O sweeter than the marriage-feast,
'Tis sweeter far to me,
To walk together to the kirk
With a goodly company!—

To walk together to the kirk,   605
And all together pray,
While each to his great Father bends,
Old men, and babes, and loving friends,
And youths and maidens gay!

and to teach, by
his own ex-
ample, love and
reverence to all
things that God
made and
loveth.

Farewell, farewell! but this I tell   610
To thee, thou Wedding-Guest!
He prayeth well, who loveth well
Both man and bird and beast.

He prayeth best, who loveth best
All things both great and small;   615
For the dear God who loveth us,
He made and loveth all.'

The Mariner, whose eye is bright,
Whose beard with age is hoar,

Is gone: and now the Wedding-Guest   620
Turned from the Bridegroom's door.

He went like one that hath been stunned,
And is of sense forlorn:
A sadder and a wiser man,
He rose the morrow morn.   625

WALTER SAVAGE LANDOR (1775–1864)

ROSE AYLMER

Ah, what avails the sceptred race!
   Ah, what the form divine!
What every virtue, every grace!
   Rose Aylmer, all were thine.

Rose Aylmer, whom these wakeful eyes
   May weep, but never see,
A night of memories and sighs
   I consecrate to thee.

THE DEATH OF ARTEMIDORA

"Artemidora! Gods invisible,
While thou art lying faint along the couch,
Have tied the sandal to thy veinèd feet
And stand beside thee, ready to convey
Thy weary steps where other rivers flow.   5
Refreshing shades will waft thy weariness
Away, and voices like thy own come nigh
Soliciting, nor vainly, thy embrace."
  Artemidora sighed, and would have pressed
The hand now pressing hers, but was too weak.   10
Fate's shears were over her dark hair unseen
While thus Elpenor spake: he looked into
Eyes that had given light and life erewhile
To those above them, those now dim with tears

And watchfulness. Again he spake of joy   15
Eternal. At that word, that sad word, joy,
Faithful and fond her bosom heaved once more:
Her head fell back; one sob, one loud deep sob
Swelled through the darkened chamber; 'twas not hers:
With her that old boat incorruptible,   20
Unwearied, undiverted in its course,
Had plashed the water up the farther strand.

DIRCE

Stand close around, ye Stygian set,
    With Dirce in one boat convey'd!
Or Charon, seeing, may forget
    That he is old, and she a shade.

TERNISSA! YOU ARE FLED!

Ternissa! you are fled!
I say not to the dead,
But to the happy ones who rest below:
    For surely, surely, where
    Your voice and graces are,
Nothing of death can any feel or know.
    Girls who delight to dwell
    Where grows most asphodel,
Gather to their calm breasts each word you speak:
    The mild Persephone
    Places you on her knee,
And your cool palm smoothes down stern Pluto's cheek.

ON HIS SEVENTY-FIFTH BIRTHDAY

I strove with none, for none was worth my strife;
    Nature I loved, and next to Nature, Art;
I warmed both hands before the fire of life;
    It sinks, and I am ready to depart.

GEORGE GORDON, LORD BYRON
(1788–1824)

SHE WALKS IN BEAUTY

She walks in beauty, like the night
   Of cloudless climes and starry skies;
And all that's best of dark and bright
   Meet in her aspect and her eyes:
Thus mellowed to that tender light   5
   Which heaven to gaudy day denies.

One shade the more, one day the less,
   Had half impaired the nameless grace
Which waves in every raven tress,
   Or softly lightens o'er her face;   10
Where thoughts serenely sweet express
   How pure, how dear, their dwelling-place.

And on that cheek, and o'er that brow,
   So soft, so calm, so eloquent,
The smiles that win, the tints that glow,   15
   But tell of days in goodness spent,
A mind at peace with all below,
   A heart whose love is innocent!

SO WE'LL GO NO MORE A-ROVING

So, we'll go no more a-roving
   So late into the night,
Though the heart be still as loving,
   And the moon be still as bright.

For the sword outwears its sheath,
   And the soul wears out the breast,
And the heart must pause to breathe,
   And love itself have rest.

Though the night was made for loving,
And the day returns too soon,
Yet we'll go no more a-roving
By the light of the moon.

SONNET ON CHILLON

Eternal Spirit of the chainless Mind!
Brightest in dungeons, Liberty! thou art,
For there thy habitation is the heart—
The heart which love of thee alone can bind;
And when thy sons to fetters are consigned—
To fetters, and the damp vault's dayless gloom,
Their country conquers with their martyrdom,
And Freedom's fame finds wings on every wind.
Chillon! thy prison is a holy place,
And thy sad floor an altar—for 'twas trod,
Until his very steps have left a trace
Worn, as if thy cold pavement were a sod,
By Bonnivard!—May none those marks efface!
For they appeal from tyranny to God.

FROM *DON JUAN*

THE ISLES OF GREECE

The isles of Greece, the isles of Greece!
    Where burning Sappho loved and sung,
Where grew the arts of War and Peace,—
    Where Delos rose, and Phoebus sprung!
Eternal summer gilds them yet,   5
But all, except their Sun, is set.

The Scian and the Teian muse,
    The Hero's harp, the Lover's lute,
Have found the fame your shores refuse:
    Their place of birth alone is mute   10
To sounds which echo further west
Than your Sires' "Islands of the Blest."

The mountains look on Marathon—
   And Marathon looks on the sea;
And musing there an hour alone,   15
   I dreamed that Greece might still be free;
For standing on the Persians' grave,
I could not deem myself a slave.

A King sate on the rocky brow
   Which looks o'er sea-born Salamis;   20
And ships, by thousands, lay below,
   And men in nations; all were his!
He counted them at break of day—
And when the Sun set, where were they?

And where are they? and where art thou,   25
   My country? On thy voiceless shore
The heroic lay is tuneless now—
   The heroic bosom beats no more!
And must thy Lyre, so long divine,
Degenerate into hands like mine?   30

'Tis something, in the dearth of Fame,
   Though linked among a fettered race,
To feel at least a patriot's shame,
   Even as I sing, suffuse my face;
For what is left the poet here?   35
For Greeks a blush—for Greece a tear.

Must we but weep o'er days more blest?
   Must we but blush?—Our fathers bled.
Earth! render back from out thy breast
   A remnant of our Spartan dead!   40
Of the three hundred grant but three,
To make a new Thermopylae!

What, silent still? and silent all?
   Ah! no;—the voices of the dead
Sound like a distant torrent's fall,   45
   And answer, "Let one living head,
But one arise,—we come, we come!"
'Tis but the living who are dumb.

In vain—in vain: strike other chords:
   Fill high the cup with Samian wine! 50
Leave battles to the Turkish hordes,
   And shed the blood of Scio's vine!
Hark! rising to the ignoble call—
How answers each bold Bacchanal!

You have the Pyrrhic dance as yet; 55
   Where is the Pyrrhic phalanx gone?
Of two such lessons, why forget
   The nobler and the manlier one?
You have the letters Cadmus gave—
Think ye he meant them for a slave? 60

Fill high the bowl with Samian wine!
   We will not think of themes like these!
It made Anacreon's song divine:
   He served—but served Polycrates—
A Tyrant; but our masters then 65
Were still, at least, our countrymen.

The Tyrant of the Chersonese
   Was Freedom's best and bravest friend;
That tyrant was Miltiades!
   Oh! that the present hour would lend 70
Another despot of the kind!
Such chains as his were sure to bind.

Fill high the bowl with Samian wine!
   On Suli's rock, and Parga's shore,
Exists the remnant of a line 75
   Such as the Doric mothers bore;
And there, perhaps, some seed is sown,
The Heracleidan blood might own.

Trust not for freedom to the Franks—
   They have a king who buys and sells; 80
In native swords and native ranks,
   The only hope of courage dwells;
But Turkish force, and **Latin fraud**,
Would break your shield, however broad.

Fill high the bowl with Samian wine! 85
   Our virgins dance beneath the shade—
I see their glorious black eyes shine;
   But gazing on each glowing maid,
My own the burning tear-drop laves,
To think such breasts must suckle slaves. 90

Place me on Sunium's marbled steep,
   Where nothing, save the waves and I,
May hear our mutual murmurs sweep;
   There, swan-like, let me sing and die:
A land of slaves shall ne'er be mine— 95
Dash down yon cup of Samian wine!

     *   *   *   *

Thus sung, or would, or could, or should have sung,
   The modern Greek, in tolerable verse:
If not like Orpheus quite, when Greece was young,
   Yet in these times he might have done much worse:
His strain displayed some feeling—right or wrong; 101
   And feeling, in a poet, is the source
Of others' feeling; but they are such liars,
And take all colours—like the hands of dyers.

But words are things, and a small drop of ink, 105
   Falling like dew, upon a thought produces
That which makes thousands, perhaps millions, think;
   'Tis strange, the shortest letter which man uses
Instead of speech, may form a lasting link
   Of ages; to what straits old Time reduces 110
Frail man when paper—even a rag like this,
Survives himself, his tomb, and all that's his!

And when his bones are dust, his grave a blank,
   His station, generation, even his nation,
Become a thing, or nothing, save to rank 115
   In chronological commemoration,
Some dull MS. oblivion long has sank,
   Or graven stone found in a barrack's station
In digging the foundation of a closet,
May turn his name up, as a rare deposit. 120

And glory long has made the sages smile;
    'Tis something, nothing, words, illusion, wind—
Depending more upon the historian's style
    Than on the name a person leaves behind:
Troy owes to Homer what whist owes to Hoyle;   125
    The present century was growing blind
To the great Marlborough's skill in giving knocks,
Until his late Life by Archdeacon Coxe.

Milton's the prince of poets—so we say;
    A little heavy, but no less divine: 130
An independent being in his day—
    Learn'd, pious, temperate in love and wine;
But his life falling into Johnson's way,
    We're told this great high priest of all the Nine
Was whipt at college—a harsh sire—odd spouse,   135
For the first Mrs. Milton left his house.

All these are, *certes*, entertaining facts,
    Like Shakespeare's stealing deer, Lord Bacon's bribes;
Like Titus' youth, and Cæsar's earliest acts;
    Like Burns (whom Doctor Currie well describes);   140
Like Cromwell's pranks;—but although truth exacts
    These amiable descriptions from the scribes,
As most essential to their hero's story,
They do not much contribute to his glory.

All are not moralists, like Southey, when   145
    He prated to the world of "Pantisocrasy":
Or Wordsworth unexcised, unhired, who then
    Season'd his pedlar poems with democracy;
Or Coleridge, long before his flighty pen
    Lent to the Morning Post its aristocracy;   150
When he and Southey, following the same path,
Espoused two partners (milliners of Bath).

Such names at present cut a convict figure,
    The very Botany Bay in moral geography;
Their royal treason, renegado rigor,   155
    Are good manure for their more bare biography.
Wordsworth's last quarto, by the way, is bigger
    Than any since the birthday of typography;

A drowsy frowzy poem, call'd the "Excursion,"
Writ in a manner which is my aversion.   160

He there builds up a formidable dyke
   Between his own and others' intellect;
But Wordsworth's poem, and his followers, like
   Joanna Southcote's Shiloh, and her sect,
Are things which in this century don't strike   165
   The public mind,—so few are the elect;
And the new births of both their stale virginities
Have proved but dropsies, taken for divinities.

But let me to my story: I must own,
   If I have any fault, it is digression,   170
Leaving my people to proceed alone,
   While I soliloquize beyond expression:
But these are my addresses from the throne,
   Which put off business to the ensuing session:
Forgetting each omission is a loss to   175
The world, not quite so great as Ariosto.

I know that what our neighbors call "longueurs,"
   (We've not so good a word, but have the thing,
In that complete perfection which insures
   An epic from Bob Southey every Spring—)   180
Form not the true temptation which allures
   The reader; but 't would not be hard to bring
Some fine examples of the epopée,
To prove its grand ingredient is ennui.

We learn from Horace, "Homer sometimes sleeps;"   185
   We feel without him, Wordsworth sometimes wakes,—
To show with what complacency he creeps,
   With his dear "Wagoners," around his lakes.
He wishes for "a boat" to sail the deeps—
   Of ocean?—No, of air; and then he makes   190
Another outcry for "a little boat,"
And drivels seas to set it well afloat.

If he must fain sweep o'er the ethereal plain,
   And Pegasus runs restive in his "Wagon,"

Could he not beg the loan of Charles's Wain? 195
Or pray Medea for a single dragon?
Or if, too classic for his vulgar brain,
He fear'd his neck to venture such a nag on,
And he must needs mount nearer to the moon,
Could not the blockhead ask for a balloon? 200

"Pedlars," and "Boats," and "Wagons!" Oh! ye shades
Of Pope and Dryden, are we come to this?
That trash of such sort not alone evades
Contempt, but from the bathos' vast abyss
Floats scumlike uppermost, and these Jack Cades 205
Of sense and song above your graves may hiss—
The "little boatman" and his "Peter Bell"
Can sneer at him who drew "Achitophel!"

PERCY BYSSHE SHELLEY (1792–1822)

THE CLOUD

I bring fresh showers for the thirsting flowers,
From the seas and the streams;
I bear light shade for the leaves when laid
In their noonday dreams.
From my wings are shaken the dews that waken 5
The sweet buds every one,
When rocked to rest on their mother's breast,
As she dances about the sun.
I wield the flail of the lashing hail,
And whiten the green plains under, 10
And then again I dissolve it in rain,
And laugh as I pass in thunder.

I sift the snow on the mountains below,
And their great pines groan aghast,
And all the night 'tis my pillow white, 15
While I sleep in the arms of the blast.
Sublime on the towers of my skiey bowers,
Lightning, my pilot, sits,

In a cavern under is fettered the thunder,
   It struggles and howls at fits;   20
Over earth and ocean, with gentle motion,
   This pilot is guiding me,
Lured by the love of the genii that move
   In the depths of the purple sea;
Over the rills, and the crags, and the hills,   25
   Over the lakes and the plains,
Wherever he dream, under mountain or stream,
   The Spirit he loves remains;
And I all the while bask in heaven's blue smile,
   Whilst he is dissolving in rains.   30

The sanguine sunrise, with his meteor eyes,
   And his burning plumes outspread,
Leaps on the back of my sailing rack,
   When the morning star shines dead,
As on the jag of a mountain crag,   35
   Which an earthquake rocks and swings,
An eagle alit one moment may sit
   In the light of its golden wings.
And when sunset may breathe, from the lit sea beneath,
   Its ardours of rest and of love,   40
And the crimson pall of eve may fall
   From the depth of heaven above,
With wings folded I rest, on mine airy nest,
   As still as a brooding dove.

That orbèd maiden with white fire laden,   45
   Whom mortals call the moon,
Glides glimmering o'er my fleece-like floor,
   By the midnight breezes strewn:
And wherever the beat of her unseen feet,
   Which only the angels hear,   50
May have broken the woof of my tent's thin roof,
   The stars peep behind her and peer;
And I laugh to see them whirl and flee,
   Like a swarm of golden bees,
When I widen the rent in my wind-built tent,   55
   Till the calm rivers, lakes, and seas,
Like strips of the sky fallen through me on high,
   Are each paved with the moon and these.

I bind the sun's throne with a burning zone,
   And the moon's with a girdle of pearl;   60
The volcanoes are dim, and the stars reel and swim,
   When the whirlwinds my banner unfurl.
From cape to cape, with a bridge-like shape,
   Over a torrent sea,
Sunbeam-proof, I hang like a roof,   65
   The mountains its columns be.
The triumphal arch through which I march
   With hurricane, fire, and snow,
When the powers of the air are chained to my chair,
   Is the million-coloured bow;   70
The sphere-fire above its soft colours wove,
   While the moist earth was laughing below.

I am the daughter of earth and water,
   And the nursling of the sky;
I pass through the pores of the ocean and shores;   75
   I change, but I cannot die.
For after the rain, when with never a stain
   The pavilion of heaven is bare,
And the winds and sunbeams, with their convex gleams,
   Build up the blue dome of air,   80
I silently laugh at my own cenotaph,
   And out of the caverns of rain,
Like a child from the womb, like a ghost from the tomb,
   I arise and unbuild it again.

ODE TO THE WEST WIND

I

O wild West Wind, thou breath of Autumn's being,
Thou, from whose unseen presence the leaves dead
Are driven, like ghosts from an enchanter fleeing,

Yellow, and black, and pale, and hectic red,
Pestilence-stricken multitudes: O thou,   5
Who chariotest to their dark wintry bed

The wingèd seeds, where they lie cold and low,
Each like a corpse within its grave, until
Thine azure sister of the spring shall blow

Her clarion o'er the dreaming earth, and fill   10
(Driving sweet buds like flocks to feed in air)
With living hues and odours plain and hill;

Wild Spirit, which art moving everywhere;
Destroyer and preserver; hear, Oh hear!

II

Thou on whose stream, 'mid the steep sky's commotion,
Loose clouds like earth's decaying leaves are shed,   16
Shook from the tangled boughs of Heaven and Ocean,

Angels of rain and lightning: there are spread
On the blue surface of thine airy surge,
Like the bright hair uplifted from the head   20

Of some fierce Mænad, even from the dim verge
Of the horizon to the zenith's height
The locks of the approaching storm. Thou dirge

Of the dying year, to which this closing night
Will be the dome of a vast sepulchre,   25
Vaulted with all thy congregated might

Of vapours, from whose solid atmosphere
Black rain, and fire, and hail will burst: Oh hear!

III

Thou who didst waken from his summer dreams
The blue Mediterranean, where he lay,   30
Lulled by the coil of his crystalline streams,

Beside a pumice isle in Baiæ's bay,
And saw in sleep old palaces and towers
Quivering within the wave's intenser day,

All overgrown with azure moss and flowers   35
So sweet, the sense faints picturing them! Thou
For whose path the Atlantic's level powers

Cleave themselves into chasms, while far below
The sea-blooms and the oozy woods which wear
The sapless foliage of the ocean, know   40

Thy voice, and suddenly grow gray with fear,
And tremble and despoil themselves: Oh hear!

IV

If I were a dead leaf thou mightest bear;
If I were a swift cloud to fly with thee;
A wave to pant beneath thy power, and share   45

The impulse of thy strength, only less free
Than thou, O uncontrollable! If even
I were as in my boyhood, and could be

The comrade of thy wanderings over heaven,
As then, when to outstrip thy skiey speed   50
Scarce seemed a vision; I would ne'er have striven

As thus with thee in prayer in my sore need.
Oh! lift me as a wave, a leaf, a cloud!
I fall upon the thorns of life! I bleed!

A heavy weight of hours has chained and bowed   55
One too like thee; tameless, and swift, and proud.

V

Make me thy lyre, even as the forest is:
What if my leaves are falling like its own!
The tumult of thy mighty harmonies

Will take from both a deep, autumnal tone,   60
Sweet though in sadness. Be thou, spirit fierce,
My spirit! Be thou me, impetuous one!

Drive my dead thoughts over the universe
Like withered leaves to quicken a new birth!
And, by the incantation of this verse,   65

Scatter, as from an unextinguished hearth
Ashes and sparks, my words among mankind!
Be through my lips to unawakened earth

The trumpet of a prophecy! O, wind,
If Winter comes, can Spring be far behind?   70

HYMN OF PAN

I

From the forests and highlands
        We come, we come;
From the river-girt islands,
        Where loud waves are dumb
            Listening to my sweet pipings.   5
The wind in the reeds and the rushes,
    The bees on the bells of thyme,
The birds on the myrtle bushes,
    The cicale above in the lime,
And the lizards below in the grass,   10
Were as silent as ever old Tmolus was
        Listening to my sweet pipings.

II

Liquid Peneus was flowing,
        And all dark Tempe lay
In Pelion's shadow, outgrowing   15
        The light of the dying day,
            Speeded by my sweet pipings.
The Sileni, and Sylvans, and Fauns,
    And the Nymphs of the woods and waves,
To the edge of the moist river-lawns,   20
    And the brink of the dewy caves,
And all that did then attend and follow
Were silent with love, as you now, Apollo,
        With envy of my sweet pipings.

III

I sang of the dancing stars,   25
    I sang of the dædal Earth,
And of Heaven—and the giant wars,
    And Love, and Death, and Birth,—
      And then I changed my pipings—
Singing how down the vale of Menalus   30
    I pursued a maiden and clasp'd a reed:
Gods and men, we are all deluded thus!
    It breaks in our bosom and then we bleed:
All wept, as I think both ye now would,
If envy or age had not frozen your blood,   35
    At the sorrow of my sweet pipings.

CHORUS FROM *HELLAS*

The world's great age begins anew,
    The golden years return,
The earth doth like a snake renew
    Her winter weeds outworn:
Heaven smiles, and faiths and empires gleam,   5
Like wrecks of a dissolving dream.

A brighter Hellas rears its mountains
    From waves serener far:
A new Peneus rolls his fountains
    Against the morning star.   10
Where· fairer Tempes bloom, there sleep
Young Cyclads on a sunnier deep.

A loftier Argo cleaves the main,
    Fraught with a later prize;
Another Orpheus sings again,   15
    And loves, and weeps, and dies.
A new Ulysses leaves once more
Calypso for his native shore.

Oh, write no more the tale of Troy,
    If Earth Death's scroll must be!   20
Nor mix with Laian rage the joy
    Which dawns upon the free:

Although a subtler Sphinx renew
Riddles of death Thebes never knew.

Another Athens shall arise,   25
   And to remoter time
Bequeath, like sunset to the skies,
   The splendour of its prime;
And leave, if nought so bright may live,
All earth can take or Heaven can give.   30

Saturn and Love their long repose
   Shall burst, more bright and good
Than all who fell, than One who rose,
   Than many unsubdued:
Not gold, not blood, their altar dowers,   35
But votive tears and symbol flowers.

Oh, cease! Must hate and death return?
   Cease! Must men kill and die?
Cease! drain not to its dregs the urn
   Of bitter prophecy.   40
The world is weary of the past,
Oh, might it die, or rest at last!

SONNET: ENGLAND IN 1819

An old, mad, blind, despised, and dying king,—
Princes, the dregs of their dull race, who flow
Through public scorn,—mud from a muddy spring,—
Rulers who neither see, nor feel, nor know,
But leech-like to their fainting country cling,
Till they drop, blind in blood, without a blow,—
A people starved and stabbed in the untilled field,—
An army, which liberticide and prey
Makes as a two-edged sword to all who wield
Golden and sanguine laws which tempt and slay;
Religion Christless, Godless—a book sealed;
A Senate,—Time's worst statute unrepealed,—
Are graves, from which a glorious Phantom may
Burst, to illumine our tempestuous day.

SONG TO THE MEN OF ENGLAND

Men of England, wherefore plough
For the lords who lay ye low?
Wherefore weave with toil and care
The rich robes your tyrants wear?

Wherefore feed, and clothe, and save,   5
From the cradle to the grave,
Those ungrateful drones who would
Drain your sweat—nay, drink your blood?

Wherefore, Bees of England, forge
Many a weapon, chain, and scourge,   10
That these stingless drones may spoil
The forced produce of your toil?

Have ye leisure, comfort, calm,
Shelter, food, love's gentle balm?
Or what is it ye buy so dear   15
With your pain and with your fear?

The seed ye sow, another reaps;
The wealth ye find, another keeps;
The robes ye weave, another wears;
The arms ye forge, another bears.   20

Sow seed,—but let no tyrant reap;
Find wealth,—let no impostor heap;
Weave robes,—let not the idle wear;
Forge arms,—in your defence to bear.

Shrink to your cellars, holes, and cells;   25
In halls ye deck, another dwells.
Why shake the chains ye wrought? Ye see
The steel ye tempered glance on ye.

With plough and spade, and hoe and loom,
Trace your grave, and build your tomb,   30
And weave your winding-sheet, till fair
England be your sepulchre.

FROM *PROMETHEUS UNBOUND*

This is the day, which down the void abysm
At the Earth-born's spell yawns for Heaven's despotism,
    And Conquest is dragged captive through the deep:
Love, from its awful throne of patient power
In the wise heart, from the last giddy hour   5
    Of dread endurance, from the slippery, steep,
And narrow verge of crag-like agony, springs
And folds over the world its healing wings.

Gentleness, Virtue, Wisdom, and Endurance,
These are the seals of that most firm assurance   10
    Which bars the pit over Destruction's strength;
And if, wth infirm hand, Eternity,
Mother of many acts and hours, should free
    The serpent that would clasp her with his length;
These are the spells by which to re-assume   15
An empire o'er the disentangled doom.

To suffer woes which Hope thinks infinite;
To forgive wrongs darker than death or night;
    To defy Power, which seems omnipotent;
To love, and bear; to hope till Hope creates   20
From its own wreck the thing it contemplates:
    Neither to change, nor falter, nor repent;
This, like thy glory, Titan! is to be
Good, great and joyous, beautiful and free;
This is alone Life, Joy, Empire, and Victory!   25

OZYMANDIAS

I met a traveller from an antique land
Who said: Two vast and trunkless legs of stone
Stand in the desert. Near them, on the sand,
Half sunk, a shattered visage lies, whose frown,
And wrinkled lip, and sneer of cold command,
Tell that its sculptor well those passions read

Which yet survive, stamped on these lifeless things,
The hand that mocked them and the heart that fed:
And on the pedestal these words appear:
"My name is Ozymandias, king of kings:
Look on my works, ye Mighty, and despair!"
Nothing beside remains. Round the decay
Of that colossal wreck, boundless and bare
The lone and level sands stretch far away.

A WIDOW BIRD SATE MOURNING FOR HER LOVE

A widow bird sate mourning for her love
   Upon a wintry bough;
The frozen wind crept on above,
   The freezing stream below.

There was no leaf upon the forest bare,
   No flower upon the ground,
And little motion in the air
   Except the mill-wheel's sound.

TO NIGHT

Swiftly walk over the western wave,
   Spirit of Night!
Out of the misty eastern cave,
Where all the long and lone daylight,
Thou wovest dreams of joy and fear,   5
Which make thee terrible and dear,—
   Swift be thy flight!

Wrap thy form in a mantle gray,
   Star-inwrought!
Blind with thine hair the eyes of Day;   10
Kiss her until she be wearied out,
Then wander o'er city, and sea, and land,
Touching all with thine opiate wand—
   Come, long-sought!

When I arose and saw the dawn, 15
    I sighed for thee;
When light rode high, and the dew was gone,
And noon lay heavy on flower and tree,
And the weary Day turned to his rest,
Lingering like an unloved guest, 20
    I sighed for thee.

Thy brother Death came, and cried,
    Wouldst thou me?
Thy sweet child Sleep, the filmy-eyed,
Murmured like a noontide bee, 25
Shall I nestle near thy side?
Wouldst thou me?—And I replied,
    No, not thee!

Death will come when thou art dead,
    Soon, too soon— 30
Sleep will come when thou art fled;
Of neither would I ask the boon
I ask of thee, beloved Night—
Swift be thine approaching flight,
    Come soon, soon! 35

TO JANE: THE INVITATION

Best and brightest, come away!
Fairer far than this fair Day,
Which, like thee to those in sorrow,
Comes to bid a sweet good-morrow
To the rough Year just awake 5
In its cradle on the brake.
The brightest hour of unborn Spring,
Through the winter wandering,
Found, it seems, the halcyon Morn
To hoar February born; 10
Bending from Heaven, in azure mirth,
It kissed the forehead of the Earth,
And smiled upon the silent sea,
And bade the frozen streams be free,

And waked to music all their fountains, 15
And breathed upon the frozen mountains,
And like a prophetess of May
Strewed flowers upon the barren way,
Making the wintry world appear
Like one on whom thou smilest, dear. 20

Away, away, from men and towns,
To the wild wood and the downs—
To the silent wilderness
Where the soul need not repress
Its music lest it should not find 25
An echo in another's mind,
While the touch of Nature's art
Harmonizes heart to heart.

Radiant Sister of the Day,
Awake! arise! and come away! 30
To the wild woods and the plains,
And the pools where winter rains
Image all their roof of leaves,
Where the pine its garland weaves
Of sapless green and ivy dun 35
Round stems that never kiss the sun;
Where the lawns and pastures be,
And the sandhills of the sea;—
Where the melting hoar-frost wets
The daisy-star that never sets, 40
And wind-flowers, and violets,
Which yet join not scent to hue,
Crown the pale year weak and new;
When the night is left behind
In the deep east, dun and blind, 45
And the blue noon is over us,
And the multitudinous
Billows murmur at our feet,
Where the earth and ocean meet,
And all things seem only one 50
In the universal sun.

JOHN CLARE (1793–1864)

MOUSE'S NEST

I found a ball of grass among the hay
And progged it as I passed and went away;
And when I looked I fancied something stirred,
And turned agen and hoped to catch the bird—
When out an old mouse bolted in the wheats
With all her young ones hanging at her teats;
She looked so odd and so grotesque to me,
I ran and wondered what the thing could be,
And pushed the knapweed bunches where I stood;
Then the mouse hurried from the craking brood.
The young ones squeaked, and as I went away
She found her nest again among the hay.
The water o'er the pebbles scarce could run
And broad old cesspools glittered in the sun.

THE HEDGEHOG

The hedgehog hides beneath the rotten hedge
And makes a great round nest of grass and sedge,
Or in a bush or in a hollow tree;
And many often stoop and say they see
Him roll and fill his prickles full of crabs
And creep away; and where the magpie dabs
His wing at muddy dyke, in aged root
He makes a nest and fills it full of fruit,
On the hedge bottom hunts for crabs and sloes
And whistles like a cricket as he goes.
It rolls up like a ball or shapeless hog
When gipsies hunt it with their noisy dog;
I've seen it in their camps—they call it sweet,
Though black and bitter and unsavoury meat.

THE MOLE

Rude architect, rich instinct's natural taste
Is thine by heritage. Thy little mounds,
Bedecking furze-clad heath and rushy waste
Betraced with sheep-tracks, shine like pleasure grounds.
No rude inelegance thy work confounds,
But scenes of picturesque and beautiful
Lie mid thy little hills of cushioned thyme,
On which the cow-boy, when his hands are full
Of wild flowers, leans upon his arm at rest,
As though his seat were feathers. When I climb
Thy little fragrant mounds, I feel thy guest,
And hail neglect thy patron, who contrives
Waste spots for thee on nature's quiet breast,
Where taste admires and thy still labour thrives.

THE FEAR OF FLOWERS

The nodding oxeye bends before the wind,
The woodbine quakes lest boys their flowers should find,
And prickly dog-rose, spite of its array,
Can't dare the blossom-seeking hand away,
While thistles wear their heavy knobs of bloom
Proud as a war-horse wears its haughty plume,
And by the roadside danger's self defy;
On commons where pined sheep and oxen lie,
In ruddy pomp and ever thronging mood
It stands and spreads like danger in a wood,
And in the village street, where meanest weeds
Can't stand untouched to fill their husks with seeds,
The haughty thistle o'er all danger towers,
In every place the very wasp of flowers.

CLOCK-A-CLAY

In the cowslip pips I lie,
Hidden from the buzzing fly,
While green grass beneath me lies,
Pearled with dew like fishes' eyes,

Here I lie, a clock-a-clay,   5
Waiting for the time of day.

While grassy forest quakes surprise,
And the wild wind sobs and sighs,
My gold home rocks as like to fall,
On its pillar green and tall;   10
When the pattering rain drives by
Clock-a-clay keeps warm and dry.

Day by day and night by night,
All the week I hide from sight;
In the cowslip pips I lie,   15
In rain and dew still warm and dry;
Day and night, and night and day,
Red, black-spotted clock-a-clay.

My home shakes in wind and showers,
Pale green pillar topped with flowers,   20
Bending at the wild wind's breath,
Till I touch the grass beneath;
Here I live, lone clock-a-clay,
Watching for the time of day.

WILLIAM CULLEN BRYANT (1794–1878)

TO A WATERFOWL

Whither, midst falling dew,
While glow the heavens with the last steps of day,
Far, through their rosy depths, dost thou pursue
    Thy solitary way?

Vainly the fowler's eye   5
Might mark thy distant flight to do thee wrong,
As, darkly seen against the crimson sky,
    Thy figure floats along.

Seek'st thou the plashy brink
Of weedy lake, or marge of river wide,   10
Or where the rocking billows rise and sink
    On the chafed ocean-side?

There is a Power whose care
Teaches thy way along that pathless coast—
The desert and illimitable air—   15
    Lone wandering, but not lost.

All day thy wings have fanned,
At that far height, the cold, thin atmosphere,
Yet stoop not, weary, to the welcome land,
    Though the dark night is near.   20

And soon that toil shall end;
Soon shalt thou find a summer home, and rest,
And scream among thy fellows; reeds shall bend,
    Soon, o'er thy sheltered nest.

Thou'rt gone, the abyss of heaven   25
Hath swallowed up thy form; yet, on my heart
Deeply hath sunk the lesson thou hast given,
    And shall not soon depart.

He who, from zone to zone,
Guides through the boundless sky thy certain flight,   30
In the long way that I must tread alone,
    Will lead my steps aright.

JOHN KEATS (1795–1821)

LA BELLE DAME SANS MERCI

"O what can ail thee, knight-at-arms,
    Alone and palely loitering?
The sedge has wither'd from the lake,
    And no birds sing.

"O what can ail thee, knight-at-arms,   5
    So haggard and so woe-begone?
The squirrel's granary is full,
    And the harvest's done.

"I see a lily on thy brow
    With anguish moist and fever dew;   10

And on thy cheek a fading rose
   Fast withereth too."

"I met a lady in the meads,
   Full beautiful—a faery's child,
Her hair was long, her foot was light,   15
   And her eyes were wild.

"I made a garland for her head,
   And bracelets too, and fragrant zone;
She look'd at me as she did love,
   And made sweet moan.   20

"I set her on my pacing steed
   And nothing else saw all day long,
For sidelong would she bend, and sing
   A faery's song.

"She found me roots of relish sweet,   25
   And honey wild, and manna dew,
And sure in language strange she said—
   'I love thee true.'

"She took me to her elfin grot,
   And there she wept, and sigh'd full sore;   30
And there I shut her wild wild eyes
   With kisses four.

"And there she lullèd me asleep,
   And there I dream'd—Ah! woe betide!
The latest dream I ever dream'd   35
   On the cold hill's side.

"I saw pale kings and princes too,
   Pale warriors, death-pale were they all;
They cried—'La Belle Dame sans Merci
   Hath thee in thrall!'   40

"I saw their starv'd lips in the gloom,
   With horrid warning gapèd wide,
And I awoke and found me here,
   On the cold hill's side.

"And this is why I sojourn here,   45
    Alone and palely loitering,
Though the sedge is wither'd from the lake,
    And no birds sing."

ODE TO A NIGHTINGALE

My heart aches, and a drowsy numbness pains
    My sense, as though of hemlock I had drunk,
Or emptied some dull opiate to the drains
    One minute past, and Lethe-wards had sunk:
'Tis not through envy of thy happy lot,   5
    But being too happy in thine happiness—
        That thou, light wingèd Dryad of the trees,
            In some melodious plot
    Of beechen green, and shadows numberless,
        Singest of summer in full-throated ease.   10

O, for a draught of vintage! that hath been
    Cool'd a long age in the deep-delvèd earth,
Tasting of Flora and the country green,
    Dance, and Provençal song, and sunburnt mirth!
O for a beaker full of the warm South,   15
    Full of the true, the blushful Hippocrene,
        With beaded bubbles winking at the brim,
            And purple-stainèd mouth;
    That I might drink, and leave the world unseen,
        And with thee fade away into the forest dim: 20

Fade far away, dissolve, and quite forget
    What thou among the leaves hast never known,
The weariness, the fever, and the fret
    Here, where men sit and hear each other groan;
Where palsy shakes a few, sad, last gray hairs,   25
    Where youth grows pale, and spectre-thin, and dies;
        Where but to think is to be full of sorrow
            And leaden-eyed despairs,
    Where Beauty cannot keep her lustrous eyes,
        Or new Love pine at them beyond to-morrow.   30

Away! away! for I will fly to thee,
    Not charioted by Bacchus and his pards,

But on the viewless wings of Poesy,
  Though the dull brain perplexes and retards:
Already with thee! tender is the night, 35
  And haply the Queen-Moon is on her throne,
    Cluster'd around by all her starry Fays;
      But here there is no light,
  Save what from heaven is with the breezes blown
    Through verdurous glooms and winding mossy ways. 40

I cannot see what flowers are at my feet,
  Nor what soft incense hangs upon the boughs,
But, in embalmèd darkness, guess each sweet
  Wherewith the seasonable month endows
The grass, the thicket, and the fruit-tree wild; 45
  White hawthorn, and the pastoral eglantine;
    Fast fading violets cover'd up in leaves;
      And mid-May's eldest child,
  The coming musk-rose, full of dewy wine,
    The murmurous haunt of flies on summer eves. 50

Darkling I listen; and, for many a time
  I have been half in love with easeful Death,
Call'd him soft names in many a musèd rhyme,
  To take into the air my quiet breath;
Now more than ever seems it rich to die, 55
  To cease upon the midnight with no pain,
    While thou art pouring forth thy soul abroad
      In such an ecstasy!
  Still wouldst thou sing, and I have ears in vain—
    To thy high requiem become a sod. 60

Thou wast not born for death, immortal Bird!
  No hungry generations tread thee down;
The voice I hear this passing night was heard
  In ancient days by emperor and clown:
Perhaps the self-same song that found a path 65
  Through the sad heart of Ruth, when, sick for home,
    She stood in tears amid the alien corn;
      The same that oft-times hath
  Charm'd magic casements, opening on the foam
    Of perilous seas, in faery lands forlorn. 70

Forlorn! the very word is like a bell
  To toll me back from thee to my sole self!
Adieu! the fancy cannot cheat so well
  As she is fam'd to do, deceiving elf.
Adieu! adieu! thy plaintive anthem fades   75
    Past the near meadows, over the still stream,
      Up the hill-side; and now 'tis buried deep
        In the next valley-glades:
  Was it a vision, or a waking dream?
    Fled is that music:—Do I wake or sleep?   80

ODE ON A GRECIAN URN

Thou still unravish'd bride of quietness,
  Thou foster-child of silence and slow time,
Sylvan historian, who canst thus express
  A flowery tale more sweetly than our rhyme:
What leaf-fring'd legend haunts about thy shape   5
    Of deities or mortals, or of both,
      In Tempe or the dales of Arcady?
What men or gods are these? What maidens loth?
  What mad pursuit? What struggle to escape?
    What pipes and timbrels? What wild ecstasy?   10

Heard melodies are sweet, but those unheard
  Are sweeter; therefore, ye soft pipes, play on;
Not to the sensual ear, but, more endear'd,
  Pipe to the spirit ditties of no tone:
Fair youth, beneath the trees, thou canst not leave   15
    Thy song, nor ever can those trees be bare;
      Bold Lover, never, never canst thou kiss
Though winning near the goal—yet, do not grieve;
    She cannot fade, though thou hast not thy bliss,
      For ever wilt thou love, and she be fair!   20

Ah, happy, happy boughs! that cannot shed
  Your leaves, nor ever bid the Spring adieu;
And, happy melodist, unwearied,
  For ever piping songs for ever new;

More happy love! more happy, happy love!   25
  For ever warm and still to be enjoy'd,
    For ever panting, and for ever young;
All breathing human passion far above,
  That leaves a heart high-sorrowful and cloy'd,
    A burning forehead, and a parching tongue.   30

Who are these coming to the sacrifice?
  To what green altar, O mysterious priest,
Lead'st thou that heifer lowing at the skies,
  And all her silken flanks with garlands dressed?
What little town by river or sea shore,   35
  Or mountain-built with peaceful citadel,
    Is emptied of this folk, this pious morn?
And, little town, thy streets for evermore
  Will silent be; and not a soul to tell
    Why thou art desolate, can e'er return.   40

O Attic shape! Fair attitude! with brede
  Of marble men and maidens overwrought
With forest branches and the trodden weed;
  Thou, silent form, dost tease us out of thought
As doth eternity: Cold Pastoral!   45
  When old age shall this generation waste,
    Thou shalt remain, in midst of other woe
Than ours, a friend to man, to whom thou say'st,
  "Beauty is truth, truth beauty,"—that is all
    Ye know on earth, and all ye need to know.   50

ODE ON MELANCHOLY

No, no, go not to Lethe, neither twist
  Wolf's-bane, tight-rooted, for its poisonous wine;
Nor suffer thy pale forehead to be kissed
  By nightshade, ruby grape of Proserpine;
Make not your rosary of yew-berries,   5
  Nor let the beetle, nor the death-moth be
    Your mournful Psyche, nor the downy owl
A partner in your sorrow's mysteries;
  For shade to shade will come too drowsily,
    And drown the wakeful anguish of the soul.   10

But when the melancholy fit shall fall
   Sudden from heaven like a weeping cloud,
That fosters the droop-headed flowers all,
   And hides the green hill in an April shroud;
Then glut thy sorrow on a morning rose,   15
   Or on the rainbow of the salt sand-wave,
      Or on the wealth of globèd peonies;
Or if thy mistress some rich anger shows,
   Emprison her soft hand, and let her rave,
      And feed deep, deep upon her peerless eyes.   20

She dwells with Beauty—Beauty that must die,
   And Joy, whose hand is ever at his lips
Bidding adieu; and aching Pleasure nigh,
   Turning to poison while the bee-mouth sips:
Ay, in the very temple of delight   25
   Veiled Melancholy has her sovran shrine,
      Though seen of none save him whose strenuous
         tongue
Can burst Joy's grape against his palate fine;
His soul shall taste the sadness of her might,
      And be among her cloudy trophies hung.   30

TO AUTUMN

Season of mists and mellow fruitfulness,
   Close bosom-friend of the maturing sun;
Conspiring with him how to load and bless
   With fruit the vines that round the thatch-eaves run;
To bend with apples the moss'd cottage-trees,   5
   And fill all fruit with ripeness to the core;
      To swell the gourd, and plump the hazel shells
With a sweet kernel; to set budding more,
   And still more, later flowers for the bees,
   Until they think warm days will never cease,   10
      For Summer has o'er-brimmed their clammy cells.

Who hath not seen thee oft amid thy store?
   Sometimes whoever seeks abroad may find
Thee sitting careless on a granary floor,
   Thy hair soft-lifted by the winnowing wind;   15

Or on a half-reap'd furrow sound asleep,
   Drows'd with the fume of poppies, while thy hook
     Spares the next swath and all its twined flowers:
And sometimes like a gleaner thou dost keep
   Steady thy laden head across a brook;   20
   Or by a cider-press, with patient look,
     Thou watchest the last oozings hours by hours.

Where are the songs of Spring? Ay, where are they?
   Think not of them, thou hast thy music too,—
While barred clouds bloom the soft-dying day,   25
   And touch the stubble-plains with rosy hue;
Then in a wailful choir the small gnats mourn
   Among the river sallows, borne aloft
     Or sinking as the light wind lives or dies;
And full-grown lambs loud bleat from hilly bourn;   30
   Hedge-crickets sing; and now with treble soft
   The red-breast whistles from a garden-croft;
     And gathering swallows twitter in the skies.

THE EVE OF ST. AGNES

I

St. Agnes' Eve—Ah, bitter chill it was!
The owl, for all his feathers, was a-cold;
The hare limped trembling through the frozen grass,
And silent was the flock in woolly fold:
Numb were the Beadsman's fingers, while he told   5
His rosary, and while his frosted breath,
Like pious incense from a censer old,
Seemed taking flight for Heaven, without a death,
Past the sweet Virgin's picture, while his prayer he saith.

II

His prayer he saith, this patient, holy man;   10
Then takes his lamp, and riseth from his knees,
And back returneth, meagre, barefoot, wan,
Along the chapel aisle by slow degrees:
The sculptured dead on each side seem to freeze,

Imprisoned in black, purgatorial rails: 15
Knights, ladies, praying in dumb orat'ries,
He passeth by; and his weak spirit fails
To think how they may ache in icy hoods and mails.

III

Northward he turneth through a little door,
And scarce three steps, ere Music's golden tongue 20
Flattered to tears this aged man and poor;
But no—already had his deathbell rung:
The joys of all his life were said and sung.
His was harsh penance on St. Agnes' Eve:
Another way he went, and soon among 25
Rough ashes sat he for his soul's reprieve,
And all night kept awake, for sinners' sake to grieve.

IV

That ancient Beadsman heard the prelude soft;
And so it chanced, for many a door was wide,
From hurry to and fro. Soon, up aloft, 30
The silver, snarling trumpets 'gan to chide:
The level chambers, ready with their pride,
Were glowing to receive a thousand guests:
The carved angels, ever eager-eyed,
Stared, where upon their heads the cornice rests, 35
With hair blown back, and wings put crosswise on their
        breasts.

V

At length burst in the argent revelry,
With plume, tiara, and all rich array,
Numerous as shadows haunting faerily
The brain, new stuffed, in youth, with triumphs gay 40
Of old romance. These let us wish away,
And turn, sole-thoughted, to one Lady there,
Whose heart had brooded, all that wintry day,
On love, and winged St. Agnes' saintly care,
As she had heard old dames full many times declare. 45

VI

They told her how, upon St. Agnes' Eve,
Young virgins might have visions of delight,

And soft adorings from their loves receive
Upon the honeyed middle of the night,
If ceremonies due they did aright;　　　　　　　　　50
As, supperless to bed they must retire,
And couch supine their beauties, lily white;
Nor look behind, nor sideways, but require
Of Heaven with upward eyes for all that they desire.

VII

Full of this whim was thoughtful Madeline:　　　　55
The music, yearning like a God in pain,
She scarcely heard: her maiden eyes divine,
Fixed on the floor, saw many a sweeping train
Pass by—she heeded not at all: in vain
Came many a tiptoe, amorous cavalier,　　　　　　60
And back retired; not cooled by high disdain,
But she saw not: her heart was otherwhere:
She sighed for Agnes' dreams, the sweetest of the year.

VIII

She danced along with vague, regardless eyes,
Anxious her lips, her breathing quick and short:　　65
The hallowed hour was near at hand: she sighs
Amid the timbrels, and the thronged resort
Of whisperers in anger, or in sport;
'Mid looks of love, defiance, hate, and scorn,
Hoodwinked with faery fancy; all amort,　　　　　70
Save to St. Agnes and her lambs unshorn,
And all the bliss to be before to-morrow morn.

IX

So, purposing each moment to retire,
She lingered still. Meantime, across the moors,
Had come young Porphyro, with heart on fire　　　75
For Madeline. Beside the portal doors,
Buttressed from moonlight, stands he, and implores
All saints to give him sight of Madeline,
But for one moment in the tedious hours,
That he might gaze and worship all unseen;　　　　80
Perchance speak, kneel, touch, kiss—in sooth such things
　　　　have been.

X

He ventures in: let no buzzed whisper tell:
All eyes be muffled, or a hundred swords
Will storm his heart, Love's fev'rous citadel:
For him, those chambers held barbarian hordes,   85
Hyena foemen, and hot-blooded lords,
Whose very dogs would execrations howl
Against his lineage: not one breast affords
Him any mercy, in that mansion foul,
Save one old beldame, weak in body and in soul.   90

XI

Ah, happy chance! the aged creature came,
Shuffling along with ivory-headed wand,
To where he stood, hid from the torch's flame,
Behind a broad hall-pillar, far beyond
The sound of merriment and chorus bland: 95
He startled her; but soon she knew his face,
And grasped his fingers in her palsied hand,
Saying, 'Mercy, Porphyro! hie thee from this place:
They are all here to-night, the whole blood-thirsty race!

XII

'Get hence! get hence! there's dwarfish Hildebrand;   100
He had a fever late, and in the fit
He cursed thee and thine, both house and land:
Then there's that old Lord Maurice, not a whit
More tame for his gray hairs—Alas me! flit!
Flit like a ghost away.'—'Ah, Gossip dear,   105
We're safe enough; here in this arm chair sit,
And tell me how'—'Good saints! not here, not here;
Follow me, child, or else these stones will be thy bier.'

XIII

He followed through a lowly archèd way,
Brushing the cobwebs with his lofty plume,   110
And as she muttered 'Well-a—well-a-day!'
He found him in a little moonlight room,
Pale, latticed, chill, and silent as a tomb.

'Now tell me where is Madeline,' said he,
'O tell me Angela, by the holy loom   115
Which none but secret sisterhood may see,
When they St. Agnes' wool are weaving piously.

XIV

'St. Agnes! Ah! it is St. Agnes' Eve—
Yet men will murder upon holy days:
Thou must hold water in a witch's sieve,   120
And be liege-lord of all the Elves and Fays,
To venture so: it fills me with amaze
To see thee, Porphyro!—St. Agnes' Eve!
God's help! my lady fair the conjuror plays
This very night: good angels her deceive!   125
But let me laugh awhile, I've mickle time to grieve.'

XV

Feebly she laugheth in the languid moon
While Porphyro upon her face doth look,
Like puzzled urchin on an aged crone
Who keepeth closed a wond'rous riddle-book,   130
As spectacled she sits in chimney nook.
But soon his eyes grew brilliant, when she told
His lady's purpose; and he scarce could brook
Tears, at the thought of those enchantments cold,
And Madeline asleep in lap of legends old.   135

XVI

Sudden a thought came like a full-blown rose,
Flushing his brow, and in his painèd heart
Made purple riot: then doth he propose
A stratagem, that makes the beldame start:
'A cruel man and impious thou art: 140
Sweet lady, let her pray, and sleep, and dream
Alone with her good angels, far apart
From wicked men like thee. Go, go!—I deem
Thou canst not surely be the same that thou didst seem.'

XVII

'I will not harm her, by all saints I swear,'   145
Quoth Porphyro: 'O may I ne'er find grace

When my weak voice shall whisper its last prayer,
If one of her soft ringlets I displace,
Or look with ruffian passion in her face:
Good Angela, believe me by these tears;   150
Or I will, even in a moment's space,
Awake, with horrid shout, my foemen's ears,
And beard them, though they be more fanged than
    wolves and bears.'

XVIII

'Ah! why wilt thou affright a feeble soul?
A poor, weak, palsy-stricken, churchyard thing,   155
Whose passing-bell may ere the midnight toll;
Whose prayers for thee, each morn and evening,
Were never missed.'—Thus plaining, doth she bring
A gentler speech from burning Porphyro;
So woful, and of such deep sorrowing,   160
That Angela gives promise she will do
Whatever he shall wish, betide her weal or woe.

XIX

Which was, to lead him, in close secrecy,
Even to Madeline's chamber, and there hide
Him in a closet, of such privacy   165
That he might see her beauty unespied,
And win perhaps that night a peerless bride,
While legioned faeries paced the coverlet,
And pale enchantment held her sleepy-eyed.
Never on such a night have lovers met,   170
Since Merlin paid his Demon all the monstrous debt.

XX

'It shall be as thou wishest,' said the Dame:
'All cates and dainties shall be storèd there
Quickly on this feast-night: by the tambour frame
Her own lute thou wilt see: no time to spare,   175
For I am slow and feeble, and scarce dare
On such a catering trust my dizzy head.
Wait here, my child, with patience; kneel in prayer
The while: Ah! thou must needs the lady wed,
Or may I never leave my grave among the dead.'   180

XXI

So saying she hobbled off with busy fear.
The lover's endless minutes slowly passed;
The dame returned, and whispered in his ear
To follow her; with aged eyes aghast
From fright of dim espial. Safe at last,   185
Through many a dusky gallery, they gain
The maiden's chamber, silken, hushed, and chaste;
Where Porphyro took covert, pleased amain.
His poor guide hurried back with agues in her brain.

XXII

Her faltering hand upon the balustrade,   190
Old Angela was feeling for the stair,
When Madeline, St. Agnes' charmèd maid,
Rose, like a missioned spirit, unaware:
With silver taper's light, and pious care,
She turned, and down the aged gossip led   195
To a safe level matting. Now prepare,
Young Porphyro, for gazing on that bed;
She comes, she comes again, like ring-dove frayed and fled.

XXIII

Out went the taper as she hurried in;
Its little smoke, in pallid moonshine, died: 200
She closed the door, she panted, all akin
To spirits of the air, and visions wide:
No uttered syllable, or, woe betide!
But to her heart, her heart was voluble,
Paining with eloquence her balmy side;   205
As though a tongueless nightingale should swell
Her throat in vain, and die, heart-stifled, in her dell.

XXIV

A casement high and triple-arched there was,
All garlanded with carven imag'ries
Of fruits, and flowers, and bunches of knot-grass,   210
And diamonded with panes of quaint device,
Innumerable of stains and splendid dyes,
As are the tiger-moth's deep-damasked wings;

And in the midst, 'mong thousand heraldries,
And twilight saints, and dim emblazonings,   215
A shielded scutcheon blushed with blood of queens and
    kings.

XXV

Full on this casement shone the wintry moon,
And threw warm gules on Madeline's fair breast,
As down she knelt for heaven's grace and boon;
Rose-bloom fell on her hands, together prest,   220
And on her silver cross soft amethyst,
And on her hair a glory, like a saint:
She seemed a splendid angel, newly drest,
Save wings, for heaven:—Porphyro grew faint:
She knelt, so pure a thing, so free from mortal taint.   225

XXVI

Anon his heart revives: her vespers done,
Of all its wreathèd pearls her hair she frees;
Unclasps her warmèd jewels one by one;
Loosens her fragrant bodice; by degrees
Her rich attire creeps rustling to her knees: 230
Half-hidden like a mermaid in sea-weed,
Pensive awhile she dreams awake, and sees,
In fancy, fair St. Agnes in her bed,
But dares not look behind, or all the charm is fled.

XXVII

Soon, trembling in her soft and chilly nest,   235
In sort of wakeful swoon, perplexed she lay,
Until the poppied warmth of sleep oppressed
Her soothèd limbs, and soul fatigued away;
Flown, like a thought, until the morrow-day;
Blissfully havened both from joy and pain;   240
Clasped like a missal where swart Paynims pray;
Blinded alike from sunshine and from rain,
As though a rose should shut, and be a bud again.

XXVIII

Stolen to this paradise, and so entranced,
Porphyro gazed upon her empty dress,   245

And listened to her breathing, if it chanced
To wake into a slumberous tenderness;
Which when he heard, that minute did he bless,
And breathed himself: then from the closet crept,
Noiseless as fear in a wide wilderness,   250
And over the hushed carpet, silent stept,
And 'tween the curtains peeped, where, lo!—how fast
    she slept.

XXIX

Then by the bedside, where the faded moon
Made a dim, silver twilight, soft he set
A table, and, half anguished, threw thereon   255
A cloth of woven crimson, gold, and jet:—
O for some drowsy Morphean amulet!
The boisterous, midnight, festive clarion,
The kettle-drum, and far-heard clarinet,
Affray his ears, though but in dying tone:—   260
The hall door shuts again, and all the noise is gone.

XXX

And still she slept an azure-lidded sleep,
In blanchèd linen, smooth, and lavendered,
While he from the closet brought a heap
Of candied apple, quince, and plum, and gourd;   265
With jellies soother than the creamy curd,
And lucent syrups, tinct with cinnamon;
Manna and dates, in argosy transferred
From Fez; and spicèd dainties, every one,
From silken Samarcand to cedared Lebanon.   270

XXXI

These delicates he heaped with glowing hand
On golden dishes and in baskets bright
Of wreathèd silver: sumptuous they stand
In the retirèd quiet of the night,
Filling the chilly room with perfume light.—   275
'And now, my love, my seraph fair, awake!
Thou art my heaven, and I thine eremite:
Open thine eyes for meek St. Agnes' sake,
Or I shall drowse beside thee, so my soul doth ache.'

XXXII

Thus whispering, his warm, unnervèd arm   280
Sank in her pillow. Shaded was her dream
By the dusk curtains:—'twas a midnight charm
Impossible to melt as icèd stream:
The lustrous salvers in the moonlight gleam;
Broad golden fringe upon the carpet lies: 285
It seemed he never, never could redeem
From such a stedfast spell his lady's eyes;
So mused awhile, entoiled in woofèd phantasies.

XXXIII

Awakening up, he took her hollow lute,—
Tumultuous,—and, in chords that tenderest be,   290
He played an ancient ditty, long since mute,
In Provence called, 'La belle dame sans mercy':
Close to her ear touching the melody;—
Wherewith disturbed, she uttered a soft moan:
He ceased—she panted quick—and suddenly   295
Her blue affrayèd eyes wide open shone:
Upon his knees he sank, pale as smooth-sculptured stone.

XXXIV

Her eyes were open, but she still beheld,
Now wide awake, the vision of her sleep:
There was a painful change, that nigh expelled   300
The blisses of her dream so pure and deep;
At which fair Madeline began to weep,
And moan forth witless words with many a sigh;
While still her gaze on Porphyro would keep;
Who knelt, with joined hands and piteous eye,   305
Fearing to move or speak, she looked so dreamingly.

XXXV

'Ah, Porphyro!' said she, 'but even now
Thy voice was at sweet tremble in mine ear,
Made tuneable with every sweetest vow;
And those sad eyes were spiritual and clear: 310

How changed thou art! how pallid, chill, and drear!
Give me that voice again, my Porphyro,
Those looks immortal, those complainings dear!
Oh leave me not in this eternal woe,
For if thou diest, my Love, I know not where to go.'   315

XXXVI

Beyond a mortal man impassioned far
At these voluptuous accents, he arose,
Ethereal, flushed, and like a throbbing star
Seen mid the sapphire heaven's deep repose;
Into her dream he melted, as the rose   320
Blendeth its odour with the violet,—
Solution sweet: meantime the frost-wind blows
Like Love's alarum pattering the sharp sleet
Against the window-panes; St. Agnes' moon hath set.

XXXVII

'Tis dark: quick pattereth the flaw-blown sleet: 325
'This is no dream, my bride, my Madeline!'
'Tis dark: the icèd gusts still rave and beat:
'No dream, alas! alas! and woe is mine!
Porphyro will leave me here to fade and pine.—
Cruel! what traitor could thee hither bring?   330
I curse not, for my heart is lost in thine,
Though thou forsakest a deceivèd thing;—
A dove forlorn and lost with sick unprunèd wing.'

XXXVIII

'My Madeline! sweet dreamer! lovely bride!
Say, may I be for ay thy vassal blest?   335
Thy beauty's shield, heart-shaped and vermeil dyed?
Ah, silver shrine, here will I take my rest
After so many hours of toil and quest,
A famished pilgrim,—saved by miracle.
Though I have found, I will not rob thy nest   340
Saving of thy sweet self; if thou think'st well
To trust, fair Madeline, to no rude infidel.

XXXIX

'Hark! 'tis an elfin-storm from faery land,
Of haggard seeming, but a boon indeed:

Arise—arise! the morning is at hand;— 345
The bloated wassaillers will never heed:—
Let us away, my love, with happy speed;
There are no ears to hear, or eyes to see,—
Drowned all in Rhenish and the sleepy mead:
Awake! arise! my love, and fearless be, 350
For o'er the southern moors I have a home for thee.'

XL

She hurried at his words, beset with fears,
For there were sleeping dragons all around,
At glaring watch, perhaps, with ready spears—
Down the wide stairs a darkling way they found.— 355
In all the house was heard no human sound.
A chain-drooped lamp was flickering by each door;
The arras, rich with horseman, hawk, and hound,
Fluttered in the besieging wind's uproar;
And the long carpets rose along the gusty floor. 360

XLI

They glide, like phantoms, into the wide hall;
Like phantoms, to the iron porch they glide;
Where lay the Porter, in uneasy sprawl,
With a huge empty flagon by his side:
The wakeful bloodhound rose, and shook his hide, 365
But his sagacious eye an inmate owns:
By one, and one, the bolts full easy slide:—
The chains lie silent on the footworn stones;—
The key turns, and the door upon its hinges groans.

XLII

And they are gone: aye, ages long ago 370
These lovers fled away into the storm.
That night the Baron dreamt of many a woe,
And all his warrior-guests, with shade and form
Of witch, and demon, and large coffin-worm
Were long be-nightmared. Angela the old 375
Died palsy-twitched, with meagre face deform;
The Beadsman, after thousand aves told,
For ay unsought for slept among his ashes cold.

LINES ON THE MERMAID TAVERN

Souls of Poets dead and gone,
What Elysium have ye known,
Happy field or mossy cavern,
Choicer than the Mermaid Tavern?
Have ye tippled drink more fine   5
Than mine host's Canary wine?
Or are fruits of Paradise
Sweeter than those dainty pies
Of venison? O generous food!
Drest as though bold Robin Hood   10
Would, with his Maid Marian,
Sup and bowse from horn and can.

  I have heard that on a day
Mine host's sign-board flew away,
Nobody knew whither, till   15
An astrologer's old quill
To a sheepskin gave the story,
Said he saw you in your glory,
Underneath a new-old sign
Sipping beverage divine,   20
And pledging with contented smack
The Mermaid in the Zodiac.

  Souls of Poets dead and gone,
What Elysium have ye known,
Happy field or mossy cavern,   25
Choicer than the Mermaid Tavern?

TO ONE WHO HAS BEEN LONG IN CITY PENT

To one who has been long in city pent,
'Tis very sweet to look into the fair
And open face of heaven,—to breathe a prayer
Full in the smile of the blue firmament.
Who is more happy, when, with heart's content,
Fatigued he sinks into some pleasant lair
Of wavy grass, and reads a debonair
And gentle tale of love and languishment?

Returning home at evening with an ear
Catching the notes of Philomel,—an eye
Watching the sailing cloudlet's bright career,
He mourns that day so soon has glided by:
E'en like the passage of an angel's tear
That falls through the clear ether silently.

ON THE GRASSHOPPER AND THE CRICKET

The poetry of earth is never dead:
When all the birds are faint with the hot sun,
And hide in cooling trees, a voice will run
From hedge to hedge about the new-mown mead;
That is the Grasshopper's—he takes the lead
In summer luxury,—he has never done
With his delights; for when tired out with fun
He rests at ease beneath some pleasant weed.
The poetry of earth is ceasing never:
On a lone winter evening, when the frost
Has wrought a silence, from the stove there shrills
The Cricket's song, in warmth increasing ever,
And seems to one in drowsiness half lost,
The Grasshopper's among some grassy hills.

ON FIRST LOOKING INTO CHAPMAN'S HOMER

Much have I travell'd in the realms of gold,
And many goodly states and kingdoms seen;
Round many western islands have I been
Which bards in fealty to Apollo hold.
Oft of one wide expanse had I been told
That deep-brow'd Homer ruled as his demesne;
Yet did I never breathe its pure serene
Till I heard Chapman speak out loud and bold:
Then felt I like some watcher of the skies
When a new planet swims into his ken;
Or like stout Cortez when with eagle eyes
He star'd at the Pacific—and all his men
Look'd at each other with a wild surmise—
Silent, upon a peak in Darien.

ON SEEING THE ELGIN MARBLES

My spirit is too weak—mortality
Weighs heavily on me like unwilling sleep,
And each imagined pinnacle and steep
Of godlike hardship, tells me I must die
Like a sick Eagle looking at the sky.
Yet 'tis a gentle luxury to weep
That I have not the cloudy winds to keep,
Fresh for the opening of the morning's eye.
Such dim-conceivèd glories of the brain
Bring round the heart an undescribable feud;
So do these wonders a most dizzy pain,
That mingles Grecian grandeur with the rude
Wasting of old Time—with a billowy main—
A sun—a shadow of a magnitude.

ON THE SEA

It keeps eternal whisperings around
Desolate shores, and with its mighty swell
Gluts twice ten thousand Caverns, till the spell
Of Hecate leaves them their old shadowy sound.
Often 'tis in such gentle temper found,
That scarcely will the very smallest shell
Be moved for days from where it sometime fell,
When last the winds of Heaven were unbound.
Oh ye! who have your eye-balls vexed and tired,
Feast them upon the wideness of the Sea;
Oh ye! whose ears are dinned with uproar rude,
Or fed too much with cloying melody—
Sit ye near some old Cavern's Mouth, and brood
Until ye start, as if the sea-nymphs quired!

WHEN I HAVE FEARS THAT I MAY CEASE TO BE

When I have fears that I may cease to be
Before my pen has glean'd my teeming brain,
Before high-piled books, in charact'ry,
Hold like rich garners the full ripen'd grain;

When I behold, upon the night's starr'd face,
Huge cloudy symbols of a high romance,
And think that I may never live to trace
Their shadows, with the magic hand of chance;
And when I feel, fair creature of an hour,
That I shall never look upon thee more,
Never have relish in the faery power
Of unreflecting love;—then on the shore
Of the wide world I stand alone, and think
Till love and fame to nothingness do sink.

BRIGHT STAR! WOULD I WERE STEADFAST
AS THOU ART

Bright star! would I were steadfast as thou art—
Not in lone splendor hung aloft the night,
And watching, with eternal lids apart,
Like Nature's patient sleepless Eremite,
The moving waters at their priestlike task
Of pure ablution round earth's human shores,
Or gazing on the new soft-fallen mask
Of snow upon the mountains and the moors—
No—yet still steadfast, still unchangeable,
Pillowed upon my fair love's ripening breast,
To feel for ever its soft fall and swell,
Awake for ever in a sweet unrest,
Still, still to hear her tender-taken breath,
  And so live ever—or else swoon to death.

PART SIX
The Victorian Age

RALPH WALDO EMERSON (1803–1882)

CONCORD HYMN

Sung at the Completion of the Battle Monument, July 4, 1837

By the rude bridge that arched the flood,
   Their flag to April's breeze unfurled,
Here once the embattled farmers stood
   And fired the shot heard round the world.

The foe long since in silence slept;   5
   Alike the conqueror silent sleeps;
And Time the ruined bridge has swept
   Down the dark stream which seaward creeps.

On this green bank, by this soft stream,
   We set to-day a votive stone;   10
That memory may their deed redeem,
   When, like our sires, our sons are gone.

Spirit, that made those heroes dare
   To die, and leave their children free,
Bid Time and Nature gently spare   15
   The shaft we raise to them and thee.

HAMATREYA

Bulkeley, Hunt, Willard, Hosmer, Meriam, Flint,
Possessed the land which rendered to their toil
Hay, corn, roots, hemp, flax, apples, wool, and wood.
Each of these landlords walked amidst his farm,
Saying, " 'Tis mine, my children's, and my name's: 5
How sweet the west wind sounds in my own trees!
How graceful climb those shadows on my hill!
I fancy these pure waters and the flags

Know me, as does my dog: we sympathize;
And, I affirm, my actions smack of the soil."   10
Where are these men? Asleep beneath their grounds;
And strangers, fond as they, their furrows plough.
Earth laughs in flowers, to see her boastful boys
Earth-proud, proud of the earth which is not theirs;
Who steer the plough, but cannot steer their feet   15
Clear of the grave.
They added ridge to valley, brook to pond,
And sighed for all that bounded their domain.
"This suits me for a pasture; that's my park;
We must have clay, lime, gravel, granite-ledge,   20
And misty lowland, where to go for peat.
The land is well,—lies fairly to the south.
'Tis good, when you have crossed the sea and back,
To find the sitfast acres where you left them."
Ah! the hot owner sees not Death, who adds   25
Him to his land, a lump of mould the more.
Hear what the Earth says:—

EARTH-SONG

"Mine and yours;
Mine, not yours.
Earth endures;   30
Stars abide—
Shine down in the old sea;
Old are the shores;
But where are old men?
I who have seen much,   35
Such have I never seen.

"The lawyer's deed
Ran sure,
In tail,
To them, and to their heirs   40
Who shall succeed,
Without fail,
Forevermore.

"Here is the land,
Shaggy with wood,   45
With its old valley,
Mound, and flood.
But the heritors?—
Fled like the flood's foam.
The lawyer, and the laws,   50
And the kingdom,
Clean swept herefrom.

"They called me theirs,
Who so controlled me;
Yet every one   55
Wished to stay, and is gone.
How am I theirs,
If they cannot hold me,
But I hold them?"

When I heard the Earth-Song,   60
I was no longer brave;
My avarice cooled
Like lust in the chill of the grave.

DAYS

Daughters of Time, the hypocritic Days,
Muffled and dumb like barefoot dervishes,
And marching single in an endless file,
Bring diadems and fagots in their hands.
To each they offer gifts after his will,
Bread, kingdoms, stars, and sky that holds them all.
I, in my pleachèd garden, watched the pomp,
Forgot my morning wishes, hastily
Took a few herbs and apples, and the Day
Turned and departed silent. I, too late,
Under her solemn fillet saw the scorn.

THE RHODORA

On Being Asked, Whence is the Flower?

In May, when sea-winds pierced our solitudes,
I found the fresh Rhodora in the woods,
Spreading its leafless blooms in a damp nook,
To please the desert and the sluggish brook.
The purple petals fallen in the pool,   5
Made the black water with their beauty gay;
Here might the red-bird come his plumes to cool,
And court the flower that cheapens his array.
Rhodora! if the sages ask thee why
This charm is wasted on the earth and sky,   10
Tell them, dear, that if eyes were made for seeing,
Then Beauty is its own excuse for being:
Why thou wert there, O rival of the rose!
I never thought to ask, I never knew;
But, in my simple ignorance, suppose   15
The self-same Power that brought me there brought
    you.

BRAHMA

If the red slayer think he slays,
    Or if the slain think he is slain,
They know not well the subtle ways
    I keep, and pass, and turn again.

Far or forgot to me is near;   5
    Shadow and sunlight are the same;
The vanished gods to me appear;
    And one to me are shame and fame.

They reckon ill who leave me out;
    When me they fly, I am the wings;   10
I am the doubter and the doubt,
    And I the hymn the Brahmin sings.

The strong gods pine for my abode,
    And pine in vain the sacred Seven;
But thou, meek lover of the good!   15
    Find me, and turn thy back on heaven.

HENRY WADSWORTH LONGFELLOW
(1807–1882)

MY LOST YOUTH

Often I think of the beautiful town
  That is seated by the sea;
Often in thought go up and down
The pleasant streets of that dear old town,
    And my youth comes back to me.   5
      And a verse of a Lapland song
      Is haunting my memory still:
      "A boy's will is the wind's will,
And the thoughts of youth are long, long thoughts."

I can see the shadowy lines of its trees,   10
  And catch, in sudden gleams,
The sheen of the far-surrounding seas,
And islands that were the Hesperides
  Of all my boyish dreams.
      And the burden of that old song,   15
      It murmurs and whispers still:
      "A boy's will is the wind's will,
And the thoughts of youth are long, long thoughts."

I remember the black wharves and the slips,
  And the sea-tides tossing free;   20
And Spanish sailors with bearded lips,
And the beauty and mystery of the ships,
  And the magic of the sea.
      And the voice of that wayward song
      Is singing and saying still: 25
      "A boy's will is the wind's will,
And the thoughts of youth are long, long thoughts."

I remember the bulwarks by the shore,
  And the fort upon the hill;
The sunrise gun, with its hollow roar,   30
The drum-beat repeated o'er and o'er,

And the bugle wild and shrill.
　And the music of that old song
　Throbs in my memory still:
　"A boy's will is the wind's will,
And the thoughts of youth are long, long thoughts." 35

I remember the sea-fight far away,
　How it thundered o'er the tide!
And the dead sea-captains, as they lay
In their graves, o'erlooking the tranquil bay 40
　Where they in battle died.
　And the sound of that mournful song
　Goes through me with a thrill:
　"A boy's will is the wind's will,
And the thoughts of youth are long, long thoughts." 45

I can see the breezy dome of groves,
　The shadows of Deering's Woods;
And the friendships old and the early loves
Come back with a Sabbath sound, as of doves
　In quiet neighborhoods. 50
　And the verse of that sweet old song,
　It flutters and murmurs still:
　"A boy's will is the wind's will,
And the thoughts of youth are long, long thoughts."

I remember the gleams and glooms that dart 55
　Across the school-boy's brain;
The song and the silence in the heart,
That in part are prophecies, and in part
　Are longings wild and vain.
　And the voice of that fitful song 60
　Sings on, and is never still:
　"A boy's will is the wind's will,
And the thoughts of youth are long, long thoughts."

There are things of which I may not speak;
　There are dreams that cannot die; 65
There are thoughts that make the strong heart weak,
And bring a pallor into the cheek,
　And a mist before the eye.

And the words of that fatal song
Come over me like a chill: 70
"A boy's will is the wind's will,
And the thoughts of youth are long, long thoughts."

Strange to me now are the forms I meet
    When I visit the dear old town;
But the native air is pure and sweet,   75
And the trees that o'ershadow each well-known street,
    As they balance up and down,
        Are singing the beautiful song,
        Are sighing and whispering still:
        "A boy's will is the wind's will,   80
And the thoughts of youth are long, long thoughts."

And Deering's Woods are fresh and fair,
    And with joy that is almost pain
My heart goes back to wander there,
And among the dreams of the days that were,   85
    I find my lost youth again.
        And the strange and beautiful song,
        The groves are repeating it still:
        "A boy's will is the wind's will,
And the thoughts of youth are long, long thoughts."   90

THREE SONNETS ON THE
DIVINA COMMEDIA

I

Oft have I seen at some cathedral door
A laborer, pausing in the dust and heat,
Lay down his burden, and with reverent feet
Enter, and cross himself, and on the floor
Kneel to repeat his paternoster o'er;
Far off the noises of the world retreat;
The loud vociferations of the street
Become an undistinguishable roar.
So, as I enter here from day to day,

And leave my burden at this minster gate,
Kneeling in prayer, and not ashamed to pray,
The tumult of the time disconsolate
To inarticulate murmurs dies away,
While the eternal ages watch and wait.

II

How strange the sculptures that adorn these towers!
This crowd of statues, in whose folded sleeves
Birds build their nests: while canopied with leaves
Parvis and portal bloom like trellised bowers,
And the vast minster seems a cross of flowers!
But fiends and dragons on the gargoyled eaves
Watch the dead Christ between the living thieves,
And, underneath, the traitor Judas lowers!
Ah! from what agonies of heart and brain,
What exultations trampling on despair,
What tenderness, what tears, what hate of wrong,
What passionate outcry of a soul in pain,
Uprose this poem of the earth and air,
This medieval miracle of song!

III

I lift mine eyes, and all the windows blaze
With forms of saints and holy men who died,
Here martyred and hereafter glorified;
And the great Rose upon its leaves displays
Christ's triumph, and the angelic roundelays,
With splendor upon splendor multiplied;
And Beatrice again at Dante's side
No more rebukes, but smiles her words of praise.
And then the organ sounds, and unseen choirs
Sing the old Latin hymns of peace and love,
And benedictions of the Holy Ghost;
And the melodious bells among the spires
O'er all the house-tops and through heaven above
Proclaim the elevation of the Host!

EDGAR ALLAN POE (1809–1849)

TO HELEN

Helen, thy beauty is to me
  Like those Nicèan barks of yore
That gently, o'er a perfumed sea,
  The weary way-worn wanderer bore
To his own native shore.   5

On desperate seas long wont to roam,
  Thy hyacinth hair, thy classic face,
Thy Naiad airs have brought me home
  To the glory that was Greece,
And the grandeur that was Rome.   10

Lo, in yon brilliant window-niche
  How statue-like I see thee stand,
  The agate lamp within thy hand,
Ah! Psyche, from the regions which
  Are holy land!   15

ANNABEL LEE

It was many and many a year ago,
  In a kingdom by the sea,
That a maiden there lived whom you may know
  By the name of Annabel Lee;—
And this maiden she lived with no other thought   5
  Than to love and be loved by me.

I was a child and she was a child,
  In this kingdom by the sea,
But we loved with a love that was more than love—
  I and my Annabel Lee—   10
With a love that the wingèd seraphs of Heaven
  Coveted her and me.

And this was the reason that, long ago,
  In this kingdom by the sea,

A wind blew out of a cloud by night   15
  Chilling my Annabel Lee;
So that her highborn kinsman came
  And bore her away from me,
To shut her up in a sepulcher
  In this kingdom by the sea.   20

The angels, not half so happy in heaven,
  Went envying her and me:—
Yes! that was the reason (as all men know,
  In this kingdom by the sea)
That the wind came out of the clouds, chilling   25
  And killing my Annabel Lee.

But our love it was stronger by far than the love
  Of those who were older than we—
  Of many far wiser than we—
And neither the angels in heaven above   30
  Nor the demons down under the sea
Can ever dissever my soul from the soul
  Of the beautiful Annabel Lee:—

For the moon never beams without bringing me dreams
  Of the beautiful Annabel Lee;   35
And the stars never rise but I feel the bright eyes
  Of the beautiful Annabel Lee;
And so, all the night-tide, I lie down by the side
Of my darling, my darling, my life and my bride,
  In her sepulcher there by the sea,   40
  In her tomb by the side of the sea.

EDWARD FITZGERALD (1809–1883)

QUATRAINS FROM
THE RUBAIYAT OF OMAR KHAYYAM

I

Wake! For the Sun, who scattered into flight
The Stars before him from the Field of Night,
  Drives Night along with them from Heav'n, and strikes
The Sultàn's Turret with a Shaft of Light.

Before the phantom of False morning died,   5
Methought a Voice within the Tavern cried,
   "When all the Temple is prepared within,
Why nods the drowsy Worshipper outside?"

And, as the Cock crew, those who stood before
The Tavern shouted—"Open then the Door!   10
   You know how little while we have to stay,
And, once departed, may return no more."

       *   *   *

Come, fill the Cup, and in the fire of Spring
Your Winter-garment of Repentance fling:
   The Bird of Time has but a little way   15
To flutter—and the Bird is on the Wing.

II

A Book of Verses underneath the Bough,
A Jug of Wine, a Loaf of Bread—and Thou
   Beside me singing in the Wilderness—
Oh, Wilderness were Paradise enow!

Some for the Glories of this World; and some   5
Sigh for the Prophet's Paradise to come;
   Ah, take the Cash, and let the Credit go,
Nor heed the rumble of a distant Drum!

Look to the blowing Rose about us—"Lo,
Laughing," she says, "into the world I blow,   10
   At once the silken tassel of my Purse
Tear, and its Treasure on the Garden throw."

And those who husbanded the Golden grain,
And those who flung it to the winds like Rain,
   Alike to no such aureate Earth are turn'd   15
As, buried once, Men want dug up again.

The Worldly Hope men set their Hearts upon
Turns Ashes—or it prospers; and anon,
   Like Snow upon the Desert's dusty Face,
Lighting a little hour or two—was gone.   20

Think, in this batter'd Caravanserai
Whose Portals are alternate Night and Day,
How Sultan after Sultan with his Pomp
Abode his destin'd Hour, and went his way.

They say the Lion and the Lizard keep   25
The Courts where Jamshyd gloried and drank deep:
And Bahram, that great Hunter—the Wild Ass
Stamps o'er his Head, but cannot break his Sleep.

I sometimes think that never blows so red
The Rose as where some buried Cæsar bled;   30
That every Hyacinth the Garden wears
Dropt in her Lap from some once lovely Head.

And this reviving Herb whose tender Green
Fledges the River-Lip on which we lean—
Ah, lean upon it lightly! for who knows   35
From what once lovely Lip it springs unseen!

Oh, my Belovèd, fill the Cup that clears
To-day of past Regret and future Fears:
To-morrow!—Why, To-morrow I may be
Myself with Yesterday's Sev'n thousand Years.   40

For some we loved, the loveliest and the best
That from his Vintage rolling Time hath prest,
Have drunk their Cup a Round or two before
And one by one crept silently to rest.

And we that now make merry in the Room   45
They left, and Summer dresses in new bloom,
Ourselves must we beneath the Couch of Earth
Descend—ourselves to make a Couch—for whom?

Ah, make the most of what we yet may spend,
Before we too into the Dust descend;   50
Dust into Dust, and under Dust, to lie,
Sans Wine, sans Song, sans Singer, and—sans End!

III

O Thou, who Man of baser Earth didst make,
  And ev'n with Paradise devised the Snake:
    For all the Sin wherewith the Face of Man
Is blackened—Man's forgiveness give—and take!

IV

Yet Ah, that Spring should vanish with the Rose
That Youth's sweet-scented manuscript should close!
    The Nightingale that in the branches sang,
Oh whence, and whither flown again, who knows!

Would but the Desert of the Fountain yield   5
One glimpse—if dimly, yet indeed, reveal'd,
    To which the fainting Traveller might spring,
As springs the trampled herbage of the field!

Would but some wingèd Angel ere too late
Arrest the yet unfolded Roll of Fate,   10
    And make the stern Recorder otherwise
Enregister, or quite obliterate!

Ah Love! could you and I with Him conspire
To grasp this sorry Scheme of Things entire,
    Would not we shatter it to bits—and then   15
Re-mould it nearer to the Heart's desire.

Yon rising Moon that looks for us again—
How oft hereafter will she wax and wane;
    How oft hereafter rising look for us
Through this same Garden—and for one in vain!   20

And when like her, oh Saki, you shall pass
Among the Guests Star-scatter'd on the Grass,
    And in your joyous errand reach the spot
Where I made One—turn down an empty Glass!

ALFRED, LORD TENNYSON (1809–1892)

THE LADY OF SHALOTT

I

On either side the river lie
Long fields of barley and of rye,
That clothe the wold and meet the sky;
And thro' the field the road runs by
  To many-tower'd Camelot;   5
And up and down the people go,
Gazing where the lilies blow
Round an island there below,
  The island of Shalott.

Willows whiten, aspens quiver,   10
Little breezes dusk and shiver
Thro' the wave that runs for ever
By the island in the river
  Flowing down to Camelot.
Four grey walls, and four grey towers, 15
Overlook a space of flowers,
And the silent isle imbowers
  The Lady of Shalott.

By the margin, willow-veil'd,
Slide the heavy barges trail'd   20
By slow horses; and unhail'd
The shallop flitteth silken-sail'd
  Skimming down to Camelot:
But who hath seen her wave her hand?
Or at the casement seen her stand? 25
Or is she known in all the land,
  The Lady of Shalott?

Only reapers, reaping early
In among the bearded barley,
Hear a song that echoes cheerly 30
From the river winding clearly,
  Down to tower'd Camelot:

And by the moon the reaper weary,
Piling sheaves in uplands airy,
Listening, whispers " 'Tis the fairy   35
      Lady of Shalott."

II

There she weaves by night and day
A magic web with colours gay.
She has heard a whisper say,
A curse is on her if she stay   40
      To look down to Camelot.
She knows not what the curse may be,
And so she weaveth steadily,
And little other care hath she,
      The Lady of Shalott.   45

And moving thro' a mirror clear
That hangs before her all the year,
Shadows of the world appear.
There she sees the highway near
      Winding down to Camelot: 50
There the river eddy whirls.
And there the surly vilage-churls,
And the red cloaks of market girls,
      Pass onward from Shalott.

Sometimes a troop of damsels glad,   55
An abbot on an ambling pad,
Sometimes a curly shepherd-lad,
Or long-hair'd page in crimson clad,
      Goes by to tower'd Camelot;
And sometimes thro' the mirror blue   60
The knights come riding two and two:
She hath no loyal knight and true,
      The Lady of Shalott.

But in her web she still delights
To weave the mirror's magic sights,   65
For often thro' the silent nights
A funeral, with plumes and lights
      And music, went to Camelot:

Or when the moon was overhead,
Came two young lovers lately wed;   70
"I am half sick of shadows," said
    The Lady of Shalott.

III

A bow-shot from her bower-eaves,
He rode between the barley-sheaves,
The sun came dazzling thro' the leaves,   75
And flamed upon the brazen greaves
    Of bold Sir Lancelot.
A red-cross knight for ever kneel'd
To a lady in his shield,
That sparkled on the yellow field,   80
    Beside remote Shalott.

The gemmy bridle glitter'd free,
Like to some branch of stars we see
Hung in the golden Galaxy.
The bridle bells rang merrily   85
    As he rode down to Camelot:
And from his blazon'd baldric slung
A mighty silver bugle hung,
And as he rode his armour rung,
    Beside remote Shalott.   90

All in the blue unclouded weather
Thick-jewell'd shone the saddle-leather,
The helmet and the helmet-feather
Burn'd like one burning flame together,
    As he rode down to Camelot.   95
As often thro' the purple night,
Below the starry clusters bright,
Some bearded meteor, trailing light,
    Moves over still Shalott.

His broad clear brow in sunlight glow'd;   100
On burnish'd hooves his war-horse trode;
From underneath his helmet flow'd
His coal-black curls as on he rode,
    As he rode down to Camelot.

From the bank and from the river 105
He flash'd into the crystal mirror,
"Tirra lirra," by the river
      Sang Sir Lancelot.

She left the web, she left the loom,
She made three paces thro' the room, 110
She saw the water-lily bloom,
She saw the helmet and the plume,
      She look'd down to Camelot.
Out flew the web and floated wide;
The mirror crack'd from side to side; 115
"The curse is come upon me," cried
      The Lady of Shalott.

IV

In the stormy east-wind straining,
The pale yellow woods were waning,
The broad stream in his banks complaining, 120
Heavily the low sky raining
      Over tower'd Camelot;
Down she came and found a boat
Beneath a willow left afloat,
And round about the prow she wrote 125
      The Lady of Shalott.

And down the river's dim expanse
Like some bold seër in a trance,
Seeing all his own mischance—
With a glassy countenance 130
      Did she look to Camelot.
And at the closing of the day
She loosed the chain, and down she lay;
The broad stream bore her far away,
      The Lady of Shalott. 135

Lying, robed in snowy white
That loosely flew to left and right—
The leaves upon her falling light—
Thro' the noises of the night
      She floated down to Camelot: 140

And as the boat-head wound along
The willowy hills and fields among,
They heard her singing her last song,
    The Lady of Shalott.

Heard a carol, mournful, holy,   145
Chanted loudly, chanted lowly,
Till her blood was frozen slowly,
And her eyes were darken'd wholly,
    Turn'd to tower'd Camelot.
For ere she reach'd upon the tide   150
The first house by the water-side,
Singing in her song she died,
    The Lady of Shalott.

Under tower and balcony,
By garden-wall and gallery,   155
A gleaming shape she floated by,
Dead-pale between the houses high,
    Silent into Camelot.
Out upon the wharfs they came,
Knight and burgher, lord and dame,   160
And round the prow they read her name,
    The Lady of Shalott.

Who is this? and what is here?
And in the lighted palace near
Died the sound of royal cheer;   165
And they cross'd themselves for fear,
    All the knights at Camelot:
But Lancelot mused a little space;
He said, "She has a lovely face;
God in His mercy lend her grace,   170
    The Lady of Shalott."

THE LOTOS-EATERS

"Courage!" he said, and pointed toward the land,
"This mounting wave will roll us shoreward soon."
In the afternoon they came unto a land
In which it seemed always afternoon.

All round the coast the languid air did swoon,   5
Breathing like one that hath a weary dream.
Full-faced above the valley stood the moon;
And like a downward smoke, the slender stream
Along the cliff to fall and pause and fall did seem.

A land of streams! some, like a downward smoke,   10
Slow-dropping veils of thinnest lawn, did go;
And some through wavering lights and shadows broke,
Rolling a slumbrous sheet of foam below.
They saw the gleaming river seaward flow
From the inner land: far off, three mountain-tops,   15
Three silent pinnacles of aged snow,
Stood sunset-flushed: and, dewed with showery drops,
Up-clomb the shadowy pine above the woven copse.

The charmed sunset lingered low adown
In the red West: through mountain clefts the dale   20
Was seen far inland, and the yellow down
Bordered with palm, and many a winding vale
And meadow, set with slender galingale;
A land where all things always seemed the same!
And round about the keel with faces pale,   25
Dark faces pale against that rosy flame,
The mild-eyed melancholy Lotos-eaters came.

Branches they bore of that enchanted stem,
Laden with flower and fruit, whereof they gave
To each, but whoso did receive of them,   30
And taste, to him the gushing of the wave
Far far away did seem to mourn and rave
On alien shores; and if his fellow spake,
His voice was thin, as voices from the grave;
And deep-asleep he seemed, yet all awake,   35
And music in his ears his beating heart did make.

They sat them down upon the yellow sand,
Between the sun and moon upon the shore;
And sweet it was to dream of Fatherland,
Of child, and wife, and slave; but evermore   40
Most weary seemed the sea, weary the oar,
Weary the wandering fields of barren foam.

Then someone said, "We will return no more";
And all at once they sang, "Our island home
Is far beyond the wave; we will no longer roam."   45

CHORIC SONG

I

There is sweet music here that softer falls
Than petals from blown roses on the grass,
Or night-dews on still waters between walls
Of shadowy granite, in a gleaming pass;
Music that gentlier on the spirit lies,   50
Than tired eyelids upon tired eyes;
Music that brings sweet sleep down from the blissful skies.
Here are cool mosses deep,
And through the moss the ivies creep,
And in the stream the long-leaved flowers weep,   55
And from the craggy ledge the poppy hangs in sleep.

II

Why are we weighed upon with heaviness,
And utterly consumed with sharp distress,
While all things else have rest from weariness?
All things have rest: why should we toil alone,   60
We only toil, who are the first of things,
And make perpetual moan,
Still from one sorrow to another thrown:
Nor ever fold our wings,
And cease from wanderings,   65
Nor steep our brows in slumber's holy balm;
Nor hearken what the inner spirit sings,
"There is no joy but calm!"—
Why should we only toil, the roof and crown of things?

III

Lo! in the middle of the wood,   70
The folded leaf is wooed from out the bud
With winds upon the branch, and there
Grows green and broad, and takes no care,
Sun-steeped at noon, and in the moon
Nightly dew-fed; and turning yellow   75
Falls, and floats adown the air.

Lo! sweetened with the summer light,
The full-juiced apple, waxing over-mellow,
Drops in a silent autumn night.
All its allotted length of days,   80
The flower ripens in its place,
Ripens and fades, and falls, and hath no toil,
Fast-rooted in the fruitful soil.

IV

Hateful is the dark-blue sky,
Vaulted o'er the dark-blue sea.   85
Death is the end of life; ah, why
Should life all labor be?
Let us alone. Time driveth onward fast,
And in a little while our lips are dumb.
Let us alone. What is it that will last?   90
All things are taken from us, and become
Portions and parcels of the dreadful past.
Let us alone. What pleasure can we have
To war with evil? Is there any peace
In ever climbing up the climbing wave?   95
All things have rest, and ripen toward the grave
In silence—ripen, fall and cease:
Give us long rest or death, dark death, or dreamful ease.

V

How sweet it were, hearing the downward stream,
With half-shut eyes ever to seem   100
Falling asleep in a half-dream!
To dream and dream, like yonder amber light,
Which will not leave the myrrh-bush on the height;
To hear each other's whispered speech;
Eating the Lotos day by day,   105
To watch the crisping ripples on the beach,
And tender curving lines of creamy spray;
To lend our hearts and spirits wholly
To the influence of mild-minded melancholy;
To muse and brood and live again in memory,   110
With those old faces of our infancy
Heaped over with a mound of grass,
Two handfuls of white dust, shut in an urn of brass!

VI

Dear is the memory of our wedded lives,
And dear the last embraces of our wives   115
And their warm tears: but all hath suffered change;
For surely now our household hearths are cold:
Our sons inherit us: our looks are strange:
And we should come like ghosts to trouble joy.
Or else the island princes over-bold   120
Have eat our substance, and the minstrel sings
Before them of the ten-years' war in Troy,
And our great deeds, as half-forgotten things.
Is there confusion in the little isle?
Let what is broken so remain.   125
The Gods are hard to reconcile:
'Tis hard to settle order once again.
There is confusion worse than death,
Trouble on trouble, pain on pain,
Long labor unto aged breath,   130
Sore task to hearts worn out with many wars
And eyes grown dim with gazing on the pilot-stars.

VII

But, propt on beds of amaranth and moly,
How sweet (while warm airs lull us, blowing lowly)
With half-dropt eyelids still,   135
Beneath a heaven dark and holy,
To watch the long bright river drawing slowly
His waters from the purple hill—
To hear the dewy echoes calling
From cave to cave through the thick-twined vine—   140
To watch the emerald-colored water falling
Through many a woven acanthus-wreath divine!
Only to hear and see the far-off sparkling brine,
Only to hear were sweet, stretched out beneath the pine.

VIII

The Lotos blooms below the barren peak: 145
The Lotos blows by every winding creek:
All day the wind breathes low with mellower tone:
Through every hollow cave and alley lone

Round and round the spicy downs the yellow Lotos-dust is
    blown.
We have had enough of action, and of motion we,   150
Rolled to starboard, rolled to larboard, when the surge was
    seething free,
Where the wallowing monster spouted his foam-fountains
    in the sea.
Let us swear an oath, and keep it with an equal mind,
In the hollow Lotos-land to live and lie reclined
On the hills like Gods together, careless of mankind.   155
For they lie beside their nectar, and the bolts are hurled
Far below them in the valleys, and the clouds are lightly
    curled
Round their golden houses, girdled with the gleaming
    world:
Where they smile in secret, looking over wasted lands,
Blight and famine, plague and earthquake, roaring deeps
    and fiery sands,   160
Clanging fights, and flaming towns, and sinking ships, and
    praying hands.
But they smile, they find a music centered in a doleful song
Steaming up, a lamentation and an ancient tale of wrong,
Like a tale of little meaning though the words are strong;
Chanted from an ill-used race of men that cleave the soil, 165
Sow the seed, and reap the harvest with enduring toil,
Storing yearly little dues of wheat, and wine and oil;
Till they perish and they suffer—some, 'tis whispered—
    down in hell
Suffer endless anguish, others in Elysian valleys dwell,
Resting weary limbs at last on beds of asphodel.   170
Surely, surely, slumber is more sweet than toil, the shore
Than labor in the deep mid-ocean, wind and wave and oar;
Oh, rest ye, brother mariners, we will not wander more.

ULYSSES

It little profits that an idle king,
By this still hearth, among these barren crags,
Matched with an aged wife, I mete and dole
Unequal laws unto a savage race,
That hoard, and sleep, and feed, and know not me.   5

I cannot rest from travel: I will drink
Life to the lees; all times I have enjoyed
Greatly, have suffered greatly, both with those
That loved me, and alone; on shore, and when
Through scudding drifts the rainy Hyades   10
Vext the dim sea: I am become a name;
For always roaming with a hungry heart
Much have I seen and known; cities of men
And manners, climates, councils, governments,
Myself not least, but honoured of them all;   15
And drunk delight of battle with my peers,
Far on the ringing plains of windy Troy.
I am a part of all that I have met;
Yet all experience is an arch wherethrough
Gleams that untravelled world, whose margin fades   20
For ever and for ever when I move.
How dull it is to pause, to make an end,
To rust unburnished, not to shine in use!
As though to breathe were life. Life piled on life
Were all too little, and of one to me   25
Little remains; but every hour is saved
From that eternal silence, something more,
A bringer of new things; and vile it were
For some three suns to store and hoard myself,
And this grey spirit yearning in desire   30
To follow knowledge like a sinking star,
Beyond the utmost bound of human thought.
          This is my son, mine own Telemachus,
To whom I leave the sceptre and the isle—
Well-loved of me, discerning to fulfil   35
This labour, by slow prudence to make mild
A rugged people, and through soft degrees
Subdue them to the useful and the good.
Most blameless is he, centered in the sphere
Of common duties, decent not to fail   40
In offices of tenderness, and pay
Meet adoration to my household gods,
When I am gone. He works his work, I mine.
          There lies the port; the vessel puffs her sail:
There gloom the dark broad seas. My mariners,   45
Souls that have toiled, and wrought, and thought
          with me—

That ever with a frolic welcome took
The thunder and the sunshine, and opposed
Free hearts, free foreheads—you and I are old;
Old age hath yet his honour and his toil;   50
Death closes all; but something ere the end,
Some work of noble note, may yet be done,
Not unbecoming men that strove with Gods.
The lights begin to twinkle from the rocks:
The long day wanes: the slow moon climbs: the deep 55
Moans round with many voices. Come, my friends,
'Tis not too late to seek a newer world.
Push off, and sitting well in order smite
The sounding furrows; for my purpose holds
To sail beyond the sunset, and the baths   60
Of all the western stars, until I die.
It may be that the gulfs will wash us down:
It may be we shall touch the Happy Isles,
And see the great Achilles, whom we knew.
Though much is taken, much abides; and though   65
We are not now that strength which in old days
Moved earth and heaven; that which we are, we are;
One equal temper of heroic hearts,
Made weak by time and fate, but strong in will
To strive, to seek, to find, and not to yield.   70

MORTE D'ARTHUR

So all day long the noise of battle roll'd
Among the mountains by the winter sea;
Until King Arthur's table, man by man,
Had fall'n in Lyonnesse about their Lord,
King Arthur: then, because his wound was deep,   5
The bold Sir Bedivere uplifted him,
Sir Bedivere, the last of all his knights,
And bore him to a chapel nigh the field,
A broken chancel with a broken cross,
That stood on a dark strait of barren land.   10
On one side lay the Ocean, and on one
Lay a great water, and the moon was full.
    Then spake King Arthur to Sir Bedivere:
'The sequel of to-day unsolders all
The goodliest fellowship of famous knights   15

Whereof this world holds record. Such a sleep
They sleep—the men I loved. I think that we
Shall never more, at any future time,
Delight our souls with talk of knightly deeds,
Walking about the gardens and the halls   20
Of Camelot, as in the days that were.
I perish by this people which I made,—
Tho' Merlin sware that I should come again
To rule once more—but let what will be, be,
I am so deeply smitten thro' the helm   25
That without help I cannot last till morn.
Thou therefore take my brand Excalibur,
Which was my pride: for thou rememberest how
In those old days, one summer noon, an arm
Rose up from out the bosom of the lake,   30
Clothed in white samite, mystic, wonderful,
Holding the sword—and how I row'd across
And took it, and have worn it, like a king:
And, wheresoever I am sung or told
In aftertime, this also shall be known: 35
But now delay not: take Excalibur,
And fling him far into the middle mere:
Watch what thou seëst, and lightly bring me word.'
    To him replied the bold Sir Bedivere:
'It is not meet, Sir King, to leave thee thus,   40
Aidless, alone, and smitten thro' the helm.
A little thing may harm a wounded man.
Yet I thy hest will all perform at full,
Watch what I see, and lightly bring thee word.'
    So saying, from the ruin'd shrine he stept   45
And in the moon athwart the place of tombs,
Where lay the mighty bones of ancient men,
Old knights, and over them the sea-wind sang
Shrill, chill, with flakes of foam. He, stepping down
By zig-zag paths, and juts of pointed rock,   50
Came on the shining levels of the lake.
    There drew he forth the brand Excalibur,
And o'er him, drawing it, the winter moon,
Brightening the skirts of a long cloud, ran forth
And sparkled keen with frost against the hilt: 55
For all the haft twinkled with diamond sparks,
Myriads of topaz-lights, and jacinth-work

Of subtlest jewellery. He gazed so long
That both his eyes were dazzled, as he stood,
This way and that dividing the swift mind, 60
In act to throw: but at the last it seem'd
Better to leave Excalibur conceal'd
There in the many-knotted waterflags,
That whistled stiff and dry about the marge.
So strode he back slow to the wounded King. 65
　　Then spake King Arthur to Sir Bedivere:
'Hast thou perform'd my mission which I gave?
What is it thou hast seen? or what hast heard?'
　　And answer made the bold Sir Bedivere:
'I heard the ripple washing in the reeds, 70
And the wild water lapping on the crag.'
　　To whom replied King Arthur, faint and pale:
'Thou hast betray'd thy nature and thy name,
Not rendering true answer, as beseem'd
Thy fëalty, nor like a noble knight: 75
For surer sign had follow'd, either hand,
Or voice, or else a motion of the mere.
This is a shameful thing for men to lie.
Yet now, I charge thee, quickly go again
As thou art lief and dear, and do the thing 80
I bade thee, watch, and lightly bring me word.'
　　Then went Sir Bedivere the second time
Across the ridge, and paced beside the mere,
Counting the dewy pebbles, fix'd in thought;
But when he saw the wonder of the hilt, 85
How curiously and strangely chased, he smote
His palms together, and he cried aloud.
　　'And if indeed I cast the brand away,
Surely a precious thing, one worthy note,
Should thus be lost for ever from the earth, 90
Which might have pleased the eyes of many men.
What good should follow this, if this were done?
What harm, undone? deep harm to disobey,
Seeing obedience is the bond of rule.
Were it well to obey then, if a king demand 95
An act unprofitable, against himself?
The King is sick, and knows not what he does.
What record, or what relic of my lord
Should be to aftertime, but empty breath

And rumours of a doubt? but were this kept, 100
Stored in some treasure-house of mighty kings,
Some one might show it at a joust of arms,
Saying, "King Arthur's sword, Excalibur,
Wrought by the lonely maiden of the Lake.
Nine years she wrought it, sitting in the deeps 105
Upon the hidden bases of the hills."
So might some old man speak in the aftertime
To all the people, winning reverence.
But now much honour and much fame were lost.'
   So spake he, clouded with his own conceit, 110
And hid Excalibur the second time,
And so strode back slow to the wounded King.
   Then spoke King Arthur, breathing heavily:
'What is it thou hast seen? or what hast heard?'
   And answer made the bold Sir Bedivere: 115
'I heard the water lapping on the crag,
And the long-ripple washing in the reeds.'
   To whom replied King Arthur, much in wrath:
'Ah, miserable and unkind, untrue,
Unknightly, traitor-hearted! Woe is me! 120
Authority forgets a dying king,
Laid widow'd of the power in his eye
That bow'd the will. I see thee what thou art,
For thou, the latest-left of all my knights,
In whom should meet the offices of all, 125
Thou wouldst betray me for the precious hilt;
Either from lust of gold, or like a girl
Valuing the giddy pleasure of the eyes.
Yet, for a man may fail in duty twice,
And the third time may prosper, get thee hence: 130
But, if thou spare to fling Excalibur,
I will arise and slay thee with my hands.'
   Then quickly rose Sir Bedivere, and ran,
And, leaping down the ridges lightly, plunged
Among the bulrush-beds, and clutch'd the sword, 135
And strongly wheel'd and threw it. The great brand
Made lightnings in the splendour of the moon,
And flashing round and round, and whirl'd in an arch,
Shot like a streamer of the northern morn,
Seen where the moving isles of winter shock 140
By night, with noises of the northern sea.

So flash'd and fell the brand Excalibur:
But ere he dipt the surface, rose an arm
Clothed in white samite, mystic, wonderful,
And caught him by the hilt, and brandish'd him   145
Three times, and drew him under in the mere.
And lightly went the other to the King.
    Then spoke King Arthur, drawing thicker breath:
'Now see I by thine eyes that this is done.
Speak out: what is it thou hast heard, or seen?'   150
    And answer made the bold Sir Bedivere:
'Sir King, I closed mine eyelids, lest the gems
Should blind my purpose, for I never saw,
Nor shall see, here or elsewhere, till I die,
Not tho' I live three lives of mortal men,   155
So great a miracle as yonder hilt.
Then with both hands I flung him, wheeling him;
But when I look'd again, behold an arm,
Clothed in white samite, mystic, wonderful,
That caught him by the hilt, and brandish'd him   160
Three times, and drew him under in the mere.'
    And answer made King Arthur, breathing hard:
'My end draws nigh; 'tis time that I were gone.
Make broad thy shoulders to receive my weight,
And bear me to the margin; yet I fear   165
My wound hath taken cold, and I shall die.'
    So saying, from the pavement he half rose,
Slowly, with pain, reclining on his arm,
And looking wistfully with wide blue eyes
As in a picture. Him Sir Bedivere   170
Remorsefully regarded thro' his tears,
And would have spoken, but he found not words,
Then took with care, and kneeling on one knee,
O'er both his shoulders drew the languid hands,
And rising bore him thro' the place of tombs.   175
    But, as he walk'd, King Arthur panted hard,
Like one that feels a nightmare on his bed
When all the house is mute. So sigh'd the King,
Muttering and murmuring at his ear, 'Quick, quick!
I fear it is too late, and I shall die.'   180
But the other swiftly strode from ridge to ridge,
Clothed with his breath, and looking, as he walk'd,
Larger than human on the frozen hills.

He heard the deep behind him, and a cry
Before. His own thought drove him like a goad.   185
Dry clash'd his harness in the icy caves
And barren chasms, and all to left and right
The bare black cliff clang'd round him, as he based
His feet on juts of slippery crag that rang
Sharp-smitten with the dint of armed heels—   190
And on a sudden, lo! the level lake,
And the long glories of the winter moon.
　Then saw they how there hove a dusky barge,
Dark as a funeral scarf from stem to stern,
Beneath them; and descending they were ware   195
That all the decks were dense with stately forms
Black-stoled, black-hooded, like a dream—by these
Three Queens with crowns of gold—and from them rose
A cry that shiver'd to the tingling stars,
And, as it were one voice, an agony   200
Of lamentation, like a wind, that shrills
All night in a waste land, where no one comes,
Or hath come, since the making of the world.
　Then murmur'd Arthur, 'Place me in the barge,'
And to the barge they came. There those three Queens   205
Put forth their hands, and took the King, and wept.
But she, that rose the tallest of them all
And fairest, laid his head upon her lap,
And loosed the shatter'd casque, and chafed his hands,
And call'd him by his name, complaining loud,   210
And dropping bitter tears against his brow
Striped with dark blood: for all his face was white
And colourless, and like the wither'd moon
Smote by the fresh beam of the springing east;
And all his greaves and cuisses dash'd with drops   215
Of onset; and the light and lustrous curls—
That made his forehead like a rising sun
High from the daïs-throne—were parch'd with dust;
Or, clotted into points and hanging loose,
Mix'd with the knightly growth that fringed his lips.   220
So like a shatter'd column lay the King;
Not like that Arthur who, with lance in rest,
From spur to plume a star of tournament,
Shot thro' the lists at Camelot, and charged
Before the eyes of ladies and of kings.   225

Then loudly cried the bold Sir Bedivere,
'Ah! my Lord Arthur, whither shall I go?
Where shall I hide my forehead and my eyes?
For now I see the true old times are dead,
When every morning brought a noble chance, 230
And every chance brought out a noble knight.
Such times have been not since the light that led
The holy Elders with the gift of myrrh.
But now the whole ROUND TABLE is dissolved
Which was an image of the mighty world; 235
And I, the last, go forth companionless,
And the days darken round me, and the years,
Among new men, strange faces, other minds.'
 And slowly answered Arthur from the barge:
'The old order changeth, yielding place to new, 240
And God fulfils Himself in many ways,
Lest one good custom should corrupt the world.
Comfort thyself: what comfort is in me?
I have lived my life, and that which I have done
May He within Himself make pure! but thou, 245
If thou shouldst never see my face again,
Pray for my soul. More things are wrought by prayer
Than this world dreams of. Wherefore, let thy voice
Rise like a fountain for me night and day.
For what are men better than sheep or goats 250
That nourish a blind life within the brain,
If, knowing God, they lift not hands of prayer
Both for themselves and those who call them friend?
For so the whole round earth is every way
Bound by gold chains about the feet of God. 255
But now farewell. I am going a long way
With these thou seëst—if indeed I go—
(For all my mind is clouded with a doubt)
To the island-valley of Avilion;
Where falls not hail, or rain, or any snow, 260
Nor ever wind blows loudly; but it lies
Deep-meadow'd, happy, fair with orchard-lawns
And bowery hollows crown'd with summer sea,
Where I will heal me of my grievous wound.'
 So said he, and the barge with oar and sail 265
Moved from the brink, like some full-breasted swan
That, fluting a wild carol ere her death,

Ruffles her pure cold plume, and takes the flood
With swarthy webs. Long stood Sir Bedivere
Revolving many memories, till the hull   270
Look'd one black dot against the verge of dawn,
And on the mere the wailing died away.

SONGS FROM *THE PRINCESS*

I

Come down, O maid, from yonder mountain heights:
What pleasure lives in height (the shepherd sang)
In height and cold, the splendour of the hills?
But cease to move so near the heavens, and cease
To glide a sunbeam by the blasted Pine,   5
To sit a star upon the sparkling spire;
And come, for Love is of the valley, come,
For Love is of the valley, come thou down
And find him; by the happy threshold, he,
Or hand in hand with Plenty in the maize,   10
Or red with spirted purple of the vats,
Or foxlike in the vine; nor cares to walk
With Death and Morning on the silver horns,
Nor wilt thou snare him in the white ravine,
Nor find him dropt upon the firths of ice   15
That huddling slant in furrow-cloven falls
To roll the torrent out of dusky doors:
But follow; let the torrent dance thee down
To find him in the valley; let the wild
Lean-headed Eagles yelp alone, and leave   20
The monstrous ledges there to slope, and spill
Their thousand wreaths of dangling water-smoke
That like a broken purpose waste in air:
So waste not thou; but come; for all the vales
Await thee; azure pillars of the hearth   25
Arise to thee; the children call, and I
Thy shepherd pipe, and sweet is every sound,
Sweeter thy voice, but every sound is sweet;
Myriads of rivulets hurrying thro' the lawn,
The moan of doves in immemorial elms,   30
And murmuring of innumerable bees.

II

Now sleeps the crimson petal, now the white;
Nor waves the cypress in the palace walk;
Nor winks the gold fin in the porphyry font:
The fire-fly wakens: waken thou with me.

Now droops the milkwhite peacock like a ghost,
And like a ghost she glimmers on to me.

Now lies the Earth all Danaë to the stars,
And all thy heart lies open unto me.

Now slides the silent meteor on, and leaves
A shining furrow, as thy thoughts in me.

Now folds the lily all her sweetness up,
And slips into the bosom of the lake:
So fold thyself, my dearest, thou, and slip
Into my bosom and be lost in me.

III

Tears, idle tears, I know not what they mean,
Tears from the depth of some divine despair
Rise in the heart, and gather to the eyes,
In looking on the happy autumn-fields,
And thinking of the days that are no more.   5

Fresh as the first beam glittering on a sail,
That brings out friends up from the underworld,
Sad as the last which reddens over one
That sinks with all we love below the verge;
So sad, so fresh, the days that are no more.   10

Ah, sad and strange as in dark summer dawns
The earliest pipe of half-awaken'd birds
To dying ears, when unto dying eyes
The casement slowly grows a glimmering square;
So sad, so strange, the days that are no more.   15

Dear as remember'd kisses after death,
And sweet as those by hopeless fancy feign'd
On lips that are for others; deep as love,
Deep as first love, and wild with all regret;
O Death in Life, the days that are no more!   20

FROM *IN MEMORIAM A. H. H.*

PROEM

Strong Son of God, immortal Love,
　　Whom we, that have not seen thy face,
　　By faith, and faith alone, embrace,
Believing where we cannot prove;

Thine are these orbs of light and shade;　　　　5
　　Thou madest Life in man and brute;
　　Thou madest Death; and lo, thy foot
Is on the skull which thou hast made.

Thou wilt not leave us in the dust;
　　Thou madest man, he knows not why,　　　10
　　He thinks he was not made to die;
And thou hast made him: thou art just.

Thou seemest human and divine,
　　The highest, holiest manhood, thou.
　　Our wills are ours, we know not how;　　　15
Our wills are ours, to make them thine.

Our little systems have their day;
　　They have their day and cease to be;
　　They are but broken lights of thee,
And thou, O Lord, art more than they.　　　　20

We have but faith: we cannot know,
　　For knowledge is of things we see;
　　And yet we trust it comes from thee,
A beam in darkness: let it grow.

Let knowledge grow from more to more,　　　25
　　But more of reverence in us dwell;
　　That mind and soul, according well,
May make one music as before,

A. H. H.: Arthur Henry Hallam, engaged to Tennyson's sister, died in Italy, 1833.

But vaster. We are fools and slight;
    We mock thee when we do not fear: 30
    But help thy foolish ones to bear;
Help thy vain worlds to bear thy light.

Forgive what seemed my sin in me;
    What seemed my worth since I began;
    For merit lives from man to man,   35
And not from man, O Lord, to thee.

Forgive my grief for one removed,
    Thy creature, whom I found so fair.
    I trust he lives in thee, and there
I find him worthier to be loved.   40

Forgive these wild and wandering cries,
    Confusions of a wasted youth;
    Forgive them where they fail in truth,
And in thy wisdom make me wise.

II

Old Yew, which graspest at the stones
    That name the under-lying dead,
    Thy fibres net the dreamless head,
Thy roots are wrapt about the bones.

The seasons bring the flower again,   5
    And bring the firstling to the flock;
    And in the dusk of thee, the clock
Beats out the little lives of men.

O not for thee the glow, the bloom,
    Who changest not in any gale,   10
    Nor branding summer suns avail
To touch thy thousand years of gloom:

And gazing on thee, sullen tree,
    Sick for thy stubborn hardihood,
    I seem to fail from out my blood   15
And grow incorporate into thee.

VII

Dark house, by which once more I stand
  Here in the long unlovely street,
  Doors, where my heart was used to beat
So quickly, waiting for a hand,

A hand that can be clasp'd no more—   5
  Behold me, for I cannot sleep,
  And like a guilty thing I creep
At earliest morning to the door.

He is not here; but far away
  The noise of life begins again,   10
  And ghastly thro' the drizzling rain
On the bald street breaks the blank day.

XI

Calm is the morn without a sound,
  Calm as to suit a calmer grief,
  And only through the faded leaf
The chestnut pattering to the ground:

Calm and deep peace on this high wold,   5
  And on these dews that drench the furze,
  And all the silvery gossamers
That twinkle into green and gold:

Calm and still light on yon great plain
  That sweeps with all its autumn bowers,   10
  And crowded farms and lessening towers,
To mingle with the bounding main:

Calm and deep peace in this wide air,
  These leaves that redden to the fall;
  And in my heart, if calm at all,   15
If any calm, a calm despair:

Calm on the seas, and silver sleep,
  And waves that sway themselves in rest,
  And dead calm in that noble breast
Which heaves but with the heaving deep.   20

LIV

Oh yet we trust that somehow good
  Will be the final goal of ill,
  To pangs of nature, sins of will,
Defects of doubt, and taints of blood;

That nothing walks with aimless feet;   5
  That not one life shall be destroyed,
  Or cast as rubbish to the void,
When God hath made the pile complete;

That not a worm is cloven in vain;
  That not a moth with vain desire   10
  Is shriveled in a fruitless fire,
Or but subserves another's gain.

Behold, we know not anything;
  I can but trust that good shall fall
  At last—far off—at last, to all,   15
And every winter change to spring.

So runs my dream: but what am I?
  An infant crying in the night:
  An infant crying for the light:
And with no language but a cry.   20

LV

The wish, that of the living whole
  No life may fail beyond the grave,
  Derives it not from what we have
The likest God within the soul?

Are God and Nature then at strife,   5
  That Nature lends such evil dreams?
  So careful of the type she seems,
So careless of the single life;

That I, considering everywhere
  Her secret meaning in her deeds,   10
  And finding that of fifty seeds
She often brings but one to bear,

I falter where I firmly trod,
   And falling with my weight of cares
   Upon the great world's altar-stairs   15
That slope thro' darkness up to God,

I stretch lame hands of faith, and grope,
   And gather dust and chaff, and call
   To what I feel is Lord of all,
And faintly trust the larger hope.   20

LVI

'So careful of the type?' but no.
   From scarpèd cliff and quarried stone
   She cries, 'A thousand types are gone:
I care for nothing, all shall go.

'Thou makest thine appeal to me: 5
   I bring to life, I bring to death:
   The spirit does but mean the breath:
I know no more.' And he, shall he,

Man, her last work, who seem'd so fair,
   Such splendid purpose in his eyes,   10
   Who roll'd the psalm to wintry skies,
Who built him fanes of fruitless prayer,

Who trusted God was love indeed
   And love Creation's final law—
   Tho' Nature, red in tooth and claw   15
With ravine, shriek'd against his creed—

Who loved, who suffer'd countless ills,
   Who battled for the True, the Just,
   Be blown about the desert dust,
Or seal'd within the iron hills?   20

No more? A monster then, a dream,
   A discord. Dragons of the prime,
   That tare each other in their slime,
Were mellow music match'd with him.

O life as futile, then, as frail!   25
  O for thy voice to soothe and bless!
  What hope of answer, or redress?
Behind the veil, behind the veil.

LXVI

When on my bed the moonlight falls,
  I know that in thy place of rest
  By that broad water of the west,
There comes a glory on the walls:

Thy marble bright in dark appears,   5
  As slowly steals a silver flame
  Along the letters of thy name,
And o'er the number of thy years.

The mystic glory swims away;
  From off my bed the moonlight dies;   10
  And closing eaves of wearied eyes
I sleep till dusk is dipt in gray;

And then I know the mist is drawn
  A lucid veil from coast to coast,
  And in the chancel like a ghost   15
Thy tablet glimmers to the dawn.

CI

Unwatch'd, the garden bough shall sway,
  The tender blossom flutter down;
  Unloved, that beech will gather brown,
This maple burn itself away;

Unloved, the sun-flower, shining fair,   5
  Ray round with flames her disk of seed,
  And many a rose-carnation feed
With summer spice the humming air;

Unloved, by many a sandy bar,
  The brook shall babble down the plain,   10
  At noon or when the lesser wain
Is twisting round the polar star;

Uncared for, gird the windy grove,
   And flood the haunts of hern and crake;
   Or into silver arrows break   15
The sailing moon in creek and cove;

Till from the garden and the wild
   A fresh association blow,
   And year by year the landscape grow
Familiar to the stranger's child;   20

As year by year the labourer tills
   His wonted glebe, or lops the glades;
   And year by year our memory fades
From all the circle of the hills.

CVI

Ring out, wild bells, to the wild sky,
   The flying cloud, the frosty light:
   The year is dying in the night;
Ring out, wild bells, and let him die.

Ring out the old, ring in the new,   5
   Ring, happy bells, across the snow:
   The year is going, let him go;
Ring out the false, ring in the true.

Ring out the grief that saps the mind,
   For those that here we see no more;   10
   Ring out the feud of rich and poor,
Ring in redress to all mankind.

Ring out a slowly dying cause,
   And ancient forms of party strife;
   Ring in the nobler modes of life,   15
With sweeter manners, purer laws.

Ring out the want, the care, the sin,
   The faithless coldness of the times;
   Ring out, ring out my mournful rhymes,
But ring the fuller minstrel in.   20

Ring out false pride in place and blood,
 The civic slander and the spite;
 Ring in the love of truth and right,
Ring in the common love of good.

Ring out old shapes of foul disease;   25
 Ring out the narrowing lust of gold;
 Ring out the thousand wars of old,
Ring in the thousand years of peace.

Ring in the valiant man and free,
 The larger heart, the kindlier hand;   30
 Ring out the darkness of the land,
Ring in the Christ that is to be.

CXV

Now fades the last long streak of snow,
 Now burgeons every maze of quick
 About the flowering squares, and thick
By ashen roots the violets blow.

Now rings the woodland loud and long,   5
 The distance takes a lovelier hue,
 And drown'd in yonder living blue
The lark becomes a sightless song.

Now dance the lights on lawn and lea,
 The flocks are whiter down the vale,   10
 And milkier every milky sail
On winding stream or distant sea;

Where now the seamew pipes, or dives
 In yonder greening gleam, and fly
 The happy birds, that change their sky   15
To build and brood; that live their lives

From land to land; and in my breast
 Spring wakens too; and my regret
 Becomes an April violet,
And buds and blossoms like the rest.   20

CXVIII

Contemplate all this work of Time,
  The giant labouring in his youth;
  Nor dream of human love and truth,
As dying Nature's earth and lime;

But trust that those we call the dead   5
  Are breathers of an ampler day
  For ever nobler ends. They say
The solid earth whereon we tread

In tracts of fluent heat began,
  And grew to seeming-random forms,   10
  The seeming prey of cyclic storms,
Till at the last arose the man;

Who throve and branch'd from clime to clime,
  The herald of a higher race,
  And of himself in higher place,   15
If so he type this work of time

Within himself, from more to more;
  Or, crown'd with attributes of woe
  Like glories, move his course, and show
That life is not as idle ore,   20

But iron dug from central gloom,
  And heated hot with burning fears,
  And dipt in baths of hissing tears,
And batter'd with the shocks of doom

To shape and use. Arise and fly   25
  The reeling Faun, the sensual feast;
  Move upward, working out the beast,
And let the ape and tiger die.

CXXIII

There rolls the deep where grew the tree.
  O earth, what changes hast thou seen!
  There where the long street roars, hath been
The stillness of the central sea.

The hills are shadows, and they flow   5
  From form to form, and nothing stands;
  They melt like mist, the solid lands,
Like clouds they shape themselves and go.

But in my spirit will I dwell,
  And dream my dream, and hold it true;   10
  For tho' my lips may breathe adieu,
I cannot think the thing farewell.

CXXVI

Love is and was my Lord and King,
  And in his presence I attend
  To hear the tidings of my friend,
Which every hour his couriers bring.

Love is and was my King and Lord,   5
  And will be, tho' as yet I keep
  Within his court on earth, and sleep
Encompass'd by his faithful guard,

And hear at times a sentinel
  Who moves about from place to place,   10
  And whispers to the worlds of space,
In the deep night, that all is well.

THE EAGLE

He clasps the crag with crooked hands;
Close to the sun in lonely lands,
Ring'd with the azure world, he stands.

The wrinkled sea beneath him crawls;
He watches from his mountain walls,
And like a thunderbolt he falls.

OLIVER WENDELL HOLMES (1809–1894)

THE LAST LEAF

I saw him once before,
As he passed by the door,
    And again
The pavement stones resound,
As he totters o'er the ground
    With his cane.   5

They say that in his prime,
Ere the pruning-knife of Time
    Cut him down,
Not a better man was found   10
By the Crier on his round
    Through the town.

But now he walks the streets,
And he looks at all he meets
    Sad and wan,   15
And he shakes his feeble head,
That it seems as if he said,
    "They are gone."

The mossy marbles rest
On the lips that he has pressed   20
    In their bloom,
And the names he loved to hear
Have been carved for many a year
    On the tomb.

My grandmamma has said—   25
Poor old lady, she is dead
    Long ago—
That he had a Roman nose,
And his cheek was like a rose
    In the snow;   30

But now his nose is thin,
And it rests upon his chin
    Like a staff,

And a crook is in his back,
And a melancholy crack   35
    In his laugh.

I know it is a sin
For me to sit and grin
    At him here;
But the old three-cornered hat,   40
And the breeches, and all that,
    Are so queer!

And if I should live to be
The last leaf upon the tree
    In the spring,   45
Let them smile, as I do now,
At the old forsaken bough
    Where I cling.

EDWARD LEAR (1812–1888)

THE JUMBLIES

1

They went to sea in a sieve, they did;
    In a sieve they went to sea:
In spite of all their friends could say,
On a winter's morn, on a stormy day,
    In a sieve they went to sea.   5
And when the sieve turned round and round,
And everyone cried, "You'll all be drowned!"
They called aloud, "Our sieve ain't big,
But we don't care a button; we don't care a fig:
    In a sieve we'll go to sea!"   10
        Far and few, far and few,
            Are the lands where the Jumblies live:
            Their heads are green, and their hands are blue;
                And they went to sea in a sieve.

2

They sailed away in a sieve, they did,   15
    In a sieve they sailed so fast,
With only a beautiful pea-green veil
Tied with a ribbon, by way of a sail,
    To a small tobacco-pipe mast.
And every one said who saw them go,   20
"Oh! won't they be soon upset; you know!
For the sky is dark, and the voyage is long;
And, happen what may, it's extremely wrong
    In a sieve to sail so fast."

3

The water it soon came in, it did;   25
    The water it soon came in:
So, to keep them dry, they wrapped their feet
In a pinky paper all folded neat;
    And they fastened it down with a pin.
And they passed the night in a crockery-jar;   30
And each of them said, "How wise we are!
Though the sky be dark, and the voyage be long,
Yet we never can think we were rash or wrong
    While round in our sieve we spin."

4

And all night long they sailed away;   35
    And, when the sun went down,
They whistled and warbled a moony song
To the echoing sound of a coppery gong,
    In the shade of the mountains brown,
"O Timballoo! how happy we are   40
When we live in a sieve and a crockery-jar!
And all night long, in the moonlight pale,
We sail away with a pea-green sail
    In the shade of the mountains brown."

5

They sailed to the Western Sea, they did,—   45
    To a land all covered with trees:
And they bought an owl, and a useful cart,
And a pound of rice, and a cranberry-tart,
    And a hive of silvery bees;

And they bought a pig, and some green jackdaws, 50
And a lovely monkey with lollipop paws,
And forty bottles of ring-bo-ree,
    And no end of Stilton cheese.

6

And in twenty years they all came back,—
    In twenty years or more; 55
And every one said, "How tall they've grown!
For they've been to the Lakes, and the Torrible Zone,
    And the hills of the Chankly Bore."
And they drank their health, and gave them a feast
Of dumplings made of beautiful yeast; 60
And every one said, "If we only live,
We, too, will go to sea in a sieve,
    To the hills of the Chankly Bore."
        Far and few, far and few,
            Are the lands where the Jumblies live. 65
        Their heads are green, and their hands are blue;
            And they went to sea in a sieve.

ROBERT BROWNING (1812–1889)

HOME-THOUGHTS FROM ABROAD

Oh, to be in England
Now that April's there,
And whoever wakes in England
Sees, some morning, unaware,
That the lowest boughs and the brush-wood sheaf 5
Round the elm-tree bole are in tiny leaf,
While the chaffinch sings on the orchard bough
In England—now!

And after April, when May follows,
And the whitethroat builds, and all the swallows! 10
Hark, where my blossomed pear-tree in the hedge
Leans to the field and scatters on the clover
Blossoms and dewdrops—at the bent spray's edge—

That's the wise thrush; he sings each song twice over,
   Lest you should think he never could recapture   15
The first fine careless rapture!
And though the fields look rough with hoary dew,
All will be gay when noontide wakes anew
The buttercups, the little children's dower
—Far brighter than this gaudy melon flower!   20

SOLILOQUY OF THE SPANISH CLOISTER

Gr-r-r—there go, my heart's abhorrence!
   Water your damned flower-pots, do!
If hate killed men, Brother Lawrence,
   God's blood, would not mine kill you!
What? your myrtle-bush wants trimming?   5
   Oh, that rose has prior claims—
Needs its leaden vase filled brimming?
   Hell dry you up with its flames!

At the meal we sit together;
   Salve tibi! I must hear   10
Wise talk of the kind of weather,
   Sort of season, time of year:
Not a plenteous cork-crop: scarcely
   Dare we hope oak-galls, I doubt;
What's the Latin name for "parsley"?   15
   What's the Greek name for Swine's Snout?

Whew! We'll have our platter burnished,
   Laid with care on our own shelf!
With a fire-new spoon we're furnished,
   And a goblet for ourself,   20
Rinsed like something sacrificial
   Ere 'tis fit to touch our chaps—
Marked with L. for our initial!
   (He-he! There his lily snaps!)

Saint, forsooth! While brown Dolores   25
   Squats outside the Convent bank

With Sanchicha, telling stories,
    Steeping tresses in the tank,
Blue-black, lustrous, thick like horsehairs,
    —Can't I see his dead eye glow,   30
Bright as 'twere a Barbary corsair's?
    (That is, if he'd let it show!)

When he finishes refection,
    Knife and fork he never lays
Cross-wise, to my recollection,   35
    As do I, in Jesu's praise.
I, the Trinity illustrate,
    Drinking watered orange-pulp—
In three sips the Arian frustrate;
    While he drains his at one gulp!   40

Oh, those melons! if he's able
    We're to have a feast; so nice!
One goes to the Abbot's table,
    All of us get each a slice.
How go on your flowers? None double?   45
    Not one fruit-sort can you spy?
Strange!—And I, too, at such trouble,
    Keep them close-nipped on the sly!

There's a great text in Galatians,
    Once you trip on it, entails   50
Twenty-nine distinct damnations,
    One sure, if another fails;
If I trip him just a-dying,
    Sure of heaven as sure can be,
Spin him round and send him flying   55
    Off to hell, a Manichee?

Or, my scrofulous French novel
    On grey paper with blunt type!
Simply glance at it, you grovel
    Hand and foot in Belial's gripe;   60
If I double down its pages
    At the woeful sixteenth print,
When he gathers his greengages,
    Ope a sieve and slip it in't?

Or, there's Satan!—one might venture 65
   Pledge one's soul to him, yet leave
Such a flaw in the indenture
   As he'd miss till, past retrieve,
Blasted lay that rose-acacia
   We're so proud of! *Hy, Zy, Hine.* . . . 70
'St, there's Vespers! *Plena gratia*
   Ave, Virgo! Gr-r-r—you swine!

MY LAST DUCHESS

Ferrara

That's my last Duchess painted on the wall,
Looking as if she were alive. I call
That piece a wonder, now: Frà Pandolf's hands
Worked busily a day, and there she stands.
Will't please you sit and look at her? I said 5
"Frà Pandolf" by design, for never read
Strangers like you that pictured countenance,
The depth and passion of its earnest glance,
But to myself they turned (since none puts by
The curtain I have drawn for you, but I) 10
And seemed as they would ask me, if they durst,
How such a glance came there; so, not the first
Are you to turn and ask thus. Sir, 'twas not
Her husband's presence only, called that spot
Of joy into the Duchess' cheek; perhaps 15
Frà Pandolf chanced to say, "Her mantle laps
Over my lady's wrist too much," or "Paint
Must never hope to reproduce the faint
Half-flush that dies along her throat": such stuff
Was courtesy, she thought, and cause enough 20
For calling up that spot of joy. She had
A heart—how shall I say?—too soon made glad,
Too easily impressed: she liked whate'er
She looked on, and her looks went everywhere.
Sir, 'twas all one! My favour at her breast, 25
The dropping of the daylight in the West,
The bough of cherries some officious fool
Broke in the orchard for her, the white mule
She rode with round the terrace—all and each

Would draw from her alike the approving speech,   30
Or blush, at least. She thanked men,—good! but thanked
Somehow—I know not how—as if she ranked
My gift of a nine-hundred-years-old name
With anybody's gift. Who'd stoop to blame
This sort of trifling? Even had you skill   35
In speech—(which I have not)—to make your will
Quite clear to such an one, and say, "Just this
Or that in you disgusts me; here you miss,
Or there exceed the mark"—and if she let
Herself be lessoned so, nor plainly set   40
Her wits to yours, forsooth, and made excuse,
—E'en then would be some stooping; and I choose
Never to stoop. Oh sir, she smiled, no doubt,
Whene'er I passed her; but who passed without
Much the same smile? This grew; I gave commands;   45
Then all smiles stopped together. There she stands
As if alive. Will't please you rise? We'll meet
The company below, then. I repeat,
The Count your master's known munificence
Is ample warrant that no just pretence   50
Of mine for dowry will be disallowed;
Though his fair daughter's self, as I avowed
At starting, is my object. Nay, we'll go
Together down, sir. Notice Neptune, though,
Taming a sea-horse, thought a rarity,   55
Which Claus of Innsbruck cast in bronze for me!

THE BISHOP ORDERS HIS TOMB AT SAINT PRAXED'S CHURCH

ROME, 15—

Vanity, saith the preacher, vanity!
Draw round my bed: is Anselm keeping back?
Nephews—sons mine . . . ah God, I know not! Well—
She, men would have to be your mother once,
Old Gandolf envied me, so fair she was!   5
What's done is done, and she is dead beside,
Dead long ago, and I am Bishop since,
And as she died so must we die ourselves,
And thence ye may perceive the world's a dream.

Life, how and what is it? As here I lie   10
In this state-chamber, dying by degrees,
Hours and long hours in the dead night, I ask,
"Do I live, am I dead?" Peace, peace seems all.
Saint Praxed's ever was the church for peace;
And so, about this tomb of mine. I fought   15
With tooth and nail to save my niche, ye know:
—Old Gandolf cozened me, despite my care;
Shrewd was that snatch from out the corner South
He graced his carrion with, God curse the same!
Yet still my niche is not so cramped but thence   20
One sees the pulpit o' the epistle-side,
And somewhat of the choir, those silent seats,
And up into the aery dome where live
The angels, and a sunbeam's sure to lurk:
And I shall fill my slab of basalt there,   25
And 'neath my tabernacle take my rest,
With those nine columns round me, two and two,
The odd one at my feet where Anselm stands:
Peach-blossom marble all, the rare, the ripe
As fresh-poured red wine of a mighty pulse.   30
—Old Gandolf with his paltry onion-stone,
Put me where I may look at him! True peach,
Rosy and flawless: how I earned the prize!
Draw close: that conflagration of my church
—What then? So much was saved if aught were missed!   35
My sons, ye would not be my death? Go dig
The white-grape vineyard where the oil-press stood,
Drop water gently till the surface sink,
And if ye find . . . Ah God, I know not, I! . . .
Bedded in store of rotten fig-leaves soft,   40
And corded up in a tight olive-frail,
Some lump, ah God, of *lapis lazuli*,
Big as a Jew's head cut off at the nape,
Blue as a vein o'er the Madonna's breast . . .
Sons, all have I bequeathed you, villas, all,   45
That brave Frascati villa with its bath,
So, let the blue lump poise between my knees,
Like God the Father's globe on both his hands
Ye worship in the Jesu Church so gay,
For Gandolf shall not choose but see and burst!   50
Swift as a weaver's shuttle fleet our years:

Man goeth to the grave, and where is he?
Did I say basalt for my slab, sons? Black—
'Twas ever antique-black I meant! How else
Shall ye contrast my frieze to come beneath?   55
The bas-relief in bronze ye promised me,
Those Pans and Nymphs ye wot of, and perchance
Some tripod, thyrsus, with a vase or so,
The Savior at his sermon on the mount,
Saint Praxed in a glory, and one Pan   60
Ready to twitch the Nymph's last garment off,
And Moses with the tables . . . but I know
Ye mark me not! What do they whisper thee,
Child of my bowels, Anselm? Ah, ye hope
To revel down my villas while I gasp   65
Bricked o'er with beggar's moldy travertine
Which Gandolf from his tomb-top chuckles at!
Nay, boys, ye love me—all of jasper, then!
'Tis jasper ye stand pledged to, lest I grieve.
My bath must needs be left behind, alas!   70
One block, pure green as a pistachio-nut,
There's plenty jasper somewhere in the world—
And have I not Saint Praxed's ear to pray
Horses for ye, and brown Greek manuscripts,
And mistresses with great smooth marbly limbs?   75
—That's if ye carve my epitaph aright,
Choice Latin, picked phrase, Tully's every word,
No gaudy ware like Gandolf's second line—
Tully, my masters? Ulpian serves his need!
And then how I shall lie through centuries,   80
And hear the blessed mutter of the mass,
And see God made and eaten all day long,
And feel the steady candle-flame, and taste
Good, strong, thick, stupefying incense-smoke!
For as I lie here, hours of the dead night,   85
Dying in state and by such slow degrees,
I fold my arms as if they clasped a crook,
And stretch my feet forth straight as stone can point,
And let the bedclothes, for a mortcloth, drop
Into great laps and folds of sculptor's-work: 90
And as yon tapers dwindle, and strange thoughts
Grow, with a certain humming in my ears,
About the life before I lived this life,

And this life too, popes, cardinals and priests,
Saint Praxed at his sermon on the mount,   95
Your tall pale mother with her talking eyes,
And new-found agate urns as fresh as day,
And marble's language, Latin pure, discreet,
—Aha, ELUCESCEBAT quoth our friend?
No Tully, said I, Ulpian at the best!   100
Evil and brief hath been my pilgrimage.
All *lapis*, all, sons! Else I give the Pope
My villas! Will ye ever eat my heart?
Ever your eyes were as a lizard's quick,
They glitter like your mother's for my soul,   105
Or ye would heighten my impoverished frieze,
Piece out its starved design, and fill my vase
With grapes, and add a visor and a Term,
And to the tripod ye would tie a lynx
That in his struggle throws the thyrsus down,   110
To comfort me on my entablature
Whereon I am to lie till I must ask,
"Do I live, am I dead?" There, leave me, there!
For ye have stabbed me with ingratitude
To death—ye wish it—God, ye wish it! Stone—   115
Gritstone, a-crumble! Clammy squares which sweat
As if the corpse they keep were oozing through—
And no more *lapis* to delight the world!
Well, go! I bless ye. Fewer tapers there,
But in a row: and, going, turn your backs   120
—Aye, like departing altar-ministrants,
And leave me in my church, the church for peace,
That I may watch at leisure if he leers—
Old Gandolf—at me, from his onion-stone,
As still he envied me, so fair she was!   125

99. ELUCESCEBAT: He was famous. Not in the pure Latin of Cicero (Tully)
but in the debased style of Ulpian.

UP AT A VILLA—DOWN IN THE CITY

(AS DISTINGUISHED BY AN ITALIAN PERSON OF QUALITY)

Had I but plenty of money, money enough and to spare,
The house for me, no doubt, were a house in the city-square;
Ah, such a life, such a life, as one leads at the window there!

Something to see, by Bacchus, something to hear, at least!
There, the whole day long, one's life is a perfect feast; 5
While up at a villa one lives, I maintain it, no more than a beast.

Well now, look at our villa! stuck like the horn of a bull
Just on a mountain-edge as bare as the creature's skull,
Save a mere shag of a bush with hardly a leaf to pull!
—I scratch my own, sometimes, to see if the hair's turned wool. 10

But the city, oh the city—the square with the houses! Why?
They are stone-faced, white as a curd, there's something to take
    the eye!
Houses in four straight lines, not a single front awry;
You watch who crosses and gossips, who saunters, who hurries by;
Green blinds, as a matter of course, to draw when the sun gets
    high; 15
And the shops with fanciful signs which are painted properly.

What of a villa? Though winter be over in March by rights,
'Tis May perhaps ere the snow shall have withered well off the
    heights:
You've the brown ploughed land before, where the oxen steam
    and wheeze,
And the hills over-smoked behind by the faint gray olive-trees. 20

Is it better in May, I ask you? You've summer all at once;
In a day he leaps complete with a few strong April suns.
'Mid the sharp short emerald wheat, scarce risen three fingers well,
The wild tulip, at end of its tube, blows out its great red bell
Like a thin clear bubble of blood, for the children to pick
    and sell. 25

Is it ever hot in the square? There's a fountain to spout and splash!
In the shade it sings and springs; in the shine such foambows flash
On the horses with curling fish-tails, that prance and paddle
    and pash
Round the lady atop in her conch—fifty gazers do not abash,
Though all that she wears is some weeds round her waist in a
    sort of sash. 30

All the year long at the villa, nothing to see though you linger,
Except yon cypress that points like death's lean lifted forefinger.

Some think fireflies pretty, when they mix i' the corn and mingle,
Or thrid the stinking hemp till the stalks of it seem a-tingle.
Late August or early September, the stunning cicala is shrill,   35
And the bees keep their tiresome whine round the resinous firs on
    the hill.
Enough of the seasons,—I spare you the months of the fever
    and chill.

Ere you open your eyes in the city, the blessed church-bells begin:
No sooner the bells leave off than the diligence rattles in:
You get the pick of the news, and it costs you never a pin.   40
By and by there's the travelling doctor gives pills, lets blood,
    draws teeth;
Or the Pulcinello-trumpet breaks up the market beneath.
At the post-office such a scene-picture—the new play, piping hot!
And a notice how, only this morning, three liberal thieves were shot.
Above it, behold the Archbishop's most fatherly of rebukes,   45
And beneath, with his crown and his lion, some little new law
    of the Duke's!
Or a sonnet with flowery marge, to the Reverend Don So-and-so,
Who is Dante, Boccaccio, Petrarca, Saint Jerome, and Cicero,
"And moreover," (the sonnet goes rhyming,) "the skirts of Saint
    Paul had reached,
Having preached us those six Lent-lectures more unctuous than
    ever he preached."   50
Noon strikes,—here sweeps the procession! our Lady borne smiling
    and smart
With a pink gauze gown all spangles, and seven swords stuck
    in her heart!
Bang-whang-whang goes the drum, tootle-te-tootle the fife;
No keeping one's haunches still: it's the greatest pleasure in life.

But bless you, it's dear—it's dear! fowls, wine, at double the
    rate.   55
They have clapped a new tax upon salt, and what oil pays passing
    the gate
It's a horror to think of. And so, the villa for me, not the city!
Beggars can scarcely be choosers: but still—ah, the pity, the pity!
Look, two and two go the priests, then the monks with cowls
    and sandals,
And the penitents dressed in white shirts, a-holding the yellow
    candles;   60

One, he carries a flag up straight, and another a cross with handles,
And the Duke's guard brings up the rear, for the better prevention
    of scandals:
Bang-whang-whang goes the drum, *tootle-te-tootle* the fife.
Oh, a day in the city-square, there is no such pleasure in life!

'CHILDE ROLAND TO THE DARK TOWER CAME'

(See Edgar's song in 'Lear')

I

My first thought was, he lied in every word,
    That hoary cripple, with malicious eye
    Askance to watch the working of his lie
On mine, and mouth scarce able to afford
Suppression of the glee that pursed and scored   5
    Its edge at one more victim gained thereby.

II

What else should he be set for, with his staff?
    What, save to waylay with his lies, ensnare
    All travellers that might find him posted there,
And ask the road? I guessed what skull-like laugh   10
Would break, what crutch 'gin write my epitaph
    For pastime in the dusty thoroughfare,

III

If at his counsel I should turn aside
    Into that ominous tract which, all agree,
    Hides the Dark Tower. Yet acquiescingly   15
I did turn as he pointed; neither pride
Nor hope rekindling at the end descried,
    So much as gladness that some end might be.

IV

For, what with my whole world-wide wandering,
    What with my search drawn out thro' years, my hope 20
    Dwindled into a ghost not fit to cope
With that obstreperous joy success would bring.—
I hardly tried now to rebuke the spring
    My heart made, finding failure in its scope.

V

As when a sick man very near to death   25
  Seems dead indeed, and feels begin and end
  The tears, and takes the farewell of each friend,
And hears one bid the other go, draw breath
Freelier outside, ('since all is o'er,' he saith,
  'And the blow fallen no grieving can amend;')   30

VI

While some discuss if near the other graves
  Be room enough for this, and when a day
  Suits best for carrying the corpse away,
With care about the banners, scarves and staves,—
And still the man hears all, and only craves   35
  He may not shame such tender love and stay.

VII

Thus, I had so long suffered in this quest,
  Heard failure prophesied so oft, been writ
  So many times among 'The Band!'—to wit,
The knights who to the Dark Tower's search addressed 40
Their steps—that just to fail as they, seemed best.
  And all the doubt was now—should I be fit.

VIII

So, quiet as despair, I turned from him,
  That hateful cripple, out of his highway
  Into the path he pointed. All the day   45
Had been a dreary one at best, and dim
Was settling to its close, yet shot one grim
  Red leer to see the plain catch its estray.

IX

For mark! no sooner was I fairly found
  Pledged to the plain, after a pace or two,   50
  Than, pausing to throw backward a last view
To the safe road, 'twas gone; grey plain all round:
Nothing but plain to the horizon's bound.
  I might go on; nought else remained to do.

X

So, on I went. I think I never saw   55
  Such starved ignoble nature; nothing throve:
  For flowers—as well expect a cedar grove!
But cockle, spurge, according to their law
Might propagate their kind, with none to awe,
  You'd think; a burr had been a treasure-trove.   60

XI

No! penury, inertness and grimace,
  In some strange sort, were the land's portion. 'See
  Or shut your eyes,' said Nature peevishly,
'It nothing skills: I cannot help my case:
'Tis the Last Judgement's fire must cure this place,   65
  Calcine its clods and set my prisoners free.'

XII

If there pushed any ragged thistle-stalk
  Above its mates, the head was chopped—the bents
  Were jealous else. What made those holes and rents
In the dock's harsh swarth leaves—bruised as to baulk   70
All hope of greenness? 'tis a brute must walk
  Pashing their life out, with a brute's intents.

XIII

As for the grass, it grew as scant as hair
  In leprosy; thin dry blades pricked the mud
  Which underneath looked kneaded up with blood.   75
One stiff blind horse, his every bone a-stare,
Stood stupefied, however he came there:
  Thrust out past service from the devil's stud!

XIV

Alive? he might be dead for aught I know,
  With that red, gaunt and colloped neck a-strain,   80
  And shut eyes underneath the rusty mane;
Seldom went such grotesqueness with such woe;
I never saw a brute I hated so;
  He must be wicked to deserve such pain.

XV

I shut my eyes and turned them on my heart.   85
  As a man calls for wine before he fights,
  I asked one draught of earlier, happier sights,
Ere fitly I could hope to play my part.
Think first, fight afterwards—the soldier's art:
  One taste of the old time sets all to rights!   90

XVI

Not it! I fancied Cuthbert's reddening face
  Beneath its garniture of curly gold,
  Dear fellow, till I almost felt him fold
An arm in mine to fix me to the place,
That way he used. Alas! one night's disgrace!   95
  Out went my heart's new fire and left it cold.

XVII

Giles, then, the soul of honour—there he stands
  Frank as ten years ago when knighted first.
  What honest men should dare (he said) he durst.
Good—but the scene shifts—faugh! what hangman's
    hands   100
Pin to his breast a parchment? his own bands
  Read it. Poor traitor, spit upon and curst!

XVIII

Better this Present than a Past like that;
  Back therefore to my darkening path again.
  No sound, no sight as far as eye could strain.   105
Will the night send a howlet or a bat?
I asked: when something on the dismal flat
  Came to arrest my thoughts and change their train.

XIX

A sudden little river crossed my path
  As unexpected as a serpent comes.   110
  No sluggish tide congenial to the glooms—
This, as it frothed by, might have been a bath
For the fiend's glowing hoof—to see the wrath
  Of its black eddy bespate with flakes and spumes.

XX

So petty yet so spiteful! all along,   115
  Low scrubby alders kneeled down over it;
  Drenched willows flung them headlong in a fit
Of mute despair, a suicidal throng:
The river which had done them all the wrong,
  Whate'er that was, rolled by, deterred no whit.   120

XXI

Which, while I forded,—good saints, how I feared
  To set my foot upon a dead man's cheek,
  Each step, or feel the spear I thrust to seek
For hollows, tangled in his hair or beard!
—It may have been a water-rat I speared,   125
  But, ugh! it sounded like a baby's shriek.

XXII

Glad was I when I reached the other bank.
  Now for a better country. Vain presage!
  Who were the strugglers, what war did they wage,
Whose savage trample thus could pad the dank   130
Soil to a plash? toads in a poisoned tank,
  Or wild cats in a red-hot iron cage—

XXIII

The fight must so have seemed in that fell cirque.
  What penned them there, with all the plain to choose?
  No footprint leading to that horrid mews,   135
None of it. Mad brewage set to work
Their brains, no doubt, like galley-slaves the Turk
  Pits for his pastime, Christians against Jews.

XXIV

And more than that—a furlong on—why, there!
  What bad use was that engine for, that wheel,   140
  Or brake, not wheel—that harrow fit to reel
Men's bodies out like silk? with all the air
Of Tophet's tool, on earth left unware,
  Or brought to sharpen its rusty teeth of steel.

XXV

Then came a bit of stubbed ground, once a wood,   145
  Next a marsh, it would seem, and now mere earth
  Desperate and done with; (so a fool finds mirth,
Makes a thing and then mars it, till his mood
Changes and off he goes!) within a rood—
  Bog, clay and rubble, sand and stark black dearth.   150

XXVI

Now blotches rankling, coloured gay and grim,
  Now patches where some leanness of the soil's
  Broke into moss or substances like boils;
Then came some palsied oak, a cleft in him
Like a distorted mouth that splits its rim   155
  Gaping at death, and dies while it recoils.

XXVII

And just as far as ever from the end!
  Nought in the distance but the evening, nought
  To point my footsteps further! At the thought,
A great black bird, Apollyon's bosom-friend,   160
Sailed past, nor beat his wide wing dragon-penned
  That brushed my cap—perchance the guide I sought.

XXVIII

For, looking up, aware I somehow grew,
  'Spite of the dusk, the plain had given place
  All round to mountains—with such name to grace   165
Mere ugly heights and heaps now stolen in view.
How thus they had surprised me,—solve it, you!
  How to get from them was no clearer case.

XXIX

Yet half I seemed to recognize some trick
  Of mischief happened to me, God knows when—   170
  In a bad dream perhaps. Here ended, then,
Progress this way. When, in the very nick
Of giving up, one time more, came a click
  As when a trap shuts—you're inside the den!

XXX

Burningly it came on me all at once, 175
  This was the place! those two hills on the right,
  Crouched like two bulls locked horn in horn in fight;
While to the left, a tall scalped mountain . . . Dunce,
Fool, to be dozing at the very nonce,
  After a life spent training for the sight! 180

XXXI

What in the midst lay but the Tower itself?
  The round squat turret, blind as the fool's heart,
  Built of brown stone, without a counterpart
In the whole world. The tempest's mocking elf
Points to the shipman thus the unseen shelf 185
  He strikes on, only when the timbers start.

XXXII

Not see? because of night perhaps?—Why, day
  Came back again for that! before it left,
  The dying sunset kindled through a cleft:
The hills, like giants at a hunting, lay, 190
Chin upon hand, to see the game at bay,—
  'Now stab and end the creature—to the heft!'

XXXIII

Not hear? when noise was everywhere! it tolled
  Increasing like a bell. Names in my ears,
  Of all the lost adventurers my peers,— 195
How such a one was strong, and such was bold,
And such was fortunate, yet each of old
  Lost, lost! one moment knelled the woe of years.

XXXIV

There they stood, ranged along the hillsides, met
  To view the last of me, a living frame 200
  For one more picture! in a sheet of flame
I saw them and I knew them all. And yet
Dauntless the slug-horn to my lips I set,
  And blew. *'Childe Roland to the Dark Tower came.'*

TWO IN THE CAMPAGNA

I wonder do you feel to-day
   As I have felt since, hand in hand,
We sat down on the grass, to stray
   In spirit better through the land,
This morn of Rome and May?   5

For me, I touched a thought, I know,
   Has tantalized me many times,
(Like turns of thread the spiders throw
   Mocking across our path) for rhymes
To catch at and let go.   10

Help me to hold it! First it left
   The yellowing fennel, run to seed
There, branching from the brickwork's cleft,
   Some old tomb's ruin; yonder weed
Took up the floating weft,   15

Where one small orange cup amassed
   Five beetles—blind and green they grope
Among the honey-meal; and last,
   Everywhere on the grassy slope
I traced it. Hold it fast!   20

The champaign with its endless fleece
   Of feathery grasses everywhere!
Silence and passion, joy and peace,
   An everlasting wash of air—
Rome's ghost since her decease.   25

Such life here, through such lengths of hours,
   Such miracles performed in play,
Such primal naked forms of flowers,
   Such letting Nature have her way
While Heaven looks from its towers!   30

How say you? Let us, O my dove,
   Let us be unashamed of soul,

As earth lies bare to heaven above!
  How is it under our control
To love or not to love?   35

I would that you were all to me,
  You that are just so much, no more,
Nor yours, nor mine, nor slave nor free!
  Where does the fault lie? What the core
Of the wound, since wound must be?   40

I would I could adopt your will,
  See with your eyes, and set my heart
Beating by yours, and drink my fill
  At your soul's springs,—your part my part
In life, for good and ill.   45

No. I yearn upward, touch you close,
  Then stand away. I kiss your cheek,
Catch your soul's warmth—I pluck the rose
  And love it more than tongue can speak—
Then the good minute goes.   50

Already how am I so far
  Out of that minute? Must I go
Still like the thistle-ball, no bar,
  Onward, whenever light winds blow,
Fixed by no friendly star?   55

Just when I seemed about to learn!
  Where is the thread now? Off again!
The old trick! Only I discern—
  Infinite passion, and the pain
Of finite hearts that yearn.   60

PROSPICE

Fear death?—to feel the fog in my throat,
  The mist in my face,
When the snows begin, and the blasts denote
  I am nearing the place,
The power of the night, the press of the storm, 5
  The post of the foe;

Where he stands, the Arch Fear in a visible form,
   Yet the strong man must go:
For the journey is done and the summit attained,
   And the barriers fall,   10
Though a battle's to fight ere the guerdon be gained,
   The reward of it all.
I was ever a fighter, so—one fight more,
   The best and the last!
I would hate that death bandaged my eyes and forbore, 15
   And bade me creep past.
No! let me taste the whole of it, fare like my peers
   The heroes of old,
Bear the brunt, in a minute pay glad life's arrears
   Of pain, darkness and cold.   20
For sudden the worst turns the best to the brave,
   The black minute's at end,
And the elements' rage, the fiend-voices that rave,
   Shall dwindle, shall blend,
Shall change, shall become first a peace, out of pain, 25
   Then a light, then thy breast,
O thou soul of my soul! I shall clasp thee again
   And with God be the rest!

WALT WHITMAN (1819–1892)

OUT OF THE CRADLE ENDLESSLY ROCKING

Out of the cradle endlessly rocking,
Out of the mocking-bird's throat, the musical shuttle,
Out of the Ninth-month midnight,
Over the sterile sands, and the fields beyond, where the child,
   leaving his bed, wander'd alone, bareheaded, barefoot,
Down from the shower'd halo,   5
Up from the mystic play of shadows, twining and twisting as if
   they were alive,
Out from the patches of briers and blackberries,
From the memories of the bird that chanted to me,
From your memories, sad brother—from the fitful risings and
   fallings I heard,
From under that yellow half-moon, late-risen, and swollen as if
   with tears,   10

From those beginning notes of sickness and love, there in the
    transparent mist,
From the thousand responses of my heart, never to cease,
From the myriad thence-aroused words,
From the word stronger and more delicious than any,
From such, as now they start, the scene revisiting,   15
As a flock, twittering, rising, or overhead passing,
Borne hither—ere all eludes me, hurriedly,
A man—yet by these tears a little boy again,
Throwing myself on the sand, confronting the waves,
I, chanter of pains and joys, uniter of here and hereafter,   20
Taking all hints to use them—but swiftly leaping beyond them,
A reminiscence sing.

Once, Paumanok,
When the snows had melted—when the lilac-scent was in the air,
    and the Fifth-month grass was growing,
Up this sea-shore, in some briers,   25
Two guests from Alabama—two together,
And their nest, and four light-green eggs, spotted with brown,
And every day the he-bird, to and fro, near at hand,
And every day the she-bird, crouch'd on her nest, silent, with
    bright eyes,
And every day I, a curious boy, never too close, never disturbing
    them,   30
Cautiously peering, absorbing, translating.

Shine! shine! shine!
Pour down your warmth, great Sun!
While we bask—we two together.

Two together!   35
Winds blow South, or winds blow North,
Day come white, or night come black,
Home, or rivers and mountains from home,
Singing all time, minding no time,
While we two keep together.   40

Till of a sudden,
May-be kill'd, unknown to her mate,
One forenoon the she-bird crouch'd not on the nest,
Nor return'd that afternoon, nor the next,

Nor ever appear'd again. 45
And thenceforward, all summer, in the sound of the sea,
And at night, under the full of the moon, in calmer weather,
Over the hoarse surging of the sea,
Or flitting from brier to brier by day,
I saw, I heard at intervals, the remaining one, the he-bird, 50
The solitary guest from Alabama.

Blow! blow! blow!
Blow up, sea-winds, along Paumanok's shore!
I wait and I wait, till you blow my mate to me.

Yes, when the stars glisten'd, 55
All night long, on the prong of a moss-scallop'd stake,
Down, almost amid the slapping waves,
Sat the lone singer, wonderful, causing tears.

He call'd on his mate;
He pour'd forth the meanings which I, of all men, know. 60

Yes, my brother, I know;
The rest might not—but I have treasured every note;
For once, and more than once, dimly, down to the beach gliding,
Silent, avoiding the moonbeams, blending myself with the shadows,
Recalling now the obscure shapes, the echoes, the sounds and
      sights after their sorts, 65
The white arms out in the breakers tirelessly tossing,
I, with bare feet, a child, the wind wafting my hair,
Listen'd long and long.

Listen'd, to keep, to sing—now translating the notes,
Following you, my brother. 70

Soothe! soothe! soothe!
Close on its wave soothes the wave behind,
And again another behind, embracing and lapping, every one close,
But my love soothes not me, not me.

Low hangs the moon—it rose late; 75
O it is lagging—O I think it is heavy with love, with love.

O madly the sea pushes, pushes upon the land,
With love—with love.

O night! do I not see my love fluttering out there among the
    breakers?

What is that little black thing I see there in the white?   80
Loud! loud! loud!
Loud I call to you, my love!
High and clear I shoot my voice over the waves;
Surely you must know who is here, is here;
You must know who I am, my love.   85

Low-hanging moon!
What is that dusky spot in your brown yellow?
O it is the shape, the shape of my mate!
O moon, do not keep her from me any longer.

Land! land! O land!   90
Whichever way I turn, O I think you could give me my mate back
    again, if you only would;
For I am almost sure I see her dimly whichever way I look.

O rising stars!
Perhaps the one I want so much will rise, will rise with some of you.

O throat! O trembling throat!   95
Sound clearer through the atmosphere!
Pierce the woods, the earth;
Somewhere listening to catch you, must be the one I want.

Shake out, carols!
Solitary here—the night's carols!   100
Carols of lonesome love! Death's carols!
Carols under that lagging, yellow, waning moon!
O, under that moon, where she droops almost down into the sea!
O reckless, despairing carols.

But soft! sink low;   105
Soft! let me just murmur;
And do you wait a moment, you husky-noised sea;
For somewhere I believe I heard my mate responding to me,
So faint—I must be still, be still to listen;
But not altogether still, for then she might not come immediately
    to me.   110

Hither, my love!
Here I am! Here!
With this just-sustain'd note I announce myself to you;
This gentle call is for you, my love, for you.

Do not be decoy'd elsewhere!   115
That is the whistle of the wind—it is not my voice;
That is the fluttering, the fluttering of the spray;
Those are the shadows of leaves.

O darkness! O in vain!
O I am very sick and sorrowful.   120

O brown halo in the sky, near the moon, drooping upon the sea!
O troubled reflection in the sea!
O throat! O throbbing heart!
O all—and I singing uselessly, uselessly all the night.

Yet I murmur, murmur on!   125
O murmurs—you yourselves make me continue to sing, I know
    not why.
O past! O life! O songs of joy!
In the air—in the woods—over fields;
Loved! loved! loved! loved! loved!
But my love no more, no more with me!   130
We two together no more.

The aria sinking;
All else continuing—the stars shining,
The winds blowing—the notes of the bird continuous echoing,
With angry moans the fierce old mother incessantly moaning,   135
On the sands of Paumanok's shore, grey and rustling;
The yellow half-moon enlarged, sagging down, drooping, the face
    of the sea almost touching;
The boy ecstatic—with his bare feet the waves, with his hair the
    atmosphere dallying,
The love in the heart long pent, now loose, now at last tumultu-
    ously bursting,
The aria's meaning, the ears, the Soul, swiftly depositing,   140
The strange tears down the cheeks coursing,
The colloquy there—the trio—each uttering,
The undertone—the savage old mother, incessantly crying,

To the boy's Soul's questions sullenly timing—some drown'd
    secret hissing,
To the outsetting bard of love.   145

Demon or bird! (said the boy's soul,)
Is it indeed toward your mate you sing? or is it mostly to me?
For I, that was a child, my tongue's use sleeping,
Now I have heard you,
Now in a moment I know what I am for—I awake,   150
And already a thousand singers—a thousand songs, clearer, louder
    and more sorrowful than yours,
A thousand warbling echoes have started to life within me,
Never to die.

O you singer, solitary, singing by yourself—projecting me;
O solitary me, listening—never more shall I cease perpetuating
    you;   155
Never more shall I escape, never more the reverberations,
Never more the cries of unsatisfied love be absent from me,
Never again leave me to be the peaceful child I was before what
    there, in the night,
By the sea, under the yellow and sagging moon,
The messenger there aroused—the fire, the sweet hell within,   160
The unknown want, the destiny of me.
O give me the clue! (it lurks in the night here somewhere;)
O if I am to have so much, let me have more!
O a word! O what is my destination? (I fear it is henceforth chaos;)
O how joys, dreads, convolutions, human shapes, and all shapes,
    spring as from graves around me!   165
O phantoms! you cover all the land and all the sea!
O I cannot see in the dimness whether you smile or frown upon me;
O vapour, a look, a word! O well-beloved!
O you dear women's and men's phantoms!
A word then, (for I will conquer it,)   170
The word final, superior to all,
Subtle, sent up—what is it?—I listen;
Are you whispering it, and have been all the time, you sea-waves?
Is that it from your liquid rims and wet sands?

Whereto answering, the sea,   175
Delaying not, hurrying not,
Whisper'd me through the night, and very plainly before daybreak,

Lisp'd to me the low and delicious word Death;
And again Death—ever Death, Death, Death,
Hissing melodious, neither like the bird, nor like my aroused
    child's heart,   180
But edging near, as privately for me, rustling at my feet,
Creeping thence steadily up to my ears, and laving me softly
    all over,
Death, Death, Death, Death, Death.

Which I do not forget,
But fuse the song of my dusky demon and brother,   185
That he sang to me in the moonlight on Paumanok's grey beach,
With the thousand responsive songs, at random,
My own songs, awaked from that hour;
And with them the key, the word up from the waves,
The word of the sweetest song, and all songs,   190
That strong and delicious word which, creeping to my feet,
The sea whisper'd me.

FOUR POEMS FROM *SONG OF MYSELF*

X

Alone far in the wilds and mountains I hunt,
Wandering amazed at my own lightness and glee,
In the late afternoon choosing a safe spot to pass the night,
Kindling a fire and broiling the fresh-kill'd game,
Falling asleep on the gather'd leaves with my dog and gun by
    my side.   5

The Yankee clipper is under her sky-sails, she cuts the sparkle
    and scud,
My eyes settle the land, I bent at her prow or shout joyously from
    the deck.

The boatmen and clam-diggers arose early and stopt for me,
I tuck'd my trowser-ends in my boots and went and had a good
    time;
You should have been with us that day round the chowder-
    kettle.   10
I saw the marriage of the trapper in the open air in the far west,
    the bride was a red girl,

Her father and his friends sat near cross-legged and dumbly smoking, they had moccasins to their feet and large thick blankets
hanging from their shoulders,
On a bank lounged the trapper, he was drest mostly in skins, his
luxuriant beard and curls protected his neck, he held his bride
by the hand,
She had long eyelashes, her head was bare, her coarse straight locks
descended upon her voluptuous limbs and reach'd to her feet.

The runaway slave came to my house and stopt outside,   15
I heard his motions crackling the twigs of the woodpile,
Through the swung half-door of the kitchen I saw him limpsy
and weak,
And went where he sat on a log and led him in and assured him,
And brought water and fill'd a tub for his sweated body and
bruis'd feet,
And gave him a room that enter'd from my own, and gave him
some coarse clean clothes,   20
And remember perfectly well his revolving eyes and his awk-
wardness,
And remember putting plasters on the galls of his neck and ankles;
He staid with me a week before he was recuperated and pass'd
north,
I had him sit next me at table, my fire-lock lean'd in the corner

XXI

I am the poet of the Body and I am the poet of the Soul,
The pleasures of heaven are with me and the pains of hell are
with me,
The first I graft and increase upon myself, the latter I translate
into a new tongue.
I am the poet of the woman the same as the man,
And I say it is as great to be a woman as to be a man,   5
And I say there is nothing greater than the mother of men.

I chant the chant of dilation or pride,
We have had ducking and deprecating about enough,
I show that size is only development.
Have you outstript the rest? are you the President?   10
It is a trifle, they will more than arrive there every one, and still
pass on.

I am he that walks with the tender and growing night,
I call to the earth and sea half-held by the night.

Press close bare-bosom'd night—press close magnetic nourishing
    night!
Night of south winds—night of the large few stars!   15
Still nodding night—mad naked summer night.

Smile O voluptuous cool-breath'd earth!
Earth of the slumbering and liquid trees!
Earth of departed sunset—earth of the mountains misty-topt!
Earth of the vitreous pour of the full moon just tinged with
    blue!   20
Earth of shine and dark mottling the tide of the river!
Earth of the limpid gray of clouds brighter and clearer for my
    sake!
Far-swooping elbow'd earth—rich apple-blossom'd earth!
Smile, for your lover comes.

Prodigal, you have given me love—therefore I to you give love!   25
O unspeakable passionate love.

XXXI

I believe a leaf of grass is no less than the journeywork of the stars,
And the pismire is equally perfect, and a grain of sand, and the
    egg of the wren,
And the tree-toad is a chef-d'œuvre for the highest,
And the running blackberry would adorn the parlors of heaven,
And the narrowest hinge in my hand puts to scorn all ma-
    chinery,   5
And the cow crunching with depress'd head surpasses any statue,
And a mouse is miracle enough to stagger sextillions of infidels.

I find I incorporate gneiss, coal, long-threaded moss, fruits, grains,
    esculent roots,
And am stucco'd with quadrupeds and birds all over,
And have distanced what is behind me for good reasons,   10
But call any thing back again when I desire it.
In vain the speeding or shyness,
In vain the plutonic rocks send their old heat against my approach,
In vain the mastodon retreats beneath its own powder'd bones,

In vain objects stand leagues off and assume manifold shapes, 15
In vain the ocean settling in hollows and the great monsters lying
    low,
In vain the buzzard houses herself with the sky,
In vain the snake slides through the creepers and logs,
In vain the elk takes to the inner passes of the woods,
In vain the razor-bill'd auk sails far north to Labrador, 20
I follow quickly, I ascend to the nest in the fissure of the cliff.

XXXV–XXXVI

Would you hear of an old-time sea-fight?
Would you learn who won by the light of the moon and stars?
List to the yarn, as my grandmother's father the sailor told it to me.

Our foe was no skulk in his ship I tell you (said he),
His was the surly English pluck, and there is no tougher or truer,
    and never was, and never will be; 5
Along the lowered eve he came horribly raking us.

We closed with him, the yards entangled, the cannon touched,
My captain lashed fast with his own hands.

We had received some eighteen pound shots under the water,
On our lower-gun-deck two large pieces had burst at the first fire,
    killing all around and blowing up overhead. 10

Fighting at sun-down, fighting at dark,
Ten o'clock at night, the full moon well up, our leaks on the gain,
    and five feet of water reported,
The master-at-arms loosing the prisoners confined in the after-hold
    to give them a chance for themselves.

The transit to and from the magazine is now stopped by the
    sentinels,
They see so many strange faces they do not know whom to
    trust. 15

Our frigate takes fire,
The other asks if we demand quarter?
If our colors are struck and the fighting done?

Now I laugh content, for I hear the voice of my little captain,
We have not struck, he composedly cries, we have just begun our
    part of the fighting.   20

Only three guns are in use,
One is directed by the captain himself against the enemy's main-
    mast,
Two well served with grape and canister silence his musketry and
    clear his decks.

The tops alone second the fire of this little battery, especially the
    main-top,
They hold out bravely during the whole of the action.   25

Not a moment's cease,
The leaks gain fast on the pumps, the fire eats toward the powder-
    magazine.

One of the pumps has been shot away, it is generally thought we
    are sinking.

Serene stands the little captain,
He is not hurried, his voice is neither high nor low,   30
His eyes give more light to us than our battle-lanterns.

Toward twelve there in the beams of the moon they surrender
    to us.

*   *   *   *

Stretch'd and still lies the midnight,
Two great hulls motionless on the breast of the darkness,
Our vessel riddled and slowly sinking, preparations to pass to the
    one we have conquer'd,   35
The captain on the quarter-deck coldly giving his orders through
    a countenance white as a sheet,
Near by the corpse of the child that serv'd in the cabin,
The dead face of an old salt with long white hair and carefully
    curl'd whiskers,
The flames spite of all that can be done flickering aloft and below,
The husky voices of the two or three officers yet fit for duty,   40
Formless stacks of bodies and bodies by themselves, dabs of flesh
    upon the masts and spars,

Cut of cordage, dangle of rigging, slight shock of the soothe of
    waves,
Black and impassive guns, litter of powder-parcels, strong scent,
A few large stars overhead, silent and mournful shining,
Delicate sniffs of sea-breeze, smells of sedgy grass and fields by the
    shore, death-messages given in charge to survivors,   45
The hiss of the surgeon's knife, the gnawing teeth of his saw,
Wheeze, cluck, swash of falling blood, short wild scream, and long,
    dull, tapering groan,
These so, these irretrievable.

WHEN LILACS LAST IN THE DOORYARD BLOOM'D

I

When lilacs last in the dooryard bloom'd,
And the great star early droop'd in the western sky in the night,
I mourn'd, and yet shall mourn with ever-returning spring.

Ever-returning spring, trinity sure to me you bring,
Lilac blooming perennial and drooping star in the west,   5
And thought of him I love.

II

O powerful western fallen star!
O shades of night—O moody, tearful night!
O great star disappear'd—O the black murk that hides the star!
O cruel hands that hold me powerless—O helpless soul of me!   10
O harsh surrounding cloud that will not free my soul.

III

In the dooryard fronting an old farm-house near the white-wash'd
    palings,
Stands the lilac-bush tall-growing with heart-shaped leaves of rich
    green,
With many a pointed blossom rising delicate, with the perfume
    strong I love,
With every leaf a miracle—and from this bush in the door-
    yard,   15
With delicate-colour'd blossoms and heart-shaped leaves of rich
    green,
A sprig with its flower I break.

IV

In the swamp in secluded recesses,
A shy and hidden bird is warbling a song.
Solitary the thrush,   20
The hermit withdrawn to himself, avoiding the settlements,
Sings by himself a song.

Song of the bleeding throat,
Death's outlet song of life (for well, dear brother, I know,
If thou wast not granted to sing thou would'st surely die).   25

V

Over the breast of the spring, the land, amid cities,
Amid lanes and through old woods, where lately the violets peep'd
    from the ground, spotting the grey débris,
Amid the grass in the fields each side of the lanes, passing the
    endless grass,
Passing the yellow-spear'd wheat, every grain from its shroud in
    the dark-brown fields uprisen,   30
Passing the apple-tree blows of white and pink in the orchards,
Carrying a corpse to where it shall rest in the grave,
Night and day journeys a coffin.

VI

Coffin that passes through lanes and streets,
Through day and night with the great cloud darkening the land,
With the pomp of the inloop'd flags with the cities draped in
    black,   35
With the show of the States themselves as of crepe-veiled women
    standing,
With processions long and winding and the flambeaus of the night,
With the countless torches lit, with the silent sea of faces and the
    unbared heads,
With the waiting depot, the arriving coffin, and the somber faces,
With dirges through the night, with the thousand voices rising
    strong and solemn,   40
With all the mournful voices of the dirges poured around the
    coffin,
The dim-lit churches and the shuddering organs—where amid these
    you journey,

With the tolling tolling bells' perpetual clang,
Here, coffin that slowly passes,
I give you my sprig of lilac.   45

VII

(Nor for you, for one alone,
Blossoms and branches green to coffins all I bring,
For fresh as the morning, thus would I chant a song for you O
    sane and sacred death.

All over bouquets of roses,
O death, I cover you over with roses and early lilies,   50
But mostly and now the lilac that blooms the first,
Copious I break, I break the sprigs from the bushes,
With loaded arms I come, pouring for you,
For you and the coffins all of you O death.)

VIII

O western orb sailing the heaven,   55
Now I know what you must have meant as a month since I walked,
As I walked in silence the transparent shadowy night,
As I saw you had something to tell as you bent to me night after
    night,
As you drooped from the sky low down as if to my side (while
    the other stars all looked on),
As we wandered together the solemn night (for something I know
    not what kept me from sleep),   60
As the night advanced, and I saw on the rim of the west how full
    you were of woe,
As I stood on the rising ground in the breeze in the cool transparent
    night,
As I watched where you passed and was lost in the netherward
    black of the night,
As my soul in its trouble dissatisfied sank, as where you, sad orb,
Concluded, dropped in the night, and was gone.   65

IX

Sing on there in the swamp,
O singer bashful and tender, I hear your notes, I hear your call,
I hear, I come presently, I understand you,
But a moment I linger, for the lustrous star has detained me,
The star, my departing comrade, holds and detains me.   70

X

O how shall I warble myself for the dead one there I loved?
And how shall I deck my song for the large sweet soul that has
gone?
And what shall my perfume be for the grave of him I love?

Sea-winds blown from east and west,
Blown from the Eastern sea and blown from the Western sea, till
there on the prairies meeting,   75
These and with these and the breath of my chant,
I'll perfume the grave of him I love.

XI

O what shall I hang on the chamber walls?
And what shall the pictures be that I hang on the walls,
To adorn the burial-house of him I love?   80

Pictures of growing spring and farms and homes,
With the Fourth-month eve at sundown, and the gray smoke lucid
and bright,
With floods of the yellow gold of the gorgeous, indolent, sinking
sun, burning, expanding the air,
With the fresh sweet herbage under foot, and the pale green leaves
of the trees prolific,
In the distance the flowing glaze, the breast of the river, with a
wind-dapple here and there,   85
With ranging hills on the banks, with many a line against the sky,
and shadows,
And the city at hand with dwellings so dense, and stacks of
chimneys,
And all the scenes of life and the workshops, and the workmen
homeward returning.

XII

Lo, body and soul—this land,
My own Manhattan with spires, and the sparkling and hurrying
tides, and the ships,   90
The varied and ample land, the South and the North in the light,
Ohio's shores and flashing Missouri,
And ever the far-spreading prairies covered with grass and corn.

Lo, the most excellent sun so calm and haughty,
The violet and purple morn with just-felt breezes,
The gentle soft-born measureless light,   95
The miracle spreading, bathing all, the fulfilled noon,
The coming eve delicious, the welcome night and the stars,
Over my cities shining all, enveloping man and land.

XIII

Sing on, sing on you gray-brown bird,
Sing from the swamps, the recesses, pour your chant from the
    bushes,   100
Limitless out of the dusk, out of the cedars and pines.

Sing on dearest brother, warble your reedy song,
Loud human song, with voice of uttermost woe.

O liquid and free and tender!
O wild and loose to my soul—O wondrous singer!   105
You only I hear—yet the star holds me (but will soon depart),
Yet the lilac with mastering odor holds me.

XIV

Now while I sat in the day and looked forth,
In the close of the day with its light and the fields of spring, and
    the farmers preparing their crops,
In the large unconscious scenery of my land with its lakes and
    forests,   110
In the heavenly aerial beauty (after the perturbed winds and the
    storms),
Under the arching heavens of the afternoon swift passing, and the
    voices of children and women,
The many-moving sea-tides, and I saw the ships how they sailed,
And the summer approaching with richness, and the fields all busy
    with labor,
And the infinite separate houses, how they all went on, each with
    its meals and minutia of daily usages,   115
And the streets how their throbbings throbb'd, and the cities pent
    —lo, then and there,
Falling upon them all and among them all, enveloping me with
    the rest,

Appear'd the cloud, appear'd the long black trail,
And I knew death, its thought, and the sacred knowledge of death.

Then with the knowledge of death as walking one side of me,   120
And the thought of death close-walking the other side of me,
And I in the middle as with companions, and as holding the hands
    of companions,
I fled forth to the hiding receiving night that talks not,
Down to the shores of the water, the path by the swamp in the
    dimness,
To the solemn shadowy cedars and ghostly pines so still.   125

And the singer so shy to the rest receiv'd me,
The gray-brown bird I know receiv'd us comrades three,
And he sang the carol of death, and a verse for him I love.

From deep secluded recesses,
From the fragrant cedars and the ghostly pines so still,   130
Came the carol of the bird.

And the charm of the carol rapt me,
As I held as if by their hands my comrades in the night,
And the voice of my spirit tallied the song of the bird.

Come lovely and soothing death,   135
Undulate round the world, serenely arriving, arriving,
In the day, in the night, to all, to each,
Sooner or later delicate death.

Prais'd be the fathomless universe,
For life and joy, and for objects and knowledge curious,   140
And for love, sweet love—but praise! praise! praise!
For the sure-enwinding arms of cool-enfolding death.

Dark mother always gliding near with soft feet,
Have none chanted for thee a chant of fullest welcome?
Then I chant it for thee, I glorify thee above all,   145
I bring thee a song that when thou must indeed come, come un-
    falteringly.

Approach strong deliveress,
When it is so, when thou hast taken them, I joyously sing the dead,

Lost in the loving floating ocean of thee,
Laved in the flood of thy bliss, O death.   150
From me to thee glad serenades,
Dances for thee I propose saluting thee, adornments and feastings
    for thee,
And the sights of the open landscape and the high-spread sky are
    fitting,
And life and the fields, and the huge and thoughtful night.

The night in silence under many a star,   155
The ocean shore and the husky whispering wave whose voice I
    know,
And the soul turning to thee, O vast and well-veil'd death,
And the body gratefully nestling close to thee.

Over the tree-tops I float thee a song,
Over the rising and sinking waves, over the myriad fields and the
    prairies wide,   160
Over the dense-pack'd cities all and the teeming wharves and ways,
I float this carol with joy, with joy to thee, O death.

                          XV

To the tally of my soul,
Loud and strong kept up the gray-brown bird,
With pure deliberate notes spreading, filling the night.   165

Loud in the pines and cedars dim,
Clear in the freshness moist and the swamp-perfume,
And I with my comrades there in the night.

While my sight that was bound in my eyes unclosed,
As to long panoramas of visions.   170

And I saw askant the armies,
I saw as in noiseless dreams hundreds of battle-flags,
Borne through the smoke of the battles and pierc'd with missiles
    I saw them,
And carried hither and yon through the smoke, and torn and
    bloody,
And at last but a few shreds left on the staffs (and all in silence),
And the staffs all splinter'd and broken.   176

I saw battle-corpses, myriads of them,
And the white skeletons of young men, I saw them,
I saw the débris and débris of all the slain soldiers of the war,
But I saw they were not as was thought,   180
They themselves were fully at rest, they suffered not,
The living remained and suffered, the mother suffered,
And the wife and the child and the musing comrade suffered,
And the armies that remained suffered.

XVI

Passing the visions, passing the night,   185
Passing, unloosing the hold of my comrades' hands,
Passing the song of the hermit bird and the tallying song of my
     soul,
Victorious song, death's outlet song, yet varying, ever-altering song,
As low and wailing, yet clear the notes, rising and falling, flooding
     the night,
Sadly sinking and fainting, as warning and warning, and yet again
     bursting with joy,   190
Covering the earth and filling the spread of the heaven,
As that powerful psalm in the night I heard from recesses,
Passing, I leave thee lilac with heart-shaped leaves,
I leave thee there in the door-yard, blooming, returning with spring.

I cease from my song for thee,   195
From my gaze on thee in the west, fronting the west, communing
     with thee,
O comrade lustrous with silver face in the night.

Yet each to keep and all, retrievements out of the night,
The song, the wondrous chant of the gray-brown bird,
And the tallying chant, the echo aroused in my soul,   200
With the lustrous and drooping star with the countenance full
     of woe,
With the holders holding my hand nearing the call of the bird,
Comrades mine and I in the midst, and their memory ever to keep,
     for the dead I loved so well,
For the sweetest, wisest soul of all my days and lands—and this for
     his dear sake,
Lilac and star and bird twined with the chant of my soul,   205
There in the fragrant pines and the cedars dusk and dim.

AS TOILSOME I WANDER'D VIRGINIA'S WOODS

As toilsome I wander'd Virginia's woods,
To the music of rustling leaves kick'd by my feet (for 'twas
    autumn),
I mark'd at the foot of a tree the grave of a soldier;
Mortally wounded he and buried on the retreat (easily all could I
    understand),
The halt of a mid-day hour, when up! no time to lose—yet this
    sign left,
On a tablet scrawl'd and nail'd on the tree by the grave,
Bold, cautious, true, and my loving comrade.

Long, long I muse, then on my way go wandering,
Many a changeful season to follow, and many a scene of life,
Yet at times through changeful season and scene, abrupt, alone, or
    in the crowded street,
Comes before me the unknown soldier's grave, comes the inscrip-
    tion rude in Virginia's woods,
Bold, cautious, true, and my loving comrade.

MATTHEW ARNOLD (1822–1888)

DOVER BEACH

The sea is calm to-night.
The tide is full, the moon lies fair
Upon the straits;—on the French coast the light
Gleams and is gone; the cliffs of England stand,
Glimmering and vast, out in the tranquil bay.   **5**
Come to the window, sweet is the night air!
Only, from the long line of spray
Where the sea meets the moon-blanched land,
Listen! you hear the grating roar
Of pebbles which the waves draw back, and fling,   **10**
At their return, up the high strand,
Begin, and cease, and then again begin,
With tremulous cadence slow, and bring
The eternal note of sadness in.

Sophocles long ago 15
Heard it on the Ægean, and it brought
Into his mind the turbid ebb and flow
Of human misery; we
Find also in the sound a thought,
Hearing it by this distant northern sea. 20
The Sea of Faith
Was once, too, at the full, and round earth's shore
Lay like the folds of a bright girdle furled.
But now I only hear
Its melancholy, long, withdrawing roar, 25
Retreating, to the breath
Of the night wind, down the vast edges drear
And naked shingles of the world.

Ah, love, let us be true
To one another! for the world, which seems 30
To lie before us like a land of dreams,
So various, so beautiful, so new,
Hath really neither joy, nor love, nor light,
Nor certitude, nor peace, nor help for pain;
And we are here as on a darkling plain 35
Swept with confused alarms of struggle and flight
Where ignorant armies clash by night.

PHILOMELA

Hark, ah, the nightingale—
The tawny-throated!
Hark, from that moonlit cedar what a burst!
What triumph! hark!—what pain!
O wanderer from a Grecian shore, 5
Still, after many years, in distant lands,
Still nourishing in thy bewildered brain
That wild, unquenched, deep-sunken, old-world pain—
Say, will it never heal?
And can this fragrant lawn 10
With its cool trees, and night,
And the sweet, tranquil Thames,
And moonshine, and the dew,
To thy racked heart and brain
Afford no balm? 15

Dost thou tonight behold,
Here, through the moonlight on this English grass,
The unfriendly palace in the Thracian wild?
Dost thou again peruse
With hot cheeks and seared eyes   20
The too clear web, and thy dumb sister's shame?
Dost thou once more assay
Thy flight, and feel come over thee,
Poor fugitive, the feathery change
Once more, and once more seem to make resound   25
With love and hate, triumph and agony,
Lone Daulis, and the high Cephissian vale?
Listen, Eugenia—
How thick the bursts come crowding through the leaves!
Again—thou hearest?   30
Eternal passion!
Eternal pain!

A SUMMER NIGHT

In the deserted, moon-blanch'd street,
How lonely rings the echo of my feet!
Those windows, which I gaze at, frown,
Silent and white, unopening down,
Repellent as the world;—but see,   5
A break between the housetops shows
The moon! and, lost behind her, fading dim
Into the dewy dark obscurity
Down at the far horizon's rim,
Doth a whole tract of heaven disclose!   10

And to my mind the thought
Is on a sudden brought
Of a past night, and a far different scene.
Headlands stood out into the moonlit deep
As clearly as at noon;   15
The spring-tide's brimming flow
Heaved dazzlingly between;
Houses, with long white sweep,
Girdled the glistening bay;
Behind, through the soft air,   20

The blue haze-cradled mountains spread away.
That night was far more fair—
But the same restless pacings to and fro,
And the same vainly throbbing heart was there,
And the same bright, calm moon.   25

And the calm moonlight seems to say:
Hast thou then still the old unquiet breast,
Which neither deadens into rest,
Nor ever feels the fiery glow
That whirls the spirit from itself away,   30
But fluctuates to and fro,
Never by passion quite possess'd
And never quite benumb'd by the world's sway?—
And I, I know not if to pray
Still to be what I am, or yield and be   35
Like all the other men I see.

For most men in a brazen prison live,
Where, in the sun's hot eye,
With heads bent o'er their toil, they languidly
Their lives to some unmeaning taskwork give,   40
Dreaming of nought beyond their prison-wall.
And as, year after year,
Fresh products of their barren labour fall
From their tired hands, and rest
Never yet comes more near,   45
Gloom settles slowly down over their breast;
And while they try to stem
The waves of mournful thought by which they are prest
Death in their prison reaches them,
Unfreed, having seen nothing, still unblest.   50

And the rest, a few,
Escape their prison and depart
On the wide ocean of life anew.
There the freed prisoner, where'er his heart
Listeth, will sail;   55
Nor doth he know how there prevail,
Despotic on that sea,
Trade-winds which cross it from eternity.
Awhile he holds some false way, undebarr'd

By thwarting signs, and braves 60
The freshening wind and blackening waves.
And then the tempest strikes him; and between
The lightning-bursts is seen
Only a driving wreck,
And the pale master on his spar-strewn deck 65
With anguish'd face and flying hair
Grasping the rudder hard,
Still bent to make some port he knows not where,
Still standing for some false, impossible shore.
And sterner comes the roar 70
Of sea and wind, and through the deepening gloom
Fainter and fainter wreck and helmsman loom,
And he too disappears, and comes no more.

Is there no life, but these alone?
Madman or slave, must man be one? 75

Plainness and clearness without shadow of stain!
Clearness divine!
Ye heavens, whose pure dark regions have no sign
Of languor, though so calm, and, though so great,
Are yet untroubled and unpassionate; 80
Who, though so noble, share in the world's toil,
And, though so task'd, keep free from dust and soil!
I will not say that your mild deeps retain
A tinge, it may be, of their silent pain
Who have long'd deeply once, and long'd in vain— 85
But I will rather say that you remain
A world above man's head, to let him see
How boundless might his soul's horizons be,
How vast, yet of what clear transparency!
How it were good to live there, and breathe free; 90
How fair a lot to fill
Is left to each man still!

TO MARGUERITE

Yes! in the sea of life enisled,
With echoing straits between us thrown,
Dotting the shoreless watery wild,
We mortal millions live *alone*.

The islands feel the enclasping flow,   5
And then their endless bounds they know.

But when the moon their hollows lights,
And they are swept by balms of spring,
And in their glens, on starry nights,
The nightingales divinely sing;   10
And lovely notes, from shore to shore,
Across the sounds and channels pour—

Oh! then a longing like despair
Is to their farthest caverns sent;
For surely once, they feel, we were   15
Parts of a single continent!
Now round us spreads the watery plain—
Oh might our marges meet again!

Who order'd, that their longing's fire
Should be, as soon as kindled, cool'd?   20
Who renders vain their deep desire?—
A God, a God their severance ruled!
And bade betwixt their shores to be
The unplumb'd, salt, estranging sea.

THE SCHOLAR-GIPSY

There was very lately a lad in the University of Oxford, who was by his poverty forced to leave his studies there, and at last to join himself to a company of vagabond gipsies. Among these extravagant people, by the insinuating subtilty of his carriage, he quickly got so much of their love and esteem as that they discovered to him their mystery. After he had been a pretty while exercised in the trade, there chanced to ride by a couple of scholars, who had formerly been of his acquaintance. They quickly spied out their old friend among the gipsies; and he gave them an account of the necessity which drove him to that kind of life, and told them that the people he went with were not such impostors as they were taken for, but that they had a traditional kind of learning among them, and could do wonders by the power of imagination, their fancy binding that of others: that himself had learned much of their art, and when he had compassed the whole secret, he intended, he said, to leave their company, and give the world an account of what he had learned.—Glanvil's *Vanity of Dogmatizing*, 1661.

Go, for they call you, shepherd, from the hill;
    Go, shepherd, and untie the wattled cotes!
        No longer leave thy wistful flock unfed,
    Nor let thy bawling fellows rack their throats,
        Nor the cropped herbage shoot another head.   5

But when the fields are still,
And the tired men and dogs all gone to rest,
And only the white sheep are sometimes seen
Cross and recross the strips of moon-blanched green,
Come, shepherd; and again begin the quest!　　　10

Here, where the reaper was at work of late,
In this high field's dark corner, where he leaves
His coat, his basket, and his earthen cruse,
And in the sun, all morning, binds the sheaves,
Then here, at noon, comes back his stores to use—　15
Here will I sit and wait,
While to my ear from uplands far away
The bleating of the folded flocks is borne,
With distant cries of reapers in the corn—
All the live murmur of a summer's day.　　　20

Screened is this nook, o'er the high half-reaped field,
And here till sun-down, shepherd! will I be.
Through the thick corn the scarlet poppies peep,
And round green roots and yellowing stalks, I see
Pale pink convolvulus in tendrils creep;　　　25
And air-swept lindens yield
Their scent, and rustle down their perfumed showers
Of bloom on the bent grass where I am laid,
And bower me from the August sun with shade;
And the eye travels down to Oxford's towers.　　　30

And near me on the grass lies Glanvil's book.
Come, let me read the oft-read tale again!
The story of the Oxford scholar poor,
Of shining parts and quick inventive brain,
Who, tired of knocking at preferment's door,　　　35
One summer morn forsook
His friends, and went to learn the gipsy-lore,
And roamed the world with that wild brotherhood,
And came, as most men deemed, to little good,
But came to Oxford and his friends no more.　　　40

But once, years after, in the country-lanes,
Two scholars, whom at college erst he knew,
Met him, and of his way of life enquired;

Whereat he answered that the gipsy-crew,
   His mates, had arts to rule as they desired   45
      The workings of men's brains,
And they can bind them to what thoughts they will.
   "And I," he said, "the secret of their art,
     When fully learned, will to the world impart;
But it needs Heaven-sent moments for this skill."   50

This said, he left them, and returned no more.
   But rumors hung about the countryside,
     That the lost scholar long was seen to stray,
   Seen by rare glimpses, pensive and tongue-tied,
     In hat of antique shape, and cloak of grey,   55
      The same the gipsies wore.
Shepherds had met him on the Hurst in spring;
   At some lone alehouse in the Berkshire moors,
   On the warm ingle-bench, the smock-frocked boors
Had found him seated at their entering;   60

But, 'mid their drink and clatter, he would fly.—
   And I myself seem half to know thy looks,
     And put the shepherds, wanderer! on thy trace;
   And boys who in lone wheatfields scare the rooks,
     I ask if thou hast passed their quiet place;   65
      Or in my boat I lie
Moored to the cool bank in the summer-heats,
   'Mid wide grass meadows which the sunshine fills,
   And watch the warm, green-muffled Cumner hills,
And wonder if thou haunt'st their shy retreats.   70

For most, I know, thou lov'st retired ground:
   Thee, at the ferry, Oxford riders blithe,
     Returning home on summer-nights, have met
   Crossing the stripling Thames at Bablockhithe,
     Trailing in the cool stream thy fingers wet,   75
      As the punt's rope chops round;
And leaning backward in a pensive dream,
   And fostering in thy lap a heap of flowers
   Plucked in shy fields and distant Wychwood bowers;
And thine eyes resting on the moonlit stream.   80

And then they land, and thou art seen no more!—
   Maidens who from the distant hamlets come

To dance around the Fyfield elm in May,
Oft through the darkening fields have seen thee roam,
    Or cross a stile into the public way.   85
        Oft thou hast given them store
Of flowers: the frail-leafed white anemony,
    Dark bluebells drenched with dews of summer eves,
    And purple orchises with spotted leaves;
But none hath words she can report of thee.   90

And, above Godstow Bridge, when haytime's here
    In June, and many a scythe in sunshine flames,
    Men who through those wide fields of breezy grass,
Where black-winged swallows haunt the glittering Thames,
    To bathe in the abandoned lasher pass,   95
        Have often passed thee near,
Sitting upon the river bank o'ergrown;
    Marked thine outlandish garb, thy figure spare,
    Thy dark vague eyes, and soft abstracted air:
But when they came from bathing, thou wast gone!   100

At some lone homestead in the Cumner hills,
    Where at her open door the housewife darns,
    Thou hast been seen; or hanging on a gate,
To watch the threshers in the mossy barns.
    Children, who early range these slopes, and late, 105
        For cresses from the rills,
Have known thee eying, all an April day,
    The springing pastures and the feeding kine;
And marked thee, when the stars come out and shine,
Through the long dewy grass move slow away.   110

In autumn, on the skirts of Bagley Wood,
    (Where most the gipsies by the turf-edged way
    Pitch their smoked tents, and every bush you see
With scarlet patches tagged, and shreds of grey,
    Above the forest-ground called Thessaly,)   115
        The blackbird, picking food,
Sees thee, nor stops his meal, nor fears at all;
    So often has he known thee past him stray,
    Rapt, twirling in thy hand a withered spray,
And waiting for the spark from heaven to fall.   120

And once, in winter, on the causeway chill,
　Where home through flooded fields foot-travellers go,
　　Have I not passed thee on the wooden bridge,
　Wrapt in thy cloak and battling with the snow,
　　Thy face toward Hinksey and its wintry ridge?　　125
　　　And thou hast climbed the hill,
　And gained the white brow of the Cumner range;
　　Turned once to watch, while thick the snowflakes fall,
　　The line of festal light in Christ-Church hall;
　Then sought thy straw in some sequestered grange.　　130

But what—I dream! Two hundred years are flown,
　Since first thy story ran through Oxford halls,
　　And the grave Glanvil did the tale inscribe
　That thou wert wandered from the studious walls
　　To learn strange arts, and join a gipsy-tribe;　　135
　　　And thou from earth art gone
　Long since, and in some quiet churchyard laid:
　　Some country-nook, where o'er thy unknown grave
　　Tall grasses and white flowering nettles wave,
　Under a dark red-fruited yew-tree's shade.　　140

No, no, thou hast not felt the lapse of hours!
　For what wears out the life of mortal men?
　　'Tis that from change to change their being rolls;
　'Tis that repeated shocks, again, again,
　　Exhaust the energy of strongest souls,　　145
　　　And numb the elastic powers.
　Till, having used our nerves with bliss and teen,
　　And tired upon a thousand schemes our wit,
　　To the just-pausing Genius we remit
　Our worn-out life, and are—what we have been.　　150

Thou hast not lived, why shouldst thou perish, so?
　Thou hadst one aim, one business, one desire;
　　Else wert thou long since numbered with the dead,
　Else hadst thou spent, like other men, thy fire!
　　The generations of thy peers are fled,　　155
　　　And we ourselves shall go;
　But thou possessest an immortal lot,
　　And we imagine thee exempt from age
　　And living as thou liv'st on Glanvil's page,
　Because thou hadst what we, alas! have not.　　160

For early didst thou leave the world, with powers
   Fresh, undiverted to the world without,
     Firm to their mark, not spent on other things;
   Free from the sick fatigue, the languid doubt,
     Which much to have tried, in much been baffled,
       brings.   165
       O life unlike to ours!
Who fluctuate idly without term or scope,
   Of whom each strives, nor knows for what he strives,
   And each half-lives a hundred different lives;
Who wait like thee, but not, like thee, in hope.   170

Thou waitest for the spark from heaven! and we,
   Light half-believers of our casual creeds,
     Who never deeply felt, nor clearly willed,
   Whose insight never has borne fruit in deeds,
     Whose vague resolves never have been fulfilled;   175
       For whom each year we see
Breeds new beginnings, disappointments new;
   Who hesitate and falter life away,
   And lose to-morrow the ground won to-day:
Ah! do not we, wanderer! await it too?   180

Yes, we await it! but it still delays,
   And then we suffer! and amongst us, one
     Who most has suffered, takes dejectedly
His seat upon the intellectual throne;
     And all his store of sad experience he   185
       Lays bare of wretched days;
Tells us his misery's birth and growth and signs,
   And how the dying spark of hope was fed,
   And how the breast was soothed, and how the head,
And all his hourly-varied anodynes.   190

This for our wisest: and we others pine,
   And wish the long unhappy dream would end,
     And waive all claim to bliss, and try to bear,
   With close-lipped patience for our only friend,
     Sad patience, too near neighbor to despair.   195
       But none has hope like thine!
Thou through the fields and through the woods dost stray,
   Roaming the country-side, a truant boy,

Nursing thy project in unclouded joy,
And every doubt long blown by time away. 200

O born in days when wits were fresh and clear,
And life ran gaily as the sparkling Thames,
Before this strange disease of modern life,
With its sick hurry, its divided aims,
Its heads o'ertaxed, its palsied hearts, was rife— 205
Fly hence, our contact fear!
Still fly, plunge deeper in the bowering wood!
Averse, as Dido did, with gesture stern,
From her false friend's approach in Hades turn,
Wave us away; and keep thy solitude! 210

Still nursing the unconquerable hope,
Still clutching the inviolable shade,
With a free onward impulse brushing through,
By night, the silvered branches of the glade,
Far on the forest-skirts, where none pursue, 215
On some mild pastoral slope
Emerge; and resting on the moonlit pales,
Freshen thy flowers, as in former years,
With dew, or listen with enchanted ears,
From the dark dingles, to the nightingales! 220

But fly our paths, our feverish contact fly!
For strong the infection of our mental strife,
Which, though it gives no bliss, yet spoils for rest;
And we should win thee from thy own fair life,
Like us distracted, and like us unblest. 225
Soon, soon thy cheer would die,
Thy hopes grow timorous, and unfixed thy powers,
And thy clear aims be cross and shifting made;
And then thy glad perennial youth would fade,
Fade, and grow old at last, and die like ours. 230

Then fly our greetings, fly our speech and smiles!
As some grave Tyrian trader, from the sea,
Descried at sunrise an emerging prow
Lifting the cool-haired creepers stealthily,
The fringes of a southward-facing brow 235
Among the Ægæan isles;

And saw the merry Grecian coaster come,
    Freighted with amber grapes and Chian wine,
    Green bursting figs, and tunnies steeped in brine,
And knew the intruders on his ancient home,   240

The young light-hearted masters of the waves!
    And snatched his rudder, and shook out more sail;
    And day and night held on indignantly
O'er the blue Midland waters with the gale,
    Betwixt the Syrtes and soft Sicily,   245
        To where the Atlantic raves
Outside the western straits, and unbent sails
    There, where down cloudy cliffs, through sheets of foam,
    Shy traffickers, the dark Iberians come;
And on the beach undid his corded bales.   250

THE BURIED LIFE

Light flows our war of mocking words, and yet,
Behold, with tears my eyes are wet!
I feel a nameless sadness o'er me roll.
Yes, yes, we know that we can jest,
We know, we know that we can smile!   5
But there's a something in this breast,
To which thy light words bring no rest,
And thy gay smiles no anodyne.
Give me thy hand, and hush awhile,
And turn those limped eyes on mine,   10
And let me read there, love, thy inmost soul.
Alas, is even love too weak
To unlock the heart, and let it speak?
Are even lovers powerless to reveal
To one another what indeed they feel?   15
I knew the mass of men concealed
Their thoughts, for fear that if revealed
They would by other men be met
With blank indifference, or with blame reproved;
I knew they lived and moved   20
Tricked in disguises, alien to the rest
Of men, and alien to themselves—and yet
The same heart beats in every human breast!

But we, my love!—does a like spell benumb
Our hearts, our voices?—must we too be dumb?   25
Ah, well for us, if even we,
Even for a moment, can get free
Our heart, and have our lips unchained;
For that which seals them hath been deep-ordained.

Fate, which foresaw   30
How frivolous a baby man would be—
By what distractions he would be possessed,
How he would pour himself in every strife,
And well-nigh change his own identity—
That it might keep from his capricious play   35
His genuine self, and force him to obey
Even in his own despite his being's law,
Bade through the deep recesses of our breast
The unregarded river of our life
Pursue with indiscernible flow its way;   40
And that we should not see
The buried stream, and seem to be
Eddying about in blind uncertainty,
Though driving on with it eternally.

But often, in the world's most crowded streets,   45
But often, in the din of strife,
There rises an unspeakable desire
After the knowledge of our buried life;
A thirst to spend our fire and restless force
In tracking out our true, original course;   50
A longing to inquire
Into the mystery of this heart that beats
So wild, so deep in us—to know
Whence our lives come, and where they go.
And many a man in his own breast then delves,   55
But deep enough, alas, none ever mines.
And we have been on many thousand lines,
And we have shown, on each, spirit and power;
But hardly have we, for one little hour,
Been on our own line, have we been ourselves—   60
Hardly had skill to utter one of all
The nameless feelings that course through our breast,
But they course on for ever unexpressed.

And long we try in vain to speak and act
Our hidden self, and what we say and do   65
Is eloquent, is well—but 'tis not true!
And then we will no more be racked
With inward striving, and demand
Of all the thousand nothings of the hour
Their stupefying power;   70
Ah yes, and they benumb us at our call!
Yet still, from time to time, vague and forlorn,
From the soul's subterranean depth upborne
As from an infinitely distant land,
Come airs, and floating echoes, and convey   75
A melancholy into all our day.

Only—but this is rare—
When a beloved hand is laid in ours,
When, jaded with the rush and glare
Of the interminable hours,   80
Our eyes can in another's eyes read clear,
When our world-deafened ear
Is by the tones of a loved voice caressed—
A bolt is shot back somewhere in our breast,
And a lost pulse of feeling stirs again.   85
The eye sinks inward, and the heart lies plain,
And what we mean, we say, and what we would, we know.
A man becomes aware of his life's flow,
And hears its winding murmur; and he sees
The meadows where it glides, the sun, the breeze.   90

And there arrives a lull in the hot race
Wherein he doth for ever chase
That flying and elusive shadow, rest.
An air of coolness plays upon his face,
And an unwonted calm pervades his breast.   95
And then he thinks he knows
The hills where his life rose,
And the sea where it goes.

DANTE GABRIEL ROSSETTI (1828–1882)

MY SISTER'S SLEEP

She fell asleep on Christmas Eve:
 At length the long-ungranted shade
 Of weary eyelids overweigh'd
The pain nought else might yet relieve.

Our mother, who had leaned all day 5
 Over the bed from chime to chime,
 Then raised herself for the first time,
And as she sat her down, did pray.

Her little work-table was spread
 With work to finish. For the glare 10
 Made by her candle, she had care
To work some distance from the bed.

Without, there was a cold moon up,
 Of winter radiance sheer and thin;
 The hollow halo it was in 15
Was like an icy crystal cup.

Through the small room, with subtle sound
 Of flame, by vents the fireshine drove
 And reddened. In its dim alcove
The mirror shed a clearness round. 20

I had been sitting up some nights,
 And my tired mind felt weak and blank;
 Like a sharp strengthening wine it drank
The stillness and the broken lights.

Twelve struck. That sound, by dwindling years 25
 Heard in each hour, crept off; and then
 The ruffled silence spread again,
Like water that a pebble stirs.

Our mother rose from where she sat:
 Her needles, as she laid them down, 30
 Met lightly, and her silken gown
Settled: no other noise than that.

"Glory unto the Newly Born!"
   So, as said angels, she did say;
   Because we were in Christmas Day,   35
Though it would still be long till morn.

Just then in the room over us
   There was a pushing back of chairs,
   As some who had sat unawares
So late, now heard the hour, and rose.   40

With anxious softly-stepping haste
   Our mother went where Margaret lay,
   Fearing the sounds o'erhead—should they
Have broken her long watched-for rest!

She stooped an instant, calm, and turned;   45
   But suddenly turned back again;
   And all her features seemed in pain
With woe, and her eyes gazed and yearned.

For my part, I but hid my face,
   And held my breath, and spoke no word: 50
   There was none spoken; but I heard
The silence for a little space.

Our mother bowed herself and wept:
   And both my arms fell, and I said,
   "God knows I knew that she was dead."   55
And there, all white, my sister slept.

Then kneeling, upon Christmas morn
   A little after twelve o'clock
   We said, ere the first quarter struck,
"Christ's blessing on the newly born!"   60

THE BLESSED DAMOZEL

The blessed Damozel leaned out
   From the gold bar of Heaven;
Her eyes were deeper than the depth
   Of waters stilled at even;
She had three lilies in her hand,   5
   And the stars in her hair were seven.

Her robe, ungirt from clasp to hem,
  No wrought flowers did adorn,
But a white rose of Mary's gift,
  For service meetly worn;   10
Her hair that lay along her back,
  Was yellow like ripe corn.

Herseemed she scarce had been a day
  One of God's choristers;
The wonder was not yet quite gone   15
  From that still look of hers;
Albeit, to them she left, her day
  Had counted as ten years.

(To one it is ten years of years:
  . . . Yet now, here in this place,   20
Surely she leaned o'er me,—her hair
  Fell all about my face. . . .
Nothing: the autumn-fall of leaves.
  The whole year sets apace.)

It was the rampart of God's house   25
  That she was standing on;
By God built over the sheer depth
  In which is Space begun;
So high, that looking downward thence,
  She scarce could see the sun.   30

It lies in Heaven, across the flood
  Of ether, as a bridge.
Beneath, the tides of day and night
  With flame and darkness ridge
The void, as low as where this earth   35
  Spins like a fretful midge.

Around her, lovers, newly met
  'Mid deathless love's acclaims,
Spoke evermore among themselves,
  Their heart-remembered names;   40
And the souls, mounting up to God,
  Went by her like thin flames.

And still she bowed herself, and stooped
   Out of the circling charm;
Until her bosom must have made   45
   The bar she leaned on warm,
And the lilies lay as if asleep
   Along her bended arm.

From the fixed place of Heaven, she saw
   Time, like a pulse, shake fierce   50
Through all the worlds. Her gaze still strove,
   Within the gulf to pierce
Its path; and now she spoke as when
   The stars sang in their spheres.

The sun was gone now; the curled moon   55
   Was like a little feather
Fluttering far down the gulf; and now
   She spoke through the still weather.
Her voice was like the voice the stars
   Had when they sang together.   60

(Ah sweet! Even now in that bird's song,
   Strove not her accents there,
Fain to be hearkened? When those bells
   Possessed the mid-day air,
Strove not her steps to reach my side   65
   Down all the echoing stair?)

"I wish that he were come to me,
   For he will come," she said.
"Have I not prayed in Heaven? on earth
   Lord, Lord, has he not prayed?   70
Are not two prayers a perfect strength?
   And shall I feel afraid?

"When round his head the aureole clings,
   And he is clothed in white,
I'll take his hand and go with him   75
   To the deep wells of light;
We will step down as to a stream,
   And bathe there in God's sight.

"We two will stand beside that shrine,
　　Occult, withheld, untrod,　　　　　　　80
Whose lamps are stirred continually
　　With prayer sent up to God;
And see our old prayers granted, melt
　　Each like a little cloud.

"We two will lie i' the shadow of　　　85
　　That living mystic tree
Within whose secret growth the Dove
　　Is sometimes felt to be,
While every leaf that His plumes touch
　　Saith His Name audibly.　　　　　　90

"And I myself will teach to him
　　I myself, lying so,
The songs I sing here; which his voice
　　Shall pause in, hushed and slow,
And find some knowledge at each pause,　95
　　Or some new thing to know."

(Alas! we two, we two, thou say'st!
　　Yea, one wast thou with me
That once of old. But shall God lift
　　To endless unity　　　　　　　　100
The soul whose likeness with thy soul
　　Was but its love for thee?)

"We two," she said, "will seek the groves
　　Where the lady Mary is,
With her five handmaidens, whose names　105
　　Are five sweet symphonies:—
Cecily, Gertrude, Magdalen,
　　Margaret and Rosalys.

"Circlewise sit they, with bound locks
　　And foreheads garlanded;　　　　110
Into the fine cloth white like flame,
　　Weaving the golden thread,
To fashion the birth-robes for them
　　Who are just born, being dead.

"He shall fear, haply, and be dumb: 115
  Then will I lay my cheek
To his, and tell about our love,
  Not once abashed or weak:
And the dear Mother will approve
  My pride, and let me speak. 120

"Herself shall bring us, hand in hand,
  To Him round whom all souls
Kneel, the clear-ranged unnumbered heads
  Bowed with their aureoles:
And angels, meeting us, shall sing 125
  To their citherns and citoles.

"There will I ask of Christ the Lord
  Thus much for him and me:—
Only to live as once on earth
  With Love,—only to be, 130
As then awhile, for ever now
  Together, I and he."

She gazed, and listened, and then said,
  Less sad of speech than mild,—
"All this is when he comes." She ceased. 135
  The light thrilled towards her, filled
With angels, in strong level lapse.
  Her eyes prayed, and she smiled.

(I saw her smile.) But soon their path
  Was vague in distant spheres. 140
And then she cast her arms along
  The golden barriers,
And laid her face between her hands,
  And wept. (I heard her tears.)

GEORGE MEREDITH (1828–1909)

THREE 'SONNETS' FROM MODERN LOVE

XLIII

Mark where the pressing wind shoots javelin-like,
Its skeleton shadow on the broad-backed wave!
Here is a fitting spot to dig Love's grave;
Here where the ponderous breakers plunge and strike,
And dart their hissing tongues high up the sand: 5
In hearing of the ocean, and in sight
Of those ribbed wind-streaks running into white.
If I the death of Love had deeply planned,
I never could have made it half so sure,
As by the unblest kisses which upbraid   10
The full-waked senses; or failing that, degrade!
'Tis morning: but no morning can restore
What we have forfeited. I see no sin:
The wrong is mixed. In tragic life, God wot,
No villain need be! Passions spin the plot: 15
We are betrayed by what is false within.

XLVII

We saw the swallows gathering in the sky
And in the osier-isle we heard them noise.
We had not to look back on summer joys,
Or forward to a summer of bright dye:
But in the largeness of the evening earth   5
Our spirits grew as we went side by side.
The hour became her husband and my bride.
Love that had robbed us so, thus blessed our dearth!
The pilgrims of the year waxed very loud
In multitudinous chatterings, as the flood   10
Full brown came from the West, and like pale blood
Expanded to the upper crimson cloud.
Love that had robbed us of immortal things,
This little moment mercifully gave,
Where I have seen across the twilight wave   15
The swan sail with her young beneath her wings.

L

Thus piteously Love closed what he begat;
The union of this ever-diverse pair!
These two were rapid falcons in a snare,
Condemned to do the flitting of the bat.
Lovers beneath the singing sky of May,   5
They wandered once; clear as the dew on flowers.
But they fed not on the advancing hours:
Their hearts held cravings for the buried day.
Then each applied to each that fatal knife,
Deep questioning, which probes to endless dole.   10
Ah! what a dusty answer gets the soul
When hot for certainties in this our life!—
In tragic hints here see what evermore
Moves dark as yonder midnight ocean's force,
Thundering like ramping hosts of warrior horse,   15
To throw that faint thin line upon the shore.

LUCIFER IN STARLIGHT

On a starred night Prince Lucifer uprose.
Tired of his dark dominion swung the fiend
Above the rolling ball in cloud part screened,
Where sinners hugged their spectre of repose.
Poor prey to his hot fit of pride were those.
And now upon his western wing he leaned,
Now his huge bulk o'er Afric's sands careened,
Now the black planet shadowed Arctic snows.
Soaring through wider zones that pricked his scars
With memory of the old revolt from Awe,
He reached a middle height, and at the stars,
Which are the brain of heaven, he looked, and sank.
Around the ancient track marched rank on rank,
The army of unalterable law.

DIRGE IN THE WOODS

A wind sways the pines,
            And below
Not a breath of wild air;
Still as the mosses that glow

On the flooring and over the lines
Of the roots here and there.
The pine-tree drops its dead;
They are quiet, as under the sea.
Overhead, overhead
Rushes life in a race,
As the clouds the clouds chase;
  And we go,
And we drop like the fruits of the tree,
   Even we,
   Even so.

EMILY DICKINSON (1830–1886)

I TASTE A LIQUOR NEVER BREWED

I taste a liquor never brewed,
From tankards scooped in pearl;
Not all the vats upon the Rhine
Yield such an alcohol!

Inebriate of air am I,   5
And debauchee of dew,
Reeling, through endless summer days,
From inns of molten blue.

When landlords turn the drunken bee
Out of the foxglove's door,   10
When butterflies renounce their drams,
I shall but drink the more!

Till seraphs swing their snowy hats,
And saints to windows run,
To see the little tippler   15
Leaning against the sun!

A BIRD CAME DOWN THE WALK

A bird came down the walk:
He did not know I saw;
He bit an angle-worm in halves
And ate the fellow, raw.

And then he drank a dew   5
From a convenient grass,
And then hopped sidewise to the wall
To let a beetle pass.

He glanced with rapid eyes
That hurried all abroad,—   10
They looked like frightened beads, I thought
He stirred his velvet head

Like one in danger; cautious,
I offered him a crumb,
And he unrolled his feathers   15
And rowed him softer home

Than oars divide the ocean,
Too silver for a seam,
Or butterflies, off banks of noon,
Leap, plashless, as they swim.   20

A NARROW FELLOW IN THE GRASS

A narrow fellow in the grass
Occasionally rides;
You may have met him,—did you not?
His notice sudden is.

The grass divides as with a comb,   5
A spotted shaft is seen;
And then it closes at your feet
And opens further on.

He likes a boggy acre,
A floor too cool for corn.   10
Yet when a child, and barefoot,
I more than once, at morn,

Have passed, I thought, a whip-lash
Unbraiding in the sun,—
When, stooping to secure it,   15
It wrinkled, and was gone.

Several of nature's people
I know, and they know me;
I feel for them a transport
Of cordiality;   20

But never met this fellow,
Attended or alone,
Without a tighter breathing,
And zero at the bone.

IN WINTER, IN MY ROOM

In winter, in my room
I came upon a worm,
Pink, lank, and warm.
But as he was a worm
And worms presume,   5
Not quite with him at home—
Secured him by a string
To something neighboring,
And went along.

A trifle afterward   10
A thing occurred,
I'd not believe it if I heard—
But state with creeping blood;
A snake, with mottles rare,
Surveyed my chamber floor,   15
In feature as the worm before,
But ringed with power.
The very string
With which I tied him, too,
When he was mean and new,   20
That string was there.

I shrank—"How fair you are!"
Propitiation's claw—
"Afraid," he hissed,
"Of me?   25
No cordiality?"
He fathomed me.

Then, to a rhythm slim
Secreted in his form,
As patterns swim,   30
Projected him.

That time I flew,
Both eyes his way,
Lest he pursue—
Nor ever ceased to run,   35
Till, in a distant town,
Towns on from mine—
I sat me down;
This was a dream.

BECAUSE I COULD NOT STOP FOR DEATH

Because I could not stop for Death,
He kindly stopped for me;
The carriage held but just ourselves
And Immortality.

We slowly drove, he knew no haste,   5
And I had put away
My labor, and my leisure too,
For his civility.

We passed the school where children played
At wrestling in a ring;
We passed the fields of gazing grain,   10
We passed the setting sun.

We paused before a house that seemed
A swelling of the ground;
The roof was scarcely visible,   15
The cornice but a mound.

Since then 'tis centuries; but each
Feels shorter than the day
I first surmised the horses' heads
Were toward eternity.   20

I HEARD A FLY BUZZ WHEN I DIED

I heard a fly buzz when I died;
The stillness in the room
Was like the stillness in the air
Between the heaves of storm.

The eyes around had wrung them dry,   5
And breaths were gathering firm
For that last onset when the king
Be witnessed in the room.

I willed my keepsakes, signed away
What portion of me be   10
Assignable—and then it was
There interposed a fly,

With blue, uncertain, stumbling buzz
Between the light and me;
And then the windows failed, and then   15
I could not see to see.

'TWAS LIKE A MAELSTROM

'Twas like a maelstrom, with a notch
That nearer every day
Kept narrowing its boiling wheel
Until the agony

Toyed cooly with the final inch   5
Of your delirious hem,
And you dropped, lost, when something broke
And let you from a dream;

As if a goblin with a gauge
Kept measuring the hours,   10
Until you felt your second weigh
Helpless in his paws,

And not a sinew, stirred, could help,
And sense was setting numb,
When God remembered, and the fiend   15
Let go then, overcome;

As if your sentence stood pronounced,
And you were frozen led
From dungeon's luxury of doubt
To gibbets and the dead;   20

And when the film had stitched your eyes,
A creature gasped "Reprieve!"
Which anguish was the utterest then,
To perish, or to live?

CHRISTINA ROSSETTI (1830–1894)

EVE

'While I sit at the door,
Sick to gaze within,
Mine eye weepeth sore
For sorrow and sin:
As a tree my sin stands   5
To darken all lands;
Death is the fruit it bore.

'How have Eden bowers grown
Without Adam to bend them!
How have Eden flowers blown,   10
Squandering their sweet breath,
Without me to tend them!
The Tree of Life was ours,
Tree twelvefold-fruited,
Most lofty tree that flowers,   15
Most deeply rooted:
I chose the Tree of Death.

'Hadst thou but said me nay,
Adam, my brother,

I might have pined away;   20
I, but none other:
God might have let thee stay
Safe in our garden
By putting me away
Beyond all pardon.   25

'I, Eve, sad mother
Of all who must live,
I, not another,
Plucked bitterest fruit to give
My friend, husband, lover.   30
O wanton eyes run over;
Who but I should grieve?—
Cain hath slain his brother:
Of all who must die mother,
Miserable Eve!'   35

Thus she sat weeping,
Thus Eve our mother,
Where one lay sleeping
Slain by his brother.
Greatest and least   40
Each piteous beast
To hear her voice
Forgot his joys
And set aside his feast.
The mouse paused in his walk   45
And dropped his wheaten stalk;
Grave cattle wagged their heads
In rumination;
The eagle gave a cry
From his cloud station: 50
Larks on thyme beds
Forbore to mount or sing;
Bees drooped upon the wing;
The raven perched on high
Forgot his ration;   55
The conies in their rock,
A feeble nation,
Quaked sympathetical;
The mocking-bird left off to mock;

Huge camels knelt as if   60
In deprecation;
The kind hart's tears were falling;
Chattered the wistful stork;
Dove-voices with a dying fall
Cooed desolation   65
Answering grief by grief.
Only the serpent in the dust,
Wriggling and crawling,
Grinned an evil grin, and thrust
His tongue out with its fork.   70

ECHO

Come to me in the silence of the night;
    Come in the speaking silence of a dream;
Come with soft rounded cheeks and eyes as bright
    As sunlight on a stream;
        Come back in tears,   5
O memory, hope, love of finished years.

O dream how sweet, too sweet, too bitter sweet,
    Whose wakening should have been in Paradise,
Where souls brimful of love abide and meet;
    Where thirsty longing eyes   10
        Watch the slow door
That opening, letting in, lets out no more.

Yet come to me in dreams, that I may live
    My very life again though cold in death:
Come back to me in dreams, that I may give   15
    Pulse for pulse, breath for breath:
        Speak low, lean low,
As long ago, my love, how long ago!

LEWIS CARROLL
(CHARLES LUTWIDGE DODGSON)
(1832–1898)

JABBERWOCKY

'Twas brillig, and the slithy toves
    Did gyre and gimble in the wabe;
All mimsy were the borogoves,
    And the mome raths outgrabe.

"Beware the Jabberwock, my son!   5
    The jaws that bite, the claws that catch!
Beware the jubjub bird, and shun
    The frumious Bandersnatch!"

He took his vorpal sword in hand:
    Long time the manxome foe he sought,—   10
So rested he by the Tumtum tree,
    And stood awhile in thought.

And as in uffish thought he stood,
    The Jabberwock, with eyes of flame,
Came whiffling through the tulgey wood,   15
    And burbled as it came!

One, two! One, two! And through and through
    The vorpal blade went snicker-snack!
He left it dead, and with its head
    He went galumphing back.   20

"And hast thou slain the Jabberwock?
    Come to my arms, my beamish boy!
O frabjous day! Callooh! Callay!"
    He chortled in his joy.

'Twas brillig, and the slithy toves   25
    Did gyre and gimble in the wabe;
All mimsy were the borogoves,
    And the mome raths outgrabe.

WILLIAM MORRIS (1834–1896)

THE HAYSTACK IN THE FLOODS

Had she come all the way for this,
To part at last without a kiss?
Yea, had she borne the dirt and rain
That her own eyes might see him slain
Beside the haystack in the floods?   5
Along the dripping leafless woods,
The stirrup touching either shoe,
She rode astride as troopers do;
With kirtle kilted to her knee,
To which the mud splashed wretchedly;   10
And the wet dripped from every tree
Upon her head and heavy hair,
And on her eyelids broad and fair;
The tears and rain ran down her face.

By fits and starts they rode apace,   15
And very often was his place
Far off from her; he had to ride
Ahead, to see what might betide
When the roads crossed; and sometimes, when
There rose a murmuring from his men,   20
Had to turn back with promises;
Ah me! she had but little ease;
And often for pure doubt and dread
She sobbed, made giddy in the head
By the swift riding; while, for cold,   25
Her slender fingers scarce could hold
The wet reins; yea, and scarcely, too,
She felt the foot within her shoe
Against the stirrup: all for this,
To part at last without a kiss   30
Beside the haystack in the floods.

For when they neared that rain-soaked hay,
They saw across the only way
That Judas, Godmar, and the three

Red running lions dismally　　　　　　　　　35
Grinned from his pennon, under which
In one straight line along the ditch,
They counted thirty heads.

　　　　　　　　　　So then,
While Robert turned round to his men,　　　40
She saw at once the wretched end,
And, stooping down, tried hard to rend
Her coif the wrong way from her head,
And hid her eyes; while Robert said:
"Nay, love, 'tis scarcely two to one,　　　45
At Poictiers where we made them run
So fast—why, sweet my love, good cheer,
The Gascon frontier is so near,
Nought after this."
　　　　　　　But, "O," she said,　　　50
"My God! my God! I have to tread
The long way back without you; then
The court at Paris; those six men;
The gratings of the Chatelet;
The swift Seine on some rainy day　　　55
Like this, and people standing by,
And laughing, while my weak hands try
To recollect how strong men swim.
All this, or else a life with him,
For which I should be damned at last.　　　60
Would God that this next hour were past!"

He answered not, but cried his cry,
"St. George for Marny!" cheerily;
And laid his hand upon her rein.
Alas! no man of all his train　　　65
Gave back that cheery cry again;
And, while for rage his thumb beat fast
Upon his sword-hilt, some one cast
About his neck a kerchief long,
And bound him.　　　　　　　　　70
　　　　　　Then they went along
To Godmar; who said: "Now, Jehane,
Your lover's life is on the wane
So fast, that, if this very hour

You yield not as my paramour, 75
He will not see the rain leave off—
Nay, keep your tongue from gibe and scoff,
Sir Robert, or I slay you now."

She laid her hand upon her brow,
Then gazed upon the palm, as though 80
She thought her forehead bled, and—"No,"
She said, and turned her head away,
As there were nothing else to say,
And everything were settled; red
Grew Godmar's face from chin to head: 85
"Jehane, on yonder hill there stands
My castle, guarding well my lands;
What hinders me from taking you,
And doing that I list to do
To your fair wilful body, while 90
Your knight lies dead?"

                    A wicked smile
Wrinkled her face, her lips grew thin,
A long way out she thrust her chin:
"You know that I should strangle you 95
While you were sleeping; or bite through
Your throat, by God's help: ah!" she said,
"Lord Jesus, pity your poor maid!
For in such wise they hem me in,
I cannot choose but sin and sin, 100
Whatever happens: yet I think
They could not make me eat or drink,
And so should I just reach my rest."

"Nay, if you do not my behest,
O Jehane! though I love you well," 105
Said Godmar, "would I fail to tell
All that I know?" "Foul lies," she said.
"Eh? lies, my Jehane? by God's head,
At Paris folks would deem them true!
Do you know, Jehane, they cry for you, 110
'Jehane the brown! Jehane the brown!
Give us Jehane to burn or drown!'
Eh—gag me Robert!—sweet my friend,

This were indeed a piteous end
For those long fingers, and long feet,   115
And long neck, and smooth shoulders sweet;
An end that few men would forget
That saw it. So, an hour yet:
Consider, Jehane, which to take
Or life or death!"   120

                         So, scarce awake,
Dismounting, did she leave that place,
And totter some yards: with her face
Turned upward to the sky she lay,
Her head on a wet heap of hay,   125
And fell asleep: and while she slept,
And did not dream, the minutes crept
Round to the twelve again; but she,
Being waked at last, sighed quietly,
And strangely childlike came, and said: 130
"I will not." Straightway Godmar's head,
As though it hung on strong wires, turned
Most sharply round, and his face burned.

For Robert—both his eyes were dry,
He could not weep, but gloomily   135
He seemed to watch the rain; yea, too,
His lips were firm; he tried once more
To touch her lips; she reached out, sore
And vain desire so tortured them,
The poor grey lips, and now the hem   140
Of his sleeve brushed them.

                                With a start
Up Godmar rose, thrust them apart;
From Robert's throat he loosed the bands
Of silk and mail; with empty hands   145
Held out, she stood and gazed, and saw,
The long bright blade without a flaw
Glide out from Godmar's sheath, his hand
In Robert's hair; she saw him bend
Back Robert's head; she saw him send   150
The thin steel down; the blow told well,
Right backward the knight Robert fell,

And moaned as dogs do, being half dead,
Unwitting, as I deem: so then
Godmar turned grinning to his men,   155
Who ran, some five or six, and beat
His head to pieces at their feet.

Then Godmar turned again and said:
"So, Jehane, the first fitte is read!
Take note, my lady, that your way   160
Lies backward to the Chatelet!"
She shook her head and gazed awhile
At her cold hands with a rueful smile,
As though this thing had made her mad.

This was the parting that they had   165
Beside the haystack in the floods.

ALGERNON CHARLES SWINBURNE
(1837–1909)

CHORUS FROM *ATALANTA IN CALYDON*

When the hounds of spring are on winter's traces,
    The mother of months in meadow or plain
Fills the shadows and windy places
    With lisp of leaves and ripple of rain;
And the brown bright nightingale amorous   5
Is half assuaged for Itylus,
For the Thracian ships and the foreign faces,
    The tongueless vigil, and all the pain.

Come with bows bent and with emptying of quivers,
    Maiden most perfect, lady of light,   10
With a noise of winds and many rivers,
    With a clamour of waters, and with might;
Bind on thy sandals, O thou most fleet,
Over the splendour and speed of thy feet;
For the faint east quickens, the wan west shivers,   15
    Round the feet of the day and the feet of the night.

Where shall we find her, how shall we sing to her,
    Fold our hands round her knees, and cling?

O that man's heart were as fire and could spring to her,
   Fire, or the strength of the streams that spring!   20
For the stars and the winds are unto her
As raiment, as songs of the harp-player;
For the risen stars and the fallen cling to her,
   And the southwest-wind and the west-wind sing.

For winter's rains and ruins are over,   25
   And all the season of snows and sins;
The days dividing lover and lover,
   The light that loses, the night that wins;
And time remember'd is grief forgotten,
And frosts are slain and flowers begotten,   30
And in green underwood and cover
   Blossom by blossom the spring begins.

The full streams feed on flower of rushes,
   Ripe grasses trammel a travelling foot,
The faint fresh flame of the young year flushes   35
   From leaf to flower and flower to fruit;
And fruit and leaf are as gold and fire,
And the oat is heard above the lyre,
And the hoofed heel of a satyr crushes
   The chestnut-husk at the chestnut-root.   40

And Pan by noon and Bacchus by night,
   Fleeter of foot than the fleet-foot kid,
Follows with dancing and fills with delight
   The Mænad and the Bassarid;
And soft as lips that laugh and hide   45
The laughing leaves of the trees divide,
And screen from seeing and leave in sight
   The god pursuing, the maiden hid.

The ivy falls with the Bacchanal's hair
   Over her eyebrows hiding her eyes;   50
The wild vine slipping down leaves bare
   Her bright breast shortening into sighs;
The wild vine slips with the weight of its leaves,
But the berried ivy catches and cleaves
To the limbs that glitter, the feet that scare   55
   The wolf that follows, the fawn that flies.

HYMN TO PROSERPINE

After the Proclamation in Rome of the Christian Faith
Vicisti, Galilæe

I have lived long enough, having seen one thing, that love hath
    an end;
Goddess and maiden and queen, be near me now and befriend.
Thou art more than the day or the morrow, the seasons that laugh
    or that weep;
For these give joy and sorrow; but thou, Proserpina, sleep.
Sweet is the treading of wine, and sweet the feet of the dove;   5
But a goodlier gift is thine than foam of the grapes or love.
Yea, is not even Apollo, with hair and harpstring of gold,
A bitter God to follow, a beautiful God to behold?
I am sick of singing: the bays burn deep and chafe: I am fain
To rest a little from praise and grievous pleasure and pain.   10
For the Gods we know not of, who give us our daily breath,
We know they are cruel as love or life, and lovely as death.
O Gods dethroned and deceased, cast forth, wiped out in a day!
From your wrath is the world released, redeemed from your chains,
    men say.
New Gods are crowned in the city; their flowers have broken your
    rods;   15
They are merciful, clothed with pity, the young compassionate
    Gods.
But for me their new device is barren, the days are bare;
Things long past over suffice, and men forgotten that were.
Time and the Gods are at strife; ye dwell in the midst thereof,
Draining a little life from the barren breasts of love.   20
I say to you, cease, take rest; yea, I say to you all, be at peace,
Till the bitter milk of her breast and the barren bosom shall cease.
Wilt thou yet take all, Galilean? but these thou shalt not take,
The laurel, the palms and the pæan, the breast of the nymphs in
    the brake;
Breasts more soft than a dove's, that tremble with tenderer
    breath;   25
And all the wings of the Loves, and all the joy before death;
All the feet of the hours that sound as a single lyre,
Dropped and deep in the flowers, with strings that flicker like fire,
More than these wilt thou give, things fairer than all these things?
Nay, for a little we live, and life hath mutable wings.   30
A little while and we die; shall life not thrive as it may?

For no man under the sky lives twice, outliving his day.
And grief is a grievous thing, and a man hath enough of his tears:
Why should he labor, and bring fresh grief to blacken his years?
Thou hast conquered, O pale Galilean; the world has grown gray
    from thy breath;   35
We have drunken of things Lethean, and fed on the fulness of
    death.
Laurel is green for a season, and love is sweet for a day;
But love grows bitter with treason, and laurel outlives not May.
Sleep, shall we sleep after all? for the world is not sweet in the
    end;
For the old faiths loosen and fall, the new years ruin and rend.   40
Fate is a sea without shore, and the soul is a rock that abides;
But her ears are vexed with the roar and her face with the foam
    of the tides.
O lips that the live blood faints in, the leavings of rack and rods!
O ghastly glories of saints, dead limbs of gibbeted Gods!
Though all men abase them before you in spirit, and all knees
    bend,   45
I kneel not neither adore you, but standing, look to the end.
All delicate days and pleasant, all spirits and sorrows are cast
Far out with the foam of the present that sweeps to the surf of
    the past:
Where beyond the extreme sea-wall, and between the remote
    sea-gates,
Waste water washes, and tall ships founder, and deep death
    waits: 50
Where, mighty with deepening sides, clad about with the seas as
    with wings,
And impelled of invisible tides, fulfilled of unspeakable things,
White-eyed and poisonous-finned, shark-toothed and serpentine-
    curled,
Rolls, under the whitening wind of the future, the wave of the
    world.
The depths stand naked in sunder behind it, the storms flee
    away;   55
In the hollow before it the thunder is taken and snared as a prey;
In its sides is the north-wind bound; and its salt is of all men's tears;
With light of ruin, and sound of changes, and pulse of years:
With travail of day after day, and with trouble of hour upon hour;
And bitter as blood is the spray; and the crests are as fangs that
    devour: 60

And its vapor and storm of its steam as the sighing of spirits to be;
And its noise as the noise in a dream; and its depth as the roots of
the sea:
And the height of its head as the height of the utmost stars of
the air:
And the ends of the earth at the might thereof tremble, and time
is made bare.
Will ye bridle the deep sea with reins, will ye chasten the high
sea with rods? 65
Will ye take her to chain her with chains, who is older than all
ye Gods?
All ye as a wind shall go by, as a fire shall ye pass and be past;
Ye are Gods, and behold, ye shall die, and the waves be upon
you at last.
In the darkness of time, in the deeps of the years, in the changes
of things,
Ye shall sleep as a slain man sleeps, and the world shall forget you
for kings. 70
Though the feet of thine high priests tread where thy lords and
our forefathers trod,
Though these that were Gods are dead, and thou being dead art
a God,
Though before thee the throned Cytherean be fallen, and hidden
her head,
Yet thy kingdom shall pass, Galilean, thy dead shall go down to
thee dead.
Of the maiden thy mother men sing as a goddess with grace clad
around; 75
Thou art throned where another was king; where another was
queen she is crowned.
Yea, once we had sight of another: but now she is queen, say these.
Not as thine, not as thine was our mother, a blossom of flowering
seas,
Clothed round with the world's desire as with raiment, and fair
as the foam,
And fleeter than kindled fire, and a goddess and mother of
Rome. 80
For thine came pale and a maiden, and sister to sorrow; but ours,
Her deep hair heavily laden with odor, and color of flowers,
White rose of the rose-white water, a silver splendor, a flame,
Bent down into us that besought her, and earth grew sweet with
her name.

For thine came weeping, a slave among slaves, and rejected; but she   85
Came flushed from the full-flushed wave, and imperial, her foot on the sea.
And the wonderful waters knew her, the winds and the viewless ways,
And the roses grew rosier, and bluer the sea-blue stream of the bays.
Ye are fallen, our lords, by what token? we wist that ye should not fall.
Ye were all so fair that are broken; and one more fair than ye all. 90
But I turn to her still, having seen she shall surely abide in the end;
Goddess and maiden and queen, be near me now and befriend.
O daughter of earth, of my mother, her crown and blossom of birth,
I am also, I also thy brother; I go as I came unto earth.
In the night where thine eyes are as moons are in heaven, the night where thou art,   95
Where the silence is more than all tunes, where sleep overflows from the heart,
Where the poppies are sweet as the rose in our world, and the red rose is white,
And the wind falls faint as it blows with the fume of the flowers of the night,
And the murmur of spirits that sleep in the shadow of Gods from afar
Grows dim in thine ears and deep as the deep dim soul of a star,   100
In the sweet low light of thy face, under heavens untrod by the sun,
Let my soul with their souls find place, and forget what is done and undone.
Thou art more than the God who number the days of our temporal breath;
For these give labor and slumber; but thou, Proserpina, death.
Therefore now at thy feet I abide for a season in silence. I know   105
I shall die as my fathers died, and sleep as they sleep; even so.
For the glass of the years is brittle wherein we gaze for a span;
A little soul for a little bears up this corpse which is man.
So long I endure, no longer; and laugh not again, neither weep.
For there is no God found stronger than death; and death is a sleep.   110

THE GARDEN OF PROSERPINE

Here, where the world is quiet;
  Here, where all trouble seems
Dead winds' and spent waves' riot
  In doubtful dreams of dreams;
I watch the green field growing   5
For reaping folk and sowing,
For harvest-time and mowing,
  A sleepy world of streams.

I am tired of tears and laughter,
  And men that laugh and weep;   10
Of what may come hereafter
  For men that sow to reap:
I am weary of days and hours,
Blown buds of barren flowers,
Desires and dreams and powers   15
  And everything but sleep.

Here life has death for neighbour,
  And far from eye or ear
Wan waves and wet winds labour,
  Weak ships and spirits steer;   20
They drive adrift, and whither
They wot not who make thither;
But no such winds blow hither,
  And no such things grow here.

No growth of moor or coppice,   25
  No heather-flower or vine,
But bloomless buds of poppies,
  Green grapes of Proserpine,
Pale beds of blowing rushes,
Where no leaf blooms or blushes   30
Save this whereout she crushes
  For dead men deadly wine.

Pale, without name or number,
  In fruitless fields of corn,

They bow themselves and slumber   35
   All night till light is born;
And like a soul belated,
In hell and heaven unmated,
By cloud and mist abated
   Comes out of darkness morn.   40

Though one were strong as seven,
   He too with death shall dwell,
Nor wake with wings in heaven,
   Nor weep for pains in hell;
Though one were fair as roses,   45
His beauty clouds and closes;
And well though love reposes,
   In the end it is not well.

Pale, beyond porch and portal,
   Crowned with calm leaves, she stands   50
Who gathers all things mortal
   With cold immortal hands;
Her languid lips are sweeter
Than love's who fears to greet her,
To men that mix and meet her   55
   From many times and lands.

She waits for each and other,
   She waits for all men born;
Forgets the earth her mother,
   The life of fruits and corn;   60
And spring and seed and swallow
Take wing for her and follow
Where summer song rings hollow
   And flowers are put to scorn.

There go the loves that wither,   65
   The old loves with wearier wings;
And all dead years draw thither,
   And all disastrous things;
Dead dreams of days forsaken,
Blind buds that snows have shaken,   70
Wild leaves that winds have taken,
   Red strays of ruined springs.

We are not sure of sorrow,
  And joy was never sure;
Today will die tomorrow;   75
  Time stoops to no man's lure;
And love, grown faint and fretful,
With lips but half regretful
Sighs, and with eyes forgetful
  Weeps that no loves endure.   80

From too much love of living,
  From hope and fear set free,
We thank with brief thanksgiving
  Whatever gods may be
That no life lives for ever;   85
That dead men rise up never;
That even the weariest river
  Winds somewhere safe to sea.

Then star nor sun shall waken,
  Nor any change of light: 90
Nor sound of waters shaken,
  Nor any sound or sight:
Nor wintry leaves nor vernal,
Nor days nor things diurnal;
Only the sleep eternal   95
  In an eternal night.

PART SEVEN
The Modern Period

THOMAS HARDY (1840–1928)

THE DARKLING THRUSH

December 1900

I leant upon a coppice gate
  When Frost was spectre-gray,
And Winter's dregs made desolate
  The weakening eye of day.
The tangled bine-stems scored the sky   5
  Like strings of broken lyres,
And all mankind that haunted nigh
  Had sought their household fires.

The land's sharp features seemed to be
  The Century's corpse outleant,   10
His crypt the cloudy canopy,
  The wind his death lament.
The ancient pulse of germ and birth
  Was shrunken hard and dry,
And every spirit upon earth   15
  Seemed fervourless as I.

At once a voice arose among
  The bleak twigs overhead
In a full-hearted evensong
  Of joy illimited;   20
An aged thrush, frail, gaunt, and small,
  In blast-beruffled plume,
Had chosen thus to fling his soul
  Upon the growing gloom.

So little cause for carollings   25
  Of such ecstatic sound
Was written on terrestrial things
  Afar or nigh around,

That I could think there trembled through
 His happy good-night air   30
Some blessed Hope, whereof he knew
 And I was unaware.

DRUMMER HODGE

They throw in Drummer Hodge, to rest
 Uncoffined—just as found:
His landmark is a kopje-crest
 That breaks the veldt around:
And foreign constellations west   5
 Each night above his mound.

Young Hodge the Drummer never knew—
 Fresh from his Wessex home—
The meaning of the broad Karoo,
 The Bush, the dusty loam,   10
And why uprose to nightly view
 Strange stars amid the gloam.

Yet portion of that unknown plain
 Will Hodge forever be;
His homely Northern breast and brain 15
 Grow to some Southern tree,
And strange-eyed constellations reign
 His stars eternally.

THE CONVERGENCE OF THE TWAIN

(Lines on the loss of the "Titanic")

I

In a solitude of the sea
Deep from human vanity,
And the Pride of Life that planned her, stilly couches she.

II

Steel chambers, late the pyres
Of her salamandrine fires,
Cold currents thrid, and turn to rhythmic tidal lyres.

III

Over the mirrors meant
To glass the opulent
The sea-worm crawls—grotesque, slimed, dumb, indifferent.

IV

Jewels in joy designed
To ravish the sensuous mind
Lie lightless, all their sparkles bleared and black and blind.

V

Dim moon-eyed fishes near
Gaze at the gilded gear
And query: "What does this vaingloriousness down here?"

VI

Well: while was fashioning
This creature of cleaving wing,
The Immanent Will that stirs and urges everything

VII

Prepared a sinister mate
For her—so gaily great—
A Shape of Ice, for the time far and dissociate.

VIII

And as the smart ship grew
In stature, grace, and hue,
In shadowy silent distance grew the Iceberg too.

IX

Alien they seemed to be;
No mortal eye could see
The intimate welding of their later history,

X

Or sign that they were bent
By paths coincident
On being anon twin halves of one august event,

XI

Till the Spinner of the Years
Said "Now!" And each one hears,
And consummation comes, and jars two hemispheres.

CHANNEL FIRING

That night your great guns unawares,
Shook all our coffins as we lay,
And broke the chancel window squares,
We thought it was the Judgment-day

And sat upright. While drearisome   5
Arose the howl of wakened hounds:
The mouse let fall the altar-crumb,
The worms drew back into the mounds,

The glebe cow drooled. Till God called, "No;
It's gunnery practice out at sea   10
Just as before you went below;
The world is as it used to be:

"All nations striving strong to make
Red war yet redder. Mad as hatters
They do no more for Christés sake   15
Than you who are helpless in such matters.

"That this is not the judgment-hour
For some of them's a blessed thing,
For if it were they'd have to scour
Hell's floor for so much threatening . . .   20

"Ha, ha. It will be warmer when
I blow the trumpet (if indeed
I ever do; for you are men,
And rest eternal sorely need)."

So down we lay again. "I wonder,   25
Will the world ever saner be,"
Said one, "than when He sent us under
In our indifferent century!"

And many a skeleton shook his head.
"Instead of preaching forty years," 30
My neighbor Parson Thirdly said,
"I wish I had stuck to pipes and beer."

Again the guns disturbed the hour,
Roaring their readiness to avenge,
As far inland as Stourton Tower, 35
And Camelot, and starlit Stonehenge.

April, 1914

IN TIME OF 'THE BREAKING OF NATIONS' (1915)

Only a man harrowing clods
  In a slow silent walk
With an old horse that stumbles and nods
  Half asleep as they stalk.

Only thin smoke without flame
  From the heaps of couch-grass;
Yet this will go onward the same
  Though Dynasties pass.

Yonder a maid and her wight
  Come whispering by:
War's annals will cloud into night
  Ere their story die.

THE RUINED MAID

"O, 'Melia, my dear, this does everything crown!
Who would have supposed I should meet you in Town?
And whence such fair garments, such prosperi-ty?"—
"O didn't you know I'd been ruined?" said she.

—"You left us in tatters, without shoes or socks, 5
Tired of digging potatoes, and spudding up docks;
And now you've gay bracelets and bright feathers three!"—
"Yes: that's how we dress when we're ruined," said she.

—"At home in the barton you said 'thee' and 'thou,'
And 'thik oon,' and 'theas oon,' and 't'other'; but now   10
Your talking quite fits 'ee for high compa-ny!"
"Some polish is gained with one's ruin," said she.

—"Your hands were like paws then, your face blue and bleak,
But now I'm bewitched by your delicate cheek,
And your little gloves fit as on any la-dy!"—   15
"We never do work when we're ruined," said she.

—"You used to call home-life a hag-ridden dream,
And you'd sigh, and you'd sock; but at present you seem
To know not of megrims or melancho-ly!"—
"True. One's pretty lively when ruined," said she.   20

—"I wish I had feathers, a fine sweeping gown,
And a delicate face, and could strut about Town!"—
"My dear—a raw country girl, such as you be,
Cannot quite expect that. You ain't ruined," said she.

DURING WIND AND RAIN

They sing their dearest songs—
He, she, all of them—yea,
Treble and tenor and bass,
   And one to play;
With the candles mooning each face. . . .   5
   Ah, no; the years O!
How the sick leaves reel down in throngs!

They clear the creeping moss—
Elders and juniors—aye,
Making the pathways neat   10
   And the garden gay;
And they build a shady seat. . . .
   Ah, no; the years, the years;
See, the white storm-birds wing across!

They are blithely breakfasting all—   15
Men and maidens—yea,

Under the summer tree,
  With a glimpse of the bay,
While pet fowl come to the knee. . . .
    Ah, no; the years O!   20
And the rotten rose is ript from the wall.

They change to a high new house,
He, she, all of them—aye,
Clocks and carpets and chairs
  On the lawn all day,   25
And brightest things that are theirs. . . .
    Ah, no; the years, the years;
Down their carved names the rain-drop ploughs.

REGRET NOT ME

  Regret not me;
Beneath the sunny tree
I lie uncaring, slumbering peacefully.

  Swift as the light
I flew my faery flight;   5
Ecstatically I moved, and feared no night.

  I did not know
That heydays fade and go,
But deemed that what was would be always so.

  I skipped at morn   10
Between the yellowing corn,
Thinking it good and glorious to be born.

  I ran at eves
Among the piled-up sheaves,
Dreaming, "I grieve not, therefore nothing grieves."   15

  Now soon will come
The apple, pear, and plum,
And hinds will sing, and autumn insects hum.

Again you will fare
To cider-makings rare,   20
And junketings; but I shall not be there.

Yet gaily sing
Until the pewter ring
Those songs we sang when we went gipsying.

And lightly dance   25
A triple-timed romance
In coupled figures, and forget mischance;

And mourn not me
Beneath the yellowing tree;
For I shall mind not, slumbering peacefully.   30

AFTERWARDS

When the Present has latched its postern behind my tremulous
    stay,
  And the May month flaps its glad green leaves like wings,
Delicate-filmed as new-spun silk, will the neighbours say,
  "He was a man who used to notice such things"?

If it be in the dusk when, like an eyelid's soundless blink,   5
  The dewfall-hawk comes crossing the shades to alight
Upon the wind-warped upland thorn, a gazer may think,
  "To him this must have been a familiar sight."

If I pass during some nocturnal blackness, mothy and warm,
  When the hedgehog travels furtively over the lawn,   10
One may say, "He strove that such innocent creatures should come
    to no harm,
  But he could do little for them; and now he is gone."

If, when hearing that I have been stilled at last, they stand at the
    door,
  Watching the full-starred heavens that winter sees,
Will this thought rise on those who will meet my face no more, 15
  "He was one who had an eye for such mysteries"?

And will any say when my bell of quittance is heard in the gloom,
   And a crossing breeze cuts a pause in its outrollings,
Till they rise again, as they were a new bell's boom,
   "He hears it not now, but used to notice such things"?   20

GERARD MANLEY HOPKINS (1844–1889)

GOD'S GRANDEUR

The world is charged with the grandeur of God.
   It will flame out, like shining from shook foil;
   It gathers to a greatness, like the ooze of oil
Crushed. Why do men then now not reck his rod?
Generations have trod, have trod, have trod;
   And all is seared with trade; bleared, smeared with toil;
   And wears man's smudge and shares man's smell: the soil
Is bare now, nor can foot feel, being shod.

And for all this, nature is never spent;
   There lives the dearest freshness deep down things;
And though the last lights off the black West went
   Oh, morning, at the brown brink eastward, springs—
Because the Holy Ghost over the bent
   World broods with warm breast and with ah! bright wings.

SPRING AND FALL: TO A YOUNG CHILD

    Márgarét, are you gríeving
    Over Goldengrove unleaving?
    Leáves, líke the things of man, you
    With your fresh thoughts care for, can you?
    Ah! ás the heart grows older   5
    It will come to such sights colder
    By and by, nor spare a sigh
    Though worlds of wanwood leafmeal lie;
    And yet you wíll weep and know why.
    Now no matter, child, the name: 10
    Sórrow's spríngs áre the same.

Nor mouth had, no nor mind, expressed
What heart heard of, ghost guessed:
It ís the blight man was born for,
It is Margaret you mourn for.   15

THE WRECK OF THE DEUTSCHLAND

*To the happy memory of five Franciscan Nuns, exiles by the Falk
Laws, drowned between midnight and morning of Dec. 7th, 1875*

PART THE FIRST

I

Thou mastering me
God! giver of breath and bread;
World's strand, sway of the sea;
Lord of living and dead;
Thou hast bound bones and veins in me, fastened me flesh,   5
And after it almost unmade, what with dread,
Thy doing: and dost thou touch me afresh?
Over again I feel thy finger and find thee.

II

I did say yes
O at lightning and lashed rod;   10
Thou heardst me truer than tongue confess
Thy terror, O Christ, O God;
Thou knowest the walls, altar and hour and night:
The swoon of a heart that the sweep and the hurl of thee trod
Hard down with a horror of height: 15
And the midriff astrain with leaning of, laced with fire of stress.

III

The frown of his face
Before me, the hurtle of hell
Behind, where, where was a, where was a place?
I whirled out wings that spell   20
And fled with a fling of the heart to the heart of the Host.
My heart, but you were dovewinged, I can tell,
Carrier-witted, I am bold to boast,
To flash from the flame to the flame then, tower from the grace
to the grace.

IV

I am soft sift   25
  In an hourglass—at the wall
Fast, but mined with a motion, a drift,
  And it crowds and it combs to the fall;
I steady as a water in a well, to a poise, to a pane,
But roped with, always, all the way down from the tall   30
  Fells or flanks of the voel, a vein
Of the gospel proffer, a pressure, a principle, Christ's gift.

V

I kiss my hand
  To the stars, lovely-asunder
Starlight, wafting him out of it; and   35
  Glow, glory in thunder;
Kiss my hand to the dappled-with-damson west:
Since, tho' he is under the world's splendour and wonder,
  His mystery must be instressed, stressed;
For I greet him the days I meet him, and bless when I under-
      stand.   40

VI

Not out of his bliss
  Springs the stress felt
Nor first from heaven (and few know this)
  Swings the stroke dealt—
Stroke and a stress that stars and storms deliver,   45
That guilt is hushed by, hearts are flushed by and melt—
  But it rides time like riding a river
(And here the faithful waver, the faithless fable and miss).

VII

It dates from day
  Of his going in Galilee;   50
Warm-laid grave of a womb-like grey;
  Manger, maiden's knee;
The dense and the driven Passion, and frightful sweat;
Thence the discharge of it, there its swelling to be,
  Though felt before, though in high flood yet—   55
What none would have known of it, only the heart, being hard
      at bay.

VIII

Is out with it! Oh,
· We lash with the best or worst
Word last! How a lush-kept plush-capped sloe
 Will, mouthed to flesh-burst,   60
Gush!—flush the man, the being with it, sour or sweet,
Brim, in a flash, full!—Hither then, last or first,
 To hero of Calvary, Christ's feet—
Never ask if meaning it, wanting it, warned of it—men go.

IX

Be adored among men,   65
 God, three-numberèd form;
Wring thy rebel, dogged in den,
 Man's malice, with wrecking and storm.
Beyond saying sweet, past telling of tongue,
Thou art lightning and love, I found it, a winter and warm;   70
 Father and fondler of heart thou hast wrung:
Hast thy dark descending and most art merciful then.

X

With an anvil-ding
 And with fire in him forge thy will
Or rather, rather then, stealing as Spring   75
 Through him, melt him but master him still:
Whether at once, as once at a crash Paul,
Or as Austin, a lingering-out sweet skill,
 Make mercy in all of us, out of us all
Mastery, but be adored, but be adored King.   80

PART THE SECOND

XI

"Some find me a sword; some
 The flange and the rail; flame,
Fang, or flood" goes Death on drum,
 And storms bugle his fame.
But wé dream we are rooted in earth—Dust!   85
Flesh falls within sight of us, we, though our flower the same,
 Wave with the meadow, forget that there must
The sour scythe cringe, and the blear share come.

XII

On Saturday sailed from Bremen,
  American-outward-bound,   90
Take settler and seamen, tell men with women,
  Two hundred souls in the round—
O Father, not under thy feathers nor ever as guessing
The goal was a shoal, of a fourth the doom to be drowned;
  Yet did the dark side of the bay of thy blessing   95
Not vault them, the millions of rounds of thy mercy not reeve
    even them in?

XIII

Into the snows she sweeps,
  Hurling the haven behind,
The Deutschland, on Sunday; and so the sky keeps,
  For the infinite air is unkind,   100
And the sea flint-flake, black-backed in the regular blow,
Sitting Eastnortheast, in cursed quarter, the wind;
  Wiry and white-fiery and whirlwind-swivellèd snow
Spins to the widow-making unchilding unfathering deeps.

XIV

She drove in the dark to leeward,   105
  She struck—not a reef or a rock
But the combs of a smother of sand: night drew her
  Dead to the Kentish Knock;
And she beat the bank down with her bows and the ride of
    her keel:
The breakers rolled on her beam with ruinous shock;   110
  And canvas and compass, the whorl and the wheel
Idle for ever to waft her or wind her with, these she endured.

XV

Hope had grown grey hairs,
  Hope had mourning on,
Trenched with tears, carved with cares,   115
  Hope was twelve hours gone;
And frightful a nightfall folded rueful a day
Nor rescue, only rocket and lightship, shone,
  And lives at last were washing away:
To the shrouds they took,—they shook in the hurling and horrible
    airs.   120

XVI

One stirred from the rigging to save
The wild woman-kind below,
With a rope's end round the man, handy and brave—
He was pitched to his death at a blow,
For all his dreadnought breast and braids of thew: 125
They could tell him for hours, dandled the to and fro
Through the cobbled foam-fleece, what could he do
With the burl of the fountains of air, buck and the flood of the
    wave?

XVII

They fought with God's cold—
And they could not and fell to the deck   130
(Crushed them) or water (and drowned them) or rolled
With the sea-romp over the wreck.
Night roared, with the heart-break hearing a heart-broke rabble,
The woman's wailing, the crying of child without check—
Till a lioness arose breasting the babble,   135
A prophetess towered in the tumult, a virginal tongue told.

XVIII

Ah, touched in your bower of bone
Are you! turned for an exquisite smart,
Have you! make words break from me here all alone,
Do you!—mother of being in me, heart.   140
O unteachably after evil, but uttering truth,
Why, tears! is it? tears; such a melting, a madrigal start!
Never-eldering revel and river of youth,
What can it be, this glee? the good you have there of your own?

XIX

Sister, a sister calling   145
A master, her master and mine!—
And the inboard seas run swirling and hawling;
The rash smart sloggering brine
Blinds her; but she that weather sees one thing, one;
Has one fetch in her: she rears herself to divine   150
Ears, and the call of the tall nun
To the men in the tops and the tackle rode over the storm's
    brawling.

XX

  She was first of a five and came
   Of a coifèd sisterhood.
  (O Deutschland, double a desperate name!   155
   O world wide of its good!
But Gertrude, lily, and Luther, are two of a town,
Christ's lily and beast of the waste wood:
   From life's dawn it is drawn down,
Abel is Cain's brother and breasts they have sucked the same.) 160

XXI

  Loathed for a love men knew in them,
   Banned by the land of their birth,
  Rhine refused them. Thames would ruin them;
   Surf, snow, river and earth
Gnashed: but thou art above, thou Orion of light;   165
Thy unchancelling poising palms were weighing the worth,
   Thou martyr-master: in thy sight
Storm flakes were scroll-leaved flowers, lily showers—sweet heaven
   was astrew in them.

XXII

  Five! the finding and sake
   And cipher of suffering Christ.   170
  Mark, the mark is of man's make
   And the word of it Sacrificed.
But he scores it in scarlet himself on his own bespoken,
Before-time-taken, dearest prizèd and priced—
   Stigma, signal, cinquefoil token   175
For lettering of the lamb's fleece, ruddying of the rose flake.

XXIII

  Joy fall to thee, father Francis,
   Drawn to the Life that died;
  With the gnarls of the nails in thee, niche of the lance, his
    Lovescape crucified
And seal of his seraph-arrival! and these thy daughters   180
And five-livèd and leavèd favour and pride,
   Are sisterly sealed in wild waters,
To bathe in his fall-gold mercies, to breathe in his all-fire glances.

XXIV

    Away in the loveable west,
      On a pastoral forehead of Wales,   185
  I was under a roof here, I was at rest,
      And they the prey of the gales;
She to the black-about air, to the breaker, the thickly
Falling flakes, to the throng that catches and quails
    Was calling "O Christ, Christ, come quickly":   190
The cross to her she calls Christ to her, christens her wild-worst
        Best.

XXV

    The majesty! what did she mean?
    Breathe, arch and original Breath.
  Is it love in her of the being as her lover had been?
    Breathe, body of lovely Death.   195
They were else-minded then, altogether, the men
Woke thee with a *we are perishing* in the weather of Genne-
      sareth.
    Or is it that she cried for the crown then,
The keener to come at the comfort for feeling the combating
    keen?

XXVI

    For how to the heart's cheering   200
    The down-dugged ground-hugged grey
  Hovers off, the jay-blue heavens appearing
    Of pied and peeled May!
Blue-beating and hoary-glow height; or night, still higher,
With belled fire and the moth-soft Milky Way,   205
    What by your measure is the heaven of desire,
The treasure never eyesight got, nor was ever guessed what for
    the hearing?

XXVII

    No, but it was not these.
    The jading and jar of the cart,
  Time's tasking, it is fathers that asking for ease   210
    Of the sodden-with-its-sorrowing heart,
Not danger, electrical horror; then further it finds
The appealing of the Passion is tenderer in prayer apart:
    Other, I gather, in measure her mind's
Burden, in wind's burly and beat of endragonèd seas.   215

XXVIII

But how shall I . . . make me room there:
Reach me a . . . Fancy, come faster—
Strike you the sight of it? look at it loom there,
Thing that she . . . there then! the Master,
Ipse, the only one, Christ, King, Head: 220
He was to cure the extremity where he had cast her;
Do, deal, lord it with living and dead;
Let him ride, her pride, in his triumph, despatch and have done
with his doom there.

XXIX

Ah! there was a heart right!
There was single eye!   225
Read the unshapeable shock night
And knew the who and the why;
Wording it how but by him that present and past,
Heaven and earth are word of, worded by?—
The Simon Peter of a soul! to the blast   230
Tarpeian-fast, but a blown beacon of light.

XXX

Jesu, heart's light,
Jesu, maid's son,
What was the feast followed the night
Thou hadst glory of this nun?—   235
Feast of the one woman without stain.
For so conceivèd, so to conceive thee is done;
But here was heart-throe, birth of a brain,
Word, that heard and kept thee and uttered thee outright.

XXXI

Well, she has thee for the pain, for the   240
Patience; but pity of the rest of them!
Heart, go and bleed at a bitterer vein for the
Comfortless unconfessed of them—
No not uncomforted: lovely-felicitous Providence
Finger of a tender of, O of a feathery delicacy, the breast of
the   245
Maiden could obey so, be a bell to, ring of it, and
Startle the poor sheep back! is the shipwrack then a harvest,
does tempest carry the grain for thee?

XXXII

I admire thee, master of the tides,
  Of the Yore-flood, of the year's fall;
    The recurb and the recovery of the gulf's sides,   250
      The girth of it and the wharf of it and the wall;
Stanching, quenching ocean of a motionable mind;
Ground of being, and granite of it: past all
    Grasp of God, throned behind
Death with a sovereignty that heeds but hides, bodes but
        abides;   255

XXXIII

  With a mercy that outrides
    The all of water, an ark
  For the listener; for the lingerer with a love glides
    Lower than death and the dark;
A vein for the visiting of the past-prayer, pent in prison,   260
The-last-breath penitent spirits—the uttermost mark
    Our passion-plungèd giant risen,
The Christ of the Father compassionate, fetched in the storm of
    his strides.

XXXIV

  Now burn, new born to the world,
    Double-naturèd name,   265
  The heaven-flung, heart-fleshed, maiden-furled
    Miracle-in-Mary-of-flame,
Mid-numbered He in three of the thunder-throne!
Not a dooms-day dazzle in his coming nor dark as he came;
  Kind, but royally reclaiming his own;   270
A released shower, let flash to the shire, not a lightning of fire
    hard-hurled.

XXXV

  Dame, at our door
    Drowned, and among our shoals,
  Remember us in the roads, the heaven-haven of the Reward:
    Our King back, oh, upon English souls!   275
Let him easter in us, be a dayspring to the dimness of us, be a
    crimson-cresseted east,
  More brightening her, rare-dear Britain, as his reign rolls,
    Pride, rose, prince, hero of us, high-priest,
Our hearts' charity's hearth's fire, our thoughts' chivalry's throng's
    Lord.

THE WINDHOVER

TO CHRIST OUR LORD

I caught this morning morning's minion, king-
    dom of daylight's dauphin, dapple-dawn-drawn Falcon,
      in his riding
Of the rolling level underneath him steady air, and striding
High there, how he rung upon the rein of a wimpling wing
In his ecstasy! then off, off forth on swing,
    As a skate's heel sweeps smooth on a bow-bend: the hurl and
      gliding
Rebuffed the big wind. My heart in hiding
Stirred for a bird,—the achieve of, the mastery of the thing!

Brute beauty and valor and act, oh, air, pride, plume, here
    Buckle! AND the fire that breaks from thee then, a billion
Times told lovelier, more dangerous, O my chevalier!

    No wonder of it: shéer plód makes plow down sillion
Shine, and blue-bleak embers, ah my dear,
    Fall, gall themselves, and gash gold-vermilion.

I WAKE AND FEEL THE FELL OF DARK

I wake and feel the fell of dark, not day.
What hours, O what black hoürs we have spent
This night! what sights you, heart, saw; ways you went!
And more must, in yet longer light's delay.
    With witness I speak this. But where I say
Hours I mean years, mean life. And my lament
Is cries countless, cries like dead letters sent
To dearest him that lives alas! away.

    I am gall, I am heartburn. God's most deep decree
Bitter would have me taste: my taste was me;
Bones built in me, flesh filled, blood brimmed the curse.
    Selfyeast of spirit a dull dough sours. I see
The lost are like this, and their scourge to be
As I am mine, their sweating selves; but worse.

ROBERT BRIDGES (1844–1930)

NIGHTINGALES

Beautiful must be the mountains whence ye come,
And bright in the fruitful valleys the streams wherefrom
    Ye learn your song:
Where are those starry woods? O might I wander there,
  Among the flowers, which in that heavenly air   5
    Bloom the year long!

Nay, barren are those mountains and spent the streams:
Our song is the voice of desire, that haunts our dreams,
    A throe of the heart,
Whose pining visions dim, forbidden hopes profound,   10
  No dying cadence nor long sigh can sound,
    For all our art.

Alone, aloud in the raptured ear of men
We pour our dark nocturnal secret; and then,
    As night is withdrawn   15
From these sweet-springing meads and bursting boughs of
    May,
  Dream, while the innumerable choir of day
    Welcome the dawn.

A PASSER-BY

Whither, O splendid ship, thy white sails crowding,
  Leaning across the bosom of the urgent West
That fearest nor sea rising, nor sky clouding,
  Whither away, fair rover, and what thy quest?
  Ah! soon, when Winter has all our vales opprest,   5
When skies are cold and misty, and hail is hurling,
  Wilt thou glide on the blue Pacific, or rest
In a summer haven asleep, thy white sails furling.

I there before thee, in the country that well thou knowest,
  Already arrived am inhaling the odorous air: 10
I watch thee enter unerringly where thou goest,
  And anchor queen of the strange shipping there,
  Thy sails for awnings spread, thy masts bare:

Nor is aught from the foaming reef to the snow-capped,
    grandest
  Peak, that is over the feathery palms more fair   15
Than thou, so upright, so stately, and still thou standest.

And yet, O splendid ship, unhailed and nameless,
  I know not if, aiming a fancy, I rightly divine
That thou hast a purpose joyful, a courage blameless,
  Thy port assured in a happier land than mine.   20
  But for all I have given thee, beauty enough is thine,
As thou, aslant with trim tackle and shrouding,
  From the proud nostril curve of a prow's line
In the offing scatterest foam, thy white sails crowding.

LONDON SNOW

When men were all asleep the snow came flying,
In large white flakes falling on the city brown,
Stealthily and perpetually settling and loosely lying,
  Hushing the latest traffic of the drowsy town;
Deadening, muffling, stifling its murmurs failing;   5
Lazily and incessantly floating down and down:
  Silently sifting and veiling road, roof and railing;
Hiding difference, making unevenness even,
Into angles and crevices softly drifting and sailing.
  All night it fell, and when full inches seven   10
It lay in the depth of its uncompacted lightness,
The clouds blew off from a high and frosty heaven;
  And all woke earlier for the unaccustomed brightness
Of the winter dawning, the strange unheavenly glare:
The eye marvelled—marvelled at the dazzling whiteness;   15
  The ear hearkened to the stillness of the solemn air;
No sound of wheel rumbling nor of foot falling,
And the busy morning cries came thin and spare.
  Then boys I heard, as they went to school, calling,
They gathered up the crystal manna to freeze   20
Their tongues with tasting, their hands with snowballing;
  Or rioted in a drift, plunging up to the knees;
Or peering up from under the white-mossed wonder,
"O look at the trees!" they cried, "O look at the trees!"
  With lessened load a few carts creak and blunder,   25

Following along the white deserted way,
A country company long dispersed asunder:
  When now already the sun, in pale display
Standing by Paul's high dome, spread forth below
His sparkling beams, and awoke the stir of the day.   30
  For now doors open, and war is waged with the snow;
And trains of sombre men, past tale of number,
Tread long brown paths, as toward their toil they go:
  But even for them awhile no cares encumber
Their minds diverted; the daily word is unspoken,   35
Their daily thoughts of labour and sorrow slumber
At the sight of the beauty that greets them, for the charm they
    have broken.

THE NORTH WIND CAME UP YESTERNIGHT

The north wind came up yesternight
  With the new year's full moon,
And rising as she gained her height,
  Grew to a tempest soon.
Yet found he not on heaven's face   5
  A task of cloud to clear;
There was no speck that he might chase
  Off the blue hemisphere;
Nor vapour from the land to drive:
  The frost-bound country held   10
Nought motionable or alive,
  That 'gainst his wrath rebelled.
There scarce was hanging in the wood
  A shrivelled leaf to reave;
No bud had burst its swathing hood   15
  That he could rend or grieve:
Only the tall tree-skeletons,
  Where they were shadowed all,
Wavered a little on the stones,
  And on the white church-wall.   20

—Like as an artist in his mood,
  Who reckons all as nought,
So he may quickly paint his nude
  Unutterable thought:
So Nature in a frenzied hour   25

By day or night will show
Dim indications of the power
   That doometh man to woe.
Ah, many have my visions been,
   And some I know full well: 30
I would that all that I have seen
   Were fit for speech to tell.—

And by the churchyard as I came,
   It seemed my spirit passed
Into a land that hath no name,   35
   Grey, melancholy and vast;
Where nothing comes: but Memory
   The widowed queen of Death,
Reigns, and with fixed, sepulchral eye
   All slumber banisheth.   40
Each grain of writhen dust, that drapes
   That sickly, staring shore,
Its old chaotic change of shapes
   Remembers evermore.
And ghosts of cities long decayed,   45
   And ruined shrines of Fate
Gather the paths, that Time hath made
   Foolish and desolate.
Nor winter there hath hope of spring,
   Nor the pale night of day,   50
Since the old king with scorpion sting
   Hath done himself away.

*   *   *

The morn was calm; the wind's last breath
   Had fall'n: in solemn hush
The golden moon went down beneath   55
   The dawning's crimson flush.

ΕΡΩΣ [1]

Why hast thou nothing in thy face?
Thou idol of the human race,
Thou tyrant of the human heart,
The flower of lovely youth that art;

1. **Eros:** god of physical passion.

Yea, and that standest in thy youth 5
An image of eternal Truth,
With thy exuberant flesh so fair,
That only Pheidias might compare,
Ere from his chaste marmoreal form
Time had decayed the colours warm; 10
Like to his gods in thy proud dress,
Thy starry sheen of nakedness.

Surely thy body is thy mind,
For in thy face is nought to find,
Only thy soft unchristen'd smile, 15
That shadows neither love nor guile,
But shameless will and power immense,
In secret sensuous innocence.

O king of joy, what is thy thought?
I dream thou knowest it is nought, 20
And wouldst in darkness come, but thou
Makest the light where'er thou go.
Ah yet no victim of thy grace,
None who e'er long'd for thy embrace,
Hath cared to look upon thy face. 25

FRANCIS THOMPSON (1859–1907)

THE KINGDOM OF GOD

"In no Strange Land"

O world invisible, we view thee;
    O world intangible, we touch thee;
O world unknowable, we know thee;
    Inapprehensible, we clutch thee!

Does the fish soar to find the ocean, 5
    The eagle plunge to find the air—
That we ask of the stars in motion
    If they have rumor of thee there?

Not where the wheeling systems darken,
    And our benumbed conceiving soars!—   10
The drift of pinions, would we hearken,
    Beats at our own clay-shuttered doors.

The angels keep their ancient places—
    Turn but a stone, and start a wing!
'Tis ye, 'tis your estrangèd faces   15
    That miss the many-splendored thing.

But (when so sad thou canst not sadder)
    Cry—and upon thy sore loss
Shall shine the traffic of Jacob's ladder
    Pitched betwixt Heaven and Charing Cross.   20

Yea, in the night, my Soul, my daughter,
    Cry,—clinging heaven by the hems:
And lo, Christ walking on the water,
    Not of Gennesareth, but Thames!

THE HOUND OF HEAVEN

I fled Him, down the nights and down the days;
    I fled Him, down the arches of the years;
I fled Him, down the labyrinthine ways
    Of my own mind; and in the mist of tears
I hid from Him, and under running laughter.   5
        Up vistaed hopes I sped;
        And shot, precipitated,
Adown Titanic glooms of chasmed fears,
    From those strong Feet that followed, followed after.
        But with unhurrying chase,   10
        And unperturbed pace,
Deliberate speed, majestic instancy,
        They beat—and a Voice beat
        More instant than the Feet—
"All things betray thee, who betrayest Me."   15

        I pleaded, outlaw-wise,
By many a hearted casement, curtained red,
    Trellised with intertwining charities;
(For, though I knew His love Who followed,

      Yet was I sore adread   20
Lest, having Him, I must have naught beside);
But, if one little casement parted wide,
    The gust of His approach would clash it to:
    Fear wist not to evade, as Love wist to pursue.
Across the margent of the world I fled,   25
    And troubled the gold gateways of the stars,
    Smiting for shelter on their clanged bars;
           Fretted to dulcet jars
And silvern chatter the pale ports o' the moon.
I said to dawn: Be sudden—to eve: Be soon;   30
    With thy young skiey blossoms heap me over
           From this tremendous Lover—
Float thy vague veil about me, lest He see!
    I tempted all His servitors, but to find
My own betrayal in their constancy,   35
In faith to Him their fickleness to me,
    Their traitorous trueness, and their loyal deceit.

To all swift things for swiftness did I sue;
    Clung to the whistling mane of every wind.
        But whether they swept, smoothly fleet,   40
      The long savannahs of the blue;
        Or whether, Thunder-driven,
        They clanged his chariot 'thwart a heaven,
Plashy with flying lightnings round the spurn o' their feet:—
    Fear wist not to evade as Love wist to pursue.   45
        Still with unhurrying chase,
        And unperturbed pace,
    Deliberate speed, majestic instancy,
        Came on the following Feet,
        And a Voice above their beat—   50
    "Naught shelters thee, who wilt not shelter Me."

I sought no more that after which I strayed
        In face of man or maid;
But still within the little children's eyes
        Seems something, something that replies,   55
They at least are for me, surely for me!
I turned me to them very wistfully;
But just as their young eyes grew sudden fair
        With dawning answers there,
Their angel plucked them from me by the hair.   60

"Come then, ye other children, Nature's—share
With me" (said I) "your delicate fellowship;
    Let me greet you lip to lip,
    Let me twine with you caresses,
      Wantoning   65
    With our Lady-Mother's vagrant tresses,
      Banqueting
    With her in her wind-walled palace,
    Underneath her azured daïs,
    Quaffing, as your taintless way is,   70
      From a chalice
Lucent-weeping out of the dayspring."
      So it was done:
I in their delicate fellowship was one—
Drew the bolt of Nature's secrecies.   75
    I knew all the swift importings
    On the willful face of skies;
    I knew how the clouds arise
    Spumed of the wild sea-snortings;
      All that's born or dies   80
      Rose and drooped with; made them shapers
Of mine own moods, or wailful or divine;
    With them joyed and was bereaven.
    I was heavy with the even,
    When she lit her glimmering tapers   85
    Round the day's dead sanctities.
    I laughed in the morning's eyes.
I triumphed and I saddened with all weather,
    Heaven and I wept together,
And its sweet tears were salt with mortal mine.   90
Against the red throb of its sunset-heart
    I laid my own to beat,
    And share commingling heat;
But not by that, by that, was eased my human smart.
In vain my tears were wet on Heaven's gray cheek.   95
For ah! we know not what each other says,
    These things and I; in sound I speak—
Their sound is but their stir, they speak by silences.
Nature, poor stepdame, cannot slake my drouth;
    Let her, if she would owe me,   100
Drop yon blue bosom-veil of sky, and show me
    The breasts o' her tenderness:

Never did any milk of hers once bless
    My thirsting mouth.
      Nigh and nigh draws the chase,   105
      With unperturbed pace,
    Deliberate speed, majestic instancy;
    And past those noised Feet
      A Voice comes yet more fleet—
  "Lo! naught contents thee, who content'st not Me."   110

Naked I wait Thy love's uplifted stroke!
My harness piece by piece Thou hast hewn from me,
    And smitten me to my knee;
    I am defenseless utterly.
    I slept, methinks, and woke,   115
And, slowly gazing, find me stripped in sleep.
In the rash lustihead of my young powers,
    I shook the pillaring hours
And pulled my life upon me; grimed with smears,
I stand amid the dust o' the mounded years—   120
My mangled youth lies dead beneath the heap.
My days have crackled and gone up in smoke,
Have puffed and burst as sun-starts on a stream.
    Yea, faileth now even dream
The dreamer, and the lute the lutanist;   125
Even the linked fantasies, in whose blossomy twist
I swung the earth a trinket at my wrist,
Are yielding; cords of all too weak account
For earth with heavy griefs so overplussed.
    Ah! is Thy love indeed   130
A weed, albeit an amaranthine weed,
Suffering no flowers except its own to mount?
    Ah! must—
    Designer infinite!—
Ah! must Thou char the wood ere Thou canst limn with it? 135
My freshness spent its wavering shower i' the dust;
And now my heart is as a broken fount,
Wherein tear-drippings stagnate, spilt down ever
    From the dank thoughts that shiver
Upon the sighful branches of my mind.   140
    Such is; what is to be?
The pulp so bitter, how shall taste the rind?
I dimly guess what Time in mists confounds;

Yet ever and anon a trumpet sounds
From the hid battlements of Eternity; 145
Those shaken mists a space unsettle, then
Round the half-glimpsed turrets slowly wash again.
  But not ere him who summoneth
  I first have seen, enwound
With glooming robes purpureal, cypress-crowned; 150
His name I know, and what his trumpet saith.
Whether man's heart or life it be which yields
  Thee harvest, must Thy harvest-fields
  Be dunged with rotten death?

   Now of that long pursuit 155
   Comes on at hand the bruit;
  That Voice is round me like a bursting sea:
   "And is thy earth so marred,
   Shattered in shard on shard?
  Lo, all things fly thee, for thou fliest Me! 160
  Strange, piteous, futile thing!

Wherefore should any set thee love apart?
Seeing none but I makes much of naught" (He said),
"And human love needs human meriting:
  How hast thou merited— 165
Of all man's clotted clay the dingiest clot?
  Alack, thou knowest not
How little worthy of any love thou art!
Whom wilt thou find to love ignoble thee
  Save Me, save only Me?
All which I took from thee I did but take,
  Not for thy harms.
But just that thou might'st seek it in My arms.
  All which thy child's mistake
Fancies as lost, I have stored for thee at home: 175
  Rise, clasp My hand, and come!"

  Halts by me that footfall:
  Is my gloom, after all,
  Shade of His hand, outstretched caressingly?
  "Ah, fondest, blindest, weakest, 180
  I am He Whom thou seekest!
Thou dravest love from thee, who dravest Me."

A. E. HOUSMAN (1859–1936)

TO AN ATHLETE DYING YOUNG

The time you won your town the race
We chaired you through the market-place;
Man and boy stood cheering by,
And home we brought you shoulder-high.

Today, the road all runners come,   5
Shoulder-high we bring you home,
And set you at your threshold down,
Townsman of a stiller town.

Smart lad, to slip betimes away
From fields where glory does not stay,   10
And early though the laurel grows
It withers quicker than the rose.

Eyes the shady night has shut
Cannot see the record cut,
And silence sounds no worse than cheers   15
After earth has stopped the ears:

Now you will not swell the rout
Of lads that wore their honors out,
Runners whom renown outran
And the name died before the man.   20

So set, before its echoes fade,
The fleet foot on the sill of shade,
And hold to the low lintel up
The still-defended challenge-cup.

And round that early-laureled head   25
Will flock to gaze the strengthless dead,
And find unwithered on its curls
The garland briefer than a girl's.

IS MY TEAM PLOWING

"Is my team plowing,
   That I was used to drive
And hear the harness jingle
   When I was man alive?"

Aye, the horses trample,   5
   The harness jingles now;
No change though you lie under
   The land you used to plow.

"Is football playing
   Along the river shore,   10
With lads to chase the leather,
   Now I stand up no more?"

Aye, the ball is flying,
   The lads play heart and soul;
The goal stands up, the keeper   15
   Stands up to keep the goal.

"Is my girl happy,
   That I thought hard to leave,
And has she tired of weeping
   As she lies down at eve?"   20

Aye, she lies down lightly,
   She lies not down to weep:
Your girl is well contented.
   Be still, my lad, and sleep.

"Is my friend hearty,   25
   Now I am thin and pine;
And has he found to sleep in
   A better bed than mine?"

Yes, lad, I lie easy,
   I lie as lads would choose;   30
I cheer a dead man's sweetheart.
   Never ask me whose.

THE DESERTER

"What sound awakened me, I wonder,
   For now 'tis dumb."
"Wheels on the road most like, or thunder:
   Lie down; 'twas not the drum."

Toil at sea and two in haven
   And trouble far:
Fly crow, away, and follow, raven,
   And all that croaks of war.

"Hark, I heard the bugle crying,
   And where am I?
My friends are up and dressed and dying,
   And I will dress and die."

"Oh, love is rare and trouble plenty
   And carrion cheap,
And daylight dear at four-and-twenty:
   Lie down again and sleep."

"Reach me my belt and leave your prattle:
   Your hour is gone;
But my day is the day of battle,
   And that comes dawning on.

"They mow the field of man in season:
   Farewell, my fair,
And, call it truth or call it treason,
   Farewell the vows that were."

"Ay, false heart, forsake me lightly;
   'Tis like the brave.
They find no bed to joy in rightly
   Before they find the grave.

"Their love is for their own undoing,
   And east and west
They scour about the world a-wooing
   The bullet to their breast.

5

10

15

20

25

30

"Sail away the ocean over,
    Oh sail away,
And lie there with your leaden lover   35
    Forever and a day."

TERENCE, THIS IS STUPID STUFF

"Terence, this is stupid stuff;
You eat your victuals fast enough;
There can't be much amiss, 'tis clear,
To see the rate you drink your beer.
But oh, good Lord, the verse you make,   5
It gives a chap the belly-ache.
The cow, the old cow, she is dead;
It sleeps well, the horned head:
We poor lads, 'tis our turn now
To hear such tunes as killed the cow.   10
Pretty friendship 'tis to rhyme
Your friends to death before their time
Moping melancholy mad:
Come, pipe a tune to dance to, lad."
Why, if 'tis dancing you would be,   15
There's brisker pipes than poetry.
Say, for what were hop-yards meant,
Or why was Burton built on Trent?
Oh, many a peer of England brews
Livelier liquor than the Muse,   20
And malt does more than Milton can
To justify God's ways to man.
Ale, man, ale's the stuff to drink
For fellows whom it hurts to think:
Look into the pewter pot   25
To see the world as the world's not.
And faith, 'tis pleasant till 'tis past:
The mischief is that 'twill not last.
Oh, I have been to Ludlow fair
And left my necktie God knows where,   30
And carried half way home, or near,
Pints and quarts of Ludlow beer:
Then the world seemed none so bad,
And I myself a sterling lad;
And down in lovely muck I've lain,   35

Happy till I woke again.
Then I saw the morning sky:
Heigho, the tale was all a lie;
The world, it was the old world yet,
I was I, my things were wet,   40
And nothing now remained to do
But begin the game anew.

Therefore, since the world has still
Much good, but much less good than ill,
And while the sun and moon endure   45
Luck's a chance, but trouble's sure,
I'd face it as a wise man would,
And train for ill and not for good.
'Tis true, the stuff I bring for sale
Is not so brisk a brew as ale: 50
Out of a stem that scored the hand
I wrung it in a weary land.
But take it: if the smack is sour,
The better for the embittered hour;
It should do good to heart and head   55
When your soul is in my soul's stead;
And I will friend you, if I may,
In the dark and cloudy day.

There was a king reigned in the East:
There, when kings will sit to feast,   60
They get their fill before they think
With poisoned meat and poisoned drink.
He gathered all that springs to birth
From the many-venomed earth;
First a little, thence to more,   65
He sampled all her killing store;
And easy, smiling, seasoned sound,
Sate the king when healths went round.
They put arsenic in his meat
And stared aghast to watch him eat;   70
They poured strychnine in his cup
And shook to see him drink it up:
They shook, they stared as white's their shirt:
Them it was their poison hurt.
—I tell the tale that I heard told.   75
Mithridates, he died old.

THE STARS HAVE NOT DEALT ME

The stars have not dealt me the worst they could do;
My pleasures are plenty, my troubles are two.
But oh, my two troubles they reave me of rest,
The brains in my head and the heart in my breast.

O grant me the ease that is granted so free,
The birthright of multitudes, give it to me,
That relish their victuals and rest on their bed
With flint in the bosom and guts in the head.

EASTER HYMN

If in that Syrian garden, ages slain,
You sleep, and know not you are dead in vain,
Nor even in dreams behold how dark and bright
Ascends in smoke and fire by day and night
The hate you died to quench and could but fan,
Sleep well and see no morning, son of man.

But if, the grave rent and the stone rolled by,
At the right hand of majesty on high
You sit, and sitting so remember yet
Your tears, your agony and bloody sweat,
Your cross and passion and the life you gave,
Bow hither out of heaven and see and save.

ALTA QUIES

Good night. Ensured release,
Imperishable peace,
  Have these for yours.
While sky and sea and land
And earth's foundations stand
  And heaven endures.

When earth's foundations flee,
Nor sky nor land nor sea
  At all is found,
Content you; let them burn,
It is not your concern:
  Sleep on, sleep sound.

RUDYARD KIPLING (1865–1936)

CITIES AND THRONES AND POWERS

Cities and Thrones and Powers,
    Stand in Time's eye,
Almost as long as flowers,
    Which daily die.
But, as new buds put forth   5
    To glad new men,
Out of the spent and unconsidered Earth
    The Cities rise again.

This season's Daffodil,
    She never hears   10
What change, what chance, what chill,
    Cut down last year's:
But with bold countenance,
    And knowledge small,
Esteems her seven days' continuance   15
    To be perpetual.

So Time that is o'erkind,
    To all that be,
Ordains us e'en as blind,
    As bold as she: 20
That in our very death,
    And burial sure,
Shadow to shadow, well persuaded, saith,
    "See how our works endure!"

THE WAY THROUGH THE WOODS

They shut the road through the woods
Seventy years ago.
Weather and rain have undone it again,
And now you would never know
There was once a road through the woods   5
Before they planted the trees.

It is underneath the coppice and heath
And the thin anemones.
Only the keeper sees
That, where the ring-dove broods,   10
And the badgers roll at ease
There was once a road through the woods.

Yet, if you enter the woods
Of a summer evening late,
When the night-air cools on the trout-ringed pools   15
Where the otter whistles his mate,
(They fear not men in the woods
Because they see so few.)
You will hear the beat of a horse's feet
And the swish of a skirt in the dew,   20
Steadily cantering through
The misty solitudes,
As though they perfectly knew
The old lost road through the woods . . .
But there is no road through the woods.   25

WILLIAM BUTLER YEATS (1865–1939)

THE HOST OF THE AIR

O'Driscoll drove with a song
The wild duck and the drake
From the tall and the tufted reeds
Of the drear Hart Lake.

And he saw how the reeds grew dark   5
At the coming of night-tide,
And he dreamed of the long dim hair
Of Bridget his bride.

He heard while he sang and dreamed
A piper piping away,   10
And never was piping so sad,
And never was piping so gay.

And he saw young men and young girls
Who danced on a level place,
And Bridget his bride among them,   15
With a sad and a gay face.

The dancers crowded about him,
And many a sweet thing said,
And a young man brought him red wine
And a young girl white bread.   20

But Bridget drew him by the sleeve,
Away from the merry bands,
To old men playing at cards
With a twinkling of ancient hands.

The bread and the wine had a doom,   25
For these were the host of the air;
He sat and played in a dream
Of her long dim hair.

He played with the merry old men
And thought not of evil chance,   30
Until one bore Bridget his bride
Away from the merry dance.

He bore her away in his arms,
The handsomest young man there,
And his neck and his breast and his arms   35
Were drowned in her long dim hair.

O'Driscoll scattered the cards
And out of his dream awoke:
Old men and young men and young girls
Were gone like a drifting smoke;   40

But he heard high up in the air
A piper piping away,
And never was piping so sad,
And never was piping so gay.

EASTER, 1916

I have met them at close of day
Coming with vivid faces
From counter or desk among grey
Eighteenth-century houses.
I have passed with a nod of the head   5
Or polite meaningless words,
Or have lingered awhile and said
Polite meaningless words,
And thought before I had done
Of a mocking tale or a gibe   10
To please a companion
Around the fire at the club,
Being certain that they and I
But lived where motley is worn:
All changed, changed utterly: 15
A terrible beauty is born.

That woman's days were spent
In ignorant good-will,
Her nights in argument
Until her voice grew shrill.   20
What voice more sweet than hers
When, young and beautiful,
She rode to harriers?
This man had kept a school
And rode our wingèd horse;   25
This other his helper and friend
Was coming into his force;
He might have won fame in the end,
So sensitive his nature seemed,
So daring and sweet his thought.   30
This other man I had dreamed
A drunken, vainglorious lout.
He had done most bitter wrong
To some who are near my heart,
Yet I number him in the song;   35
He, too, has resigned his part
In the casual comedy;
He, too, has been changed in his turn,
Transformed utterly:
A terrible beauty is born.   40

Hearts with one purpose alone
Through summer and winter seem
Enchanted to a stone
To trouble the living stream.
The horse that comes from the road,   45
The rider, the birds that range
From cloud to tumbling cloud,
Minute by minute they change;
A shadow of cloud on the stream
Changes minute by minute;   50
A horse-hoof slides on the brim,
And a horse plashes within it;
The long-legged moor-hens dive,
And hens to moor-cocks call;
Minute by minute they live: 55
The stone's in the midst of all.

Too long a sacrifice
Can make a stone of the heart.
O when may it suffice?
That is Heaven's part, our part   60
To murmur name upon name,
As a mother names her child
When sleep at last has come
On limbs that had run wild.
What is it but nightfall?   65
No, no, not night but death;
Was it needless death after all?
For England may keep faith
For all that is done and said.
We know their dream; enough   70
To know they dreamed and are dead;
And what if excess of love
Bewildered them till they died?
I write it out in a verse—
MacDonagh and MacBride   75
And Connolly and Pearse
Now and in time to be,
Wherever green is worn,
Are changed, changed utterly:
A terrible beauty is born.   80

September 25, 1916

LEDA AND THE SWAN

A sudden blow: the great wings beating still
Above the staggering girl, her thighs caressed
By the dark webs, her nape caught in his bill,
He holds her helpless breast upon his breast.

How can those terrified vague fingers push
The feathered glory from her loosening thighs?
And how can body, laid in that white rush,
But feel the strange heart beating where it lies?

A shudder in the loins engenders there
The broken wall, the burning roof and tower
And Agamemnon dead.
                   Being so caught up,
So mastered by the brute blood of the air,
Did she put on his knowledge with his power
Before the indifferent beak could let her drop?

THE SECOND COMING

Turning and turning in the widening gyre
The falcon cannot hear the falconer;
Things fall apart; the center cannot hold;
Mere anarchy is loosed upon the world,
The blood-dimmed tide is loosed, and everywhere   5
The ceremony of innocence is drowned;
The best lack all conviction, while the worst
Are full of passionate intensity.

Surely some revelation is at hand;
Surely the Second Coming is at hand.   10
The Second Coming! Hardly are those words out
When a vast image out of *Spiritus Mundi*
Troubles my sight: somewhere in sands of the desert
A shape with lion body and the head of a man,
A gaze blank and pitiless as the sun,   15
Is moving its slow thighs, while all about it
Reel shadows of the indignant desert birds.

The darkness drops again; but now I know
That twenty centuries of stony sleep
Were vexed to nightmare by a rocking cradle,   20
And what rough beast, its hour come round at last,
Slouches towards Bethlehem to be born?

TWO SONGS FROM A PLAY

I

I saw a staring virgin stand
Where holy Dionysus died,
And tear the heart out of his side,
And lay the heart upon her hand
And bear that beating heart away;   5
And then did all the Muses sing
Of Magnus Annus at the spring,
As though God's death were but a play.

Another Troy must rise and set,
Another lineage feed the crow,   10
Another Argo's painted prow
Drive to a flashier bauble yet.
The Roman Empire stood appalled:
It dropped the reins of peace and war
When that fierce virgin and her Star   15
Out of the fabulous darkness called.

II

In pity for man's darkening thought
He walked that room and issued thence
In Galilean turbulence;
The Babylonian starlight brought
A fabulous, formless darkness in;   5
Odor of blood when Christ was slain
Made all Platonic tolerance vain
And vain all Doric discipline.

Everything that man esteems
Endures a moment or a day.   10
Love's pleasure drives his love away,
The painter's brush consumes his dreams;

The herald's cry, the soldier's tread
Exhaust his glory and his might:
Whatever flames upon the night   15
Man's own resinous heart has fed.

FOR ANNE GREGORY

"Never shall a young man,
Thrown into despair
By those great honey-coloured
Ramparts at your ear,
Love you for yourself alone   5
And not your yellow hair."

"But I can get a hair-dye
And set such colour there,
Brown, or black, or carrot,
That young men in despair   10
May love me for myself alone
And not my yellow hair."

"I heard an old religious man
But yesternight declare
That he had found a text to prove   15
That only God, my dear,
Could love you for yourself alone
And not your yellow hair."

THE TOWER

I

What shall I do with this absurdity—
O heart, O troubled heart—this caricature,
Decrepit age that has been tied to me
As to a dog's tail?

           Never had I more   5
Excited, passionate, fantastical
Imagination, nor an ear and eye
That more expected the impossible—
No, not in boyhood when with rod and fly,

Or the humbler worm, I climbed Ben Bulben's back   10
And had the livelong summer day to spend.
It seems that I must bid the Muse go pack,
Choose Plato and Plotinus for a friend
Until imagination, ear and eye,
Can be content with argument and deal   15
In abstract things; or be derided by
A sort of battered kettle at the heel.

II

I pace upon the battlements and stare
On the foundations of a house, or where
Tree, like a sooty finger, starts from the earth;   20
And send imagination forth
Under the day's declining beam, and call
Images and memories
From ruin or from ancient trees,
For I would ask a question of them all.   25

Beyond that ridge lived Mrs. French, and once
When every silver candlestick or sconce
Lit up the dark mahogany and the wine,
A serving man that could divine
That most respected lady's every wish,   30
Ran and with the garden shears
Clipped an insolent farmer's ears
And brought them in a little covered dish.

Some few remembered still when I was young,
A peasant girl commended by a song,   35
Who'd lived somewhere upon that rocky place,
And praised the color of her face,
And had the greater joy in praising her,
Remembering that, if walked she there,
Farmers jostled at the fair   40
So great a glory did the song confer.

And certain men, being maddened by those rhymes,
Or else by toasting her a score of times,
Rose from the table and declared it right
To test their fancy by their sight;   45

But they mistook the brightness of the moon
For the prosaic light of day—
Music had driven their wits astray—
And one was drowned in the great bog of Cloone.

Strange, but the man who made the song was blind,   50
Yet, now I have considered it, I find
That nothing strange; the tragedy began
With Homer that was a blind man,
And Helen has all living hearts betrayed.
O may the moon and sunlight seem   55
One inextricable beam,
For if I triumph I must make men mad.

And I myself created Hanrahan
And drove him drunk or sober through the dawn
From somewhere in the neighboring cottages,   60
Caught by an old man's juggleries
He stumbled, tumbled, fumbled to and fro
And had but broken knees for hire
And horrible splendor of desire;
I thought it all out twenty years ago: 65

Good fellows shuffled cards in an old bawn;
And when that ancient ruffian's turn was on
He so bewitched the cards under his thumb
That all, but the one card, became
A pack of hounds and not a pack of cards,   70
And that he changed into a hare.
Hanrahan rose in frenzy there
And followed up those baying creatures towards—

O towards I have forgotten what—enough!
I must recall a man that neither love   75
Nor music nor an enemy's clipped ear
Could, he was so harried, cheer;
A figure that has grown so fabulous
There's not a neighbor left to say
When he finished his dog's day: 80
An ancient bankrupt master of this house.

Before that ruin came, for centuries,
Rough men-at-arms, cross-gartered to the knees
Or shod in iron, climbed the narrow stairs,
And certain men-at-arms there were   85
Whose images, in the Great Memory stored,
Come with loud cry and panting breast
To break upon a sleeper's rest
While their great wooden dice beat on the board.

As I would question all, come all who can;   90
Come old, necessitous, half-mounted man;
And bring beauty's blind rambling celebrant;
The red man the juggler sent
Through God-forsaken meadows; Mrs. French,
Gifted with so fine an ear;   95
The man drowned in a bog's mire,
When mocking muses chose the country wench.

Did all old men and women, rich and poor,
Who trod upon these rocks or passed this door,
Whether in public or in secret rage   100
As I do now against old age?
But I have found an answer in those eyes
That are impatient to be gone;
Go therefore; but leave Hanrahan,
For I need all his mighty memories.   105

Old lecher with a love on every wind
Bring up out of that deep considering mind
All that you have discovered in the grave,
For it is certain that you have
Reckoned up every unforeknown, unseeing   110
Plunge, lured by a softening eye,
Or by a touch or a sigh,
Into the labyrinth of another's being;

Does the imagination dwell the most
Upon a woman won or woman lost?   115
If on the lost, admit you turned aside
From a great labyrinth out of pride,

Cowardice, some silly over-subtle thought
Or anything called conscience once;
And that if memory recur, the sun's   120
Under eclipse and the day blotted out.

III

It is time that I wrote my will;
I choose upstanding men,
That climb the streams until
The fountain leap, and at dawn   125
Drop their cast at the side
Of dripping stone; I declare
They shall inherit my pride,
The pride of people that were
Bound neither to Cause nor to State,   130
Neither to slaves that were spat on,
Nor to the tyrants that spat,
The people of Burke and of Grattan
That gave, though free to refuse—
Pride, like that of the morn,   135
When the headlong light is loose,
Or that of the fabulous horn,
Or that of the sudden shower
When all streams are dry,
Or that of the hour   140
When the swan must fix his eye
Upon a fading gleam,
Float out upon a long
Last reach of glittering stream
And there sing his last song.   145
And I declare my faith;
I mock Plotinus' thought
And cry in Plato's teeth,
Death and life were not
Till man made up the whole,   150
Made lock, stock and barrel
Out of his bitter soul,
Aye, sun and moon and star, all,
And further add to that
That, being dead, we rise,   155
Dream and so create
Translunar Paradise.

I have prepared my peace
With learned Italian things
And the proud stones of Greece,   160
Poet's imaginings
And memories of love,
Memories of the words of women,
All those things whereof
Man makes a superhuman,   165
Mirror-resembling dream.

As at the loophole there,
The daws chatter and scream,
And drop twigs layer upon layer.
When they have mounted up,   170
The mother bird will rest
On their hollow top,
And so warm her wild nest.

I leave both faith and pride
To young upstanding men   175
Climbing the mountain side,
That under bursting dawn
They may drop a fly;
Being of that metal made
Till it was broken by   180
This sedentary trade.

Now shall I make my soul
Compelling it to study
In a learned school
Till the wreck of body   185
Slow decay of blood,
Testy delirium
Or dull decrepitude,
Or what worse evil come—
The death of friends, or death   190
Of every brilliant eye
That made a catch in the breath—
Seem but the clouds of the sky
When the horizon fades;
Or a bird's sleepy cry   195
Among the deepening shades.

AMONG SCHOOL CHILDREN

I walk through the long schoolroom questioning,
A kind old nun in a white hood replies;
The children learn to cipher and to sing,
To study reading-books and history,
To cut and sew, be neat in everything   5
In the best modern way—the children's eyes
In momentary wonder stare upon
A sixty year old smiling public man.

I dream of a Ledæan body, bent
Above a sinking fire, a tale that she   10
Told of a harsh reproof, or trivial event
That changed some childish day to tragedy—
Told, and it seemed that our two natures blent
Into a sphere from youthful sympathy,
Or else, to alter Plato's parable,   15
Into the yolk and white of the one shell.

And thinking of that fit of grief or rage
I look upon one child or t'other there
And wonder if she stood so at that age—
For even daughters of the swan can share   20
Something of every paddler's heritage—
And had that color upon cheek or hair;
And thereupon my heart is driven wild:
She stands before me as a living child.

Her present image floats into the mind—   25
Did quattrocento finger fashion it
Hollow of cheek as though it drank the wind
And took a mess of shadows for its meat?
And I though never of Ledæan kind
Had pretty plumage once—enough of that,   30
Better to smile on all that smile, and show
There is a comfortable kind of old scarecrow.

What youthful mother, a shape upon her lap
Honey of generation had betrayed,
And that must sleep, shriek, struggle to escape   35
As recollection or the drug decide,

Would think her son, did she but see that shape
With sixty or more winters on its head,
A compensation for the pang of his birth,
Or the uncertainty of his setting forth?   40

Plato thought nature but a spume that plays
Upon a ghostly paradigm of things;
Solider Aristotle played the taws
Upon the bottom of a king of kings;
World-famous golden-thighed Pythagoras   45
Fingered upon a fiddle stick or strings
What a star sang and careless Muses heard:
Old clothes upon old sticks to scare a bird.

Both nuns and mothers worship images,
But those the candles light are not as those   50
That animate a mother's reveries,
But keep a marble or a bronze repose.
And yet they too break hearts—O Presences
That passion, piety or affection knows,
And that all heavenly glory symbolize—   55
O self-born mockers of man's enterprise;

Labor is blossoming or dancing where
The body is not bruised to pleasure soul,
Nor beauty born out of its own despair,
Nor blear-eyed wisdom out of midnight oil.   60
O chestnut tree, great rooted blossomer,
Are you the leaf, the blossom or the bole?
O body swayed to music, O brightening glance,
How can we know the dancer from the dance?

SAILING TO BYZANTIUM

That is no country for old men. The young
In one another's arms, birds in the trees
—Those dying generations—at their song,
The salmon-falls, the mackerel-crowded seas,
Fish, flesh, or fowl, commend all summer long   5
Whatever is begotten, born, and dies.
Caught in that sensual music all neglect
Monuments of unaging intellect.

An aged man is but a paltry thing,
A tattered coat upon a stick, unless   10
Soul clap its hands and sing, and louder sing
For every tatter in its mortal dress,
Nor is there singing school but studying
Monuments of its own magnificence;
And therefore I have sailed the seas and come   15
To the holy city of Byzantium.

O sages standing in God's holy fire
As in the gold mosaic of a wall,
Come from the holy fire, perne in a gyre,
And be the singing-masters of my soul.   20
Consume my heart away; sick with desire
And fastened to a dying animal
It knows not what it is; and gather me
Into the artifice of eternity.

Once out of nature I shall never take   25
My bodily form from any natural thing,
But such a form as Grecian goldsmiths make
Of hammered gold and gold enameling
To keep a drowsy Emperor awake;
Or set upon a golden bough to sing   30
To lords and ladies of Byzantium
Of what is past, or passing, or to come.

BYZANTIUM

The unpurged images of day recede;
The Emperor's drunken soldiery are abed;
Night resonance recedes, night-walkers' song
After great cathedral gong;
A starlit or a moonlit dome disdains   5
All that man is,
All mere complexities,
The fury and the mire of human veins.

Before me floats an image, man or shade,
Shade more than man, more image than a shade;   10
For Hades' bobbin bound in mummy-cloth
May unwind the winding path;

A mouth that has no moisture and no breath
Breathless mouths may summon;
I hail the superhuman;   15
I call it death-in-life and life-in-death.

Miracle, bird or golden handiwork,
More miracle than bird or handiwork,
Planted on the star-lit golden bough,
Can like the cocks of Hades crow,   20
Or, by the moon embittered, scorn aloud
In glory of changeless metal
Common bird or petal
And all complexities of mire or blood.

At midnight on the Emperor's pavement flit   25
Flames that no fagot feeds, nor steel has lit,
Nor storm disturbs, flames begotten of flame,
Where blood-begotten spirits come
And all complexities of fury leave,
Dying into a dance,   30
An agony of trance,
An agony of flame that cannot singe a sleeve.

Astraddle on the dolphin's mire and blood,
Spirit after spirit! The smithies break the flood,
The golden smithies of the Emperor!   35
Marbles of the dancing floor
Break bitter furies of complexity,
Those images that yet
Fresh images beget,
That dolphin-torn, that gong-tormented sea.   40

EDWIN ARLINGTON ROBINSON
(1869–1935)

FLAMMONDE

The man Flammonde, from God knows where,
With firm address and foreign air,
With news of nations in his talk
And something royal in his walk,

With glint of iron in his eyes,   5
But never doubt, nor yet surprise,
Appeared, and stayed, and held his **head**
As one by kings accredited.

Erect, with his alert repose
About him, and about his clothes,   10
He pictured all tradition hears
Of what we owe to fifty years.
His cleansing heritage of taste
Paraded neither want nor waste;
And what he needed for his fee   15
To live, he borrowed graciously.

He never told us what he was,
Or what mischance, or other cause,
Had banished him from better days
To play the Prince of Castaways.   20
Meanwhile he played surpassing well
A part, for most, unplayable;
In fine, one pauses, half afraid
To say for certain that he played.

For that, one may as well forego   25
Conviction as to yes or no;
Nor can I say just how intense
Would then have been the difference
To several, who, having striven
In vain to get what he was given,   30
Would see the stranger taken on
By friends not easy to be won.

Moreover, many a malcontent
He soothed and found munificent;
His courtesy beguiled and foiled   35
Suspicion that his years were soiled;
His mien distinguished any crowd,
His credit strengthened when he bowed;
And women, young and old, were fond
Of looking at the man Flammonde.   40

There was a woman in our town
On whom the fashion was to frown;

But while our talk renewed the tinge
Of a long-faded scarlet fringe,
The man Flammonde saw none of that,   45
And what he saw we wondered at—
That none of us, in her distress,
Could hide or find our littleness.

There was a boy that all agreed
Had shut within him the rare seed   50
Of learning. We could understand,
But none of us could lift a hand.
The man Flammonde appraised the youth,
And told a few of us the truth;
And thereby, for a little gold,   55
A flowered future was unrolled.

There were two citizens who fought
For years and years, and over nought;
They made life awkward for their friends,
And shortened their own dividends.   60
The man Flammonde said what was wrong
Should be made right; nor was it long
Before they were again in line,
And hath each other in to dine.

And these I mention are but four   65
Of many out of many more.
So much for them. But what of him—
So firm in every look and limb?
What small satanic sort of kink
Was in his brain? What broken link   70
Withheld him from the destinies
That came so near to being his?

What was he, when we came to sift
His meaning, and to note the drift
Of incommunicable ways   75
That make us ponder while we praise?
Why was it that his charm revealed
Somehow the surface of a shield?
What was it that we never caught?
What was he, and what was he not?   80

How much it was of him we met
We cannot ever know: nor yet
Shall all he gave us quite atone
For what was his, and his alone;
Nor need we now, since he knew best,   85
Nourish an ethical unrest:
Rarely at once will nature give
The power to be Flammonde and live.

We cannot know how much we learn
From those who never will return,   90
Until a flash of unforeseen
Remembrance falls on what has been.
We've each a darkening hill to climb;
And this is why, from time to time
In Tilbury Town, we look beyond   95
Horizons for the man Flammonde.

MINIVER CHEEVY

Miniver Cheevy, child of scorn,
    Grew lean while he assailed the seasons;
He wept that he was ever born,
    And he had reasons.

Miniver loved the days of old   5
    When swords were bright and steeds were prancing;
The vision of a warrior bold
    Would set him dancing.

Miniver sighed for what was not,
    And dreamed, and rested from his labors;   10
He dreamed of Thebes and Camelot,
    And Priam's neighbors.

Miniver mourned the ripe renown
    That made so many a name so fragrant;
He mourned Romance, now on the town,   15
    And Art, a vagrant.

Miniver loved the Medici,
  Albeit he had never seen one;
He would have sinned incessantly
  Could he have been one.   20

Miniver cursed the commonplace
  And eyed a khaki suit with loathing;
He missed the mediæval grace
  Of iron clothing.

Miniver scorned the gold he sought,   25
  But sore annoyed was he without it;
Miniver thought, and thought, and thought,
  And thought about it.

Miniver Cheevy, born too late,
  Scratched his head and kept on thinking;   30
Miniver coughed, and called it fate,
  And kept on drinking.

CASSANDRA

I heard one who said: "Verily,
  What word have I for children here?
Your Dollar is your only Word,
  The wrath of it your only fear.

"You build it altars tall enough   5
  To make you see, but you are blind;
You cannot leave it long enough
  To look before you or behind.

"When Reason beckons you to pause,
  You laugh and say that you know best;   10
But what it is you know, you keep
  As dark as ingots in a chest.

"You laugh and answer, 'We are young;
  Oh, leave us now, and let us grow:'
Not asking how much more of this   15
  Will Time endure or Fate bestow.

"Because a few complacent years
   Have made your peril of your pride,
Think you that you are to go on
   Forever pampered and untried?   20

"What lost eclipse of history,
   What bivouac of the marching stars,
Has given the sign for you to see
   Millenniums and last great wars?

"What unrecorded overthrow   25
   Of all the world has ever known,
Or ever been, has made itself
   So plain to you, and you alone?

"Your Dollar, Dove and Eagle make
   A Trinity that even you   30
Rate higher than you rate yourselves;
   It pays, it flatters, and it's new.

"And though your very flesh and blood
   Be what your Eagle eats and drinks,
You'll praise him for the best of birds,   35
   Not knowing what the Eagle thinks.

"The power is yours, but not the sight;
   You see not upon what you tread;
You have the ages for your guide,
   But not the wisdom to be led.   40

"Think you to tread forever down
   The merciless old verities?
And are you never to have eyes
   To see the world for what it is?

"Are you to pay for what you have   45
   With all you are?"—No other word
We caught, but with a laughing crowd
   Moved on. None heeded, and few heard.

MR. FLOOD'S PARTY

Old Eben Flood, climbing alone one night
Over the hill between the town below
And the forsaken upland hermitage
That held as much as he should ever know
On earth again of home, paused warily.   5
The road was his with not a native near;
And Eben, having leisure, said aloud,
For no man else in Tilbury Town to hear:

"Well, Mr. Flood, we have the harvest moon
Again, and we may not have many more;   10
The bird is on the wing, the poet says,
And you and I have said it here before.
Drink to the bird." He raised up to the light
The jug that he had gone so far to fill,
And answered huskily: "Well, Mr. Flood,   15
Since you propose it, I believe I will."

Alone, as if enduring to the end
A valiant armor of scarred hopes outworn,
He stood there in the middle of the road
Like Roland's ghost winding a silent horn.   20
Below him, in the town among the trees,
Where friends of other days had honored him,
A phantom salutation of the dead
Rang thinly till old Eben's eyes were dim.

Then, as a mother lays her sleeping child   25
Down tenderly, fearing it may awake,
He set the jug down slowly at his feet
With trembling care, knowing that most things break;
And only when assured that on firm earth
It stood, as the uncertain lives of men   30
Assuredly did not, he paced away,
And with his hand extended paused again:

"Well, Mr. Flood, we have not met like this
In a long time; and many a change has come

To both of us, I fear, since last it was   35
We had a drop together. Welcome home!"
Convivially returning with himself,
Again he raised the jug up to the light
And with an acquiescent quaver said:
"Well, Mr. Flood, if you insist, I might.   40

"Only a very little, Mr. Flood—
For auld lang syne. No more, sir; that will do."
So, for the time, apparently it did,
And Eben evidently thought so too;
For soon amid the silver loneliness   45
Of night he lifted up his voice and sang,
Secure, with only two moons listening,
Until the whole harmonious landscape rang—

"For auld lang syne." The weary throat gave out,
The last word wavered; and the song being done,   50
He raised again the jug regretfully
And shook his head, and was again alone.
There was not much that was ahead of him,
And there was nothing in the town below—
Where strangers would have shut the many doors   55
That many friends had opened long ago.

EDGAR LEE MASTERS (1869–1950)

THE HILL

Where are Elmer, Herman, Bert, Tom and Charley,
The weak of will, the strong of arm, the clown, the boozer, the fighter?
All, all, are sleeping on the hill.

One passed in a fever,
One was burned in a mine,   5
One was killed in a brawl,
One died in a jail,
One fell from a bridge toiling for children and wife—
All, all, are sleeping, sleeping, sleeping on the hill.

Where are Ella, Kate, Mag, Lizzie and Edith,   10
The tender heart, the simple soul, the loud, the proud, the
    happy one?—
All, all, are sleeping on the hill.

One died in shameful childbirth,
One of a thwarted love,
One at the hands of a brute in a brothel,   15
One of a broken pride, in the search for heart's desire,
One after life in far-away London and Paris
Was brought to her little space by Ella and Kate and Mag—
All, all, are sleeping, sleeping, sleeping on the hill.

Where are Uncle Isaac and Aunt Emily,   20
And old Towny Kincaid and Sevigne Houghton,
And Major Walker who had talked
With venerable men of the revolution?—
All, all, are sleeping on the hill.

They brought them dead sons from the war,   25
And daughters whom life had crushed,
And their children fatherless, crying—
All, all, are sleeping, sleeping, sleeping on the hill.

Where is Old Fiddler Jones
Who played with life all his ninety years,   30
Braving the sleet with bared breast,
Drinking, rioting, thinking neither of wife nor kin,
Nor gold, nor love, nor heaven?
Lo! he babbles of the fish-frys of long ago,
Of the horse races of long ago at Clary's Grove,   35
Of what Abe Lincoln said
One time at Springfield.

RALPH HODGSON (1872–   )

EVE

Eve, with her basket, was
Deep in the bells and grass,
Wading in bells and grass
Up to her knees,

Picking a dish of sweet   5
Berries and plums to eat,
Down in the bells and grass
Under the trees.

Mute as a mouse in a
Corner the cobra lay,   10
Curled round a bough of the
Cinnamon tall. . . .
Now to get even and
Humble proud heaven and—
Now was the moment or   15
Never at all.

"Eva!" Each syllable
Light as a flower fell,
"Eva!" he whispered the
Wondering maid,   20
Soft as a bubble sung
Out of a linnet's lung,
Soft and most silverly
"Eva!" he said.

Picture that orchard sprite,   25
Eve, with her body white,
Supple and smooth to her
Slim finger tips,
Wondering, listening,
Listening, wondering,   30
Eve with a berry
Half-way to her lips.

Oh, had our simple Eve
Seen through the make-believe!
Had she but known the   35
Pretender he was!
Out of the boughs he came,
Whispering still her name,
Tumbling in twenty rings
Into the grass.   40

Here was the strangest pair
In the world anywhere,
Eve in the bells and grass
Kneeling, and he
Telling his story low. . . .   45
Singing birds saw them go
Down the dark path to
The Blasphemous Tree.

Oh, what a clatter when
Titmouse and Jenny Wren   50
Saw him successful and
Taking his leave!
How the birds rated him!
How they all hated him!
How they all pitied   55
Poor motherless Eve!

Picture her crying
Outside in the lane,
Eve, with no dish of sweet
Berries and plums to eat,   60
Haunting the gate of the
Orchard in vain. . . .
Picture the lewd delight
Under the hill to-night—
"Eva!" the toast goes round,   65
"Eva!" again.

WALTER DE LA MARE (1873–1956)

THE LISTENERS

'Is there anybody there?' said the Traveller,
    Knocking on the moonlit door;
And his horse in the silence champed the grasses
    Of the forest's ferny floor:
And a bird flew up out of the turret,   5
    Above the Traveller's head:
And he smote upon the door again a second time;
    'Is there anybody there?' he said.

But no one descended to the Traveller;
    No head from the leaf-fringed sill   10
Leaned over and looked into his grey eyes,
    Where he stood perplexed and still.
But only a host of phantom listeners
    That dwelt in the lone house then
Stood listening in the quiet of the moonlight   15
    To that voice from the world of men:
Stood thronging the faint moonbeams on the dark stair,
    That goes down to the empty hall,
Hearkening in an air stirred and shaken
    By the lonely Traveller's call.   20
And he felt in his heart their strangeness,
    Their stillness answering his cry,
While his horse moved, cropping the dark turf,
    'Neath the starred and leafy sky;
For he suddenly smote on the door, even   25
    Louder, and lifted his head:—
'Tell them I came, and no one answered,
    That I kept my word!' he said.
Never the least stir made the listeners,
    Though every word he spake   30
Fell echoing through the shadowiness of the still house
    From the one man left awake;
Ay, they heard his foot upon the stirrup,
    And the sound of iron on stone,
And how the silence surged softly backward,   35
    When the plunging hoofs were gone.

THE SLEEPER

As Ann came in one summer's day,
    She felt that she must creep,
So silent was the clear cool house,
    It seemed a house of sleep.
And sure, when she pushed open the door,   5
    Rapt in the stillness there,
Her mother sat with stooping head,
    Asleep upon a chair;
Fast—fast asleep; her two hands laid
    Loose-folded on her knee,   10

So that her small unconscious face
   Looked half unreal to be:
So calmly lit with sleep's pale light
   Each feature was; so fair
Her forehead—every trouble was   15
   Smooth'd out beneath her hair.
But though her mind in dream now moved,
   Still seemed her gaze to rest
From out beneath her fast-sealed lids,
   Above her moving breast,   20
On Ann, as quite, quite still she stood;
   Yet slumber lay so deep
Even her hands upon her lap
   Seemed saturate with sleep.
And as Ann peeped, a cloudlike dread   25
   Stole over her, and then,
On stealthy, mouselike feet she trod,
   And tiptoed out again.

ECHO

"Who called?" I said, and the words
   Through the whispering glades,
Hither, thither, baffled the birds—
   "Who called? Who called?"

The leafy boughs on high   5
   Hissed in the sun;
The dark air carried my cry
   Faintingly on:

Eyes in the green, in the shade,
   In the motionless brake,   10
Voices that said what I said,
   For mockery's sake:

"Who cares?" I bawled through my tears;
   The wind fell low:
In the silence, "Who cares? who cares?"   15
   Wailed to and fro.

ALL THAT'S PAST

Very old are the woods;
    And the buds that break
Out of the brier's boughs,
    When March winds wake,
So old with their beauty are—   5
    Oh, no man knows
Through what wild centuries
    Roves back the rose.

Very old are the brooks;
    And the rills that rise   10
Where snow sleeps cold beneath
    The azure skies
Sing such a history
    Of come and gone,
Their every drop is as wise   15
    As Solomon.

Very old are we men;
    Our dreams are tales
Told in dim Eden
    By Eve's nightingales;   20
We wake and whisper awhile,
    But, the day gone by,
Silence and sleep like fields
    Of amaranth lie.

G. K. CHESTERTON (1874–1936)

THE ROLLING ENGLISH ROAD

Before the Roman came to Rye or out to Severn strode,
The rolling English drunkard made the rolling English road.
A reeling road, a rolling road, that rambles round the shire,
And after him the parson ran, the sexton and the squire;
A merry road, a mazy road, and such as we did tread   5
The night we went to Birmingham by way of Beachy Head.

I knew no harm of Bonaparte and plenty of the Squire,
And for to fight the Frenchman I did not much desire;
But I did bash their baggonets because they came arrayed
To straighten out the crooked road an English drunkard
    made,   10
Where you and I went down the lane with ale-mugs in our
    hands,
The night we went to Glastonbury by way of Goodwin Sands.

His sins they were forgiven him; or why do flowers run
Behind him; and the hedges all strengthening in the sun?
The wild thing went from left to right and knew not which
    was which,   15
But the wild rose was above him when they found him in the
    ditch.
God pardon us, nor harden us; we did not see so clear
The night we went to Bannockburn by way of Brighton Pier.

My friends, we will not go again or ape an ancient rage,
Or stretch the folly of our youth to be the shame of age,   20
But walk with clearer eyes and ears this path that wandereth,
And see undrugged in evening light the decent inn of death;
For there is good news yet to hear and fine things to be seen,
Before we go to Paradise by way of Kensal Green.

Kensal Green: a large cemetery in the suburbs of London.

ROBERT FROST (1875–   )

THE TUFT OF FLOWERS

I went to turn the grass once after one
Who mowed it in the dew before the sun.

The dew was gone that made his blade so keen
Before I came to view the leveled scene.

I looked for him behind an isle of trees;   5
I listened for his whetstone on the breeze.

But he had gone his way, the grass all mown,
And I must be, as he had been,—alone,

'As all must be,' I said within my heart,
'Whether they work together or apart.'   10

But as I said it, swift there passed me by
On noiseless wing a bewildered butterfly,

Seeking with memories grown dim o'er night
Some resting flower of yesterday's delight.

And once I marked his flight go round and round,   15
As where some flower lay withering on the ground.

And then he flew as far as eye could see,
And then on tremulous wing came back to me.

I thought of questions that have no reply,
And would have turned to toss the grass to dry;   20

But he turned first, and led my eye to look
At a tall tuft of flowers beside a brook,

A leaping tongue of bloom the scythe had spared
Beside a reedy brook the scythe had bared.

I left my place to know them by their name,   25
Finding them butterfly-weed when I came.

The mower in the dew had loved them thus,
By leaving them to flourish, not for us,

Nor yet to draw one thought of ours to him,
But from sheer morning gladness at the brim.   30

The butterfly and I had lit upon,
Nevertheless, a message from the dawn,

That made me hear the wakening birds around,
And hear his long scythe whispering to the ground,

And feel a spirit kindred to my own;   35
So that henceforth I worked no more alone;

But glad with him, I worked as with his aid,
And weary, sought at noon with him the shade;

And dreaming, as it were, held brotherly speech
With one whose thought I had not hoped to reach.   40

'Men work together,' I told him from the heart,
'Whether they work together or apart.'

MENDING WALL

Something there is that doesn't love a wall,
That sends the frozen-ground-swell under it,
And spills the upper boulders in the sun;
And makes gaps even two can pass abreast.
The work of hunters is another thing: 5
I have come after them and made repair
Where they have left not one stone on a stone,
But they would have the rabbit out of hiding,
To please the yelping dogs. The gaps I mean,
No one has seen them made or heard them made,   10
But at spring mending-time we find them there.
I let my neighbour know beyond the hill;
And on a day we meet to walk the line
And set the wall between us once again.
We keep the wall between us as we go.   15
To each the boulders that have fallen to each.
And some are loaves and some so nearly balls
We have to use a spell to make them balance:
"Stay where you are until our backs are turned!"
We wear our fingers rough with handling them.   20
Oh, just another kind of out-door game,
One on a side. It comes to little more:
There where it is we do not need the wall:
He is all pine and I am apple orchard.
My apple trees will never get across   25
And eat the cones under his pines, I tell him.
He only says, "Good fences make good neighbours."
Spring is the mischief in me, and I wonder
If I could put a notion in his head:
"Why do they make good neighbours? Isn't it   30

Where there are cows? But here there are no cows.
Before I built a wall I'd ask to know
What I was walling in or walling out,
And to whom I was like to give offence.
Something there is that doesn't love a wall,   35
That wants it down." I could say "Elves" to him,
But it's not elves exactly, and I'd rather
He said it for himself. I see him there
Bringing a stone grasped firmly by the top
In each hand, like an old-stone savage armed.   40
He moves in darkness as it seems to me,
Not of woods only and the shade of trees.
He will not go behind his father's saying,
And he likes having thought of it so well
He says again, "Good fences make good neighbours."   45

THE ROAD NOT TAKEN

Two roads diverged in a yellow wood,
And sorry I could not travel both
And be one traveler, long I stood
And looked down one as far as I could
To where it bent in the undergrowth;   5

Then took the other, as just as fair,
And having perhaps the better claim,
Because it was grassy and wanted wear;
Though as for that the passing there
Had worn them really about the same,   10

And both that morning equally lay
In leaves no step had trodden black.
Oh, I kept the first for another day!
Yet knowing how way leads on to way,
I doubted if I should ever come back.   15

I shall be telling this with a sigh
Somewhere ages and ages hence:
Two roads diverged in a wood, and I—
I took the one less traveled by,
And that has made all the difference.   20

THE DEATH OF THE HIRED MAN

Mary sat musing on the lamp-flame at the table
Waiting for Warren. When she heard his step,
She ran on tip-toe down the darkened passage
To meet him in the doorway with the news
And put him on his guard. "Silas is back."   5
She pushed him outward with her through the door
And shut it after her. "Be kind," she said.
She took the market things from Warren's arms
And set them on the porch, then drew him down
To sit beside her on the wooden steps.   10

"When was I ever anything but kind to him?
But I'll not have the fellow back," he said.
"I told him so last haying, didn't I?
'If he left then,' I said, 'that ended it.'
What good is he? Who else will harbor him   15
At his age for the little he can do?
What help he is there's no depending on.
Off he goes always when I need him most.
'He thinks he ought to earn a little pay,
Enough at least to buy tobacco with,   20
So he won't have to beg and be beholden.'
'All right,' I say, 'I can't afford to pay
Any fixed wages, though I wish I could.'
'Some one else can.' 'Then some one else will have to.'
I shouldn't mind his bettering himself   25
If that was what it was. You can be certain,
When he begins like that, there's some one at him
Trying to coax him off with pocket-money,—
In haying time, when any help is scarce.
In winter he comes back to us. I'm done."   30

"Sh! not so loud: he'll hear you," Mary said.

"I want him to: he'll have to soon or late."

"He's worn out. He's asleep beside the stove.
When I came up from Rowe's I found him here,
Huddled against the barn-door fast asleep,   35
A miserable sight, and frightening, too—

You needn't smile—I didn't recognize him—
I wasn't looking for him—and he's changed.
Wait till you see."

   "Where did you say he'd been?"

"He didn't say. I dragged him to the house,   40
And gave him tea and tried to make him smoke.
I tried to make him talk about his travels.
Nothing would do: he just kept nodding off."

"What did he say? Did he say anything?"

"But little."

   "Anything? Mary, confess   45
He said he'd come to ditch the meadow for me."

"Warren!"

   "But did he? I just want to know."

"Of course he did. What would you have him say?
Surely you wouldn't grudge the poor old man
Some humble way to save his self-respect.   50
He added, if you really care to know,
He meant to clear the upper pasture, too.
That sounds like something you have heard before?
Warren, I wish you could have heard the way
He jumbled everything. I stopped to look   55
Two or three times—he made me feel so queer—
To see if he was talking in his sleep.
He ran on Harold Wilson—you remember—
The boy you had in haying four years since.
He's finished school, and teaching in his college.   60
Silas declares you'll have to get him back.
He says they two will make a team for work.
Between them they will lay this farm as smooth!
The way he mixed that in with other things.
He thinks young Wilson a likely lad, though daft   65
On education—you know how they fought
All through July under the blazing sun,

Silas up on the cart to build the load,
Harold along beside to pitch it on."

"Yes, I took care to keep well out of earshot."   70

"Well, those days trouble Silas like a dream.
You wouldn't think they would. How some things linger!
Harold's young college boy's assurance piqued him.
After so many years he still keeps finding
Good arguments he sees he might have used.   75
I sympathize. I know just how it feels
To think of the right thing to say too late.
Harold's associated in his mind with Latin.
He asked me what I thought of Harold's saying
He studied Latin like the violin   80
Because he liked it—that an argument!
He said he couldn't make the boy believe
He could find water with a hazel prong—
Which showed how much good school had ever done him.
He wanted to go over that. But most of all   85
He thinks if he could have another chance
To teach him how to build a load of hay—"

"I know, that's Silas' one accomplishment.
He bundles every forkful in its place,
And tags and numbers it for future reference,   90
So he can find and easily dislodge it
In the unloading. Silas does that well.
He takes it out in bunches like big birds' nests.
You never see him standing on the hay
He's trying to lift, straining to lift himself."   95

"He thinks if he could teach him that, he'd be
Some good perhaps to some one in the world.
He hates to see a boy the fool of books.
Poor Silas, so concerned for other folk,
And nothing to look backward to with pride,   100
And nothing to look forward to with hope,
So now and never any different."

Part of a moon was falling down the west,
Dragging the whole sky with it to the hills.

Its light poured softly in her lap. She saw   105
And spread her apron to it. She put out her hand
Among the harp-like morning-glory strings,
Taut with the dew from garden bed to eaves,
As if she played unheard the tenderness
That wrought on him beside her in the night.   110
"Warren," she said, "he has come home to die:
You needn't be afraid he'll leave you this time."

"Home," he mocked gently.

      "Yes, what else but home?
It all depends on what you mean by home.
Of course he's nothing to us, any more   115
Than was the hound that came a stranger to us
Out of the woods, worn out upon the trail."

"Home is the place where, when you have to go there,
They have to take you in."

     "I should have called it
Something you somehow haven't to deserve."   120

Warren leaned out and took a step or two,
Picked up a little stick, and brought it back
And broke it in his hand and tossed it by.
"Silas has better claim on us, you think,
Than on his brother? Thirteen little miles   125
As the road winds would bring him to his door.
Silas has walked that far no doubt today.
Why didn't he go there? His brother's rich,
A somebody—director in the bank."

"He never told us that."

     "We know it though."   130

"I think his brother ought to help, of course.
I'll see to that if there is need. He ought of right
To take him in, and might be willing to—
He may be better than appearances.
But have some pity on Silas. Do you think   135

If he'd had any pride in claiming kin
Or anything he looked for from his brother,
He'd keep so still about him all this time?"

"I wonder what's between them."

                              "I can tell you.
Silas is what he is—we wouldn't mind him—   140
But just the kind that kinsfolk can't abide.
He never did a thing so very bad.
He don't know why he isn't quite as good
As any one. He won't be made ashamed
To please his brother, worthless though he is."   145

"I can't think Si ever hurt any one."

"No, but he hurt my heart the way he lay
And rolled his old head on that sharp-edged chair-back.
He wouldn't let me put him on the lounge.
You must go in and see what you can do.   150
I made the bed up for him there tonight.
You'll be surprised at him—how much he's broken.
His working days are done; I'm sure of it."

"I'd not be in a hurry to say that."

"I haven't been. Go, look, see for yourself.   155
But, Warren, please remember how it is:
He's come to help you ditch the meadow.
He has a plan. You mustn't laugh at him.
He may not speak of it, and then he may.
I'll sit and see if that small sailing cloud   160
Will hit or miss the moon."

                        It hit the moon.
Then there were three there, making a dim row,
The moon, the little silver cloud, and she.

Warren returned—too soon, it seemed to her,
Slipped to her side, caught up her hand and waited.   165

"Warren," she questioned.

                      "Dead," was all he answered.

THE WOOD-PILE

Out walking in the frozen swamp one gray day
I paused and said, "I will turn back from here.
No, I will go on farther—and we shall see."
The hard snow held me, save where now and then
One foot went through. The view was all in lines   5
Straight up and down of tall slim trees
Too much alike to mark or name a place by
So as to say for certain I was here
Or somewhere else: I was just far from home.
A small bird flew before me. He was careful   10
To put a tree between us when he lighted,
And say no word to tell me who he was
Who was so foolish as to think what *he* thought.
He thought that I was after him for a feather—
The white one in his tail; like one who takes   15
Everything said as personal to himself.
One flight out sideways would have undeceived him.
And then there was a pile of wood for which
I forgot him and let his little fear
Carry him off the way I might have gone,   20
Without so much as wishing him good-night.
He went behind it to make his last stand.
It was a cord of maple, cut and split
And piled—and measured, four by four by eight.
And not another like it could I see.   25
No runner tracks in this year's snow looped near it.
And it was older sure than this year's cutting,
Or even last year's or the year's before.
The wood was gray and the bark warping off it
And the pile somewhat sunken. Clematis   30
Had wound strings round and round it like a bundle.
What held it though on one side was a tree
Still growing, and on one a stake and prop,
These latter about to fall. I thought that only
Someone who lived in turning to fresh tasks   35
Could so forget his handiwork on which
He spent himself, the labour of his axe,
And leave it there far from a useful fireplace
To warm the frozen swamp as best it could
With the slow smokeless burning of decay.   40

A SOLDIER

He is that fallen lance that lies as hurled,
That lies unlifted now, come dew, come rust,
But still lies pointed as it ploughed the dust.
If we who sight along it round the world,
See nothing worthy to have been its mark,
It is because like men we look too near,
Forgetting that as fitted to the sphere,
Our missiles always make too short an arc.
They fall, they rip the grass, they intersect
The curve of earth, and striking, break their own;
They make us cringe for metal-point on stone.
But this we know, the obstacle that checked
And tripped the body, shot the spirit on
Farther than target ever showed or shone.

DIRECTIVE

Back out of all this now too much for us,
Back in a time made simple by the loss
Of detail, burned, dissolved, and broken off
Like a graveyard marble sculpture in the weather,
There is a house that is no more a house   5
Upon a farm that is no more a farm
And in a town that is no more a town.
The road there, if you'll let a guide direct you
Who only has at heart your getting lost,
May seem as if it should have been a quarry—   10
Great monolithic knees the former town
Long since gave up pretence of keeping covered.
And there's a story in a book about it:
Besides the wear of iron wagon wheels
The ledges show lines ruled southeast northwest, 15
The chisel work of an enormous Glacier
That braced his feet against the Arctic Pole.
You must not mind a certain coolness from him
Still said to haunt this side of Panther Mountain.
Nor need you mind the serial ordeal   20

Of being watched from forty cellar holes
As if by eye pairs out of forty firkins.
As for the woods' excitement over you
That sends light rustle rushes to their leaves,
Charge that to upstart inexperience. 25
Where were they all not twenty years ago?
They think too much of having shaded out
A few old pecker-fretted apple trees.
Make yourself up a cheering song of how
Someone's road home from work this once was, 30
Who may be just ahead of you on foot
Or creaking with a buggy load of grain.
The height of the adventure is the height
Of country where two village cultures faded
Into each other. Both of them are lost. 35
And if you're lost enough to find yourself
By now, pull in your ladder road behind you
And put a sign up CLOSED to all but me.
Then make yourself at home. The only field
Now left's no bigger than a harness gall. 40
First there's the children's house of make believe,
Some shattered dishes underneath a pine,
The playthings in the playhouse of the children.
Weep for what little things could make them glad.
Then for the house that is no more a house, 45
But only a belilaced cellar hole,
Now slowly closing like a dent in dough.
This was no playhouse but a house in earnest.
Your destination and your destiny's
A brook that was the water of the house, 50
Cold as a spring as yet so near its source,
Too lofty and original to rage.
(We know the valley streams that when aroused
Will leave their tatters hung on barb and thorn.)
I have kept hidden in the instep arch 55
Of an old cedar at the waterside
A broken drinking goblet like the Grail
Under a spell so the wrong ones can't find it,
So can't get saved, as Saint Mark says they mustn't.
(I stole the goblet from the children's playhouse.) 60
Here are your waters and your watering place.
Drink and be whole again beyond confusion.

DESIGN

I found a dimpled spider, fat and white,
On a white heal-all, holding up a moth
Like a white piece of rigid satin cloth—
Assorted characters of death and blight
Mixed ready to begin the morning right,
Like the ingredients of a witch's broth—
A snow-drop spider, a flower like froth,
And dead wings carried like a paper kite.

What had that flower to do with being white,
The wayside blue and innocent heal-all?
What brought the kindred spider to that height,
Then steered the white moth thither in the night?
What but design of darkness to appall?—
If design govern in a thing so small.

JOHN MASEFIELD (1878–   )

THE YARN OF THE LOCH ACHRAY

The "Loch Achray" was a clipper tall
With seven-and-twenty hands in all.
Twenty to hand and reef and haul,
A skipper to sail and mates to bawl
"Tally on to the tackle-fall,   5
Heave now 'n' start her, heave 'n' pawl!"
        Hear the yarn of a sailor,
        An old yarn learned at sea.

Her crew were shipped and they said "Farewell,
So-long, my Tottie, my lovely gell;   10
We sail to-day if we fetch to hell,
It's time we tackled the wheel a spell."
        Hear the yarn of a sailor,
        An old yarn learned at sea.

The dockside loafers talked on the quay 15
The day that she towed down to sea:
"Lord, what a handsome ship she be!
Cheer her, sonny boys, three times three!"
And the dockside loafers gave her a shout
As the red-funnelled tug-boat towed her out; 20
They gave her a cheer as the custom is,
And the crew yelled "Take our loves to Liz—
Three cheers, bullies, for old Pier Head
'N' the bloody stay-at-homes!" they said.
  Hear the yarn of a sailor, 25
  An old yarn learned at sea.

In the grey of the coming on of night
She dropped the tug at the Tuskar Light,
'N' the topsails went to the topmast head
To a chorus that fairly awoke the dead. 30
She trimmed her yards and slanted South
With her royals set and a bone in her mouth.
  Hear the yarn of a sailor,
  An old yarn learned at sea.

She crossed the Line and all went well, 35
They ate, they slept, and they struck the bell
And I give you a gospel truth when I state
The crowd didn't find any fault with the Mate,
But one night off the River Plate.
  Hear the yarn of a sailor, 40
  An old yarn learned at sea.

It freshened up till it blew like thunder
And burrowed her deep lee-scuppers under.
The old man said, "I mean to hang on
Till her canvas busts or her sticks are gone"— 45
Which the blushing looney did, till at last
Overboard went her mizzen-mast.
  Hear the yarn of a sailor,
  An old yarn learned at sea.

Then a fierce squall struck the "Loch Achray" 50
And bowed her down to her water-way;

Her main-shrouds gave and her forestay,
And a green sea carried her wheel away;
Ere the watch below had time to dress,
She was cluttered up in a blushing mess.   55
  Hear the yarn of a sailor,
  An old yarn learned at sea.

She couldn't lay to nor yet pay-off,
And she got swept clean in the bloody trough;
Her masts were gone, and afore you knowed   60
She filled by the head, and down she goed.
Her crew made seven-and-twenty dishes
For the big jack-sharks and the little fishes,
And over their bones the water swishes.
  Hear the yarn of a sailor,   65
  An old yarn learned at sea.

The wives and girls they watch in the rain
For a ship as won't come home again.
"I reckon it's them head-winds," they say,
"She'll be home to-morrow, if not to-day.   70
I'll just nip home 'n' I'll air the sheets
'N' buy the fixins 'n' cook the meats
As my man likes 'n' as my man eats."
So home they goes by the windy streets,
Thinking their men are homeward bound   75
With anchors hungry for English ground,
And the bloody fun of it is, they're drowned!
  Hear the yarn of a sailor,
  An old yarn learned at sea.

CARGOES

Quinquireme of Nineveh from distant Ophir,
Rowing home to haven in sunny Palestine,
With a cargo of ivory,
And apes and peacocks,
Sandalwood, cedarwood, and sweet white wine.   5

Stately Spanish galleon coming from the Isthmus,
Dipping through the Tropics by the palm-green shores,
With a cargo of diamonds,
Emeralds, amethysts,
Topazes, and cinnamon, and gold moidores.   10

Dirty British coaster with a salt-caked smoke-stack,
Butting through the Channel in the mad March days,
With a cargo of Tyne coal,
Road-rails, pig-lead,
Firewood, iron-ware, and cheap tin trays.   15

CARL SANDBURG (1878–   )

FOUR PRELUDES ON PLAYTHINGS OF THE WIND

"The past is a bucket of ashes."

1

The woman named To-morrow
sits with a hairpin in her teeth
and takes her time
and does her hair the way she wants it
and fastens at last the last braid and coil   5
and puts the hairpin where it belongs
and turns and drawls: Well, what of it?
My grandmother, Yesterday, is gone.
What of it? Let the dead be dead.

2

The doors were cedar   10
and the panels strips of gold
and the girls were golden girls
and the panels read and the girls chanted:
      We are the greatest city,
      the greatest nation: 15
      nothing like us ever was.

The doors are twisted on broken hinges.
Sheets of rain swish through on the wind
where the golden girls ran and the panels read:
    We are the greatest city,   20
    the greatest nation:
    nothing like us ever was.

3

It has happened before.
Strong men put up a city and got
    a nation together,   25
And paid singers to sing and women
    to warble: We are the greatest city,
        the greatest nation:
        nothing like us ever was.

And while the singers sang   30
and the strong men listened
and paid the singers well
and felt good about it all,
    there were rats and lizards who listened
    . . . and the only listeners left now   35
    . . . are . . . the rats . . . and the lizards.

And there are black crows
crying, "Caw, caw,"
bringing mud and sticks
building a nest   40
    over the words carved
    on the doors where the panels were cedar
    and the strips on the panels were gold
    and the golden girls came singing:
        We are the greatest city,   45
        the greatest nation:
        nothing like us ever was.

The only singers now are crows crying, "Caw, caw,"
And the sheets of rain whine in the wind and doorways.
And the only listeners now are . . . the rats . . . and   50
    the lizards.

4

The feet of the rats
scribble on the doorsills;
the hieroglyphs of the rat footprints
chatter the pedigrees of the rats   55
and babble of the blood
and gabble of the breed
of the grandfathers and the great-grandfathers
of the rats.

And the wind shifts   60
and the dust on a doorsill shifts
and even the writing of the rat footprints
tells us nothing, nothing at all
about the greatest city, the greatest nation
where the strong men listened   65
and the women warbled: Nothing like us ever was.

VACHEL LINDSAY (1879–1931)

GENERAL WILLIAM BOOTH ENTERS INTO HEAVEN

To be sung to the tune of THE BLOOD OF THE LAMB
with indicated instruments.

[*Bass drum beaten loudly*]
Booth led boldly with his big bass drum,
    Are you washed in the blood of the Lamb?
The saints smiled gravely, and they said,
        "He's come."
    Are you washed in the blood of the Lamb?   5
Walking lepers followed, rank on rank,
Lurching bravos from the ditches dank,
Drabs from the alleyways and drug-fiends pale—
Minds still passion-ridden, soul-powers frail!

[*Banjos*]
Vermin-eaten saints with moldy breath   10
Unwashed legions with the ways of death—
    Are you washed in the blood of the Lamb?

Every slum had sent its half-a-score
The round world over—Booth had groaned for more.
Every banner that the wide world flies   15
Bloomed with glory and transcendent dyes.
Big-voiced lasses made their banjos bang!
Tranced, fanatical, they shrieked and sang,
    Are you washed in the blood of the Lamb?
Hallelujah! It was queer to see   20
Bull-necked convicts with that land make free!
Loons with bazoos blowing blare, blare, blare—
On, on, upward through the golden air.
    Are you washed in the blood of the Lamb?

[*Bass drum slower and softer*]
Booth died blind, and still by faith he trod,   25
Eyes still dazzled by the ways of God.
Booth led boldly and he looked the chief:
Eagle countenance in sharp relief,
Beard a-flying, air of high command
Unabated in that holy land.   30

[*Sweet flute music*]
Jesus came from out the Courthouse door,
Stretched his hands above the passing poor.
Booth saw not, but led his queer ones there
Round and round the mighty Courthouse square.
Yet in an instant all that blear review   35
Marched on spotless, clad in raiment new.
The lame were straightened, withered limbs uncurled,
And blind eyes opened on a new sweet world.

[*Bass drum louder*]
Drabs and vixens in a flash made whole!
Gone was the weasel-head, the snout, the jowl;   40
Sages and sibyls now, and athletes clean,
Rulers of empires, and of forests green!

[*Grand chorus of all instruments. Tambourines to
    the foreground*]
The hosts were sandaled and their wings were fire—
    Are you washed in the blood of the Lamb?
But their noise played havoc with the angel-choir.   45

Are you washed in the blood of the Lamb?
Oh, shout Salvation! it was good to see
Kings and princes by the Lamb set free.
The banjos rattled and the tambourines
Jing-jing-jingled in the hands of queens!   50

[Reverently sung, no instruments]
And when Booth halted by the curb for prayer
He saw his Master through the flag-filled air.
Christ came gently with a robe and crown
For Booth the soldier while the throng knelt down.
He saw King Jesus—they were face to face,   55
And he knelt a-weeping in that holy place.
Are you washed in the blood of the Lamb?

WALLACE STEVENS (1879–1955)

SUNDAY MORNING

I

Complacencies of the peignoir, and late
Coffee and oranges in a sunny chair,
And the green freedom of a cockatoo
Upon a rug mingle to dissipate
The holy hush of ancient sacrifice.   5
She dreams a little, and she feels the dark
Encroachment of that old catastrophe,
As a calm darkens among water-lights.
The pungent oranges and bright, green wings
Seem things in some procession of the dead,   10
Winding across wide water, without sound.
The day is like wide water, without sound,
Stilled for the passing of her dreaming feet
Over the seas, to silent Palestine,
Dominion of the blood and sepulchre.   15

II

Why should she give her bounty to the dead?
What is divinity if it can come
Only in silent shadows and in dreams?
Shall she not find in comforts of the sun,

In pungent fruit and bright, green wings, or else   20
In any balm or beauty of the earth,
Things to be cherished like the thought of heaven?
Divinity must live within herself:
Passions of rain, or moods in falling snow;
Grievings in loneliness, or unsubdued   25
Elations when the forest blooms; gusty
Emotions on wet roads on autumn nights;
All pleasures and all pains, remembering
The bough of summer and the winter branch.
These are the measures destined for her soul.   30

III

Jove in the clouds had his inhuman birth.
No mother suckled him, no sweet land gave
Large-mannered motions to his mythy mind.
He moved among us, as a muttering king,
Magnificent, would move among his hinds,   35
Until our blood, commingling, virginal,
With heaven, brought such requital to desire
The very hinds discerned it in a star.
Shall our blood fail? Or shall it come to be
The blood of paradise? And shall the earth   40
Seem all of paradise that we shall know?
The sky will be much friendlier then than now,
A part of labor and a part of pain,
And next in glory to enduring love,
Not this dividing and indifferent blue.   45

IV

She says, "I am content when wakened birds,
Before they fly, test the reality
Of misty fields, by their sweet questionings;
But when the birds are gone, and their warm fields
Return no more, where, then, is paradise?"   50
There is not any haunt of prophecy,
Nor any old chimera of the grave,
Neither the golden underground, nor isle
Melodious, where spirits gat them home,
Nor visionary south, nor cloudy palm   55
Remote on heaven's hill, that has endured

As April's green endures; or will endure
Like her remembrance of awakened birds,
Or her desire for June and evening, tipped
By the consummation of the swallow's wings.   60

V

She says, "But in contentment I still feel
The need of some imperishable bliss."
Death is the mother of beauty; hence from her,
Alone, shall come fulfilment to our dreams
And our desires. Although she strews the leaves   65
Of sure obliteration on our paths,
The path sick sorrow took, the many paths
Where triumph rang its brassy phrase, or love
Whispered a little out of tenderness,
She makes the willow shiver in the sun   70
For maidens who were wont to sit and gaze
Upon the grass, relinquished to their feet.
She causes boys to pile new plums and pears
On disregarded plate. The maidens taste
And stray impassioned in the littering leaves.   75

VI

Is there no change of death in paradise?
Does ripe fruit never fall? Or do the boughs
Hang always heavy in that perfect sky,
Unchanging, yet so like our perishing earth,
With rivers like our own that seek for seas   80
They never find, the same receding shores
That never touch with inarticulate pang?
Why set the pear upon those river-banks
Or spice the shores with odors of the plum?
Alas, that they should wear our colors there,   85
The silken weavings of our afternoons,
And pick the strings of our insipid lutes!
Death is the mother of beauty, mystical,
Within whose burning bosom we devise
Our earthly mothers waiting, sleeplessly.   90

VII

Supple and turbulent, a ring of men
Shall chant in orgy on a summer morn

Their boisterous devotion to the sun,
Not as a god, but as a god might be,
Naked among them, like a savage source.   95
Their chant shall be a chant of paradise,
Out of their blood, returning to the sky;
And in their chant shall enter, voice by voice,
The windy lake wherein their lord delights,
The trees, like serafim, and echoing hills,   100
That choir among themselves long afterward.
They shall know well the heavenly fellowship
Of men that perish and of summer morn.
And whence they came and whither they shall go
The dew upon their feet shall manifest.   105

VIII

She hears, upon that water without sound,
A voice that cries, "The tomb in Palestine
Is not the porch of spirits lingering.
It is the grave of Jesus, where he lay."
We live in an old chaos of the sun,   110
Or old dependency of day and night,
Or island solitude, unsponsored, free,
Of that wide water, inescapable.
Deer walk upon our mountains, and the quail
Whistle about us their spontaneous cries;   115
Sweet berries ripen in the wilderness;
And, in the isolation of the sky,
At evening, casual flocks of pigeons make
Ambiguous undulations as they sink,
Downward to darkness, on extended wings.   120

BANTAMS IN PINE WOODS

Chieftain Iffucan of Azcan in caftan
Of tan with henna hackles, halt!

Damned universal cock, as if the sun
Was blackamoor to bear your blazing tail.

Fat! Fat! Fat! Fat! I am the personal.
Your world is you. I am my world.

You ten-foot poet among inchlings. Fat!
Begone! An inchling bristles in these pines,

Bristles, and points their Appalachian tangs,
And fears not portly Azcan nor his hoos.

DANCE OF THE MACABRE MICE

In the land of turkeys in turkey weather
At the base of the statue, we go round and round.
What a beautiful history, beautiful surprise!
Monsieur is on horseback. The horse is covered with mice.

This dance has no name. It is a hungry dance.
We dance it out to the tip of Monsieur's sword,
Reading the lordly language of the inscription,
Which is like zithers and tambourines combined:

The Founder of the State. Whoever founded
A state that was free, in the dead of winter, from mice?
What a beautiful tableau tinted and towering,
The arm of bronze outstretched against all evil!

WILLIAM CARLOS WILLIAMS (1883–   )

A SORT OF A SONG

Let the snake wait under
his weed
and the writing
be of words, slow and quick, sharp
to strike, quiet to wait,
sleepless.

—through metaphor to reconcile
the people and the stones.
Compose. (No ideas
but in things) Invent!
Saxifrage is my flower that splits
the rocks.

THE YACHTS

contend in a sea which the land partly encloses
shielding them from the too heavy blows
of an ungoverned ocean which when it chooses

tortures the biggest hulls, the best man knows
to pit against its beating, and sinks them pitilessly.   5
Mothlike in mists, scintillant in the minute

brilliance of cloudless days, with broad bellying sails
they glide to the wind tossing green water
from their sharp prows while over them the crew crawls

ant-like, solicitously grooming them, releasing,   10
making fast as they turn, lean far over and having
caught the wind again, side by side, head for the mark.

In a well guarded arena of open water surrounded by
lesser and greater craft which, sycophant, lumbering
and flittering follow them, they appear youthful, rare   15

as the light of a happy eye, live with the grace
of all that in the mind is feckless, free and
naturally to be desired. Now the sea which holds them

is moody, lapping their glossy sides, as if feeling
for some slightest flaw but fails completely.   20
Today no race. Then the wind comes again. The yachts

move, jockeying for a start, the signal is set and they
are off. Now the waves strike at them but they are too
well made, they slip through, though they take in canvas.

Arms with hands grasping seek to clutch at the prows.   25
Bodies thrown recklessly in the way are cut aside.
It is a sea of faces about them in agony, in despair

until the horror of the race dawns staggering the mind,
the whole sea become an entanglement of watery bodies
lost to the world bearing what they cannot hold. Broken,   30

beaten, desolate, reaching from the dead to be taken up
they cry out, failing, failing! their cries rising
in waves still as the skillful yachts pass over.

A UNISON

The grass is very green, my friend,
and tousled, like the head of—
your grandson, yes? And the mountain,
the mountain we climbed
twenty years since for the last   5
time (I write this thinking
of you) is saw-horned as then
upon the sky's edge—an old barn
is peaked there also, fatefully,
against the sky. And there it is   10
and we can't shift it or change
it or parse it or alter it
in any way. Listen! Do you not hear
them? the singing? There it is and
we'd better acknowledge it and   15
write it down that way, not otherwise.
Not twist the words to mean
what we should have said but to mean
—what cannot be escaped: the
mountain riding the afternoon as   20
it does, the grass matted green,
green underfoot and the air—
rotten wood. Hear! Hear them!
the Undying. The hill slopes away,
then rises in the middleground,   25
you remember, with a grove of gnarled
maples centering the bare pasture,
sacred, surely—for what reason?
I cannot say. Idyllic!
a shrine cinctured there by   30
the trees, a certainty of music!
a unison and a dance, joined
at this death's festival: Something
of a shed snake's skin, the beginning
goldenrod. Or, best, a white stone,   35

you have seen it: *Mathilda Maria*
Fox—and near the ground's lip,
all but undecipherable, *Aet Suae,*
Anno 9—still there, the grass
dripping of last night's rain—and   40
welcome! The thin air, the near,
clear brook water!—and could not,
and died, unable; to escape
what the air and the wet grass—
through which, tomorrow, bejewelled,   45
the great sun will rise—the
unchanging mountains, forced on them—
and they received, willingly!
Stones, stones of a difference
joining the others at peace. Hear!   50
Hear the unison of their voices. . . .

TO A DOG INJURED IN THE STREET

IT IS MYSELF,
     not the poor beast lying there
          yelping with pain
that brings me to myself with a start—
     as at the explosion   5
          of a bomb, a bomb that has laid
all the world waste.
     I can do nothing
          but sing about it
and so I am assuaged   10
     from my pain.

A DROWSY NUMBNESS drowns my sense
     as if of hemlock
          I had drunk. I think
of the poetry   15
     of René Char
          and all he must have seen
and suffered
     that has brought him
          to speak only of   20

sedgy rivers,
    of daffodils and tulips
        whose roots they water,
even to the freeflowing river
    that laves the rootlets   25
        of those sweet scented flowers
that people the
    milky
        way

I REMEMBER Norma   30
    our English setter of my childhood
        her silky ears
and expressive eyes.
    She had a litter
        of pups one night   35
in our pantry and I kicked
    one of them
        thinking, in my alarm,
that they
    were biting her breasts
        to destroy her.

I REMEMBER also
    a dead rabbit
        lying harmlessly   45
on the outspread palm
    of a hunter's hand.
        As I stood by
watching
    he took a hunting knife   50
        and with a laugh
thrust it
    up into the animal's private parts.
        I almost fainted.

WHY SHOULD I think of that now?   55
    The cries of a dying dog
        are to be blotted out
as best I can.
    René Char
        you are a poet who believes   60

> in the power of beauty
> > to right all wrongs.
> > > I believe it also.
> With invention and courage
> > we shall surpass 65
> > > the pitiful dumb beasts,
> let all men believe it,
> > as you have taught me also
> > > to believe it.

D. H. LAWRENCE (1885–1930)

SONG OF A MAN WHO HAS COME THROUGH

Not I, not I, but the wind that blows through me!
A fine wind is blowing the new direction of Time.
If only I let it bear me, carry me, if only it carry me!
If only I am sensitive, subtle, oh, delicate, a winged gift!
If only, most lovely of all, I yield myself and am borrowed   5
By the fine, fine wind that takes its course through the
    chaos of the world
Like a fine, an exquisitive chisel, a wedge-blade inserted;
If only I am keen and hard like the sheer tip of a wedge
Driven by invisible blows,
The rock will split, we shall come at the wonder, we shall
    find the Hesperides.   10

Oh, for the wonder that bubbles into my soul,
I would be a good fountain, a good well-head,
Would blur no whisper, spoil no expression.

What is the knocking?
What is the knocking at the door in the night?   15
It is somebody wants to do us harm.

No, no, it is the three strange angels.
Admit them, admit them.

SNAKE

A snake came to my water-trough
On a hot, hot day, and I in pyjamas for the heat,
To drink there.

In the deep, strange-scented shade of the great dark
    carob-tree
I came down the steps with my pitcher   5
And must wait, must stand and wait, for there he was at
    the trough before me.

He reached down from a fissure in the earth-wall in the
    gloom
And trailed his yellow-brown slackness soft-bellied down,
    over the edge of the stone trough
And rested his throat upon the stone bottom,
And where the water had dripped from the tap, in a
    small clearness,   10
He sipped with his straight mouth,
Softly drank through his straight gums, into his slack long
    body,
Silently.

Someone was before me at my water-trough,
And I, like a second comer, waiting.   15

He lifted his head from his drinking, as cattle do,
And looked at me vaguely, as drinking cattle do,
And flickered his two-forked tongue from his lips, and
    mused a moment,
And stooped and drank a little more,
Being earth-brown, earth-golden from the burning burning
    bowels of the earth   20
On the day of Sicilian July, with Etna smoking.

The voice of my education said to me
He must be killed,
For in Sicily the black, black snakes are innocent, the gold
    are venomous.

And voices in me said, If you were a man   25
You would take a stick and break him now, and finish
    him off.

But must I confess how I liked him,
How glad I was he had come like a guest in quiet, to drink
    at my water-trough
And depart peaceful, pacified, and thankless,
Into the burning bowels of this earth?   30

Was it cowardice, that I dared not kill him?
Was it perversity, that I longed to talk to him?
Was it humility, to feel so honoured?
I felt so honoured.

And yet those voices: 35
If you were not afraid, you would kill him!

And truly I was afraid, I was most afraid,
But even so, honoured still more
That he should seek my hospitality
From out the dark door of the secret earth.   40

He drank enough
And lifted his head, dreamily, as one who has drunken,
And flickered his tongue like a forked night on the air, so
    black,
Seeming to lick his lips,
And looked around like a god, unseeing, into the air,   45
And slowly turned his head,
And slowly, very slowly, as if thrice adream,
Proceeded to draw his slow length curving round
And climb again the broken bank of my wall-face.

And as he put his head into that dreadful hole,   50
And as he slowly drew up, snake-easing his shoulders, and
    entered farther,
A sort of horror, a sort of protest against his withdrawing
    into that horrid black hole,
Deliberately going into the blackness, and slowly drawing
    himself after,
Overcame me now his back was turned.

I looked round, I put down my pitcher,   55
I picked up a clumsy log
And threw it at the water-trough with a clatter.

I think it did not hit him,
But suddenly that part of him that was left behind convulsed
    in undignified haste,
Writhed like lightning, and was gone   60
Into the black hole, the earth-lipped fissure in the wallfront,
At which, in the intense still noon, I stared with fascination.

And immediately I regretted it.
I thought how paltry, how vulgar, what a mean act!
I despised myself and the voices of my accursed human
    education.   65

And I thought of the albatross,
And I wished he would come back, my snake.

For he seemed to me again like a king,
Like a king in exile, uncrowned in the underworld,
Now due to be crowned again.   70

And so, I missed my chance with one of the lords
Of life.
And I have something to expiate;
A pettiness.

BAVARIAN GENTIANS

Not every man has gentians in his house
in Soft September, at slow, Sad Michaelmas.

Bavarian gentians, big and dark, only dark
darkening the day-time torch-like with the smoking
    blueness of Pluto's gloom,
ribbed and torch-like, with their blaze of darkness
    spread blue   5
down flattening into points, flattened under the sweep
    of white day
torch-flower of the blue-smoking darkness, Pluto's
    dark-blue daze,

black lamps from the halls of Dio, burning dark blue,
giving off darkness, blue darkness, as Demeter's pale
    lamps give off light,
lead me then, lead me the way.   10

Reach me a gentian, give me a torch
let me guide myself with the blue, forked torch of this
    flower
down the darker and darker stairs, where blue is darkened
    on blueness,
even where Persephone goes, just now, from the frosted
    September
to the sightless realm where darkness is awake upon the
    dark   15
and Persephone herself is but a voice
or a darkness invisible enfolded in the deeper dark
of the arms Plutonic, and pierced with the passion of
    dense gloom,
among the splendour of torches of darkness, shedding
    darkness on the lost bride and her groom.

EZRA POUND (1885–   )

EXILE'S LETTER

To So-Kin of Rakuyo, ancient friend, Chancellor of Gen.
Now I remember that you built me a special tavern
By the south side of the bridge at Ten-Shin.
With yellow gold and white jewels, we paid for songs and
    laughter
And we were drunk for month on month, forgetting the
    kings and princes.   5
Intelligent men came drifting in from the sea and from
    the west border,
And with them, and with you especially
There was nothing at cross purpose,
And they made nothing of sea-crossing or of mountain-
    crossing,
If only they could be of that fellowship,   10
And we all spoke out our hearts and minds, and without
    regret.
And then I was sent off to South Wei,
    smothered in laurel groves,

And you to the north of Raku-hoku
Till we had nothing but thoughts and memories in common.
And then, when separation had come to its worst,   15
We met, and travelled into Sen-Go,
Through all the thirty-six folds of the turning and twisting
    waters,
Into a valley of the thousand bright flowers,
That was the first valley;
And into ten thousand valleys full of voices and pine-
    winds.   20
And with silver harness and reins of gold,
Out came the East of Kan foreman and his company.
And there came also the 'True man' of Shi-yo to meet me,
Playing on a jewelled mouth-organ.
In the storied houses of San-Ko they gave us more
    Sennin music,   25
Many instruments, like the sound of young phoenix broods.
The foreman of Kan Chu, drunk, danced
        because his long sleeves wouldn't keep still
With that music playing,
And I, wrapped in brocade, went to sleep with my head
    on his lap,
And my spirit so high it was all over the heavens,   30
And before the end of the day we were scatttered like
    stars, or rain.
I had to be off to So, far away over the waters,
You back to your river-bridge.
And your father, who was brave as a leopard,
Was governor in Hei Shu, and put down the barbarian
    rabble.   35
And one May he had you send for me,
        despite the long distance.
And what with broken wheels and so on, I won't say it
    wasn't hard going,
Over roads twisted like sheep's guts.
And I was still going, late in the year,
        in the cutting wind from the North,
And thinking how little you cared for the cost,
        and you caring enough to pay it.   40
And what a reception:
Red jade cups, food well set on a blue jewelled table,
And I was drunk, and had no thought of returning.

And you would walk out with me to the western
   corner of the castle,
To the dynastic temple, with water about it clear as blue
   jade,   45
With boats floating, and the sound of mouth-organs and
   drums,
With ripples like dragon-scales, going grass-green on the
   water,
Pleasure lasting, with courtesans, going and coming without
   hindrance,
With the willow flakes falling like snow,
And the vermilioned girls getting drunk about sunset,   50
And the water, a hundred feet deep, reflecting green
   eyebrows
—Eyebrows painted green are a fine sight in young moon-
   light,
Gracefully painted—
And the girls singing back at each other,   55
Dancing in transparent brocade,
And the wind lifting the song, and interrupting it,
Tossing it up under the clouds.
     And all this comes to an end.
     And is not again to be met with.
I went up to the court for examination,   60
Tried Layu's luck, offered the Choyo song,
And got no promotion,
     and went back to the East Mountains
     White-headed.
And once again, later, we met at the South bridgehead.   65
And then the crowd broke up, you went north to San
   palace,
And if you ask how I regret that parting:
It is like the flowers falling at Spring's end
     Confused, whirled in a tangle.
What is the use of talking, and there is no end of
   talking,
There is no end of things in the heart.   70
I call in the boy,
Have him sit on his knees here
     To seal this,
And send it a thousand miles, thinking.   75

                     By Rihaku

HUGH SELWYN MAUBERLEY

(LIFE AND CONTACTS)

"VOCAT AESTUS IN UMBRAM"
Nemesianus, Ec. IV

I

E. P. ODE POUR L'ELECTION DE SON SEPULCHRE

For three years, out of key with his time,
He strove to resuscitate the dead art
Of poetry; to maintain "the sublime"
In the old sense. Wrong from the start—

No hardly, but seeing he had been born   5
In a half savage country, out of date;
Bent resolutely on wringing lilies from the acorn;
Capaneus; trout for factitious bait;

Ἴδμεν γάρ τοι πάνθ', ὅσ ἐνὶ Τροίη
Caught in the unstopped ear;   10
Giving the rocks small lee-way
The chopped seas held him, therefore, that year.

His true Penelope was Flaubert,
He fished by obstinate isles;
Observed the elegance of Circe's hair   15
Rather than the mottoes on sun-dials.

Unaffected by "the march of events,"
He passed from men's memory in l'an trentiesme
De son eage; the case presents
No adjunct to the Muses' diadem.   20

8. **Capaneus:** one of the seven heroes who attacked Thebes, struck by a thunderbolt from Zeus.
9. **For we know all things that in Troy [the heroes endured]:** part of the song of the Sirens, Odyssey xii, 189.
18-19. In the thirtieth year of his life—paraphrased from Villon.

II

The age demanded an image
Of its accelerated grimace,
Something for the modern stage,
Not, at any rate, an attic grace;

Not, not certainly, the obscure reveries   25
Of the inward gaze;
Better mendacities
Than the classics in paraphrase!

The 'age demanded' chiefly a mould in plaster,
Made with no loss of time,   30
A prose kinema, not, not assuredly, alabaster
Or the 'sculpture' of rhyme.

III

The tea-rose tea-gown, etc.
Supplants the mousseline of Cos,   35
The pianola 'replaces'
Sappho's barbitos.

Christ follows Dionysus,
Phallic and ambrosial
Made way for macerations;   40
Caliban casts out Ariel.

All things are a flowing,
Sage Heracleitus says;
But a tawdry cheapness
Shall outlast our days.

Even the Christian beauty   45
Defects—after Samothrace;
We see τὸ καλὸν
Decreed in the market place.

Faun's flesh is not to us,
Nor the saint's vision.   50
We have the press for wafer;
Franchise for circumcision.

47. **To Kalon:** the Beautiful

All men, in law, are equals.
Free of Pisistratus,
We choose a knave or an eunuch   55
To rule over us.

O bright Apollo,
τίν' ἄνδρα, τίν ἥρωα, τίνα θεὸν,
What god, man, or hero
Shall I place a tin wreath upon!   60

IV

These fought in any case,
and some believing,
                              pro domo, in any case . . .

Some quick to arm,   65
some for adventure,
some from fear of weakness,
some from fear of censure,
some for love of slaughter, in imagination,
learning later . . .
some in fear, learning love of slaughter;   70

Died some, pro patria,
                    non "dulce" non "et decor" . . .
walked eye-deep in hell
believing in old men's lies, then unbelieving
came home, home to a lie,   75
home to many deceits,
home to old lies and new infamy;
usury age-old and age-thick
and liars in public places.

Daring as never before, wastage as never before.   80
Young blood and high blood,
fair cheeks, and fine bodies;

fortitude as never before

58. **Tin andra, tin heroa, tina theon:** what man, what hero, what god? (note the bitter pun on "tin wreath").

71–72. A reference to Horace's famous lines "*Dulce et decorum est pro patria mori*" (Sweet and fitting it is to die for one's country), *Odes III*, ii, 13.

frankness as never before,
disillusions as never told in the old days,   85
hysterias, trench confessions,
laughter out of dead bellies.

V

There died a myriad,
And of the best, among them,
For an old bitch gone in the teeth,   90
For a botched civilization,

Charm, smiling at the good mouth,
Quick eyes gone under earth's lid,

For two gross of broken statues,
For a few thousand battered books.   95

CANTO I

And then went down to the ship,
Set keel to breakers, forth on the godly sea, and
We set up mast and sail on that swart ship,
Bore sheep aboard her, and our bodies also
Heavy with weeping, and winds from sternward   5
Bore us out onward with bellying canvas,
Circe's this craft, the trim-coifed goddess.
Then sat we amidships, wind jamming the tiller,
Thus with stretched sail, we went over sea till day's end.
Sun to his slumber, shadows o'er all the ocean,   10
Came we then to the bounds of deepest water,
To the Kimmerian lands, and peopled cities
Covered with close-webbed mist, unpierced ever
With glitter of sun·ray
Nor with stars stretched, nor looking back from heaven   15
Swartest night stretched over wretched men there.
The ocean flowing backward, came we then to the place
Aforesaid by Circe.
Here did they rites, Perimedes and Eurylochus,
And drawing sword from my hip   20
I dug the ell-square pitkin;
Poured we libations unto each the dead,

First mead and then sweet wine, water mixed with white flour.
Then prayed I many a prayer to the sickly death's-heads;
As set in Ithaca, sterile bulls of the best   25
For sacrifice, heaping the pyre with goods,
A sheep to Tiresias only, black and a bell-sheep.
Dark blood flowed in the fosse,
Souls out of Erebus, cadaverous dead, of brides
Of youths and of the old who had borne much;   30
Souls stained with recent tears, girls tender,
Men many, mauled with bronze lance heads,
Battle spoil, bearing yet dreory arms,
These many crowded about me; with shouting,
Pallor upon me, cried to my men for more beasts;   35
Slaughtered the herds, sheep slain of bronze;
Poured ointment, cried to the gods,
To Pluto the strong, and praised Proserpine;
Unsheathed the narrow sword,
I sat to keep off the impetuous impotent dead,   40
Till I should hear Tiresias.
But first Elpenor came, our friend Elpenor,
Unburied, cast on the wide earth,
Limbs that we left in the house of Circe,
Unwept, unwrapped in sepulcher, since toils urged other.   45
Pitiful spirit. And I cried in hurried speech:
"Elpenor, how art thou come to this dark coast?
"Cam'st thou afoot, outstripping seamen?"
              And he in heavy speech:
"Ill fate and abundant wine. I slept in Circe's ingle.   50
"Going down the long ladder unguarded,
"I fell against the buttress,
"Shattered the nape-nerve, the soul sought Avernus.
"But thou, O King, I bid remember me, unwept, unburied,
"Heap up mine arms, be tomb by sea-bord, and inscribed: 55
" 'A man of no fortune and with a name to come.'
"And set my oar up, that I swung mid fellows."

And Anticlea came, whom I beat off, and then Tiresias Theban,
Holding his golden wand, knew me, and spoke first:
"A second time? why? man of ill star,   60
"Facing the sunless dead and this joyless region?
"Stand from the fosse, leave me my bloody bever
"For soothsay."

And I stepped back,
And he strong with the blood, said then: "Odysseus
"Shalt return through spiteful Neptune, over dark seas,　　　65
"Lose all companions." And then Anticlea came.
Lie quiet Divus. I mean, that is Andreas Divus,
In officina Wecheli, 1538, out of Homer.
And he sailed, by Sirens and thence outward and away
And unto Circe.　　　70
　　　　　Venerandam,
In the Cretan's phrase, with the golden crown, Aphrodite,
Cypri munimenta sortita est, mirthful, oricalchi, with golden
Girdles and breast bands, thou with dark eyelids
Bearing the golden bough of Argicida.

FROM CANTO LXXXI

What thou lovest well remains,
　　　　　　　　the rest is dross
What thou lov'st well shall not be reft from thee
What thou lov'st well is thy true heritage
Whose world, or mine or theirs　　　5
　　　　　　　　or is it of none?
First came the seen, then thus the palpable
　Elysium, though it were in the halls of hell,
What thou lovest well is thy true heritage.

The ant's a centaur in his dragon world.　　　10
Pull down thy vanity, it is not man
Made courage, or made order, or made grace,
　Pull down thy vanity, I say pull down.
Learn of the green world what can be thy place
In scaled invention or true artistry,　　　15
Pull down thy vanity,
　　　　　　Paquin pull down!
The green casque has outdone your elegance.

"Master thyself, then others shall thee beare"
　Pull down thy vanity　　　20
Thou art a beaten dog beneath the hail,
A swollen magpie in a fitful sun,
Half black half white

17. **Paquin:** famous Paris fashion designer.

Nor knowst'ou wing from tail
Pull down thy vanity   25
      How mean thy hates
Fostered in falsity,
      Pull down thy vanity,
Rathe to destroy, niggard in charity,
Pull down thy vanity,   30
      I say pull down.

But to have done instead of not doing
      this is not vanity
To have, with decency, knocked
That a Blunt should open   35
      To have gathered from the air a live tradition
or from a fine old eye the unconquered flame
This is not vanity.
    Here error is all in the not done,
all in the diffidence that faltered.

35. **Blunt:** Wilfrid Scawen Blunt (1840–1922), English poet, scholar, and
    traveler.

EDWARD THOMAS (1878–1917)

OLD MAN

Old Man, or Lad's-love,—in the name there's nothing
To one that knows not Lad's-love, or Old Man,
The hoar-green feathery herb, almost a tree,
Growing with rosemary and lavender.
Even to one that knows it well, the names   5
Half decorate, half perplex, the thing it is:
At least, what that is clings not to the names
In spite of time. And yet I like the names.

The herb itself I like not, but for certain
I love it, as some day the child will love it   10
Who plucks a feather from the door-side bush
Whenever she goes in or out of the house.
Often she waits there, snipping the tips and shrivelling
The shreds at last on to the path, perhaps

Thinking, perhaps of nothing, till she sniffs   15
Her fingers and runs off. The bush is still
But half as tall as she, though it is as old;
So well she clips it. Not a word she says;
And I can only wonder how much hereafter
She will remember, with that bitter scent,   20
Of garden rows, and ancient damson trees
Topping a hedge, a bent path to a door,
A low thick bush beside the door, and me
Forbidding her to pick.

              As for myself,
Where first I met the bitter scent is lost.   25
I, too, often shrivel the grey shreds,
Sniff them and think and sniff again and try
Once more to think what it is I am remembering,
Always in vain. I cannot like the scent,
Yet I would rather give up others more sweet,   30
With no meaning, than this bitter one.

I have mislaid the key. I sniff the spray
And think of nothing; I see and I hear nothing;
Yet seem, too, to be listening, lying in wait
For what I should, yet never can, remember: 35
No garden appears, no path, no hoar-green bush
Of Lad's-love, or Old Man, no child beside,
Neither father nor mother, nor any playmate;
Only an avenue, dark, nameless, without end.

THE MANOR FARM

The rock-like mud unfroze a little and rills
Ran and sparkled down each side of the road
Under the catkins wagging in the hedge.
But earth would have her sleep out, spite of the sun;
Nor did I value that thin gilding beam   5
More than a pretty February thing
Till I came down to the old Manor Farm,
And church and yew-tree opposite, in age
Its equals and in size. The church and yew
And farmhouse slept in a Sunday silentness.   10

The air raised not a straw. The steep farm roof,
With tiles duskily glowing, entertained
The mid-day sun; and up and down the roof
White pigeons nestled. There was no sound but one.
Three cart-horses were looking over a gate   15
Drowsily through their forelocks, swishing their tails
Against a fly, a solitary fly.

The Winter's cheek flushed as if he had drained
Spring, Summer, and Autumn at a draught
And smiled quietly. But 'twas not Winter—   20
Rather a season of bliss unchangeable
Awakened fom farm and church where it had lain
Safe under tile and thatch for ages since
This England, Old already, was called Merry.

THE BROOK

Seated once by a brook, watching a child
Chiefly that paddled, I was thus beguiled.
Mellow the blackbird sang and sharp the thrush
Not far off in the oak and hazel brush,
Unseen. There was a scent like honeycomb   5
From mugwort dull. And down upon the dome
Of the stone the cart-horse kicks against so oft
A butterfly alighted. From aloft
He took the heat of the sun, and from below,
On the hot stone he perched contented so,   10
As if never a cart would pass again
That way; as if I were the last of men
And he the first of insects to have earth
And sun together and to know their worth.
I was divided between him and the gleam,   15
The motion, and the voices, of the stream,
The waters running frizzled over gravel,
That never vanish and for ever travel.
A grey flycatcher silent on a fence
And I sat as if we had been there since   20
The horseman and the horse lying beneath
The fir-tree-covered barrow on the heath,
The horseman and the horse with silver shoes,

Galloped the downs last. All that I could lose
I lost. And then the child's voice raised the dead.   25
"No one's been here before" was what she said
And what I felt, yet never should have found
A word for, while I gathered sight and sound.

RUPERT BROOKE (1887–1915)

THE FUNERAL OF YOUTH: THRENODY

The day that Youth had died,
There came to his grave-side,
In decent mourning, from the county's ends,
Those scattered friends
Who had lived the boon companions of his prime,   5
And laughed with him and sung with him and wasted,
In feast and wine and many-crown'd carouse,
The days and nights and dawnings of the time
When Youth kept open house,
Nor left untasted   10
Aught of his high emprise and ventures dear,
No quest of his unshar'd—
All these, with loitering feet and sad head bar'd,
Followed their old friend's bier.
Folly went first,   15
With muffled bells and coxcomb still revers'd;
And after trod the bearers, hat in hand—
Laughter, most hoarse, and Captain Pride with tanned
And martial face all grim, and fussy Joy,
Who had to catch a train, and Lust, poor snivelling boy;   20
These bore the dear departed.
Behind them, broken-hearted,
Came Grief, so noisy a widow, that all said,
"Had he but wed
Her elder sister Sorrow, in her stead."   25
And by her, trying to soothe her all the time,
The fatherless children, Colour, Tune, and Rhyme
(The sweet lad Rhyme), ran all-uncomprehending.
Then, at the way's sad ending,
Round the raw grave they stay'd. Old Wisdom read,   30
In mumbling tone, the Service for the Dead.

There stood *Romance*,
The furrowing tears had mark'd her rougéd cheek;
Poor old *Conceit*, his wonder unassuag'd;
Dead *Innocency's* daughter, *Ignorance*;   35
And shabby, ill-dress'd *Generosity*;
And *Argument*, too full of woe to speak;
Passion, grown portly, something middle-aged;
And *Friendship*—not a minute older, she;
Impatience, ever taking out his watch;   40
Faith, who was deaf, and had to lean to catch
Old *Wisdom's* endless drone.
Beauty was there,
Pale in her black; dry-eyed; she stood alone.
Poor maz'd *Imagination*; *Fancy* wild;   45
Ardour, the sunlight on his greying hair;
Contentment, who had known *Youth* as a child
And never seen him since. And *Spring* came too,
Dancing over the tombs, and brought him flowers—
She did not stay for long.   50
And *Truth*, and *Grace*, and all the merry crew,
The laughing *Winds* and *Rivers*, and lithe *Hours*;
And *Hope*, the dewy-eyed; and sorrowing *Song*;—
Yes, with much woe and mourning general,
At dead *Youth's* funeral,   55
Even these were met once more together, all,
Who erst the fair and living *Youth* did know;
All, except only *Love*. *Love* had died long ago.

TIARE TAHITI

Mamua, when our laughter ends,
And hearts and bodies, brown as white
Are dust about the doors of friends,
Or scent ablowing down the night,
Then, oh! then, the wise agree,   5
Comes our immortality.
Mamua, there waits a land
Hard for us to understand.
Out of time, beyond the sun,
All are one in Paradise,   10

You and Pupure are one,
And Tau, and the ungainly wise.
There the Eternals are, and there
The Good, the Lovely, and the True,
And Types, whose earthly copies were   15
The foolish broken things we knew;
There is the Face, whose ghosts we are;
The real, the never-setting Star;
And the Flower, of which we love
Faint and fading shadows here;   20
Never a tear, but only Grief;
Dance, but not the limbs that move;
Songs in Song shall disappear;
Instead of lovers, Love shall be;
For hearts, Immutability;   25
And there, on the Ideal Reef,
Thunders the Everlasting Sea!

   And my laughter, and my pain,
Shall home to the Eternal Brain;
And all lovely things, they say,   30
Meet in Loveliness again;
Mirri's laugh, Teipo's feet,
And the hands of Matua.
Stars and sunlight there shall meet.
Coral's hues and rainbows there,   35
And Teüra's braided hair;
And with the starred *tiare's* white,
And white birds in the dark ravine,
And *flamboyants* ablaze at night,
And jewels, and evening's after-green,   40
And dawns of pearl and gold and red,
Mamua, your lovelier head!
And there'll no more be one who dreams
Under the ferns, of crumbling stuff,
Eyes of illusion, mouth that seems,   45
All time-entangled human love.
And you'll no longer swing and sway
Divinely down the scented shade,
Where feet to Ambulation fade,
And moons are lost in endless Day.   50
How shall we wind these wreaths of ours,

Where there are neither heads nor flowers?
Oh, Heaven's Heaven!—but we'll be missing
The palms, and sunlight, and the south;   55
And there's an end, I think, of kissing,
When our mouths are one with Mouth . . .

    Taü here, Mamua,
Crown the hair, and come away!
Hear the calling of the moon,   60
And the whispering scents that stray
About the idle warm lagoon.
Hasten, hand in human hand,
Down the dark, the flowered way,
Along the whiteness of the sand,   65
And in the water's soft caress,
Wash the mind of foolishness,
Mamua, until the day.
Spend the glittering moonlight there
Pursuing down the soundless deep   70
Limbs that gleam and shadowy hair,
Or floating lazy, half-asleep.
Dive and double and follow after,
Snare in flowers, and kiss, and call,
With lips that fade, and human laughter,   75
With faces individual,
Well this side of Paradise! . . .
There's little comfort in the wise.

HEAVEN

Fish (fly-replete, in depth of June
Dawdling away their wat'ry noon)
Ponder deep wisdom, dark or clear,
Each secret fishy hope or fear.
Fish say, they have their Stream and Pond;   5
But is there anything Beyond?
This life cannot be All, they swear,
For how unpleasant, if it were!
One may not doubt that, somehow, good
Shall come of Water and of Mud;   10
And, sure, the reverent eye must see
A Purpose in Liquidity.

We darkly know, by Faith we cry,
The future is not Wholly Dry.
Mud unto Mud!—Death eddies near—   15
Not here the appointed End, not here!
But somewhere, beyond Space and Time,
Is wetter water, slimier slime!
And there (they trust) there swimmeth One
Who swam ere rivers were begun,   20
Immense, of fishy form and mind,
Squamous, omnipotent, and kind;
And under that Almighty Fin
The littlest fish may enter in.
Oh! never fly conceals a hook,   25
Fish say, in the Eternal Brook,
But more than mundane weeds are there,
And mud, celestially fair;
Fat caterpillars drift around,
And Paradisal grubs are found;   30
Unfading moths, immortal flies,
And the worm that never dies.
And in that Heaven of all their wish,
There shall be no more land, say fish.

THE DEAD

These hearts were woven of human joys and cares,
   Washed marvellously with sorrow, swift to mirth.
The years had given them kindness. Dawn was theirs,
   And sunset, and the colours of the earth.

These had seen movement, and heard music; known
   Slumber and waking; loved; gone proudly friended;
Felt the quick stir of wonder; sat alone;
   Touched flowers and furs and cheeks. All this is ended.

There are waters blown by changing winds to laughter
And lit by the rich skies, all day. And after,
   Frost, with a gesture, stays the waves that dance
And wandering loveliness. He leaves a white
   Unbroken glory, a gathered radiance,
A width, a shining peace, under the night.

ROBINSON JEFFERS (1887–   )

APOLOGY FOR BAD DREAMS

I

In the purple light, heavy with redwood, the slopes drop seaward,
Headlong convexities of forest, drawn in together to the steep
  ravine. Below, on the sea-cliff,
A lonely clearing; a little field of corn by the streamside; a roof
  under spared trees. Then the ocean
Like a great stone someone has cut to a sharp edge and polished to
  shining. Beyond it, the fountain
And furnace of incredible light flowing up from the sunk sun. In
  the little clearing a woman   5
Is punishing a horse; she had tied the halter to a sapling at the
  edge of the wood, but when the great whip
Clung to the flanks the creature kicked so hard she feared he
  would snap the halter; she called from the house
The young man her son; who fetched a chain tie-rope, they work-
  ing together
Noosed the small rusty links round the horse's tongue
And tied him by the swollen tongue to the tree.   10
Seen from this height they are shrunk to insect size,
Out of all human relation. You cannot distinguish
The blood dripping from where the chain is fastened,
The beast shuddering; but the thrust neck and the legs
Far apart. You can see the whip fall on the flanks. . . .   15
The gesture of the arm. You cannot see the face of the woman.
The enormous light beats up out of the west across the cloud-bars
  of the trade-wind. The ocean
Darkens, the high clouds brighten, the hills darken together.
  Unbridled and unbelievable beauty
Covers the evening world . . . not covers, grows apparent out of
  it, as Venus down there grows out
From the lit sky. What said the prophet? "I create good; and I
  create evil: I am the Lord."   20

II

This coast crying out for tragedy like all beautiful places,
(The quiet ones ask for quieter suffering; but here the granite cliff
  the gaunt cypresses' crown

Demands what victim? The dykes of red lava and black what Titan?
    The hills like pointed flames
Beyond Soberanes, the terrible peaks of the bare hills under the
    sun, what immolation?)
This coast crying out for tragedy like all beautiful places: and like
    the passionate spirit of humanity   25
Pain for its bread: God's, many victims', the painful deaths, the
    horrible transfigurements: I said in my heart,
"Better invent than suffer: imagine victims
Lest your own flesh be chosen the agonist, or you
Martyr some creature to the beauty of the place." And I said,
"Burn sacrifices once a year to magic   30
Horror away from the house, this little house here
You have built over the ocean with your own hands
Beside the standing bowlders: for what are we,
The beast that walks upright, with speaking lips
And little hair, to think we should always be fed,   35
Sheltered, intact, and self-controlled? We sooner more liable
Than the other animals. Pain and terror, the insanities of desire;
    not accidents but essential,
And crowd up from the core." I imagined victims for those wolves,
    I made them phantoms to follow.
They have hunted the phantoms and missed the house. It is not
    good to forget over what gulfs the spirit
Of the beauty of humanity, the petal of a lost flower blown sea-
    ward by the night-wind, floats to its quietness.   40

III

Bowlders blunted like an old bear's teeth break up from the head-
    land; below them
All the soil is thick with shells, the tide-rock feasts of a dead people.
Here the granite flanks are scarred with ancient fire, the ghosts of
    the tribe
Crouch in the nights beside the ghost of a fire, they try to remem-
    ber the sunlight,
Light has died out of their skies. These have paid something for
    the future   45
Luck of the country, while we living keep old griefs in memory:
    though God's
Envy is not a likely fountain of ruin, to forget evils calls down
Sudden reminders from the cloud: remembered deaths be our
    redeemers;

Imagined victims our salvation: white as the half moon at midnight
Someone flamelike passed me, saying, "I am Tamar Cauldwell, I
   have my desire,"   50
Then the voice of the sea returned, when she had gone by, the stars
   to their towers.
. . . Beautiful country, burn again, Point Pinos down to the
   Sur Rivers
Burn as before with bitter wonders, land and ocean and the
   Carmel water.

IV

He brays humanity in a mortar to bring the savor
From the bruised root: a man having bad dreams, who invents vic-
   tims, is only the ape of that God.   55
He washes it out with tears and many waters, calcines it with fire
   in the red crucible,
Deforms it, makes it horrible to itself: the spirit flies out and stands
   naked, he sees the spirit.
He takes it in the naked ecstasy; it breaks in his hand, the atom is
   broken, the power that massed it
Cries to the power that moves the stars, "I have come home to
   myself, behold me.
I bruised myself in the flint mortar and burnt me   60
In the red shell, I tortured myself, I flew forth,
Stood naked of myself and broke me in fragments,
And here am I moving the stars that are me."
I have seen these ways of God: I know of no reason
For fire and change and torture and the old returnings.   65
He being sufficient might be still. I think they admit no reason;
   they are the ways of my love.
Unmeasured power, incredible passion, enormous craft: no thought
   apparent but burns darkly
Smothered with its own smoke in the human brain-vault: no
   thought outside: a certain measure in phenomena:
The fountains of the boiling stars, the flowers on the foreland, the
   ever-returning roses of dawn.

MARIANNE MOORE (1887–   )

A GRAVE

Man looking into the sea,
taking the view from those who have as much right to it as
  you have to it yourself,
it is human nature to stand in the middle of a thing,
but you cannot stand in the middle of this;
the sea has nothing to give but a well excavated grave.   5
The firs stand in a procession, each with an emerald turkey-
  foot at the top,
reserved as their contours, saying nothing;
repression, however, is not the most obvious characteristic of
  the sea;
the sea is a collector, quick to return a rapacious look.
There are others besides you who have worn that look—   10
whose expression is no longer a protest; the fish no longer
  investigate them
for their bones have not lasted:
men lower nets, unconscious of the fact that they are
  desecrating a grave,
and row quickly away—the blades of the oars
moving together like the feet of water-spiders as if there were
  no such thing as death.   15
The wrinkles progress among themselves in a phalanx—
  beautiful under networks of foam,
and fade breathlessly while the sea rustles in and out of the
  seaweed;
the birds swim through the air at top speed, emitting catcalls
  as heretofore—
the tortoise-shell scourges about the feet of the cliffs, in
  motion beneath them;
and the ocean, under the pulsation of lighthouses and noise
  of bell-buoys,   20
advances as usual, looking as if it were not that ocean in
  which dropped things are bound to sink—
in which if they turn and twist, it is neither with volition
  nor consciousness.

THE MONKEYS

winked too much and were afraid of snakes. The zebras,
    supreme in
their abnormality; the elephants with their fog-coloured
    skin
    and strictly practical appendages
      were there, the small cats; and the parrakeet—
        trivial and humdrum on examination, destroying   5
      bark and portions of the food it could not eat.

I recall their magnificence, now not more magnificent
than it is dim. It is difficult to recall the ornament,
    speech, and precise manner of what one might
      call the minor acquaintances twenty   10
        years back; but I shall not forget him—that Gilga-
        mesh
          among
    the hairy carnivora—that cat with the

wedge-shaped, slate-grey marks on its forelegs and the
    resolute tail,
astringently remarking, "They have imposed on us with   15
      their pale
    half-fledged protestations, trembling about
      in inarticulate frenzy, saying
        it is not for us to understand art; finding it
    all so difficult, examining the thing

as if it were inconceivably arcanic, as symmet-   20
rically frigid as if it had been carved out of chrysoprase
    or marble—strict with tension, malignant
      in its power over us and deeper
        than the sea when it proffers flattery in exchange for
        hemp,
        rye, flax, horses, platinum, timber, and fur."   25

IN DISTRUST OF MERITS

Strengthened to live, strengthened to die for
   medals and positioned victories?
They're fighting, fighting, fighting the blind
   man who thinks he sees,—
who cannot see that the enslaver is   5
enslaved; the hater, harmed. O shining O
      firm star, O tumultuous
         ocean lashed till small things go
    as they will, the mountainous
        wave makes us who look, know   10

depth. Lost at sea before they fought! O
    star of David, star of Bethlehem,
O black imperial lion
    of the Lord—emblem
of a risen world—be joined at last, be   15
joined. There is hate's crown beneath which all is
      death; there's love's without which none
        is king; the blessed deeds bless
    the halo. As contagion
      of sickness makes sickness,   10

contagion of trust can make trust. They're
    fighting in deserts and caves, one by
one, in battalions and squadrons;
    they're fighting that I   15
may yet recover from the disease, My
Self; some have it lightly; some will die. 'Man
      wolf to man' and we devour
        ourselves. The enemy could not
    have made a greater breach in our
        defences. One pilot-   20

ing a blind man can escape him, but
    Job disheartened by false comfort knew
that nothing can be so defeating
    as a blind man who
can see. O alive who are dead, who are   25
proud not to see, O small dust of the earth

that walks so arrogantly,
　　　trust begets power and faith is
an affectionate thing. We
　　　vow, we make this promise　　　　　　　　　30

to the fighting—it's a promise—'We'll
　　　never hate black, white, red, yellow, Jew,
Gentile, Untouchable.' We are
　　　not competent to
make our vows. With set jaw they are fighting,　　　35
fighting, fighting,—some we love whom we know,
　　　some we love but know not—that
　　　　　hearts may feel and not be numb.
　　　It cures me; or am I what
　　　　I can't believe in? Some　　　　　　　　　40

in snow, some on crags, some in quicksands,
　　　little by little, much by much, they
are fighting fighting fighting that where
　　　there was death there may
be life. 'When a man is prey to anger,　　　　　　45
he is moved by outside things; when he holds
　　　his ground in patience patience
　　　　patience, that is action or
　　　beauty', the soldier's defence
　　　　and hardest armour for　　　　　　　　　50

the fight. The world's an orphans' home. Shall
　　　we never have peace without sorrow?
without pleas of the dying for
　　　help that won't come? O
quiet form upon the dust, I cannot　　　　　　　　55
look and yet I must. If these great patient
　　　dyings—all these agonies
　　　　and woundbearings and bloodshed—
　　　can teach us how to live, these
　　　　dyings were not wasted.　　　　　　　60

Hate-hardened heart, O heart of iron,
　　　iron is iron till it is rust.
There never was a war that was
　　　not inward; I must

fight till I have conquered in myself what 65
causes war, but I would not believe it.
           I inwardly did nothing.
                 O Iscariotlike crime!
           Beauty is everlasting
                 and dust is for a time. 70

NEVERTHELESS

you've seen a strawberry
        that's had a struggle; yet
        was, where the fragments met,

a hedgehog or a star-
        fish for the multitude 5
        of seeds. What better food

than apple-seeds—the fruit
        within the fruit—locked in
        like counter-curved twin

hazel-nuts? Frost that kills 10
        the little rubber-plant-
        leaves of *kok-saghyz*-stalks, can't

harm the roots; they still grow
        in frozen ground. Once where
        there was a prickly-pear- 15

leaf clinging to barbed wire,
        a root shot down to grow
        in earth two feet below;

as carrots form mandrakes
        or a ram's-horn root some- 20
        times. Victory won't come

to me unless I go
        to it; a grape-tendril
        ties a knot in knots till

knotted thirty times,—so   25
    the bound twig that's under-
    gone and over-gone, can't stir.

The weak overcomes its
    menace, the strong over-
    comes itself. What is there   30

like fortitude! What sap
    went through that little thread
    to make the cherry red!

T. S. ELIOT (1888–   )

THE LOVE SONG OF J. ALFRED PRUFROCK

S'io credesse che mia risposta fosse
A persona che mai tornasse al mondo,
Questa fiamma staria senza piu scosse.
Ma perciocche giammai di questo fondo
Non torno vivo alcum, s'i'odo il vero,
Senza tema d'infamia ti rispondo.[1]

Let us go then, you and I,
When the evening is spread out against the sky
Like a patient etherized upon a table;
Let us go, through certain half-deserted streets,
The muttering retreats   5
Of restless nights in one-night cheap hotels
And sawdust restaurants with oyster-shells:
Streets that follow like a tedious argument
Of insidious intent
To lead you to an overwhelming question. . . .   10
Oh, do not ask, 'What is it?'
Let us go and make our visit.

In the room the women come and go
Talking of Michelangelo.

1. *S'io credesse*, etc.: If I believed that my answer were to a person who should ever return to the world, this flame would stand without further movement; but since never one returns alive from this deep, if I hear true, I answer you without fear of infamy. *Inferno*, xxvii.

The yellow fog that rubs its back upon the window-panes,   15
The yellow smoke that rubs its muzzle on the window-panes,
Licked its tongue into the corners of the evening,
Lingered upon the pools that stand in drains,
Let fall upon its back the soot that falls from chimneys,
Slipped by the terrace, made a sudden leap,   20
And seeing that it was a soft October night,
Curled once about the house, and fell asleep.

And indeed there will be time
For the yellow smoke that slides along the street,
Rubbing its back upon the window-panes;   25
There will be time, there will be time
To prepare a face to meet the faces that you meet;
There will be time to murder and create,
And time for all the works and days of hands
That lift and drop a question on your plate;   30
Time for you and time for me,
And time yet for a hundred indecisions,
And for a hundred visions and revisions,
Before the taking of a toast and tea.

In the room the women come and go   35
Talking of Michelangelo.

And indeed there will be time
To wonder, 'Do I dare?' and, 'Do I dare?'
Time to turn back and descend the stair,
With a bald spot in the middle of my hair—   40
[They will say: 'How his hair is growing thin!']
My morning coat, my collar mounting firmly to the chin,
My necktie rich and modest, but asserted by a simple pin—
[They will say: 'But how his arms and legs are thin!']
Do I dare
Disturb the universe?   45
In a minute there is time
For decisions and revisions which a minute will reverse.

For I have known them all already, known them all:—
Have known the evenings, mornings, afternoons,   50
I have measured out my life with coffee spoons;
I know the voices dying with a dying fall

Beneath the music from a farther room.
    So how should I presume?

And I have known the eyes already, known them all—   55
The eyes that fix you in a formulated phrase,
And when I am formulated, sprawling on a pin,
When I am pinned and wriggling on the wall,
Then how should I begin
To spit out all the butt-ends of my days and ways?   60
    And how should I presume?

And I have known the arms already, known them all—
Arms that are braceleted and white and bare
[But in the lamplight, downed with light brown hair!]
Is it perfume from a dress   65
That makes me so digress?
Arms that lie along a table, or wrap about a shawl.
    And should I then presume?
    And how should I begin?

      .   .   .

Shall I say, I have gone at dusk through narrow streets   70
And watched the smoke that rises from the pipes
Of lonely men in shirt-sleeves, leaning out of windows? . . .

I should have been a pair of ragged claws
Scuttling across the floors of silent seas.

      .   .   .

And the afternoon, the evening, sleeps so peacefully!   75
Smoothed by long fingers,
Asleep . . . tired . . . or it malingers,
Stretched on the floor, here beside you and me.
Should I, after tea and cakes and ices,
Have the strength to force the moment to its crisis?   80
But though I have wept and fasted, wept and prayed,
Though I have seen my head [grown slightly bald] brought
    in upon a platter,
I am no prophet—and here's no great matter;
I have seen the moment of my greatness flicker,
And I have seen the eternal Footman hold my coat, and
    snicker,   85
And in short, I was afraid.

And would it have been worth it, after all,
After the cups, the marmalade, the tea,
Among the porcelain, among some talk of you and me,
Would it have been worth while,   90
To have bitten off the matter with a smile,
To have squeezed the universe into a ball
To roll it toward some overwhelming question,
To say: 'I am Lazarus, come from the dead,
Come back to tell you all, I shall tell you all'—   95
If one, settling a pillow by her head,
     Should say: 'That is not what I meant at all.
     That is not it, at all.'

And would it have been worth it, after all,
Would it have been worth while,   100
After the sunsets and the dooryards and the sprinkled streets,
After the novels, after the teacups, after the skirts that trail
     along the floor—
And this, and so much more?—
It is impossible to say just what I mean!
But as if a magic lantern threw the nerves in patterns on a
     screen: 105
Would it have been worth while
If one, settling a pillow or throwing off a shawl,
And turning toward the window, should say:
     'That is not it at all,
     That is not what I meant, at all.'   110

        .   .   .

No! I am not Prince Hamlet, nor was meant to be;
Am an attendant lord, one that will do
To swell a progress, start a scene or two,
Advise the prince; no doubt, an easy tool,
Deferential, glad to be of use,   115
Politic, cautious, and meticulous;
Full of high sentence, but a bit obtuse;
At times, indeed, almost ridiculous—
Almost, at times, the Fool.

I grow old. . . . I grow old. . . .   120
I shall wear the bottoms of my trousers rolled.

Shall I part my hair behind? Do I dare to eat a peach?
I shall wear white flannel trousers, and walk upon the beach.
I have heard the mermaids singing, each to each.

I do not think that they will sing to me.   125

I have seen them riding seaward on the waves
Combing the white hair of the waves blown back
When the wind blows the water white and black.

We have lingered in the chambers of the sea
By sea-girls wreathed with seaweed red and brown   130
Till human voices wake us, and we drown.

GERONTION

> *Thou hast nor youth nor age*
> *But as it were an after dinner sleep*
> *Dreaming of both.* [1]

Here I am, an old man in a dry month,
Being read to by a boy, waiting for rain.
I was neither at the hot gates
Nor fought in the warm rain
Nor knee deep in the salt marsh, heaving a cutlass,   5
Bitten by flies, fought.
My house is a decayed house,
And the jew squats on the window sill, the owner,
Spawned in some estaminet of Antwerp,
Blistered in Brussels, patched and peeled in London.   10
The goat coughs at night in the field overhead;
Rocks, moss, stonecrop, iron, merds.
The woman keeps the kitchen, makes tea,
Sneezes at evening, poking the peevish gutter.
                              I an old man,
A dull head among windy spaces.   15

Signs are taken for wonders. "We would see a sign!"
The word within a word, unable to speak a word,

[1] **Thou hast nor youth nor age, etc.:** Shakespeare, *Measure for Measure*, III, i.

Swaddled with darkness. In the juvescence of the year
Came Christ the tiger

In depraved May, dogwood and chestnut, flowering judas,   20
To be eaten, to be divided, to be drunk
Among whispers; by Mr. Silvero
With caressing hands, at Limoges
Who walked all night in the next room;
By Hakagawa, bowing among the Titians;   25
By Madame de Tornquist, in the dark room
Shifting the candles; Fräulein von Kulp
Who turned in the hall, one hand on the door.
        Vacant shuttles
Weave the wind. I have no ghosts,   30
An old man in a draughty house
Under a windy knob.

After such knowledge, what forgiveness? Think now
History has many cunning passages, contrived corridors
And issues, deceives with whispering ambitions,   35
Guides us by vanities. Think now
She gives when our attention is distracted
And what she gives, gives with such supple confusions
That the giving famishes the craving. Gives too late
What's not believed in, or if still believed,   40
In memory only, reconsidered passion. Gives too soon
Into weak hands, what's thought can be dispensed with
Till the refusal propagates a fear. Think
Neither fear nor courage saves us. Unnatural vices
Are fathered by our heroism. Virtues   45
Are forced upon us by our impudent crimes.
These tears are shaken from the wrath-bearing tree.

The tiger springs in the new year. Us he devours.
        Think at last
We have not reached conclusion, when I   50
Stiffen in a rented house. Think at last
I have not made this show purposelessly
And it is not by any concitation
Of the backward devils.
I would meet you upon this honestly.
I that was near your heart was removed therefrom   55

To lose beauty in terror, terror in inquisition.
I have lost my passion: why should I need to keep it
Since what is kept must be adulterated?
I have lost my sight, smell, hearing, taste, and touch: 60
How should I use them for your closer contact?

These with a thousand small deliberations
Protract the profit of their chilled delirium,
Excite the membrane, when the sense has cooled,
With pungent sauces, multiply variety   65
In a wilderness of mirrors. What will the spider do,
Suspend its operations, will the weevil
Delay? De Bailhache, Fresca, Mrs. Cammel, whirled
Beyond the circuit of the shuddering Bear
In fractured atoms. Gull against the wind, in the windy
    straits
Of Belle Isle, or running on the Horn,
White feathers in the snow, the Gulf claims,
And an old man driven by the Trades
To a sleepy corner.

                    Tenants of the house,
Thoughts of a dry brain in a dry season.   75

SWEENEY AMONG THE NIGHTINGALES

ὤμοι, πέπληγμαι καιρίαν πληγὴν ἔσω [1]

Apeneck Sweeney spreads his knees
Letting his arms hang down to laugh,
The zebra stripes along his jaw
Swelling to maculate giraffe.

The circles of the stormy moon   5
Slide westward toward the River Plate,
Death and the Raven drift above
And Sweeney guards the hornèd gate.

1. Ay me! I am smitten with a mortal blow. Aeschylus, *Agamemnon*.

Gloomy Orion and the Dog
Are veiled; and hushed the shrunken seas;   10
The person in the Spanish cape
Tries to sit on Sweeney's knees

Slips and pulls the table cloth
Overturns a coffee-cup,
Reorganized upon the floor   15
She yawns and draws a stocking up;

The silent man in mocha brown
Sprawls at the window-sill and gapes;
The waiter brings in oranges
Bananas figs and hothouse grapes;   20

The silent vertebrate in brown
Contracts and concentrates, withdraws;
Rachel née Rabinovitch
Tears at the grapes with murderous paws;

She and the lady in the cape   25
Are suspect, thought to be in league;
Therefore the man with heavy eyes
Declines the gambit, shows fatigue,

Leaves the room and reappears
Outside the window, leaning in,   30
Branches of wistaria
Circumscribe a golden grin;

The host with someone indistinct
Converses at the door apart,
The nightingales are singing near   35
The Convent of the Sacred Heart,

And sang within the bloody wood
When Agamemnon cried aloud,
And let their liquid siftings fall
To stain the stiff dishonored shroud.   40

ASH WEDNESDAY

I

Because I do not hope to turn again
Because I do not hope
Because I do not hope to turn
Desiring this man's gift and that man's scope
I no longer strive to strive towards such things   5
(Why should the agèd eagle stretch its wings?)
Why should I mourn
The vanished power of the usual reign?

Because I do not hope to know again
The infirm glory of the positive hour   10
Because I do not think
Because I know I shall not know
The one veritable transitory power
Because I cannot drink
There, where trees flower, and springs flow, for there is
    nothing again   15

Because I know that time is always time
And place is always and only place
And what is actual is actual only for one time
And only for one place
I rejoice that things are as they are and   20
I renounce the blessèd face
And renounce the voice
Because I cannot hope to turn again
Consequently I rejoice, having to construct something
Upon which to rejoice   25

And pray to God to have mercy upon us
And I pray that I may forget
These matters that with myself I too much discuss
Too much explain
Because I do not hope to turn again   30
Let these words answer
For what is done, not to be done again
May the judgement not be too heavy upon us

Because these wings are no longer wings to fly
But merely vans to beat the air   35
The air which is now thoroughly small and dry
Smaller and dryer than the will
Teach us to care and not to care
Teach us to sit still.

Pray for us sinners now and at the hour of our death   40
Pray for us now and at the hour of our death.

II

Lady, three white leopards sat under a juniper-tree
In the cool of the day, having fed to satiety
On my legs my heart my liver and that which had been
    contained
In the hollow round of my skull. And God said   45
Shall these bones live? shall these
Bones live? And that which had been contained
In the bones (which were already dry) said chirping:
Because of the goodness of this Lady
And because of her loveliness, and because   50
She honours the Virgin in meditation,
We shine with brightness. And I who am here dissembled
Proffer my deeds to oblivion, and my love
To the posterity of the desert and the fruit of the gourd.
It is this which recovers   55
My guts the strings of my eyes and the indigestible portions
Which the leopards reject. The Lady is withdrawn
In a white gown, to contemplation, in a white gown.
Let the whiteness of bones atone to forgetfulness.
There is no life in them. As I am forgotten   60
And would be forgotten, so I would forget
Thus devoted, concentrated in purpose. And God said
Prophesy to the wind, to the wind only for only
The wind will listen. And the bones sang chirping
With the burden of the grasshopper, saying   65

Lady of silences
Calm and distressed
Torn and most whole
Rose of memory
Rose of forgetfulness   70

Exhausted and life-giving
Worried reposeful
The single Rose
Is now the Garden
Where all loves end 75
Terminate torment
Of love unsatisfied
The greater torment
Of love satisfied
End of the endless 80
Journey to no end
Conclusion of all that
Is inconclusible
Speech without word and
Word of no speech 85
Grace to the Mother
For the Garden
Where all love ends.

Under a juniper-tree the bones sang, scattered and shining
We are glad to be scattered, we did little good to each other, 90
Under a tree in the cool of the day, with the blessing of sand,
Forgetting themselves and each other, united
In the quiet of the desert. This is the land which ye
Shall divide by lot. And neither division nor unity
Matters. This is the land. We have our inheritance. 95

III

At the first turning of the second stair
I turned and saw below
The same shape twisted on the banister
Under the vapour in the fetid air
Struggling with the devil of the stairs who wears 100
The deceitful face of hope and of despair.

At the second turning of the second stair
I left them twisting, turning below;
There were no more faces and the stair was dark,
Damp, jaggèd, like an old man's mouth drivelling, beyond
    repair,
Or the toothed gullet of an agèd shark. 105

At the first turning of the third stair
Was a slotted window bellied like the fig's fruit
And beyond the hawthorn blossom and a pasture scene
The broadbacked figure drest in blue and green   110
Enchanted the maytime with an antique flute.
Blown hair is sweet, brown hair over the mouth blown,
Lilac and brown hair;
Distraction, music of the flute, stops and steps of the mind
        over the third stair,
Fading, fading; strength beyond hope and despair   115
Climbing the third stair.

Lord, I am not worthy
Lord, I am not worthy

        but speak the word only.

IV

Who walked between the violet and the violet   120
Who walked between
The various ranks of varied green
Going in white and blue, in Mary's colour,
Talking of trivial things
In ignorance and in knowledge of eternal dolour   125
Who moved among the others as they walked,
Who then made strong the fountains and made fresh the
        springs

Made cool the dry rock and made firm the sand
In blue of larkspur, blue of Mary's colour,
Sovegna vos   130

Here are the years that walk between, bearing
Away the fiddles and the flutes, restoring
One who moves in the time between sleep and waking,
        wearing

White light folded, sheathed about her, folded.
The new years walk, restoring   135
Through a bright cloud of tears, the years, restoring
With a new verse the ancient rhyme. Redeem
The time. Redeem

The unread vision in the higher dream
While jewelled unicorns draw by the gilded hearse.   140

The silent sister veiled in white and blue
Between the yews, behind the garden god,
Whose flute is breathless, bent her head and signed but
    spoke no word

But the fountain sprang up and the bird sang down
Redeem the time, redeem the dream   145
The token of the word unheard, unspoken

Till the wind shake a thousand whispers from the yew

And after this our exile

v

If the lost word is lost, if the spent word is spent
If the unheard, unspoken   150
Word is unspoken, unheard;
Still is the unspoken word, the Word unheard,
The Word without a word, the Word within
The world and for the world;
And the light shone in darkness and   155
Against the Word the unstilled world still whirled
About the centre of the silent Word.

      O my people, what have I done unto thee.

Where shall the word be found, where will the word
Resound? Not here, there is not enough silence   160
Not on the sea or on the islands, not
On the mainland, in the desert or the rain land,
For those who walk in darkness
Both in the day time and in the night time
The right time and the right place are not here   165
No place of grace for those who avoid the face
No time to rejoice for those who walk among noise and
    deny the voice

Will the veiled sister pray for
Those who walk in darkness, who chose thee and oppose thee,

Those who are torn on the horn between season and season,
    time and time, between   170
Hour and hour, word and word, power and power, those
    who wait
In darkness? Will the veiled sister pray
For children at the gate
Who will not go away and cannot pray:
Pray for those who chose and oppose   175

        O my people, what have I done unto thee.

Will the veiled sister between the slender
Yew trees pray for those who offend her
And are terrified and cannot surrender
And affirm before the world and deny between the rocks   180
In the last desert between the last blue rocks
The desert in the garden the garden in the desert
Of drouth, spitting from the mouth the withered apple-seed.

        O my people.

VI

Although I do not hope to turn again   185
Although I do not hope
Although I do not hope to turn

Wavering between the profit and the loss
In this brief transit where the dreams cross
The dreamcrossed twilight between birth and dying   190
(Bless me father) though I do not wish to wish these things
From the wide window towards the granite shore
The white sails still fly seaward, seaward flying
Unbroken wings

And the lost heart stiffens and rejoices   195
In the lost lilac and the lost sea voices
And the weak spirit quickens to rebel
For the bent golden-rod and the lost sea smell
Quickens to recover
The cry of quail and the whirling plover   200
And the blind eye creates
The empty forms between the ivory gates
And smell renews the salt savour of the sandy earth

This is the time of tension between dying and birth
The place of solitude where three dreams cross   205
Between blue rocks
But when the voices shaken from the yew-tree drift away
Let the other yew be shaken and reply.

Blessèd sister, holy mother, spirit of the fountain, spirit of
    the garden,
Suffer us not to mock ourselves with falsehood   210
Teach us to care and not to care
Teach us to sit still
Even among these rocks,
Our peace in His will
And even among these rocks   215
Sister, mother
And spirit of the river, spirit of the sea,
Suffer me not to be separated

And let my cry come unto Thee.

THE DRY SALVAGES

(The Dry Salvages—presumably *les trois sauvages*—is a small group of rocks,
with a beacon, off the N. E. coast of Cape Ann, Massachusetts. *Salvages* is
pronounced to rhyme with *assuages*.)

I

I do not know much about gods; but I think that the river
Is a strong brown god—sullen, untamed and intractable,
Patient to some degree, at first recognised as a frontier;
Useful, untrustworthy, as a conveyor of commerce;
Then only a problem confronting the builder of bridges.   5
The problem once solved, the brown god is almost forgotten
By the dwellers in cities—ever, however, implacable,
Keeping his seasons and rages, destroyer, reminder
Of what men choose to forget. Unhonoured, unpropitiated
By worshippers of the machine, but waiting, watching and
    waiting.   10
His rhythm was present in the nursery bedroom,
In the rank ailanthus of the April dooryard,
In the smell of grapes on the autumn table,
And the evening circle in the winter gaslight.

The river is within us, the sea is all about us;   15
The sea is the land's edge also, the granite
Into which it reaches, the beaches where it tosses
Its hints of earlier and other creation:
The starfish, the hermit crab, the whale's backbone;
The pools where it offers to our curiosity   20
The more delicate algae and the sea anemone.
It tosses up our losses, the torn seine,
The shattered lobsterpot, the broken oar
And the gear of foreign dead men. The sea has many voices,
Many gods and many voices.
                      The salt is on the briar rose,   25
The fog is in the fir trees.
                The sea howl
And the sea yelp, are different voices
Often together heard; the whine in the rigging,
The menace and caress of wave that breaks on water,   30
The distant rote in the granite teeth,
And the wailing warning from the approaching headland
Are all sea voices, and the heaving groaner
Rounded homewards, and the seagull:
And under the oppression of the silent fog   35
The tolling bell
Measures time not our time, rung by the unhurried
Ground swell, a time
Older than the time of chronometers, older
Than time counted by anxious worried women   40
Lying awake, calculating the future,
Trying to unweave, unwind, unravel
And piece together the past and the future,
Between midnight and dawn, when the past is all deception,
The future futureless, before the morning watch   45
When time stops and time is never ending;
And the ground swell, that is and was from the beginning,
Clangs
The bell.

II

Where is there an end of it, the soundless wailing,   50
The silent withering of autumn flowers
Dropping their petals and remaining motionless;
Where is there an end to the drifting wreckage,

33. **Groaner:** a whistling buoy.

The prayer of the bone on the beach, the unprayable
Prayer at the calamitous annunciation?   55

There is no end, but addition: the trailing
Consequence of further days and hours,
While emotion takes to itself the emotionless
Years of living among the breakage
Of what was believed in as the most reliable—   60
And therefore the fittest for renunciation.

There is the final addition, the failing
Pride or resentment at failing powers,
The unattached devotion which might pass for devotionless,
In a drifting boat with a slow leakage,   65
The silent listening to the undeniable
Clamour of the bell of the last annunciation.

Where is the end of them, the fishermen sailing
Into the wind's tail, where the fog cowers?
We cannot think of a time that is oceanless   70
Or of an ocean not littered with wastage
Or of a future that is not liable
Like the past, to have no destination.

We have to think of them as forever bailing,
Setting and hauling, while the North East lowers   75
Over shallow banks unchanging and erosionless
Or drawing their money, drying sails at dockage;
Not as making a trip that will be unpayable
For a haul that will not bear examination.

There is no end of it, the voiceless wailing,   80
No end to the withering of withered flowers,
To the movement of pain that is painless and motionless,
To the drift of the sea and the drifting wreckage
The bone's prayer to Death its God. Only the hardly, barely
      prayable
Prayer of the one Annunciation.   85

It seems, as one becomes older,
That the past has another pattern, and ceases to be a mere
      sequence—
Or even development: the latter a partial fallacy

Encouraged by superficial notions of evolution,
Which becomes, in the popular mind, a means of disowning
    the past.   90
The moments of happiness—not the sense of well-being,
Fruition, fulfilment, security or affection,
Or even a very good dinner, but the sudden illumination—
We had the experience but missed the meaning,
And approach to the meaning restores the experience   95
In a different form, beyond any meaning
We can assign to happiness. I have said before
That the past experience revived in the meaning
Is not the experience of one life only
But of many generations—not forgetting   100
Something that is probably quite ineffable:
The backward look behind the assurance
Of recorded history, the backward half-look
Over the shoulder, towards the primitive terror.
Now, we come to discover that the moments of agony   105
(Whether, or not, due to misunderstanding,
Having hoped for the wrong things or dreaded the wrong things,
Is not in question) are likewise permanent
With such permanence as time has. We appreciate this better
In the agony of others, nearly experienced,   110
Involving ourselves, than in our own.
For our own past is covered by the currents of action,
But the torment of others remains an experience
Unqualified, unworn by subsequent attrition.
People change, and smile: but the agony abides.   115
Time the destroyer is time the preserver,
Like the river with its cargo of dead negroes, cows and chicken
    coops,
The bitter apple and the bite in the apple.
And the ragged rock in the restless waters,
Waves wash over it, fogs conceal it;   120
On a halcyon day it is merely a monument,
In navigable weather it is always a seamark
To lay a course by: but in the sombre season
Or the sudden fury, is what it always was.

III

I sometimes wonder if that is what Krishna meant—   125
Among other things—or one way of putting the same thing:

That the future is a faded song, a Royal Rose or a lavender
    spray
Of wistful regret for those who are not yet here to
    regret,
Pressed between yellow leaves of a book that has never been
    opened.
And the way up is the way down, the way forward is the
    way back.   130
You cannot face it steadily, but this thing is sure,
That time is no healer: the patient is no longer here.
When the train starts, and the passengers are settled
To fruit, periodicals and business letters
(And those who saw them off have left the platform)   135
Their faces relax from grief into relief,
To the sleepy rhythm of a hundred hours.
Fare forward, travellers! not escaping from the past
Into different lives, or into any future;
You are not the same people who left that station   140
Or who will arrive at any terminus,
While the narrowing rails slide together behind you;
And on the deck of the drumming liner
Watching the furrow that widens behind you,
You shall not think 'the past is finished'   145
Or 'the future is before us'.
At nightfall, in the rigging and the aerial,
Is a voice descanting (though not to the ear,
The murmuring shell of time, and not in any
    language)
'Fare forward, you who think that you are voyaging;   150
You are not those who saw the harbour
Receding, or those who will disembark.
Here between the hither and the farther shore
While time is withdrawn, consider the future
And the past with an equal mind.   155
At the moment which is not of action or inaction
You can receive this: "on whatever sphere of being
The mind of a man may be intent
At the time of death"—that is the one action
(And the time of death is every moment)   160
Which shall fructify in the lives of others:
And do not think of the fruit of action.
Fare forward.

O voyagers, O seamen,
You who come to port, and you whose bodies   165
Will suffer the trial and judgement of the sea,
Or whatever event, this is your real destination.'
So Krishna, as when he admonished Arjuna
On the field of battle.
                              Not fare well,   170
But fare forward, voyagers.

                              IV

Lady, whose shrine stands on the promontory,
Pray for all those who are in ships, those
Whose business has to do with fish, and
Those concerned with every lawful traffic   175
And those who conduct them.

Repeat a prayer also on behalf of
Women who have seen their sons or husbands
Setting forth, and not returning: 180
Figlia del tuo figlio,
Queen of Heaven.

Also pray for those who were in ships, and
Ended their voyage on the sand, in the sea's lips
Or in the dark throat which will not reject them
Or wherever cannot reach them the sound of the sea bell's   185
Perpetual angelus.

                              V

To communicate with Mars, converse with spirits,
To report the behaviour of the sea monster,
Describe the horoscope, haruspicate or scry,
Observe disease in signatures, evoke   190
Biography from the wrinkles of the palm
And tragedy from fingers; release omens
By sortilege, or tea leaves, riddle the inevitable
With playing cards, fiddle with pentagrams
Or barbituric acids, or dissect   195
The recurrent image into pre-conscious terrors—
To explore the womb, or tomb, or dreams; all these are usual
Pastimes and drugs, and features of the press:
And always will be, some of them especially

When there is distress of nations and perplexity 200
Whether on the shores of Asia, or in the Edgware Road.
Men's curiosity searches past and future
And clings to that dimension. But to apprehend
The point of intersection of the timeless
With time, is an occupation for the saint— 205
No occupation either, but something given
And taken, in a lifetime's death in love,
Ardour and selflessness and self-surrender.
For most of us, there is only the unattended
Moment, the moment in and out of time, 210
The distraction fit, lost in a shaft of sunlight,
The wild thyme unseen, or the winter lightning
Or the waterfall, or music heard so deeply
That it is not heard at all, but you are the music
While the music lasts. These are only hints and guesses, 215
Hints followed by guesses; and the rest
Is prayer, observance, discipline, thought and action.
The hint half guessed, the gift half understood, is Incarnation.
Here the impossible union
Of spheres of existence is actual, 220
Here the past and future
Are conquered, and reconciled,
Where action were otherwise movement—
Of that which is only moved
And has in it no source of movement 225
Driven by daemonic, chthonic
Powers. And right action is freedom
From past and future also.
For most of us, this is the aim
Never here to be realised; 230
Who are only undefeated
Because we have gone on trying;
We, content at the last
If our temporal reversion nourish
(Not too far from the yew-tree) 235
The life of significant soil.

JOHN CROWE RANSOM (1888–   )

CAPTAIN CARPENTER

Captain Carpenter rose up in his prime
Put on his pistols and went riding out
But had got wellnigh nowhere at that time
Till he fell in with ladies in a rout.

It was a pretty lady and all her train
That played with him so sweetly but before
An hour she'd taken a sword with all her main
And twined him of his nose for evermore.

Captain Carpenter mounted up one day
And rode straightway into a stranger rogue   10
That looked unchristian but be that as may
The Captain did not wait upon prologue.

But drew upon him out of his great heart
The other swung against him with a club
And cracked his two legs at the shinny part
And let him roll and stick like any tub.

Captain Carpenter rode many a time
From male and female took he sundry harms
He met the wife of Satan crying "I'm
The she-wolf bids you shall bear no more arms."   20

Their strokes and counters whistled in the wind
I wish he had delivered half his blows
But where she should have made off like a hind
The bitch bit off his arms at the elbows.

And Captain Carpenter parted with his ears
To a black devil that used him in this wise
O Jesus ere his threescore and ten years
Another had plucked out his sweet blue eyes.

Captain Carpenter got up on his roan
And sallied from the gate in hell's despite   30

I heard him asking in the grimmest tone
If any enemy yet there was to fight?

"To any adversary it is fame
If he risk to be wounded by my tongue
Or burnt in two beneath my red heart's flame
Such are the perils he is cast among.

"But if he can he has a pretty choice
From an anatomy with little to lose
Whether he cut my tongue and take my voice
Or whether it be my round red heart he choose."   40

It was the neatest knave that ever was seen
Stepping in perfume from his lady's bower
Who at this word put in his merry mien
And fell on Captain Carpenter like a tower.

I would not knock old fellows in the dust
But there lay Captain Carpenter on his back
His weapons were the old heart in his bust
And a blade shook between rotten teeth alack.

The rogue in scarlet and grey soon knew his mind
He wished to get his trophy and depart   50
With gentle apology and touch refined
He pierced him and produced the Captain's heart.

God's mercy rest on Captain Carpenter now
I thought him Sirs an honest gentleman
Citizen husband soldier and scholar enow
Let jangling kites eat of him if they can.

But God's deep curses follow after those
That shore him of his goodly nose and ears
His legs and strong arms at the two elbows
And eyes that had not watered seventy years   60

The curse of hell upon the sleek upstart
That got the Captain finally on his back
And took the red red vitals of his heart
And made the kites to whet their beaks clack clack.

EDNA ST. VINCENT MILLAY (1892–1950)

OH, SLEEP FOREVER IN THE LATMIAN CAVE

Oh, sleep forever in the Latmian cave,
Mortal Endymion, darling of the Moon!
Her silver garments by the senseless wave
Shouldered and dropped and on the shingle strewn,
Her fluttering hand against her forehead pressed,
Her scattered looks that trouble all the sky,
Her rapid footsteps running down the west—
Of all her altered state, oblivious lie!
Whom earthen you, by deathless lips adored,
Wild-eyed and stammering to the grasses thrust,
And deep into her crystal body poured
The hot and sorrowful sweetness of the dust:
Whereof she wanders mad, being all unfit
For mortal love, that might not die of it.

ARCHIBALD Mac LEISH (1892–   )

THE TOO-LATE BORN

We too, we too, descending once again
The hills of our own land, we too have heard
Far off—Ah, que ce cor a longue haleine—
The horn of Roland in the passages of Spain,
The first, the second blast, the failing third,
And with the third turned back and climbed once more
The steep road southward, and heard faint the sound
Of swords, of horses, the disastrous war,
And crossed the dark defile at last, and found
At Roncevaux upon the darkening plain
The dead against the dead and on the silent ground
The silent slain—

WILFRED OWEN (1893–1918)

STRANGE MEETING

It seemed that out of the battle I escaped
Down some profound dull tunnel, long since scooped
Through granites which Titanic wars had groined.
Yet also there encumbered sleepers groaned,
Too fast in thought or death to be bestirred.   5
Then, as I probed them, one sprang up, and stared
With piteous recognition in fixed eyes,
Lifting distressful hands as if to bless.
And by his smile, I knew that sullen hall;
By his dead smile I knew I stood in Hell.   10
With a thousand pains that vision's face was grained;
Yet no blood reached there from the upper ground,
And no guns thumped, or down the flues made moan.
"Strange, friend," I said, "here is no cause to mourn."
"None," said the other, "save the undone years,   15
The hopelessness. Whatever hope is yours
Was my life also; I went hunting wild
After the wildest beauty in the world,
Which lies not calm in eyes, or braided hair,
But mocks the steady running of the hour,   20
And if it grieves, grieves richlier than here.
For by my glee might many men have laughed,
And of my weeping something had been left,
Which must die now. I mean the truth untold,
The pity of war, the pity war distilled.   25
Now men will go content with what we spoiled,
Or, discontent, boil bloody, and be spilled.
They will be swift with swiftness of the tigress,
None will break ranks, though nations trek from progress.
Courage was mine, and I had mystery,   30
Wisdom was mine, and I had mastery;
To miss the march of this retreating world
Into vain citadels that are not walled.
Then when much blood had clogged their chariot-wheels
I would go up and wash them from sweet wells,   35
Even with truths that lie too deep for taint.
I would have poured my spirit without stint

But not through wounds; not on the cess of war.
Foreheads of men have bled where no wounds were.
I am the enemy you killed, my friend.   40
I knew you in this dark; for so you frowned
Yesterday through me as you jabbed and killed.
I parried; but my hands were loth and cold.
Let us sleep now. . . ."

GREATER LOVE

Red lips are not so red
  As the stained stones kissed by the English dead.
Kindness of wooed and wooer
Seems shame to their love pure.
O Love, your eyes lose lure   5
  When I behold eyes blinded in my stead!

Your slender attitude
  Trembles not exquisite like limbs knife-skewed,
Rolling and rolling there
Where God seems not to care;   10
Till the fierce love they bear
  Cramps them in death's extreme decrepitude.

Your voice sings not so soft,—
  Though even as wind murmuring through raftered loft,—
Your dear voice is not dear,   15
Gentle, and evening clear,
As theirs whom none now hear
  Now earth has stopped their piteous mouths that coughed.

Heart, you were never hot,
  Nor large, nor full like hearts made great with shot;   20
And though your hand be pale,
Paler are all which trail
Your cross through flame and hail:
  Weep, you may weep, for you may touch them not.

INSENSIBILITY

I

Happy are men who yet before they are killed
Can let their veins run cold.
Whom no compassion fleers
Or makes their feet
Sore on the alleys cobbled with their brothers.   5
The front line withers,
But they are troops who fade, not flowers,
For poets' tearful fooling:
Men, gaps for filling:
Losses who might have fought   10
Longer; but no one bothers.

II

And some cease feeling
Even themselves or for themselves.
Dullness best solves
The tease and doubt of shelling,   15
And Chance's strange arithmetic
Comes simpler than the reckoning of their shilling.
They keep no check on armies' decimation.

III

Happy are these who lose imagination:
They have enough to carry with ammunition.   20
The spirit drags no pack,
Their old wounds save with cold can not more ache.
Having seen all things red,
Their eyes are rid
Of the hurt of the colour of blood for ever.   25
And terror's first constriction over,
Their hearts remain small-drawn.
Their senses in some scorching cautery of battle
Now long since ironed,
Can laugh among the dying, unconcerned.   30

IV

Happy the soldier home, with not a notion
How somewhere, every dawn, some men attack,
And many sighs are drained.
Happy the lad whose mind was never trained:
His days are worth forgetting more than not.   35
He sings along the march
Which we march taciturn, because of dusk,
The long, forlorn, relentless trend
From larger day to huger night.

V

We wise, who with a thought besmirch   40
Blood over all our soul,
How should we seek our task
But through his blunt and lashless eyes?
Alive, he is not vital overmuch;
Dying, not mortal overmuch;   45
Nor sad, nor proud,
Nor curious at all.
He cannot tell
Old men's placidity from his.

VI

But cursed are dullards whom no cannon stuns,   50
That they should be as stones;
Wretched are they, and mean
With paucity that never was simplicity.
By choice they made themselves immune
To pity and whatever moans in man   55
Before the last sea and the hapless stars;
Whatever mourns when many leave these shores;
Whatever shares
The eternal reciprocity of tears.

E. E. CUMMINGS (1894–   )

WHO'S MOST AFRAID OF DEATH? THOU

who's most afraid of death? thou
                                art of him

utterly afraid, i love of thee
(beloved) this

                and truly i would be
near when his scythe takes crisply the whim
of thy smoothness.   and mark the fainting
murdered petals.   with the caving stem.

But of all most would i be one of them

round the hurt heart which do so frailly cling . . .)
i who am but imperfect in my fear

Or with thy mind against my mind, to hear
nearing our hearts' irrevocable play—
through the mysterious high futile day

an enormous stride
                    (and drawing thy mouth toward

my mouth, steer our lost bodies carefully downward)

ROBERT GRAVES (1895–   )

TO JUAN AT THE WINTER SOLSTICE

There is one story and one story only
That will prove worth your telling,
Whether as learned bard or gifted child;
To it all lines or lesser gauds belong
That startle with their shining   5
Such common stories as they stray into.

Is it of trees you tell, their months and virtues,
Of strange beasts that beset you,
Of birds that croak at you the Triple will?
Or of the Zodiac and how slow it turns   10
Below the Boreal Crown,
Prison of all true kings that ever reigned?

Water to water, ark again to ark,
From woman back to woman:
So each new victim treads unfalteringly   15
The never altered circuit of his fate,
Bringing twelve peers as witness
Both to his starry rise and starry fall.

Or is it of the Virgin's silver beauty,
All fish below the thighs?   20
She in her left hand bears a leafy quince;
When with her right she crooks a finger, smiling,
How may the King hold back?
Royally then he barters life for love.

Or of the undying snake from chaos hatched,   25
Whose coils contain the ocean,
Into whose chops with naked sword he springs,
Then in black water, tangled by the reeds,
Battles three days and nights,
To be spewed up beside her scalloped shore?   30

Much snow is falling, winds roar hollowly,
The owl hoots from the elder,
Fear in your heart cries to the loving-cup:
Sorrow to sorrow as the sparks fly upward.
The log groans and confesses   35
There is one story and one story only.

Dwell on her graciousness, dwell on her smiling,
Do not forget what flowers
The great boar trampled down in ivy time.
Her brow was creamy as the long ninth wave,   40
Her sea-blue eyes were wild.
But nothing promised that is not performed.

OGRES AND PYGMIES

Those famous men of old, the Ogres—
They had long beards and stinking arm-pits.
They were wide-mouthed, long-yarded and great-bellied
Yet of not taller stature, Sirs, than you.
They lived on Ogre-Strand, which was no place   5
But the churl's terror of their proud extent,
Where every foot was three-and-thirty inches
And every penny bought a whole sheep.
Now of their company none survived, not one,
The times being, thank God, unfavourable   10
To all but nightmare memory of them.
Their images stand howling in the waste,
(The winds enforced against their wide mouths)
Whose granite haunches king and priest must yearly
Buss, and their cold knobbed knees.   15
So many feats they did to admiration:
With their enormous lips they sang louder
Than ten cathedral choirs, with their grand yards
Stormed the most rare and obstinate maidenheads,
With their strong-gutted and capacious bellies   20
Digested stones and glass like ostriches.
They dug great pits and heaped great cairns,
Deflected rivers, slew whole armies
And hammered judgements for posterity—
For the sweet-cupid-lipped tassel-yarded   25
Delicate-stomached dwellers
In Pygmy Alley, where with brooding on them
A foot is shrunk to seven inches
And twelve-pence will not buy a spare rib.
And who would choose between Ogres and Pygmies—   30
The thundering text, the snivelling commentary—
Reading between such covers he will likely
Prove his own disproportion and not laugh.

ALLEN TATE (1899–   )

THE MEDITERRANEAN

Quem das finem, rex magne, dolorum? [1]

Where we went in the boat was a long bay
A slingshot wide, walled in by towering stone—
Peaked margin of antiquity's delay,
And we went there out of time's monotone:

Where we went in the black hull no light moved   5
But a gull white-winged along the feckless wave,
The breeze, unseen but fierce as a body loved,
That boat drove onward like a willing slave:

Where we went in the small ship the seaweed
Parted and gave to us the murmuring shore   10
And we made feast and in our secret need
Devoured the very plates Aeneas bore:

Where derelict you see through the low twilight
The green coast that you, thunder-tossed, would win,
Drop sail, and hastening to drink all night   15
Eat dish and bowl—to take that sweet land in!

Where we feasted and caroused on the sandless
Pebbles, affecting our day of piracy,
What prophecy of eaten plates could landless
Wanderers fulfil by the ancient sea?   20

We for that time might taste the famous age
Eternal here yet hidden from our eyes
When lust of power undid its stuffless rage;
They, in a wineskin, bore earth's paradise.

Let us lie down once more by the breathing side   25
Of Ocean, where our live forefathers sleep
As if the Known Sea still were a month wide—
Atlantis howls but is no longer steep!

[1] **Quem das finem etc.:** When, great King, will you bring an end to our griefs? Vergil, *Aeneid.*

What country shall we conquer, what fair land
Unman our conquest and locate our blood?   30
We've cracked the hemispheres with careless hand!
Now, from the gates of Hercules we flood

Westward, westward, till the barbarous brine
Whelms us to the tired world where tasseling corn,
Fat beans, grapes sweeter than muscadine   35
Rot on the vine: in that land were we born.

ODE TO THE CONFEDERATE DEAD

Row after row with strict impunity
The headstones yield their names to the element,
The wind whirrs without recollection;
In the riven troughs the splayed leaves
Pile up, of nature the casual sacrament   5
To the seasonal eternity of death;
Then driven by the fierce scrutiny
Of heaven to their election in the vast breath,
They sough the rumor of mortality.

Autumn is desolation in the plot   10
Of a thousand acres where these memories grow
From the inexhaustible bodies that are not
Dead, but feed the grass row after rich row.
Think of the autumns that have come and gone!—
Ambitious November with the humors of the year,   15
With a particular zeal for every slab,
Staining the uncomfortable angels that rot
On the slabs, a wing chipped here, an arm there:
The brute curiosity of an angel's stare
Turns you, like them, to stone,   20
Transforms the heaving air
Till plunged to a heavier world below
You shift your sea-space blindly
Heaving, turning like the blind crab.

Dazed by the wind, only the wind   25
The leaves flying, plunge

You know who have waited by the wall
The twilight certainty of an animal,
Those midnight restitutions of the blood
You know—the immitigable pines, the smoky frieze   30
Of the sky, the sudden call: you know the rage,
The cold pool left by the mounting flood,
Of muted Zeno and Parmenides.
You who have waited for the angry resolution
Of those desires that should be yours tomorrow,   35
You know the unimportant shrift of death
And praise the vision
And praise the arrogant circumstance
Of those who fall
Rank upon rank, hurried beyond decision—   40
Here by the sagging gate, stopped by the wall.

    Seeing, seeing only the leaves
    Flying, plunge and expire

Turn your eyes to the immoderate past,
Turn to the inscrutable infantry rising   45
Demons out of the earth—they will not last.
Stonewall, Stonewall, and the sunken fields of hemp,
Shiloh, Antietam, Malvern Hill, Bull Run.
Lost in that orient of the thick and fast
You will curse the setting sun.   50

    Cursing only the leaves crying
    Like an old man in a storm

You hear the shout, the crazy hemlocks point
With troubled fingers to the silence which
Smothers you, a mummy, in time.   55

               The hound bitch
Toothless and dying, in a musty cellar
Hears the wind only.

             Now that the salt of their blood
Stiffens the saltier oblivion of the sea,   60
Seals the malignant purity of the flood,
What shall we who count our days and bow
Our heads with a commemorial woe
In the ribboned coats of grim felicity,

What shall we say of the bones, unclean,   65
Whose verdurous anonymity will grow?

The raged arms, the ragged heads and eyes
Lost in these acres of the insane green?
The gray lean spiders come, they come and go;
In a tangle of willows without light   70
The singular screech-owl's tight
Invisible lyric seeds the mind
With the furious murmur of their chivalry.

    We shall say only the leaves
    Flying, plunge and expire   75

We shall say only the leaves whispering
In the improbable mist of nightfall
That flies on multiple wing:
Night is the beginning and the end
And in between the ends of distraction   80
Waits mute speculation, the patient curse
That stones the eyes, or like the jaguar leaps
For his own image in a jungle pool, his victim.

What shall we say who have knowledge
Carried to the heart? Shall we take the act   85
To the grave? Shall we, more hopeful, set up the grave
In the house? The ravenous grave?
                     Leave now
The shut gate and the decomposing wall:
The gentle serpent, green in the mulberry bush,   90
Riots with his tongue through the hush—
Sentinel of the grave who counts us all!

HART CRANE (1899–1932)

TO BROOKLYN BRIDGE

How many dawns, chill from his rippling rest
The seagull's wings shall dip and pivot him,
Shedding white rings of tumult, building high
Over the chained bay waters Liberty—

Then, with inviolate curve, forsake our eyes 5
As apparitional as sails that cross
Some page of figures to be filed away;
—Till elevators drop us from our day . . .

I think of cinemas, panoramic sleights
With multitudes bent toward some flashing scene 10
Never disclosed, but hastened to again,
Foretold to other eyes on the same screen;

And Thee, across the harbor, silver-paced
As though the sun took step of thee, yet left
Some motion ever unspent in thy stride,— 15
Implicitly thy freedom staying thee!

Out of some subway scuttle, cell or loft
A bedlamite speeds to thy parapets,
Tilting there momently, shrill shirt ballooning,
A jest falls from the speechless caravan. 20

Down Wall, from girder into street noon leaks,
A rip-tooth of the sky's acetylene;
All afternoon the cloud-flown derricks turn . . .
Thy cables breathe the North Atlantic still.

And obscure as that heaven of the Jews, 25
Thy guerdon . . . Accolade thou dost bestow
Of anonymity time cannot raise:
Vibrant reprieve and pardon thou dost show.

O harp and altar, of the fury fused,
(How could mere toil align thy choiring strings!) 30
Terrific threshold of the prophet's pledge,
Prayer of pariah, and the lover's cry,—

Again the traffic lights that skim thy swift
Unfractioned idiom, immaculate sigh of stars,
Beading thy path—condense eternity: 35
And we have seen night lifted in thine arms.

Under thy shadow by the piers I waited;
Only in darkness is thy shadow clear.

The City's fiery parcels all undone,
Already snow submerges an iron year . . .   40

O Sleepless as the river under thee,
Vaulting the sea, the prairies' dreaming sod,
Unto us lowliest sometime sweep, descend
And of the curveship lend a myth to God.

REPOSE OF RIVERS

The willows carried a slow sound,
A sarabande the wind mowed on the mead.
I could never remember
That seething, steady leveling of the marshes
Till age had brought me to the sea.   5

Flags, weeds. And remembrance of steep alcoves
Where cypresses shared the noon's
Tyranny; they drew me into hades almost.
And mammoth turtles climbing sulphur dreams
Yielded, while sun-silt rippled them   10
Asunder . . .

How much I would have bartered! the black gorge
And all the singular nestings in the hills
Where beavers learn stitch and tooth.
The pond I entered once and quickly fled—   15
I remember now its singing willow rim.

And finally, in that memory all things nurse;
After the city that I finally passed
With scalding unguents spread and smoking darts
The monsoon cut across the delta   20
At gulf gates . . . There, beyond the dykes

I heard wind flaking sapphire, like this summer,
And willows could not hold more steady sound.

THE DANCE

(from *The Bridge*)

The swift red flesh, a winter king—
Who squired the glacier woman down the sky?
She ran the neighing canyons all the spring;
She spouted arms; she rose with maize—to die.

And in the autumn drouth, whose burnished hands   5
With mineral wariness found out the stone
Where prayers, forgotten, streamed the mesa sands?
He holds the twilight's dim, perpetual throne.

Mythical brows we saw retiring—loth,
Disturbed and destined, into denser green.   10
Greeting they sped us, on the arrow's oath:
Now lie incorrigibly what years between . . .

There was a bed of leaves, and broken play;
There was a veil upon you, Pocahontas, bride—
O Princess whose brown lap was virgin May;   15
And bridal flanks and eyes hid tawny pride.

I left the village for dogwood. By the canoe
Tugging below the mill-race, I could see
Your hair's keen crescent running, and the blue
First moth of evening take wing stealthily.   20

What laughing chains the water wove and threw!
I learned to catch the trout's moon whisper; I
Drifted how many hours I never knew,
But, watching, saw that fleet young crescent die,—

And one star, swinging, take its place, alone,   25
Cupped in the larches of the mountain pass—
Until, immortally, it bled into the dawn.
I left my sleek boat nibbling margin grass . . .

I took the portage climb, then chose
A further valley-shed; I could not stop.   30
Feet nozzled wat'ry webs of upper flows;
One white veil gusted from the very top.

O Appalachian Spring! I gained the ledge;
Steep, inaccessible smile that eastward bends
And northward reaches in that violet wedge   35
Of Adirondack!—wisped of azure wands,

Over how many bluffs, tarns, streams I sped!
—And knew myself within some boding shade:
Grey tepees tufting the blue knolls ahead,
Smoke swirling through the yellow chestnut glade . . . 40

A distant cloud, a thunder-bud—it grew,
That blanket of the skies: the padded foot
Within,—I heard it; 'til its rhythm drew,
—Siphoned the black pool from the heart's hot root!

A cyclone threshes in the turbine crest,   45
Swooping in eagle feathers down your back;
Know, Maquokeeta, greeting; know death's best;
—Fall, Sachem, strictly as the tamarack!

A birch kneels. All her whistling fingers fly.
The oak grove circles in a crash of leaves;   50
The long moan of a dance is in the sky.
Dance, Maquokeeta: Pocahontas grieves . . .

And every tendon scurries toward the twangs
Of lightning deltaed down your saber hair.
Now snaps the flint in every tooth; red fangs   55
And splay tongues thinly busy the blue air . . .

Dance, Maquokeeta! snake that lives before,
That casts his pelt, and lives beyond! Sprout, horn!
Spark, tooth! Medicine-man, relent, restore—
Lie to us—dance us back the tribal morn!   60

Spears and assemblies: black drums thrusting on—
O yelling battlements,—I, too, was liege
To rainbows currying each pulsant bone:
Surpassed the circumstance, danced out the siege!

And buzzard-circleted, screamed from the stake;   65
I could not pick the arrows from my side.

Wrapped in that fire, I saw more escorts wake—
Flickering, sprint up the hill groins like a tide.

I heard the hush of lava wrestling your arms,
And stag teeth foam about the raven throat;   70
Flame cataracts of heaven in seething swarms
Fed down your anklets to the sunset's moat.

O, like the lizard in the furious noon,
That drops his legs and colors in the sun,
—And laughs, pure serpent, Time itself, and moon   75
Of his own fate, I saw thy change begun!

And saw thee dive to kiss that destiny
Like one white meteor, sacrosanct and blent
At last with all that's consummate and free
There, where the first and last gods keep thy tent.   80

                    *   *   *

Thewed of the levin, thunder-shod and lean,
Lo, through what infinite seasons dost thou gaze—
Across what bivouacs of thine angered slain,
And see'st thy bride immortal in the maize!

Totem and fire-gall, slumbering pyramid—   85
Though other calendars now stack the sky,
Thy freedom is her largesse, Prince, and hid
On paths thou knewest best to claim her by.

High unto Labrador the sun strikes free
Her speechless dream of snow, and stirred again,   90
She is the torrent and the singing tree;
    And she is virgin to the last of men . . .

West, west and south! winds over Cumberland
And winds across the llano grass resume
Her hair's warm sibilance. Her breasts are fanned—   95
O stream by slope and vineyard—into bloom!

And when the caribou slant down for salt
Do arrows thirst and leap? Do antlers shine
Alert, star-triggered in the listening vault
Of dusk?—And are her perfect brows to thine?   100

We danced, O Brave, we danced beyond their farms,
In cobalt desert closures made our vows . . .
Now is the strong prayer folded in thine arms,
The serpent with the eagle in the boughs.

VOYAGES (VI)

Where icy and bright dungeons lift
Of swimmers their lost morning eyes,
And ocean rivers, churning, shift
Green borders under stranger skies,

Steadily as a shell secretes   5
Its beating leagues of monotone,
Or as many waters trough the sun's
Red kelson past the cape's wet stone;

O rivers mingling toward the sky
And harbor of the phoenix' breast—   10
My eyes pressed black against the prow,
—Thy derelict and blinded guest

Waiting, afire, what name, unspoke,
I cannot claim: let thy waves rear
More savage than the death of kings,   15
Some splintered garland for the seer.

Beyond siroccos harvesting
The solstice thunders, crept away,
Like a cliff swinging or a sail
Flung into April's inmost day—   20

Creation's blithe and petalled word
To the lounged goddess when she rose
Conceding dialogue with eyes
That smile unsearchable repose—

Still fervid covenant, Belle Isle,   25
—Unfolding floating dais before
Which rainbows twine continual hair—
Belle Isle, white echo of the oar!

The imaged Word, it is, that holds
Hushed willows anchored in its glow.   30
It is the unbetrayable reply
Whose accent no farewell can know.

RICHARD EBERHART (1904–   )

THE GROUNDHOG

In June, amid the golden fields,
I saw a groundhog lying dead.
Dead lay he; my senses shook,
And mind outshot our naked frailty.
There lowly in the vigorous summer   5
His form began its senseless change,
And made my senses waver dim
Seeing nature ferocious in him.
Inspecting close his maggots' might
And seething cauldron of his being,   10
Half with loathing, half with a strange love,
I poked him with an angry stick.
The fever arose, became a flame
And Vigour circumscribed the skies,
Immense energy in the sun,   15
And through my frame a sunless trembling.
My stick had done nor good nor harm.
Then stood I silent in the day
Watching the object, as before;
And kept my reverence for knowledge   20
Trying for control, to be still,
To quell the passion of the blood;
Until I had bent down on my knees
Praying for joy in the sight of decay.
And so I left; and I returned   25
In Autumn strict of eye, to see
The sap gone out of the groundhog,
But the bony sodden hulk remained.
But the year had lost its meaning,
And in intellectual chains   30
I lost both love and loathing,
Mured up in the wall of wisdom.

Another summer took the fields again
Massive and burning, full of life,
But when I chanced upon the spot   35
There was only a little hair left,
And bones bleaching in the sunlight
Beautiful as architecture;
I watched them like a geometer,
And cut a walking stick from a birch.   40
It has been three years, now.
There is no sign of the groundhog.
I stood there in the whirling summer,
My hand capped a withered heart,
And thought of China and of Greece,   45
Of Alexander in his tent;
Of Montaigne in his tower,
Of Saint Theresa in her wild lament.

W. H. AUDEN (1907-   )

MUSEE DES BEAUX ARTS

About suffering they were never wrong,
The Old Masters: how well they understood
Its human position; how it takes place
While someone else is eating or opening a window or just
    walking dully along;
How, when the aged are reverently, passionately waiting   5
For the miraculous birth, there always must be
Children who did not specially want it to happen, skating
On a pond at the edge of the wood:
They never forgot
That even the dreadful martyrdom must run its course   10
Anyhow in a corner, some untidy spot
Where the dogs go on with their doggy life and the tor-
    turer's horse
Scratches its innocent behind on a tree.
In Brueghel's *Icarus*, for instance: how everything turns away
Quite leisurely from the disaster; the ploughman may   15
Have heard the splash, the forsaken cry,

But for him it was not an important failure; the sun shone
As it had to on the white legs disappearing into the green
Water; and the expensive delicate ship that must have seen
Something amazing, a boy falling out of the sky,   20
Had somewhere to get to and sailed calmly on.

SEPTEMBER 1, 1939

I sit in one of the dives
On Fifty-Second Street
Uncertain and afraid
As the clever hopes expire
Of a low dishonest decade: 5
Waves of anger and fear
Circulate over the bright
And darkened lands of the earth,
Obsessing our private lives;
The unmentionable odour of death   10
Offends the September night.

Accurate scholarship can
Unearth the whole offence
From Luther until now
That has driven a culture mad,   15
Find what occurred at Linz,
What huge imago made
A psychopathic god:
I and the public know
What all schoolchildren learn,   20
Those to whom evil is done
Do evil in return.

Exiled Thucydides knew
All that a speech can say
About Democracy,
And what dictators do,   25
The elderly rubbish they talk

16. **Linz:** Where Hitler spent his   24. **Speech:** the famous funeral ora-
    childhood   tion of Pericles

To an apathetic grave;
Analysed all in his book,
The enlightenment driven away,   30
The habit-forming pain,
Mismanagement and grief:
We must suffer them all again.

Into this neutral air
Where blind skyscrapers use   35
Their full height to proclaim
The strength of Collective Man,
Each language pours its vain
Competitive excuse:
But who can live for long   40
In an euphoric dream;
Out of the mirror they stare,
Imperialism's face
And the international wrong.

Faces along the bar   45
Cling to their average day:
The lights must never go out,
The music must always play,
All the conventions conspire
To make this fort assume   50
The furniture of home;
Lest we should see where we are,
Lost in a haunted wood,
Children afraid of the night
Who have never been happy or good.   55

The windiest militant trash
Important Persons shout
It is not so crude as our wish:
What mad Nijinsky wrote
About Diaghilev   60
Is true of the normal heart;
For the error bred in the bone
Of each woman and each man
Craves what it cannot have,
Not universal love   65
But to be loved alone.

From the conservative dark
Into the ethical life
The dense commuters come,
Repeating their morning vow;   70
"I *will* be true to the wife,
I'll concentrate more on my work,"
And helpless governors wake
To resume their compulsory game:
Who can release them now,   75
Who can reach the deaf,
Who can speak for the dumb?

All I have is a voice
To undo the folded lie,
The romantic lie in the brain   80
Of the sensual man-in-the-street
And the lie of Authority
Whose buildings grope the sky:
There is no such thing as the State
And no one exists alone;   85
Hunger allows no choice
To the citizen or the police;
We must love one another or die.

Defenceless under the night
Our world in stupor lies;   90
Yet dotted everywhere,
Ironic points of light
Flash out wherever the Just
Exchange their messages:
May I, composed like them   95
Of Eros and of dust,
Beleaguered by the same
Negation and despair,
Show an affirming flame.

AS I WALKED OUT ONE EVENING

As I walked out one evening,
    Walking down Bristol Street,
The crowds upon the pavement
    Were fields of harvest wheat.

And down by the brimming river   5
  I heard a lover sing
Under an arch of the railway
  "Love has no ending.

"I'll love you, dear, I'll love you
  Till China and Africa meet   10
And the river jumps over the mountain
  And the salmon sing in the street.

"I'll love you till the ocean
  Is folded and hung up to dry
And the seven stars go squawking   15
  Like geese about the sky.

"The years shall run like rabbits,
  For in my arms I hold
The Flower of the Ages
  And the first love of the world."   20

But all the clocks in the city
  Began to whirr and chime:
"O let not Time deceive you,
  You cannot conquer Time.

"In the burrows of the nightmare   25
  Where Justice naked is,
Time watches from the shadow
  And coughs when you would kiss.

"In headaches and in worry
  Vaguely life leaks away,   30
And Time will have his fancy
  To-morrow or to-day.

"Into many a green valley
  Drifts the appalling snow;
Time breaks the threaded dances   35
  And the diver's brilliant bow.

"O plunge your hands in water,
  Plunge them in up to the wrist;

Stare, stare in the basin
  And wonder what you've missed.   40

"The glacier knocks in the cupboard,
  The desert sighs in the bed,
And the crack in the tea-cup opens
  A lane to the land of the dead.

"Where the beggars raffle the banknotes   45
  And the Giant is enchanting to Jack,
And the Lily-white Boy is a Roarer
  And Jill goes down on her back.

"O look, look in the mirror,
  O look in your distress;   50
Life remains a blessing
  Although you cannot bless.

"O stand, stand at the window
  As the tears scald and start;
You shall love your crooked neighbour   55
  With your crooked heart."

It was late, late in the evening,
  The lovers they were gone;
The clocks had ceased their chiming
  And the deep river ran on.   60

PREFACE [to *The Sea and the Mirror*]
  (The Stage Manager to the Critics)

The aged catch their breath,
For the nonchalant couple go
Waltzing across the tightrope
As if there were no death
Or hope of falling down;   5
The wounded cry as the clown
Doubles his meaning, and O
How the dear little children laugh
When the drums roll and the lovely
Lady is sawn in half.   10

O what authority gives
Existence its surprise?
Science is happy to answer
That the ghosts who haunt our lives
Are handy with mirrors and wire,   15
That song and sugar and fire,
Courage and come-hither eyes
Have a genius for taking pains.
But how does one think up a habit?
Our wonder, our terror remains.   20

Art opens the fishiest eye
To the Flesh and the Devil who heat
The Chamber of Temptation
Where heroes roar and die.
We are wet with sympathy now;   25
Thanks for the evening; but how
Shall we satisfy when we meet,
Between Shall-I and I-Will,
The lion's mouth whose hunger
No metaphors can fill?   30

Well, who in his own backyard
Has not opened his heart to the smiling
Secret he cannot quote?
Which goes to show that the Bard
Was sober when he wrote   35
That this world of fact we love
Is unsubstantial stuff:
All the rest is silence
On the other side of the wall;
And the silence ripeness,   40
And the ripeness all.

FUGAL CHORUS

(from *For the Time-Being*)

Great is Caesar: He has conquered Seven Kingdoms.
The First was the Kingdom of Abstract Idea:
Last night it was Tom, Dick and Harry; tonight it is
     S's with P's:

Instead of inflexions and accents
There are prepositions and word-order;   5
Instead of aboriginal objects excluding each other
There are specimens reiterating a type;
Instead of wood-nymphs and river-demons,
There is one unconditioned ground of Being.
Great is Caesar: God must be with Him.   10

Great is Caesar: He has conquered Seven Kingdoms.
The Second was the Kingdom of Natural Cause:
Last night it was Sixes and Sevens; tonight it is One and Two;
Instead of saying, "Strange are the whims of the Strong,"
We say, "Harsh is the Law but it is certain";   15
Instead of building temples, we build laboratories;
Instead of offering sacrifices, we perform experiments;
Instead of reciting prayers, we note pointer-readings;
Our lives are no longer erratic but efficient.
Great is Caesar: God must be with Him.   20

Great is Caesar: He has conquered Seven Kingdoms.
The Third was the Kingdom of Infinite Number:
Last night it was Rule-of-Thumb, tonight it is To-a-T;
Instead of Quite-a-lot, there is Exactly-so-many;
Instead of Only-a-few, there is Just-these;   25
Instead of saying, "You must wait until I have counted,"
We say, "Here you are. You will find this answer correct";
Instead of a nodding acquaintance with a few integers
The Transcendentals are our personal friends.
Great is Caesar: God must be with Him.   30

Great is Caesar: He has conquered Seven Kingdoms.
The Fourth was the Kingdom of Credit Exchange:
Last night it was Tit-for-Tat, Tonight it is C.O.D.;
When we have a surplus, we need not meet someone with a
    deficit;
When we have a deficit, we need not meet someone with a
    surplus;   35
Instead of heavy treasures, there are paper symbols of value;
Instead of Pay at Once, there is Pay when you can;
Instead of My Neighbour, there is Our Customers;
Instead of Country Fair, there is World Market.
Great is Caesar: God must be with Him.   40

Great is Caesar: He has conquered Seven Kingdoms.
The Fifth was the Kingdom of Inorganic Giants:
Last night it was Heave-Ho, tonight it is Whee-Spree;
When we want anything, They make it;
When we dislike anything, They change it;   45
When we want to go anywhere, They carry us;
When the Barbarian invades us, They raise immovable
    shields;
When we invade the Barbarian, They brandish irresistible
    swords;
Fate is no longer a fiat of Matter, but a freedom of Mind.
Great is Caesar: God must be with Him.   50

Great is Caesar: He has conquered Seven Kingdoms.
The Sixth was the Kingdom of Organic Dwarfs:
Last night it was Ouch-Ouch, tonight it is Yum-Yum;
When diseases waylay us, They strike them dead;
When worries intrude on us, They throw them out;   55
When pain accosts us, They save us from embarrassment;
When we feel like sheep, They make us lions;
When we feel like geldings, They make us stallions;
Spirit is no longer under Flesh, but on top.
Great is Caesar: God must be with Him.   60

Great is Caesar: He has conquered Seven Kingdoms.
The Seventh was the Kingdom of Popular Soul:
Last night it was Order-Order, tonight it is Hear-Hear;
When he says, You are happy, we laugh;
When he says, You are wretched, we cry;   65
When he says, It is true, everyone believes it;
When he says, It is false, no one believes it;
When he says, This is good, this is loved;
When he says, That is bad, that is hated.
Great is Caesar: God must be with Him.   70

LOUIS Mac NEICE (1907–   )

BAGPIPE MUSIC

It's no go the merrygoround, it's no go the rickshaw,
All we want is a limousine and a ticket for the peepshow.
Their knickers are made of crêpe-de-chine, their shoes are made of
    python,

Their halls are lined with tiger rugs and their walls with heads of
    bison.

John MacDonald found a corpse, put it under the sofa,   5
Waited till it came to life and hit it with a poker,
Sold its eyes for souvenirs, sold its blood for whiskey,
Kept its bones for dumb-bells to use when he was fifty.

It's no go the Yogi-Man, it's no go Blavatsky,
All we want is a bank balance and a bit of skirt in a taxi.   10

Annie MacDougall went to milk, caught her foot in the heather,
Woke to hear a dance record playing of Old Vienna.
It's no go your maidenheads, it's no go your culture,
All we want is a Dunlop tyre and the devil mend the puncture.

The Laird o'Phelps spent Hogmannay declaring he was sober;   15
Counted his feet to prove the fact and found he had one foot over.
Mrs. Carmichael had her fifth, looked at the job with repulsion,
Said to the midwife 'Take it away; I'm through with over-
    production.'

It's no go the gossip column, it's no go the Ceilidh,
All we want is a mother's help and a sugar-stick for the baby.   20

Willie Murray cut his thumb, couldn't count the damage,
Took the hide of an Ayrshire cow and used it for a bandage.
His brother caught three hundred cran when the seas were lavish,
Threw the bleeders back in the sea and went upon the parish.

It's no go the Herring Board, it's no go the Bible,   25
All we want is a packet of fags when our hands are idle.

It's no go the picture palace, it's no go the stadium,
It's no go the country cot with a pot of pink geraniums.
It's no go the Government grants, it's no go the elections,
Sit on your arse for fifty years and hang your hat on a pension.   30

It's no go my honey love, it's no go my poppet;
Work your hands from day to day, the winds will blow the profit.
The glass is falling hour by hour, the glass will fall for ever,
But if you break the bloody glass you won't hold up the weather.

STEPHEN SPENDER (1909–   )

THE EXPRESS

After the first powerful plain manifesto
The black statement of pistons, without more fuss
But gliding like a queen, she leaves the station.
Without bowing and with restrained unconcern
She passes the houses which humbly crowd outside,   5
The gasworks and at last the heavy page
Of death, printed by gravestones in the cemetery.
Beyond the town there lies the open country
Where, gathering speed, she acquires mystery,
The luminous self-possession of ships on ocean.   10
It is now she begins to sing—at first quite low
Then loud, and at last with a jazzy madness—
The song of her whistle screaming at curves,
Of deafening tunnels, brakes, innumerable bolts.
And always light, aerial, underneath   15
Goes the elate metre of her wheels.
Steaming through metal landscape on her lines
She plunges new eras of wild happiness
Where speed throws up strange shapes, broad curves
And parallels clean like the steel of guns.   20
At last, further than Edinburgh or Rome,
Beyond the crest of the world, she reaches night
Where only a low streamline brightness
Of phosphorus on the tossing hills is white.
Ah, like a comet through flame she moves entranced   25
Wrapt in her music no bird song, no, nor bough
Breaking with honey buds, shall ever equal.

TWO ARMIES

Deep in the winter plain, two armies
Dig their machinery, to destroy each other.
Men freeze and hunger. No one is given leave
On either side, except the dead, and wounded.
These have their leave; while new battalions wait   5
On time at last to bring them violent peace.

All have become so nervous and so cold
That each man hates the cause and distant words
Which brought him here, more terribly than bullets.
Once a boy hummed a popular marching song,   10
Once a novice hand flapped the salute;
The voice was choked, the lifted hand fell,
Shot through the wrist by those of his own side.

From their numb harvest all would flee, except
For discipline drilled once in an iron school   15
Which holds them at the point of a revolver.
Yet when they sleep, the images of home
Ride wishing horses of escape
Which herd the plain in a mass unspoken poem.

Finally, they cease to hate: for although hate   20
Bursts from the air and whips the earth like hail
Or pours it up in fountains to marvel at,
And although hundreds fall, who can connect
The inexhaustible anger of the guns
With the dumb patience of these tormented animals?   25

Clean silence drops at night when a little walk
Divides the sleeping armies, each
Huddled in linen woven by remote hands.
When the machines are stilled, a common suffering
Whitens the air with breath and makes both one   30
As though these enemies slept in each other's arms.

Only the lucid friend to aerial raiders,
The brilliant pilot moon, stares down
Upon the plain she makes a shining bone
Cut by the shadow of many thousand bones.   35
Where amber clouds scatter on no-man's land
She regards death and time throw up
The furious words and minerals which kill life.

KARL SHAPIRO (1913–   )

SCYROS

snuffle and sniff and handkerchief

The doctor punched my vein
The captain called me Cain
Upon my belly sat the sow of fear
　　With coins on either eye
　　The President came by
And whispered to the braids what none could hear

　　High over where the storm
　　Stood steadfast cruciform
The golden eagle sank in wounded wheels
　　White negroes laughing still   10
　　Crept fiercely on Brazil
Turning the navies upward on their keels

　　Now one by one the trees
　　Stripped to their naked knees
To dance upon the heaps of shrunken dead   15
　　The roof of England fell
　　Great Paris tolled her bell
And China staunched her milk and wept for bread

　　No island singly lay
　　But lost its name that day   20
The Ainu dived across the plunging sands
　　From dawn to dawn to dawn
　　King George's birds came on
Strafing the tulips from his children's hands

　　Thus in the classic sea   25
　　Southeast from Thessaly
The dynamited mermen washed ashore
　　And tritons dressed in steel
　　Trolled heads with rod and reel
And dredged potatoes from the Aegean floor   30

Hot is the sky and green
Where Germans have been seen
The moon leaks metal on the Atlantic fields
Pink boys in birthday shrouds
Look lightly through the clouds 35
Or coast the peaks of Finland on their shields

That prophet year by year
Lay still but could not hear
Where scholars tapped to find his new remains
Gog and Magog ate pork 40
In vertical New York
And war began next Monday on the Danes.

DYLAN THOMAS (1914–1953)

IN MY CRAFT OR SULLEN ART

In my craft or sullen art
Exercised in the still night
When only the moon rages
And the lovers lie abed
With all their griefs in their arms, 5
I labour by singing light
Not for ambition or bread
Or the strut and trade of charms
On the ivory stages
But for the common wages 10
Of their most secret heart.

Not for the proud man apart
From the raging moon I write
On these spindrift pages
Nor for the towering dead 15
With their nightingales and psalms
But for the lovers, their arms
Round the griefs of the ages,
Who pay no praise or wages
Nor heed my craft or art. 20

BALLAD OF THE LONG-LEGGED BAIT

The bows glided down, and the coast
Blackened with birds took a last look
At his thrashing hair and whale-blue eye;
The trodden town rang its cobbles for luck.

Then good-bye to the fishermanned   5
Boat with its anchor free and fast
As a bird hooking over the sea,
High and dry by the top of the mast,

Whispered the affectionate sand
And the bulwarks of the dazzled quay.   10
For my sake sail, and never look back,
Said the looking land.

Sails drank the wind, and white as milk
He sped into the drinking dark;
The sun shipwrecked west on a pearl   15
And the moon swam out of its hulk.

Funnels and masts went by in a whirl.
Good-bye to the man on the sea-legged deck
To the gold gut that sings on his reel
To the bait that stalked out of the sack,   20

For we saw him throw to the swift flood
A girl alive with his hooks through her lips;
All the fishes were rayed in blood,
Said the dwindling ships.

Good-bye to chimneys and funnels,   25
Old wives that spin in the smoke,
He was blind to the eyes of candles
In the praying windows of waves

But heard his bait buck in the wake
And tussle in a shoal of loves.   30
Now cast down your rod, for the whole
Of the sea is hilly with whales,

She longs among horses and angels,
The rainbow-fish bend in her joys,
Floated the lost cathedral   35
Chimes of the rocked buoys.

Where the anchor rode like a gull
Miles over the moonstruck boat
A squall of birds bellowed and fell,
A cloud blew the rain from its throat;   40

He saw the storm smoke out to kill
With fuming bows and ram of ice,
Fire on starlight, rake Jesu's stream;
And nothing shone on the water's face

But the oil and bubble of the moon,   45
Plunging and piercing in his course
The lured fish under the foam
Witnessed with a kiss.

Whales in the wake like capes and Alps
Quaked the sick sea and snouted deep,   50
Deep the great bushed bait with raining lips
Slipped the fins of those humpbacked tons

And fled their love in a weaving dip.
Oh, Jericho was falling in their lungs!
She nipped and dived in the nick of love,   55
Spun on a spout like a long-legged ball

Till every beast blared down in a swerve
Till every turtle crushed from his shell
Till every bone in the rushing grave
Rose and crowed and fell!   60

Good luck to the hand on the rod,
There is thunder under its thumbs;
Gold gut is a lightning thread,
His fiery reel sings off its flames,

The whirled boat in the burn of his blood   65
Is crying from nets to knives,

Oh the shearwater birds and their boatsized brood
Oh the bulls of Biscay and their calves

Are making under the green, laid veil
The long-legged beautiful bait their wives.   70
Break the black news and paint on a sail
Huge weddings in the waves,

Over the wakeward-flashing spray
Over the gardens of the floor
Clash out the mounting dolphin's day,   75
My mast is a bell-spire,

Strike and smoothe, for my decks are drums,
Sing through the water-spoken prow
The octopus walking into her limbs
The polar eagle with his tread of snow.   80

From salt-lipped beak to the kick of the stern
Sing how the seal has kissed her dead!
The long, laid minute's bride drifts on
Old in her cruel bed.

Over the graveyard in the water   85
Mountains and galleries beneath
Nightingale and hyena
Rejoicing for that drifting death

Sing and howl through sand and anemone
Valley and sahara in a shell,   90
Oh all the wanting flesh his enemy
Thrown to the sea in the shell of a girl

Is old as water and plain as an eel;
Always good-bye to the long-legged bread
Scattered in the paths of his heels   95
For the salty birds fluttered and fed

And the tall grains foamed in their bills;
Always good-bye to the fires of the face,
For the crab-backed dead on the sea-bed rose
And scuttled over her eyes,   100

The blind, clawed stare is cold as sleet
The tempter under the eyelid
Who shows to the selves asleep
Mast-high moon-white women naked

Walking in wishes and lovely for shame   105
Is dumb and gone with his flame of brides.
Susannah's drowned on the bearded stream
And no-one stirs at Sheba's side

But the hungry kings of the tides;
Sin who had a woman's shape   110
Sleeps till Silence blows on a cloud
And all the lifted waters walk and leap.

Lucifer that bird's dropping
Out of the sides of the north
Has melted away and is lost   115
Is always lost in her vaulted breath,

Venus lies star-struck in her wound
And the sensual ruins make
Seasons over the liquid world,
White springs in the dark.   120

Always good-bye, cried the voices through the shell,
Good-bye always for the flesh is cast
And the fisherman winds his reel
With no more desire than a ghost.

Always good luck, praised the finned in the feather   125
Bird after dark and the laughing fish
As the sails drank up the hail of thunder
And the long-tailed lightning lit his catch.

The boat swims into the six-year weather,
A wind throws a shadow and it freezes fast.   130
See what the gold gut drags from under
Mountains and galleries to the crest!

See what clings to hair and skull
As the boat skims on with drinking wings!

The statues of great rain stand still,   135
And the flakes fall like hills.

Sing and strike his heavy haul
Toppling up the boatside in a snow of light!
His decks are drenched with miracles.
Oh miracle of fishes! The long dead bite!   140

Out of the urn the size of a man
Out of the room the weight of his trouble
Out of the house that holds a town
In the continent of a fossil

One by one in dust and shawl,   145
Dry as echoes and insect-faced,
His fathers cling to the hand of the girl
And the dead hand leads the past,

Leads them as children and as air
On to the blindly tossing tops;   150
The centuries throw back their hair
And the old men sing from newborn lips:

Time is bearing another son.
Kill Time! She turns in her pain!
The oak is felled in the acorn   155
And the hawk in the egg kills the wren.

He who blew the great fire in
And died on a hiss of flames
Or walked on the earth in the evening
Counting the denials of the grains   160

Clings to her drifting hair, and climbs;
And he who taught their lips to sing
Weeps like the risen sun among
The liquid choirs of his tribes.

The rod bends low, divining land,   165
And through the sundered water crawls
A garden holding to her hand
With birds and animals

With men and women and waterfalls
Trees cool and dry in the whirlpool of ships   170
And stunned and still on the green, laid veil
Sand with legends in its virgin laps

And prophets loud on the burned dunes;
Insects and valleys hold her thighs hard,
Time and places grip her breast bone,   175
She is breaking with seasons and clouds;

Round her trailed wrist fresh water weaves,
With moving fish and rounded stones
Up and down the greater waves
A separate river breathes and runs;   180

Strike and sing his catch of fields
For the surge is sown with barley,
The cattle graze on the covered foam,
The hills have footed the waves away,

With wild sea fillies and soaking bridles   185
With salty colts and gales in their limbs
All the horses of his haul of miracles
Gallop through the arched, green farms,

Trot and gallop with gulls upon them
And thunderbolts in their manes.   190
O Rome and Sodom to-morrow and London
The country tide is cobbled with towns,

And steeples pierce the cloud on her shoulder
And the streets that the fisherman combed
When his long-legged flesh was a wind on fire   195
And his loin was a hunting flame

Coil from the thoroughfares of her hair
And terribly lead him home alive
Lead her prodigal home to his terror,
The furious ox-killing house of love.   200

Down, down, down, under the ground,
Under the floating villages,

Turns the moon-chained and water-wound
Metropolis of fishes,

There is nothing left of the sea but its sound,   205
Under the earth the loud sea walks,
In deathbeds of orchards the boat dies down
And the bait is drowned among hayricks,

Land, land, land, nothing remains
Of the pacing, famous sea but its speech,   210
And into its talkative seven tombs
The anchor dives through the floors of a church.

Good-bye, good luck, struck the sun and the moon,
To the fisherman lost on the land.
He stands alone at the door of his home,   215
With his long-legged heart in his hand.

A WINTER'S TALE

It is a winter's tale
That the snow blind twilight ferries over the lakes
And floating fields from the farm in the cup of the vales,
Gliding windless through the hand folded flakes,
The pale breath of cattle at the stealthy sail,   5

And the stars falling cold,
And the smell of hay in the snow, and the far owl
Warning among the folds, and the frozen hold
Flocked with the sheep white smoke of the farm house cowl
In the river wended vales where the tale was told.   10

Once when the world turned old
On a star of faith pure as the drifting bread,
As the food and flames of the snow, a man unrolled
The scrolls of fire that burned in his heart and head,
Torn and alone in a farm house in a fold   15

Of fields. And burning then
In his firelit island ringed by the winged snow

And the dung hills white as wool and the hen
Roosts sleeping chill till the flame of the cock crow
Combs through the mantled yards and the morning men   20

        Stumble out with their spades,
The cattle stirring, the mousing cat stepping shy,
The puffed birds hopping and hunting, the milk maids
Gentle in their clogs over the fallen sky,
And all the woken farm at its white trades,   25

        He knelt, he wept, he prayed,
By the spit and the black pot in the log bright light
And the cup and the cut bread in the dancing shade,
In the muffled house, in the quick of night,
At the point of love, forsaken and afraid.   30

        He knelt on the cold stones,
He wept from the crest of grief, he prayed to the veiled sky
May his hunger go howling on bare white bones
Past the statues of the stables and the sky roofed sties
And the duck pond glass and the blinding byres alone   35

        Into the home of prayers
And fires where he should prowl down the cloud
Of his snow blind love and rush in the white lairs.
His naked need struck him howling and bowed
Though no sound flowed down the hand folded air   40

        But only the wind strung
Hunger of birds in the fields of the bread of water, tossed
In high corn and the harvest melting on their tongues.
And his nameless need bound him burning and lost
When cold as snow he should run the wended vales among   45

        The rivers mouthed in night,
And drown in the drifts of his need, and lie curled caught
In the always desiring centre of the white
Inhuman cradle and the bride bed forever sought
By the believer lost and the hurled outcast of light.   50

        Deliver him, he cried,
By losing him all in love, and cast his need

Alone and naked in the engulfing bride,
Never to flourish in the fields of the white seed
Or flower under the time dying flesh astride.   55

       Listen. The minstrels sing
In the departed villages. The nightingale,
Dust in the buried wood, flies on the grains of her wings
And spells on the winds of the dead his winter's tale.
The voice of the dust of water from the withered spring   60

       Is telling. The wizened
Stream with bells and baying water bounds. The dew rings
On the gristed leaves and the long gone glistening
Parish of snow. The carved mouths in the rock are wind swept
    strings.
Time sings through the intricately dead snow drop. Listen.   65

       It was a hand or sound
In the long ago land that glided the dark door wide
And there outside on the bread of the ground
A she bird rose and rayed like a burning bride.
A she bird dawned, and her breast with snow and scarlet
    downed.   70

       Look. And the dancers move
On the departed, snow bushed green, wanton in moon light
As a dust of pigeons. Exulting, the grave hooved
Horses, centaur dead, turn and tread the drenched white
Paddocks in the farms of birds. The dead oak walks for love.   75

       The carved limbs in the rock
Leap, as to trumpets. Calligraphy of the old
Leaves is dancing. Lines of age on the stones weave in a flock.
And the harp shaped voice of the water's dust plucks in a fold
Of fields. For love, the long ago she bird rises. Look.   80

       And the wild wings were raised
Above her folded head, and the soft feathered voice
Was flying through the house as though the she bird praised
And all the elements of the slow fall rejoiced
That a man knelt alone in the cup of the vales,   85

In the mantle and calm,
By the spit and the black pot in the log bright light.
And the sky of birds in the plumed voice charmed
Him up and he ran like a wind after the kindling flight
Past the blind barns and byres of the windless farm.　　　90

In the poles of the year
When black birds died like priests in the cloaked hedge row
And over the cloth of counties the far hills rode near,
Under the one leaved trees ran a scarecrow of snow
And fast through the drifts of the thickets antlered like deer.　95

Rags and prayers down the knee-
Deep hillocks and loud on the numbed lakes,
All night lost and long wading in the wake of the she-
Bird through the times and lands and tribes of the slow flakes.
Listen and look where she sails the goose plucked sea,　　　100

The sky, the bird, the bride,
The cloud, the need, the planted stars, the joy beyond
The fields of seed and the time dying flesh astride,
The heavens, the heaven, the grave, the burning font,
In the far ago land the door of his death glided wide,　　　105

And the bird descended.
On a bread white hill over the cupped farm
And the lakes and floating fields and the river wended
Vales where he prayed to come to the last harm
And the home of prayers and fires, the tale ended.　　　110

The dancing perishes
On the white, no longer growing green, and, minstrel dead,
The singing breaks in the snow shoed villages of wishes
That once cut the figures of birds on the deep bread
And over the glazed lakes skated the shapes of fishes　　　115

Flying. The rite is shorn
Of nightingale and centaur dead horse. The springs wither
Back. Lines of age sleep on the stones till trumpeting dawn.
Exultation lies down. Time buries the spring weather
That belled and bounded with the fossil and the dew reborn.　120

For the bird lay bedded
In a choir of wings, as though she slept or died,
And the wings glided wide and he was hymned and wedded,
And through the thighs of the engulfing bride,
The woman breasted and the heaven headed   125

Bird, he was brought low,
Burning in the bride bed of love, in the whirl-
Pool at the wanting centre, in the folds
Of Paradise, in the spun bud of the world.
And she rose with him flowering in her melting snow.   130

DO NOT GO GENTLE INTO THAT GOOD NIGHT

Do not go gentle into that good night,
Old age should burn and rave at close of day;
Rage, rage against the dying of the light.

Though wise men at their end know dark is right,
Because their words had forked no lightning they   5
Do not go gentle into that good night.

Good men, the last wave by, crying how bright
Their frail deeds might have danced in a green bay,
Rage, rage against the dying of the light.

Wild men who caught and sang the sun in flight,   10
And learn, too late, they grieved it on its way,
Do not go gentle into that good night.

Grave men, near death, who see with blinding sight
Blind eyes could blaze like meteors and be gay,
Rage, rage against the dying of the light   15

And you, my father, there on the sad height,
Curse, bless, me now with your fierce tears, I pray.
Do not go gentle into that good night.
Rage, rage against the dying of the light.

ROBERT LOWELL (1917–   )

AFTER THE SURPRISING CONVERSIONS

September twenty-second, Sir: today
I answer. In the latter part of May,
Hard on our Lord's Ascension, it began
To be more sensible. A gentleman
Of more than common understanding, strict   5
In morals, pious in behavior, kicked
Against our goad. A man of some renown,
An useful, honored person in the town,
He came of melancholy parents; prone
To secret spells, for years they kept alone—   10
His uncle, I believe, was killed of it:
Good people, but of too much or little wit.
I preached one Sabbath on a text from Kings;
He showed concernment for his soul. Some things
In his experience were hopeful. He   15
Would sit and watch the wind knocking a tree
And praise this countryside our Lord has made.
Once when a poor man's heifer died, he laid
A shilling on the doorsill; though a thirst
For loving shook him like a snake, he durst   20
Not entertain much hope of his estate
In heaven. Once we saw him sitting late
Behind his attic window by a light
That guttered on his Bible; through that night
He meditated terror, and he seemed   25
Beyond advice or reason, for he dreamed
That he was called to trumpet Judgment Day
To Concord. In the latter part of May
He cut his throat. And though the coroner
Judged him delirious, soon a noisome stir   30
Palsied our village. At Jehovah's nod
Satan seemed more let loose amongst us: God
Abandoned us to Satan, and he pressed
Us hard, until we thought we could not rest
Till we had done with life. Content was gone.   35
All the good work was quashed. We were undone.
The breath of God had carried out a planned

And sensible withdrawal from this land;
The multitude, once unconcerned with doubt,
Once neither callous, curious nor devout,   40
Jumped at broad noon, as though some peddler groaned
At it in its familiar twang: "My friend,
Cut your own throat. Cut your own throat. Now! Now!"
September twenty-second, Sir, the bough
Cracks with the unpicked apples, and at dawn   45
The small-mouth bass breaks water, gorged with spawn.

MR. EDWARDS AND THE SPIDER

I saw the spiders marching through the air,
Swimming from tree to tree that mildewed day
   In latter August when the hay
   Came creaking to the barn. But where
     The wind is westerly,   5
Where gnarled November makes the spiders fly
Into the apparitions of the sky,
They purpose nothing but their ease and die
Urgently beating east to sunrise and the sea;

What are we in the hands of the great God?   10
It was in vain you set up thorn and brier
   In battle array against the fire
   And treason crackling in your blood;
     For the wild thorns grow tame
And will do nothing to oppose the flame;   15
Your lacerations tell the losing game
You play against a sickness past your cure.
How will the hands be strong? How will the heart endure?

A very little thing, a little worm,
Or hourglass-blazoned spider, it is said,   20
   Can kill a tiger. Will the dead
   Hold up his mirror and affirm
     To the four winds the smell
And flash of his authority? It's well
If God who holds you to the pit of hell,   25
Much as one holds a spider, will destroy,
Baffle and dissipate your soul. As a small boy

On Windsor Marsh, I saw the spider die
When thrown into the bowels of fierce fire:
  There's no long struggle, no desire 30
    To get up on its feet and fly—
      It stretches out its feet
And dies. This is the sinner's last retreat;
Yes, and no strength exerted on the heat
Then sinews the abolished will, when sick
And full of burning, it will whistle on a brick. 35

But who can plumb the sinking of that soul?
Josiah Hawley, picture yourself cast
  Into a brick-kiln where the blast
    Fans your quick vitals to a coal— 40
      If measured by a glass,
How long would it seem burning! Let there pass
A minute, ten, ten trillion; but the blaze
Is infinite, eternal: this is death,
To die and know it. This is the Black Widow, death.

THE DRUNKEN FISHERMAN

Wallowing in this bloody sty,
I cast for fish that pleased my eye
(Truly Jehovah's bow suspends
No pots of gold to weight its ends);
Only the blood-mouthed rainbow trout 5
Rose to my bait. They flopped about
My canvas creel until the moth
Corrupted its unstable cloth.

A calendar to tell the day;
A handkerchief to wave away 10
The gnats; a couch unstuffed with storm
Pouching a bottle in one arm;
A whiskey bottle full of worms;
And bedroom slacks: are these fit terms
To mete the worm whose molten rage 15
Boils in the belly of old age?

Once fishing was a rabbit's foot—
O wind blow cold, O wind blow hot,
Let suns stay in or suns step out:
Life danced a jig on the sperm-whale's spout—   20
The fisher's fluent and obscene
Catches kept his conscience clean.
Children, the raging memory drools
Over the glory of past pools.

Now the hot river, ebbing, hauls   25
Its bloody waters into holes;
A grain of sand inside my shoe
Mimics the moon that might undo
Man and Creation too; remorse
Stinking, has puddled up its source;   30
Here tantrums thrash to a whale's rage.
This is the pot-hole of old age.

Is there no way to cast my hook
Out of this dynamited brook?
The Fisher's sons must cast about   35
When shallow waters peter out.
I will catch Christ with a greased worm,
And when the Prince of Darkness stalks
My bloodstream to its Stygian term . . .
On water the Man-Fisher walks.   40

APPENDIX ONE

POETRY: ITS NATURE AND PURPOSE
A SERIES OF STATEMENTS BY POETS AND CRITICS

1. SIR PHILIP SIDNEY: The Poet's World

There is no Art delivered to mankind that hath not the works of Nature for his principal object, without which they could not consist, and on which they so depend, as they become actors and players, as it were, of what Nature will have set forth. . . . Only the poet, disdaining to be tied to any such subjection, lifted up with the vigor of his own Invention, doth grow in effect another nature, in making things either better than Nature bringeth forth, or, quite anew, forms such as never were in Nature, as the *Heroes, Demigods, Cyclops, Chimeras, Furies,* and such like . . . He goeth hand in hand with Nature, not enclosed within the narrow warrant of' her gifts, but freely ranging only within the Zodiac of his own wit.

Nature never set forth the earth in so rich a tapestry as divers Poets have done, neither with pleasant rivers, fruitful trees, sweet-smelling flowers, nor whatsoever else may make the too much loved earth more lovely. Her world is brazen, the Poets only deliver a golden.

from An Apologie for Poetrie (1595)

2. WILLIAM SHAKESPEARE: Theseus on Imagination

> Lovers and madmen have such seething brains,
> Such shaping fantasies, that apprehend
> More than cool reason ever comprehends.
> The lunatic, the lover, and the poet
> Are of imagination all compact:—
> One sees more devils than vast hell can hold,—
> That is the madman: the lover, all as frantic,
> Sees Helen's beauty in a brow of Egypt:
> The poet's eye, in a fine frenzy rolling,
> Doth glance from heaven to earth, from earth to heaven;
> And, as imagination bodies forth

The forms of things unknown, the poet's pen
Turns them to shapes, and gives to airy nothing
A local habitation and a name.
Such tricks hath strong imagination,
That, if it would but apprehend some joy,
It comprehends some bringer of that joy;
Or in the night, imagining some fear,
How easy is a bush supposed a bear!

from *A Midsummer Night's Dream* (1595?, 1600)

3. BEN JONSON: Of the Poet

. . . I would lead you to the knowledge of our poet by a perfect information, what he is, or should be, by nature, by exercise, by imitation, by study . . .

1. *Ingenium*. First, we require in our poet, or maker (for that title our language affords him elegantly with the Greek), a goodness of natural wit. For, whereas all other arts consist of doctrine and precepts, the poet must be able, by nature and instinct, to pour out the treasure of his mind . . .

2. *Exercitatio*. To this perfection of nature in our poet, we require exercise of those parts, and frequent. If his wit will not arrive suddenly at the dignity of the ancients, let him not yet fall out with it, quarrel, or be over-hastily angry, offer to turn it away from study, in a humour; but come to it again upon better cogitation, try another time, with labour. . . . The common rhymers pour forth verses, such as they are, extempore, but there never comes from them one sense worth the life of a day. A rhymer and a poet are two things. It is said of the incomparable Virgil that he brought forth his verses like a bear, and after formed them with licking. . . . I have met many of these rattles, that made a noise and buzzed. They had their hum, and no more. Indeed, things wrote with labour deserve to be so read.

3. *Imitatio*. The third requisite in our poet, or maker, is imitation: to be able to convert the substance or riches of another poet to his own use. To make choice of one excellent man above the rest, and so to follow him till he grow very he. or so like him that the copy may be mistaken for the principal. Not a creature that swallows what it takes in, crude, raw, or undigested; but that feeds with an appetite, and hath a stomach to concoct, divide, and turn all into nourishment. Not to imitate servilely, as Horace saith, and

catch at vices for virtue; but to draw forth out of the best and choicest flowers, with the bee, and turn all into honey; work it into one relish and savour; make our imitation sweet; observe how the best writers have imitated, and follow them. How Virgil and Statius have imitated Homer; how Horace, Archilochus; how Alcaeus and the other Lyrics; and so of the rest.

4. *Lectio*. But that which we especially require in him is an exactness of study and multiplicity of reading, which maketh a full man; not alone enabling him how to know the history or argument of a poem, and to report it; but so to master the matter and style as to show he knows how to handle, place, or dispose of either with elegancy, when need shall be. And not think he can leap forth suddenly a poet by dreaming he hath been in Parnassus, or having washed his lips—as they say—in Helicon.

from *Discoveries* (1641)

4. JOHN MILTON: A True Poem

. . . And long it was not after, when I was confirm'd in this opinion, that he who would not be frustrate of his hope to write well hereafter in laudable things, ought himself to be a true Poem; that is, a composition and pattern of the best and honourablest things; not presuming to sing high praises of heroic men or famous Cities, unless he have in himself the experience and the practice of all that which is praiseworthy.

from *Apology for Smectymnuus* (1642)

5. JOHN MILTON: The Troublesome Bondage of Riming

The measure [of *Paradise Lost*] is English Heroic Verse without Rime, as that of Homer in Greek, and of Virgil in Latin; Rime being no necessary adjunct or true ornament of a Poem or good verse, in longer works especially, but the invention of a barbarous age, to set off wretched matter and lame meter; graced indeed since by the use of some famous modern poets, carried away by custom, but much to their own vexation, hindrance, and constraint to express many things otherwise, and for the most part worse than else they would have exprest them. Not without cause therefore some both Italian and Spanish poets of prime note have rejected Rime both in longer and shorter works, as have also long since our best

English Tragedies, as a thing of itself, to all judicious ears, trivial and of no true musical delight; which consists only in apt numbers, fit quantity of syllables, and the sense variously drawn out from one verse into another, not in the jingling sound of like endings, a fault avoided by the learned Ancients both in Poetry and all good Oratory. This neglect then of Rime so little is to be taken for a defect, though it may seem so perhaps to vulgar readers, that it rather is to be esteem'd an example set, the first in English, of ancient liberty recover'd to Heroic Poem from the troublesome and modern bondage of Riming.

Note added to *Paradise Lost*, 1668

6. JOHN DRYDEN: The Function of Imagination in Poetical Composition

The composition of all poems is, or ought to be, of wit; and wit in the poet, or wit writing (if you will give me leave to use a School distinction) is no other than the faculty of imagination in the writer, which, like a nimble spaniel, beats over and ranges thro' the field of memory, till it springs the quarry it hunted after; or, without metaphor, which searches over all the memory for the species or ideas of those things which it designs to represent. Wit written is that which is well defined, the happy result of thought, or product of imagination.
. . . The first happiness of the poet's imagination is properly invention, or finding of the thought; the second is fancy, or the variation, deriving, or molding of that thought, as the judgment represents it proper to the subject; the third is elocution, or the art of clothing and adorning that thought, so found and varied, in apt, significant, and sounding words: the quickness of the imagination is seen in the invention, the fertility in the fancy, and the accuracy in the expression.

from *An Account of the Ensuing Poem* (*Annus Mirabilis*, 1666)

7. JOHN DRYDEN: The Accomplishments Necessary to a Poet

Mere poets are as sottish as mere drunkards are, who live in a continual mist, without seeing or judging anything clearly. A man should be learned in several sciences, and should have a reasonable, philosophical, and in some measure a mathematical head, to be a complete and excellent poet; and besides this, should have experience in all sorts of humours and manners of men. . . . Mr. Settle having never studied any sort of learning but poetry . . . must make very lame work on 't.

> from *Notes and Observations on The Empress of Morocco*
> (1674)

8. ALEXANDER POPE: Nature, the Rules, and Art

> First follow Nature, and your judgment frame
> By her just standard, which is still the same:
> Unerring Nature, still divinely bright,
> One clear, unchang'd, and universal light,
> Life, force, and beauty, must to all impart,
> At once the source, and end, and test, of Art.
> Art from that fund each just supply provides,
> Works without show, and without pomp presides. . . .
>
> 'Tis more to guide, than spur the Muse's steed;
> Restrain his fury, than provoke his speed;
> The winged courser, like a gen'rous horse,
> Shows most true mettle when you check his course.
>   Those RULES of old discovered, not devis'd,
> Are Nature still, but Nature methodiz'd. . . .
>
> Learn hence for ancient rules a just esteem;
> To copy Nature is to copy them.
>   Some beauties yet no Precepts can declare,
> For there's a happiness as well as care.
> Music resembles Poetry, in each
> Are nameless graces which no methods teach,
> And which a master hand alone can reach.
> If, where the rules not far enough extend,
> (Since rules were made but to promote their end)
> Some lucky License answer to the full
> Th'intent propos'd, that License is a rule.
> Thus Pegasus, a nearer way to take,
> May boldly deviate from the common track;
> From vulgar bounds with brave disorder part,
> And snatch a grace beyond the reach of art,

Which, without passing thro' the judgment, gains
The heart, and all its end at once attains. . . .

True Wit is Nature to advantage dress'd,
What oft was thought, but ne'er so well express'd;
Something, whose truth convinc'd at sight we find,
That gives us back the image of our mind.

from *An Essay on Criticism* (1711)

). SAMUEL JOHNSON: A Dissertation upon Poetry

"Wherever I went, [it is Imlac, a young Persian traveler speaking to Rasselas, the prince of Abyssinia] I found that poetry was considered as the highest learning, and regarded with a veneration somewhat approaching to that which man would pay to the Angelic Nature. And yet it fills me with wonder, that in almost all countries the most ancient poets are considered as the best; whether it be that every other kind of knowledge is an acquisition gradually attained, and poetry is a gift conferred at once; or that the first poetry of every nation surprised them as a novelty, and retained the credit by consent which it received by accident at first; or whether as the province of poetry is to describe nature and passion, which are always the same, the first writers took possession of the most striking objects for description, and the most probable occurrences for fiction, and left nothing to those that followed them, but transcription of the same events, and new combinations of the same images. Whatever be the reason, it is commonly observed, that the early writers are in possession of nature, and their followers of art; that the first excel in strength and invention, and the latter in elegance and refinement.

"I was desirous to add my name to this illustrious fraternity. I read all the poets of Persia and Arabia, and was able to repeat by memory the volumes that are suspended in the mosque of Mecca; but I soon found that no man was ever great by imitation. My desire of excellence impelled me to transfer my attention to nature and to life. Nature was to be my subject, and men to be my auditors. I could never describe what I had not seen; I could not hope to move those with delight or terror, whose interests and opinions I did not understand.

"Being now resolved to be a poet, I saw everything with a new purpose; my sphere of attention was suddenly magnified; no kind of knowledge was to be overlooked. I ranged mountains and deserts for images and resemblances, and pictured upon my mind every tree of the forest and flower of the valley. I observed with equal care the crags of the rock and the pinnacles of the palace. Sometimes I wandered along the mazes of the rivulet, and sometimes watched the changes of the summer clouds. To a poet nothing can be useless. Whatever is beautiful and whatever is dreadful, must be familiar to his imagination; he must be conversant with all that is awfully vast or elegantly little. The plants of the garden, the animals of the wood, the minerals of the earth and meteors of the sky, must all concur to store his mind with inexhaustible variety, for every idea is useful for the enforcement or decoration of moral or religious truths; and he who knows most will have most power of diversifying his scenes, and of gratifying his reader with remote allusions and unexpected instruction.

"All the appearances of nature I was therefore careful to study, and every country which I have surveyed has contributed something to my poetical powers."

"In so wide a survey," said the prince, "you must have left much unobserved. I have lived till now within the circuit of these mountains, and yet cannot walk abroad without the sight of something which I had never beheld before or never heeded."

"The business of a poet," said Imlac, "is to examine, not the individual, but the species; to remark general properties and large appearances; he does not number the streaks of the tulip, or describe the different shades in the verdure of the forest. He is to exhibit in his portraits of nature such prominent and striking features, as recall the original to every mind; and must neglect the minuter discriminations which one may have remarked and another have neglected, for those characteristics which are alike obvious to vigilance and carelessness.

"But the knowledge of nature is only half the task of a poet; he must be acquainted likewise with all the modes of life. His character requires that he estimate the happiness and misery of every condition; observe the power of all the passions in all their combinations, and trace the changes of the human mind as they are modified by various institutions and accidental influences of climate or custom, from the sprightliness of infancy to the despondence of decrepitude. He must divest himself of the prejudices of his age or country; he must consider right and wrong in their abstracted and invariable state; he must disregard present laws and opinions, and rise to general and transcendental truths, which will always be the same; he must therefore content himself with the slow progress of his name, contemn the applause of his own time, and commit his claims to the justice of posterity. He must write as the interpreter of nature, and the legislator of mankind, and consider himself as presiding over the thoughts and manners of future generations, as a being superior to time and place.

"His labour is not yet at an end: he must know many languages and many sciences; and that his style may be worthy of his thoughts, must, by incessant practice, familiarise to himself every delicacy of speech and grace of harmony."

Imlac now felt the enthusiastic fit and was proceeding to aggrandize his own profession, when the prince cried out, "Enough! thou hast convinced me that no human being can ever be a poet. . . ."

from The History of Rasselas (1759)

10. SAMUEL JOHNSON: The Wit of the Metaphysical Poets

Wit, abstracted from its effects upon the hearer, may be more rigorously and philosophically considered as a kind of *discordia concors*; a combination of dissimilar images, or discovery of occult resemblances in things apparently unlike. Of wit, thus defined, they [the metaphysical poets] have more than enough. The most heterogeneous ideas are yoked by violence together; nature and art are ransacked for illustrations, comparisons, and allusions; their learning instructs, and their subtlety surprises; but the reader commonly thinks his improvement dearly bought, and, though he sometimes admires, is seldom pleased. . . .

Their attempts were always analytic; they broke every image into fragments; and could no more represent, by their slender conceits and laboured particularities, the prospects of nature, or the scenes of life, than he who dissects a sunbeam with a prism can exhibit the wide effulgence of a summer noon.

Yet great labour, directed by great abilities, is never wholly lost: if they frequently threw away their wit upon false conceits, they likewise sometimes struck out unexpected truth: if their conceits were far-fetched, they were often worth the carriage. To write on their plan, it was at least necessary to read and think. No man could be born a metaphysical poet, nor assume the dignity of a writer by descriptions borrowed from descriptions, by imitations borrowed from imitations, by traditional imagery, and hereditary similes, by readiness of rhyme and volubility of syllables.

from Life of Cowley (1779)

11. WILLIAM WORDSWORTH: What is a Poet?

What is a Poet? To whom does he address himself? And what language is to be expected from him?—He is a man speaking to men: a man, it is true, endowed with more lively sensibility, more enthusiasm and tenderness, who has a greater knowledge of human nature, and a more comprehensive soul, than are supposed to be common among mankind; a man pleased with his own passions and volitions, and who rejoices more than other men in the spirit of life that is in him; delighting to contemplate similar volitions and passions as manifested in the goings-on of the Universe, and habitually impelled to create them where he does not find them. To these qualities he has added a disposition to be affected more than other men by absent things as if they were present; an ability of conjuring up in himself passions, which are indeed far from being the same as those produced by real events, yet (especially in those parts of the general sympathy which are pleasing and delightful) do more nearly resemble the passions produced by real events, than anything which, from the motions of their own minds merely, other men are accustomed to feel in themselves:—whence, and from practice, he has acquired a greater readiness and power in expressing what he thinks and feels, and especially those thoughts and feelings which, by his own choice, or from the structure of his own mind, arise in him without immediate external excitement.

from the Preface to *Lyrical Ballads*, Second Edition (1800)

12. WILLIAM WORDSWORTH: The Object of Poetry

Aristotle, I have been told, has said that Poetry is the most philosophic of all writing: it is so: its object is truth, not individual and local, but general and operative; not standing upon external testimony, but carried alive into the heart by passion; truth which is its own testimony, which gives competence and confidence to the tribunal to which it appeals, and receives them from the same tribunal. Poetry is the image of man and nature. . . .

Poetry is the breath and finer spirit of all knowledge; it is the impassioned expression which is in the countenance of all Science. Emphatically may it be said of the Poet, as Shakespeare hath said of man, "that he looks before and after." He is the rock of defence for human nature; an upholder and preserver, carrying everywhere with him relationship and love. In spite of difference of soil and climate, of language and manners, of laws and customs; in spite of things silently gone out of mind, and things violently destroyed; the Poet binds together by passion and knowledge the vast empire of human society, as it is spread over the whole earth, and over all time. The objects of the Poet's thoughts are everywhere; though the eyes and senses of man are, it is true, his favourite guides, yet he will follow wheresoever he can find an atmosphere of sensation in which to move his wings. Poetry is the first and last of all knowledge—it is as immortal as the heart of man. . . .

from the Preface to *Lyrical Ballads*, Second Edition (1800)

13. WILLIAM WORDSWORTH: A Definition of Poetry

. . . Poetry is the spontaneous overflow of powerful feelings: it takes its origin from emotion recollected in tranquility: the emotion is contemplated till, by a species of reaction, the tranquillity gradually disappears, and an emotion, kindred to that which was before the subject of contemplation, is gradually produced, and does itself actually exist in the mind. In this mood successful composition generally begins, and in a mood similar to this it is carried on; but the emotion, of whatever kind, and in whatever degree, from various causes, is qualified by various pleasures, so that in describing any passions whatsoever, which are voluntarily described, the mind will, upon the whole, be in a state of enjoyment. If Nature be thus cautious to preserve in a state of enjoyment a being so employed, the Poet ought to profit by the lesson held forth to him, and ought especially to take care that, whatever passions he communicates to his Reader, those passions, if his Reader's mind be sound and vigorous, should always be accompanied with an overbalance of pleasure. Now the music of harmonious metrical language, the sense of difficulty overcome, and the blind association of pleasure which has been previously received from works of rhyme or metre of the same or similar construction, an indistinct perception perpetually renewed of language closely resembling that of real life, and yet, in the circumstance of metre, differing from it so widely—all these imperceptibly make up a complex feeling of delight, which is of the most important use in tempering the painful feeling always found intermingled with powerful descriptions of the deeper passions. This effect is always produced in pathetic and impassioned poetry;

while, in lighter compositions, the ease and gracefulness with which the Poet manages his numbers are themselves confessedly a principal source of the gratification of the Reader.

from the Preface to *Lyrical Ballads*, Second Edition (1800)

14. S. T. COLERIDGE: The Power of the Poet

What is poetry?—is so nearly the same question with, what is a poet?—that the answer to the one is involved in the solution of the other. For it is a distinction resulting from the poetic genius itself, which sustains and modifies the images, thoughts, and emotions of the poet's own mind.

The poet, described in ideal perfection, brings the whole soul of man into activity, with the subordination of its faculties to each other according to their relative worth and dignity. He diffuses a tone and spirit of unity, that blends, and (as it were) *fuses*, each into each, by that synthetic and magical power, to which I would exclusively appropriate the name of Imagination. This power, first put in action by the will and understanding, and retained under their irremissive, though gentle and unnoticed, control, *laxis effertur habenis*, reveals itself in the balance or reconcilement of opposite or discordant qualities: of sameness, with difference; of the general with the concrete; the idea with the image; the individual with the representative; the sense of novelty and freshness with old and familiar objects; a more than usual state of emotion with more than usual order; judgment ever awake and steady; self-possession with enthusiasm and feeling profound or vehement; and while it blends and harmonizes the natural and the artificial, still subordinates art to nature; the manner to the matter; and our admiration of the poet to our sympathy with the poetry. Doubtless, as Sir John Davies observes of the soul—(and his words may with slight alteration be applied, and even more appropriately, to the poetic Imagination)—

> Doubtless this could not be, but that she turns
>   Bodies to *spirit* by sublimation strange,
> As fire converts to fire the things it burns,
>   As we our food into our nature change.
>
> From their gross matter she abstracts *their* forms,
>   And draws a kind of quintessence from things;

Which to her proper nature she transforms
To bear them light on her celestial wings.

Thus does she, when from *individual states*
She doth abstract the universal kinds;
Which then re-clothed in divers names and fates
Steal access through the senses to our minds.

Finally, Good Sense is the Body of poetic genius, Fancy its Drapery, Motion its Life, and Imagination the Soul that is everywhere, and in each; and forms all into one graceful and intelligent whole.

from *Biographia Literaria*, Chapter XIV (1817)

15. JOHN KEATS: Imagination and Truth

. . . What the Imagination seizes as Beauty must be truth—whether it existed before or not,—for I have the same idea of all our passions as of Love: they are all, in their sublime, creative of essential Beauty. . . . The Imagination may be compared to Adam's dream,—he awoke and found it truth. . . .

. . . O for a life of Sensations rather than of Thoughts! . . .

. . . the simple Imaginative Mind may have its rewards in the repetition of its own silent Working coming continually on the Spirit with a fine Suddenness.

. . . if a Sparrow come before my window, I take part in its existence and pick about the gravel. . . .

from a letter to Benjamin Bailey, November 22, 1817

16. JOHN KEATS: A Few Axioms

In poetry I have a few axioms, and you will see how far I am from their centre.

1st. I think poetry should surprise by a fine excess, and not by singularity; It should strike the reader as a wording of his own highest thoughts, and appear almost a remembrance.

2nd. Its touches of beauty should never be half way, thereby making the reader breathless, instead of content. The rise, the progress, the setting of imagery should, like the sun, come natural to him, and set soberly, although in magnificence, leaving him in the luxury of twilight. But it is easier to think what poetry should be than to write it—And this leads me to

Another axiom—That if poetry comes not as naturally as the leaves to a tree, it had better not come at all.

from a letter to John Taylor, February 27, 1818

17. PERCY BYSSHE SHELLEY: The Utility of Poetry

Poetry lifts the veil from the hidden beauty of the world, and makes familiar objects be as if they were not familiar . . .

A man to be greatly good, must imagine intensely and comprehensively; he must put himself in the place of another and of many others; the pains and pleasures of his species must become his own. The great instrument of moral good is the imagination; and poetry administers to the effect by acting upon the cause. Poetry enlarges the circumference of the imagination by replenishing it with thoughts of ever new delight, which have the power of attracting and assimilating to their own nature all other thoughts. . . . Poetry strengthens the faculty which is the organ of the moral nature of man, in the same manner as exercise strengthens a limb. . . . Whatever strengthens and purifies the affections, enlarges the imagination, and adds spirit to sense, is useful.

from A Defence of Poetry (1821)

18. MATTHEW ARNOLD: Poetry and the Present Age

The present age makes great claims upon us: we owe it service, it will not be satisfied without our admiration. I know not how it is, but their commerce with the ancients appears to me to produce, in those who constantly practise it, a steadying and composing effect upon their judgment, not of literary works only, but of men and events in general. . . . If they are endeavoring to practise any art, they remember the plain and simple proceedings of the old artists, who attained their grand results by penetrating themselves with some noble and significant action, not by inflating themselves with a belief in the preeminent importance and greatness of their own times. They do not talk of their mission, nor of interpreting their age, nor of the coming Poet; all this, they know, is the mere delirium of vanity; their business is not to praise their age, but to afford to the men who live in it the highest pleasure which they are capable of feeling. If asked to afford this by means of subjects drawn from the age itself, they ask what special fitness the present age has for supplying them: they are told that it is an era of progress, an age commissioned to carry out the great ideas of industrial development and social amelioration. They reply that with all this they can do nothing; that the elements they need for the exercise of their art are great actions, calculated powerfully and delightfully to affect what is permanent in the human soul; that so far as the present age can supply such actions, they will gladly make use of them; but that an age wanting in moral grandeur can with difficulty supply such, and an age of spiritual discomfort with difficulty be powerfully and delightfully affected by them.

from Preface to Poems (1854)

19. MATTHEW ARNOLD: The Future of Poetry

The future of poetry is immense, because in poetry, where it is worthy of its high destinies, our race, as time goes on, will find an ever surer and surer stay. There is not a creed which is not shaken, not an accredited dogma which is not shown to be questionable, not a received tradition which does not threaten to dissolve. Our religion has materialised itself in the fact, in the supposed fact; it has attached its emotion to the fact, and now the fact is failing it. But for poetry the idea is everything; the rest is a world of illusion, of divine illusion. Poetry attaches its emotion to the idea; the idea *is* the fact. The strongest part of our religion to-day is its unconscious poetry.

from General Introduction to The English Poets,
edited by T. H. Ward (1880)

20. W. B. YEATS: The Purpose of Rhythm

The purpose of rhythm, it has always seemed to me, is to prolong the moment of contemplation, the moment when we are both asleep and awake, which is the one moment of creation, by hushing us with an alluring monotony, while it holds us waking by variety, to keep us in that state of perhaps real trance, in which the mind liberated from the pressure of the will is unfolded in symbols.

from The Symbolism of Poetry (1900)

21. GEORGE SANTAYANA: The Great Function of Poetry

The great function of poetry is precisely this: to repair to the material of experience, seizing hold of the reality of sensation and fancy beneath the surface of conventional ideas, and then out of that living but indefinite material to build new structures, richer, finer, fitter to the primary tendencies of our nature, truer to the ultimate possibilities of the soul. Our descent into the elements of our being is then justified by our subsequent freer ascent toward its goal; we revert to sense only to find food for reason; we destroy conventions only to construct ideals.

from *Interpretations of Poetry and Religion* (1900)

22. GEORGE SANTAYANA: The Innocence of the Eye

The poet retains by nature the innocence of the eye, or recovers it easily; he disintegrates the fictions of common perception into their sensuous elements, gathers these together again into chance groups as the accidents of his environment or the affinities of his temperament may conjoin them; and this wealth of sensation and this freedom of fancy, which makes an extraordinary ferment in his ignorant heart, presently bubble over into some kind of utterance.

from *Interpretations of Poetry and Religion* (1900)

23. GEORGE SANTAYANA: The Primitive, Radical Form of Poetry

Memorable nonsense, or sound with a certain hypnotic power, is the really primitive and radical form of poetry. Nor is such poetry yet extinct: children still love and compose it, and every genuine poet, on one side of his genius, reverts to it from explicit speech. As all language has acquired its meaning, and did not have it in the beginning, so the man who launches a new locution, the poet who creates a symbol, must do so without knowing what significance it may eventually acquire, and conscious at best only of the emotional background from which it emerged. Pure poetry is pure experiment; and it is not strange that nine-tenths of it should be pure failure.

from *Reason in Art* (1905)

24. T. S. ELIOT: Poetry and Personal Emotion

It is not in his personal emotions, the emotions provoked by particular events in his life, that the poet is in any way remarkable or interesting. His particular emotions may be simple, or crude, or flat. The emotion in his poetry will be a very complex thing, but not with the complexity of the emotions of people who have very complex or unusual emotions in life. One error, in fact, of eccentricity in poetry is to seek for new human emotions to express; and in this search for novelty in the wrong place it discovers the perverse. The business of the poet is not to find new emotions, but to use the ordinary ones and, in working them up into poetry, to express feelings which are not in actual emotions at all. And emotions which he has never experienced will serve his turn as well as those familiar to him. Consequently, we must believe that "emotion recollected in tranquillity" is an inexact formula. For it is neither emotion, nor recollection, nor, without distortion of meaning, tranquillity. It is a concentration, and a new thing resulting from the concentration, of a very great number of experiences which to the practical and active person would not seem to be experiences at all; it is a concentration which does not happen consciously or of deliberation. These experiences are not "recollected," and they finally unite in an atmosphere which is "tranquil" only in that it is a passive attending upon the event. Of course this is not quite the whole story. There is a great deal, in the writing of poetry, which must be conscious and deliberate. In fact, the bad poet is usually unconscious where he ought to be conscious, and conscious where he ought to be unconscious. Both errors tend to make him "personal." Poetry is not a turning loose of emotion, but an escape from emotion; it is not the expression of personality, but an escape from personality. But, of course, only those who have personality and emotions know what it means to want to escape from these things.

from *Tradition and the Individual Talent* (1917)

25. T. S. ELIOT: The Chief Use of Meaning

The chief use of the "meaning" of a poem, in the ordinary sense, may be (for here again I am speaking of some kinds of poetry and not all) to satisfy one habit of the reader, to keep his mind diverted and quiet, while the poem does its work upon him: much as the imaginary burglar is always provided with a bit of nice meat for the house-dog. This is a normal situation of which I approve. But the minds of all poets do not work that way; some of them, assuming that there are other minds like their own, become impatient of this "meaning" which seems superfluous, and perceive possibilities of intensity through its elimination. I am not asserting that this situation is ideal; only that we must write our poetry as we can, and take it as we find it. It may be that for some periods of society a more relaxed form of writing is right, and for others a more concentrated.

from *The Use of Poetry and the Use of Criticism:*
Conclusion (1933)

26. MARIANNE MOORE: Poetry

I, too, dislike it: there are things that are important beyond
        all this fiddle.
    Reading it, however, with a perfect contempt for it, one
        discovers in
    it after all, a place for the genuine.
        Hands that can grasp, eyes
        that can dilate, hair that can rise
            if it must, these things are important not because a

high-sounding interpretation can be put upon them but
        because they are
    useful. When they become so derivative as to become
        unintelligible,
    the same thing may be said for all of us, that we
        do not admire what
        we cannot understand: the bat
            holding on upside down or in quest of something to

eat, elephants pushing, a wild horse taking a roll, a tireless
        wolf under
    a tree, the immovable critic, twitching his skin like a
        horse that feels a flea, the base-
    ball fan, the statistician—
        nor is it valid
            to discriminate against 'business documents and

school-books'; all these phenomena are important. One
              must make a distinction
    however: when dragged into prominence by half poets,
          the result is not poetry,
    nor till the poets among us can be
      'literalists of
      the imagination'—above
        insolence and triviality and can present

for inspection, imaginery gardens with real toads in them,
          shall we have
    it. In the meantime, if you demand on the one hand,
    the raw material of poetry in
      all its rawness and
      that which is on the other hand
        genuine, then you are interested in poetry.

from Poems (1921)

27. ARCHIBALD MACLEISH: Ars Poetica

A poem should be palpable and mute
As a globed fruit

Dumb
As old medallions to the thumb

Silent as the sleeve-worn stone
Of casement ledges where the moss has grown—

A poem should be wordless
As the flight of birds

                *   *   *

A poem should be motionless in time
As the moon climbs

Leaving, as the moon releases
Twig by twig the night-entangled trees,

Leaving, as the moon behind the winter leaves,
Memory by memory the mind—

A poem should be motionless in time
As the moon climbs

*   *   *

A poem should be equal to:
Not true

For all the history of grief
An empty doorway and a maple leaf

For love
The leaning grasses and two lights above the sea—

A poem should not mean
But be.

(1926)

28. W. H. Auden and John Garrett: Memorable Speech

Of the many definitions of poetry, the simplest is still the best: 'memorable speech.' That is to say, it must move our emotions, or excite our intellect, for only that which is moving or exciting is memorable, and the stimulus is the audible spoken word and cadence, to which in all its power of suggestion and incantation we must surrender, as we do when talking to an intimate friend. We must, in fact, make exactly the opposite kind of mental effort to that we make in grasping other verbal uses, for in the case of the latter the aura of suggestion round every word through which, like the atom radiating lines of force through the whole of space and time, it becomes ultimately a sign for the sum of all possible meanings, must be rigorously suppressed and its meaning confined to a single dictionary one. For this reason the exposition of a scientific theory is easier to read than to hear. No poetry, on the other hand, which when mastered is not better heard than read is good poetry.

from *The Poet's Tongue*, Introduction (1935)

29. Louis Macneice: The Modern Poet

I consider that the poet is a blend of the entertainer and the critic or informer; he is not a legislator, however unacknowledged, nor yet, essentially, a prophet. As informer, he is not a photographic or scientific informer, but more like the "informer," in the derogatory sense. His object is not merely to record a fact but to record a fact *plus and therefore modified by* his own emotional reaction to it; this involves mannerism in its presentation—hence the tricks of poetry. . . .

I would have a poet able-bodied, fond of talking, a reader of the newspapers, capable of pity and laughter, informed in economics, appreciative of women, involved in personal relationships, actively interested in politics, susceptible to physical impressions.

from *Modern Poetry* (1938)

APPENDIX TWO

VERSIFICATION AND KINDRED TOPICS

1. VERSIFICATION

RHYTHM is characteristic of prose and of everyday speech, but its units are too variable to be conveniently described in terms of any recurring pattern. Verse is distinguished from prose by the more or less regular repetition of an evenly spaced series of beats or accents. Such a pattern of beats is called METER, and verse is said to be metrical.

The metrical unit in English verse is the FOOT. It consists of two or of three syllables. The commonest feet in English are the following:

IAMB: two syllables, an unaccented one followed by an accented one (afraid, accept, oppose).

TROCHEE: two syllables, an accented one followed by an unaccented one (beauty, trochee, trouble).

SPONDEE: two syllables, both accented (bookcase, heartbreak, tongue-tied).

ANAPEST: three syllables, two unaccented ones followed by an accented one (introduce, ascertain, anapest).

DACTYL: three syllables, one accented syllable followed by two unaccented ones (merrily, poverty, syllable).

Those feet in which the unstressed syllables come first (iamb and anapest) are the units of a RISING METER; those in which the stress comes first (trochee and dactyl) are units of a FALLING METER.

In Greek and Latin poetry the rhythm is not measured in terms of stress or accent but in terms of length, and the foot is made up of various combinations not of accented and unaccented syllables but of long and short syllables. Much of the sensitiveness and

735

variety of English verse depends on the fact that all accented syllables are not equally heavy nor all unaccented ones equally light, but vary somewhat according to the length of the syllable. However, in establishing a normal pattern accent alone is taken into consideration.

The LINE is a larger unit. It is named according to the number of feet it contains:—

MONOMETER: one foot   TETRAMETER: four feet
DIMETER: two feet   PENTAMETER: five feet
TRIMETER: three feet   HEXAMETER (or Alexandrine): six feet
                  HEPTAMETER: seven feet

A line is described by naming the kind of feet and the number of feet it contains. Here are some illustrations:—

The line

Now sleeps/the crim/son pet/al, now/the white

is an IAMBIC PENTAMETER. The iambic is the commonest of meters, a series of unrhymed iambic pentameters being the form most often adopted in dramatic poetry and for longer narrative or reflective poems. Such unrhymed lines are called BLANK VERSE.

The line

Tyger,/tyger,/burning/bright

is a TROCHAIC TETRAMETER. It should be noticed that the final unaccented syllable of the last foot has been omitted. This is a slight variation that is very commonly found. An unstressed syllable may be dropped from the end of a line of falling meter or added at the end of a line of rising meter, as in the following eleven-syllable iambic pentameter:—

A thing/of beau/ty is/a joy/for ev/er

This addition of an extra unstressed syllable is called a FEMININE ENDING.

A line made up of three anapests—

I am mon/arch of all/I survey—

is an ANAPESTIC TRIMETER. In Browning's line

Grind away/moisten and/mash up thy/paste

we have four dactyls, although the two unstressed syllables at the end of the last foot have been dropped. This line is a DACTYLLIC TETRAMETER.

The IAMBIC HEXAMETER (or ALEXANDRINE) is the commonest measure in French poetry, and in English is often used for a special effect along with iambic pentameters. Thus, it is used to conclude and sum up the Spenserian stanza (for which, see below) and was sometimes introduced into a series of iambic pentameter couplets. Pope illustrated the Alexandrine in the second line of the following couplet:—

A needless Alexandrine ends the song,

That like/a wound/ed snake/drags its/slow length/along.

This last line illustrates a device of great importance in English metrics, the device known as SUBSTITUTION. Notice that two of the six feet depart from the established iambic pattern of the line and the poem. The fourth foot is a trochee and the fifth is a spondee. This line is called an iambic hexameter, nevertheless, for the kind of foot that is in the majority gives its name to the line. Here the purpose of substitution is obviously and effectively to slow up the speed of the line and bring its rhythm into harmony with its meaning.

A trochee is frequently substituted for an iamb, especially at the beginning of a line, and often the speed of a line is checked and an added emphasis is gained by the substitution of a spondee. Some examples of substitution are found in the following lines:—

Bright star,/would I/were stead/fast as/thou art

Not in/lone splen/dour hung/aloft/the night

*

All day/thy wings/have fanned

At that/far height/the thin/cold at/mosphere

*

The lone/and lev/el sands/stretch far/away

Substitution is only one of many ways in which the mechanical sing-song effect of perfect regularity is avoided. The logical meaning of any line imposes upon it a rhetorical rhythm that is subtly interwoven with the meter in such a way that some of the stressed syllables are given a greater weight than others. In the three examples just above, the stresses on the key words *star, thou, fanned, that, height, thin, cold,* and *stretch* are a little heavier than on the other accented syllables.

Another important element in the rhythmical effect of a line or passage of verse is the position of the pauses required by the sense (and by the lungs of the reader). The line is a metrical unit, and this unit may coincide with a unit of thought (phrase, clause, or sentence), but more often it does not. More often the sense requires a pause (or pauses) within the line. The most important of such pauses is called a CAESURA; others are called secondary pauses. Lines in which the caesura comes at the end of the line are called END-STOPT; those in which the sense runs on into the next line without a break are called RUN-ON LINES.

A metrical analysis of Coleridge's famous little rhyme will serve to sum up and illustrate what has been said about versification:—

1. Trochee/trips from/long to/short. (ᵘ)

2. From long/to long/in sol/emn sort

3. Slow Spon/dee stalks;/strong foot!/yet ill/able

4. Ever to/come up with/Dactyl tri/syllable.

5. Iamb/ics march/from short/to long;—

6. With a leap/and a bound/the swift An/apests throng.

Line 1 is a trochaic tetrameter, with the final unaccented syllable dropped. Line 2 is iambic tetrameter, preparing for the shift into spondees in line 3. Line 3 is a spondaic pentameter, though the fifth foot is a trochee. It should be noted that a line is rarely made up of a majority of spondees. The spondee is used principally for purposes of substitution. Line 4 is a dactyllic tetrameter; 5 is an iambic tetrameter; and 6 is an anapestic tetrameter. Lines 2 and 3 are run-on lines; the others are end-stopt.

2. SOUND AND SENSE

IT IS in accordance with a law of human nature that expression and communication adapt themselves as far as possible to the sense of what is being expressed and to the emotional excitement that accompanies it. Thus the rhythm of a song of victory will be quick and joyful; that of a funeral dirge, slow and mournful. This fact has been stated with great precision and illustrated with great skill by Alexander Pope in a well-known passage of his *Essay on Criticism.* If we examine it carefully we shall see what "devices of sound"—including variations in the speed and evenness of rhythm —are utilized by the practised craftsman to bring the sound and sense of a poem into the greatest possible harmony. Here are Pope's lines:—

> True ease in writing comes from art, not chance,
> As those move easiest who have learn'd to dance.
> 'Tis not enough no harshness gives offense,
> The sound must seem an echo to the sense:
> Soft is the strain when Zephyr gently blows,
> And the smooth stream in smoother numbers flow;
> But when loud surges lash the sounding shore,
> The hoarse, rough verse should like the torrent roar:
> When Ajax strives some rock's vast weight to throw,
> The line too labours, and the words move slow:
> Not so, when swift Camilla scours the plain,
> Flies o'er th'unbending corn, and skims along the main.

It can be seen that even within the strict pattern of the closed iambic pentameter couplet there is room (when handled by a master) for considerable rhythmic variation. The simplest variation is that of speed, and the sharpest contrast is between the line about Ajax and the last line quoted. In the former, the first and last feet only are iambs, the rest are spondees; in the latter, not even the stressed syllables are very heavily stressed, and the line, which is an Alexandrine, flies along because it contains no sounds or stresses that clash with one another in any way. But such effects are not gained by ingenious variations in the meter alone. We must consider the way in which the vowels and consonants making up the sounds of the words have been intermingled in subtle patterns to produce a final sound-effect in harmony with the sense. Let us first define these devices:—

RHYME: The repetition of vowel and consonantal sounds. The beginning sound of rhyming syllables must be different, but the middle (vowel) sound and the ending (consonant) sound must be the same. The following words are perfect rhymes: *old, bold, cold; older, bolder* (or *bowlder*), *colder; Birmingham, confirming 'em.*

When the rhyme falls on a single stressed syllable (as in the first series just given) it is called MASCULINE RHYME; when it falls upon a stressed syllable followed by one or more unstressed syllables (as in the second and third groups of words) it is called FEMININE RHYME.

Many poets have modulated the sound of their rhymes by the use of what has been misleadingly called IMPERFECT RHYME, that is, rhyme based upon an approximation, not an identity, of vowel sounds: *love, grove; lost, most; heaven, given.* Such rhymes are usually chosen deliberately for a definite effect and are not to be regarded as a sign of incompetence.

Rhymes are usually placed at the end of a line; INTERNAL RHYME, however, is sometimes made use of, either with great regularity, as in Shelley's *The Cloud,* or more often as an occasional sound-device. A good illustration is afforded by the following two lines in Dryden's *Secular Masque:*

> A very merry, dancing, drinking,
> Laughing, quaffing, and unthinking time.

CONSONANTAL RHYME (*grave, grieve; scope, skip*) has been used effectively by some modern poets. Wilfred Owen experimented with this device in a number of powerful poems, and his poem *Strange Meeting* is a good illustration of the effective use of consonantal rhymes.

ONOMATOPOEIA: a general name for the expression of meaning by the imitation of a sound, whether in a single word or a group of words. *Buzz, crash, whir* are simple and obvious examples of onomatopoetic words; *lush, lucent, syrop* are others, though not so obvious.

Some of the devices that result in a general onomatopoetic effect are concerned with the manipulation of vowels and some with the manipulation of consonants.

ASSONANCE: the special effect resulting from the juxtaposition of identical or closely similar vowel sounds. Note the effect in Pope's lines of the chiming together of such words as *loud* and *sounding*; *shore*, *hoarse*, and *torrent*; *lash*, *Ajax*, and *vast*.

ALLITERATION: the special effect resulting from the repetition of consonants, particularly at the beginnings of words and at the beginnings of stressed syllables. However, a repeated consonant at the end of a word or in the unstressed part of a foot makes a contribution to the total effect. Consider the pattern of alliteration in the following couplet:

> 'Tis not enough no harshness gives offense,
> 1 2   2 3 2   2 1   3 1   3 2 1
> The sound must seem an echo to the sense.
> 1   4   1   4   2   1 2 1

Note that the *m* at the end of *seem* and the *n* at the end of *an* make their effect felt in the alliterative pattern because they are followed by a vowel. "Imperfect" alliteration, such as *v* with *f* or *b* with *p* must also be taken into consideration. There are other slighter effects due to the pattern of the *t*'s and *d*'s (and perhaps due to the *g* of *gives* and the *ch* of *echo*) but these have not been marked.

Alliteration was an essential feature of Anglo-Saxon poetry, taking the place of rhyme. It persisted until the 14th century. The sonnets of Shakespeare and the poems of Donne, Dryden, Browning, and Tennyson afford many subtle examples of skilful alliteration. It is a favorite device of Milton; in Swinburne it became a mannerism. But in Gerard Manley Hopkins it was made a powerful and effective element in creative expression. One or two more obvious examples of "apt alliteration's artful aid" may be quoted:—

> The breezes blew, the fair foam flew,
> The furrow followed free.

*

> High there, how he rung upon the rein of a wimpling wing

*

> An Austrian army awfully arrayed
> Boldly by battery besieged Belgrade.

There are three points which remain to be made about the so-called "devices" of sound: rhythm, rhyme, assonance, and alliteration, and they must be stated clearly and emphatically, so as to clear up a rather widespread confusion.

1. These devices are not really devices or tricks at all. They are not mere mechanical manipulations introduced by the poet as an ornament and imposed on his verse as something extra, like the icing on a cake. They are a natural and inseparable part of the expression, and they arise, when they are successful, because excitement, passion, and emotion of any sort finds its most spontaneous expression in language that conveys half its meaning in its sound. The cursing of a fishwife is an instance of this; so is the outburst Shakespeare puts into the mouth of Othello at a moment of intensest passion:

> Never, Iago. Like to the Pontic sea
> Whose icy current and compulsive course
> Ne'er feels retiring ebb, but keeps due on
> To the Propontic and the Hellespont:
> Even so my bloody thoughts, with violent pace,
> Shall ne'er look back, ne'er ebb to humble love,
> Till that a capable and wide revenge
> Swallow them up.

Here the rhythm, alliteration, assonance, and an almost Miltonic use of high-sounding proper names, all grow out of the passion of the dramatic moment and out of the character of the speaker; and they all fuse to express and communicate the situation and the character. The sound and the sense are one and indivisible.

2. The effect of none of these devices, rhythm, rhyme, assonance, and alliteration, is an isolated one. They all interact upon one another, so that in considering the effect of sound upon sense, we must consider all of them, though in most cases some of them will be more important than others. Let us see some examples of special successes in the identification of sound and sense, and we will see that this is the case.

Here is how Milton describes or, rather, imitates; i.e., recreates, the fall of the rebel Angel:

> Him the Almighty Power
> Hurled headlong flaming from th'ethereal sky
> With hideous ruin and combustion down

> To bottomless perdition, there to dwell
> In adamantine chains and penal fire,
> Who durst defy th'Omnipotent to arms.

Here the reversed order of words, the syntax, and the rhythm of the sentence, regarded simply as prose, without reference to its place in the rhythmical pattern of the line, contribute to the modification of the blank verse rhythm. Note that only the last two lines are end-stopt, and that the caesura is in varying positions. The most striking metrical variation is in the line

> Hurlèd head/long flam/ing from/th'ether/eal sky.

The *the* before *ethereal* is elided so that it is not sounded as a separate syllable. The last three letters of *ethereal* are treated as half a foot, one syllable, though actually this has the value of a little more than a syllable, and is heard as a faint tremor in the rhythm of the line.

The vowel music of the passage is not mainly due to assonance, although assonance is present in the juxtaposition of *almighty* and *sky* at the beginning with *fire* and *defy* at the end,—and there are some other instances as well. The special effect of this passage is gained, not by *repeating* vowel sounds, but by varying them as richly and widely as possible.

Alliteration is frequent, but subtle and complex. It allies itself with the variation in the speed of the rhythm (and contributes to it) in order to imitate and suggest, in the first part the movement of a heavy body flung with irresistible force through the air, which gives and tears as it is forced apart by the passage of the falling body. The spondees in the second line and the *h* alliteration in the first three lines play an important part in giving this effect. Then the heavily accented beat on *down* and the alliteration on the hard consonants *d, b, t, p, m*, and *n*, change the effect completely. Now the resisting force is not air, which tears, but adamantine chains and inescapable perdition, which resist.

An example of the effective use of rhythm, alliteration, and assonance to suggest not sound but movement is afforded in two lines by a little-known Canadian poet of the last century, John Hunter Duvar:

> The largest game were sandpipers, whose feet
> In dancing step stamped deltas on the sand.

Here both alliteration and assonance have been arranged in an alternating series that neatly imitates the mincing and complicated quickstep of the hopping bird.

A striking example of the way in which a poet can combine all these devices for the purpose of communicating his meaning in terms of sensation can be found in Keats' *Eve of St. Agnes*:

> And still she slept an azure-lidded sleep,
> In blanched linen, smooth, and lavender'd,
> While he from forth the closet brought a heap
> Of candied apple, quince, and plum, and gourd;
> With jellies soother than the creamy curd,
> And lucent syrops, tinct with cinnamon;
> Manna and dates, in argosy transferr'd
> From Fez; and spiced dainties, every one,
> From silken Samarcand to cedared Lebanon.

In this stanza, as Lascelles Abercrombie has pointed out, the intricate interweavings of hard and soft consonants and of open vowels compel the reader to a nimbleness of tongue that actually makes the mouth water.

Tennyson is famous for the virtuosity with which he has utilized the various onomatopoetic devices. Here are a few of his most striking successes. The reader should need no help in discovering the part played by assonance and alliteration in achieving the total effect; but he should note carefully the variations in meter, the effect of spondees, the contrasts in speed afforded by a series of short words followed by polysyllables. The position and heaviness of the caesura are also of importance.

> The long day wanes; the slow moon climbs; the deep
> Moans round with many voices.

*

> The bare black cliff clang'd round him, as he based
> His feet on juts of slippery crag that rang
> Sharp-smitten with the din of armed heels—

And on a sudden, lo! the level lake
And the long glories of the winter moon.

*

Myriads of rivulets hurrying thro' the lawn,
The moan of doves in immemorial elms,
And murmuring of innumerable bees.

But the poet is concerned with the whole of life, and he cannot
limit himself to imitating the sound of doves in immemorial elms.
This brings us to the last of the three points we have been making
about these technical devices.

3. Devices of sound are not limited to the expression of pretty,
pleasant, or euphonious sounds. They do not exist for their own
sake but are means to an end, and that end is the interpretation
of experience—any experience. When the aspect of reality presented (the "sense") is harsh, ugly, cruel, or painful, then the
sound too must become harsh and sometimes cacaphonous. A few
illustrations should make this clear.

Keats can make our mouths water with his lucent syrops and his
creamy curds, but Milton, when he has occasion to, can fill our
mouths with ashes:—

> . . . greedily they pluck'd
> The fruitage fair to sight, like that which grew
> Near that bituminous lake where Sodom flam'd;
> This mere delusive, not the touch, but taste
> Deceiv'd; they, fondly thinking to allay
> Their appetite with gust, instead of fruit
> Chew'd bitter ashes, which th'offended taste
> With spattering noise rejected; oft they assay'd,
> Hunger and thirst constraining, drugg'd as oft,
> With hatefullest disrelish writh'd their jaws
> With soot and cinders fill'd.

Pope wants to pillory noisy, talkative, empty-headed critics, so he
describes the sound of a roomful of them in breathless, shouting,
self-assertive argument—the argument of superficial theorists,
among whom, by the way, he is careful to name one or two of his
enemies—and the vociferous speed of the cacaphonous couplets

does more than half the work of making the point the author wishes us to accept:—

> Now thousand tongues are heard in one loud din;
> The monkey-mimics rush discordant in;
> 'Twas chatt'ring, grinning, mouthing, jabb'ring all,
> And noise and Norton, brangling and Breval,
> Dennis and dissonance, and captious art,
> And snip-snap short, and interruption smart,
> And demonstration thin, and theses thick,
> And major, minor, and conclusion quick.

Browning combines pictures and sounds to convey an impression of the godforsaken wasteland through which Childe Roland travels to his doom:—

> If there pushed any ragged thistle-stalk
> Above its mates, the head was chopped; the bents
> Were jealous else. What made those holes and rents
> In the dock's harsh swarth leaves, bruised as to baulk
> All hope of greenness? 'tis a brute must walk
> Pashing their life out, with a brute's intents.

3. FIGURATIVE LANGUAGE

ONE OF the essential distinctions between poetry and prose is that a great part of the language of poetry is figurative language; that is, many of the statements made, or their implications, or the assumptions on which they are based, must be interpreted imaginatively and figuratively, not literally. When Shelley writes in his *Adonais* that

> Life, like a dome of many-coloured glass,
> Stains the white radiance of eternity

he is using sensuous images and figures of speech to say something to the understanding and the emotions that could not be expressed at all in the language of logical matter-of-fact statement. The literal-minded must be warned against the error of thinking that the truth here presented is any the less truth and any less precise than that expressed by the statement

$$g = tv^2.$$

It is directed to a different faculty and makes use of a different method—the method of figurative language. To understand this it will be helpful to define and illustrate some of the most frequently used FIGURES OF SPEECH. The commonest are the two "figures of likeness":—SIMILE: A statement by which a thing or action or quality is directly compared (usually by means of *like* or *as*) to some unlike thing, action, or quality.

My Luve is like a red, red rose (Burns)

*

'Twas like a maelstrom with a notch (Dickinson)

*

Thy soul was like a Star; and dwelt apart (Wordsworth)

are similes. Note that the simile is a *figurative* comparison, not a literal one. Compare the above similes with the following literal statements:—

A carnation is like a rose

*

The center of a cyclone is like a maelstrom

*

A planet is like a star.

These statements are wholly or in part either true or false. A simile is either appropriate or inappropriate, accurate or vague, useful or distracting. Its purpose is to make something unknown clearer and more familiar by likening it—or some significant aspect of it—to something already known. Thus in the three lines of poetry quoted above the poet wished to bring vividly before our attention the sweetness, delicacy, and fragrance of his beloved; the irresistible centrifugal pull of a terrifying experience; and the lonely grandeur and fixed steadiness of will that makes the poet Milton a guide and inspiration to later poets; and he does so by choosing an image that is distinguished by the qualities he wishes transferred to the main object of our attention.

METAPHOR: A statement of identity, in which a thing, an action, or a quality is directly or by implication affirmed to be some other unlike thing, quality, or action. For example:—

> There is a garden in her face (Campion)
>
> *
>
> Sweet spring, full of sweet days and roses,
> A box where sweets compacted lie (Herbert)
>
> *
>
> When the hounds of spring are on winter's traces (Swinburne)
>
> *
>
> Queen rose of the rosebud garden of girls (Tennyson).

Similes and metaphors, like some other figures, are usually rich in concrete sensuous perceptions and it requires a nice discrimination to distinguish what is to be interpreted literally from what is to be taken figuratively. The following stanza from Rossetti's *My Sister's Sleep* affords an interesting illustration of this point:

> Twelve struck. The sound, by dwindling years
>   Heard in each hour, crept off; and then
>   The ruffled silence spread again
> Like water that a pebble stirs.

The last line is hardly a simile; but when taken in conjunction with the whole sentence it appears as part of a metaphor in which the abstract non-being of sound—"silence"—is presented as a concrete thing—"ruffled" water.

One of the most frequent and effective uses of figurative language is this presentation of an abstraction as a concrete sensuous image. Herbert's lines

> I took, without more thinking, in good part
>   Time's gentle admonition:
> Who did so sweetly death's sad *taste* convey,
> Making my mind to *smell* my fatal day,
>   Yet *sug'ring* the suspicion

afford a good example; and Shakespeare's sonnets show many such: "Nativity, once in the main of light, Crawls to maturity"; "Incertainties now crown themselves assured"; "It (Love) is the star to every wand'ring bark"; "the glowing of such fire That on the ashes of his youth doth lie"; these and many more might be cited. Sometimes such figures are so sensuously and psychologically realistic that we need hardly be aware of them as figurative. Keats's image in stanza xvi of The Eve of St. Agnes,

> Sudden a thought came like a full blown rose,
> Flushing his brow

is of this kind.

While it is necessary to warn the reader of poetry not to interpret too literally what is intended to have the richness and multiplicity of figurative language, it is necessary also to add that even quite literal statements demand tact and intelligence for their proper interpretation. A witty commentator once pointed out that the famous lines in Keats' Ode on a Grecian Urn,

> Heard melodies are sweet, but those unheard
> Are sweeter

do not mean "It's nice to listen to music, but it's nicer not to."

An extended comparison making use of similes and metaphors in especially unexpected, surprising, or fantastic ways is called a CONCEIT (the word is an older form of concept: a thought or idea). This is a form of wit, much practised in the 17th century and in some modern poetry, in which an intellectual element is predominant and (when successful) is made the source of powerful emotion. It has been defined by Dr. Johnson, as "a kind of discordia concors; a combination of dissimilar images, or discovery of occult resemblances in things apparently unlike." (See p. 722.) Characteristic examples are to be found in the comparison of absent lovers' souls to the feet of a pair of compasses in Donne's A Valediction forbidding Mourning (p. 133); or of united lovers to phoenix in Shakespeare's Phoenix and the Turtle (p. 115) and in Donne's The Canonization (p. 126). The development of the metaphor "There is a garden in her face" in Campion's lyric (p. 117) through all the fantastic but consistent details of cherry lips, eyes like angels, and frowns like bended bows is another instance of the use of conceits. The poet needs faultless taste to manage the conceit without falling into bathos or the ridiculous or the repulsive. Examples of such failure among the followers of Donne did much to discredit the conceit in the 18th and 19th centuries, and such examples as the following were often held up to ridicule:

> Upwards thou dost weep.
> Heaven's bosom drinks the gentle stream,
> Where the milky rivers creep,
> Thine floats above; & is the cream.

> > Richard Crashaw describing the pious tears
> > of Mary Magdalene

*

> Each little pimple had a tear in it
> To weep the fault its rising did commit.

> > John Dryden (in an early poem) lamenting the
> > death of a nobleman who died of smallpox.

*

A famous, and successful, modern use of the conceit is found in the opening lines of T. S. Eliot's *Love Song of J. Alfred Prufrock* (p. 643):

> The evening is spread out against the sky
> Like a patient etherised upon a table.

Another very common figure of speech related to the metaphor is PERSONIFICATION. Here abstract qualities, lifeless things, objects in nature, etc. are spoken of as persons, either directly, by being given a name and shown as acting or feeling as a person, or indirectly by being given some attribute or power of a human being or of a god or other mythological being. Milton's *L'Allegro* and *Il Penseroso*, Gray's *Ode on a Distant Prospect of Eton College*, Shakespeare's *Sonnet LXVI*, and Rupert Brooke's *The Funeral of Youth* offer many examples. Here are a number of brief examples:—

> Daughters of Time, the hypocrite Days (Emerson)

*

> See Scandal praying with her sharp knees up
> And Virtue stood at Weeping Cross (Auden)

*

There Honour comes, a pilgrim gray (Collins)

*

This sea that bares her bosom to the moon (Wordsworth)

*

Fair Quiet, have I found thee here,
And Innocence, thy sister dear? (Marvell)

A very significant figure, and one which may be as concentrated as a single epithet or extend as a kind of pervading spirit through the tone of a whole passage or a complete poem is IRONY. This is the figure which implies the opposite of what is actually said. Marvell's couplet

> The grave's a fine and private place,
> But none, I think, do there embrace—

is a classic example of irony. Note how the "I think" of the second line converts a plain truism into ironic understatement. Understatement or innuendo is a subtle and effective form of irony and can be found in such a line as Robert Frost's "Something there is that doesn't love a wall" or Chaucer's seeming praise of the Prioress,

> But sikerly she hadde a fair forheed,

followed immediately by a line which translates the irony into the literal fact—

> It was almoost a spanne brood, I trowe.

And this is followed at once by another bit of ironic understatement:

> For, hardily, she was nat undergrowe.

Though not always used in a satiric manner, irony is one of the most effective and widely used devices in SATIRE, a method of exposing folly to the ridicule of reasonable men and vice to the condemnation of virtuous and responsible men.

Among poems which are pervaded by an ironic tone, achieved by a variety of figurative devices, we might cite, in addition to Marvell's *Coy Mistress* and Chaucer's *Prologue*, such poems as

Shakespeare's sonnet "My mistress' eyes are nothing like the sun," (p. 106) Dryden's *Prologue to Aurengzebe* (p. 222), Pope's *Rape of the Lock* (p. 240), Blake's *"I asked a thief"* (p. 287), Robinson's *Miniver Cheevy* (p. 575) and Ransom's *Captain Carpenter* (p. 664).

It will be noted that the MOCK-HEROIC—of which *The Rape of the Lock* affords us the perfect example—might be described as "ironic overstatement." All the imagery and grandeur of style appropriate to a great subject are here applied to the ordinary and the familiar—a game of cards, for example, described in the language used by the epic poets to describe battles of heroes and gods. This has the ironic (and surprising) effect, not of magnifying the grandeur of the commonplace but of making us more aware than ever of its littleness, as we grow conscious of the amusing discrepancy between the thing described and the method used to describe it. BURLESQUE is a converse device. What is really grand and great (or what ought to be) is described in a language and imagery suitable to mean, humble, or vulgar subjects. For a more general note on the uses of satire see below, p. 761.

4. VERSE-FORMS AND STANZA PATTERNS

BLANK VERSE: a series of unrhymed iambic pentameters. It is the verse form of the Elizabethan drama, of Milton's *Paradise Lost*, Wordsworth's *Tintern Abbey*, and Robert Frost's *Death of the Hired Man*, to name but a few examples, and is the commonest of all forms in English for longer narrative and reflective poems. The name is sometimes given to any unrhymed poem, in whatever meter. There are a number of beautiful unrhymed lyrics, among them Campion's *Laura*, Collins' *Ode to Evening*, and Tennyson's *Tears, Idle Tears*.

FREE VERSE, or *vers libre:* unrhymed verse in which the rhythmical unit is larger and looser than the foot. The units here are the cadence or strophe rather than the foot, and the verse paragraph rather than the line. The *Psalms* and the *Song of Solomon* in the Authorized Version of the English Bible are in free verse. So are some of the prophetic books of William Blake in the 18th century. Matthew Arnold's *Philomela* is free verse, although an occasional rhyme is introduced. Such unrhymed poems as Campion's *Laura*, Collins' *Ode to Evening*, and Tennyson's *Tears, Idle Tears* are metrically regular and should not be confused with free verse. The

modern revival of interest in free verse is largely due to the influence of Walt Whitman, whose *Leaves of Grass* (first edition
1855) is the largest and finest body of free verse in the language.
In the 20th century free verse of great formal beauty has been
written by T. S. Eliot and Ezra Pound. Carl Sandburg's *Four
Preludes on Playthings of the Wind* is a good illustration of the
successful union of the colloquial and the lyrical in free verse.

COUPLET, or Distich: two lines linked by a rhyme. The commonest
couplets are those of four feet (tetrameters) and of five feet
(pentameters). A series of iambic pentameter couplets is known
as HEROIC COUPLETS. This form rivals blank verse in popularity,
and is especially suitable for satiric and didactic poetry. It was
most highly regarded in the 18th century, but there has never been
a time when it has not been widely used for a variety of purposes.
The following poems are written in heroic couplets: Chaucer's
Prologue and many of the *Canterbury Tales*, Marlowe's *Hero and
Leander*, Jonson's *Lines on Shakespeare*, Dryden's *Mac Flecknoe*,
Pope's *Rape of the Lock*, Keats' *Lamia*, Browning's *My Last
Duchess*. The student should note the difference between the
somewhat tightly restricted end-stopt couplets of Dryden and
Pope and the freer movement of the run-on lines in Keats and
Browning. The difference is chiefly due to a difference in purpose:
the 18th century poems are satirical and intellectual, the 19th are
narrative and dramatic. The octosyllabic couplet is used by
Chaucer, Milton, Marvell, Herrick, Blake, Burns, Coleridge,
Rupert Brooke, and many other poets. It is particularly suitable
for light elegant, witty poetry, though it is by no means limited to
such verse.

TERCETS: three lines linked by a single rhyme. Tennyson's *The
Eagle* is a little poem made up of two tercets.

TERZA-RIMA: a series of three-line stanzas connected by an interlocking rhyme, *aba, bcb, cdc,* etc. Dante's *Divine Comedy* and
Shelley's *Ode to the West Wind* are terza rimas.

QUATRAINS: any four-line stanza: the lines may be of any length,
and the possible rhyme patterns are *abcb, abab, abba, aaba,* and
aabb. Examples of each of these are (in order): *Sir Patrick Spens,*
Gray's *Elegy in a Country Churchyard*, Tennyson's *In Memoriam*,
Fitzgerald's *Omar Khayam*, and Blake's *The Tyger*.

Rime Royal: a stanza composed of seven iambic pentameters rhyming *ababbcc*. Chaucer's *Troilus and Criseyde* and Shakespeare's *Rape of Lucrece* are in this stanza, as are some of John Masefield's narrative poems.

Ottava-Rima: A stanza composed of eight iambic pentameters rhyming *abababcc*. It was brought from Italy in the 16th century by Sir Thomas Wyatt. It is the stanza used by Byron in his great satires *Don Juan* and *The Vision of Judgment*.

Spenserian Stanza: A nine-line stanza, the first eight being iambic pentameters and the last an Alexandrine. The rhyme scheme is *ababbcbcc*. This stanza was first used by Edmund Spenser in his *Faerie Queene*. It was used with remarkable success in a number of poems in the late 18th and early 19th centuries: Shenstone's *The Schoolmistress*, Thomson's *The Castle of Indolence*, Byron's *Childe Harold*, Keats' *Eve of St. Agnes*, and Shelley's *Adonais*. The opening stanzas of Tennyson's *Lotos-Eaters* are Spenserian.

5. SOME TYPES OF POETRY

Lyric: a general name given to all poetry that is predominantly musical and emotional. It excludes poems that are primarily narrative, didactic, satirical, or conversational; but such reflective poems as sonnets, elegies, and odes are usually included. The name is derived from the Greek lyre, which was used as an accompaniment to the ode and elegy. The term is sometimes limited to the song, a brief, unified poem intended to be sung to a musical accompaniment. Among such poems included here are the songs in Shakespeare's plays, Ben Jonson's *Drink to me only with thine eyes*, Burns' *A Red, Red Rose*, and Byron's *She walks in beauty*.

Epic: A long narrative poem constructed on a grand scale, and celebrating in lofty verse the heroic deeds of men and gods. The ancient epic is of primitive origin, having taken form from cycles of ballads and lays preserved in an oral tradition. The popular epic is a reflection of racial and national ideals, a repository of myth and aspiration, the crystallization of the religious and patriotic ideals of a people. The finest examples are the Greek epics assigned to Homer, the *Iliad* and the *Odyssey*, and, in English literature, the Germanic epic *Beowulf*. Sophisticated literary imitations of the popular epic have, in the hands of poets of genius, been made the richest and most serious of all the types of poetry, with the possible exception of tragedy. Virgil's *Aeneid* and Dante's *Divine Comedy* represent the highest point reached by two great literatures; while Milton's *Paradise Lost* and *Paradise Regained* have a seriousness and magnificence shared only by the greatest of Shakespeare's tragedies. The MOCK-HEROIC epic is a satirical poem in which the grandeur of style and machinery appropriate to a lofty subject is applied to trivial, mean, or vulgar material. Pope's *Rape of the Lock* is the most brilliant example of the achievement of comedy and satire by the deliberate misapplication of all the characteristic devices of epic poetry. BURLESQUE is a misapplication of a diametrically opposite kind: it employs a familiar or vulgar style to treat of a noble and lofty subject.

BALLAD: A poem meant for singing, which tells a story. The popular ballad, while probably originating with a single author, has been so added to and changed in the course of its passage by word of mouth from one place to another and from generation to generation that it can be considered a communal production of the folk. The characteristics of the ballad are impersonality, directness, conciseness, concreteness, and intensity. The story is told dramatically, often by means of dialogue. Explanation or comment is rarely offered, and the reader is often, as at the beginning of *Edward* or in the whole of *The Twa Corbies*, left to infer a dramatic situation from what he *overhears*. The stories are such as would impress themselves on the minds of the common folk living in a primitive society and in an age of faith. They are stories of the supernatural; of faithful, ill-starred, or sinful love; of feats of strength or cunning; and of magic and religion. The old ballads were part of an oral tradition long before they were written down. So that the audience, as well as the bard or song-leader, could take part in the singing of them, many of them have a repeated chorus or refrain. These refrains are often meaningless, but sometimes they are built into the structure and form an essential part of the developing plot. Such a development is called "incremental repetition," and can be seen in *Lord Randal* and *Edward*. The popular ballads present a tragic view of life, and their interpretation of experience is characterized by an absence of squeamishness, a sharp realism, and an acceptance of the consequences of evil, which give them a tragic dignity. It should not be forgotten that genuine folk ballads still appear in the modern world. Examples of these are *Casey Jones, Frankie and Johnny,* and *St. James' Infirmary.*

ART BALLAD: Modern imitations of the folk ballad have sometimes succeeded in catching the spirit of popular poetry, and even sophisticated and elaborate poems like *The Rime of the Ancient Mariner* have recaptured the romantic spirit of ballads like *Sir Patrick Spens* and *True Thomas.* Other successful art ballads are Longfellow's *The Wreck of the Hesperus* and *The Skeleton in Armor,* and Keats' *La Belle Dame sans Merci,* perhaps the finest of all. Wordsworth's *Lucy Gray* is a domestic ballad, which aims to reproduce the artless simplicity of humble poetry. Burns' *John Barleycorn* is the re-working of a genuine old ballad. Two modern poems which are unusually successful in recreating the spirit and form of the popular ballad in terms of the modern world are Housman's *The Deserter* and Auden's *As I walked out one evening.*

DRAMATIC MONOLOGUE: A dynamic form of narrative in which a rigorously limited kind of dramatic unity is utilised to achieve a maximum effect with the most economical means. The characteristic device of the dramatic monologue is the presentation of *everything*—setting, motivation, characterisation, and action alike—from the single point of view of one of the persons involved. To whom he is speaking, why, and under what circumstances, we are left to piece together as we read on through the poem. Any descriptive or explanatory material comes from this source alone, whose soliloquy or one-sided conversation we overhear, much as if we had picked up the receiver on a party line in the middle of an interesting conversation, though it is the voice of only one speaker we can hear. At the beginning of the poem we are presented with a situation in unstable equilibrium—just what it is we pick up as we go along as details begin to fall into place. This moves through a series of minor crises until with the final denouement we are left with the original situation shifted and altered into another which was implicit in the beginning. This technique lends itself to subtlety and speed and is an excellent vehicle for dramatic irony. The speaker who occupies the center of the stage often unconsciously reveals his own weakness, folly, or wickedness, as, for instance, in Browning's *My Last Duchess, Soliloquy of the Spanish Cloister,* and *The Bishop Orders his Tomb.* Browning is the great master of the dramatic monologue, but many other poets, including Tennyson, Edwin Arlington Robinson, Robert Frost, and Ezra Pound, have demonstrated the richness of the form. The student might find it interesting to compare Tennyson's dramatic monologue *Ulysses* with a modern treatment of a similar theme— T. S. Eliot's *Love Song of J. Alfred Prufrock*. Many effective modern short stories have been constructed on the principle of the dramatic monologue, Ring Lardner's *Haircut* being a particularly neat example.

SONNET: a fourteen-line poem in which a rather rigorous conventional pattern has been used to give added weight to the thought and feeling. The sonnet form might be described as a "rhetorical shape," and the effectiveness with which the writer integrates the development of his idea and its accompanying emotions is a measure of its success. Although many slight variations are found in each, there are two chief types of sonnet: the Italian, or Petrarchan, and the English, or Shakespearean. The meter is usually iambic and the line a pentameter.

The ITALIAN SONNET: two stanzas, the first of eight lines, called an octave, and rhyming *abbaabba*, and the second of six lines, called a sestet. The rhyme scheme of the sestet has been so widely varied in modern times that it is accurate enough to say that the sestet may consist of any combination of two or three rhymes, *cdecde* and *cdcdcd* being two of the commonest. There is usually a logical and emotional relationship between the two parts of the Italian sonnet: a progression from the general to the particular, from cause to effect, or from a concrete experience to its interpretation or application. This double form makes the sonnet particularly effective for the powerful presentation of contrast. The student should study the way in which the form conditions the expression of thought and feeling in the following sonnets: Keats' *On First Looking into Chapman's Homer*, Wordsworth's *Upon Westminster Bridge*, Brooke's *The Dead* (the rhyme scheme in this is irregular, but the relationship between the parts is of much interest). Milton introduced a variation into the Petrarchan sonnet that many later sonnet writers followed him in. He disregarded the break between the octave and sestet, and (while keeping the rhyme scheme intact) made the sonnet a single developing entity culminating in a climax at the end. A fine example of this is Milton's sonnet *On his Deceased Wife*.

The ENGLISH SONNET: Three quatrains, rhyming *abab, cdcd, efef,* followed by a couplet, *gg.* Here the major division in the poem is at the end of the twelfth line. The concluding couplet is a dramatic climax, an epigrammatic close, an intense and concentrated statement of the "point" of the whole poem, or a summing-up of the consequences of what has been presented. Here the poet focuses the application of the experience developed in the three quatrains, criticizes, modifies, or expands it, and at once unifies and evaluates the experience out of which the sonnet has been made. This is a general description of the method of Shakespeare's sonnets. Perhaps the most striking example of the surprise ending is in sonnet cxxx. While Shakespeare was the greatest and most prolific writer of English sonnets, many poets have used the form with conspicuous success. Sidney's *Leave me, O love,* Drayton's *The Parting,* Donne's *Death, be not proud,* are characteristic examples of the English sonnet.

Edmund Spenser varied the form of the English sonnet by linking his three quatrains more closely together by means of an interlocking rhyme. The rhyme scheme of the Spenserian sonnet is *abab, bcbc, cdcd, ee.*

Experiments in varying the form and particularly the metrical structure of the sonnet have been made by Gerard Manley Hopkins (cf. *The Windhover*) and E. E. Cummings (cf. *who's most afraid of Death*). Meredith in *Modern Love* and Wallace Stevens in *Sunday Morning* wrote sonnet-like poems of 16 and of 15 lines respectively.

ODE: A reflective and more or less formal poem, usually of some length, exalted in tone and elaborate in manner. Originally a choral interlude in Greek dramatic poetry, the ode was divided into three parts, the strophe, epode, and antistrophe, in accordance with the conventional movements of a chorus of singers and dancers. The Greek poet Pindar developed the ode as an independent composition, and imitations in English of this form are called Pindaric odes. They are divided into three parts, the strophe and antistrophe being similar in their often very elaborate stanza pattern, while the middle part, the epode, is different. In long odes this sequence of three parts may be repeated, either completely or partially. Dryden and Gray are masters of this form.

A second kind of ode is the homostrophic, i.e., odes written in a single stanza type. As the theme is lofty and the style elaborate, the stanza form is usually large and complex. Examples of this type of ode are Spenser's *Epithalamium*, Milton's *On the Morning of Christ's Nativity*, Shelley's *Ode to the West Wind*, and the odes of Keats. The Roman poet Horace wrote a large number of personal reflective poems addressed to his friends, his patron, or his mistress. These were written in regular stanzas and were called odes. The Horatian ode in English is a simpler form of the homostrophic ode. Its diction tends to be more homely and the style in general is less elaborate and lofty than in the odes named above. Some examples are Ben Jonson's *An Ode to Himself*, Marvell's *An Horatian Ode on Cromwell's Return from Ireland*, and Pope's *Ode on Solitude*.

A third form of the ode is the irregular. Here every sort of freedom in length, rhyme-scheme, and meter is permitted in the various parts of the ode. This allows the greatest possible equivalence between the changing thought and feeling and the form of the expression. Wordsworth's *Ode on Intimations of Immortality* is the finest example of this type of ode. Others are Dryden's *Alexander's Feast*, Tennyson's *Ode on the Death of the Duke of Wellington*, and Allen Tate's *Ode on the Confederate Dead*.

ELEGY: Originally a classic form of serious meditative verse dealing with some aspect of death, war, or love; in 16th and 17th century English poetry the name "elegy" was given to epistles and love poems. In modern times the name is restricted to a lyrical or reflective poem on the subject of death. Gray's *Elegy written in a Country Churchyard* is the best known of all English elegies. Collins' *Ode written in 1746* is actually an elegy. Tennyson's *In Memoriam* is a sequence of elegies—the longest and most sustained in the language.

A number of the finest elegies in English make use of the conventional "machinery" of classical pastoral poetry and are called PASTORAL ELEGIES. These return to the imagery and characters of the ancient Sicilian poet Theocritus and the Roman poet Virgil, presenting an idealized and somewhat artificial countryside, peopled by nymphs and shepherds and visited by the Pagan deities. The person whose death is mourned is given a classical name and is often lamented by the poet in the guise of a fellow shepherd.

Lycidas is the best example of the pastoral elegy, and it is interesting because Milton has mingled figures from Hebrew and Christian mythology with the Greek shepherds and gods. Other well-known pastoral elegies are Shelley's *Adonais*, mourning the death of Keats, and Matthew Arnold's *Thyrsis*, a lament for the poet Arthur Hugh Clough.

EPIGRAM: A short poem leading up to a witty or ingenious turn of thought, often satirical, sometimes sententious. It has been defined and illustrated in a couplet by Coleridge:

> What is an Epigram? A dwarfish whole;
> Its body brevity, and wit its soul.

Some of the couplets in Pope's didactic poems can stand by themselves as perfect epigrams, as, for example, this memorable statement of neo-classic poetic theory:

> True Wit is Nature to advantage dress'd;
> What oft was thought, but ne'er so well express'd.

Sometimes an epigram is frankly comic, as is this couplet by John Donne in his poem, "The Anagram":

> Though all her parts be not in th'usual place,
> She'hath yet an Anagram of a good face.

Occasionally it has a lyrical quality in which wit and beauty are curiously allied, as in this little poem of Herrick's upon *Julia Weeping*:

> She by the river sate, and sitting there
> She wept, and made it deeper by a tear.

Other characteristic, and famous, epigrams are the Earl of Rochester's quatrain on Charles II:

> Here lies our Sovereign Lord the King,
>   Whose word no man relies on,
> Who never said a foolish thing,
>   Nor ever did a wise one.

and Sir John Harington's still pertinent observation, *Of Treason:*

> Treason doth never prosper—what's the reason?
> If it doth prosper, none dare call it treason.

EPITAPH: A memorial verse intended to be carved on a tomb, or at least to commemorate the dead; and usually, whether dignified and serious or satirical and humorous, partaking of the characteristics of the epigram. William Browne's *On the Countess Dowager of Pembroke* and Pope's *Epitaph Intended for Sir Isaac Newton* are characteristic examples. Gray's *Elegy written in a Country Churchyard* is concluded by an epitaph.

DIDACTIC POETRY and SATIRE: In the literature of ancient Rome, in the Renaissance, and in the neo-Classic literature of the 18th Century we find that poetry was put to many more practical and homely uses than most poets seem to think possible today. Since the Romantic revival at the beginning of the 19th Century we have tended to narrow our conception of poetry to the expression of what is inexpressible in any other way, to what is exalted, intense, powerful, and imaginative. Romantic poetry is a poetry of ecstasy and crisis. This is (though the uninstructed student may be surprised to hear it) a new and eccentric idea. Virgil wrote a treatise on agriculture in verse, and the result was poetry. Lucretius made poetry out of a serious work of philosophy. Horace wrote personal letters, Martial stinging epigrams. The English poets of the 16th and 17th centuries wrote many poems in the form of letters to friends, or patrons, or cultivated women. Sometimes they discussed philosophical or religious problems, or paid tribute to a great poet whose works were being collected after his death, or invited a friend to supper. Many writers in whom a moral conscience was combined with wit and a sense of the ridiculous wrote satires to expose and lash the evils of the time and more particularly the folly or vice of individuals. The great medieval poem *The Vision of Piers Plowman* is a political and religious satire. Ben Jonson, John Donne, and Samuel Butler, the author of *Hudibras*, wrote satire in the 17th century. The finest flowering of satiric poetry came with the work of Dryden in the last half of the 17th century and Pope in the first half of the 18th. These poets made the heroic couplet into a superb vehicle, weighty and fast, for the expression of ideas and for the creation of sharply etched characters. Matthew Arnold's contention that Dryden and Pope are classics of our prose but not of our poetry has been made untenable by the criticism of Lytton Strachey, Edith Sitwell, T. S. Eliot, Mark van Doren, Louis Bredvold, George Sherburne, if indeed it could have survived an unprejudiced reading of *Mac Flecknoe* and *The Rape of the Lock* or *The Dunciad*. Byron, in *The Vision of Judgment* and *Don Juan* was the last great satirist in the classical tradition. There has been an awakening of interest in satire and didactic poetry in modern times: this is being given its most powerful expression in the poetry of W. H. Auden.

INDEX